Federal Land Series

Federal Land Series

A CALENDAR OF ARCHIVAL MATERIALS
ON THE LAND PATENTS ISSUED BY THE
UNITED STATES GOVERNMENT, WITH
SUBJECT, TRACT, AND NAME INDEXES

Volume 1 • 1788–1810

Clifford Neal Smith

AMERICAN LIBRARY ASSOCIATION · CHICAGO 1972

KF
5675
.S6
1972
v.1

International Standard Book Number 0-8389-0138-7 (1972)
Library of Congress Catalog Card Number 72-3238

Printed in the United States of America

Contents

Maps

Introduction

The purpose of the *Federal Land Series* is to calendar
and index part of the great mass of archival material on the
early land grants of the United States, thus making the material
available to historians, genealogical researchers, and land-
title guarantors. Emphasis is placed upon the land *patents*--
the first transfers of title from governmental (mainly federal)
entities to private persons--for land in states other than the
thirteen original ones. Since much of the land was granted for
military service in the Revolutionary War and the War of 1812,
military bounty-land warrants are basic documents upon which
many patents were granted; as a consequence, these warrants
become of interest in this Series. In addition, early volumes
of the Series will contain material taken from the records of
land companies, because speculators, many of them prominent in
governmental affairs, played a major role in the first stages
of the development of federal land distribution. Further
classes of documents included in the Series are the governmental policy directives to district land offices; through them,
the effects of changing laws and public policy can be more accur-
ately gauged than through the analysis of laws and official
statements.

Historians have given only occasional attention to the
activities of the General Land Office and its predecessor agen-
cies, despite the fact that land speculation was, from early
colonial times, the main commercial interest of both the powerful
political figures of England and the colonies and the humblest of
the emigrants. The *Federal Land Series* should be useful to historians in the sense that it makes a great mass of documentation
accessible to researchers. Particular thought has been given to
the kinds of subject matter likely to interest historians. As a
model, the indexes to the printed *Territorial Papers of the United
States* have been followed, even elaborated upon. The format of
the Series has been set up particularly with a view to the possible needs of quantitative historians.

Genealogical researchers will almost certainly find the
Federal Land Series useful, because it offers a means of locating
persons before the first decennial federal censuses were taken in
sparsely settled areas. Even when such persons can be found in
the censuses, the areas covered by original counties frequently
comprised half a state and places of residence were often ambigu-
ously described in the censuses. The Series usually locates these
early settlers precisely, making it possible to identify the modern
county of settlement and, consequently, to enter the many county
records of interest to genealogists.

The Series should also be useful to land-title searchers
and guarantors, for, despite the very great importance of land
patents as the first transactions in ever-lengthening chains of
title to land tracts, patents were rarely recorded in county land
records. The reason is simply that the patents antedate the
organization of most counties and little attempt was made, upon
establishing county land records, to begin these records by

registering first ownership of land within the newly formed counties. As a consequence, patent information has remained buried
and, for the most part, inaccessible within the records of the
General Land Office and of the district land offices.

The Archival Source Materials

The amount of source material on land grants of the United
States is vast; it is hardly catalogued; none has been calen-
dared and indexed heretofore; much of it is entirely unknown.
There are several distinct bodies of material:

¶ The records of the central office in Washington (variously,
in the early files of the U.S. Treasury, the U.S. Department
of State, and the General Land Office).

¶ The records of the many district land offices, now usually
to be found in state archives or historical collections.

¶ The miscellaneous records, particularly those of early func-
tionaries, such as Rufus Putnam and Richard Clough Anderson,
and of land companies, now scattered among many collections.

¶ The legislative records of the U.S. Senate and U.S. House of
Representatives, too, have much material of general interest,
and it is likely that many petitions from early settlers and
speculators will be found among the records which escaped the
burning of Washington during the War of 1812. No doubt, the
personal papers of early-day legislators, especially those
representing frontier districts, contain much more material
of this nature.

The first patents to western lands were issued, either by
the Treasury Department or the Department of State, following

schedules received from persons authorized to sell lands in the
Seven Ranges (eastern Ohio) at public auction. The first such
auction was held at New York between 21 September and 9 October
1787; the second auction was held at Pittsburgh between 24 October and 3 December 1796. Sales schedules for both these auc-
tions were long overlooked and their whereabouts were not known
to the custodians of land records in the National Archives. A
search for them was made by the present writer, and both have
been found. They are summarized in serial entries 2526 and 2527
of this volume. There is some reference to a third public auction of land at Philadelphia, probably held concurrently with
the Pittsburgh sale, but, so far, the original sales record has
not been found. The Pittsburgh sales schedule (serial entry
2527 herein) bears several notations that payment was to be
made in Philadelphia. Perhaps these are the tracts auctioned
at Philadelphia for which no separate record has been found.

Although the records of the Treasury Department probably
contain material pertaining to land matters almost from the
beginning, the first registers specifically dedicated to the subject seem to date from 1796, just prior to the Pittsburgh sale.
Thereafter, various series of letter books were kept; the following have so far been microfilmed by the National Archives:

Microcopy
Number

25   *Miscellaneous Letters Sent by the General Land
            Office, 1796-1889*, 228 microfilm rolls

27   *Letters Sent by the General Land Office to Sur-
            veyors General, 1796-1901*, 31 microfilm rolls

477   *Letters Sent by the Surveyor General of the
            Territory Northwest of the River Ohio, 1797-
            1854*, 10 microfilm rolls

Microcopy
Number

478 *Letters Received by the Secretary of the Treasury and the Commissioner of the General Land Office from the Surveyor General of the Territory Northwest of the River Ohio, 1797-1849*, 10 microfilm rolls

479 *Letters Received by the Surveyor General of the Territory Northwest of the River Ohio, 1797-1856*, 43 microfilm rolls

733 *Letters Sent by the Secretary of the Treasury Relating to Public Lands ("N" Series), 1801-1878*, 7 microfilm rolls

735 *Circular Letters of the Secretary of the Treasury ("T" Series), 1795-1878*, 5 microfilm rolls [of limited usefulness, excepting for some financial reports from Receivers of Public Monies at district land offices]

T-1008 *Register of Revolutionary War Land Warrants [U.S.] Military District of Ohio, 1795-1805*; a forthcoming microcopy publication will expand the series to include an index of warrants under Congressional acts of 1803 and 1806, and a recently discovered "Register of Military Land Warrants . . . 1804-1835"

The above list by no means exhausts the likely manuscript sources of information on land transactions. The *Papers of the Continental Congress* (National Archives microcopy M-247, 204 microfilm rolls) contain numerous petitions, memorials, and reports regarding land matters; serial entries 2521 through 2526 in this volume are examples of the items of value to be found in this important collection, now being indexed by the National Archives. The records of the United States Senate, *Territorial Papers, 1789-1873* (National Archives microcopy M-200, 20 microfilm rolls) likewise contain many memorials and petitions of interest, as do the several published volumes of *The Territorial Papers of the United States*. Since the affairs of the various territories were supervised by the U.S. Department of State until 1873, there are also numerous series of microfilmed territorial documents having a bearing on early land transactions; see in particular the series for Florida, 1777-1824 (National Archives microcopy M-116, 11 rolls), the series for the Territory Northwest of the River Ohio, 1787-1801 (National Archives microcopy M-470, 1 roll), the series for the Territory Southwest of the River Ohio, 1790-1795 (National Archives microcopy M-471, 1 roll), and the Orleans series, 1764-1813 (National Archives microcopy T-260, 13 rolls).

There is one enormous mass of manuscripts which cannot be calendared in the *Federal Land Series* until it has been microfilmed, thus fixing the location of individual documents for all time. This is the correspondence received by the General Land Office from the public, now in the National Archives. There are over 1700 drawers full of these letters, plus 35 bound volumes (over 25,000 pages). A cursory examination discloses that there is much of value therein for social historians, genealogists, and land-title searchers. Unlike the outgoing correspondence of the General Land Office analyzed in the *Federal Land Series*, which is in chronological order, the incoming correspondence is in alphabetical order under name of sender. The present writer hopes to motivate the National Archives to microfilm the incoming correspondence, so that some of it may eventually be included in the *Federal Land Series*. As a first step, the bound volumes, containing much confidential material on personnel matters, field intelligence reports, and the like, should be microfilmed.

The likelihood of uncovering valuable information on land transactions among the personal papers of officials is great. This volume contains two such examples: serial entry 2527, taken from the papers of General John Nevill(e), and serial entries 2537 through 2543, taken from the papers of Richard Clough Anderson, surveyor of the Virginia Military District of Ohio, specially microfilmed for inclusion in this Series. Other microfilm series of potential usefulness are the *Baynton, Wharton, Morgan Papers* [1757-1787], which contain information on Morgan's early land speculations in the Illinois country, the *Winthrop Sargent Papers* [1785-1948], revealing Sargent's interest in Ohio lands, and the extensive *Albert Gallatin Papers*. In truth, a list of manuscript collections containing materials of general interest would be quite large; the papers of every President, Senator, and Representative of the period are likely to contain material of value on land matters, particularly memorials and petitions from early settlers. The only comprehensive guide to such collections is the *National Union Catalog of Manuscript Collections* and, for the early Presidents, the guides published under the auspices of the National Archives or the Library of Congress.

Arrangement of the *Federal Land Series*

The first volume of the *Federal Land Series* is divided into four sections: the serial entries which calendar the original documents, a name index, a subject index, and a tract index. The name and subject indexes need no comment, but the serial entries and the tract descriptions (and index thereto) require some explanation.

The mass of documentation included in the *Federal Land Series* requires a precise, somewhat cryptic, format for the serial entries. As a rule, all names of persons (and their addresses, when given), tract descriptions, and subject matter are set forth in the serial entries. Within each entry, information is given in a specific position in order to conserve space and to eliminate ambiguity. Most serial entries follow the format described in figure 1.

Tract descriptions used in the *Federal Land Series* differ in the following manner from descriptions found in the correspondence itself:

(1) A prefix has been added to denote the district land office where the application for land was originally made and in whose records the details of payment, survey, etc., are presumed to be located.

(2) The tract description is shown in an order reverse to that normally found in deeds. For example, one usually finds a tract of land described by section, township, range, and meridian. When looking for the tract on a plat, however, one has first to reverse the description, finding first the meridian, then the range, then the township, then the section, necessitating an awkward mental transposition. It has been thought more convenient to the reader to arrange tract descriptions in the latter order, particularly since the order is the normal one by which a computer

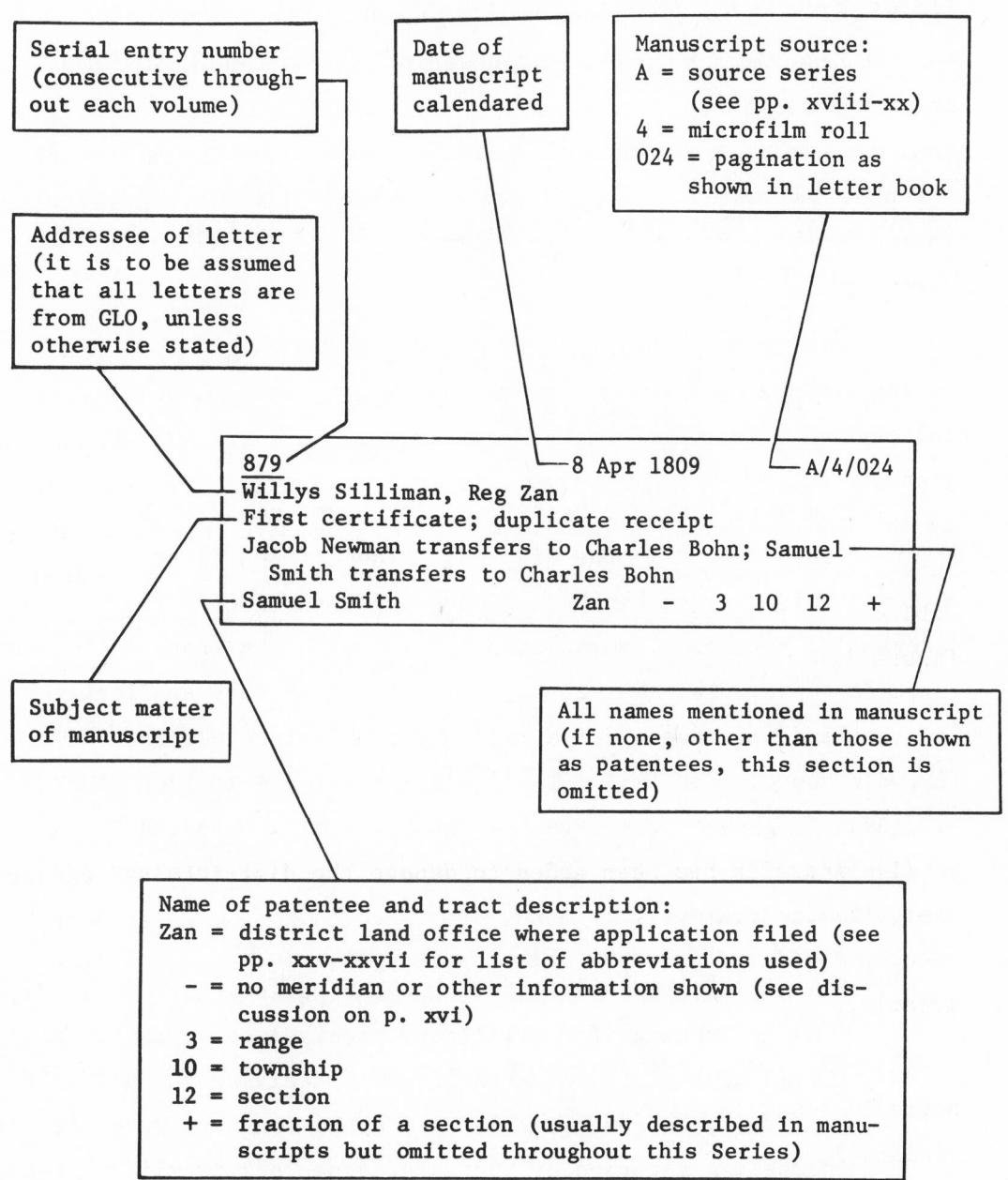

Serial entry number
(consecutive through-
out each volume)

Date of
manuscript
calendared

Manuscript source:
A = source series
    (see pp. xviii-xx)
4 = microfilm roll
024 = pagination as
    shown in letter book

Addressee of letter
(it is to be assumed
that all letters are
from GLO, unless
otherwise stated)

879   8 Apr 1809   A/4/024
Willys Silliman, Reg Zan
First certificate; duplicate receipt
Jacob Newman transfers to Charles Bohn; Samuel
    Smith transfers to Charles Bohn
Samuel Smith   Zan   -   3 10 12   +

Subject matter
of manuscript

All names mentioned in manuscript
(if none, other than those shown
as patentees, this section is
omitted)

Name of patentee and tract description:
Zan = district land office where application filed (see
    pp. xxv-xxvii for list of abbreviations used)
  - = no meridian or other information shown (see dis-
    cussion on p. xvi)
  3 = range
 10 = township
 12 = section
  + = fraction of a section (usually described in manu-
    scripts but omitted throughout this Series)

Fig. 1. Serial entry format

would read such descriptions from a punched card. Thus, the
Federal Land Series shows tract descriptions in the following
manner:

District Land Office Where Application Papers Were Filed	Meridian	Range	Township	Section	Fraction or Lot
Zan	Mil	1	1	3	9
Stu	–	2	3	6	–
Cin	EML	2	7	–	35
Cin	Pre	4	2	8	+
Chl	WS	21	11	34	+

Since meridians, or base lines, were not used in the earliest
descriptions (except in the Cincinnati land office district), the
meridian column above has been frequently used to note the survey
(Langham's, Matthew's, Worthington's) in which the tract is located
(example above: Chl WS 21 11 34 +) or whether application
for the land was made under a military bounty-land warrant *Mil*
(example above: Zan Mil 1 1 3 9) or pre-emption right
Pre (example above: Cin Pre 4 2 8 +). Genealogists, in
particular, will find the *Mil* and *Pre* notations of interest for
the following reasons:

¶ The *Mil* notation indicates that the patentee received his
land in exchange for a military bounty-land warrant. Although most of these warrants were freely bought and sold
and, thus, were frequently used by persons who were not
themselves veterans of the wars, genealogists will want to
consider the possibility that patentees of interest may
have been veterans. If so, a military service record
should be sought elsewhere in the National Archives
collections.

¶ The *Pre* notation also has significance to genealogists. Patentees receiving land under pre-emption rights very likely were settlers on the land before the land was surveyed by the federal government. In the eyes of the government, they were considered "squatters" or "intruders," occasionally with solemn consequences (see serial entries 2524 and 2525, this volume, as cases in point). A *Pre* notation probably indicates settlement in Northwest Territory at an early date--very likely before the first decennial census was taken in the area. An exception to this occurs in the Cincinnati land office district, where claimants to land under deeds issued by John Cleeves Symmes were shown on the books of the federal government as having pre-emptive right to the land, when Judge Symmes' tangled affairs were taken over by the government.

(3) Normally, tract descriptions specify the fraction of a section (as, for example, the north half of the southeast quarter of section 3, etc.). These fractional parts of a section have been indicated in the *Federal Land Series* simply by a plus sign (+) in the fraction or lot column in order to conserve space and to minimize transcription errors. Persons who have found the section in question can refer to the original microfilm source for the fractional description, if needed. Copies of the microfilm rolls are readily available from the National Archives.

Frequently, a number will be shown in the fraction or lot column of a tract description. If the land described is within the U.S. Military District of Ohio or within the Refugee Tract, the number indicates a lot number. A number placed in this column in any other land office district indicates a complete, but fractional, section--one which, because of natural topographic features (usually a river), is less than the standard 640 acres in size. Under the original land laws, such fractional sections could only be purchased by persons buying an adjacent full section.

Sources Calendared in This Volume

The material calendared in this volume of the *Federal Land Series* covers a period from about 1788 to 1810. There is much material not included, notably the voluminous records of federal bounty-land warrants and the grants made by several of the original thirteen states, particularly Virginia. Because of their length and similarity of subject matter, these records will be presented together in a forthcoming second volume. Another group of records from this early period which has not been analyzed herein are the records of early land companies and the grantees under John Cleeves Symmes. The records, likewise, must await another volume.

In this volume of the *Federal Land Series* the following sources are calendared and indexed:

Source	Serial Entries	Title
A	1 - 1200	National Archives Record Group 49, "Records of the Bureau of Land Management," *Miscellaneous Letters Sent by the General Land Office* (National Archives microcopy 25), rolls 3 [completely calendared] and 4 [partially calendared]. Roll 3 begins a subseries of letter books mainly, but not exclusively, devoted to letters transmitting land patents.
	1201 - 2109	_____, roll 1 [completely calendared]. This roll (with roll 2) constitutes a subseries of letter books concerning matters of general policy in the administration of the public land policy.

Source	Serial Entries	Title
B	2110 - 2380	National Archives Record Group 49, "Records of the Bureau of Land Management," *Letters Sent by the General Land Office to Surveyors General* (National Archives microcopy 27), roll 1 [completely calendared].
C	2381 - 2520	National Archives Record Group 56, "General Records of the Department of the Treasury," *Letters Sent by the Secretary of the Treasury Relating to Public Lands ("N" Series)* (National Archives microcopy M-733), roll 1 [partially calendared].
D	2521 - 2526	National Archives Record Group 360, "Records of the Continental Congress and the Constitutional Convention," *Papers of the Continental Congress, 1774-1789,* selections from several microfilm rolls, as noted in the serial entries.
E	2527	Pittsburgh, Pennsylvania. Carnegie Library of Pittsburgh. Register of the Pittsburgh land sale of 24 October through 3 December 1796, to be found among the personal papers of General John Nevill(e).
F	2528 - 2536	*A Compilation of Laws, Treaties, Resolutions, and Ordinances of the General and State Government which Relate to Lands in the State of Ohio.* Columbus, O.: Printed

Source	Serial Entries	Title
		by G. Nashee, State Printer, 1825. Reproduced from this work is the list of "Connecticut Sufferers" whose property was destroyed by British troops during the Revolutionary War. Indemnification was in the form of rights to land in the Connecticut Western Reserve of Ohio.
G	2537 - 2543	Urbana, Illinois. University of Illinois. Illinois Historical Survey. Richard Clough Anderson Collection. The lists of Canadian and Nova Scotian refugee grants will be found toward the end of an unpaginated ledger, entitled "Benj. Hough's Book," which has been accessioned as Ledger 11 in the Collection. (Benjamin Hough was a surveyor in the U.S. Military District of Ohio and elsewhere; see the name index, this volume, for references to him.) See also Clifford Neal Smith, "The Revolutionary War Refugees from Canada and Nova Scotia," *National Genealogical Society Quarterly*, LIX (1971), 266-273.
H	2544 - 2643	*Laws, Treaties, and Other Documents Having Operation and Respect to the Public Lands. Collected and Arranged Pursuant to an Act of Congress Passed April 27, 1810.* Washington, [D.C.]: Roger C. Weightman, 1811. Both the Library of Congress and the Newberry Library, Chicago, have copies of this

rare book and it seems likely that copies
are to be found in other collections. No
further copies are listed in the Library
of Congress union catalog, however.

Locating Tract Citations

Included in this first volume of the *Federal Land Series*
is a tract map of the lower two-thirds of the state of Ohio
(plates 1, 2, and 3). Some explanation of their use is necessary because of the changing manner in which tracts were sold
and the land offices from which they were sold.

Plate 1 covers the eastern and southeastern part of Ohio,
particularly the original Seven Ranges, surveyed shortly after
the American Revolution. In the Tract Index the auction sales
of land in this area are shown under Seven Ranges (7Rg); after
the establishment of the federal land system all other tracts
in the area were sold through the Steubenville land office,
and are so indexed. Thus it is that tract descriptions under
7Rg and *Stu* pertain to tracts in the same general area. (Note,
however, that the Steubenville land office also sold land in
ranges above the seventh.)

The upper portion of the plate includes the eastern portion (ranges 1 through 9) of the U.S. Military District. Some
of the land on the Military District was sold in large tracts
directly from Washington and these sales will be recorded in
volume 2 of the *Federal Land Series*; smaller tracts were sold
through the Zanesville land office. As a consequence, researchers will note that tract descriptions for the Military District
may be listed under *Mil* or *Zan* prefixes in the Tract Index.

Similarly, the southern portion of plate 1 includes part
of the Marietta land office district. To complicate matters,
Marietta also sold some land in an area later covered by the

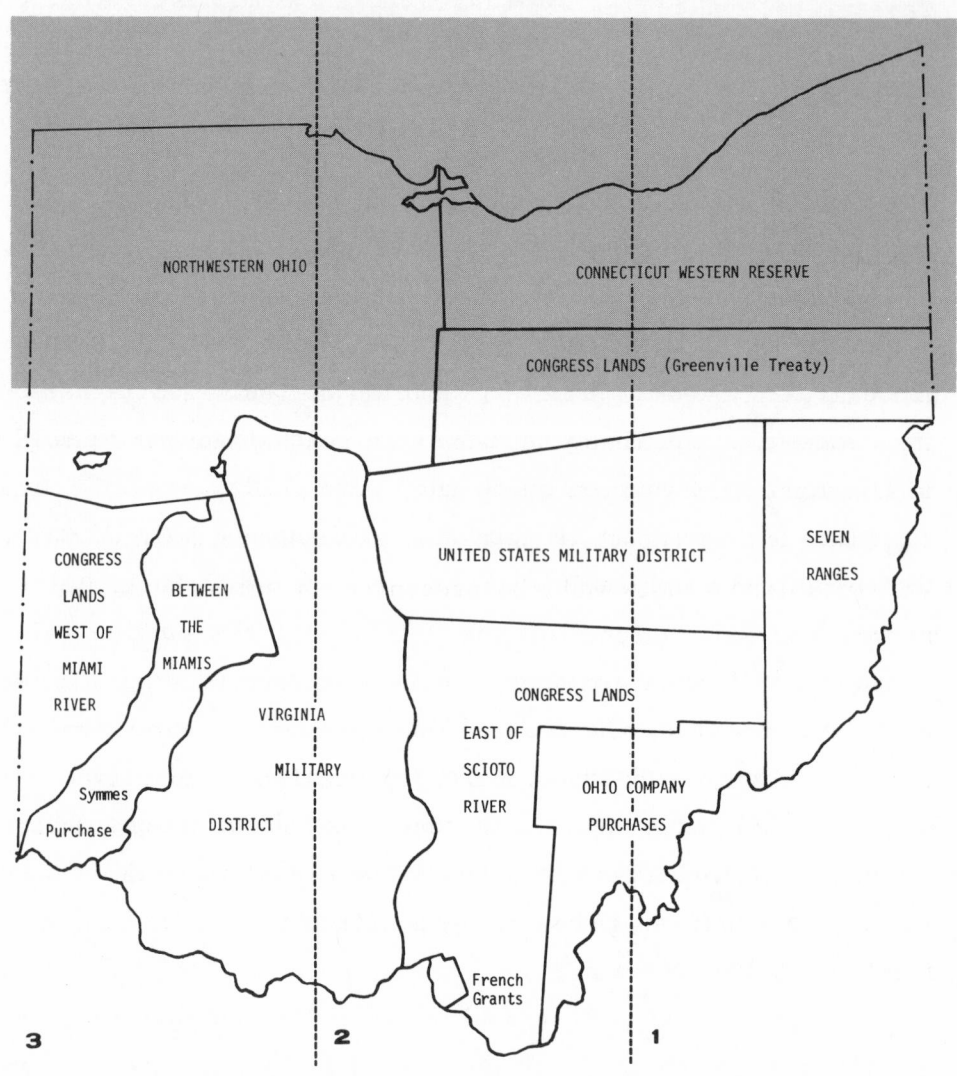

Orientation map of Ohio: Details of the areas
numbered 1-3 are the three plates inserted elsewhere. Shaded area indicates the part of the
state of Ohio that is not shown on the plates.

Zanesville land office district—cause for a jurisdictional dispute between the Registers of the Marietta and Zanesville land offices.

Plate 2 covers central and south-central Ohio, continuing the U.S. Military District and Zanesville land office district in the northern portion and the Marietta land office district in the southeastern portion of the plate. In addition, the plate includes the Chillicothe land office district. A large portion of the central and southwestern part of the land shown in the plate pertains to the Virginia Military District of Ohio, not covered in volume 1 of the *Federal Land Series*. (It is expected that some material pertaining to the Virginia land grants will be presented in volume 2 of the Series.)

Plate 3 covers western and southwestern Ohio, including the bulk of the Cincinnati land office district tract citations. The area west of the Great Miami River is also included. In Cincinnati district tract citations the designations *EML* and *WML* are often included. They refer to a meridian line drawn through the middle of fractional range II, as shown on the plate.[1]

---

[1]Ohio Cooperative Topographic Survey, *Original Ohio Land Subdivisions*, volume 3 (Ohio State Reformatory Press, 1925), p.74. The complications of tract designations in the Cincinnati land office district are best described in chapter 6 of this publication, to which the researcher will wish to refer for further information.

Abbreviations

Can   Canton (Ohio) land office district

Chl   Chillicothe (Ohio) land office district

Cin   Cincinnati (Ohio) land office district

Det   Detroit (Michigan) land office district

E   East

EML   East Meridian Line; used in Cin tract descriptions only

EOr   East Orleans land office district; office located at New Orleans

EPR   East Pearl River land office district; office located at Fort St. Stephen

frac   Fraction; fractional section

GLO   General Land Office, Washington, D.C.; some early correspondence included in GLO files is actually that of the Secretary of the U.S. Treasury, of which the GLO became a dependency

Jef   Jeffersonville (Indiana) land office district; see also Vin

Kas   Kaskaskia (Illinois) land office district

LS   Langham's Survey;   this could also refer to Ludlow's Survey in some instances, but no distinction was made in the correspondence

LO   District land office

Mar   Marietta (Ohio) land office district;   see also Zan

Mil   U.S. Military District of Ohio, if appearing in the land office column of a tract description;   if appearing in the meridian column of a tract description, it indicates that the tract was obtained under a military bounty land warrant

MR   Miami rivers;   Miami Reserve;   between the two Miami rivers

MS   Matthew's Survey

N   North

NA   National Archives, Washington, D.C.

Nas   Nashville (Tennessee) land office district, covering land in Mississippi Territory

+   Plus sign in tract description indicates fraction of a section

Pre   Pre-emption;   claimed under pre-emption right

Rec   Receiver of public monies, the official having the responsibility for accepting payments for land;   each land office had such an official

Ref   Canadian and Nova Scotian Refugee Tract (Ohio)

Reg   Register, the official in charge of a district land office

Rg   Range

S   South

Sec   Section (usually 640 acres)

SecTreas   Secretary of the U.S. Treasury

7Rg	Seven Ranges, a large tract of land in Ohio near the Pennsylvania border sold at public auction in New York, Pittsburgh, and Philadelphia in 1788 and 1796; later sales in the tract are shown under Stu
SG	Surveyor General of the United States
Stu	Steubenville (Ohio) land office district; see also 7Rg
Twp	Township
Unk	Unknown; used where land office district could not be determined from context or addressee of letter; researchers can often determine from other evidence (such as cross-indexed names) the probable land office where tract application was made
Vin	Vincennes (Indiana) land office district; note that before the establishment of Jef, the Vincennes district land office recorded all patent applications in Indiana Territory, including those for lands later assigned to Jef
W	West
War	Warrant; usually a military bounty land warrant
WML	West Meridian Line; used in Cin tract descriptions only
WOr	West Orleans land office district; office located at Opelousas
WPR	West Pearl River land office district; office located at Washington, Mississippi Territory
WS	Worthington's Survey
Zan	Zanesville (Ohio) land office district; before the establishment of Zan, applications for land in this district were accepted at Mar

CALENDAR OF
ARCHIVAL MATERIAL

<u>1</u>   7 Jan 1802   A/3/001
SecTreas
Payment for land in stock of U.S. stated by Com-
  missioner of Loans, State of Pennsylvania
Jacob Burnet of Cin.

<u>2</u>   3 Feb 1802   A/3/002
Thomas Worthington, Reg Chl
Correction of errors
John Nealey; Abraham Miller; John Shoemaker;
  Solomon Cox.

<u>3</u>   8 Mar 1802   A/3/002
Zaccheus Biggs, Rec Stu
Land payments
Zaccheus A. Beatty; John McConnell.

<u>4</u>   24 Mar 1802   A/3/002
James Ross
Payment for Stu lands
Bezaliel Wells.

<u>5</u>   6 Apr 1802   A/3/003
Albert Gallatin, SecTreas
Overpayment for Cin lands
Major David Ziegler.

<u>6</u>   8 May 1802   A/3/004
Rufus Putnam, SG
Plat of portion of Mar district
-- Mathers and Levi Whipple

Mar	- 14	16	12	-
Mar	- 14	12	12	-
Mar	- 13	12	-	+

<u>7</u>   12 Jun 1802   A/3/005
Albert Gallatin, SecTreas
Canadian and Nova Scotian refugees; plat of Chl
  township 5, range 22; Matthew's survey; Langham's survey
-- Van Meter and -- Branson, of Hardy County, Virginia

Edward Faulkner	Chl	- 22	5	1	-
Martha Walker	Chl	- 22	5	2	-
Martha Walker	Chl	- 22	5	3	-
John Starr	Chl	- 22	5	4	-
John Starr	Chl	- 22	5	5	-
Lt. Col. -- Bradford	Chl	- 22	5	6	-
John Halsted	Chl	- 22	5	9	-
Martha Walker	Chl	- 22	5	10	-
I. Van Meter & Branson	Chl	- 22	5	7	-
-- Massey & -- McCoy					
(of Chl)	Chl	- 22	5	15	-
John Derush (of Ross					
County)	Chl	- 22	5	7	-

<u>8</u>   13 May 1801   A/3/009
No addressee
Receipt of money
Isaac Van Meter and Lyonel Branson, of Hardy Coun-
  ty, Virginia.

<u>9</u>   3 Oct 1801   A/3/009
No addressee

Receipt of money
Henry Massie & James McCoy of Chl.

<u>10</u>   12 Mar 1802   A/3/009
No addressee
Receipt of money
John Derush of Ross County.

<u>11</u>   18 Jun 1802   A/3/009
Rufus Putnam, SG
Error in map Chl district

	Chl	- 22	all	-	-
	Chl	- 21	all	-	-

<u>12</u>   18 Jun 1802   A/3/010
Thomas Worthington, Reg Chl
Error in map Chl district

	Chl	- 22	all	-	-
	Chl	- 21	all	-	-

<u>13</u>   7 Jul 1802   A/3/010
Zaccheus Biggs, Rec Stu
Payment in U.S. stock
Thomas McEwen; James Johnston.

<u>14</u>   10 Jul 1802   A/3/012
Thomas Worthington, Reg Chl
Final certificates
Henry Myer; David Wright; Conrad Stump; Solo-
  mon Cox; William Ward.

<u>15</u>   27 Jul 1802   A/3/012
David Hoge, Reg Stu
Land transactions
Bazaliel Wells; James Johnston; James Ross;
  John Crumbacher; John Neidigh.

<u>16</u>   4 Aug 1802   A/3/016
Albert Gallatin, SecTreas
Transmittal of complaint
Mr. -- Boudinot.

<u>17</u>   12 Aug 1802   A/3/016
Richard C. Anderson, Surveyor of Virginia Military
  Lands, Louisville, Kentucky
Virginia Military District of Ohio.

<u>18</u>   13 Aug 1802   A/3/018
Abraham Plummer, Frederickstown, Maryland
Patent to be forwarded to President's residence
  in Virginia for signature.

<u>19</u>   6 Dec 1802   A/3/020
Zaccheus A. Beatty, Stu
Policy regarding assignees of original purchasers
William Satterthwaite,

assignee of James John-					
son	Stu	- 3	7	13	-

<u>20</u>   15 Dec 1802   A/3/020
David Hoge, Reg Stu

Richard Ridgeway	Stu	- 4	8	4	-
Richard Ridgeway	Stu	- 4	8	11	-

21   7 Jan 1803   A/3/022
Albert Gallatin, SecTreas
Canadian and Nova Scotian refugees
John Derush; Mr. -- Mills, attorney for refugees;
  Robert Culbertson; Lucas Sullivant; John Blair
Not stated   Ch1 - 22   5   7   -

22   Undated   A/3/024
Statement
Isaac Van Meter & Lyonel
  Branson   Ch1 - 22   4   2   -
Isaac Van Meter & Lyonel
  Branson   Ch1 - 22   5   7   -

23   19 Jan 1803   A/3/026
Rufus Putnam, SG
Land sales of J. C. Symmes and Associates.

24   17 Jan 1803   A/3/026
Thomas Worthington, Reg Ch1
Statement
William McCoy; John Derush
--   Ch1 - 21   9 19   -
--   Ch1 - 22   2   -   +

25   25 Jan 1803   A/3/028
SecTreas
Land sales of J. C. Symmes and Associates
Mr. -- Cadbury.

26   7 Apr 1803   A/3/030
Hon. Lucas Elmendorf
Answering query on behalf of constituents. Elmen-
  dorf to receive 4000 acres with certificates of
  100 acreas each in his name
David Hawkins
Jonathan Verry   Unk -   3   1   1   +
Thomas Smalley   Unk -   3   1   1   +
Isaac Beatley   Unk -   3   1   1   +

27   17 Mar 1803   A/3/030
Albert Gallatin, SecTreas
Lucas Elmendorf's 4000-acre grant; requests per-
  mission to grant patents of 100 acres each
David Hawkins; Peter Townsend.

28   9 Apr 1803   A/3/030
Albert Gallatin, SecTreas
Lucas Elmendorf grant?
--   Unk - 13   7   4   +
--   Unk - 13   7   1   +

29   No date   A/3/032
No addressee
Schedule, possibly of Lucas Elmendorf grant
Andrew Gregg; W. Dana; John Davenport; Lucas
  Elmendorf; Uriah Tracy; Elias B. Caldwell;
  Theodore Foster; Samuel Hambleton; John David-
  son; J. Fearing; J. Windgate; Charles McManas;
  James Hutton; Solomon P. Goodrich; Ezekiel
  Lovejoy; -- Ford; William McCloy; Isaac Pitt-
  man; Joshua Woodman.

30   12 Apr 1803   A/3/034
Albert Gallatin, SecTreas
Military District;   Society of United Brethren for
  Propagating the Gospel Among the Heathens;
  Gnadenhuetten; Salem; Schoenbrunn; Zane's
  grant; long schedule of vacant lands appended.

31   27 Apr 1803   A/3/038
Joseph Wood, Reg Mar
Increase Mathews; Levi Whipple; Rufus Putnam;
  John McIntire
--   Mar - 14 16   1   -

32   10 May 1803   A/3/039
David Hoge, Reg Stu
Land transaction
Henry Keller   Stu -   2 13 17   -
Henry Keller   Stu -   1   8 33   -

33   26 May 1803   A/3/039
Lucas Elmendorf
Elmendorf grant
John Davidson; John Clark.

34   16 Jul 1803   A/3/040
Jesse Spencer, Reg Ch1
Explains land patenting procedure.

35   18 Jul 1803   A/3/041
Jesse Spencer, Reg Ch1
Transmits patent
Charles Friend   Ch1 - 20 12 12   +

36   20 Jul 1803   A/3/042
Jesse Spencer, Reg Ch1
Transmits patents
Ludwick Bonsey   Ch1 - 23 15 23   +
Felix Renick & Benjamin
  Kerns   Ch1 - 21   7   5   +
Felix Renick & Benjamin
  Kerns   Ch1 - 21   7   6   +
Felix Renick & Benjamin
  Kerns   Ch1 - 21   7   7   -

37   9 Aug 1803   A/3/043
Stephen Thomas Cooper, York Town, Pennsylvania
Transmits patent
Stephen Thomas Cooper Stu - 21   7   7   -

38   29 Jul 1803   A/3/043
SecTreas
Letter from James Ross, Pittsburgh, copied; sale
  of public lands at Pittsburgh in October 1796;
  sale of public lands in New York
James Ross; Bazaliel Wells; Nathan McFarland,
  surveyor
Bazaliel Wells   Unk -   3   2 15   -
George Douglass   Unk -   3   2   9   -
Richard Platt   Unk -   3   2 14   -
James Ross   Unk -   3   2 15   -
Levi Whipple   Unk -   3   2   8   -
  [Probably tracts in Seven Ranges.]

<u>39</u>   9 Aug 1803   A/3/046
David Hoge, Reg Stu; Joseph Wood, Reg Mar
Instructions regarding fractional sections.

<u>40</u>   30 Sep 1803   A/3/048
Albert Gallatin, SecTreas
Discusses various discount policies in practice.

<u>41</u>   3 Oct 1803   A/3/050
David Hoge, Reg Stu
Transmits patent
Bezaliel Wells   Stu   -   2   4   20   -

<u>42</u>   - Oct 1803   A/3/051
SecTreas
Statement of land sales in the various disctricts
   from opening date to 31 Aug 1803.

<u>43</u>   18 Oct 1803   A/3/053
Zaccheus Biggs, Rec Stu (at Zan)
Military land warrants.

<u>44</u>   26 Oct 1803   A/3/054
No addressee
Certificate incorrect
Samuel Dick.

<u>45</u>   2 Nov 1803   A/3/054
SecTreas (from David Hoge, Reg Stu)
Reporting sales
--   Stu   -   1   2   33   -
--   Stu   -   4   7   5   -
--   Stu   -   2   5   23   -
--   Stu   -   4   9   8   -

<u>46</u>   17 Nov 1803   A/3/055
David Hoge, Reg Stu
Explains errors; Pittsburgh land sale of 1796;
   incomplete sales and reversion to U.S.
--   Stu   -   1   2   33   -
--   Stu   -   1   2   5   -
--   Stu   -   2   5   23   -
--   Stu   -   4   7   8   -

<u>47</u>   17 Nov 1803   A/3/056
David Hoge, Reg Stu
Transmits patents
Bazaliel Wells   Stu   -   3   11   19   -
James Ross   Stu   -   3   7   20   -

<u>48</u>   23 Nov 1803   A/3/057
Zaccheus Biggs, Rec Stu
Discount calculation
Henry Keller.

<u>49</u>   14 Dec 1803   A/3/058
J. Ludlow
Mentions Mr. -- Miller.

<u>50</u>   13 Dec 1803   A/3/058
SecTreas
Statement of account
Daniel Miller   Cin   -   6   2   30   -

<u>51</u>   14 Dec 1803   A/3/060
James Findlay, Rec Cin
Requests evidence of repayment
James Ross   Cin   -   3   7   20   -
B. Wells   Cin   -   3   11   19   -

<u>52</u>   29 Dec 1803   A/3/061
Zaccheus Biggs, Rec Stu
Underpayment
Noah Linsley, assignee of Noah Zane
Noah Linsley   Stu   -   19   15   17   -

<u>53</u>   5 Jan 1804   A/3/063
Thomas Tudor Tucker, SecTreas
Application requested
Jeremiah French   Cin   -   5   2   1   +

<u>54</u>   6 Feb 1804   A/3/064
David Meriwether, U.S. Representative
Ensign John Harding Foster of Virginia Line does
   not appear in list of military land warrants.

<u>55</u>   9 Feb 1804   A/3/064
David Hoge, Reg Stu
Underpayment (see also letter which follows on
   microfilm)
Joseph Stier   Stu   -   6   9   8   -

<u>56</u>   20 Feb 1804   A/3/066
Stephen Wooley & Daniel Miller
Transmits patents
J. Ludlow
Stephen Wooley & Daniel
   Miller   Unk   -   6   2   30   -

<u>57</u>   28 Feb 1804   A/3/066
No addressee
Policy statement regarding apportionment and cal-
   culation of surplus pre-emption lands.

<u>58</u>   1 Mar 1804   A/3/067
Charles Killgore, Reg Cin
Error in account (see also letter which follows
   on microfilm)
John Roads   Cin   -   5   1   -   +
John Roads   Cin   -   4   3   22   +

<u>59</u>   15 Mar 1804   A/3/070
Elias Boudinot, Philadelphia
Statement of account
Jonathan Dayton, U.S. Representative.

<u>60</u>   20 Mar 1804   A/3/072
Jonathan Dayton
Boudinot accounts
Elias Boudinot.

<u>61</u>   19 Mar 1804   A/3/072
James Findlay, Rec Cin
Boudinot accounts
Elias Boudinot.

<u>62</u>   29 Mar 1804   A/3/075
Zaccheus Biggs, Rec Stu
Computation of discount
William Rowls   Stu - 1 7 23 -

<u>63</u>   30 Mar 1804   A/3/077
Thomas Worthington, Reg Chl
Military land warrants
Noah Zane; John Rounsavell "late a soldier of the
  New Jersey line"; Robert Smiley "late a soldier
  in the New Jersey line"; George Beymer; Ezekial
  Tophand "late a soldier in the Connecticut Line";
  John Welch "late a soldier in the Maryland Line".

<u>64</u>   30 Mary 1804   A/3/079
Noah Zane, Zanesville, Ohio
Lots can be located only in the names of original
  warrant holders; Warrant 8684, John Rounsavell
  of New Jersey Line; Warrant 8724, Robert Smiley
  of New Jersey Line
--   Mil - 9 1 - +

<u>65</u>   1 Apr 1804   A/3/079
David Thomas, Salem, New York
Land must be registered in name of original mili-
  tary warrant holder, except when assignee can
  locate 4000 acres
Warrant 7759, Joseph McCracken.

<u>66</u>   1 Apr 1804   A/3/080
William Kennedy, Washington, North Carolina
Same information as in entry 65 above
Military land warrant 4351, Anthony Dyer.

<u>67</u>   1 Apr 1804   A/3/081
Hon. -- Van Horne
Same information as in entry 65 above
Military land warrant 4078, Origen Eaton, "late a
  private in the Massachusetts Line"; Military
  land warrant 9537, Evan Stolt, "late a soldier
  in the Pennsylvania Line."

<u>68</u>   1 Apr 1804   A/3/082
John Hanna, Harrisburg, Pennsylvania
Same information as in entry 65 above
Old military land warrant 10,621, Samuel Berryhill;
  Henry Weaver, "a soldier in the late Pennsylvania
  Line."

<u>69</u>   1 Apr 1804   A/3/083
Israel Smith, Rutland, Vermont
Same information as in entry 65 above
Old military land warrant 3656, William Woodward;
  Richard Barnard "late a soldier in the Massachu-
  setts Line."

<u>70</u>   1 May 1804   A/3/085
George Beemer
Same information as in entry 65 above
Anthony Miller; Military land warrant 6538, Ezek-
  ial Tophand, "late a soldier of the Connecticut
  Line"; Military land warrant 11,829, John Welch
  of the Maryland Line
George Beemer   Mil - 2 3 4 +
George Beemer   Mil - 2 3 4 +

<u>71</u>   3 May 1804   A/3/086
T. M. Thompson, Lancaster, Pennsylvania
Same information as in entry 65 above; suggests
  he collect enough warrants to cover 4000 acres;
  "I am very much disposed to serve my friends;
  and your introduction to me, altho' not person-
  ally known, by your Friend Mr. Miller, places
  you among the number."

<u>72</u>   27 Mar 1804   A/3/087
No addressee
Policy letter from SecTreas regarding construction
  of Act of 19 Mar 1804 respecting the location of
  military land warrants.

<u>73</u>   26 May 1804   A/3/088
George Beemer, Wheeling, Virginia
Military land warrants 6538 and 11,829; William
  Talbot, assignee of heirs of Nathaniel Richy
  (Talbot left instructions to send patent to him
  at Mar)
George Beemer   Mil - 2 3 4 +
George Beemer   Mil - 2 2 3 -

<u>74</u>   29 May 1804   A/3/089
Albert Gallatin
Calculation of payment on newly discovered frac-
  tion
Bazaliel Wells   Mar - 3 2 8 -

<u>75</u>   29 May 1804   A/3/090
Albert Gallatin
Identification of "newly discovered" land tracts;
  land sale at New York, 20 Mar 1788
George Douglass   Mar - 3 2 9 -
Richard Platt   Mar - 3 2 14 -
B. Wells   Mar - 3 2 15 -

<u>76</u>   26 Mar 1804   A/3/091
SecTreas
Interpretation of Act of 26 Mar 1804
Elias Boudinot.

<u>77</u>   1 Jun 1804   A/3/093
Hon. P. V. Cortlandt, New York
Reissuance of military land warrant
Captain Mason Wattles.

<u>78</u>   1 Jun 1804   A/3/094
James Findlay, Rec Cin
Interpretation of Act of 26 Mar 1804
Elias Boudinot.

<u>79</u>   1 Jun 1804   A/3/094
Zaccheus Biggs, Rec Stu
Cover letter
Joshua Budd, original purchaser, sold to Martin &
  Renaman by deed dated 14 Nov 1803
Simon Martin & William
  Renaman   Stu - 1 9 3 -

<u>80</u>   8 Jun 1804   A/3/095
James Madison
Certificate that no warrant for 200 acres land had
  been issued to Isaac Hite, lieutenant, Virginia.

81   16 Jun 1804   A/3/096
Andrew Gregg, Aaronsburg, Pennsylvania
Delay in issuing patents
Evan Holt; Mr. -- Vanhorne; Rev. -- Wiley.

82   16 Jun 1804   A/3/097
Col. -- Armstrong, Cin
Application for Virginia Reservation lands to be
   made to Department of State, "this department
   having no cognizance therein"
Military land warrants 155 & 156, Mr. -- Vanhorne.

83   6 Jul 1804   A/3/097
Alexander Graydon, Harrisburg, Pennsylvania
Answers queries regarding certain land warrants
   and assignments thereof
Andrew Forrest; William Coleman; James Miles;
   Samuel C. Vance.

84   13 July 1804   A/3/098
William Dickson, Nashville, Tennessee
Assumes no personal responsibility for land war-
   rants received.

85   13 Jul 1804   A/3/098
Thomas Worthington, Reg Chl
Acknowledges receipt of an "original or new land
   land warrant"
William Lytle; William Dickson; land warrants
   84 and 2095.

86   13 Jul 1804   A/3/099
Richard Gernon, Philadelphia
Location to be made to holders of 4000 acres in
   military land warrants.

87   20 Jul 1804   A/3/099
Alexander Graydon, Harrisburg, Pennsylvania
Assignment of military land warrant 2576
Robert Finley for Alexander Graydon; James Miles;
   Arthur John O'Neill.

88   24 Jul 1804   A/3/100
Albert Gallatin
Method of computing interest on instalment payments
   under Act of 26 Mar 1804 (SecTreas answer copied
   in serial entry 101 below).

89   26 Jul 1803   A/3/103
Noah Zane, Wheeling, Virginia
Location of land
John Rounsavell; Robert Smiley.

90   30 Jul 1804   A/3/103
Albert Gallatin
Statement of sale of lands from 30 Sep 1803 to
   "period of latest return" for Stu, Cin, Chl, and
   Mar districts.

91   30 Jul 1804   A/3/104
T. M. Thompson, Lancaster, Pennsylvania
Warrant thought to be a forgery

Edward Armstrong "late a Lieutenant in one of the
   additional regiments commanded by Col. William
   Malcom;" Thomas Madding.

92   30 Jul 1804   A/3/105
Col. -- Armstrong, Cin
Transmits patents (Easton and Fowler had been
   soldiers)
Moses Easton   Cin - 15 8 4 +
Robert Fowler   Cin - 15 8 4 +

93   30 Jul 1804   A/3/105
William Kennedy, Washington, North Carolina
Transmits patent (Howard had been "a fife major
   in the late Army")
John Howard   Mil - 2 3 4 +

94   30 Jul 1804   A/3/106
George Beemer, Wheeling, Virginia
Transmits patents
Ezekial Tophand   Mil - 2 3 4 +
John Welch   Mil - 2 3 4 +

95   30 Jul 1804   A/3/106
Andrew Gregg, Aaronsburg, Pennsylvania
Transmits patent
Evan Holt   Mil - 15 7 4 +

96   30 Jul 1804   A/3/107
William Talbot, Mar
Transmits patent (Talbot was assignee of the heirs
   of Nathaniel Rich, "a soldier in the late army")
William Talbot   Mil - 2 2 3 +

97   1 Aug 1804   A/3/107
Charles Killgore, Reg Cin; James Findlay, Rec Cin
Deficiency in payments
John Hormel   Cin - 4 4 32 -
John Hormel   Cin - 4 4 33 -

98   1 Aug 1804   A/3/108
Jesse Spencer, Rec Chl
Closing of account
Henry Markle   Chl - 17 16 10 +

99   2 Aug 1804   A/3/110
David Hoge, Reg Stu
Closing of account
John Shanenfelt   Stu - 2 13 2 -

100   3 Aug 1804   A/3/111
Joseph Wood, Reg Mar
Discrepancy to be explained
Hooker & McCluney of Brooke County, Virginia;
   Peel of Washington County
Richard Hooker & William
   McCluney   Mar - 12 13 30 +
Truman Peel   Mar - 12 13 30 +

101   30 Jul 1804   A/3/112
Joseph Nourse, Reg of Treasury (from SecTreas)
Method of computing interest on instalment pay-
   ments; see serial entry 88 above.

102   6 Aug 1804   A/3/114
Charles Killgore, Reg Cin
Interpretation of Act of 26 Mar 1804; correction
  of calculations

Name						
Joab Comstock	Cin	-	-	2	8	-
David E. Wade	Cin	-	-	3	27	-
David E. Wade	Cin	-	-	3	26	+
David E. Wade	Cin	-	-	3	35	+
David E. Wade	Cin	-	-	3	36	+
Joab Comstock	Cin	-	-	2	9	+
Isaac Gildersleeve	Cin	-	-	2	14	-
Isaac Gildersleeve	Cin	-	-	2	23	+

103   6 Aug 1804   A/3/115
Jesse Spencer, Reg Chl
Interpretation of Act of 26 Mar 1804; correction
  of calculations

Name						
Abraham Ream	Chl	-	18	13	3	+
Frederick Overley	Chl	-	21	9	33	+
Jacob Berry	Chl	-	17	16	19	+

104   7 Aug 1804   A/3/118
Joseph Wood, Reg Mar; Benjamin Tupper, Rec Mar;
  David Hoge, Reg Stu; Zaccheus Biggs, Rec Stu
Interpretation of Act of 26 Mar 1804.

105   7 Aug 1804   A/3/118
Samuel Finley, Rec Chl
Interpretation of Act of 26 Mar 1804; correction
  of calculations.

106   7 Aug 1804   A/3/119
James Findlay, Rec Cin
Interpretation of Act of 26 Mar 1804; correction
  of computations.

107   16 Aug 1804   A/3/120
Charles Killgore, Reg Cin

Name						
James & Thomas Newton	Cin	E	2	6	33	+

108   16 Aug 1804   A/3/121
Richard Gernon, Philadelphia
Lists entire quarter townships (4000 acres) remain-
  ing free for selection, as follows:

-	-	16	7	2	-
-	-	16	7	4	-
-	-	15	7	3	-
-	-	11	8	1	-
-	-	11	6	1	-
-	-	10	1	2	-
-	-	8	9	3	-
-	-	8	7	3	-
-	-	7	4	2	-
-	-	6	2	1	-
-	-	5	9	3	-
-	-	5	7	1	-
-	-	5	3	3	-
-	-	4	4	3	-
-	-	3	8	4	-
-	-	3	7	1	-

109   16 Aug 1804   A/3/121
Albert Gallatin
Land office records in arrears due to subdivision
  into quarter sections, causing greatly in-
  creased business. Recommends hiring additional
clerk; summarizes business in arrears
Joshua J. Moore; Michael Nourse.

110   18 Mar 1804   A/3/122
Elias Boudinot, Philadelphia
Transmittal of certificate for pre-emption lands.

111   20 Aug 1804   A/3/123
Charles Killgore, Reg Cin
Transmits patent

Name						
Nathaniel Knotts	Cin	-	5	3	30	-

112   20 Aug 1804   A/3/123
David Hoge, Reg Stu
Transmits patents

Name						
Rudolph Bair	Stu	-	1	8	7	-
Henry Forney	Stu	-	1	8	10	-

113   20 Aug 1804   A/3/124
Henry Hilger, Myer's Town, Dauphin County, Penna.
Discusses misunderstood objection; "you are de-
  signated as 'Corporal Henry Hilger, of Hazen's
  Regiment'"; objection to warrant granted 24
  Jun 1793 "to Edward Osborn, assignee of 'Andrew
  Hilger, soldier in Kazin's Regiment'"

114   21 Aug 1804   A/3/124
David Hoge, Reg Stu
Transmits patents

Name						
John Adams	Stu	-	1	2	32	-
George Atkinson	Stu	-	4	11	27	-
Anthony Pricker	Stu	-	4	9	24	-

115   21 Aug 1804   A/3/125
Charles Killgore, Reg Cin
Transmits patents

Name						
Edmund & John Richardson	Cin	E	2	3	20	-
Jacob Miller	Cin	E	1	4	25	-
Oliver Smith	Cin	E	3	3	30	+

116   24 Aug 1804   A/3/125
Jesse Spencer, Reg Chl
Transmits patents

Name						
John Ewing	Chl	-	18	15	20	+
George Arnold	Chl	-	18	15	19	+
Ezekiel Morris	Chl	-	21*	10	4	+
Henry Huddle, Sr. & Jr.	Chl	-	17	17	17	-

*Worthington's survey

117   25 Aug 1804   A/3/126
Charles Killgore, Reg Cin
Transmits patents for pre-emption lands

Name						
John Hormel	Cin	-	4	4	32	-
John Hormel	Cin	-	4	4	33	-

118   29 Aug 1804   A/3/126
Joseph Wood, Reg Mar
Transmits patent

Name						
Bazaliel Wells	Mar	-	3	2	8	+

119   30 Aug 1804   A/3/126
Samuel Finley, Rec Chl
Overpayment
George Nigh

120   3 Sep 1804   A/3/127
Jesse Spencer, Reg Chl
Error noted [both paries assigned same tract];
   originally assigned to Jonathan Holmes

George Hoffman & H. Fullerton	Chl	MS	22	2	34	−

121   12 Sep 1804   A/3/128
Jesse Spencer, Reg Chl
Overpayment
George Nigh.

122   12 Sep 1804   A/3/128
Charles Killgore, Reg Cin
Overpayment
Isaac Gildersleeve.

123   13 Sep 1804   A/3/129
William McCluney, Brooke Court House, Virginia
Military land warrants 13,780 & 6,428 can only be
   located in a parcel of 4000 acres; ". . . had
   they been of the description of original land
   warrants they might have been located on the lots
   you have designated"; many such warrants submitted in same situation and "it is my intention
   if practicable to put them together. . . ."

124   13 Sep 1804   A/3/130
Zaccheus Biggs, Rec Stu
Claim for repayment of interest denied
Bazaliel Wells.

125   14 Sep 1804   A/3/130
Jesse Spencer, Reg Chl
Transmits patent

Henry Markle	Chl	−	17	16	10	+

126   14 Sep 1804   A/3/130
David Hoge, Reg Stu
Transmits patent

John Shanenfelt	Stu	−	2	13	2	−

127   18 Sep 1804   A/3/131
Albert Gallatin
Military land warrants to be located only in 4000-
   acre sections; warrants must be submitted before
   1 Apr 1805, or they are barred
David Jones; land warrant 16 for 803 acres to
   Sampson Davis, dated 10 Mar 1800, equivalent to
   military land warrant; lists quarter townships
   remaining free for selection [see serial entry
   108].

128   19 Sep 1804   A/3/132
Richard Gernon, Philadelphia
The 1300 acres in military land warrants submitted
   is insufficient; GLO hopes to obtain further
   warrants in order to make up required 4000-acre
   section.

129   24 Sep 1804   A/3/133
David Hoge, Reg Stu

Lists discrepancies wherein same tracts were
   sold to two different persons

Bazaliel Wells vs Henry Hare	Stu	−	3	11	2	+
Bazaliel Wells vs Henry Hare	Stu	−	3	13	14	+
Henry Aten vs Benjamin Hough	Stu	−	4	10	4	+
Bazaliel Wells vs John Campbell	Stu	−	1	4	31	+
Obadiah Jennings vs William Crawford	Stu	−	1	6	7	+

130   3 Oct 1804   A/3/134
Charles Killgore, Reg Cin
Transmits patents

John Chamberlain	Cin	EML	5	2	32	−
Jacob Kuns	Cin	EML	5	4	17	−
James Porter	Cin	EML	4	3	13	+
Ezekiel Hughes	Cin	EML	1	1	15	+
Ezekiel Hughes	Cin	EML	1	1	16	−
George Statler	Cin	EML	5	2	15	+
George Statler	Cin	EML	5	2	16	−

131   9 Oct 1804   A/3/134
Charles Killgore, Reg Cin
Transmits patents

George Sinks	Cin	EML	5	5	2	+
Joseph Ely	Cin	EML	5	1	5	−
Joseph Ely	Cin	EML	5	1	8	+

132   31 Oct 1804   A/3/135
Zaccheus Biggs, Rec Stu
Corrected statement of account

John Christmas	Stu	−	3	8	36	−

133   19 Nov 1804   A/3/137
Thomas McKean Thompson, Lancaster, Pennsylvania
Land warrant 35, in name of Edward Armstrong, for
   200 acres; selection of land to be made.

134   19 Nov 1804   A/3/137
David Hoge, Reg Stu
Overpayment; patent to issue
John Taggert.

135   19 Nov 1804   A/3/137
Zaccheus Biggs, Rec Stu
Correction of account

John Taggert	Stu	−	1	8	25	−

136   4 Dec 1804   A/3/138
David Hoge, Reg Stu
Transmits patents

John Taggert	Stu	−	1	8	25	−
Emanuel Dixon	Stu	−	1	8	19	−
William Hogg	Stu	−	2	9	11	−

137   5 Dec 1804   A/3/138
Charles Killgore, Reg Cin
Transmits patent

Isaac Gildersleeve	Cin	EML	3	2	14	−
Isaac Gildersleeve	Cin	EML	3	2	23	+

138   5 Dec 1804   A/3/138
Hon. Erastus Root, U.S. House of Representatives
Canadian & Nova Scotian refugees; Act of 18 Feb
1801, referred to Col. Thomas Worthington
Heirs of Simon Chester.

139   6 Dec 1804   A/3/139
Charles Killgore, Reg Cin
Transmits duplicate patent
Nathaniel Knotts.

140   6 Dec 1804   A/3/139
Albert Gallatin, SecTreas
Interpretation of Act of 1 Jun 1796 regarding right
& mode of locating military land warrants; Act
of 2 Mar 1799; Act of 11 Feb 1800; Act of 1 Mar
1800; fractional townships on Scioto River and
Muskingum River; grant to Ebenezer Zane; Moravian settlements at Salem, Gnadenhutten, &
Schoenbrunn; Act of 26 Apr 1802; Act of 3 Mar
1803 allowing holders of new warrants to locate on lands reserved for original warrants;
distinction between old, or original, warrants
& new warrants discussed; David Jones, only
applicant to qualify for 4000-acre grant; in
an endorsement to this letter, Gallatin doubts
whether interpretation placed heretofore was
correct & directs that both old and new warrants
be admitted on equal footing.

141   12 Dec 1804   A/3/143
William Findlay, U.S. House of Representatives
Questions whether patents to be issued in name of
James McClurg (Findlay's constituent) or of Adam
Wallis
James McClurg; land warrant 10,734 to John Cook,
100 acres; land warrant 10,692 to William Al-
corn, 100 acres; both warrants assigned to Adam
Wallis.

142   12 Dec 1804   A/3/143
Albert Gallatin, Sec Treas
Statement of facts concerning purchases of land in
Mar district by Increase Mathews, Levi Whipple &
Company; stock of United States
Mr. -- Silliman of Zanesville; R. Putnam (associ-
ated with Mathews & Whipple)

Increase Mathews & Levi Whipple	Mar	–	14	16	12	–
Increase Mathews & Levi Whipple	Mar	–	14	16	1	+
Increase Mathews & Levi Whipple	Mar	–	13	12	5	+
Increase Mathews & Levi Whipple	Mar	–	13	12	6	+
John McIntire	Mar	–	13	12	4	–
John McIntire	Mar	–	13	12	5	+
John McIntire	Mar	–	14	16	1	+

143   13 Dec 1804   A/3/146
Charles Killgore, Reg Cin
Transmits patent for land "between Great Miami
River and Virginia Reservation"

James Morehouse	Cin	–	4	2	10	+

144   20 Dec 1804   A/3/146
Charles Killgore, Reg Cin

Transmits patent

Henry Null (Nutt?)	Cin	–	5	2	10	+

145   21 Dec 1804   A/3/146
William McCluney, Brooke Court House, Virginia
Selection of 100-acre lots now possible; military
land warrants 13,780 & 6,428

William McCluney	Mil	–	2	3	4	3
William McCluney	Mil	–	2	3	4	19
William McCluney	Mil	–	2	3	4	20
William McCluney	Mil	–	2	3	4	21
William McCluney	Mil	–	2	3	4	28
William McCluney	Mil	–	3	1	2	3

146   21 Dec 1804   A/3/147
Hon. David Thomas, U.S. House of Representatives
Now possible to obtain separate patent for military land warrant 7759 to Jacob Spicer; patent cannot be issued to Joseph McCracken unless
warrant properly assigned by Spicer.

147   26 Dec 1804   A/3/148
Richard Gernon, Philadelphia
Now possible to issue patents for 100-acre lots
by submitting military land warrants.

148   29 Dec 1804   A/3/148
Hon. Israel Smith, U.S. Senate
Now possible to issue patent for old military
land warrant 3656, for 100 acres, to Richard
Barnard, assigned to William Woodward.

149   3 Jan 1805   A/3/149
Richard Gernon, Philadelphia
Location of land under thirteen military land
warrants; military land warrant 8821 to
Joseph Sloan not correctly assigned

Richard Gernon	Mil	–	2	6	1	3
Richard Gernon	Mil	–	2	6	1	4
Richard Gernon	Mil	–	2	6	1	6
Richard Gernon	Mil	–	11	8	1	6
Richard Gernon	Mil	–	11	8	1	7
Richard Gernon	Mil	–	11	8	1	8
Richard Gernon	Mil	–	11	8	1	9
Richard Gernon	Mil	–	11	8	1	10
Richard Gernon	Mil	–	11	8	1	11
Richard Gernon	Mil	–	11	8	1	22
Richard Gernon	Mil	–	11	8	1	23
Richard Gernon	Mil	–	11	8	1	24
Richard Gernon	Mil	–	11	8	1	25

150   7 Jan 1805   A/3/150
Hon. Samuel Tenney, U.S. House of Representatives
Transmits patent in name of Abiel Chandler, 100
acres "in consideration of military services,"
location not stated.

151   12 Jan 1805   A/3/150
Reverend David Jones, to be left at the Spread
Eagle Turnpike office, Lancaster Road, Penn.
John Matthews of Springfield, Muskingum County,
Ohio to arrive with survey.

152   22 Jan 1805   A/3/151
Historical statement (no addressee)

Letter from Benjamin Hough of Stu; Congressional Ordinance of 20 May 1785 regarding division of Western Territory into townships; beginning points defined; internal divisions within townships not provided for; rules for giving notice of sales; provision for alternate whole & fractional township sales; price; Congressional Ordinance of 21 Apr 1787; conditions of sale; Seven Ranges; -- Hutchins, Geographer; Sales at Pittsburgh; Act of 18 May 1796 requiring sales of remaining sections in Seven Ranges; four center sections of Seven Ranges to be reserved

William Bowne (1788 patent)	-	-	2	9	7	-
John Foulks (1788 patent)	-	-	2	9	1	-
Bazill Wells		-	-	1	4	34	-
Bazill Wells		-	-	1	4	35	-
Bazill Wells		-	-	1	4	36	-

153 22 Jan 1805 A/3/158
Albert Gallatin, SecTreas
Probably transmittal letter to preceding Historical Statement; Seven Ranges; Sales at New York & Pittsburgh
Benjamin Hough.

154 21 Jan 1805 A/3/158
Thomas M. Thompson, Lancaster, Pennsylvania
Warrant in favor of E. Armstrong, 50 acres, located as near Thompson's tract as could be found; patent delivered to Thompson's agent, Mr. Findley of U.S. House of Representatives; Maddin's claim

E. Armstrong	Mil	-	1	8	3	23
E. Armstrong	Mil	-	1	8	3	24

155 23 Jan 1805 A/3/158
Henry Hilger, Myer's Town, Dauphin County, Penna.
Hilger's claim to be the subject of a report to Congress.

156 23 Jan 1805 A/3/159
Thomas M. Thompson
Transmits sketch and notes on persons locating lots thereon

--	Mil	-	1	8	3	-

157 29 Jan 1805 A/3/159
Hon. G. Worthington, U.S. Senate
Military land warrant 11,219 issued to Philip Reed & Josiah Johnson, administrators of estate of William Foreman; patent must issue in name of heirs.

158 29 Jan 1805 A/3/160
Hon. W. Nelson, U.S. House of Representatives
Military land warrant 11,501 in name of Hugh McMullin; patent must issue in name of heirs.

159 31 Jan 1805 A/3/160
Charles Killgore, Reg Cin
Errors in returns for September 1804

William Hatfield	Cin	MR	5	3	29	+
Samuel Gregg	Cin	MR	5	2	8	+
Alexander Tillford	Cin	MR	7	2	11	+
Jonathan Crane	Cin	MR	4	3	8	+

James Findlay	Cin	MR	7	2	29	+
Robert Gilkey	Cin	EML	3	3	18	+
John Bigger	Cin	*	4	3	25	+
George Kuns	Cin	EML	5	4	19	+
George Kuns	Cin	EML	5	4	18	+
Benjamin Willson	Cin	EML	2	4	23	+
David Beatty	Cin	EML	2	4	33	+

*"Lying between Miami Rivers"

160 4 Feb 1805 A/3/162
David Hoge, Reg Stu
Error in computation of discount noted.

161 4 Feb 1805 A/3/162
Zaccheus Biggs, Rec Stu
Errors in accounts
Joseph Vantaw, assignee of Samuel Haines

Joseph Vantaw	Stu	-	4	8	17	-
Jonathan Taylor	Stu	-	6	9	32	-

162 9 Feb 1805 A/3/163
Charles Killgore, Reg Cin
Errors in accounts

Thomas Butler vs Charles Noffsinger	Cin	EML	5	3	14	+
James Vanderen	Cin	*	5	2	11	+

*"Between the Miami Rivers"

163 20 Feb 1805 A/3/164
Hon. Ebenezer Seaver, U.S. House of Representatives
Military land warrants 76 & 77 (grantees not named).

164 21 Feb 1805 A/3/165
Hon. J. A. Bayard, U.S. Senate
Old military land warrant 1473 (grantee not named).

165 22 Feb 1805 A/3/165
Charles Killgore, Reg Cin
Transmits final certificate

Matthew Swartzel	Cin	EML	5	2	20	-

166 22 Feb 1805 A/3/166
James Findlay, Rec Cin
Statement of account

Matthew Swartzel	Cin	EML	5	2	20	-

167 23 Feb 1805 A/3/166
Hon. Roger Nelson, Frederick Town, Maryland
Transmits patent to bounty land
Thomas McMullin.

168 28 Feb 1805 A/3/166
Charles Killgore, Reg Cin
Correction of accounts

--	Cin	-	4	3	35	+
--	Cin	-	3	4	35	+
--	Cin	-	3	5	12	+

169 2 Mar 1805 A/3/167
Hon. C. A. Rodney
Warrant 10,736 in name of Catharine Cochran, administratrix of estate of Daniel Cochran; patent must issue in name of heirs.

170   6 Mar 1805   A/3/167
Hon. William Blackledge, Newbern, North Carolina
Letter concerning John Matthews.

171   2 Apr 1805   A/3/168
Joseph Vance, Franklinton, Ohio
Military land warrant 9027 cannot be located on
   below described land
--   Unk - 16 2 4 -

172   2 Apr 1805   A/3/168
Hon. John Archier, Bellair, Hartford County, Md.
Transmits patent
Captain E. Prall.

173   5 Apr 1805   A/3/168
James Denny, Chl
Military land warrant 10,389 in favor of Richard
   Stack
Anthony Baucher; Anthony Weaver; George Green;
John Davidson, broker for military land war-
rants in Washington, D. C.

174   9 Apr 1805   A/3/169
Samuel Finley, Rec Chl
Land transactions
George Louder; Isaac Snyder.

175   9 Apr 1805   A/3/170
Jesse Spencer, Reg Chl
Transmits patents
C. Cagy   Chl - 17 18 30 +
A. Kelley   Chl - 20 8 9 +

176   10 Apr 1805   A/3/170
Samuel Finley, Rec Chl
Mathew's survey; U.S. stock
Isaac Van Horne   Chl - 22 4 4 -

177   17 Apr 1805   A/3/170
Reverend David Jones
Concerning patents
John Mathews (Mathew's survey); Owl Creek
Rev. David Jones (4000 a.) Unk - 15 7 3 -
Rev. David Jones   Unk - 17 7 1 16

178   10 May 1805   A/3/171
Rev. David Jones, to be left at the Spread Eagle
  Post Office, Turnpike Road, Delaware County,
  Pennsylvania
Transmits patents
David Jones (4000 acres) Unk - 15 7 3 -
David Jones   Unk - 17 7 1 16

179   11 May 1805   A/3/171
Hon. David Holmes, Rockingham Court House, Va.
Transmits patent
Lewis Boyer   Mil - 8 2 - 25

180   11 May 1805   A/3/171
Hon. Joseph Hiester, Reading, Pennsylvania
Transmits patent
Stephen Barth   Mil - 15 7 4 5

181   13 May 1805   A/3/172
William Bierce, Cornwall, Connecticut
Transmits patent
William Bierce   Mil - 3 1 1 18

182   13 May 1805   A/3/172
Messrs. Dundas & Hepburn, Alexandria, Va.
Transmits patents
Dundas & Hepburn   Mil - 15 1 3 31
Dundas & Hepburn   Mil - 15 1 3 32

183   13 May 1805   A/3/172
Peter Miller, Mar
Transmits patent
Peter Miller   Mil? - 11 9 4 24

184   25 May 1805   A/3/173
John Nicodemus, to be left at Post Office, Win-
  chester, Maryland
Transmits patent
John Nicodemus   Stu - 4 10 2 -

185   25 May 1805   A/3/173
Charles Killgore, Reg Cin
Transmits patent
Matthias Swartzell   Cin EML 5 2 20 -

186   17 Jun 1805   A/3/173
Joseph A. Wood, Reg Mar
Act of 26 Mar 1804
William Dusinberry.

187   12 Jul 1805   A/3/174
George Beymer, to be left at Post Office, Zanes-
  ville, Ohio
Military land warrant 2498, George Rice, captain;
  military land warrant 9949, John McNair, sol-
  dier; military land warrant 2445, William
  Walton, captain
Ezekiel Tophand; John Welch; Henry Mullin (pat-
  ents for these persons directed to Beymer at
  Wheeling)
William Walton   Mil - 2 2 3 15
William Walton   Mil - 2 2 3 16
William Walton   Mil - 2 2 3 17
George Rice   Mil - 2 2 3 5
George Rice   Mil - 2 2 3 6
George Rice   Mil - 2 2 3 7
John McNair   Mil - 3 1 1 10

188   18 July 1805   A/3/175
Certificate without addressee (see serial entry
  189 following)
Following military land warrants were located by
  Ebenezer Pierce but not assigned by original
  warrant holders:

Mil. Land War.	Issued to	Acres
1632	John Patterson	850
2141	Thaddeus Thompson	400
1929	Enos Stone	300
1352	Ebenezer Williams et al	300
2308	Ebenezer Williams	200
4801	Benjamin Winchell	100

Mil. Land War.	Issued to	Acres
2297	Robert Walker	300
1885	Thaddeus Thompson	300
2112	William Satterlee	300
2307	Charles Parsons	200
651	Azariah Eggleston	200
4858	Grove Pomeroy	100
1901	Ebenezer Smith	300

Ebenezer Pierce Mil - 18 4 1 -

189 18 July 1805 A/3/175

Certificate given to Moses Bysche, agent for the heirs of Ebenezer Pierce, deceased
Military land warrants, located by Ebenezer Pierce on 26 Mar 1800, not assigned by following original holders:

Mil. Land War.	Issued to	Acres
1348	Thomas Marshall	500
923	John Holdridge	200
4452	David Jewett	100
1898	Henry Sewall	300
6409	Jacob Rash	100
5066	Israel Smith	100
4506	Charles Kilburn	100
13876	William Woodward	100
2175	Isaiah Tiffany	200
4120	Samuel Phipps	100
4683	Peter Maynard	100
6323	Abraham Parker	100
5478	Pharez Barnard	100
4107	Thaddeus Frisbie	100
127	Ebenezer Ballatine	300
4627	Elijah Murray	100
4338	William Hawkins	100
5163	Samuel Tilley	100
519	Walter Dean	300
4580	Moses Ashley	100
4401	Zebulon Herrick	100
4478	Nathan Jackson	100
11	Moses Ashley	400
4576	Benjamin Winchell	100
3727	Benjamin Winchell	100

Ebenezer Pierce Mil - 17 4 2 -

190 22 July 1805 A/3/176

Charles Killgore, Reg Cin
Transmits patents & points out discrepancies
John Garrard

Jacob Kent vs Jacob Arnold	Cin	-	7	3	22	+
Not stated (discrepancy)	Cin	-	3	4	35	-
Not stated (discrepancy)	Cin	-	4	3	35	-
John Smith	Cin	-	6	2	7	+
Thomas Irwin	Cin	-	6	2	7	1
Samuel Beck	Cin	-	6	2	7	2
James Snodgrass	Cin	-	6	2	7	3
John Ewing	Cin	-	6	2	7	4
John Stetler	Cin	E	6	6	29	+
Joseph Bedle	Cin	E	6	6	32	+
Arthur Vandever	Cin	E	5	2	28	+
Joab Comstock	Cin	E	2	3	28	-
John Ozias	Cin	E	3	6	3	-
Joab Comstock	Cin	E	2	2	8	+
William Stuart	Cin	E	2	4	32	-

191 25 July 1805 A/3/178

Charles Killgore, Reg Cin
Transmits patents

John MacKaig	Cin	Pre	7	2	12	+
John Ozias	Cin	Pre	5	3	32	+
Edward Mitchell	Cin	Pre	5	3	24	+
Samuel Hueston	Cin	Pre	7	2	2	+
William C. Schenck	Cin	Pre	5	2	-	31
Benjamin Robbins	Cin	Pre	6	2	25	+
John Hains	Cin	Pre	5	4	-	31
John Hains	Cin	Pre	4	4	-	6
John Hains	Cin	Pre	5	3	1	+
John Patterson	Cin	Pre	7	2	14	+
Henry Yount	Cin	Pre	4	4	27	+
Asa Kitchell	Cin	EML	1	1	5	-
Culbertson Park	Cin	EML	2	3	4	-
David E. Wade	Cin	EML	2	3	27	25
David E. Wade	Cin	EML	2	3	27	26
David E. Wade	Cin	EML	2	3	27	35
David E. Wade	Cin	EML	2	3	27	36
Joshua Delaplaine	Cin	EML	2	4	25	+
Asa Kitchell	Cin	EML	1	2	32	-
William Barkalow	Cin	EML	5	2	33	34
William Barkalow	Cin	EML	5	1	-	3
William Barkalow	Cin	EML	5	1	-	4

192 25 Jul 1805 A/3/179

David Hoge, Reg Stu
Transmits patents

John Bever	Stu	-	1	6	26	-
Michael Castner	Stu	-	3	9	9	-
Joseph Applegate	Stu	-	4	9	1	-
Bezaliel Wells	Stu	-	2	4	14	+
John Bever	Stu	-	1	6	25	-
Elisha Teitors	Stu	-	1	8	14	-

193 25 Jul 1805 A/3/179

Jesse Spencer, Reg Chl
Transmits patents
Mathew's survey; Worthington's survey

William Gessell & Jacob Meissa	Chl	-	19	15	13	-
James Ramsey	Chl	-	21	11	18	+
Abraham Ream	Chl	-	18	13	3	+
Jacob Berry	Chl	-	17	16	19	+
H. Abrams & J. Spencer	Chl	-	19	15	26	+
John Barr	Chl	-	21	10	4	+
Henry Tomlinson	Chl	-	20	14	12	+
Andrew Hite	Chl	-	18	15	14	+
Edward Tiffin	Chl	-	20	8	-	31
Edward Tiffin	Chl	-	20	8	-	32
Edward Tiffin	Chl	-	21	7	-	17
Edward Tiffin	Chl	-	20	7	-	5
Edward Tiffin	Chl	-	20	7	-	6

194 29 Jul 1805 A/3/180

Jesse Spencer, Reg Chl
Discrepancy
George Nigh.

195 31 Jul 1805 A/3/180

James Ratckin, to be left at post office, Waterford, Loudon County, Virginia
Transmits patent

James Ratckin	Stu	-	5	7	24	-

196   31 Jul 1805   A/3/181
Joseph Wood, Reg Mar
Transmits patent.

William Dusinberry	Mar	-	15	17	29	-

197   31 Jul 1805   A/3/181
George Nigh, Hagar's Town, Washington County, Mary-
    land
Transmits patents
John Christy

George Nigh	Ch1	-	20	12	3	+
George Nigh	Ch1	-	20	12	4	+
John Hanna	Ch1	-	19	15	4	-

198   8 Aug 1805   A/3/182
David Hoge, Reg Stu
Transmits patent

William B. Randolph	Stu	-	3	14	19	+

199   12 Aug 1805   A/3/182
Willys Silliman, Reg Zan
Unappropriated portion of U.S. Military District
    attached to Zan district to carry designation
    "Military".

200   21 Aug 1805   A/3/183
Thomas Worthington, Reg Ch1
Guardian of child cannot have land placed in guard-
    ian's name. Guardian has no other right over real
    property of his ward than to put him in possession
    when of age of his estate
Vincent Redman, legal guardian of Winifred B. Bel-
    field, "only child & heir of John Belfield, de-
    ceased, late a Major in the Virginia Line during
    the late war. . . ."

201   22 Aug 1805   A/3/183
Hon. Edward Tiffin
Transmits patents

Edward Tiffin	Ch1	-	20	8	32	-
Edward Tiffin	Ch1	-	20	8	-	31
Edward Tiffin	Ch1	-	21	7	-	17
Edward Tiffin	Ch1	-	20	7	-	5
Edward Tiffin	Ch1	-	20	7	-	6

202   22 Aug 1805   A/3/184
Jesse Spencer, Reg Ch1
Col. -- Worthington; Henry Abrams; Mr. -- Win-
    ship.

203   22 Aug 1805   A/3/184
Jesse Spencer, Reg Ch1
Transmits patents

Jacob Showley	Ch1	-	19	16	14	+
Nicholas Bauder	Ch1	-	19	16	23	+
Andrew & George Pontius	Ch1	-	20	11	4	+

204   22 Aug 1805   A/3/185
Charles Killgore, Reg Cin
Transmits patent

Ebenezer Paddock	Cin	EML	5	3	36	-

205   27 Aug 1805   A/3/185
Albert Gallatin, SecTreas

Transmits forms for issuing certificates of
    U.S. Treasury, or the Loan Office, on the
    transfer of public stock in payment for
    land; submits prospective form for assig-
    nee of original holder of stock.

206   3 Sep 1805   A/3/187
Thomas Fawcett, to be left at post office at Win-
    chester, Frederick County, Virginia
Transmits patent

Thomas Fawcett	Stu	-	1	6	30	-

207   4 Sep 1805   A/3/187
David Hoge, Reg Stu
Transmits patents

Rudolph Bair	Stu	-	1	9	18	-
John Morris	Stu	-	2	11	10	-
Absalom Kent	Stu	-	6	12	1	-
Christopher Winter	Stu	-	6	9	25	-
Benjamin Dilworth	Stu	-	1	8	2	-
Daniel Slagle	Stu	-	6	17	14	-
Jacob Kuhn	Stu	-	4	8	14	-
Peter Shriver	Stu	-	1	9	34	-

208   4 Sep 1805   A/3/188
George Nigh, Hagar's Town, Washington County,
    Maryland
Transmits patents
John Christy

George Nigh	Ch1	-	20	12	3	+
George Nigh	Ch1	-	20	12	4	+
John Hanna	Ch1	-	19	15	4	-
George Nigh	Ch1	-	20	12	14	+

209   9 Sep 1805   A/3/188
George Nigh
Further regarding patent

George Nigh	Ch1	-	20	12	14	+

210   10 Sep 1805   A/3/188
Jesse Spencer, Reg Ch1
Transmits patent

John Christy	Ch1	-	20	13	34	-

211   11 Sep 1805   A/3/189
Charles Killgore, Reg Cin
Final certificate returned, because heirs are not
    specified by name
Heirs of Asa Harvey of Colerain [state not given].

212   21 Sep 1805   A/3/189
Albert Gallatin, SecTreas
Estimate of probable amount of funds accruing to
    State of Ohio from 1 Jul 1804 to 30 Jun 1805,
    under Act of 3 Mar 1803.

213   2 Oct 1805   A/3/190
Charles Killgore, Reg Cin
Returns final certificate for inclusion of heirs
    by name. Heir of age may hold shares in trust
    for minors
Heirs of Robert Ross.

214   9 Oct 1805   A/3/191
James Findlay, Rec Cin

Thomas McKinney	Cin	MR	12	1	-	32

215   15 Oct 1805   A/3/191
Albert Gallatin, SecTreas
Transmits letter of Obadiah Jennings, attorney for
    William & Thomas Thorn, requesting patent be
    issued to them by devise from father, Isaac
    Thorn, deceased, testament dated 26 Jun 1805

Isaac Thorn	Stu	–	4	9	14	–

216   16 Oct 1805   A/3/192
Jesse Spencer, Reg Chl
Land granted as mill-right pre-emption under Act
    of 10 May 1800

John Derush	Chl	–	22	5	7	+

217   5 Nov 1805   A/3/193
Charles Killgore, Reg Cin
Transmits patents

Joseph Dodds	Cin	Pre	6	1	14	+
Joseph Dodds	Cin	Pre	6	1	15	–
Israel Harris	Cin	Pre	5	3	22	+
Benjamin Robbins	Cin	Pre	5	3	30	+
Edmund Munger	Cin	Pre	5	2	4	+
Edmund Munger	Cin	Pre	5	2	5	+
Benjamin Van Cleve	Town of Dayton				8	
Benjamin Van Cleve	Town of Dayton				14	
Benjamin Van Cleve	Town of Dayton				46	
Benjamin Van Cleve	Town of Dayton				51	
Benjamin Van Cleve	Town of Dayton				52	
Benjamin Van Cleve	Town of Dayton				78	

218   6 Nov 1805   A/3/193
David Hoge, Reg Stu
U.S. stock in payment for lands by John Roth of
    York Town, Pennsylvania

John Roth	Stu	–	1	4	17	–

219   13 Nov 1805   A/3/194
David Hoge, Reg Stu
Transmits patents

Daniel Slagle	Stu	–	6	17	12	–	
Peter Oyster	Stu	–	1	8	11	–	
James Hammond	Stu	–	3	8	18	–	
Michael Kepley	Stu	–	1	8	8	–	
George Atterholt	Stu	–	2	11	9	+	
William Brown	Stu	–	4	9	3	–	
Daniel Marrit	Stu	–	4	8	31	–	
Francis Fast	Stu	–	4	11	23	–	
Michael Ringer	Stu	–	7	19	7	+	
Michael Ringer	Stu	–	7	19	10	+	
Peter Keller	Stu	–	2	4	–	18	
Peter Keller	Stu	–	2	4	–	12	
Robert Smith	Stu	–	3	9	28	–	
Absalom Kent	Stu	–	5	10	29	+	
Absalom Kent	Stu	–	5	10	24	+	
John Richardson	Stu	–	1	7	12	–	
Henry Bachman	Stu	–	1	8	12	–	
William Kirk	Stu	–	3	8	4	–	
Andrew Brinker	Stu	–	2	12	12	–	
Borden Stanton (Stanlyn?)	Stu	–	3	7	7	–	
Frederick Sheitz	Stu	–	1	8	23	–	
Samuel Hanna	Stu	–	5	9	10	–	
Rudolph Bair	Stu	–	2	12	6	–	
Rudolph Bair	Stu	–	3	15	2	–	
Alexander McCleery	Stu	–	3	9	26	–	
Joseph Janney	Stu	–	5	9	2	–	
Peter Shriver	Stu	–	1	9	33	–	
Peter Shriver	Stu	–	1	9	28	–	
John Woods	Stu	–	2	12	26	–	
Lewis Kenney	Stu	–	3	14	14	–	

220   15 Nov 1805   A/3/195
Jesse Spencer, Reg Chl
U.S. stock transfer
Mathew's survey; assignment from Van Horne to
    John Stewart

Isaac Van Horne	Chl	–	22	4	4	–
Isaac Van Horne	Chl	–	22	4	–	5
John Harr, Jr.	Chl	–	21	11	6	+

221   19 Nov 1805   A/3/196
Samuel Finley, Rec Chl
U.S. stock transfer

John Shoemaker	Chl	–	20	11	22	+

222   21 Nov 1805   A/3/196
Jesse Spencer, Reg Chl
U.S. stock transfer
Mathew's survey

Jacob Algier	Chl	–	21	11	12	+

223   4 Dec 1805   A/3/197
David Hoge, Reg Stu
Transmits patents

John Heald	Stu	–	2	12	25	–
Alexander Rogers	Stu	–	2	12	33	–
Isaac James & Enos Ellis	Stu	–	2	12	34	–
Samuel Coope	Stu	–	2	5	35	–
Andrew Johnston	Stu	–	1	7	25	+
William Johnson	Stu	–	3	6	8	–
James Gilcreast Harah	Stu	–	3	9	31	–
Hugh McPike	Stu	–	2	11	8	–
Charles Long	Stu	–	8	10	3	+
Samuel Coope	Stu	–	3	8	12	–
James Johnston	Stu	–	1	8	35	+
Joshua Hatcher	Stu	–	5	8	9	–
William Heald	Stu	–	1	8	30	–
William Gillespie	Stu	–	3	8	29	–
Nathan Updegraff	Stu	–	3	7	2	–
William Hodgin	Stu	–	6	8	8	–
George West	Stu	–	2	12	14	–
John Hanna	Stu	–	7	19	8	–
Henry Wersheler	Stu	–	8	11	14	–
Thomas Hawkins	Stu	–	2	11	7	–
Jesse Edginton	Stu	–	3	9	33	–
Henry Wersheler	Stu	–	8	11	13	–
Zaccheus Test	Stu	–	4	16	23	–

224   4 Dec 1805   A/3/198
Charles Killgore, Reg Cin
Transmits patents

Jacob Case & Thomas Pound	Cin	EML	3	3	27	+	
Michael Williams	Cin	EML	5	7	19	+	
Samuel Davis	Cin	EML	3	3	19	+	
Tobias & Derick Barkalow	Cin	EML	4	2	–	14	
Tobias & Derick Barkalow	Cin	EML	4	2	11	–	
Abiathar Davis	Cin	EML	5	6	17	–	
John Allen	Cin	WML	1	7	24	+	

225   4 Dec 1805   A/3/198
Jesse Spencer, Reg Chl
Transmits patents

Michael Shallenberger	Chl	–	20	12	1	+
Adam Ansbaugh	Chl	–	17	17	1	–
Noah Zane	Chl	–	19	15	36	–
Noah Zane	Chl	–	19	14	–	1
Frederick Overley	Chl	WS	21	9	33	+
Andrew Hite	Chl	–	18	15	14	+
John & Samuel Carpenter	Chl	–	19	14	32	+

[15]

Joseph Barr	Chl	–	18	15	34	+
Emanuel & Samuel Carpenter	Chl	–	19	13	10	–
Gaspar Hufford	Chl	–	17	16	20	+
Jacob Pebler	Chl	–	18	15	35	+
Robert Culbertson & Samuel McCullock	Chl	MS	22	4	22	–
Henry Hosher	Chl	–	20	8	19	–
Abraham Hite	Chl	–	17	17	6	–
Conrad Fedder	Chl	–	18	15	33	+
Michael Shalinberger	Chl	–	19	14	31	+
Samuel Thompson	Chl	–	19	14	19	+
Benjamin Kerns & James Kilgore	Chl	–	21	7	2	–
Benjamin Kerns & James Kilgore	Chl	–	21	7	–	3
Benjamin Kerns & James Kilgore	Chl	–	21	7	–	4
James Short	Chl	MS	22	2	–	16
James Short	Chl	MS	22	2	15	–
William McCoy	Chl	WS	21	9	8	–
John Crouse	Chl	WS	21	9	20	–
Regnal Green	Chl	–	19	14	8	+
Nathaniel Wilson, Sr.	Chl	–	19	14	10	+
Nathaniel Wilson, Sr.	Chl	–	19	15	33	+
Adam Fosnough	Chl	–	20	12	5	+
Emanuel Ruffner	Chl	–	17	17	20	–
Jacob Zeiger	Chl	WS	21	11	–	19
Jacob Zeiger	Chl	WS	21	11	20	–
Jacob Zeiger	Chl	WS	22	4	–	5
William Trimble	Chl	–	18	15	26	–
George Miller	Chl	–	17	17	3	+
Henry Bowman	Chl	–	17	18	20	+
Thomas Morris	Chl	MS	22	4	27	–
Christian Binkley	Chl	–	16	16	6	+
Henry Musselman	Chl	WS	21	8	7	–
Henry Musselman	Chl	WS	22	1	–	3
Henry Musselman	Chl	WS	22	1	–	4
Jacob Slingley	Chl	WS	21	10	8	+
Thomas Cole	Chl	–	20	13	8	–
Abraham Claypoole	Chl	–	20	8	17	–
John Boyd	Chl	–	19	15	7	–

226   6 Dec 1805   A/3/200
Jesse Spencer, Reg Chl

Samuel & Christian Saygar	Chl	–	19	16	5	+

227   21 Dec 1805   A/3/200
Joseph Nourse (from Andrew Gregg)
Committee on Public Lands asks whether any land in township 14, range 15, sold at Mar by public sale on 28 May 1801, other than the following:

John McIntire	Mar	–	15	14	19	–

228   23 Dec 1805   A/3/201
Andrew Gregg, Chairman, Committee on Public Lands
Answers inquiry by submitting copy of original return.

229   24 Dec 1805   A/3/201
James Findlay, Rec Cin
Transfer of U.S. stock
James Ferguson of Maryland; Martin Baum of Cin

James Ferguson	Cin	–	7	3	35	–
Martin Baum	Cin	–	7	3	24	–
Martin Baum	Cin	–	8	3	7	–
Martin Baum	Cin	–	8	4	5	–
Martin Baum	Cin	–	8	4	17	–
Martin Baum	Cin	–	8	4	23	–
Martin Baum	Cin	–	9	4	7	–

230   24 Dec 1805   A/3/202
Samuel Finley, Rec Chl
Receipt

John Stover	Chl	–	18	1*	26	–
John Stover	Chl	–	18	1*	–	27
John Stover	Chl	–	18	1*	–	28
John Stover	Chl	–	18	1*	–	29
John Stover	Chl	–	18	1*	–	30
John Stover	Chl	–	18	1*	–	3

*May read township 7.

231   6 Jan 1806   A/3/202
David Hoge, Reg Stu
Transmits patent

Alexander McConnell	Stu	–	4	8	7	–

232   20 Jan 1806   A/3/202
James Findlay, Rec Cin
Transfers U.S. stock

James Ferguson	Cin	Pre	7	3	35	–

233   24 Jan 1806   A/3/203
Samuel Finley, Rec Chl
Transfers U.S. stock

John Pickens	Chl	–	21	8	21	+

234   30 Jan 1806   A/3/203
David Hoge, Reg Stu
Transmits patent
Benjamin Brown of Alexandria

Benjamin Brown	Stu	–	4	15	13	+

235   4 Feb 1806   A/3/204
Hon. Phanuel Bishop, U.S. House of Representatives
Military land warrant 76, in name of Barnabas Barker, cannot be patented in name of attorney, Timothy Walker.

236   4 Feb 1806   A/3/204
David Hoge, Reg Stu
Transmits patents
Jonathan Jessop, assignee of Josiah Updegraff

Josiah Updegraff	Stu	–	4	9	31	–
Samuel Brown	Stu	–	4	14	10	+

237   5 Feb 1806   A/3/205
Samuel Finley, Rec Chl
Requests duplicate of receipt
Edward Teal.

238   6 Feb 1806   A/3/205
Jared Mansfield, SG
Plat of pre-emption lands between Miami Rivers shows complete only for 4th, 5th, 6th, & 7th ranges; vast number of accounts suspended for land in 8th, 9th, & 10th ranges because books are incomplete.

239   10 Feb 1806   A/3/206
James McWhirter, St. George's, Newcastle County, Delaware
Military land warrant 10,824; Act of 1 Mar 1800

--	Mil	–	12	2	3	–

240   8 Feb 1806   A/3/207
William McCluney, Brooke Court House, Virginia
Military land warrants 6428 & 13,780; patent cor-
   responding to warrant 69 to be handed to General
   Hamilton.

241   21 Feb 1806   A/3/208
David Hoge, Reg Stu
Transmits patents

Aaron Brown	Stu	–	3	7	23	–
George Humphrey	Stu	–	3	8	8	–
William Harah	Stu	–	1	8	1	–
Peter Mosser	Stu	–	1	9	25	–
Joseph Holmes	Stu	–	4	9	25	–
Mordecai Yarnall	Stu	–	3	6	28	–
Horton Howard	Stu	–	3	7	9	–
Horton Howard	Stu	–	3	6	10	–
Horton Howard	Stu	–	3	7	17	–
George Stump	Stu	–	1	9	4	–
Cadwalader Evans	Stu	–	3	8	17	–
Samuel Mosser	Stu	–	1	9	13	–
Isaac James	Stu	–	2	12	35	–

242   25 Feb 1806   A/3/208
David Hoge, Reg Stu
Transmits patents

James Flennicken	Stu	–	3	10	29	–
James McDowel	Stu	–	5	9	24	+
Thomas Parviance	Stu	–	3	8	6	–
W. B. Randolph	Stu	–	3	14	19	+
Henry Heister	Stu	–	4	11	9	–
Joseph McConnell	Stu	–	3	15	8	–
Joseph Dorsey	Stu	–	3	9	10	–
Joseph Dorsey	Stu	–	3	9	8	–

243   25 Feb 1806   A/3/209
Jesse Spencer, Reg Chl
Transmits patents

Philip Kammerer	Chl	–	18	15	18	+
Frederick Overley	Chl	–	20	10	20	+
George Hosher	Chl	–	20	15	34	–
John Zeager	Chl	W	21	11	26	+
Jacob Strouse & Adam Def- fenbaugh	Chl	–	19	12	31	+
James Martin	Chl	M	21	9	28	+
Jacob Zeller	Chl	–	17	14	6	+
John McCorley	Chl	–	16	6	13	+
Gabriel Steely	Chl	W	21	10	29	+
John Anderson	Chl	W	21	11	10	–

244   28 Feb 1806   A/3/209
Phanuel Bishop of Rehoboth, Massachusetts, to be
   left at post office, Providence, R. I.
Transmits patent

Barnabas Barker	Mil	–	11	8	1	–

245   3 Mar 1806   A/3/210
James M. Broome, U.S. House of Representatives
Answers inquiry
Heirs of Daniel Cochran; James Cochran; Zacharia
   Rosell.

246   7 Mar 1806   A/3/210
Hon. John Smith, Committee on Land, U.S. Senate
Certified list of land purchasers.

247   14 Mar 1806   A/3/211
Samuel Finley, Rec Chl
Final certificate

Edward Teal	Chl	–	18	15	2	+

248   18 Mar 1806   A/3/211
David Hoge, Reg Stu
Transmits patents

John Crague	Stu	–	3	9	32	–
Robert McCready	Stu	–	2	10	32	+
John Bever	Stu	–	1	6	26	–
Peter Mosser	Stu	–	1	9	26	–
Peter Mosser	Stu	–	1	9	36	–
Peter Mosser	Stu	–	1	9	27	–
Bazaliel Wells	Stu	–	1	2	34	–
Daniel Longanacker	Stu	–	5	16	5	–
Daniel Longanacker	Stu	–	3	15	25	+
James B. Megrew	Stu	–	4	11	13	–
Samuel Stewart	Stu	–	6	8	35	+
William Lodge	Stu	–	4	7	35	–
William Hogg	Stu	–	3	8	36	–
Adam Rubert	Stu	–	1	8	17	–
John Taggert	Stu	–	3	7	5	–
Joseph Sharpe	Stu	–	4	8	32	–
Jacob Webb	Stu	–	5	9	6	–
Valentine Priste	Stu	–	5	16	6	–
John McCoy	Stu	–	5	10	1	–
Hugh Tease	Stu	–	4	10	7	–
Jacob Kitt	Stu	–	7	18	18	+
George Burns	Stu	–	4	16	11	–
Benjamin Stanton	Stu	–	3	7	29	–
George Augustine	Stu	–	1	8	24	–
Nathan Shepherd	Stu	–	3	8	19	–
Saiah Chambers	Stu	–	4	8	30	–
Christopher Cox	Stu	–	3	9	20	–
William Piper	Stu	–	1	8	26	–
James Sharron	Stu	–	2	5	33	–
Abel Walker	Stu	–	2	5	34	–
Asa Cadwallader	Stu	–	2	4	30	–
Thomas Mitchell	Stu	–	3	7	3	–
Notley Hayes	Stu	–	3	6	34	–
John McCollock	Stu	–	6	9	4	–
Michael Darragh	Stu	–	3	16	7	–

249   18 Mar 1806   A/3/213
Jesse Spencer, Reg Chl
Transmits patents

Joseph Cox	Chl	–	20	8	14	–
Gabriel Steely	Chl	–	21	10	20	+
Jacob Bowser	Chl	–	19	15	12	+
Nicholas Bolonback	Chl	–	19	16	29	+
Christian Binckley	Chl	–	16	17	31	–
Christian Binckley	Chl	–	17	17	13	–
Andrew Smith	Chl	–	16	17	20	+
William Craig, Sr.	Chl	–	21	10	11	+
William Martin	Chl	–	18	15	36	+
Skinner & Barber	Chl	–	16	5	11	–
Paul Bean	Chl	–	16	17	19	+

250   18 Mar 1806   A/3/213
Samuel Brown, Newmarket, Frederick County, Md.
Transmits patent

Samuel Brown	Stu	–	4	14	10	+

251   18 Mar 1806   A/3/214
No addressee
Transmits patents "both living in Newmarket, Va."

Christian Saygar	Chl?	–	19	16	5	+
Samuel Saygar	Chl?	–	19	16	5	+

252   24 Mar 1806   A/3/214
James H. Broome, U.S. House of Representatives
Discusses land applications
Zachariah Rossell
Heirs of Daniel Cochran   Mil - 15 7 4 7

253   25 Mar 1806   A/3/214
Paul Fearing, Mar
Land applications
Major E. Sproat; Messrs. Skinner & Barber (errone-
   ously sent to Chl).

254   26 Mar 1806   A/3/215
Luke Tiernan, Merchant, Market Street, Baltimore,
   Maryland
Transmits patent
Jeremiah Evans
Henry Welchaus   Unk - 19 12 30 -

255   26 Mar 1806   A/3/215
Jesse Spencer, Reg Chl
Transmits patents
Sebastian Foush   Chl - 20 11   8 -
Nathaniel Wilson   Chl - 21   9 25 +
Joseph Harness   Chl - 21   7   9 -
Joseph Harness   Chl - 21   7 10 -
Joseph Harness   Chl - 21   7 - 11
Joseph Harness   Chl - 21   7 - 12
Emanuel Carpenter   Chl - 19 13   5 -
Conrad Broucher   Chl - 20 11 35 -
John Harrison   Chl - 18 15   3 +
Samuel Lee   Chl - 20 14 11 +

256   26 Mar 1806   A/3/216
David Hoge, Reg Stu
Transmits patents
Borden Stanton   Stu -   3   6 11 -
Michael Hirley?   Stu -   5 16   4 -
Jonathan Taylor   Stu -   3   7 24 -
John McCollock   Stu -   6   9   9 -
Joseph Dorsey   Stu -   2   6 24 -
Henry Grier   Stu -   6   8 28 -
Abner Hutton   Stu -   3   8 23 -

257   26 Mar 1806   A/3/216
Charles Killgore, Reg Cin
Transmits patents
Jesse Hunt; Moses Miller
James Wetherow   Cin EML 3 3 28 +
Bowser & Waggoner   Cin EML 5 3 26 -
Bowser & Waggoner   Cin EML 5 3 - 25
Oliver Smith   Cin EML 3 3 31 +
Joseph Evans   Cin EML 3 3 20 +
Jacob Michael   Cin EML 5 3 19 -
Cyrus Lockett   Cin Pre 5 3   6 +

258   28 Mar 1806   A/3/217
Nathan Williams, U.S. House of Representatives
Transmits patents (not listed)
Devised by Frederick William, Baron de Steuben,
   Major General & Inspector General in late Army
   of the United States, to Benjamin Walker &
   William North.

259   28 Mar 1806   A/3/217
Jesse Spencer, Reg Chl

Transmits patents
Jacob Knipper   Chl MS 21 10 26 -
Jacob Miller   Chl MS 19 16   2 +
Robert Culbertson   Chl MS 22   4 15 -
Robert Culbertson   Chl MS 22   4 16 +
Robert Culbertson   Chl MS 22   4 17 +
Benjamin Ruffner   Chl - 18 15 12 +
Benjamin Ruffner   Chl - 18 15 11 -
Lewis Sites   Chl - 18 14   2 -
Joshua Hedges   Chl MS 21   9   8 -
Jesse Hedges   Chl - 19 14   4 +

260   3 Apr 1806   A/3/218
David Hoge, Reg Stu
Transmits patents
Abraham Vail   Stu -   5   8   2 -
Malachi Jolly   Stu -   3   8 10 -
Elias Aduddel   Stu -   7 10   9 +
Solomon Fisher   Stu -   3 10 26 -
John Hanna   Stu -   3 11 13 -
Jacob Christ   Stu -   1   9 29 -
John Johnson   Stu -   8 12 29 +

261   7 Apr 1806   A/3/218
Jonathan Jessop, York Town, Pennsylvania
Transmits patent
Jonathan Jessop   Stu -   4   9 31 -

262   9 Apr 1806   A/3/218
Zaccheus Biggs, Rec Stu
Transfers U.S. stock
William Moore   Stu -   6   9   1 +

263   9 Apr 1806   A/3/219
Samuel Finley, Rec Chl
Transfers U.S. stock
Stephen Moylan, Commissioner of Loans, State of
   Pennsylvania; George Harness
Abraham Miller   Chl - 21   3 19 -
Abraham Miller   Chl - 22   3 -   7

264   9 Apr 1806   A/3/219
Jesse Spencer, Reg Chl
Transmits patents
Jacob Algier   Chl - 20 15   7 +
Jacob Algier   Chl - 20 15   8 +
Jacob Algier   Chl MS 21 11 12 +

265   11 Apr 1806   A/3/220
James Findlay, Rec Cin
Transfers U.S. stock
Henry Rhea   Cin EML 3   2 20 -
Henry Rhea   Cin EML 3   2 30 -
Henry Rhea   Cin EML 3   2 - 29

266   11 Apr 1806   A/3/220
Zaccheus Biggs, Rec Stu
Transfers U.S. stock
Joseph Thompson   Stu -   3   7   5 -

267   11 Apr 1806   A/3/220
Charles Killgore, Reg Cin
Regarding assignment by John Buckles to Seth Kel-
   log.

268   12 Apr 1806   A/3/221
Joseph Wood, Reg Mar
Transmits patent
William Hill   Mar   -   7   2   36   -

269   12 Apr 1806   A/3/221
General John Smith (of Virginia)
Transmits patent
Peter Babb   Stu   -   3   7   27   -

270   12 Apr 1806   A/3/221
Peter Ratckin, to be left at post office, Water-
    ford, Loudon County, Virginia
Transmits patent
Peter Ratckin   Stu   -   7   14   6   -

271   15 Apr 1806   A/3/221
Charles Killgore, Reg Cin
Transmits patents

John Ozias	Cin	EML	3	6	10	-
Henry Yount	Cin	EML	5	5	25	+
John Hoover	Cin	EML	5	6	33	-
John Matson, Jr.	Cin	EML	2	3	31	-
Edward Bebb	Cin	EML	1	3	27	+
Seth Gard	Cin	EML	2	4	2	+
Daniel Chrilie?	Cin	EML	5	3	17	-

272   15 Apr 1806   A/3/222
Jesse Spencer, Reg Chl
Transmits patents

Conrad Rudy	Chl	WS	21	9	12	-
John Book	Chl	-	18	15	9	+
William Gass	Chl	-	18	15	33	+
John Augustis	Chl	-	20	12	25	+
Christian Binkley	Chl	-	17	17	10	+
John Finck	Chl	-	16	16	10	+
Adam Brandt	Chl	-	19	15	10	-
John Gay, Sr.	Chl	WS	21	10	8	+
Edward Teal, Jr.	Chl	-	18	15	1	+
Geehr & Shoemaker	Chl	-	20	10	18	+
Thomas Bowen	Chl	-	20	8	18	-

273   15 Apr 1806   A/3/222
David Hoge, Reg Stu
Transmits patents

Carothers & Armstrong	Stu	-	3	13	11	-
Asher Woolman	Stu	-	5	18	36	+
Samuel Woolman	Stu	-	5	8	19	+
Thomas Ball	Stu	-	3	16	29	-
Benjamin Stanton	Stu	-	4	8	5	-
Richard Kinney	Stu	-	5	7	27	+
Robert Jackman	Stu	-	1	6	11	-
John Fuller	Stu	-	4	8	10	-
Benjamin Stanton	Stu	-	5	7	34	+

274   17 Apr 1806   A/3/223
Joseph Wood, Reg Mar
Comments on form
Robert Latta & George
    Lemley   Mar   -   3   4   14   +

275   17 Apr 1806   A/3/223
Samuel Finley, Rec Chl
Transfers U.S. stock

Felix & George Renicks	Chl	MS	22	2	3	-
Felix & George Renicks	Chl	MS	22	2	-	4

Abraham Miller	Chl	-	21	3	19	-
Abraham Miller	Chl	-	22	3	-	7

276   18 Apr 1806   A/3/224
Hon. Robert Wright, U.S. Senate
Military land warrants
George Scoone

Philip Reed	Mil	-	13	8	4	1
Philip Reed	Mil	-	13	8	4	2
Philip Reed	Mil	-	13	8	4	3
William Rasin	Mil	-	13	8	4	4
William Rasin	Mil	-	13	8	4	5

277   24 Apr 1806   A/3/224
Henry Hilger, Myer's Town, Dauphin County, Penna.
Military land warrant.

278   28 Apr 1806   A/3/225
Circular letter to Rec Stu, Mar, Chl, Cin
Proceeds to State of Ohio; Act of 3 Mar 1803;
    opening roads.

279   2 May 1806   A/3/225
Zaccheus Biggs, Rec Stu
Transfer of U.S. stock
William Hough of Loudon County, Virginia

William Hough	Stu	-	4	7	25	-
William Hough	Stu	-	3	6	30	-
William Hough	Stu	-	3	7	25	-
William Hough	Stu	-	3	7	26	-

280   2 May 1806   A/3/226
Samuel Finley, Rec Chl
Transfers U.S. stock

John Valentine	Chl	-	20	12	8	+
John Valentine	Chl	-	20	12	22	+
William Lucas	Chl	LS	21	3	32	-
William Lucas	Chl	LS	21	3	31	19
Abraham Miller	Chl	-	21	3	19	-
Abraham Miller	Chl	-	22	3	7	+

281   5 May 1806   A/3/226
Willys Silliman, Reg Zan
Instructions.

282   6 May 1806   A/3/227
Samuel Finley, Rec Chl
Transfers U.S. stock

--	Chl	-	18	14	5	-
--	Chl	-	18	14	-	6

283   15 May 1806   A/3/227
Abraham Bell, Morristown, New Jersey
Military land warrant 6915, in favor of David Cole,
    "late a soldier of the New York Line"; military
    land warrant 6795, in favor of Thomas Brooks,
    "late a soldier in the New York Line."

284   15 May 1806   A/3/228
Samuel Finley, Rec Chl
Receipts

Jonathan Nave	Chl	-	19	16	35	+
Jonathan Nave	Chl	-	18	16	17	+

Henry Keller	Chl	-	19	16	1	+
Henry Keller	Chl	-	19	16	5	+
Henry Keller	Chl	-	18	15	15	-

285   15 May 1806   A/3/228
Isaac Van Horne, Rec Zan
Receipts

George Hampshire	Zan?	-	14	15	14	+
George Hampshire	Zan?	-	14	15	5	-

286   20 May 1806   A/3/229
Zaccheus Biggs, Rec Stu
Certificates

Frederick Herpster	Stu	-	6	18	20	+
Frederick Herpster	Stu	-	6	18	29	+

287   20 May 1806   A/3/230
Samuel Finley, Rec Chl
Receipts

Jacob Coffelt	Chl	-	20	15	6	+
Jacob Coffelt	Chl	-	20	15	5	+
Jacob Coffelt	Chl	-	20	14	8	-

288   22 May 1806   A/3/230
James Findlay, Rec Cin
Receipts

John Fossett	Cin	Pre	4	3	28	-

289   23 May 1806   A/3/231
Samuel Finley, Rec Chl
Certificate
Mathew's Survey

Nicholas Delong	Chl	-	21	11	34	+

290   20 May 1806   A/3/232
James Findlay, Rec Cin
Error noted
Peyton Short; Hugh Andrews

William Graham	Cin	-	4	4	28	+

291   26 May 1806   A/3/233
James M. Broom, Wilmington, Delaware
Transmits patent

Zachariah Roswell	Mil	-	8	2	1	17

292   26 May 1806   A/3/233
Joseph Vance, Franklinton, Ohio
Transmits patents
Jeremiah Morrow

John Rudduck	Mil	-	18	7	2	1
John Rudduck	Mil	-	18	7	2	2
Elias N. de Lashmutt	Mil	-	15	1	3	39

293   27 May 1806   A/3/234
Frederick Conrad, Norristown, Pennsylvania
Transmits patents
Christopher Bauman &

Barbara Schelbachin	Mil	-	17	7	4	39
Samuel Gilbert?	Mil	-	17	7	4	19

294   27 May 1806   A/3/234
Zaccheus Biggs, Rec Stu
Certificate

Christian Mishey	Stu	-	1	9	8	-

295   27 May 1806   A/3/235
Col. William Alexander, Carlisle, Cumberland
   County, Pennsylvania
Transmits patents
William Findlay

John McGinnis	Mil	-	15	1	3	1
Edward McCaley	Mil	-	15	1	3	2
Martin Yost	Mil	-	15	1	3	15
John McAllister	Mil	-	15	1	3	16
Mary Doyle	Mil	-	15	1	3	18
William Bryan	Mil	-	15	1	3	17

296   28 May 1806   A/3/235
William Findley, Westmoreland County, Pennsylvania
Transmits patent

Godfroy Kerns	Mil	-	15	1	3	19

297   30 May 1806   A/3/235
John Rice? near Chambersburg, Pennsylvania
Transmits patents

Jonathan Trickle	Mil	-	17	7	4	24
John Nulton	Mil	-	17	7	4	23

298   30 May 1806   A/3/235
Willys Silliman, Reg Zan
Returns assigned certificate as there was no con-
   sideration mentioned for the assignment
James Loverick

James Sharrock	Mil	-	1	2	22	+

299   3 June 1806   A/3/236
James Findlay, Rec Cin
Certificate; U.S. stock; Loan Office, Pennsyl-
   vania

Robert Piatt	Cin	EML	1	1	19	-

300   3 June 1806   A/3/236
William McCluney, Brooke Court House, Virginia
Transmits patents
General Hamilton of Pennsylvania

William Helannen	Mil	-	2	3	4	27
George Beemer	Mil	-	2	3	4	22

301   No date   A/3/237
General Samuel Smith, Baltimore
Transmits patents

John Sears	Mil	-	18	7	1	20
John Sears	Mil	-	18	7	1	21

302   4 June 1806   A/3/237
David Hoge, Reg Stu
Transmits patents

Henry Beeson	Stu	-	1	8	32	-
Thomas Sharpe	Stu	-	5	9	9	-
John Stapler	Stu	-	4	9	5	-
Ezra Wharton	Stu	-	4	8	6	-
John Neff	Stu	-	4	7	13	-
James McCaughey	Stu	-	9	10	23	+
Zaccheus Biggs	Stu	-	5	10	10	-
Michael Easterly	Stu	-	3	16	2	+
Henry Beeson	Stu	-	1	7	11	-
Thomas Green	Stu	-	2	11	20	-
Jacob Neff	Stu.	-	3	6	20	+
Christian Fox	Stu	-	2	13	31	-

Jacob Springer	Stu	-	4	11	30	+
Christian Clinker	Stu	-	8	12	32	+
Matthew McCall	Stu	-	5	8	18	-
Isaiah Myers	Stu	-	4	15	6	-
Hugh Rogers	Stu	-	4	9	19	-

303 4 Jun 1806 A/3/238
General Van Cortlandt, Van Cortlandt's Manor, New York
Transmits patents

John Lesuer	Mil	-	15	1	3	7
John Lesuer	Mil	-	17	7	1	1

304 4 Jun 1806 A/3/238
William Findley, Westmoreland County, Pennsylvania
Transmits patent

David Davis	Mil	-	15	1	3	20

305 5 Jun 1806 A/3/238
Robert Whitehill, Harrisburg, Pennsylvania
Mary Barkley "for the services of James Chambers, deceased"

Mary Barkley	Mil	-	17	7	2	21
Thomas & Margaret Henderson	Mil	-	17	7	2	9
John McMullin	Mil	-	17	7	2	20

306 5 Jun 1806 A/3/239
Joseph Woods, Reg Mar
Notes discrepancy
Parcel thought to have been sold to H. W. Livingston at sale in 1787

John McBride vs H. W. Livingston	Mar	-	3	1	-	26

307 6 Jun 1806 A/3/239
Joseph Budd, Hatter, North Front Street, Philadelphia, Pennsylvania
Transmits patent

Hinchman Haines	Stu	-	4	17	28	+

308 7 Jun 1806 A/3/239
Henry Hilger, Myer's Town, Dauphin County, Pennsylvania
Transmits patent

Henry Hilger	Mil	-	2	2	3	2

309 10 Jun 1806 A/3/240
David Hoge, Reg Stu
Transmits patents

John McConnell	Stu	-	2	6	32	-
Daniel Dunlevy	Stu	-	2	6	33	-
Thomas Ball	Stu	-	3	15	4	-
Thomas Ball	Stu	-	3	8	35	-
Joseph Green	Stu	-	2	11	19	-
John Oldshoe	Stu	-	4	9	28	-
James Sinclair	Stu	-	4	7	34	-
William McCloskey	Stu	-	1	8	35	+

310 10 Jun 1806 A/3/240
Charles Killgore, Reg Cin
Transmits patents

Heirs of Asa Harvey	Cin	EML	2	2	5	-
Heirs of Asa Harvey	Cin	EML	2	2	-	3
Heirs of Asa Harvey	Cin	EML	2	2	-	4
Jonas Crane	Cin	EML	1	2	19	-

311 13 Jun 1806 A/3/241
Zaccheus Biggs, Rec Stu
Receipt

Adam Seebert	Stu	-	4	8	9	-

312 19 Jun 1806 A/3/241
Charles Killgore, Reg Cin
Assignments
Joseph Lorimore to William Goudy; William Kirkpatrick to Jacob Coy

Joseph Lorimore & William Goudy	Cin	Pre	5	4	36	+
William Kirkpatrick & Jacob Coy	Cin	Pre	7	3	31	+

313 27 Jun 1806 A/3/241
John Kerr, Chl
Lots mentioned below already located by others
Philip Hobaugh

--	Mil	-	18	7	1	20
--	Mil	-	18	7	1	21

314 27 Jun 1806 A/3/242
Joel Barlow
Military land warrants
Mr. -- Wells

Joel Barlow	Mil	-	15	7	4	28
Joel Barlow	Mil	-	15	7	4	33
Joel Barlow	Mil	-	15	7	4	34
Joel Barlow	Mil	-	15	7	4	35
Joel Barlow	Mil	-	15	7	4	36
Joel Barlow	Mil	-	15	7	4	37

315 27 Jun 1806 A/3/242
Samuel Finley, Rec Chl
Error in accounts
Mathew's survey

Richard Hooker	Chl	-	20	13	18	-
Daniel Cloud	Chl	-	22	3	3	-
Daniel Cloud	Chl	-	22	3	-	4
Daniel Cloud	Chl	-	22	3	-	5

316 1 Jul 1806 A/3/243
Jesse Spencer, Reg Chl
Certificate

David Shelby	Chl	WS	21	10	3	+

317 2 Jul 1806 A/3/243
Zaccheus Biggs, Rec Stu
Receipt

James Ratckin	Stu	-	4	11	10	-

318 11 Jul 1806 A/3/244
David Hoge, Reg Stu
Certificate

James Ratckin	Stu	-	4	11	10	-
Thomas Orr	Stu	-	2	7	10	+

319 15 July 1806 A/3/244
Joseph Wood, Reg Mar
Transmits patents

Hugh Bryson	Mar	-	3	4	33	-
Henry Huffman	Mar	-	3	4	27	-

320   15 Jul 1806 A/3/244
Jesse Spencer, Reg Chl
Transmits patents
Mathew's survey

Henry Johns	Chl	–	19	15	5	+
George Johns	Chl	–	19	16	17	–
William Wilson	Chl	–	17	17	30	–
John Berry	Chl	–	18	13	10	+
Valentine Keffer	Chl	–	22	4	24	+
Duncan & Ewings	Chl	–	18	15	20	+
Nathaniel Johnson	Chl	–	21	9	32	+
Michael Stine	Chl	–	20	14	7	+
Jacob Gregg	Chl	–	20	8	1	+
Jacob Famuliner	Chl	–	20	10	6	+
Peter Humburger	Chl	–	17	18	35	+
Andrew Sherrick	Chl	–	18	15	24	+
Andrew Hite	Chl	–	18	15	24	+

321   16 Jul 1806 A/3/245
David Hoge, Reg Stu
Transmits patents

Richard Dildine	Stu	–	1	8	20	–
James Sinclair	Stu	–	5	7	17	–
Henry Ferguson	Stu	–	4	10	3	–
Joshua Dixson	Stu	–	2	12	3	–
John Henderson	Stu	–	4	8	27	–

322   19 Jul 1806 A/3/246
Albert Gallatin, SecTreas
Symmes grant boundaries; Fort Washington; Fort
 Loftus; Fort Wayne; Vincennes
Mr. -- Mansfield; Israel Ludlow.

323   21 Jul 1806 A/3/247
David Hoge, Reg Stu
Mentions Charles J. Nourse.

324   4 Aug 1806 A/3/247
Col. -- Worthington
Military land warrant 176
General Thomas Sumter; Charles Barber.

325   5 Aug 1806 A/3/248
General Thomas Sumter
Military land warrant 176, in favor of Charles Bar-
 ber, administrator of estate of Michael Buckley
Col. -- Worthington.

326   6 Aug 1806 A/3/248
Zaccheus Biggs, Rec Stu
Receipts
Michael Nourse, attorney for Adam Seebert

Frederick Herpster	Stu	–	6	18	29	+
Adam Seebert	Stu	–	4	8	9	–

327   7 Aug 1806 A/3/248
Memorandum
Sent patent for military land to Benjamin Brown,
 post office, Alexandria.

328   8 Aug 1806 A/3/249
William Hough, Waterford, Loudon County, Virginia
Transmits patents; Act of 27 Mar 1804

William Hough?	Stu	–	4	7	25	–
William Hough?	Stu	–	3	7	25	–
William Hough?	Stu	–	3	6	30	–
William Hough?	Stu	–	3	7	26	–

329   14 Aug 1806 A/3/249
Memorandum
Remittance to State of Ohio; statement of proceeds from sales of land (important accounting
 statement).

330   16 Aug 1806 A/3/250
John G. Jackson
Lots sold in U.S. Military District since adjourn-
 ment of Congress:

--	Mil	–	2	2	3	2
--	Mil	–	2	2	3	10
--	Mil	–	2	3	4	22
--	Mil	–	2	3	4	27
--	Mil	–	2	7	4	25
--	Mil	–	2	7	4	26
--	Mil	–	2	10	2	4
--	Mil	–	3	10	2	4
--	Mil	–	3	10	2	5
--	Mil	–	7	6	1	29
--	Mil	–	7	6	1	30
--	Mil	–	7	6	1	31
--	Mil	–	7	6	1	32
--	Mil	–	7	6	1	33
--	Mil	–	7	6	1	34
--	Mil	–	7	6	1	35
--	Mil	–	7	6	1	36
--	Mil	–	8	2	1	24
--	Mil	–	15	1	3	7
--	Mil	–	15	1	3	20
--	Mil	–	15	1	3	26
--	Mil	–	15	1	3	39
--	Mil	–	15	7	4	28
--	Mil	–	15	7	4	33
--	Mil	–	15	7	4	34
--	Mil	–	15	7	4	35
--	Mil	–	15	7	4	36
--	Mil	–	15	7	4	37
--	Mil	–	17	7	2	9
--	Mil	–	17	7	2	20
--	Mil	–	17	7	2	21
--	Mil	–	17	7	2	23
--	Mil	–	17	7	2	24
--	Mil	–	18	7	2	7
--	Mil	–	18	7	2	8
--	Mil	–	18	7	2	10

331   20 Aug 1806 A/3/251
Nicholas Lind, Taneytown, Maryland
Transmits patent
Conrad Dudderer.

332   5 Sep 1806 A/3/251
Isaac Van Horne, Rec Zan
Military land warrant

--	Mil?	–	8	4	3	3
--	Mil?	–	8	4	3	4
--	Mil?	–	8	4	3	5
--	Mil?	–	8	4	3	6

333   9 Sep 1806 A/3/251
David Hoge, Reg Stu
Transmits patent

Samuel Boyd	Stu	–	5	10	12	–

334		9 Sep 1806		A/3/252

David Hoge, Reg Stu
Transmits patents

Mary Newbold, Jr.	Stu	–	5	16	27	+
Jacob Nessley	Stu	–	1	8	5	–
Henry Dixon, Jr.	Stu	–	3	15	14	–
Daniel Crawford	Stu	–	2	10	12	+
William Ferguson	Stu	–	3	9	5	–
John Coffee	Stu	–	5	7	5	–
Caleb Coope	Stu	–	2	12	18	–
John Doudna	Stu	–	7	9	1	+
Reasin Beall	Stu	–	3	15	34	–
John Firestone	Stu	–	5	17	36	+
Isaac Siddall	Stu	–	2	11	9	+
Thomas Mansfield	Stu	–	2	6	31	–
John Paxton	Stu	–	5	10	14	+

---

335   4 Jun 1806   A/3/252

Thomas Worthington, Reg Chl
Copies of papers relating to erroneous patent

John Eaton; Mr. -- Moore; Israel Smith; General
   Sumter.

---

336   11 Aug 1806   A/3/254

W. Alston (from Thomas Worthington, Reg Chl)
Land of John Eaton.

---

337   11 Sep 1806   A/3/255

W. Alston, Halifax County Court House, North Carolina
Land of John Eaton.

---

338   31 Mar 1806   A/3/256

Indenture
Land of John Eaton
John Eaton & wife Elizabeth, of Halifax, North Caro-
   lina; Thomas Worthington, Ross County, Ohio;
   William Burt, justice of the peace; Richard
   Eppes, justice of the peace; L. Long, clerk

--	Mil	–	19	6	3	1
--	Mil	–	19	6	3	2
--	Mil	–	19	6	3	11
--	Mil	–	19	6	3	12

---

339   11 Sep 1806   A/3/258

Certificate
Corrects deed description given in serial entry
  338:

John Eaton	Mil	–	19	2	3	1
John Eaton	Mil	–	19	2	3	2
John Eaton	Mil	–	19	2	3	11
John Eaton	Mil	–	19	2	3	12

---

340   11 Sep 1806   A/3/259

Thomas Worthington
General Sumpter; John Eaton; W. Alston.

---

341   13 Sep 1806   A/3/260

Charles Killgore, Reg Cin
Transmits patents
Jacob Herron, assignee of Benjamin Whiteman

John Lucas	Cin	EML	4	2	1	–
John Lucas	Cin	EML	4	2	–	12
John Lucas	Cin	EML	4	2	–	13

---

342   15 Sep 1806   A/3/261

Yates Plummer, to be left at post office at Frederick Town, Maryland
Application

Yate Plummer	Unk	–	5	7	33	+

---

343   15 Sep 1806   A/3/261

David Hoge, Reg Stu
Transmits patents

John Stoneman	Stu	–	3	8	33	–
John Lamb	Stu	–	6	10	11	+
William Laughlin	Stu	–	4	14	11	+
Matthew Mitchell	Stu	–	5	10	32	+
William Spencer	Stu	–	6	9	7	–
Horton Howard	Stu	–	4	17	32	+
Horton Howard	Stu	–	4	17	31	+
Horton Howard	Stu	–	3	7	8	–
Thomas Dickerson	Stu	–	4	9	32	–
Nathan Updegraff	Stu	–	3	7	6	–
Garret Snediker	Stu	–	5	9	1	–
Thomas Thompson	Stu	–	4	15	36	+
Joseph Huff	Stu	–	4	8	36	–
James Roberts	Stu	–	4	9	13	–
Philip Deleny	Stu	–	4	10	9	–
James Taylor	Stu	–	1	9	14	–
Asa Holloway	Stu	–	2	12	29	–
Alexander Cassil	Stu	–	4	9	23	–
Campbell Lefever	Stu	–	3	6	14	–

---

344   22 Sep 1806   A/3/262

Jesse Spencer, Reg Chl
Transmits patents

Jesse Spurgeon	Chl	–	19	14	3	+
Kalback & Shaffer	Chl	–	18	15	12	+
John Bashear	Chl	–	16	17	29	+
Abraham Hagerman	Chl	MS	21	9	12	+
Christian Stukey	Chl	–	20	12	23	+
Peter Stukey	Chl	–	19	14	32	+
Jacob Beery	Chl	–	18	15	36	+
Henry Himbaugh	Chl	–	20	15	35	+

---

345   22 Sep 1806   A/3/262

David Hoge, Reg Stu
Transmits patents

Enos Ellis	Stu	–	2	11	3	–
Horton Howard	Stu	–	4	17	32	+
John T. Parker	Stu	–	3	13	9	–
John Hammond	Stu	–	3	9	17	–
Joseph Vanlaw	Stu	–	4	7	32	–
James Finney	Stu	–	4	9	27	–
Samuel Kernaghan	Stu	–	5	10	6	–
Andrew Ritchey, Jr.	Stu	–	4	8	28	–
David Parviance	Stu	–	3	8	5	–
John Siddall	Stu	–	2	11	9	+
Adam Hahn	Stu	–	5	17	25	–
John Craig	Stu	–	4	9	29	–
Thomas Dunn	Stu	–	5	8	11	–
Samuel Hanna	Stu	–	4	8	24	–
John Fulton	Stu	–	4	9	35	–
John Fugat	Stu	–	4	15	12	–

---

346   24 Sep 1806   A/3/263

John Kerr, Chl
Application

John Kerr	Mil?	–	19	7	1	7

347	26 Sep 1806		A/3/263			
Isaac Van Horne						
Transmits patents						
Isaac Van Horne?	Mil	–	8	4	3	3
Isaac Van Horne?	Mil	–	8	4	3	4
Isaac Van Horne?	Mil	–	8	4	3	5
Isaac Van Horne?	Mil	–	8	4	3	6

348	30 Sep 1806		A/3/263		
Samuel Finley, Rec Chl					
Receipts; U.S. stock					
George Harness					
John Adams	Chl	–	20	12	11	+
John Adams	Chl	–	20	12	14	+

349	30 Sep 1806		A/3/264		
Zaccheus Biggs, Rec Stu					
Receipts					
Benjamin Wright, Jr.	Stu	–	6	19	8	+
Francis Wright	Stu	–	6	19	3	+
Ann Wright	Stu	–	6	19	9	+

350	1 Oct 1806		A/3/264		
Charles Killgore, Reg Cin					
Transmits patents					
Jacob Herron, assignee of Benjamin Whiteman					
Henry Bowman	Cin	EML	5	5	28	+
Henry Bowman	Cin	EML	5	5	30	–

351	3 Oct 1806		A/3/265		
Zaccheus Biggs, Rec Stu					
Certificates					
Caleb Merryman	Stu	–	4	10	25	–

352	4 Oct 1806		A/3/265			
John Eaton, Halifax, North Carolina						
Answers inquiry						
Non-existent description	Mil	–	19	6	3	1
Non-existent description	Mil	–	19	6	3	2
Non-existent description	Mil	–	19	6	3	11
Non-existent description	Mil	–	19	6	3	12
John Eaton	Mil	–	19	2	3	1
John Eaton	Mil	–	19	2	3	2
John Eaton	Mil	–	19	2	3	11
John Eaton	Mil	–	19	2	3	12

353	8 Oct 1806		A/3/266		
Charles Killgore, Reg Cin					
Transmits patents					
John Lucas	Cin	EML	4	2	1	–
John Lucas	Cin	EML	4	2	–	12
John Lucas	Cin	EML	4	2	–	13
Calvin Ball	Cin	Pre	4	4	30	+
Moses Miller	Cin	Pre	8	4	36	+
Seth Kellog	Cin	Pre	5	3	34	+
William Thomas	Cin	Pre	5	3	9	+
Charles Williams	Cin	Pre	7	2	2	+
Joseph Perks?	Cin	Pre	5	2	15	+
Mordecai Walker	Cin	Pre	5	3	1	+
Benjamin Maltbie	Cin	Pre	5	2	4	+
Thomas Clayton	Cin	Pre	4	4	31	+
William Chapman	Cin	Pre	10	4	10	–
William Chapman	Cin	Pre	10	4	4	+
William Graham	Cin	Pre	4	4	28	+
John Hamilton	Cin	Pre	9	4	6	–
Nathan Lamme	Cin	Pre	6	3	34	–

Jacob Coy	Cin	Pre	6	2	6	+
Jacob Coy	Cin	Pre	6	2	12	+
Jacob Coy	Cin	Pre	6	3	36	+
John Webb	Cin	Pre	7	2	7	+
James McDonald	Cin	Pre	4	4	24	+
Abraham Vaneaton	Cin	Pre	6	2	1	+
Arthur Vandever	Cin	Pre	5	2	36	+

354	10 Oct 1806		A/3/267		
David Hoge, Reg Stu					
Transmits patents					
Benjamin Stanton	Stu	–	5	7	33	+
Philip Smith	Stu	–	2	6	26	–
Adam Winkleplech	Stu	–	3	10	20	–
William Millhous	Stu	–	4	17	33	+
John Robertson	Stu	–	3	16	19	–
William Ferrell	Stu	–	2	12	27	–
Mary Newbold, Jr.	Stu	–	5	16	27	+
Jacob Holmes	Stu	–	3	8	25	–

355	10 Oct 1806		A/3/267		
Jesse Spencer, Reg Chl					
Transmits patents					
Henry Bishop	Chl	WS	21	10	9	+
George Sharpe	Chl	MS	21	10	2	+
John Feeman	Chl	–	18	15	17	+
Nicholas Cox	Chl	–	20	8	10	–
John Justice	Chl	WS	21	11	5	+
Isaac Sheaffer & Abram Ream	Chl	–	18	14	33	–
Henry Humburger	Chl	–	17	18	34	+
Abraham Sheaffer	Chl	–	19	13	20	–
John Green	Chl	–	19	14	9	+
Jacob Vanmetre	Chl	–	18	14	3	–

356	10 Oct 1806		A/3/268		
Charles Killgore, Reg Cin					
Transmits patents					
Samuel Smith	Cin	EML	2	5	4	–
Stephen Vail	Cin	EML	4	2	21	–
Stephen Vail	Cin	EML	4	2	–	22

357	10 Oct 1806		A/3/268		
Willys Silliman, Reg Zan					
Application					
John Derwater	Zan	–	13	11	5	+

358	15 Oct 1806		A/3/268		
David Hoge, Reg Stu					
Transmits patents					
David Drake	Stu	–	5	9	11	–
Samuel Gregg	Stu	–	4	7	33	–
Michael Stephen	Stu	–	2	13	6	–
William Pumphrey	Stu	–	3	8	14	–
Philip Crabs	Stu	–	3	10	36	–
John Bradfield	Stu	–	2	12	36	–
William Anderson	Stu	–	6	8	29	+
Philip Willyard	Stu	–	4	14	12	–
Samuel Meek	Stu	–	1	8	27	–
Moses Blackburn	Stu	–	1	8	3	–

359	16 Oct 1806	A/3/269

Frederick Herpster, near Westminster, Frederick County, Maryland
Answers inquiry regarding patent issuance.

360		16 Oct 1806		A/3/270		

David Hoge, Reg Stu
Statement of account and request for patent issuance

Frederick Herpster	Stu	–	6	18	29	+

361		21 Oct 1806		A/3/271		

David Hoge, Reg Stu
Transmits patents

Barnet Groves	Stu	–	6	9	3	–
Samuel Dunlap	Stu	–	5	13	24	–
Robert Hanna	Stu	–	2	12	10	–
James Estop	Stu	–	5	17	14	–
William Pumphrey	Stu	–	4	9	4	–
John Pontious, Sr.	Stu	–	1	9	35	–
Joseph Sproat	Stu	–	3	10	19	+
Michael Easterly	Stu	–	2	12	5	–
Henry Williams	Stu	–	6	8	1	+
Job Cook	Stu	–	4	16	1	+
Rudolph Bair	Stu	–	3	15	13	–
Rudolph Bair	Stu	–	3	16	10	–
John Summer	Stu	–	5	17	24	–
John Summer	Stu	–	1	9	5	–
John Summer	Stu	–	5	16	23	–
John Harman	Stu	–	2	13	36	–
Thomas Lawson	Stu	–	4	6	23	+
Elisha Schooley	Stu	–	3	15	7	–
James Hoge	Stu	–	3	13	8	–
Chris Laitner	Stu	–	2	13	13	–
Joseph Hall	Stu	–	4	16	35	–
Isaac Davis	Stu	–	5	16	28	–

362		21 Oct 1806		A/3/272		

Jesse Spencer, Reg Chl
Transmits patent

John Wills	Chl	–	3	16	6	+

363		23 Oct 1806		A/3/272		

George Zeigler
Answers inquiries from Zan & Pittsburgh

Already patented	Mil?	–	19	7	1	7
Available	Mil?	–	19	7	1	5
Available	Mil?	–	19	7	1	6

364		29 Oct 1806		A/3/273		

Joseph Wood, Reg Mar
Transmits patent

John Chandler	Mar	–	12	13	14	–

365		31 Oct 1806		A/3/273		

Willys Silliman, Reg Zan
Transmits patents
Gibbons patent not signed by U.S. President and
withdrawn, per note

John Kepler	Zan	–	13	12	2	+
Joseph Peirce	Zan	–	12	13	17	+
John Larrison	Zan	–	12	12	17	+
George W. Gibbons	Zan	–	13	12	7	+
Peter Fauley	Zan	–	14	15	30	+

366		7 Nov 1806		A/3/274		

David Hoge, Reg Stu
Transmits patents

Michael Jenkins	Stu	–	4	8	20	–
Henry Beeson	Stu	–	2	12	7	–
Nathan Updegraffe	Stu	–	4	9	26	–

Joseph Clarke	Stu	–	4	9	18	–
Camm Thomas	Stu	–	6	8	1	+
Thomas Mills	Stu	–	3	5	32	+
Frederick Oldfather	Stu	–	4	7	19	–

367			7 Nov 1806		A/3/274		

Charles Killgore, Reg Cin
Transmits patents

Thomas Miller	Cin	WML	1	6	36	–
Thomas Miller	Cin	WML	1	5	–	1
John Kelsey	Cin	Pre	5	3	33	+
Nathan Lamme	Cin	Pre	6	3	33	+
Nathan Lamme	Cin	Pre	6	3	–	27
Nathan Lamme	Cin	Pre	6	3	–	28
Jonathan Garwood	Cin	Pre	4	4	34	+
Abraham Vaneaton	Cin	Pre	5	3	6	–
John Van Nest	Cin	Pre	4	2	18	+
James Cunningham	Cin	Pre	5	4	24	+
Timothy Sewell	Cin	Pre	4	2	10	+
James Scott	Cin	Pre	5	3	24	+
Daniel Doty	Cin	Pre	4	2	28	+
John Riddle	Cin	Pre	9	3	1	+
John Riddle	Cin	Pre	9	3	2	+
Martin Keever	Cin	Pre	4	4	30	+
Joseph Lorimore	Cin	Pre	5	4	36	+
Jacob Coy	Cin	Pre	7	3	31	+
Alexander Hueston	Cin	Pre	6	2	30	+
Joseph Parks	Cin	Pre	4	2	2	+
Edward Dearth	Cin	Pre	4	3	23	+
Peter Keever	Cin	Pre	4	4	22	+
Philip Siler	Cin	Pre	9	2	18	+
Thomas Vineyard	Cin	Pre	4	4	23	+
Andrew Hoover	Cin	Pre	4	4	27	+
Isaac Pedrick	Cin	Pre	5	3	9	+
Robert Wead	Cin	Pre	7	2	32	+
Andrew Hocker	Cin	Pre	7	2	9	+
Thomas Hatfield	Cin	Pre	5	3	28	+
Samuel Brewster	Cin	Pre	6	2	1	+
Stephen Vineyard	Cin	Pre	4	4	22	+
William Maddens	Cin	Pre	10	2	25	+
John Bradford	Cin	Pre	7	2	19	+
Martin Keever	Cin	Pre	5	3	25	+
Jacob Holloway	Cin	Pre	4	3	7	+
Joshua Carman	Cin	Pre	5	3	9	+
Joshua Carman	Cin	Pre	5	3	10	–
Daniel Antrim	Cin	Pre	4	4	15	+
John John, in trust for						
heirs of Thomas John	Cin	Pre	7	2	1	–
Edward Dearth	Cin	Pre	4	3	23	+
Absalom Thomas	Cin	Pre	5	3	4	+

368		7 Nov 1806		A/3/276		

James Ratckin, to be left at post office at Waterford, Loudon County, Virginia
Transmits patent

James Ratckin	Unk	–	4	11	10	–

369		13 Nov 1806		A/3/276		

Isaac Van Horne, Rec Zan
Certificates

Christian Kore	Zan	–	3	9	13	+
Henry Thomas	Zan	–	3	9	18	+
Michael Kore	Zan	–	3	9	8	+
Michael Kore & Henry						
Thomas	Zan	–	3	9	1	+

370		17 Nov 1806		A/3/276		

James Findlay, Rec Cin
Certificate

Henry Medsker	Cin	–	5	3	5	+

371		17 Nov 1806			A/3/277

Zaccheus Biggs, Rec Stu
Receipts
Peter Koffle;   Henry Benner.

372			18 Nov 1806				A/3/277

Charles Killgore, Reg Cin
Transmits patents

Joseph Lorimore	Cin	Pre	4	2	14	+
Joseph Parks	Cin	Pre	4	2	10	+
John Hueston	Cin	Pre	6	2	18	+
John McGrew	Cin	Pre	6	1	9	+
Moses Crane	Cin	Pre	4	3	15	+
James Snowden	Cin	Pre	6	2	2	+
Jacob Coy	Cin	Pre	7	2	9	+
Jacob Coy	Cin	Pre	7	3	31	+
Nicholas Petro	Cin	Pre	7	3	30	+
William Waagh	Cin	Pre	6	1	3	+
William Waagh	Cin	Pre	6	1	4	−
James McClelland	Cin	Pre	4	2	15	+
Thomas Irwin	Cin	−	4	2	9	+
Henry Null	Cin	−	5	2	7	+
George Harlin	Cin	−	5	3	20	+

373			21 Nov 1806				A/3/278

Charles Killgore, Reg Cin
Requests plats

William Ruffin	Cin	EML	3	1	−	7
William Ruffin	Cin	EML	3	1	−	8
William Ruffin	Cin	EML	3	1	−	18
John Fullenwider & Henry Cruse	Cin	EML	3	1	−	7
John Fullenwider & Henry Cruse	Cin	EML	3	1	−	8

374		21 Nov 1806		A/3/278

Jesse Spencer, Reg Chl
Land transaction
Jacob Dittoe to George Arnold;   Jacob Arnold.

375			26 Nov 1806			A/3/278

Memorandum (forwarded to Rec Stu)
First certificate

Joseph Smith	Stu	−	5	7	7	+

376		26 Nov 1806		A/3/279

David Hoge, Reg Stu
Transmits patents and request for final certificate
  for David Moore

David Moore	Stu	−	5	7	13	+
Jacob Crumbacher	Stu	−	5	16	7	−
Jacob Gilbert	Stu	−	2	13	11	−
Samuel Grimes	Stu	−	4	8	12	−
Rudolph Bair	Stu	−	6	17	5	+
William Davidson	Stu	−	4	11	5	−
Rudolph Bair, Jr.	Stu	−	8	10	12	+
Thomas Miles	Stu	−	3	5	32	+
Rudolph Bair	Stu	−	3	15	23	+
Adam Huhn	Stu	−	1	9	6	−

377			28 Nov 1806			A/3/279

James Findlay, Rec Cin
Certificate

Samuel Haines	Cin	EML	5	6	31	−

378		5 Dec 1806				A/3/280

Jesse Spencer, Reg Chl
Transmits patents

John Stover	Chl	−	18	1	−	27
John Stover	Chl	−	18	1	−	28
John Stover	Chl	−	18	1	−	29
John Stover	Chl	−	18	1	−	30
John Stover	Chl	−	18	1	26	−
John Stover	Chl	−	18	1	3	+
Nathan Willis	Chl	−	21	2	−	19
Nathan Willis	Chl	−	21	2	−	20
Adam Onsbaugh	Chl	−	17	17	12	−
Nicholas Tippal	Chl	−	18	14	24	+
Peter Walcer, assignee of Henry Claughbaugh	Chl	−	16	17	4	+
John Miller	Chl	−	19	12	6	+
Arthur Teal & Walter Teal	Chl	−	18	15	2	+
Joseph Cooper	Chl	−	17	18	2	+
Martin Falkner	Chl	−	20	14	13	−
Frederick Heck	Chl	−	16	16	18	+
James Smith	Chl	−	19	15	11	+
Thomas Davis	Chl	−	17	16	4	+
Henry Arnold	Chl	−	19	15	1	+
Mathias Kesler	Chl	−	20	12	13	+
Conrad Fedder	Chl	−	18	15	32	+
Zachariah Welsh	Chl	−	21	8	26	+
John Young	Chl	−	19	13	8	+
Thomas Selby	Chl	−	20	13	13	+
Philip King	Chl	MS	21	10	5	+
Adam Carne	Chl	WS	21	9	6	+
Emanuel Carpenter	Chl	−	19	14	14	+
Isaac Coldron	Chl	−	20	12	34	+
Samuel Spurgeon	Chl	−	20	14	2	+
Charles McClung	Chl	−	17	16	5	+
Abraham Bolanback	Chl	−	19	16	27	+
Henry Kraner & Michael Kraner	Chl	−	20	15	24	+
John Adam Sala de Ulrich Wagner & Andreas Wagner	Chl	−	18	16	31	+

379		5 Dec 1806				A/3/281

Charles Killgore, Reg Cin
Transmits patents

George Christ & Henry Hardin	Cin	WML	1	5	2	−
William Hixon	Cin	EML	3	4	9	+
Philip Gunkle	Cin	EML	4	3	13	+
William Willis	Cin	EML	5	5	4	+
Zachariah Selby & Walter Cox	Cin	EML	4	3	36	+
William Harbour	Cin	MR	12	4	13	+
Henry Stoddam	Cin	MR	4	4	−	8
Henry Stoddam	Cin	MR	4	4	2	−
Jacob Lawras	Cin	MR	5	2	30	−

380		5 Dec 1806				A/3/281

Willys Silliman, Reg Zan
Transmits patents

Thomas King	Zan	−	14	14	4	+

381		8 Dec 1806				A/3/282

Jesse Spencer, Reg Chl
Transmits patents

Jacob Allspach & George Graul	Chl	−	20	14	26	+
John Bashore	Chl	−	16	17	28	+
Abraham Ream	Chl	−	18	14	27	−

Thomas Buffington	Chl	-	16	1	-	25
Thomas Buffington	Chl	-	16	1	24	-
John Hite	Chl	-	18	15	4	-

382   8 Dec 1806   A/3/282
Jared Mansfield, SG
Act of 10 May 1800; requests all office papers be
    forwarded

Jesse Spencer (as grantee)	Chl?	MS	21	11	7	-

383   8 Dec 1806   A/3/283
Jesse Spencer, Reg Chl
Joseph Ruffner; Noah Zane; Winn Winship; Jacob
    Baylor

All of the above-named persons?	Chl	-	19	15	27	-

384   9 Dec 1806   A/3/283
Charles Killgore, Reg Cin
Error [tract presumed to lie between Miami River
    & Virginia Military Reservation]

Adam Wise	Cin	EML	12	4	1	-

385   15 Dec 1806   A/3/284
Jesse Spencer, Reg Chl
Statement of account

--	Chl	-	19	15	18	-

386   15 Dec 1806   A/3/285
Charles Killgore, Reg Cin
Statement of account
Thomas Rawlinson, agent for John Bucknall, con-
    veyed to Thomas Ewing; John Brown, assigned to
    Thomas Pursell, who reassigned to John Allen

Daniel Richardson	Cin	Pre	4	3	30	-
John Bucknall	Cin	EML	1	1	21	-
John Bucknall	Cin	EML	1	1	-	22
John Bucknall	Cin	EML	1	1	-	27
John Bucknall	Cin	EML	1	1	-	28
John Brown	Cin	WML	1	7	11	+
Jared Mansfield (as grantee)	Cin	-	2*	3	11	+

*Second fractional range.

387   22 Dec 1806   A/3/286
Charles Killgore, Reg Cin
Statement of account
James Brownlee.

388   22 Dec 1806   A/3/287
Willys Silliman, Reg Zan
Transmits patents

John Bush	Zan	-	15	17	23	+
John Bush	Zan	-	15	17	24	+
John Bush	Zan	-	15	17	25	+
George W. Gibbons	Zan	-	12	13	7	+
John Paxton, Sr.	Zan	-	2	3	10	+
William Thomas	Zan	-	1	1	1	+
John Porter	Zan	-	15	17	23	+
Henry Hoover	Zan	-	14	15	28	+
Henry Hoover	Zan	-	14	15	27	+
William Elliot	Zan	-	12	13	28	+
John Derwater	Zan	-	13	11	-	4
William Herron	Zan	-	18	13	18	-
James Sharrock	Zan Mil		1	2	21	+
Tobias Lent	Zan Mil		1	1	9	+
William Elliot	Zan	-	12	13	33	+

389   22 Dec 1806   A/3/287
Charles Killgore, Reg Cin
Transmits patents

Roger Brown	Cin	WML	1	4	-	36
Roger Brown	Cin	WML	1	4	35	-
Richard Manwaring	Cin	WML	1	7	10	-
William McClelland	Cin	EML	3	2	19	-
Williams & Vaughan	Cin	EML	1	2	24	-
Williams & Vaughan	Cin	EML	2	2	-	19
John McDonald	Cin	Pre	5	3	19	+
James Ruglass	Cin	Pre	4	2	7	+
Jacob Crissman	Cin	Pre	4	3	6	+
Leonard Hanes	Cin	Pre	9	3	31	+
John Wetherow	Cin	-	3	3	27	+
John Wetherow	Cin	-	3	3	34	+

390   22 Dec 1806   A/3/288
Nathan Harper, Frankford, Pennsylvania
Transmits patent
Dr. -- Porter

Nathan Harper	Stu	-	2	8	30	-
Nathan Harper	Stu	-	2	8	24	-

391   22 Dec 1806   A/3/288
Moses Gillingham, Frankford, Pennsylvania
Transmits patent
Dr. -- Porter

Moses Gillingham	Stu	-	2	9	19	-

392   22 Dec 1806   A/3/288
Samuel Hedges, Martinsburgh, Virginia
Transmits patent

Samuel Hedges	Zan	-	14	15	11	+

393   22 Dec 1806   A/3/289
Frederick Herpster, near Westminster, Frederick
    County, Maryland
Transmits patent

Frederick Herpster	Unk	-	6	18	29	-

394   22 Dec 1806   A/3/289
David Hoge, Reg Stu
Expedite final certificate
Mr. -- Smilie, member of Congress from Pennsyl-
    vania

Hugh Rankin	Stu	-	3	8	30	-

395   29 Dec 1806   A/3/290
Zaccheus Biggs, Rec Stu
Final certificate

Lewis Lyden	Stu	-	1	7	6	+

396   29 Dec 1806   A/3/290
David Hoge, Reg Stu
Transmits patents

John Hoopes	Stu	-	5	18	2	+
Isaac Siddall	Stu	-	2	11	13	+
Andrew Patterson	Stu	-	4	8	2	+
Horton Howard	Stu	-	7	9	7	+

397   29 Dec 1806   A/3/291
Jesse Spencer, Reg Chl
Transmits patents

Major -- Bright	Chl	-	20	14	12	+
Shiplor & Hammon	Chl	-	18	15	1	+

| Daniel Stephenson | Chl | - | 17 | 17 | 19 | - |
| Abraham Ream | Chl | - | 18 | 14 | 34 | - |

398 29 Dec 1806 A/3/291
William Davison, Winchester, Virginia
Transmits patent

| Angus McKeever | Mil | - | 1 | 8 | 4 | 16 |

399 1 Jan 1807 A/3/292
John Smilie
Transmits patents
Hugh Rankin

| James McDowel | Stu | - | 5 | 9 | 18 | - |
| Semeon Gard | Cin | EML | 1 | 7 | 36 | + |

400 1 Jan 1807 A/3/292
Charles Killgore, Reg Cin
Transmits patents

Nathanial Bell	Cin	EML	3	3	1	+
John Riddle	Cin	MR	2	3	11	+
Samuel Dick	Cin	MR	4	3	26	+

401 5 Jan 1807 A/3/293
Zaccheus Biggs Rec Stu
Query regarding

Benjamin, Francis, & Ann Wright	Stu	-	6	19	8	+
Benjamin, Francis, & Ann Wright	Stu	-	6	19	3	+
Benjamin, Francis, & Ann Wright	Stu	-	6	19	9	+

402 5 Jan 1807 A/3/293
Jesse Spencer, Reg Chl
Error in computation
Winn Winship, assignee of Radcliff & Crouch.

403 6 Jan 1807 A/3/294
Robert Whitehill
Military land warrant 365, in favor of Elizabeth Moyer, heir at law of Daniel Hummiston.

404 7 Jan 1807 A/3/294
John Hanna, Hagerstown, Maryland
Information regarding patent

| Job McNamee | Chl | - | 18 | 16 | 27 | + |

405 7 Jan 1807 A/3/295
Jesse Spencer, Reg Chl
Transmits patents

William Miller	Chl	ML	22	2	-	1
William Miller	Chl	ML	22	2	-	21
William Miller	Chl	ML	22	2	23	-
Felix & George Renick	Chl	ML	22	2	-	4
Felix & George Renick	Chl	ML	22	2	3	-
Christopher Ernst	Chl	WL	21	11	14	+
William Trimble	Chl	-	17	16	6	+
William Green	Chl	-	19	13	2	+
William Springer	Chl	-	18	15	32	+
Adam Wagener	Chl	-	19	15	3	+
Michael Cryder	Chl	-	21	8	5	-
Abraham Moyer	Chl	-	17	14	13	+
Philip Senft	Chl	-	17	17	26	-
Nathaniel Johnson	Chl	ML	21	9	32	+

406 8 Jan 1807 A/3/295
Zaccheus Biggs, Rec Stu
Duplicate receipt
James McGregor.

407 8 Jan 1807 A/3/296
Thomas Worthington, Rec Chl
Transmits patents

Jesse Spencer	Chl	-	17	18	17	+
Thomas Worthington	Chl	-	19	15	30	-
Jeremiah Strode	Chl	-	19	14	6	+
George Gibson	Chl	ML	21	10	32	-
Joseph Yates	Chl	ML	22	2	36	+
Joseph Yates	Chl	ML	21	11	6	+

408 14 Jan 1807 A/3/296
Jesse Spencer, Reg Chl
Transmits patents

Philip Herrink	Chl	-	20	13	14	-
Michael Cryder	Chl	WL	21	8	6	-
Michael Cryder	Chl	WL	22	1	-	1
Michael Cryder	Chl	WL	22	1	-	2
Daniel Miessa	Chl	-	20	13	25	+
Daniel Miessa	Chl	-	20	13	27	+
John Sharp	Chl	WL	21	10	32	+
John Homan	Chl	-	18	14	12	-

409 14 Jan 1807 A/3/297
Charles Killgore, Reg Cin
Transmits patents

Leven Hatfield	Cin	Pre	5	3	6	+
Daniel Richardson	Cin	Pre	5	2	13	+
Daniel Richardson	Cin	Pre	5	2	14	+
Jacob Reeder	Cin	Pre	5	2	-	23
Jacob Reeder	Cin	Pre	5	2	27	+
George Newcom	Cin	Pre	7	2	27	+
George Newcom	Cin	Pre	7	2	28	+
Thomas Horner	Cin	Pre	6	2	14	-
Samuel Robb	Cin	Pre	4	3	35	+
Robert Ross, devisee of	Cin	Pre	5	2	31	+
David Faulkner	Cin	Pre	4	4	6	+
David Faulkner	Cin	Pre	5	3	1	+

410 15 Jan 1807 A/3/297
Samuel Finley, Rec Chl
First certificate; "request you forward final certificate to me," signed by Nourse, GLO

| James Buchanan | Chl | - | 17 | 18 | 10 | + |

411 15 Jan 1807 A/3/298
Christian Mishey, Carlisle, Cumberland County, Pennsylvania
Isaac Jenkinson, broker at Stu.

412 23 Jan 1807 A/3/298
Peter Miller, Post Office, Baltimore, Maryland
Canadian & Nova Scotian refugees

| Ambrose Cole | * | - | 18 | 17 | 5 | + |

*Refugee tract.

413 23 Jan 1807 A/3/299
F. Herpster
Transmits patent

| F. Herpster | Stu | - | 6 | 18 | 20 | + |

414   23 Jan 1807   A/3/299
Zaccheus Biggs, Rec Stu
Final certificate
Frederick Herpster   Stu -   6 18 20   +

415   23 Jan 1807   A/3/300
Samuel Finley, Rec Chl
Accounts
Worthington survey
Samuel Hill   Chl - 21 11 29   -

416   27 Jan 1807   A/3/300
General John Hamilton, U.S. House of Representatives
Transmits patent
Thomas Liggit   Mil -   1   8   4   17

417   28 Jan 1807   A/3/301
Samuel Finley, Rec Chl
Audit of accounts; "a difference so considerable
  has suggested the propriety of acting no fur-
  ther in this case"
Joseph Jefferies; Samuel Arrowsmith.

418   28 Jan 1807   A/3/302
Jesse Spencer, Reg Chl
Audit of account; discrepancy noted
Jesse Spencer (as grantee)
Jesse Spencer   Chl MS 21 11   7   +

419   30 Jan 1807   A/3/302
Isaac Van Horne, Rec Zan
Explanation of policy regarding discounts for pay-
  ments in full on date of purchase; Act of 10
  May 1800
Christian Kore; Henry Thomas; Michael Kore; Kore
  & Thomas; Copeland, assignee of George Baymer;
  Michael Nourse; Samuel H. Smith.

420   2 Feb 1807   A/3/303
Jesse Spencer, Reg Chl
Final certificate
Isaac Larimer   Chl - 17 16 18   +

421   4 Feb 1807   A/3/304
No addressee (but to one of the land offices)
Corrections required
Heirs of Thomas Smith; Jacob Herron, assignee of
  Benjamin Whiteman.

422   6 Feb 1806   A/3/305
Joseph Smith, to be left at Chatham post office,
  Chester County, Pennsylvania
Transmits patents
Thomas Thompson (Stu), agent of David Moore
Joseph Smith   Stu -   5   7   8   +
Joseph Smith   Stu -   5   7   7   +

423   16 Feb 1807   A/3/305
Charles Killgore, Reg Cin
Transmits patents
James Harris Robison   Cin Pre 4   2   1   +
Edmund Richardson   Cin Pre 4   4 27   +
Joseph Evans   Cin Pre 6   3   -   1
Joseph Evans   Cin Pre 6   3   -   2

424   16 Feb 1807   A/3/306
Jesse Spencer, Reg Chl
Transmits patents
Philip Shortle   Chl -   20 12 26   +
Edward Tiffin   Chl -   21   8   - 30
Edward Tiffin   Chl -   21   8   - 31
Lewis Lites [Sites?]   Chl -   18 14 11   -
Thomas Hinton   Chl -   20 10 10   +
Felix Renick   Chl MS 22   3 15   -
Felix Renick   Chl MS 22   3 16   +
Henry Musselman   Chl WS 21   9 34   +
Richard Morris   Chl WS 21 10   9   +
William Mooberry   Chl MS 22   4   1   +
Rezin Ricketts   Chl -   20 15 33   +
Jacob Miller   Chl -   16 16   9   +

425   20 Feb 1807   A/3/306
John Smith
First certificate
Fielding Lowry; Richard Carr
John Smith   Cin Pre 3   1 18   -

426   23 Feb 1807   A/3/307
John Smith
First certificate.

427   21 Feb 1807   A/3/308
No addressee
Statement of funds accruing to the State of Ohio,
  1 Jul 1802 to 31 Dec 1806; Act of 3 Mar 1803.

428   27 Feb 1807   A/3/308
Robert Whitehill
Transmits patent
Elizabeth Moyer   Mil - 10   3   4 36

429   27 Feb 1807   A/3/309
Frederick Conrad
Transmits patent
Abel Lovering   Mil -   8   2   1 15

430   27 Feb 1807   A/3/309
Gurden S. Mumford
Transmits patents
Zephaniah Brown   Mil - 15   7   4 11
Zephaniah Brown   Mil - 15   7   4 21
Zephaniah Brown   Mil - 15   7   4 22

431   3 Mar 1807   A/3/309
Memorandum
Patents transmitted
John Dawson; Andrew Gregg
Churchill Jones   Mil -   9   1   3 23
Churchill Jones   Mil -   9   1   3 24
Churchill Jones   Mil -   9   1   3 39
Alexander Parker   Mil -   5   3   3 34
Alexander Parker   Mil -   5   3   3 35
Alexander Parker   Mil -   5   3   3 36

432   6 Mar 1807   A/3/310
Winn Winship, [Reg?] Chl
Transmits patents
Samuel Miller   Chl - 18 15   4   +
John Shawser, Sr.   Chl - 20 10 17   +
Nicholas Yeager   Chl - 17   1   1   +
Benjamin Duncan   Chl WS 21 10 18   +

Isaac Brink	Chl	WS	22	2	1	+
Samuel Lee [See?]	Chl	-	20	14	3	+
John Shawser, Sr.	Chl	-	20	10	17	+
John Poorman	Chl	-	16	16	8	+

433 6 Mar 1807 A/3/310
David Hoge, Reg Stu
Transmits patents

John McElroy	Stu	-	4	14	9	+
Jacob Shively	Stu	-	6	18	29	+
Jacob Shively	Stu	-	6	18	30	+
William Lacey	Stu	-	4	6	4	+
John Conkle	Stu	-	1	6	6	-
Benjamin Stanton	Stu	-	3	5	36	+
Andrew Griffin	Stu	-	3	11	28	-
Thomas Rankin	Stu	-	4	9	30	-
John Young	Stu	-	6	8	36	-
Thomas Rogers	Stu	-	1	7	13	-
Martin Adams	Stu	-	3	12	2	+
Stephen Morlaw	Stu	-	2	12	17	-
Jacob Kupplens	Stu	-	1	9	9	-
Samuel Gilmore	Stu	-	5	10	3	-
John Agnew	Stu	-	5	10	11	-
William Ferrell	Stu	-	3	15	17	-
John Hoopes	Stu	-	4	17	27	+
Emanuel Kuntz	Stu	-	4	15	26	+
Hans Wilson	Stu	-	7	17	20	+
John Henderson	Stu	-	3	11	26	+
Daniel Carter	Stu	-	8	10	14	+
Frederick Reed	Stu	-	4	10	30	-
John Myers	Stu	-	2	13	32	-

434 6 Mar 1807 A/3/311
Thomas Thompson, Stu
Transmits patents

John Bower	Stu	-	7	19	32	+
John Bower	Stu	-	6	18	32	+
John Bower	Stu	-	7	19	17	+
John Bower	Stu	-	7	19	5	+

435 -- Mar 1807 A/3/312
Winn Winship [Reg] Chl
Transmits patents

Philip Macland	Chl	-	18	15	6	+
Benjamin Duncan	Chl	WS	21	10	7	+
Jeremiah? Conway	Chl	-	16	16	19	+
Adam Wagner	Chl	-	19	15	3	+
Emmer Cox	Chl	WS	22	3	1	-
John McNaghton	Chl	-	18	16	36	-
Philip Speace	Chl	-	16	16	7	+
George Swartz	Chl	-	18	14	36	+
John Beery	Chl	-	18	14	1	-
John Murphy	Chl	-	17	17	31	-
William Rail	Chl	-	16	16	10	+
Jacob Vanmetre	Chl	-	18	14	4	-
Joseph Dixon	Chl	-	19	9	6	+
John Dill	Chl	MS	22	4	-	8
John Dill	Chl	MS	22	4	-	9
John Dill	Chl	MS	22	4	10	-
Andrew Flick	Chl	-	20	14	10	+
John Adams	Chl	-	20	12	11	+
George Kinser	Chl	WS	21	10	23	+
John Shoemaker	Chl	-	20	12	25	+
Lewis Smires	Chl	-	19	12	9	+
William Morrell	Chl	MS	21	9	28	+
Samuel Shaffer	Chl	-	19	13	18	-
Samuel Cox	Chl	-	18	9	7	+
Andrew Buckhannon	Chl	-	17	18	11	+
Christian Beery	Chl	-	17	15	7	+
Jacob Leitz [Lutz?]	Chl	-	20	11	20	-

436 9 Mar 1807 A/3/313
James Ewing, Commissioner of Loans, New Jersey
Act of the State of New York authorizing State
  Surveyor General to sell military land war-
  rants
Ezra Darby; Dr. -- Stanbery.

437 9 Mar 1807 A/3/313
N. Williams, care of Benjamin Walker, Utica, New
  York
Military land warrant 5558 in favor of William
  Cook, "late a soldier of the Connecticut Line."

438 10 Mar 1807 A/3/314
John G. Jackson, Clarkesburgh, Va.
Report on lots in U.S. Military District which
  have been located since last communication.

439 13 Mar 1807 A/3/315
Charles Killgore, Reg Cin
Method of calculating interest due on instalment
  payments.

440 17 Mar 1807 A/3/317
John McWhorter, St. Georges, Newcastle County,
  Delaware
Virginia military warrant 679; U.S. military land
  warrant 10,824.

John McWhorter	Mil	-	15	1	-	-

441 19 Mar 1807 A/3/318
Memorandum
Transmits patent

Georg Simley [Lemley?]	Mar	-	3	4	14	-

442 19 Mar 1807 A/3/319
Charles Killgore, Reg Cin
Transmits patents

Abraham Bledsoe	Cin	WML	1	8	2	+
Henry Coleman Smith	Cin	WML	1	6	27	+
Peter Parham	Cin	EML	4	3	29	+
John Miller	Cin	EML	5	3	32	-
Frederick Laum [Saum?]	Cin	MR	6	2	29	+

443 27 Mar 1807 A/3/319
Isaac Van Horne, Rec Zan
Instructions.

444 27 Mar 1807 A/3/320
Charles Killgore, Reg Cin
Correction of accounts

Stephen Vail	Cin	Pre	4	2	22	+
Martha Davis, assignee of James Hamilton	Cin	EML	3	3	34	+
Martha Davis, assignee of James Hamilton	Cin	EML	3	2	4	-
Joseph Reynolds	Cin	MR	11	3	9	+
Theodore Saunder, assignee of John Smith	Cin	Pre	10	1	4	+
Ludwick Kemp, assignee of Thomas Thompson	Cin	-	7	2	22	+

445 27 Mar 1807 A/3/320
General John Smith
Transmits patent

[30] Jacob & Samuel Pickering	Stu	-	6	9	13	

446   27 Mar 1807   A/3/321
Charles Killgore, Reg Cin
Transmits patents

Name						
David Fouts	Cin	EML	4	3	11	+
Aaron Richardson	Cin	EML	4	3	1	+
Frederick Wolf	Cin	EML	5	2	8	-
Benjamin Iddings	Cin	EML	5	5	4	+
Thomas Pottinger	Cin	EML	3	3	28	+
John Noffsinger	Cin	EML	5	3	14	-
Adam & Martin Sheivey	Cin	EML	5	2	19	-
Leonard Wolf	Cin	EML	5	3	8	-
Samuel Tibbals	Cin	EML	5	2	-	22
Samuel Tibbals	Cin	EML	5	2	-	23
Samuel Tibbals	Cin	EML	5	2	21	-
Stephen Ludlow	Cin	EML	2	2	-	16
Stephen Ludlow	Cin	EML	2	2	-	17
Searing Marsh	Cin	EML	5	2	29	-
Jacob Pouts	Cin	EML	4	3	1	+
Abia Martin	Cin	MR	11	2	13	+

447   27 Mar 1807   A/3/321
David Hoge, Reg Stu
Transmits patents

Joab Gaskill	Stu	-	6	19	29	+
Nathan Gaskill	Stu	-	6	19	14	+
Nathan Gaskill	Stu	-	6	19	13	+
Thomas Evans	Stu	-	3	8	7	-

448   27 Mar 1807   A/3/322
Jesse Spencer, Reg Chl
Transmits patents

John Fisher	Chl	-	17	18	36	-
Peter Saunders	Chl	-	17	14	13	+
George Zimmer	Chl	WS	21	11	17	-
Frederick Arnold	Chl	-	19	15	1	+
Charles Friend	Chl	-	20	12	13	+
Boston Overly	Chl	-	20	10	20	+
Nicholas Earhart	Chl	WS	21	10	3	+
Joshua Moffet	Chl	-	20	8	33	-
Joshua Moffet	Chl	-	20	7	-	+
Richard Courtwright	Chl	MS	21	11	36	+
John Lutz	Chl	-	20	11	13	-
William Gassell	Chl	-	19	15	14	-
William Brown, Sr.	Chl	-	18	15	24	+
Samuel Breckenridge	Chl	MS	22	4	26	-
Peter Hairrauf	Chl	-	20	14	11	+
Christian Miller	Chl	-	18	15	10	+
Moses Wright	Chl	MS	21	10	18	-
John Stombach	Chl	MS	22	4	3	+
Abraham Ream	Chl	-	18	14	28	-

449   27 Mar 1807   A/3/322
Winn Winship [Reg?] Chl
Transmits patents

Jacob Knipper	Chl	-	19	16	31	+
Elnathan Schofield	Chl	-	19	14	3	+
Daniel Mayer	Chl	-	18	14	14	+
Reuben Newkirk & Samuel Harper	Chl	-	20	14	36	+

450   28 Mar 1807   A/3/323
Isaac Van Horne, Rec Zan
Employment of clerk.

451   3 Apr 1807   A/3/323
James Findlay, Rec Cin
First certificate

Benjamin Chambers	Cin	WML	1	5	-	13
Benjamin Chambers	Cin	WML	1	5	-	14
Benjamin Chambers	Cin	WML	1	5	15	-

452   3 Apr 1807   A/3/324
John Archer, Bellair, Hartford County, Maryland
Transmits patent

Patrick Doran	Mil	-	15	7	4	12

453   3 Apr 1807   A/3/324
John McWhorter, St. Georges, Newcastle County,
  Delaware
Transmits patent

John McWhorter	Mil	-	15	1	3	25

454   3 Apr 1807   A/3/324
Daniel Reinzel, George Town, District of Columbia
Transmits patent

Kennedy Robinson	Mil	-	15	1	3	24

455   8 Apr 1807   A/3/325
George North, Charlestown, Jefferson County, Vir-
  ginia
Transmits patent

Polly Hall North	Chl	-	19	14	19	+

456   9 Apr 1807   A/3/325
David Hoge, Reg Stu
Transmits patents
W. McPherrin

Thomas McPherrin	Stu	-	7	15	18	+
Henry Emens	Stu	-	2	9	13	-
William Hervey	Stu	-	3	9	27	-
John Webb	Stu	-	3	16	30	-
Francis Johnson	Stu	-	3	10	30	+
Jacob Painter	Stu	-	3	16	32	-

457   9 Apr 1807   A/3/326
Frederick Herpster, near Westminster, Frederick
  County, Maryland
Transmits patent

Frederick Herpster	Stu	-	6	18	20	+

458   9 Apr 1807   A/3/326
William Phillips, to be left at post office,
  Wilmington, Delaware
Transmits patents

William Phillips	Unk	-	6	19	28	+
William Phillips	Unk	-	5	17	4	+
William Phillips	Unk	-	6	18	4	-
James Phillips	Unk	-	6	19	33	-

459   11 Apr 1807   A/3/327
John Millidge, near Augusta, Georgia
Transmits patents

Captain John Milton	Mil	-	16	7	4	33
Captain John Milton	Mil	-	16	7	4	34
Captain John Milton	Mil	-	16	7	4	35

460   13 Apr 1807   A/3/327
Jesse Spencer, Reg Chl
Certificates
Joseph Jeffries; Samuel Arrowsmith

Mathias Kester	Chl	-	20	13	35	+
Mathias Kester	Chl	-	20	13	32	+
Jacob Claypool	Chl	-	19	15	21	+

461 1 May 1807 A/3/328
David Hoge, Reg Stu
Transmits patents

John Doudna	Stu	-	6	8	19	+
Knowis Doudna	Stu	-	6	8	7	+
Knowis Doudna	Stu	-	6	8	3	+
Henry Fulton	Stu	-	2	8	29	+
James McQuilkin	Stu	-	4	14	3	+
Thomas Stanley	Stu	-	5	17	8	-
Samuel Davis	Stu	-	3	16	33	-

462 1 May 1807 A/3/328
Isaac Van Horne, Rec Zan
First certificate
Final certificate to be delivered to George Hampshire, post office, Baltimore; Christian Kore; Michael Kore; Henry Thomas

George Hampshire, assignee	Zan	-	14	15	14	+
George Hampshire, assignee	Zan	-	15	16	5	+

463 1 May 1807 A/3/329
James Findlay, Rec Cin
First certificate
Final certificate to be sent to Fred Baker, post office, Hagerstown, Maryland

Fred Baker	Cin	EML	5	3	30	+

464 1 May 1807 A/3/329
David Holmes, Rockingham Court House, Virginia
Final certificate
George Cline, prospective assignee

Samuel Kratzer	Unk	-	18	15	28	+

465 2 May 1807 A/3/329
Zaccheus Biggs, Rec Stu
Receipt

Fielder Richardson	Stu	-	3	14	18	+

466 2 May 1807 A/3/330
Mr. -- Hardy, New York
Method of assigning military land warrants.

467 2 May 1807 A/3/331
Jesse Spencer, Reg Chl
Correction of account

Andrew Barr	Chl	-	20	13	33	-
John Stine [in postscript]	Chl	-	21	11	9	+

468 -- May 1807 A/3/332
Samuel Finley, Rec Chl
First certificate

John Stine	Chl	WS	21	11	9	+
John Stine	Chl	WS	21	11	8	+
John Dunkil	Chl	WS	21	11	8	+

469 8 May 1807 A/3/332
David Hoge, Reg Stu
Transmits patents

Frederick Harman	Stu	-	2	13	19	-

Daniel Welch	Stu	-	4	10	1	-
John Thomas, Sr.	Stu	-	5	17	27	-
John Thomas, Sr.	Stu	-	5	17	29	-
John Thomas, Sr.	Stu	-	5	17	28	-
Moses Middleswart	Stu	-	4	16	10	+
Samuel McWilliams	Stu	-	5	8	28	-
Daniel Welch	Stu	-	4	9	6	-
Micajah Macy	Stu	-	6	19	11	+
Robert Simison	Stu	-	3	14	10	-
Christian Knagy	Stu	-	5	12	26	+
Rudolph Bair	Stu	-	6	17	5	+
Andrew Altman	Stu	-	3	15	1	-
Andrew Simons	Stu	-	3	15	35	-
Steuart McClave	Stu	-	4	11	6	-
Jacob Knagy	Stu	-	5	12	32	+
George Alterholt	Stu	-	3	14	9	+
Jonathan Haines	Stu	-	3	15	18	-
Michael Boyer	Stu	-	7	17	3	+
Richard Beeson	Stu	-	7	20	26	+
Thomas Haines	Stu	-	6	11	9	+
John Pugh	Stu	-	6	11	9	+
Christopher Laitner [Saitner?]	Stu	-	8	12	29	+
John Pugh	Stu	-	6	11	3	+
Ebenezer Shaw	Stu	-	8	10	14	+
John Pugh	Stu	-	6	11	10	+

470 8 May 1807 A/3/333
Charles Killgore, Reg Cin
Transmits patents

Arthur St. Clair, Jr.	Cin	EML	3	2	-	21
Arthur St. Clair, Jr.	Cin	EML	3	2	-	27
Arthur St. Clair, Jr.	Cin	EML	3	2	-	28
Arthur St. Clair, Jr.	Cin	EML	3	2	16	-
Nathan Stubbs	Cin	EML	3	4	35	+
Duncan McVickers	Cin	EML	2	4	3	+
Thomas Cooch	Cin	EML	2	5	32	-

471 8 May 1807 A/3/334
Charles Killgore, Reg Cin
Certificates

Henry Bowman	Cin	EML	5	5	28	+
Henry Bowman	Cin	EML	5	5	30	+

472 11 May 1807 A/3/334
James Findlay, Rec Cin
Correction of account

Robert Edgar	Cin	Pre	7	2	33	+

473 14 May 1807 A/3/335
Charles Killgore, Reg Cin
Final certificate, error and query

Henry Pence	Cin	EML	12	3	36	+
Henry Pence	Cin	MR	12	3	36	+
David Wolverton	Cin	EML	2	8	7	+

474 10 May 1807 A/3/336
Jesse Spencer, Reg Chl
First certificate; attestation

Samuel Sheaffer	Chl	-	19	13	19	-
James Smith	Chl	-	19	15	12	+

475 13 May 1807 A/3/336
Zaccheus Biggs, Rec Stu
First certificate correction

William Wood	Stu	-	6	17	1	+
William Meridith	Stu	-	5	8	10	-

476   21 May 1807   A/3/337
David Hoge, Reg Stu
Final certificate
Obadiah Jennings, attorney for executors of Isaac
  Thorn, deceased; assignment to Henry Beeson
  [will of Isaac Thorn enclosed but not reproduced
  in register].

477   25 May 1807   A/3/338
Charles Killgore, Reg Cin
Final certificates; errors noted
Benjamin Whiteman assigns to Jacob Heron

Name						
Benjamin Bell	Cin	EML	3	3	11	+
William Shenk	Cin	/MR	?	?	35	+
William Shenk	Cin	MR	?	?	36	+
Philip Nagley	Cin	EML	5	2	18	-
Jacob Heron	Cin	Pre	7	3	20	+
Jacob Heron	Cin	Pre	7	3	21	+

478   25 May 1807   A/3/339
James Findlay, Rec Cin
Receipt

Adam Coblance	Cin	MR	6	1	6	-

479   27 May 1807   A/3/339
Samuel Finley, Rec Chl
Corrects errors

--	Chl	WS	22	3	-	2
--	Chl	WS	22	3	-	3
--	Chl	WS	22	3	-	4
--	Chl	WS	22	3	5	-
--	Chl	-	20	9	19	-
Job Inskeep	Chl	-	20	8	6	+
Robert Hunter	Chl	-	20	13	32	-

480   30 May 1807   A/3/340
Charles Killgore, Reg Cin
Correction of errors

Name						
Robert Ewing & David Sampson	Cin	EML	5	5	9	+
William McDonald	Cin	Pre	5	3	25	+
Daniel Ingersoll	Cin	EML	2	1	-	6
Daniel Ingersoll	Cin	EML	2	1	-	7
Daniel Ingersoll	Cin	EML	1	1	-	12
Daniel Ingersoll	Cin	EML	1	1	1	-
Jacob Burnet	Cin	EML	4	1	8	-
Jacob Burnet	Cin	EML	4	1	18	-
Jacob Burnet	Cin	EML	4	1	-	9
Jacob Burnet	Cin	EML	4	1	-	19
Jacob Burnet	Cin	EML	4	1	-	17
Jacob Burnet	Cin	EML	4	1	-	16
Matthew Huston	Cin	EML	2	4	1	-

481   29 May 1807   A/3/341
Henry Bowman, Hagar's Town, Maryland
Delay in forwarding final certificate.

482   1 Jun 1807   A/3/341
James Findlay, Rec Cin
Correction of errors

--	Cin	EML	6	2	-	33
--	Cin	EML	6	2	32	-
--	Cin	EML	3	2	2	-
--	Cin	EML	11	10	24	+

483   5 Jun 1807   A/3/342
Jesse Spencer, Reg Chl
Certificates

Ruffner, Zane, & Winship	Chl	-	19	15	27	-
George Arnold & Abraham Fink	Chl	-	18	15	30	-

484   5 Jun 1807   A/3/342
John G. Jackson
List of locations made in Mil lands since 10 Mar
  1807, when last reported.

485   6 Jun 1807   A/3/343
Charles Killgore, Reg Cin
Transmits patents

Jacob Miller	Cin	EML	5	3	-	35
Jacob Miller	Cin	EML	5	3	-	36
Jacob Miller	Cin	EML	5	3	34	-
John Gray	Cin	EML	3	2	6	-
Thomas Frost	Cin	EML	1	2	4	+

486   6 Jun 1807   A/3/343
David Hoge, Reg Stu
Transmits patents

Horton Howard	Stu	-	6	9	20	+
John Hoopes	Stu	-	4	17	29	+
Simeon Martin	Stu	-	1	6	31	+
Joab Gaskitt	Stu	-	3	14	25	+
Thomas Frederick	Stu	-	3	14	3	-

487   13 Jun 1807   A/3/344
Colonel Thomas Worthington
Canadian & Nova Scotian refugee lands
Colonel John Allen.

488   16 Jun 1807   A/3/344
James Findlay, Rec Cin
Resale of land due to failure to pay for recently-
  discovered fraction

--	Cin	EML	5	5	2	+

489   29 Jun 1807   A/3/345
Charles Killgore, Reg Cin
Correction of errors

John Scott	Cin	EML	2	5	25	-
George Harner	Cin	Pre	7	3	17	+
Benjamin Chambers	Cin	WML	1	5	-	13
Benjamin Chambers	Cin	WML	1	5	-	14
Benjamin Chambers	Cin	WML	1	5	15	-

490   6 Jul 1807   A/3/346
Samuel Finley, Rec Chl
Accounting statement

Andrew Barr	Chl	-	20	13	33	-

491   6 Jul 1807   A/3/346
Michael Boyer, Creiger's Town, Frederick County,
  Maryland
Military land warrant 861, granted to Michael
  Boyer, administrator of estate of Jacob Gro-
  math, late a lieutenant, deceased; Military
  land warrant 237, granted to Michael Boyer,
  late a captain in the German Regiment

James Johnston, assignee
James Johnston   Mil - 14   2   1   -

492   2 Jul 1807   A/3/347
Jesse Spencer, Reg Chl
Transmits patent
Samuel & William Denny   Chl WS 21 10 29   +

493   2 Jul 1807   A/3/347
David Hoge, Reg Stu
Transmits patents
Horton Howard   Stu -   6   8 30   +
Horton Howard   Stu -   6   8 18   +
Thomas Frederick   Stu -   3 14 12   -

494   2 Jul 1807   A/3/348
Charles Killgore, Reg Cin
Transmits patents
Joseph Howlings   Cin MR 13   4   7   +
William Ramsay   Cin MR   9   5 30   +
William Ramsay   Cin MR 10   5 25   +

495   6 Jul 1807   A/3/348
Charles Killgore, Reg Cin
Correction of errors
Stephen Wood   Cin EML   1   1   2   -
Stephen Wood   Cin EML   1   1   - 11
Martin Kever, Jr.   Cin Pre   4   4 24   +

496   7 Jul 1807   A/3/349
Willys Silliman, Reg Zan
Military lands annexed to Zan? district to be
    designated in final certificates.

497   11 Jul 1807   A/3/350
James Findlay, Rec Cin
Correction of errors
James Irvin Nesbit   Cin EML   5   2   6   -

498   11 Jul 1807   A/3/350
Charles Killgore, Reg Cin
Correction of errors
James & Thomas Newton   Cin EML   2   6 33   +
William Allensworth &
    William Ramey [Ramsey?] Cin WML   1   7 13   +
William, Robert, James L.
    & Alexander McConnels   Cin EML   6   2 31   -

499   16 Jul 1807   A/3/351
Jesse Spencer, Reg Chl
Transmits patents
Henry Wister   Chl - 20 11 32   +
Henry Wister   Chl - 20 11 30   +
Henry Wister   Chl - 20 11 31   +
Samuel Denny   Chl WS 21 10 32   +
David Denny   Chl MS 22   2 10   -
David Denny   Chl MS 22   2   -   9
Joseph Hunter   Chl - 19 14   2   -
Frederick Harman   Chl - 18 15 27   +
David Martin & Henry
    Sellers   Chl - 17 16   7   +
David List   Chl WS 21 11 23   +
David Shalenburger   Chl - 19 13 17   -
John Martin   Chl MS 22   3 22   +

Jacob Pebler?   Chl - 18 15 35   -
Elizabeth Clark   Chl - 20 11 12   +
David Shalenburger   Chl - 18 14 17   -
Woollery Coonrod   Chl MS 22   2 26   -
Woollery Coonrod   Chl MS 22   2   - 27
Conrad Brougher   Chl - 20 10   4   +

500   16 Jul 1807   A/3/352
Charles Killgore, Reg Cin
Transmits patents
Israel Loring   Cin WML   1   4   - 25
Israel Loring   Cin WML   1   4 26   -
Frederick Weymier   Cin EML   5   5 23   -
Jacob White   Cin EML   1   2 11   -
William Low   Cin EML   5   5   5   +
Samuel Compton   Cin EML   6   3 10   +
Adam Brown   Cin EML   3   7 28   +
George Yount   Cin EML   5   5   3   +
David Sidwell   Cin EML   5   5 24   +
John Garrison   Cin EML   3   3 19   +
John Quinn   Cin EML   3   6 31   +
Peter Artherton   Cin EML   1   2   2   -

501   23 Jul 1807   A/3/353
Lewis Cass, Zan
Answers inquiry regarding tracts still not taken
--   Mil? -   8   2   1   1
--   Mil? -   7   4   2   7
--   Mil? -   7   4   2   8
--   Mil? -   7   4   2 13
--   Mil? -   7   4   2 14
--   Mil? -   7   4   2 15
--   Mil? -   7   4   2 16
--   Mil? -   7   4   2 17
--   Mil? -   7   4   2 18
--   Mil? -   7   4   2 23
--   Mil? -   7   4   2 24
--   Mil? -   7   4   2 25
--   Mil? -   7   4   2 26
--   Mil? -   7   4   2 27
--   Mil? -   7   4   2 28
--   Mil? -   7   4   2 33
--   Mil? -   7   4   2 34
--   Mil? -   7   4   2 35
--   Mil? -   7   4   2 36
--   Mil? -   7   4   2 37
--   Mil? -   7   4   2 38

502   28 Jul 1807   A/3/354
David Hoge, Reg Stu
Transmits patents
Edward S. Hall   Stu -   3   8   3   -
David Kampf   Stu -   4 16 36   -
Anthony Pricker   Stu -   4 10 24   -
Daniel Miller, Sr.   Stu -   5 18 31   +
Samuel Smith   Stu -   5 17   1   +
Samuel Davis   Stu -   4 17 20   +
John Dever   Stu -   5   9 13   -
Thomas Ball   Stu -   3 15   5   -
Amos Holloway   Stu -   6 19 11   +
Jason Morlan   Stu -   2 11 12   -
William Wurtenbe   Stu -   4 10 33   -
Henry Schaeffer   Stu -   7 18   4   +

503   28 Jul 1807   A/3/354
Charles Killgore, Reg Cin
Transmits patents
Thomas Hopkins & James
    Taylor   Cin WML   2   1   3   +

Thomas Hopkins & James Taylor	Cin	WML	1	2	36	+
Shadrach Henderson	Cin	WML	1	13	18	+
John McEwen	Cin	EML	3	3	7	+
Philip Stoner	Cin	EML	4	4	33	-
Joseph Spencer & Jacob Whitinger	Cin	EML	3	3	30	+

504   1 Aug 1807   A/3/355
William Campbell
Transmits patent

James McGregor	Stu	-	2	3	32	+

505   3 Aug 1807   A/3/355
Hon. William Findley
Transmits patent

Thomas Jones	Chl	-	17	14	14	+

506   3 Aug 1807   A/3/355
Joseph Wood, Reg Mar
Transmits patent

James Edgerton & George Starbuck	Mar	-	4	5	4	-

507   3 Aug 1807   A/3/356
Charles Killgore, Reg Cin
Transmits patents

Garret Vannimann	Cin	EML	5	7	1	+
Abraham Demott	Cin	EML	4	2	6	-
Matthew Winton	Cin	EML	3	3	32	-
Joseph McMaken	Cin	EML	1	2	10	-
James Vannimann	Cin	EML	5	8	36	+
Caspar Bottorf	Cin	EML	2	7	23	+
Cave Johnston	Cin	EML	1	1	-	29
Cave Johnston	Cin	EML	1	1	20	-
James McClelland	Cin	EML	2	4	28	+
Samuel Pottinger & James Withrow	Cin	EML	3	3	33	-
William Harborn	Cin	MR	12	4	13	-
Abner Harborn	Cin	MR	11	4	18	+
John Whistler	Cin	MR	11	1	3	+

508   5 Aug 1807   A/3/356
Henry Bowman
Transmits patent; overpayment

Henry Bowman	Cin	EML	5	5	28	+

509   5 Aug 1807   A/3/357
Colonel -- Worthington,
Canadian & Nova Scotian refugee land [forwards plat only]

--	*	-	16	18	-	18

*Refugee tract.

510   6 Aug 1807   A/3/357
Obadiah Jennings, Attorney, Stu
Transmits patent
Stephen Ford & Peter Hesser, executors of estate of Nicholas France, deceased.

511   15 Aug 1807   A/3/358
Charles Killgore, Reg Cin
Transmits patents

Daniel Miller	Cin	WML	1	10	24	+
Peter Davis	Cin	WML	1	10	8	+
Peter Davis	Cin	WML	1	10	7	+
Abraham Miller	Cin	WML	1	10	24	+
Alexander & Isaac Dubois	Cin	WML	2	10	12	+
George Hoffman	Cin	EML	3	2	2	-
William King	Cin	EML	6	2	-	33
William King	Cin	EML	6	2	32	-
Sutherland & Brown	Cin	EML	2	4	2	+
James M. Kane	Cin	EML	3	3	20	+
Cassady & Phillips	Cin	EML	3	5	35	+
Robert Willson	Cin	EML	5	4	23	-

512   15 Aug 1807   A/3/358
David Hoge, Reg Stu
Transmits patent

Jonathan Taylor	Stu	-	3	6	12	-

513   15 Aug 1807   A/3/359
Jesse Spencer, Reg Chl
Transmits patents

George Henninger	Chl	-	20	10	3	+
Henry Wister	Chl	-	20	11	32	+
David Shelby	Chl	WS	21	10	3	+
George Deverbaugh	Chl	-	19	12	19	+
Patrick Lusk	Chl	-	19	15	18	-
John Trimble	Chl	-	18	15	25	+
Henry Hottle	Chl	-	17	17	14	-
Griffith Pearce	Chl	-	20	8	26	-
John Nolind	Chl	-	21	5	26	+
Adam Rickabaugh	Chl	-	16	6	26	+
Carlile & Winship	Chl	-	20	12	1	+
John Williams	Chl	-	20	13	17	-
William Baye	Chl	MS	21	11	3	+

514   20 Aug 1807   A/3/359
Hon. H. Dearborn, Secretary of War
Answers inquiry regarding military land warrants placed in hands of Colonel William Alexander S. Smith of Baltimore; Christian Myers; Colonel William Alexander, Carlisle, Pennsylvania; Major H. Rodgers.

515   22 Aug 1807   A/3/360
Memorandum
Transmitted patent to Colonel -- Worthington, Chl

Edward Strode	Chl	-	19	14	5	+

516   25 Aug 1807   A/3/360
David Hoge, Reg Stu
Transmits patents

Jonathan Ellis	Stu	-	5	9	3	-
Nathan Shepherd	Stu	-	4	8	35	-
Jacob Ong	Stu	-	3	9	12	-
John Myers	Stu	-	2	13	33	-
Basil Perry	Stu	-	4	17	5	+
Joseph Eaton	Stu	-	5	8	14	-
Philip Choler? [Oholer?]	Stu	-	2	13	9	-

517   25 Aug 1807   A/3/361
Charles Killgore, Reg Cin
Transmits patents

William Ogle	Cin	EML	2	5	28	-
Andrew McQuisten	Cin	EML	1	6	36	+
John Young	Cin	EML	2	5	10	-
Enoch Everingham	Cin	EML	1	4	13	+

518   26 Aug 1807   A/3/361
Seth Pease
Error in numbering plat; plat sketch enclosed

--		Unk	W	4	4	-	-
--		Unk	W	4	5	-	-

519   27 Aug 1807   A/3/362
David Hoge, Reg Stu
First certificate

Nathan Gregg		Stu	-	4	16	14	-

520   28 Aug 1807   A/3/362
David Hoge, Reg Stu
Transmits patents

John Gillis	Stu	-	3	10	35	-
Alexander Gray	Stu	-	3	7	32	-
Samuel Porter	Stu	-	5	10	8	-
Joseph Curle	Stu	-	4	17	25	-
John Johnson	Stu	-	4	8	29	-
James McCoy	Stu	-	1	4	-	26
James Galbreath	Stu	-	1	4	32	-
James Galbreath	Stu	-	4	15	2	-

521   28 Aug 1807   A/3/363
Charles Killgore, Reg Cin
Transmits patents; ". . . so importunately urged
   by an agent here . . . that I shall be greatly
   obliged, if you will . . . prepare and forward
   his final certificate"

Benjamin Chambers	Cin	WML	1	5	13	-
Benjamin Chambers	Cin	WML	1	5	14	-
Benjamin Chambers	Cin	WML	1	5	15	-

522   14 Sep 1807   A/3/363
David Hoge, Reg Stu
Transmits patents

Robert Martin	Stu	-	2	9	23	-
Rudolph Bair	Stu	-	7	18	12	+
Nathan Updegraff	Stu	-	3	8	34	-
James Wilson	Stu	-	3	16	18	-
John Boyd	Stu	-	1	6	13	-
Samuel Huston	Stu	-	1	6	28	-
John McMillan	Stu	-	5	10	2	-
James Caldwell	Stu	-	4	7	2	-
Enoch Harris	Stu	-	3	8	20	-

523   14 Sep 1807   A/3/364
Charles Killgore, Reg Cin
Transmits patents

Christian Myers	Cin	EML	5	3	20	-
Thomas Buck	Cin	EML	1	4	26	+
John Miksell	Cin	EML	5	3	28	-
Abraham Chase	Cin	EML	1	4	5	+
James Brown	Cin	EML	1	6	23	+
Henry Myer	Cin	EML	4	4	36	-
William Dubois	Cin	WML	2	10	11	+

524   14 Sep 1807   A/3/364
Jesse Spencer, Reg Chl

Noah & John Zane	Chl	-	19	14	14	+
Jesse Spencer (as grantee)	Chl	MS	21	11	7	+

525   14 Sep 1807   A/3/364
Willys Silliman, Reg Zan
Transmits patent

John Adair?	Zan	-	1	3	5	+

526   29 Sep 1807   A/3/365
Charles Killgore, Reg Cin
Transmits patents

Conrad Sayrs	Cin	WML	2	8	3	+
John Sailor	Cin	WML	1	8	18	+
John Starr	Cin	WML	1	12	19	+

527   29 Sep 1807   A/3/365
Joseph Wood, Reg Mar
Overpayment; Act of 18 Apr 1806

Isaac Hall	Mar	-	5	6	33	+

528   30 Sep 1807   A/3/365
James Findlay, Rec Cin
Error in computation; Act of 18 Apr 1806

John Neff	Cin	EML	6	2	-	12
John Neff	Cin	EML	6	2	-	13
John Neff	Cin	EML	6	2	-	14
John Neff	Cin	EML	6	2	11	-
John Neff	Cin	EML	6	2	15	-

529   1 Oct 1807   A/3/366
Samuel Finley, Rec Chl
Duplicate receipt

John Adams	Chl	-	20	12	14	+

530   1 Oct 1807   A/3/367
Charles Killgore, Reg Cin
Transmits patents

Michael Pierce	Cin	EML	4	1	-	4
Michael Pierce	Cin	EML	4	1	-	5
Michael Pierce	Cin	EML	4	1	6	-
Samuel Payne	Cin	EML	3	3	9	+
Nathan Stubbs	Cin	EML	3	3	3	+
Moris Wiley	Cin	WML	1	7	11	+
Jared Mansfield (as grantee)	Cin	*	2	3	11	+

*Fractional range.

531   1 Oct 1807   A/3/367
Charles Killgore, Reg Cin
Final certificate; underpayment

Samuel Dickey	Cin	EML	4	2	7	-

532   2 Oct 1807   A/3/368
General John Smith
Transmits patent

William Ball	Mil	-	3	10	2	6

533   3 Oct 1807   A/3/368
Jesse Spencer, Reg Chl
Final certificate; underpayment

James Frazier	Chl	WS	21	10	11	+

534   3 Oct 1807   A/3/369
Charles Killgore, Reg Cin
Final certificate; overpayment

John Vennimman	Cin	EML	5	4	33	-
Samuel Dick	Cin	EML	2	2	-	30
Samuel Dick	Cin	EML	2	2	-	31

535   15 Oct 1807   A/3/370
Transmits patents

James Armstrong	Stu	-	4	15	27	+

William Smith	Stu	–	6	10	13	–
Samuel Vail	Stu	–	5	7	27	+
Thomas Stanley	Stu	–	5	17	10	+

536 15 Oct 1807 A/3/370
Jesse Spencer, Reg Chl
Transmits patents

Joseph Shaver	Chl	–	16	16	17	+
David Sweezy	Chl	–	17	17	18	–

537 15 Oct 1807 A/3/370
Willys Silliman, Reg Zan
Transmits patents

Joseph W. Satterthwaite	Zan	–	9	8	3	+
Joseph W. Satterthwaite	Zan	Mil	1	1	9	+
Joseph W. Satterthwaite	Zan	Mil	1	1	10	+
Joseph Smith	Zan	Mil	1	2	19	+

538 15 Oct 1807 A/3/371
Charles Killgore, Reg Cin
Transmits patents

David Sidwell	Cin	EML	1	8	8	+
John Vaughan	Cin	EML	1	3	25	+
John Seybold	Cin	EML	3	4	28	+
William Emrich	Cin	EML	4	3	24	+

539 19 Oct 1807 A/3/371
Willys Silliman, Reg Zan
Transmits patents

Beal Adams	Zan	Mil	7	4	25	+
George Adair	Zan	MIL	1	3	24	+
James Taylor	Zan	Mil	8	2	18	+
James Taylor	Zan	Mil	8	2	4	+
James Taylor	Zan	Mil	8	2	13	+

540 22 Oct 1807 A/3/371
Jesse Spencer, Reg Chl
Transmits patents

Peter Trumball	Chl	–	16	17	6	–
Adam Ansbaugh	Chl	–	17	18	25	+
Samuel Arrowsmith	Chl	WS	21	9	27	–

541 22 Oct 1807 A/3/372
Charles Killgore, Reg Cin
Transmits patents

Isaac Anderson	Cin	EML	2	3	23	+
Peter Weaver	Cin	EML	5	3	7	–
David Mast	Cin	EML	5	5	3	+
Jeremiah Mote	Cin	EML	5	5	5	+

542 22 Oct 1807 A/3/372
David Hoge, Reg Stu
Transmits patents

Caleb Antrim	Stu	–	7	20	9	+
Arthur Morrison	Stu	–	5	8	4	–
John Hoopes	Stu	–	4	17	29	+
John Hoopes	Stu	–	7	20	10	+

543 17 Oct 1807 A/3/372
Henry Bowman, Hagar's Town, Maryland
Transmits patent

Henry Bowman	Unk	–	5	5	30	+

544 24 Oct 1807 A/3/373
Acting Clerk, Reg Cin
Transmits patents

Jacob Shungletaker?	Cin	Pre	7	3	27	+
Solomon McCulley	Cin	Pre	7	4	34	+
Peter Thorn	Cin	Pre	4	4	21	+
Ichabod Corwin?	Cin	Pre	4	4	25	+
Amos Cook	Cin	Pre	4	4	17	–
John Brownson	Cin	Pre	11	2	20	+
Theodore Saunder	Cin	Pre	10	1	4	+
Ludwick Kemp	Cin	Pre	7	2	22	+
John Blackford	Cin	–	5	3	19	+
John Blackford	Cin	–	5	3	20	+
Thomas Trowsel	Cin	Pre	4	2	2	+
John Brownson	Cin	Pre	11	2	21	+
Robert Edgar	Cin	Pre	7	2	33	+
Daniel Richardson	Cin	Pre	4	3	30	–
William Law	Cin	Pre	5	3	15	+
Jacob Coy	Cin	Pre	6	3	36	+
Richard Palmer	Cin	Pre	10	2	36	+
Richard Palmer	Cin	Pre	10	2	30	+
Thomas Newman	Cin	Pre	10	4	7	+
Joseph Park	Cin	Pre	4	3	34	+
John Allen	Cin	Pre	5	2	25	+
Jacob Siler	Cin	Pre	9	2	18	+
Benjamin Evans	Cin	Pre	4	4	18	–
Isaac Spinning	Cin	Pre	7	2	12	+
George Harmer	Cin	Pre	7	3	17	+
William Miller	Cin	Pre	6	3	31	+
J. Harris Robison	Cin	Pre	4	3	27	+

545 27 Oct 1807 A/3/374
David Hoge, Reg Stu
First certificate
Phillips' final certificate to include the address: Kennett Township, Chester County, Pennsylvania

John Phillips	Stu	–	4	17	5	+
Henry Bowman	Stu	–	7	18	5	+
Philip Smith	Stu	–	7	18	3	+
Philip Smith	Stu	–	7	18	4	+

546 27 Oct 1807 A/3/374
Samuel Finley, Rec Chl
Duplicate receipt
Thomas Ritter & John Leef?

547 6 Nov 1807 A/3/375
Acting Clerk, Reg Cin
Transmits patents

Newton Jones	Cin	EML	3	4	34	+
Conrad Ireley	Cin	EML	4	3	14	+
Lewis Davis & Benjamin Chambers	Cin	WML	1	3	–	1
Lewis Davis & Benjamin Chambers	Cin	WML	1	3	–	2
Lewis Davis & Benjamin Chambers	Cin	WML	1	3	3	–
Drake, Pritchard, & Drake	Cin	EML	3	3	25	+

548 6 Nov 1807 A/3/375
David Hoge, Reg Stu
Transmits patents

Edward Carroll	Stu	–	1	6	29	–
John Grayble	Stu	–	4	11	11	–
Thomas Ferguson	Stu	–	4	14	3	+

549   6 Nov 1807   A/3/376
James Findlay, Rec Cin
Transmits patents

| William Ramsey | Cin | MR | 9 | 5 | 30 | + |

550   7 Nov 1807   A/3/376
Jesse Spencer, Reg Chl
First certificates; requests expediting of final
   certificates because of desire of a U.S. Representative

| Daniel Buck | Chl | - | 20 | 11 | 33 | + |
| Daniel Buck | Chl | - | 19 | 12 | 27 | + |

551   7 Nov 1807   A/3/377
James Findlay, Rec Cin
Inquiry regarding patent
Jeremiah Morrow, U.S. Representative "from your
   state"

| Robert Park | Cin | Pre | 5 | 2 | 1 | + |

552   5 Nov 1807   A/3/378
James Buckhannon, Lanceford Township, York County,
   Pennsylvania
Transmits patent

| James Buckhannon | Chl | - | 17 | 18 | 10 | + |

553   9 Nov 1807   A/3/378
James Findlay, Rec Cin
First certificate

| Henry Medsker | Cin | - | 5 | 3 | 5 | + |

554   14 Nov 1807   A/3/378
David Hoge, Reg Stu
Transmits patents

John Hooper	Stu	-	4	17	28	+
Jacob Haycock	Stu	-	1	7	20	+
Horton Howard	Stu	-	4	16	6	+
Jonah Robinson	Stu	-	2	10	10	-
Peter Hout	Stu	-	3	10	5	-
Horton Howard	Stu	-	6	8	2	+

555   14 Nov 1807   A/3/379
Acting Clerk, Reg Cin
Transmits patents

Thomas Hopkins & James Taylor	Cin	EML	1	1	-	31
Mathew Huston	Cin	EML	3	2	9	-
George Harner	Cin	MR	8	3	8	+
Mathew Brown & John Harlin	Cin	EML	1	2	17	-

556   19 Nov 1807   A/3/379
James Findlay, Rec Cin
Final certificate; underpayment
Morter's final certificate to be sent to him at
   post office, Brownsburgh, Rockbridge County,
   Virginia

John Hole, assignee of	Cin	Pre	6	1	31	+
John Hole, assignee of	Cin	Pre	6	1	35	+
Jacob Shiveley	Cin	-	5	4	32	+
Jacob Morter	Cin	EML	2	7	23	+

557   25 Nov 1807   A/3/380
Nathan Gregg, at the post office, Hillsborough,
   Loudon County, Virginia
Transmits patents

| Nathan Gregg | Stu | - | 1 | 8 | 31 | - |
| Nathan Gregg | Stu | - | 4 | 16 | 14 | - |

558   25 Nov 1807   A/3/381
Affidavit
Military land warrant 2492, in favor of John
   Mountjoy, Captain of Virginia Line, registered,
   with others, on 25 Feb 1800 for William Steele,
   4000-acre tract
Joseph Smith; John Dice; Samuel Denman; Joseph
   Nourse, Reg of Treasury

| William Wells | * | - | 17 | 6 | 3 | - |

*4000-acre tracts.

559   26 Nov 1807   A/3/381
Joseph Wood, Rec Mar
Transmits patents

| David Lockwood | Mar | - | 3 | 4 | - | 5 |
| David Lockwood | Mar | - | 3 | 4 | - | 11 |

560   26 Nov 1807   A/3/382
James Findley, Rec Cin
Overpayments; receipt
Haines certificate to be sent to him at post
   office, Taneytown, Frederick County, Maryland

David Lee	Cin	EML	1	5	24	+
John W. Miles	Cin	EML	1	3	26	+
James Conn	Cin	WML	1	5	-	27
James Conn	Cin	WML	1	5	-	28
James Conn	Cin	WML	1	5	29	-
John Hanna & George Levingston	Cin	WML	2	11	-	16
Samuel Haines	Cin	EML	5	6	31	-

561   26 Nov 1807   A/3/383
Zaccheus Biggs, Rec Stu
Duplicate receipts

| William Murdaugh | Stu | - | 3 | 10 | 19 | + |
| Michael Snider | Stu | - | 8 | 12 | 33 | + |

562   26 Nov 1807   A/3/383
Willys Silliman, Reg Zan
First certificate
Final receipt to be sent to him at post office,
   Hagar's Town, Maryland

| Jacob Thomas | Zan | - | 4 | 8 | 1 | + |

563   25 Nov 1807   A/3/383
Samuel Finley, Rec Chl
Duplicate receipt

| Jacob Claypool | Chl | - | 19 | 15 | 21 | + |

564   28 Nov 1807   A/3/384
Hon. Edward Tiffin
Transmits patent

| John Reichsterffer | Chl | - | 20 | 11 | 23 | + |

565   30 Nov 1807   A/3/384
Acting Clerk, Reg Cin
Transmits patents

Liston & Thomas	Cin	EML	3	2	1	-
Michael Myers	Cin	EML	5	3	27	-
Robert McClure	Cin	EML	5	9	3	+
Abraham Miller	Cin	EML	1	6	34	+

Jonathan Miles	Cin	EML	5	7	31	+
Jacob Melendore	Cin	EML	3	5	18	+
James Findlay (as grantee)	Cin	EML	5	1	–	7
James Findlay (as grantee)	Cin	EML	5	1	6	–
John Fox	Cin	EML	2	8	9	+
Emanuel Flory	Cin	EML	5	5	33	–

566   30 Nov 1807   A/3/385
David Hoge, Reg Stu
Transmits patents

John Gregg, Sr.	Stu	–	5	7	6	–
James Oliver	Stu	–	7	15	28	–
Alexander Young	Stu	–	4	7	18	–
Samuel Lippin	Stu	–	7	15	35	–
William Milhous	Stu	–	4	17	33	+
William McIntosh	Stu	–	2	10	26	+
Caleb Merryman	Stu	–	4	10	25	–
Thomas Marques	Stu	–	5	9	7	–
Andrew McPherson	Stu	–	2	10	36	–

567   2 Dec 1807   A/3/385
David Hoge, Reg Stu
Inquiry regarding application
Anne Mifflin; Samuel Emlen Mifflin.

568   3 Dec 1807   A/3/386
Jared Mansfield, SG
Transmits patent

Jared Mansfield (as grantee)	Cin?	EML	6	3	31	–

569   3 Dec 1807   A/3/386
David Hoge, Reg Stu
Transmits patents

Isaac Siddall	Stu	–	1	7	18	+
Daniel Stratton	Stu	–	2	12	20	–
Zadok Street	Stu	–	4	17	8	+
Daniel Straughan	Stu	–	4	17	34	–

570   3 Dec 1807   A/3/386
Acting Clerk, Reg Cin
Transmits patents

Christian Shiveley	Cin	EML	5	3	5	+
Christian Shiveley	Cin	EML	5	3	4	–
Daniel Shiveley	Cin	EML	5	4	27	+
Andrew Scott	Cin	EML	2	2	–	18
Andrew Scott	Cin	EML	2	2	7	–

571   3 Dec 1807   A/3/387
James Findlay, Rec Cin
Transmits patents

Henry Sellars	Cin	–	17	16	18	+
Josiah Shakford	Cin	–	21	2	32	+

572   5 Dec 1807   A/3/387
James Findlay, Rec Cin
Underpayment

Thomas Wilson	Cin	MR	11	2	14	–

573   9 Dec 1807   A/3/387
Jesse Spencer, Reg Chl
Final certificate; underpayment

Isaiah Strawn	Chl	–	16	17	5	–

574   18 Dec 1807   A/3/387
David Hoge, Reg Stu
Correction of final certificate to include assignee
Howard Horton

575   12 Dec 1807   A/3/388
Jesse Spencer, Reg Chl
First certificate for correction
Isaac Schaeffer; Joseph Tiffin; Samuel & James Schaeffer.

576   17 Dec 1807   A/3/388
James Findlay, Rec Cin
Transmits patents

Peter Parham	Cin	EML	4	3	20	+
Peter Parham	Cin	EML	2	8	28	+
Nathan Powell	Cin	WML	2	5	26	–
Alexander Pugh	Cin	EML	3	4	13	+

577   18 Dec 1807   A/3/388
James Findlay, Rec Cin
Transmits patents

Emanuel Flory	Cin	EML	5	4	20	+
John Brown	Cin	EML	2	3	32	+
Jeremiah Beatty	Cin	EML	2	4	24	+
Joseph Bedle	Cin	EML	6	5	5	–
Joseph Bedle	Cin	EML	6	5	–	4
David Beaty	Cin	EML	2	4	33	–
Jonas Randle [Kandle?]	Cin	EML	3	4	31	+
Isaac Bates	Cin	WML	1	10	18	+
John Brown	Cin	WML	2	9	33	+
James Gallaway	Cin	Pre	7	4	34	+
James Gallaway	Cin	Pre	7	4	–	28
James Gallaway	Cin	Pre	7	3	5	+
Jacob Saum	Cin	Pre	6	2	23	+
Joseph Reynolds	Cin	MR	11	3	15	+
Joseph Smith Reynolds	Cin	MR	11	3	2	+
John Shitaker	Cin	MR	10	2	13	+

578   18 Dec 1807   A/3/389
David Hoge, Reg Stu
Transmits patents

John Koop	Stu	–	3	10	27	–
Samuel Reeder	Stu	–	4	15	33	+
Baltzer Roller	Stu	–	3	16	36	–
Israel French, Jr.	Stu	–	6	8	17	+
Samuel Reeder [Keeder?]	Stu	–	4	15	31	+
Elias Pegg	Stu	–	2	5	28	–

579   18 Dec 1807   A/3/390
Elijah Brush, Det
Transmits patent; issuing of patents in your district to be suspended pending return of SG
Matthew Ernest.

580   18 Dec 1807   A/3/390
Jesse Spencer, Reg Chl
First certificate
Assignment to Jacob Kershner found defective

James Crain	Chl	–	20	10	1	+

581   22 Dec 1807   A/3/391
Hon. John Smilie
Transmits patent

George Riffel	Unk	–	16	1	31	+

<table>
<tr><td colspan="7">582   30 Dec 1807   A/3/391</td></tr>
</table>

582 30 Dec 1807 A/3/391
David Hoge, Reg Stu
First certificate; duplicate receipt
Forward final certificate to Hutchison at the post
   office, New London Crossroads, Chester County,
   Pennsylvania

John Hutchison	Stu	-	4	8	3	+

583 31 Dec 1807 A/3/391
James Findlay, Rec Cin
Transmits patents

Peter Shull	Cin	EML	1	2	33	+
George Shidler	Cin	EML	5	3	33	-
Alexander Pugh	Cin	EML	3	4	24	+
John Willson	Cin	EML	3	3	35	+
Joseph Kelly	Cin	EML	3	4	35	+
Henry Coleman Smith	Cin	WML	1	6	27	+
John Snavely Potter	Cin	MR	9	4	4	+

584 1 Jan 1808 A/3/392
Adam Seebert, Winchester, Virginia
Transmits patent [letter was returned unclaimed]

Adam Seebert	Stu	-	4	8	9	-

585 1 Jan 1808 A/3/392
Christian Mishey, to be left at post office, Car-
   lile, Cumberland County, Pennsylvania
Transmits patent

Christian Mishey	Stu	-	1	9	8	-

586 1 Jan 1808 A/3/392
James Findlay, Rec Cin
Transmits patents

John Sutherland & Henry Brown	Cin	EML	3	2	-	31
John Sutherland & Henry Brown	Cin	EML	3	2	32	-
John Sutherland & Henry Brown	Cin	EML	2	4	36	-
Frederick Woolf	Cin	EML	4	3	12	+
Matthew Winton	Cin	EML	3	2	5	-

587 1 Jan 1808 A/3/393
David Hoge, Reg Stu
Transmits patents

William Smith	Stu	-	5	18	3	-
David Parkhill	Stu	-	3	9	35	+
John Pugh	Stu	-	6	11	33	+
George Pfautz	Stu	-	4	11	33	-
Abraham Plummer, Sr.	Stu	-	6	9	1	+
Thomas Stanley	Stu	-	5	18	33	+
Thomas Stanley	Stu	-	7	20	33	+
Henry Sill	Stu	-	8	10	24	+
Jonathan Stanley	Stu	-	4	17	17	+
Thomas Stanley	Stu	-	5	17	12	+
Henry Stofer	Stu	-	3	16	25	-
Waddy Stanley	Stu	-	5	17	11	+
Waddy Stanley	Stu	-	5	17	2	+

588 4 Jan 1808 A/3/393
John Rathbone
Military land warrant, presumably in name of Robert
   Allyn [bankruptcy case]
Lyman Law & David Coit, assignees

John Rathbone	Mil?	-	18	7	1	10
John Rathbone	Mil?	-	18	7	1	11

589 5 Jan 1808 A/3/394
Zaccheus Biggs, Rec Stu
Duplicate receipts

Parmenas Lambourn	Stu	-	5	17	13	+
Parmenas Lambourn	Stu	-	5	17	7	+

590 13 Jan 1808 A/3/394
James Findlay, Rec Cin
Transmits patents

Daniel Shively	Cin	EML	5	4	27	+
William Wells	Cin	EML	6	6	19	+
Leonard Wolf?	Cin	EML	5	4	24	-
William Cooley	Cin	EML	2	5	33	-
Joseph Kelly	Cin	EML	3	3	1	+
Jacob Weaver	Cin	EML	5	2	-	2
Jacob Weaver	Cin	EML	5	2	3	-
George Drybread	Cin	EML	1	3	27	+
John Wolf	Cin	MR	8	3	10	+
John Wolf	Cin	MR	8	3	9	+
Adam Wise	Cin	MR	12	4	1	+
Cave Johnston	Cin	WML	1	7	13	+
Henry Coleman Smith	Cin	WML	1	6	27	+
Charles Null	Cin	Pre	4	3	12	+

591 13 Jan 1808 A/3/395
David Hoge, Reg Stu
Transmits patents

Isaac James	Stu	-	2	11	1	-
Henry Winrode	Stu	-	4	16	8	-
David Wallace	Stu	-	4	8	8	-
John Straughan	Stu	-	3	16	9	+

592 13 Jan 1808 A/3/395
Joseph Wood, Reg Mar
Transmits patents

William Dana, Jr.	Mar	-	6	1	29	-
Robert Carpenter	Mar	-	7	7	18	+
Peter Danford	Mar	-	4	5	23	+
Ambron Danford	Mar	-	4	5	34	+
Jacob Moore	Mar	-	5	6	17	+
Seth Ward	Mar	-	4	5	23	+
David Ruble	Mar	-	3	4	20	-

593 16 Jan 1808 A/3/395
James Findlay, Rec Cin
Transmits patents

Henry Jones	Cin	EML	3	4	33	+
Mehalah Johnston	Cin	EML	1	4	6	+
James Martin, et al	Cin	EML	2	5	23	-
Archibald Armstrong, Commissioner? & William Henry?	Cin	EML	2	5	9	-

594 16 Jan 1808 A/3/396
David Hoge, Reg Stu
Transmits patents

Benjamin Wheeler, Jr.	Stu	-	3	9	36	+
Benjamin Wheeler, Jr.	Stu	-	4	10	6	+
Griffith John	Stu	-	4	15	20	+
John Cox	Stu	-	6	8	17	+
William Chapline	Stu	-	5	8	20	-
Conrad Neff	Stu	-	3	6	20	+
Evan Jenkins	Stu	-	5	8	24	-

595 18 Jan 1808 A/3/396
Winn Winship
Final certificate

Henry Shock, assignee of Edmund Mace, assignee of Jesse Spencer (as grantee).

| 596 | | 19 Jan 1808 | | | | | A/3/397 |

Willys Silliman, Reg Zan
Final certificate
George Olinger, assignee of John Zane; John McIntire, assignee of John Zane

| John Zane? | Zan | - | 15 | 17 | 17 | + |

| 597 | | 21 Jan 1808 | | | | | A/3/397 |

Jesse Spencer, Reg Chl
Final certificate
James Land

| Peter Ruffner, heirs & legal representatives | Chl | - | 17 | 17 | 32 | - |

| 598 | | 23 Jan 1808 | | | | | A/3/398 |

James Findlay, Rec Cin
Duplicate receipt

| -- | Cin | Pre | 8 | 4 | 25 | - |

| 599 | | 23 Jan 1808 | | | | | A/3/398 |

David Hoge, Reg Stu
Transmits patents

Thomas Webster	Stu	-	7	9	26	+
John Webster	Stu	-	7	9	19	+
John Webster	Stu	-	7	9	14	+
John Webster	Stu	-	7	9	25	+
Edward Taylor	Stu	-	3	11	2	+
John Eskey	Stu	-	2	6	9	-
John Montgomery	Stu	-	3	11	1	-
Israel French, Sr.	Stu	-	6	8	17	+
Ralph Cowgill	Stu	-	6	10	8	+

| 600 | | 23 Jan 1808 | | | | | A/3/398 |

Jesse Spencer, Reg Chl
Transmits patents

Christopher Cagy	Chl	-	18	15	13	+
George Ritchey	Chl	WS	21	9	17	-
Nathaniel Teal	Chl	-	17	18	5	+
Robert Barron & Peter Bugh? [Pugh?]	Chl	-	16	16	6	+
George Arnold	Chl	-	18	15	30	+

| 601 | | 23 Jan 1808 | | | | | A/3/399 |

Daniel Symmes, Reg Cin
Transmits patents

David Ulrick	Cin	EML	5	4	34	-
Mauries Jones	Cin	EML	2	3	30	-
Josephus Gard	Cin	WML	1	12	36	+

| 602 | | 23 Jan 1808 | | | | | A/3/399 |

Samuel Finley, Rec Chl
Duplicate receipts

| James Claypoole | Chl | Mil | 14 | 8 | 22 | + |
| Branson & Claypoole | Chl | Mil | 14 | 8 | 21 | + |

| 603 | | 26 Jan 1808 | | | | | A/3/399 |

David Hoge, Reg Stu
Surpluses and deficiencies in acreage to be compensated for in last instalment payment
Horton Howard

Tunis & Annesley, assignees	Stu	-	9	9	-	5
Tunis & Annesley, assignees	Stu	-	9	9	-	6
Tunis & Annesley, assignees	Stu	-	9	9	-	8

| 604 | | 26 Jan 1808 | | | | | A/3/400 |

Daniel Symmes, Reg Cin
Final certificate
John Osborne, assignee; heirs of Michael Kever

| Samuel Highway & Michael Kever | Cin | Pre | 4 | 4 | 23 | - |

| 605 | | 27 Jan 1808 | | | | | A/3/401 |

Joseph Eaton, Washington County, Pennsylvania

| John Eaton | Stu | - | 5 | 8 | 14 | - |

| 606 | | 27 Jan 1808 | | | | | A/3/401 |

Jesse Spencer, Reg Chl
Requests expediting application because of inquiry by U.S. Representative

| Daniel Buck | Chl | - | 20 | 11 | 33 | + |
| Daniel Buck | Chl | - | 19 | 12 | 27 | + |

| 607 | | 28 Jan 1808 | | | | | A/3/402 |

Joseph Wood, Reg Mar
Insufficiencies of various assignments
Jacob Baker; William Bates; Robert Latta; -- Coalman, Justice of Peace; Isaac Moore, Justice of Peace.

| 608 | | 3 Feb 1808 | | | | | A/3/403 |

John Badollet, Reg Vin
Final certificate
Richard Stillwell.

| 609 | | 5 Feb 1808 | | | | | A/3/403 |

Daniel Symmes, Reg Cin
Transmits patents
James? Morrow

Joel Wright	Cin	MR	7	4	35	+
Conkling Miller	Cin	EML	6	3	34	+
John Miller	Cin	EML	5	3	29	-
Robert Park	Cin	Pre	5	2	1	+

| 610 | | 4 Feb 1808 | | | | | A/3/404 |

Jesse Spencer, Reg Chl
First certificate; duplicate recipt
Final certificate to be sent to Johns at post office, Lancaster, Pennsylvania

| Henry Johns | Chl | - | 20 | 15 | 27 | + |

| 611 | | 24 Feb 1808 | | | | | A/3/404 |

Henry Bowman, care of postmaster, McAlester's Town, York County, Pennsylvania
Transmits patent

| Henry Bowman | Stu | - | 7 | 18 | 5 | + |

| 612 | | 24 Feb 1808 | | | | | A/3/404 |

John Philips, to be left at post office, Wilmington, Delaware
Transmits patent

| John Philips | Stu | - | 4 | 17 | 5 | + |

613 25 Feb 1808 A/3/405
David Hoge, Reg Stu
Transmits patents

Name					
Jacob Black, Sr.	Stu	-	5	9	12	-
Arthur Barrett, Sr.	Stu	-	5	10	26	-
Rudolph Bair, Jr.	Stu	-	7	18	12	+
Rudolph Bair	Stu	-	6	17	8	+
David Parkhill	Stu	-	3	9	35	+
Harin? Bentley	Stu	-	3	14	23	-
Abraham Blackledge	Stu	-	3	15	29	+
Andrew Brinker	Stu	-	4	16	9	-

614 25 Feb 1808 A/3/405
Daniel Symmes, Reg Cin
Transmits patents

Andrew Black	Cin	MR	10	3	25	+
John Brown	Cin	WML	1	7	9	+
Ephraim Brown	Cin	EML	1	6	8	+
Ephraim Brown	Cin	EML	1	6	17	+
Philip Bowser	Cin	EML	5	4	13	+
Philip Bowser	Cin	EML	5	3	30	-
James Brown	Cin	EML	2	4	13	+
James Brown, Jr.	Cin	EML	3	2	18	+
Caspar Bottorf	Cin	EML	2	7	26	+
Caspar Bottorf	Cin	EML	2	7	27	-
James Robinson	Cin	MR	4	2	8	+
Joseph Brown	Cin	EML	1	1	17	-

615 25 Feb 1808 A/3/406
Jesse Spencer, Reg Chl
Transmits patents

Alexander McIntire	Chl	-	20	12	24	+
Susannah Bibler	Chl	-	17	18	30	+
Philip Ross	Chl	-	21	8	25	+
Richard Ritter	Chl	-	20	15	10	+

616 25 Feb 1808 A/3/406
Willys Silliman, Reg Zan
Transmits patents

Nicholas Sartchell	Zan	-	9	8	5	+
John Bush	Zan	-	15	17	35	+
Gideon Jennings	Zan	-	1	9	4	+
John Brummage	Zan	-	14	14	9	+

617 25 Feb 1808 A/3/406
George Hampshire, Baltimore, Maryland
Final certificate
William A. Smith & Thomas Dowden, assignors.

618 26 Feb 1808 A/3/407
Willys Silliman, Reg Zan
Final certificate
George Hampshire, assignee; Jacob Thomas
William A. Smith & Thomas
Dowden Zan - 14 15 14 +

619 29 Feb 1808 A/3/408
Elisha Hunt, Brownsville, Fayette County, Pennsylvania
Status of accounts

Elisha Hunt	Stu	-	4	17	23	-
Thomas French	Stu	-	4	16	4	-

620 9 Mar 1808 A/3/408
David Hoge, Reg Stu
Transmits patents

Randolph Cook	Stu	-	3	16	13	-
Edward Stewart	Stu	-	3	10	14	+
Levi Haines	Stu	-	5	16	36	+

621 9 Mar 1808 A/3/408
Noah Zane
Transmits patents
Col. -- Worthington

Samuel Y. Keene	Chl?	-	5	3	3	13
Samuel Y. Keene	Chl?	-	5	3	3	16
Samuel Y. Keene	Chl?	-	5	3	3	33

622 14 Mar 1808 A/3/409
John Rathbone
Military land warrant 29.

623 25 Mar 1808 A/3/409
Samuel Finley, Rec Chl
Duplicate receipt
Jacob Binckley Chl - 17 17 3 +

624 25 Mar 1808 A/3/409
Zaccheus Biggs, Rec Stu
Duplicate receipt
Joseph Matthias Stu - 5 17 13 +

625 28 Mar 1808 A/3/409
Elisha Hunt, Brownsville, Fayette County, Pennsylvania
Transmits patents

Thomas French	Stu	-	4	16	4	-
Elisha Hunt	Stu	-	4	17	23	-

626 29 Mar 1808 A/3/410
Isaac Vanhorne, Rec Zan
Transmits patents

Andrew Gregg	Zan	Mil	7	4	2	39
Andrew Gregg	Zan	Mil	7	4	2	40

627 1 Apr 1808 A/3/410
John Rathbone, Merchant, New York
Transmits patents

John Rathbone	Mil	-	18	7	1	10
John Rathbone	Mil	-	18	7	1	11

628 6 Apr 1808 A/3/410
Jacob Bonnett, Bedford, Pennsylvania
Transmits patents
Hon. John Rea

Frederick Hentze	Mil	-	18	2	2	11
Christopher Hite	Mil	-	18	2	2	12

629 7 Apr 1808 A/3/411
Jesse Spencer, Reg Chl
Transmits patents

Jacob Baylor	Chl	-	19	15	27	-
Nathan Rawlings & B. Lambert	Chl	-	22	3	14	-
Peter Frederick & A. C. Eyrstone?	Chl	WS	21	9	14	-
Nathanial Brundige	Chl	-	19	7	23	+
John Beech	Chl	-	19	16	27	+
Jacob Dittoe [Beech?]	Chl	-	16	16	9	+

Robert McTeer	Chl	–	18	15	25	+
Joseph McDill	Chl	WS	21	19	25	+
John Dindore	Chl	–	18	15	13	+
James McDill	Chl	WS	21	9	25	+

630 15 Apr 1808 A/3/411
Hon. James Sloane
Transmits patents

Jeremiah Paul	Stu	–	14	17	2	+
Jeremiah Paul	Stu	–	9	9	11	+

631 15 Apr 1808 A/3/411
Hon. W. Findley
Transmits patents

Jacob Machling	Chl	–	16	17	8	–
Jacob Machling	Chl	–	16	17	17	–

632 15 Apr 1808 A/3/412
Hon. Benjamin Parker
Transmits patent

Pierre Bordeleau	Vin	*	–	–	–	25

*Militia Donation Tract.

633 15 Apr 1808 A/3/412
Jesse Spencer, Reg Chl
Requests return of patent in order to transmit it
to U.S. Representative

Peter Trumball	Chl	–	16	17	6	–

634 15 Apr 1808 A/3/412
David Hoge, Reg Stu
Transmits patents

William Ramage	Stu	–	6	10	4	–
William Whinney	Stu	–	4	16	27	–
Allen Bond	Stu	–	5	8	13	–
John Aytencier?	Stu	–	4	15	25	+
Robert Jackman	Stu	–	1	6	2	–
Andrew Wise	Stu	–	6	18	33	+
John Kupplins	Stu	–	2	13	25	–
John Jackman	Stu	–	4	12	33	+

635 15 Apr 1808 A/3/413
Jesse Spencer, Reg Chl
Transmits patents

Nicholas Conrad	Chl	–	20	12	28	+
Daniel Helser	Chl	–	16	17	32	+
Abraham Jones	Chl	WS	21	9	5	–
George Akert	Chl	–	18	14	21	+
Jacob Shoemaker	Chl	WS	21	11	25	+
Henry Hughes	Chl	–	21	3	17	+
Jacob Dittoe [Hughes?]	Chl	–	16	16	20	+
Samuel Dixon	Chl	–	20	8	24	–
William Ward	Chl	–	20	13	23	–
Samuel Ramsey	Chl	MS	22	4	24	+

636 15 Apr 1808 A/3/413
John Johns, Lancaster, Pennsylvania
Transmits patent

Henry & John Johns	Unk	–	20	15	27	+

637 16 Apr 1808 A/3/413
Daniel Symmes, Reg Cin
Transmits patents

Georg Irminger	Cin	EML	1	3	34	+
David McDill	Cin	EML	1	6	26	+
Henry Pence	Cin	MR	12	3	36	+
Benjamin Kell	Cin	MR	4	3	11	+

638 20 Apr 1808 A/3/414
James Findlay, Rec Cin
Duplicate receipt

Achary Berry	Cin	MR	12	3	1	–

639 20 Apr 1808 A/3/414
Zaccheus Biggs, Rec Stu
Duplicate receipts

John Hannam	Stu	–	7	18	5	+
John Hannam	Stu	–	8	11	33	–
Joseph Wright	Stu	–	4	16	12	–

640 21 Apr 1808 A/3/414
David Hoge, Reg Stu
Transmits patent

James Cellar	Stu	–	2	6	29	–

641 23 Apr 1808 A/3/415
Samuel Finley, Rec Chl
Duplicate receipts

Job McNamee	Chl	–	18	16	29	–
Job McNamee	Chl	–	18	16	27	+

642 23 Apr 1808 A/3/415
David Hoge, Reg Stu
Inquires regarding final certificate

Mordecai Yarnall	Stu	–	3	6	29	–
Mordecai Yarnall	Stu	–	5	9	14	–

643 27 Apr 1808 A/3/415
David Hoge, Reg Stu
Patent application
Simon Martin & William Renaman, assignees

Joshua Budd	Stu	–	1	9	3	–

644 27 Apr 1808 A/3/416
Jesse Spencer, Reg Chl
First certificate; duplicate receipts

Job McNamee	Chl	–	18	16	29	–

645 7 Aug 1805 A/3/416
Affidavit [no explanation of date given]
Appointment of agency & assignment of military
land warrant
John Colter [also Coulter], Jefferson County,
Ohio, "soldier in Lieutenant David Linn's
company in the fifth Maryland Regiment" [dur-
ing Revolution]; Michael Nourse, Washington,
D. C.; John Barrington, assignee; Benjamin
Hough & Thomas Elliot, witnesses; John Ward,
clerk of Court of Common Pleas; Thomas Herty
& Robert King, witnesses.

646 no date A/3/418
Statement
Three-percent fund to State of Ohio, from 1 Jul
1802 to 30 Sep 1807; Act of 3 mar 1803; advances to State of Ohio in 1804, 1805, 1806,
& 1807.

647   19 May 1808   A/3/418
Jesse Spencer, Reg Chl
First certificate
Frazier assigned to Henry Kalback; Kalback
  assigned to David Landis [both patents]

Alexander Frazier	Chl	–	17	17	13 +
Henry Kalback	Chl	–	16	16	7 +
Henry Kalback	Chl	–	16	16	8 +

648   28 May 1808   A/3/419
William Findley
Transmits patent

Peter Trumball	Chl	–	16	17	6 –

649   28 May 1808   A/3/419
Jesse Spencer, Reg Chl
Answers query regarding payment
[Samuel?] Finley; Job McNamee.

650   25 May 1808   A/3/420
Daniel Symmes, Reg Cin
Correction of final certificates
McCoy assigns to Jacob Hackleman; Samuel McClary

James McCoy (error)	Cin	WML	1	8	4	+
James McCoy (correct)	Cin	WML	2	8	4	+
Matthew Houston (error)	Cin	EML	4	4	1	–
Matthew Houston (correct)	Cin	EML	2	4	1	–
John Smith	Cin	MR	10	1	– 11	
Fred[erick] Miller	Cin	EML	3	6	34	–
Daniel Perry	Cin	EML	2	5	3	–

651   30 May 1808   A/3/422
Yate Plummer, Fredericktown, Maryland
Transmits patent; Ohio taxes; Act of 30 Apr 1802
  quoted

Yate Plummer	Chl	Mil	14	8	23	+
Yate Plummer	Chl	Mil	14	8	22	+

652   1 Jun 1808   A/3/422
Jesse Spencer, Reg Chl
Error corrected

John Nealy	Chl	–	17	16	7? +

653   2 Jun 1808   A/3/423
Daniel Symmes, Reg Cin
Final certificates
James Brownlee assigns to -- Jennings

Aaron Martin	Cin	WML	1	13	30	+
Levi Jennings, assignee	Cin	EML	4	2	– 32	
Levi Jennings, assignee	Cin	EML	4	2	– 33	
Levi Jennings, assignee	Cin	EML	4	2	31	–

654   2 Jun 1808   A/3/423
Samuel Finley, Rec Chl
Duplicate receipts

Conrad Wallick	Chl	–	20	12	5	+
Conrad Wallick	Chl	–	20	12	18	+
Jacob Claypool	Chl	–	19	15	21	+

655   2 Jun 1808   A/3/423
Zaccheus Biggs, Rec Stu
Duplicate receipts

Joseph Thompson	Stu	–	1	7	5	–
Andrew Newman	Stu	–	9	10	27	+
Jacob McKay	Stu	–	6	10	7	+
Jacob Mischler	Stu	–	3	11	7	–

656   10 Jun 1808   A/3/424
John Hutchison, New London Crossroads, Chester
  County, Pennsylvania
Transmits patent

John Hutchison	Unk	–	4	8	3	+

657   22 Jun 1808   A/3/424
Daniel Symmes, Reg Cin
Transmits patents

Abel Appleton	Cin	EML	1	3	26	+
John Miller	Cin	EML	5	8	31	+
John Miller	Cin	EML	1	5	14	+
Joseph Gripe	Cin	EML	4	5	36	+
William Arnett	Cin	WML	2	8	4	+
William Wilson	Cin	WML	2	8	3	+
Joseph Stewart	Cin	MR	8	5	9	+

658   20 Jun 1808   A/3/424
Daniel Symmes, Reg Cin
Returns patent after correction

John Brownson	Cin	EML	6	6	19	+

659   22 Jun 1808   A/3/425
Memorandum
Sent Hon. Edward Tiffin, Chl, an abstract of all
  locations of 100-acre lots from commencement of
  separate location to 2 Jun 1808.

660   24 Jun 1808   A/3/425
Jesse Spencer, Reg Chl
Final certificate to be corrected; duplicate
  receipt
Benjamin (not Henry) Bowman

John Kerlin	Chl	–	17	17	21	+

661   29 Jun 1808   A/3/425
David Hoge, Reg Stu
Transmits patents

Hinchman Haines	Stu	–	4	17	24	+
Thomas Hoey [Horey?]	Stu	–	3	13	13	+
Peter Raab	Stu	–	1	9	11	–
Enock Harris	Stu	–	4	16	24	–
Jesse Holloway	Stu	–	6	19	4	+
George Humphreys	Stu	–	2	5	25	–
Michael Roller	Stu	–	3	16	35	–
Thomas Reeder, Sr.	Stu	–	5	16	24	+

662   29 Jun 1808   A/3/426
Jesse Spencer, Reg Chl
Transmits patents

Daniel Miller	Chl	–	19	15	31	+
Job Inskeep	Chl	–	20	8	6	+
John Huber	Chl	–	20	13	5	–
Adam Snyder, Jr.	Chl	–	20	14	29	+
John Vanatta	Chl	–	16	16	32	+
William Willson	Chl	–	16	16	3	+
John Hagar	Chl	MS	21	9	14	–
Andrew Hite	Chl	–	17	18	20	+
Andrew Hite	Chl	–	18	15	11	+

663   29 Jun 1808   A/3/426
Daniel Symmes, Reg Cin

Transmits patents

Amos Hawkins	Cin	EML	3	3	6 +
Jonathan Roberts	Cin	EML	3	3	8 +
John Hanna & George Levingston	Cin	WML	2	11	16 +

664   29 Jun 1808   A/3/427
Joseph Wood, Reg Mar
Final certificates to be corrected.

665   29 Jun 1808   A/3/428
Jesse Spencer, Reg Chl
Final certificates for correction
William Wilson; Abraham Lorance, assignee of Jacob Bumgarner; Joseph Cooper, assignee of John Moorhead & Barnabas Golding

Abraham Lorance	Chl	-	21	5	23 +
Abraham Lorance	Chl	-	21	5	33 +

666   30 Jun 1808   A/3/429
Obadiah Jennings, Stu
Transmits patent

Angus McBean	Stu	-	2	9	6 -

667   6 Jul 1808   A/3/429
Samuel Gwathney
Final certificates.

668   7 Jul 1808   A/3/429
John Badollet, Reg Vin
Patent application; Act of 3 Mar 1807; private claimants
James Patton, assignee of Jonathan Conger who claims under court deed.

669   7 Jul 1808   A/3/430
Jesse Spencer, Reg Chl
Duplicate receipt
Adam Smith's will devises land to son, Isaac Smith

Isaac Smith	Chl	MS	21	10	2 +

670   7 Jul 1808   A/3/430
David Hoge, Reg Stu
First certificate; duplicate receipt

Joseph Thompson	Stu	-	1	7	5 -
Richard Morrow	Stu	-	8	12	35 +

671   7 Jul 1808   A/3/431
James Findlay, Rec Cin
Duplicate receipt

Peter Ingleman	Cin	EML	3	4	12 +

672   9 Jul 1808   A/3/431
Thomas M. Thompson
Military land warrant claim
-- Greenwald.

673   9 Jul 1808   A/3/432
J. G. Jackson, Clarksburgh, Virginia
Answers inquiry regarding vacant lots, apparently in the U.S. Military District

J. G. Jackson	Mil?	-	9	7	3	28

J. G. Jackson	Mil?	-	9	7	3	38
Peter Mills	Mil?	-	9	7	3	16
Peter Mills	Mil?	-	9	7	3	39
Peter Mills	Mil?	-	9	7	3	40
S. H. Smith	Mil?	-	10	7	1	2
S. H. Smith	Mil?	-	10	7	1	3
John Slauter?	Mil?	-	10	7	1	14
Azor Sturdavant	Mil?	-	10	7	1	15

674   9 Jul 1808   A/3/432
Willys Silliman, Reg Zan
Final certificate
Noah Zane, executor of will of John Zane; George Olinger, assignee; John McIntire

John Zane	Zan	-	15	17	17 +

675   13 Jul 1808   A/3/433
John Badollet, Reg Vin
Transmits patents

John Waller	Vin	-	13W	4S	3	+
Thomas Jones	Vin	-	14W	8S	21	+
Thomas Jones	Vin	-	13W	8S	30	-
Thomas Jones	Vin	-	13W	8S	-	29
James Farris	Vin	-	13W	4S	3	+
Thomas Jones, Jr.	Vin	-	14W	8S	-	18

676   19 Jul 1808   A/3/433
T. M. Thompson
Notification that Thompson is registered as assignee of -- Greenwald's military land warrant.

677   22 Jul 1808   A/3/434
J. G. Jackson
Available lots in Mil? district; military land warrants 67, 195, 398, 408, 2692; list of locations made since 5 Jun 1807

William Foreman, heirs of	Mil?	-	8	2	3	22
Vacant	Mil?	-	8	4	3	7
Vacant	Mil?	-	6	6	2	6
Vacant	Mil?	-	6	6	2	7
Vacant	Mil?	-	7	4	2	16
Vacant	Mil?	-	7	4	2	17
Robert Means	Mil?	-	10	7	1	25
Vacant?	Mil?	-	10	7	1	26
James Morrison	Mil?	-	10	7	1	40
-- [locations made]	Mil?	-	2	10	2	17
--	Mil?	-	3	10	1	22
--	Mil?	-	3	10	2	3
--	Mil?	-	3	10	1	23
--	Mil?	-	3	10	1	24
--	Mil?	-	3	10	1	14
--	Mil?	-	3	10	2	6
--	Mil?	-	1	1	3	37
--	Mil?	-	16	7	4	39
--	Mil?	-	16	7	2	40
--	Mil?	-	16	7	2	25
--	Mil?	-	15	8	4	2
--	Mil?	-	13	8	2	10
--	Mil?	-	2	10	2	2
--	Mil?	-	13	8	4	26
--	Mil?	-	15	8	3	11
--	Mil?	-	15	8	3	17
--	Mil?	-	15	8	3	18
--	Mil?	-	15	8	3	9
--	Mil?	-	15	2	2	18
--	Mil?	-	1	6	2	5
--	Mil?	-	7	4	2	40

-- [locations made]	Mil?	-	7	4	2	39
--	Mil?	-	7	4	2	38
--	Mil?	-	1	1	3	7
--	Mil?	-	15	2	2	11
--	Mil?	-	15	2	2	12
--	Mil?	-	3	10	1	15
--	Mil?	-	2	7	4	27
--	Mil?	-	15	8	3	12
--	Mil?	-	4	4	3	9
--	Mil?	-	10	7	1	14
--	Mil?	-	10	7	1	15
--	Mil?	-	8	9	1	2
--	Mil?	-	10	7	1	25
--	Mil?	-	7	7	2	2
--	Mil?	-	18	7	1	16
--	Mil?	-	16	8	4	5
--	Mil?	-	8	5	1	22
--	Mil?	-	8	5	1	21
--	Mil?	-	3	5	1	6
--	Mil?	-	2	10	2	3
--	Mil?	-	9	7	3	28
--	Mil?	-	9	7	3	38
--	Mil?	-	10	3	4	1
--	Mil?	-	3	10	1	18
--	Mil	-	3	10	1	19
--	Mil?	-	15	1	3	5
--	Mil?	-	15	1	3	6
--	Mil?	-	15	1	3	11
--	Mil?	-	15	1	3	12
--	Mil?	-	16	7	4	30
--	Mil?	-	16	7	4	31
--	Mil?	-	16	7	4	32
--	Mil?	-	16	7	4	36
--	Mil?	-	16	7	4	37
--	Mil?	-	16	7	4	38
--	Mil?	-	16	7	4	5
--	Mil?	-	16	7	4	6
--	Mil?	-	16	7	4	7
--	Mil?	-	16	7	4	8
--	Mil?	-	16	7	4	1
--	Mil?	-	16	7	4	2
--	Mil?	-	16	7	4	3
--	Mil?	-	16	7	4	4
--	Mil?	-	16	7	4	16
--	Mil?	-	16	7	4	17
--	Mil?	-	4	4	3	7
--	Mil?	-	4	4	3	23
--	Mil?	-	4	4	3	24
--	Mil?	-	15	8	4	24
--	Mil?	-	15	8	4	25
--	Mil?	-	15	8	4	11
--	Mil?	-	15	8	4	12
--	Mil?	-	15	8	4	15
--	Mil?	-	15	8	4	16
--	Mil?	-	15	8	4	22
--	Mil?	-	15	8	4	23
--	Mil?	-	15	8	4	27
--	Mil?	-	10	3	4	9
--	Mil?	-	10	3	4	23
--	Mil?	-	10	3	4	27
--	Mil?	-	10	3	4	29
--	Mil?	-	10	3	4	22
--	Mil?	-	10	3	4	7
--	Mil?	-	10	3	4	8
--	Mil?	-	10	3	4	19?
--	Mil?	-	8	2	3	37
--	Mil?	-	10	3	4	21
--	Mil?	-	3	10	1	9
--	Mil?	-	3	10	1	12
--	Mil?	-	16	8	4	1
--	Mil?	-	16	8	4	2

-- [locations made]	Mil?	-	15	2	2	16
--	Mil?	-	15	2	2	17
--	Mil?	-	15	2	2	1
--	Mil?	-	15	2	2	2
--	Mil?	-	15	2	2	15
--	Mil?	-	15	8	3	19
--	Mil?	-	15	8	3	20
--	Mil?	-	15	1	3	8
--	Mil?	-	15	1	3	9
--	Mil?	-	2	8	4	11
--	Mil?	-	2	8	4	12
--	Mil?	-	7	9	2	25
--	Mil?	-	7	9	2	37
--	Mil?	-	7	9	2	38
--	Mil?	-	7	9	2	39
--	Mil?	-	15	7	2	22
--	Mil?	-	15	7	2	23
--	Mil?	-	15	7	2	30
--	Mil?	-	15	7	2	31
--	Mil?	-	19	7	1	3
--	Mil?	-	19	7	1	4
--	Mil?	-	19	7	1	5
--	Mil?	-	19	7	1	6
--	Mil?	-	19	7	1	1
--	Mil?	-	15	8	3	10
--	Mil?	-	17	7	2	19
--	Mil?	-	17	7	2	18
--	Mil?	-	17	7	2	10
--	Mil?	-	17	7	2	11
--	Mil?	-	18	7	1	10
--	Mil?	-	18	7	1	11
--	Mil?	-	3	10	1	16
--	Mil?	-	3	10	1	17
--	Mil?	-	10	7	1	2
--	Mil?	-	10	7	1	3
--	Mil?	-	10	7	1	4
--	Mil?	-	17	7	2	6
--	Mil?	-	17	7	2	5
--	Mil?	-	17	7	2	4
--	Mil?	-	17	7	2	3
--	Mil?	-	4	4	3	10
--	Mil?	-	4	4	3	11
--	Mil?	-	4	4	3	6
--	Mil?	-	4	4	3	22
--	Mil?	-	3	10	2	7
--	Mil?	-	3	10	2	8
--	Mil?	-	3	10	2	9
--	Mil?	-	8	9	1	16
--	Mil?	-	8	9	1	17
--	Mil?	-	8	9	1	18
--	Mil?	-	8	9	1	14
--	Mil?	-	8	9	1	15
--	Mil?	-	10	7	1	23
--	Mil?	-	8	9	1	11
--	Mil?	-	8	9	1	12
--	Mil?	-	8	9	1	13
--	Mil?	-	9	7	3	16
--	Mil?	-	9	7	3	39
--	Mil?	-	9	7	3	40
--	Mil?	-	4	4	3	12
--	Mil?	-	4	4	3	21
--	Mil?	-	4	4	3	25
--	Mil?	-	10	7	1	26
--	Mil?	-	10	7	1	39
--	Mil?	-	10	7	1	40

678   2 Aug 1808   A/3/435
Daniel Symmes, Reg Cin
Final certificate (error in location)

John Pence (error)	Cin	Pre	11	4	8	-
John Pence (correct?)	Cin	MR	11	4	8	-

679   2 Aug 1808   A/3/436
Isaac Van Horn, Rec Zan
Transmits patents

Isaac Van Horn (as grantee)	Mil	–	8 5 1 21		
Isaac Van Horn (as grantee)	Mil	–	8 5 1 22		

680   4 Aug 1808   A/3/436
Memorandum
Patent forwarded to Joseph Wood, Reg Mar

John McIntire & Henry Crooks	Mar	–	14 16 16 –

681   16 Aug 1808   A/3/436
Jesse Spencer, Reg Chl
Final certificate; first certificate
John Valentine transfers to George Valentine

John Stine	Chl	–	21 11 9 +
John Stine	Chl	–	21 11 8 +
John Valentine	Chl	–	20 12 29 +
John Valentine	Chl	–	20 12 8 +

682   15 Aug 1805   A/3/436
Nathaniel Ewing, Rec Vin
Instructions regarding discounts.

683   16 Aug 1808   A/3/437
David Hoge, Reg Stu
First certificate; duplicate receipts

Peter Walter	Stu	–	5 16 30 –
Jacob Miller	Stu	–	8 11 7 –
George Grows? [Grous?]	Stu	–	8 9 11 –
George Grows? [Grous?]	Stu	–	8 10 5 –

684   24 Aug 1808   A/3/437
Job McNamara, Hagarstown, Maryland
Transmits patent

Job McNamara	Chl	–	18 16 29 –

685   19 Aug 1808   A/3/438
Daniel Symmes, Reg Cin
Transmits patents

Jonathan Hollingsworth	Cin	EML	2 11 14 +	
Maxwell Parkinson	Cin	EML	3 3 24 +	
Henry Gaines	Cin	EML	1 4 35 +	
Joseph Greene	Cin	EML	3 3 4 +	
William Tyner	Cin	WML	2 9 33 +	
Samuel Arnett	Cin	WML	2 9 32 +	

686   19 Aug 1808   A/3/438
David Hoge, Reg Stu
Transmits patents

John Mason, Sr.	Stu	–	1 8 28 –
Reuben Griffith	Stu	–	4 15 1 +
Moses Giffin	Stu	–	5 9 26 +
Joseph Gans	Stu	–	3 11 20 +

687   24 Aug 1808   A/3/438
Christopher Haars, Sugar Refiner, Philadelphia, Pennsylvania
Transmits patents

Henry Landis	Chl	–	16 16 8 +
David Landis	Chl	–	16 16 7 +
Henry Kalback	Chl	–	17 17 13 +

688   25 Aug 1808   A/3/439
James Findlay, Rec Cin
Inquires regarding alleged forfeiture

John Smith	Cin	Pre	5 3 28 +

689   30 Aug 1808   A/3/440
John H. Brinton, 279 Market Street, Philadelphia, Pennsylvania
Draft on Bank of United States, Baltimore branch; duplicate receipts
[Robert] Annesley; [Isaac] Bonsall; John H. Brinton.

690   5 Sep 1808   A/3/440
Isaac Van Horn, Rec Zan
Military land warrant 338

Previously patented	Zan	Mil?	9 1 3 23
Previously patented	Zan	Mil?	9 1 3 24

691   5 Sep 1808   A/3/440
David Hoge, Reg Stu
Inquires regarding patent

Mahlon Smith "of St. Clairsville"	Stu	–	5 8 10 –

692   5 Sep 1808   A/3/440
Mahlon Smith, St. Clairsville, Ohio
Final certificate

Mahlon Smith	Stu	–	5 8 10 –

693   9 Sep 1808   A/3/441
Jesse Spencer, Reg Chl
Transmits patents

William Thompson	Chl	–	17 16 5 +

694   9 Sep 1808   A/3/441
Daniel Symmes, Reg Cin
Transmits patents

Thomas Patten	Cin	MR	9 5 13 +
James Turner	Cin	MR	12 4 9 +
John Forney	Cin	EML	5 3 10 –
John Fouts	Cin	EML	4 3 17 +
Samuel Dick	Cin	EML	2 3 8 +
Samuel Dick	Cin	EML	3 3 18 +
Samuel Davis	Cin	EML	3 3 18 +

695   9 Sep 1808   A/3/441
Daniel Symmes, Reg Cin
Transmits patent

Matthew Huston	Cin	EML	3 2 9 –

696   9 Sep 1808   A/3/441
David Hoge, Reg Stu
First certificate; duplicate receipt
Assignment to Samuel Russell, New Lisbon [state not given]

George Johnston	Stu	–	2 10 11 +

697   9 Sep 1808   A/3/442
Isaac Van Horn, Rec Zan
First certificate
Assignment to Charles Bohn

Samuel Smith	Zan	–	3 10 12 +

Bohn, Slingluff, & Deardorff	Zan	–	3	8	1	+
Bohn, Slingluff, & Deardorff	Zan	–	3	8	3	+
Bohn, Slingluff, & Deardorff	Zan	–	3	8	2	+

698 9 Sep 1808 A/3/442
Obadiah Jennings, Stu
Transmits patents

Henry Aten	Stu	–	6	16	20	+
Henry Aten	Stu	–	3	12	23	–
Henry Aten	Stu	–	3	12	5	+
Henry Aten	Stu	–	6	17	36	+
Henry Aten	Stu	–	3	12	17	+
Obadiah Jennings	Stu	–	3	13	28	+
Aaron Brook	Stu	–	1	6	10	–
Ephraim Holloway	Stu	–	3	15	25	+
Henry Aten	Stu	–	3	13	27	–

699 9 Sep 1808 A/3/443
David Hoge, Reg Stu
Transmits patents

Nathan Fisher	Stu	–	4	6	5	+
William Fife	Stu	–	4	15	36	+
George Fink	Stu	–	1	9	2	–
David Endsley	Stu	–	5	11	4	+
Thomas Farquhar	Stu	–	5	16	25	+

700 10 Sep 1808 A/3/443
William Ritchie, Clerk of Frederick County Court, Maryland
Comments regarding succession of patent right
Henry Kaher, Justice of Peace, Frederick County, Maryland; David Delanter, heir of Jacob Delanter who died intestate.

701 12 Sep 1808 A/3/444
Jesse Spencer, Reg Chl

James Stewart	Chl	WS	21	10	5	+
Edward Berry	Chl	–	18	16	13	+

702 14 Sep 1808 A/3/444
John Baird, Petersburgh, Virginia
Final certificate

John Baird	Town of Cin, sq. 1, 10
John Baird	Town of Cin, sq. 1, 11
John Baird	Town of Cin, sq. 1, 12
John Baird	Town of Cin, sq. 2, 16
John Baird	Town of Cin, sq. 2, 17

703 14 Sep 1808 A/3/445
Zaccheus Biggs, Rec Stu
Duplicate receipts
Robert Annesley; Isaac Bonsall; John H. Brinton

Horton Howard	Stu	–	9	9	–	26
Horton Howard	Stu	–	9	9	–	22
Horton Howard	Stu	–	10	1	–	4
Horton Howard	Stu	–	10	1	–	9
Horton Howard	Stu	–	10	1	–	5
Horton Howard	Stu	–	10	1	–	6
Tunis & Annesley	Stu	–	7	15	14	+
Tunis & Annesley	Stu	–	9	9	2	+
Tunis & Annesley	Stu	–	9	9	3	+
Tunis & Annesley	Stu	–	9	9	4	+
Tunis & Annesley	Stu	–	9	9	23	+
Tunis & Annesley	Stu	–	9	9	23	+
Tunis & Annesley	Stu	–	4	17	4	+
Tunis & Annesley	Stu	–	4	17	9	+
Tunis & Annesley	Stu	–	4	17	14	+
Tunis & Annesley	Stu	–	5	17	30	+
Tunis & Annesley	Stu	–	6	17	10	+
Tunis & Annesley	Stu	–	6	18	34	+
Tunis & Annesley	Stu	–	7	20	25	+

704 14 Sep 1808 A/3/445
John H. Brinton
Duplicate receipt
Robert Annesley; Isaac Bonsall

John H. Brinton?	Stu	–	7	20	25	+

705 23 Sep 1808 A/3/446
Daniel Symmes, Reg Cin
Answers inquiry regarding patent issuance
Short assigned to Hugh Andrews; Charles Killgore, former Reg Cin

Payton Short	Cin	Pre	8	15	14	+

706 24 Sep 1808 A/3/448
General John Smith, Winchester, Virginia
Answers inquiry regarding account; Act of 10 May 1800

Lewis Walker, Jr.	Stu	–	4	16	28	–

707 24 Sep 1808 A/3/448
Zaccheus Biggs, Rec Stu
Duplicate receipts

Anthony Wright	Stu	–	6	13	30	+
Thomas Thompson	Stu	–	9	9	14	+

708 24 Sep 1808 A/3/448
Jesse Spencer, Reg Chl
Transmits patents

Jesse Spencer (as grantee)	Chl	MS	22	2	24	–	
John Sheaffer & Martin Sheaffer	Chl	MS	19	13	19	–	
Thomas Massie	Chl	–	21	8	27	–	
Thomas Massie	Chl	–	21	8	–	28	
Thomas Massie	Chl	–	21	8	–	29	

709 27 Sep 1808 A/3/448
Willys Silliman, Reg Zan
Final certificate

Joshua W. Satterthwaite	Zan	Mil	3	1	21	+

710 27 Sep 1808 A/3/449
T. M. Thompson
Military land warrants
Thompson, assignee of Matthias Young, 200 acres, and Abraham Greenwalt, 100 acres.

711 27 Sep 1808 A/3/449
Daniel Symmes, Reg Cin
Transmits patents

King Dearman	Cin	EML	1	3	26	+
Zachariah P. Dewitt	Cin	EML	1	5	24	+
Amos Davis	Cin	EML	2	8	28	+
Thomas Dobrow	Cin	EML	2	4	4	+
Jonah Wilson	Cin	EML	2	3	–	13
Jonah Wilson	Cin	EML	2	3	24	–

712   27 Sep 1808   A/3/449
Jesse Spencer, Reg Chl
First certificate; duplicate receipt
Thomas Ritter, post office, Baltimore; John Adams,
  Hagarstown, Maryland

Thomas Ritter & John Leef	Chl	–	20	15	13	–
John Adams	Chl	–	20	12	14	+

713   27 Sep 1808   A/3/450
James Findlay, Rec Cin
Duplicate receipt

William Eaker	Cin	EML	6	5	29	+

714   10 Oct 1808   A/3/450
Peter Walter, post office, Gettysburgh, Adams
  County, Pennsylvania
Transmits patent

Peter Walter	Stu	–	5	16	30	–

715   10 Oct 1808   A/3/450
Abraham Bradley, Jr., Deputy Postmaster General
Transmits patents

William Ruffin "of Cin"	Cin	MR?	8	3	26	–

716   10 Oct 1808   A/3/450
Daniel Symmes, Reg Cin
Transmits patent; duplicate receipt
-- Heidler *et al*; Benjamin (not Henry) Bowman;
  heirs of Jacob Delader [who died intestate in
  Frederick County, Maryland]; brother of Jacob
  Delader mentioned

Henry Yount (assigned)	Cin	EML	4	4	34	–

717   11 Oct 1808   A/3/451
Willys Silliman, Reg Zan
Transmits patents

Charles Franklin	Zan	–	15	18	15	+
John Forsyth	Zan	–	15	16	17	+
Chauncey Ford	Zan	–	14	15	33	+
Peter Corbet	Zan	–	3	1	20	+

718   11 Oct 1808   A/3/451
David Hoge, Reg Stu
Transmits patents

Jacob Ferris	Stu	–	1	5	–	35
Jacob Ferris	Stu	–	1	5	36	–
Andrew Ferrier	Stu	–	5	11	27	+
James Ford	Stu	–	4	9	34	–
John Coffey	Stu	–	4	16	13	–
Lemuel Terrell	Stu	–	5	17	1	+
John Cook	Stu	–	2	10	25	–

719   11 Oct 1808   A/3/452
Daniel Symmes, Reg Cin
Transmits patents

Matthew Caldwell	Cin	EML	6	6	19	+
Matthew Caldwell	Cin	EML	6	6	20	+
Matthew Caldwell	Cin	EML	6	6	–	18
William Cooper	Cin	EML	2	5	2	+
James Cook	Cin	EML	3	3	5	+
Benjamin Greenwood	Cin	EML	2	5	5	+

720   11 Oct 1808   A/3/452
Jesse Spencer, Reg Chl
Transmits patents

Elijah Friend	Chl	–	20	12	26	+
Robert Clendenin, Sr.	Chl	–	20	12	36	+

721   21 Oct 1808   A/3/452
David Hoge, Reg Stu
First certificates; duplicate receipts
Philip Swick, to be left at post office, Hanover,
  York County, Pennsylvania

Philip Swick?	Stu	–	7	18	3	+
Philip Swick?	Stu	–	7	18	4	+

722   17 Oct 1808   A/3/453
Zaccheus Biggs, Rec Stu
Duplicate receipts

Lewis Walker	Stu	–	4	16	28	–
George Austine	Stu	–	5	16	18	+

723   19 Oct 1808   A/3/453
Daniel Symmes, Reg Cin
Final certificates
John Paul for pre-emption lands

Jacob Huffman	Cin	Pre	9	14	21	+
Jacob Huffman (error)	Cin	Pre	9	4	21	+

724   20 Oct 1808   A/3/454
David Hoge, Reg Stu
First certificate

George Austine	Stu	–	5	16	18	+

725   20 Oct 1808   A/3/454
Jesse Spencer, Reg Chl
First certificate; duplicate receipts
Haines lived at Summer Hill, Cecil County, Mary-
  land

Eli Haines	Chl	–	14	8	20	+
Eli Haines	Chl	–	14	8	19	+

726   25 Oct 1808   A/3/455
David Hoge, Reg Stu
Transmits patents

Ezekiel Cole	Stu	–	3	9	19	–
Isaac Coppock	Stu	–	7	9	20	+
John Cock [Cook?]	Stu	–	5	18	35	+
John Cock [Cook?]	Stu	–	6	19	20	+
Caleb Pumphrey	Stu	–	5	9	17	–
William Campbell	Stu	–	6	9	1	+
Lewis Cobbs	Stu	–	5	17	2	+
John Crumbacher	Stu	–	2	13	28	–
Frederick Reese	Stu	–	2	13	10	–
William Pettit	Stu	–	4	15	20	+
William Craighead	Stu	–	2	11	32	+
John Richardson	Stu	–	4	16	33	–

727   1 Nov 1808   A/3/455
Zaccheus Biggs, Reg Stu
Duplicate receipts

Joseph Reeves	Stu	–	3	15	15	+

728   1 Nov 1808   A/3/456
Jesse Spencer, Reg Chl
Final certificate; duplicate receipt
Patent to be forwarded to Reg Chl where Harsh-
  burger "expects to find it on his settling in

"your country"

Abraham Harshburger	Chl	-	18	16	24	-

---

729   1 Nov 1808   A/3/456
Jesse Spencer, Reg Chl
First certificate; duplicate receipts
Eby asked that patent be sent to him at post off-
ice, Baltimore

Christian Eby	Chl	-	18	16	17	+
Christian Eby	Chl	-	18	16	8	+
Christian Eby	Chl	-	18	15	10	-

---

730   2 Nov 1808   A/3/456
Daniel Symmes, Reg Cin
Transmits patents

Samuel Maddock	Cin	EML	3	4	29	+
John Neff	Cin	EML	2	15	-	12
John Neff	Cin	EML	2	15	-	13
John Neff	Cin	EML	2	15	-	14
John Neff	Cin	EML	2	15	11	-
Michael Myers	Cin	EML	5	3	31	+

---

731   2 Nov 1808   A/3/457
David Hoge, Reg Stu
Transmits patents

Angus McBean	Stu	-	1	5	-	29
Angus McBean	Stu	-	1	5	30	-
John Eckey	Stu	-	2	6	1	-
Peter Oyster	Stu	-	6	17	11	-

---

732   3 Nov 1808   A/3/457
Paul Fearing, Mar
Military land warrant of Captain Guy Young.

---

733   7 Nov 1808   A/3/457
Isaac Van Horn, Rec Zan
First certificate; duplicate receipt
Hon. John Rhea, U.S. Representative from Pennsyl-
vania

John Gilmer	Zan	-	7	1	13	+

---

734   7 Nov 1808   A/3/458
Dnaiel Symmes, Reg Cin
First certificate
Abigail Bigger & James Bigger, administrators of
the estate of Joseph Bigger; assignment by Wil-
liam Griffin to Frederick Fox

Joseph Bigger	Cin	Pre	5	2	12	+

---

735   7 Nov 1808   A/3/458
Joseph Wood, Reg Mar
Final certificate
Richard Hooker & William McCluney; Trueman Peet

Trueman Peet	Mar	-	?	?	19	30

---

736   8 Nov 1808   A/3/459
Samuel Gathmey, Register at Jeffersonville
Discrepancy noted

Peter Covert	?	-	9E	4N	3	+
Peter Covert	?	-	9E	1N	3	+

---

737   9 Nov 1808   A/3/460
Samuel Moorer, care of John Heckewelder, Post Mas-
ter, Muskingum [Ohio]
Transmits patent

Samuel Moorer	Mil	-	2	10	2	14
Encloses plats for	Mil	-	7	7	2	-
Encloses plats for	Zan	*	10	8	-	-

    *"not appropriated for the satisfying of mili-
tary land warrants"

---

738   10 Nov 1808   A/3/460
Jesse Spencer, Reg Chl
First certificate; duplicate receipt
Assignee requests patent to be sent to post off-
ice, Baltimore; Smith patent requested by a
U.S. Representative

John Fowble	Chl	-	21	11	12	+
F. C. Smith	Chl	MS	21	9	29	+

---

739   14 Nov 1808   A/3/461
John Badollet, Reg Vin
First certificate; duplicate receipt

Jacob Kentner?	Vin	-	3E	4S	2	+

---

740   14 Nov 1808   A/3/461
James Findlay, Rec Cin
First certificate
Seaman assigns to Samuel Gallagher who is aided
by U.S. Representative; William Eakin

Jonas Seaman	Cin	Pre	4	3	7	+

---

741   22 Nov 1808   A/3/461
Andrew Johnston, post office, Beaver Town, Penn-
sylvania
Transmits patent

Andrew Johnston	Stu	-	1	7	2	+

---

742   22 Nov 1808   A/3/462
Daniel Symmes, Reg Cin
Errors of assignment to be corrected
[Jared Mansfield] Surveyor General; Arthur Orr,
assignee of Daniel Ingersoll

-- Henrie	Cin	EML	1	1	1	-
-- Henrie	Cin	EML	1	1	-	2

---

743   22 Nov 1808   A/3/462
Lemuel Hering, Rec EPR
Transmits patent ("donation by right of occupancy")
Lorenzow Dow

Francis Steel	EPR	-	-	-	*	-

    *"on Tensaw Lake"

---

744   22 Nov 1808   A/3/462
David Hoge, Reg Stu
First certificate; duplicate receipt
Patent to be sent to John Dudderer, post office,
Petersburgh, Adams County, Pennsylvania

Conrad Dudderer	Stu	-	2	13	15	+
William Murdaugh	Stu	-	3	10	19	+
Izak Proctor	Stu	-	6	18	23	+
Michael Snider	Stu	-	8	12	33	+

---

745   22 Nov 1808   A/3/463
James Findlay, Rec Cin
Duplicate receipt

--	Cin	-	19	6	12	+

746		24 Nov 1808		A/3/463

Daniel Symmes, Reg Cin
First certificates
Assigned to David Putterbaugh, post office, Hagar's
   Town, Maryland

William & John Folkerith	Cin	MR	8	2	30	+

747		30 Nov 1808		A/3/464

Jesse Spencer, Reg Chl
Transmits patents

William Lane	Chl	–	20	14	32	+
John & James Love	Chl	–	17	16	13	+
Jacob Lamb	Chl	–	18	15	3	+
Frederick Leather	Chl	–	20	13	36	–
John Douglass	Chl	–	16	15	7	+
John Lytle? [Lyle?]	Chl	MS	22	4	24	+

748		30 Nov 1808		A/3/464

Daniel Symmes, Reg Cin
Transmits patents

James Conn	Cin	WML	1	5	–	27
James Conn	Cin	WML	1	5	–	28
James Conn	Cin	WML	1	5	29	–
Lewis Little	Cin	WML	1	12	6	+
John Logan	Cin	WML	2	9	9	+
William Logan	Cin	WML	2	10	28	+
James Lamb	Cin	WML	2	13	25	+
Thomas Cooch	Cin	EML	2	5	29	–
Samuel Cane	Cin	EML	2	6	12	+
Robert Lytle	Cin	EML	2	5	24	–
Andrew Leazure?	Cin	EML	4	6	33	+

749		30 Nov 1808		A/3/464

David Hoge, Reg Stu
Transmits patents

Samuel Quigley	Stu	–	1	6	32	–
James Edgerton	Stu	–	6	8	13	+
Harmon Davis	Stu	–	6	8	14	–
Clement Vallandigham	Stu	–	2	11	17	+
John Emrey, Sr.	Stu	–	4	16	17	–
Samuel Davis	Stu	–	4	17	20	+

750		30 Nov 1808		A/3/465

Hon. Daniel Montgomery
Transmits patent
"Heirs and legal representatives of Archibald
   Anderson, late a Major. . ."

Archibald Anderson, heirs	Mil	–	11	9	4	25
Archibald Anderson, heirs	Mil	–	11	9	4	26
Archibald Anderson, heirs	Mil	–	11	9	4	27
Archibald Anderson, heirs	Mil	–	11	9	4	28

751		30 Nov 1808		A/3/465

Hon. John Smilie, U.S. House of Representatives
Transmits patent

Peter Gary	Mil	–	6	6	2	22

752		30 Nov 1808		A/3/465

Hon. Edward Tiffin, U.S. Senate
Transmits patent
Richard Shotte

John Lamme	Mil	–	16	8	4	7

753		30 Nov 1808		A/3/465

David Hoge, Reg Stu

Final certificate

Peter Kail	Stu	–	5	11	18	+

754		1 Dec 1808		A/3/466

Daniel Symmes, Reg Cin
Final certificate
Leah Corey, wife or widown of Christopher Corey;
assigns to Isaac Vannest

Leah Corey	Cin	Pre	4	2	17	+

755		2 Dec 1808		A/3/466

David Hoge, Reg Stu
Final certificate [see also reply attached from
   Hoge and subsequent rejoinder by Albert Galla-
   tin, SecTreas]
Jacob Nessly, claimant

John Johnston	Stu	–	1	4	–	27
John Johnston	Stu	–	1	4	–	33

756		12 Dec 1808		A/3/467

David Hoge, Reg Stu
Transmits patents

Benjamin Hanna	Stu	–	7	20	12	+
Stephen Hodgin	Stu	–	6	8	11	–
Paul Halprunner	Stu	–	3	14	34	–
George Hammond	Stu	–	4	11	4	+
Edward Huston	Stu	–	1	7	28	+
James Armstrong	Stu	–	4	15	27	+
John Pickering	Stu	–	5	9	26	+
Ralph Cowgill	Stu	–	6	9	31	–

757		13 Dec 1808		A/3/467

Edmund H. Taylor
Explains delay in settlement of account.

758		15 Dec 1808		A/3/468

Daniel Symmes, Reg Cin
Transmits patents

Henry Hoover	Cin	EML	4	3	17	+
Peter Helmick	Cin	EML	1	2	5	–
Samuel Job	Cin	WML	1	12	17	+
Jacob Hackleman	Cin	WML	1	7	10	–
Eli Henderson	Cin	WML	2	11	25	+
Christian Hansell	Cin	WML	1	10	25	+
Eli Cook	Cin	EML	3	3	5	+
James Coat	Cin	EML	5	7	32	+
Noah Harborn	Cin	MR	9	6	18	+

759		15 Dec 1808		A/3/468

David Hoge, Reg Stu
Transmits patents
Obadiah Jennings inquired regarding Henry Beeson's
   patent

Reasin Beall	Stu	–	2	11	29	+
John Henderson	Stu	–	4	12	32	+
Robert Humphrey	Stu	–	2	5	27	–
Samuel Dunlap	Stu	–	5	10	20	+
Richard Jackman, Jr.?	Stu	–	3	11	14	+
John Yoder	Stu	–	8	10	20	+
Henry Beeson	Stu	–	2	12	8	–

760		15 Dec 1808		A/3/468

Jesse Spencer, Reg Chl
Transmits patents

Peter Jones	Chl	–	20	10	7	+

J. & S. Hopkins & N. Frame	Chl	WS	22	3	-	9
J. & S. Hopkins & N. Frame	Chl	WS	22	3	8	-
Robert Hunter	Chl	-	20	13	30	+

761   15 Dec 1808   A/3/469
T. M. Thompson, Lancaster, Pennsylvania
Transmits patents
Abraham Greenwalt

T. M. Thompson	Mil	-	8	9	1	30
T. M. Thompson	Mil	-	8	9	1	31

762   17 Dec 1808   A/3/469
Hon. John Love, U.S. Representative
Transmits patent

Joshua Woodrow	Unk	-	6	10	3	+

763   17 Dec 1808   A/3/469
Daniel Symmes, Reg Cin
Transmits patents

John Harvey	Cin	WML	1	14	34	+
John Hanna	Cin	WML	2	11	27	+
Solomon Hartman	Cin	EML	4	5	26	+
Benjamin Hawkins	Cin	EML	3	3	8	+
Benjamin Hawkins	Cin	EML	3	3	5	+
Joseph Hawkins	Cin	EML	3	3	4	+
Eli Cook	Cin	EML	3	4	32	+
Daniel Hoover	Cin	EML	5	5	10	+
Jonathan Cooper	Cin	EML	2	5	2	+
Matthew Caldwell	Cin	EML	6	6	30	+
Abraham Hackleman	Cin	WML	2	9	34	+

764   10 Dec 1808   A/3/470
Reg of Treasury (from James Moore, Front Royal)
Sends remittance on Bank of Potomac, Bank of Alex-
    andria, Bank of Virginia
E. Wilson; -- Bonifield

William Boniface	Zan	-	9	1	12	+

765   no date   A/3/471
Important "Statement relative to purchase of cer-
    tain lands . . . in the district of Marietta"
Public sale, Mar, May & Jun 1801
Rufus Putnam, former SG; Peregrine Foster, former
    Reg Mar; Joseph Wood, Reg Mar; Willys Silliman,
    consel for John McIntire

Increase Mathews & Levi Whipple	Mar	-	14	16	12	-
Increase Mathews & Levi Whipple	Mar	-	14	16	-	1
Increase Mathews & Levi Whipple	Mar	-	13	12	-	5W
Increase Mathews & Levi Whipple	Mar	-	13	12	-	6W
John McIntire	Mar	-	13	12	4	-
John McIntire	Mar	-	13	12	-	5E
John McIntire	Mar	-	14	16	-	1E

766   21 Dec 1808   A/3/473
Borden Stanton, St. Clairsville, Ohio
Status of application

Borden Stanton	Unk	-	3	7	1	-

767   21 Dec 1808   A/3/473
Isaac Van Horn, Rec Zan
Duplicate receipt

William Bornfield	Zan	-	9	1	12	+

768   22 Dec 1808   A/3/474
Willys Silliman, Reg Zan
Final certificate returned; assignment invalid.

769   21 Dec 1808   A/3/474
Henry Sidwell, St. Clairsville, Ohio
Transmits patent

Henry Sidwell	Unk	-	7	9	13	-
John Hall	Unk	-	7	9	7	-

770   21 Dec 1808   A/3/474
Jesse Spencer, Reg Chl
Deed of transfer
Transfers to Harman Moore

Michael Moore (error)	Chl	-	20	12	25	+
Michael Moore (correct)	Chl	-	20	12	35	+

771   24 Dec 1808   A/3/475
Borden Stanton, St. Clairsville, Ohio
Transmits patent

Borden Stanton	Stu	-	3	7	1	+

772   26 Dec 1808   A/3/475
Hon. William Hoge
Transmits patents

Jacob Kintner	Vin	-	4E	3S	30	+
Frederick Swinehart	Zan	-	3	8	9	+
Frederick Swinehart	Zan	-	3	9	11	+
George Wilhelm	Zan	-	2	7	11	+

773   26 Dec 1808   A/3/476
Hon. John Morrow
Transmits patent

John Vanusdle?	Cin?	EML	3	5	17	+

774   28 Dec 1808   A/3/476
David Hoge, Reg Stu
Transmits patents

Henry Benner	Stu	-	3	13	3	+
Thomas Ball	Stu	-	3	15	29	+
Samuel Knight	Stu	-	5	10	7	-
Moses Bartholomew	Stu	-	3	10	34	+
Henry Mayer	Stu	-	1	9	12	-
Rudolph Bair	Stu	-	6	17	1	+
Rudolph Bair	Stu	-	2	12	31	-
Rudolph Bair	Stu	-	6	17	4	+
Rudolph Bair	Stu	-	7	18	2	+
Rudolph Bair, Jr.	Stu	-	6	17	9	+
Thomas Henderson	Stu	-	7	9	29	-

775   28 Dec 1808   A/3/476
Jesse Spencer, Reg Chl
Transmits patents

John Beckler	Chl	-	17	17	25	+
David Evans	Chl	MS	21	9	31	+
Abram Deffenbaugh & -- Strouse	Chl	-	20	11	36	-
Conrad Bryan	Chl	-	17	14	12	+
John Anderson	Chl	WS	21	11	3	+
Henry Ashbaugh	Chl	-	20	14	4	+
Elijah Austin	Chl	MS	20	10	11	+

776   28 Dec 1808   A/3/477
Daniel Symmes, Reg Cin
Transmits patents

Henry Yount	Cin	EML	4	4	29	+

Peter Banta	Cin	EML	3	5	10	+
John Golding & Jesse Merit	Cin	EML	1	2	28	−
John Emrick	Cin	EML	5	2	5	−
Benjamin Evans	Cin	EML	1	7	29	+
Benjamin Evans	Cin	EML	1	7	30	+

777   28 Dec 1808   A/3/477
Willys Silliman, Reg Zan
Transmits patents

Nicholas Borden	Zan	−	13	12	2	+
George Adams	Zan	−	7	3	18	+
Arthur Adair	Zan	−	1	2	4	+
Rice Beggs	Zan	−	10	9	6	+
James Miskeman	Zan	−	4	4	7	+

778   30 Dec 1808   A/3/477
John Badollet, Reg Vin
Transmits patents
Jones was in Washington "last summer" but GLO
  lost his forwarding address

Thomas Jones	Vin	− 14W	8S	21	+
Thomas Jones	Vin	− 14W	8S	20	+

779   30 Dec 1808   A/3/478
[Daniel Symmes], Reg Cin
Transmits patents

Jaco Coy	Cin	MR	6	2	5	+
John Bradford	Cin	MR	7	2	26	+
Samuel Pence	Cin	MR	11	4	2	+
Hary Martin	Cin	MR	9	2	20	+
William Ramsey, Sr.	Cin	EML	1	6	14	+
Henry Yount	Cin	EML	6	3	30	+
James Denniston	Cin	EML	3	5	27	+
Andrew McQueston	Cin	EML	1	6	23	+
Samuel Maddock	Cin	EML	3	4	32	+
Andrew Robison & Jacob Barnet	Cin	EML	6	2	5	−
John Allen	Cin	WML	2	9	29	+
David Hansel?	Cin	WML	1	10	24	+
William Majors	Cin	WML	1	7	12	+
Hugh Reed	Cin	WML	2	11	24	+
John Allen	Cin	WML	1	8	32	−

780   30 Dec 1808   A/3/478
David Hoge, Reg Stu
Transmits patents

Henry Mayers	Stu	−	1	9	1	−
William Milhous	Stu	−	4	17	33	+
Robert Moore	Stu	−	8	11	8	+
Thomas McCamis	Stu	−	3	11	7	−
Patrick McKaig	Stu	−	3	13	7	−
John Bockins	Stu	−	4	12	34	+
David Barton	Stu	−	4	8	13	−
Absalom Kent	Stu	−	6	16	19	+

781   30 Dec 1808   A/3/479
Jesse Spencer, Reg Chl
Transmits patents

Nicholas Radabaugh	Chl	−	18	13	6	−
Abraham Monnett	Chl	−	20	11	34	−
Jacob Bearey	Chl	MS	21	9	1	−
John William Miller & Isaac Van Meter	Chl	LS?	22	3	1	−
John William Miller & Isaac Van Meter	Chl	LS?	22	3	−	2

Jacob Brunner	Chl	−	20	12	18	+
Jacob Bearey	Chl	MS	21	10	36	+

782   3 Jan 1809   A/3/479
[David Hoge], Reg Stu
Transmits patents

John Howard	Stu	−	4	15	13	+
Amos Holloway	Stu	−	6	19	14	+
Nathan Heald, Sr.	Stu	−	1	7	9	+
Henry Hinchman	Stu	−	4	17	30	+
Benjamin Harrison	Stu	−	5	16	13	+
Berriman McLaughlin	Stu	−	7	12	19	+
Aden Moreland	Stu	−	1	7	8	+
Amos Holloway	Stu	−	6	19	12	+
Amos Holloway	Stu	−	6	19	14	+

783   7 Jan 1809   A/3/479
John Fowler
Answers inquiry regarding patent application;
  military land warrant in name of Walker Baylor
Benjamin Howard, U.S. Representative; General --
  Worthington.

784   3 Jan 1809   A/3/479
[Jesse Spencer], Reg Chl
Transmits patents

John Huff	Chl	MS	22	3	12	+
Robert Hunter	Chl	−	20	13	32	+
John Hufler	Chl	−	20	13	29	−
Jesse Hedges	Chl	−	19	14	5	+
Philip Helsell	Chl	−	22	4	11	+
Gay, Moorhead & Heller	Chl	WS	21	10	6	+
Benjamin Morris	Chl	WS	21	11	35	+
Christian Hollougher	Chl	WS	20	14	34	+
Jonathan Holmes	Chl	MS	22	3	22	+
George Hill	Chl	−	18	16	23	+

785   3 Jan 1809   A/3/480
[Willys Silliman], Reg Zan
Transmits patents

Matthias Hummel	Zan	−	15	17	26	+
Richard & Andrew McBride	Zan	−	14	16	13	+

786   3 Jan 1809   A/3/480
[Daniel Symmes], Reg Cin
Transmits patents

Hugh McQueston	Cin	EML	1	6	24	+
William McCreary	Cin	EML	1	6	36	+
Jesse Henley	Cin	WML	1	12	18	+
Elijah Mendenhall	Cin	EML	3	4	34	+
Isaac Hart	Cin	EML	3	3	4	+
Shadrach Henderson	Cin	WML	2	13	13	+
Henry Hormell	Cin	EML	3	3	23	+
Elijah Mendenhall	Cin	EML	6	3	18	+
Jonathan Hollingsworth	Cin	WML	2	11	11	+
Richard Rice	Cin	WML	1	13	17	+
Samuel Black	Cin	MR	10	3	25	+
Margaret McCoy	Cin	EML	1	13	18	+

787   7 Jan 1809   A/3/481
General Thomas Worthington
Military land warrant in name of Walker Baylor,
  for 500 acres
John Fowler.

788		7 Jan 1809			A/3/481		
[David Hoge], Reg Stu							
Transmits patents							
William Milhous	Stu	–	4	17	33	+	
Alexander McDonald	Stu	–	2	10	26	+	
Hugh McGinnis	Stu	–	2	10	11	+	
William McLachlan	Stu	–	3	12	6	+	
Cornelius Van Horne	Stu	–	4	12	19	+	

789		7 Jan 1809			A/3/481	
[Jesse Spencer], Reg Chl						
Transmits patents						
John Rees	Chl	–	20	13	2	+
John Needles	Chl	–	20	15	4	+
George Needles	Chl	–	20	14	2	+

790		7 Jan 1809			A/3/481	
[Daniel Symmes], Reg Cin						
Transmits patents						
Garret Vanneman	Cin	EML	6	7	18	+
James Irwin Nesbit	Cin	EML	5	2	6	–
Thomas & James Newton	Cin	EML	2	6	33	+
Thomas & James Newton	Cin	EML	2	6	34	+
Simeon Vanwinkle	Cin	EML	3	6	27	–
Samuel Robinson	Cin	EML	1	4	2	+
Noah Harbour? [Harborn?]	Cin	MR	12	4	19	–

791		10 Jan 1809			A/3/482	
[Jesse Spencer], Reg Chl						
Transmits patents						
Jacob Dittoe	Chl	–	16	16	14	+
Jacob Dittoe	Chl	–	17	16	1	+

792		10 Jan 1809			A/3/482	
[David Hoge], Reg Stu						
Transmits patents						
Caleb Engle	Stu	–	4	6	30	+
Ebenezer Zane	Stu	–	2	3	– 28	
Ebenezer Zane	Stu	–	2	3	29	–
Caleb Dille	Stu	–	3	5	35	–
Joseph Morgan Eldridge	Stu	–	4	17	2	+

793		10 Jan 1809			A/3/482	
[Daniel Symmes], Reg Cin						
Transmits patents						
Hezekiah Phillips	Cin	EML	3	4	4	+
Williams & Gordon	Cin	EML	5	4	25	–
John Newman	Cin	MR	11	4	30	+
Zachariah Clevenger	Cin	Pre	4	3	4	+
Arthur Vandever	Cin	Pre	11	1	– 27	
Arthur Vandever	Cin	Pre	11	1	21	+
John Johnston	Cin	Pre	11	2	27	+
John Johnston	Cin	Pre	10	2	9	+
John Johnston	Cin	Pre	11	2	21	+
Robert & Andrew Robertson	Cin	Pre	4	3	33	+
Owen Davis	Cin	Pre	7	3	19	+
Conrad Horisberger	Cin	Pre	4	3	6	+
William Sloan	Cin	Pre	4	3	10	+

794		10 Jan 1809			A/3/483	
Gerard Topkin, Baltimore						
First certificate						
Gerard Topkin	Zan	–	5	1	10	+

795   10 Jan 1809   A/3/483
Willys Silliman, Reg Zan

Final certificate
Topkin, assignee of William Roberts

Gerard Topkin	Zan	–	5	1	10	+

796		14 Jan 1809			A/3/484	
Jacob Griffith, post office, Brownsville, Pennsylvania						
Transmits patents						
Jacob Griffith	Stu	–	4	15	5	–
Joseph Griest	Stu	–	7	26	13	+

797		16 Jan 1809			A/3/484	
John Badollet, Reg Vin						
Assignment						
Hervey Hoth transfers to Eli Wright; Walter Taylor, Judge						
Eli Wright	Vin	–	4E	4S	4	+

798		17 Jan 1809			A/3/484	
Willys Silliman, Reg Zan						
Transmits patents						
Frederick Dorner	Zan	Mil	4	8	3	+
George Dorner	Zan	Mil	4	8	13	+
Jacob Dorner	Zan	Mil	4	8	8	+

799		17 Jan 1809			A/3/484	
[Jesse Spencer], Reg Chl						
Transmits patents						
John Patton & George Bright	Chl	–	17	16	17	+
Abraham Pope	Chl	–	18	15	8	+
Jacob Dittoe	Chl	–	16	16	23	+
Anthony Dittoe	Chl	–	19	15	11	+
Anthony Dittoe	Chl	–	19	15	2	+
Anthony Dittoe	Chl	–	17	16	2	–

800		17 Jan 1809			A/3/485	
[Daniel Symmes], Reg Cin						
Transmits patents						
Rice Price	Cin	EML	1	8	33	+
Benjamin Enyrt	Cin	EML	3	2	12	–
James Porter	Cin	EML	4	3	18	+
Joshua Palmer, Sr.	Cin	WML	2	11	11	+
Thomas Patton	Cin	MR	9	5	19	–

801		17 Jan 1809			A/3/485	
Hon. Nathan Wilson, U.S. Representative						
Transmits patent						
Joseph Gamble	Mil?	–	15	2	2	20

802		18 Jan 1809			A/3/485	
Joel Ferree, Peter Creek, Allegheny County, Pennsylvania						
Patent sent to Reg Stu						
Joel Ferree?	Stu	–	1	5	– 35	
Joel Ferree?	Stu	–	1	5	36	–

803		25 Jan 1809			A/3/485	
Peter Wilson						
Duplicate receipts						
Matthew Mitchel	Unk	–	4	17	5	+
Richard Schooley	Unk	–	4	15	17	+

804   25 Jan 1809   A/3/486
James Findlay, Rec Cin

Duplicate receipts

Jacob Humbert	Cin	EML	5	4	15	+
Jacob Humbert	Cin	EML	3	5	15	+
Jacob Humbert	Cin	EML	4	4	5	-
Jacob Humbert	Cin	EML	3	5	22	-

805   25 Jan 1809   A/3/486
Jesse Spencer, Reg Ch1
First certificate; duplicate receipts

William Miller	Ch1	MS	21	10	29	+
Henry Orts	Ch1	-	18	16	8	+

806   1 Feb 1809   A/3/486
[Jesse Spencer], Reg Ch1
Transmits patents

George Fryback & John W. Loofborrow	Ch1	WS	22	3	-	1
George Fryback & John W. Loofborrow	Ch1	WS	22	3	6	-
John McNeal	Ch1	WS	22	4	-	3
John McNeal	Ch1	WS	22	4	-	4
Thomas Barr	Ch1	WS	21	10	19	+
Jacob Backard	Ch1	MS	21	10	1	+
Elisha Decker	Ch1	MS	21	10	11	+
John Marakle?	Ch1	-	17	16	28	+
Jacob Dittoe	Ch1	-	16	16	13	+
George Bowman	Ch1	-	16	16	19	+
Elizabeth Bonet?	Ch1	-	21	5	31	+
John Bashore	Ch1	-	16	17	28	+
Andrew Barr	Ch1	-	20	13	33	-
Henry Boyer	Ch1	-	17	18	23	+
George Bowman	Ch1	-	16	16	18	+
William Burrus?	Ch1	-	16	7	35	+
Thomas Buffington	Ch1	-	16	1	23	+
John Rees	Ch1	-	20	13	2	+

807   1 Feb 1809   A/3/489
[David Hoge], Reg Stu
Transmits patents

Henry Bard, Sr.	Stu	-	3	16	4	-
Henry Barricklaw	Stu	-	5	10	13	+
Stephen Bryan	Stu	-	5	7	36	+
George Burrier?	Stu	-	4	11	28	+
Philip Bowman	Stu	-	3	16	6	-
Rudolph Bair	Stu	-	6	17	9	+
Rudolph Bair	Stu	-	7	18	2	+
Nathan Burditt	Stu	-	3	5	36	+
Robert Beal	Stu	-	5	8	26	+
Peter Baker	Stu	-	3	16	24	-
Stephen Ford	Stu	-	3	9	36	+
Russell Blair	Stu	-	5	10	23	-
Abraham Betz	Stu	-	1	8	34	+
James Caldwell	Stu	-	4	6	11	+
Caleb Cope	Stu	-	5	17	5	-
Henry Fitz	Stu	-	1	7	28	+
James Douglass	Stu	-	6	18	28	+
John Garwood	Stu	-	2	12	28	-
Francis Gilmore	Stu	-	5	10	14	+
David Bower	Stu	-	2	10	1	+
David Bower	Stu	-	1	6	5	+
John Bower	Stu	-	6	13	27	+
Benjamin Barton?	Stu	-	7	9	12	+
Jacob Brandenburgh	Stu	-	3	14	30	+

808   13 Nov 1807   A/3/487
Memorandum [at foot of page, reversed]
First instalment payment for 640 acres "on the

waters of Bayou Pierre.—Mr. Williams the
Register's certificate . . . dated 29 Dec
1806."

809   27 Feb 1806   A/3/*
Account
John Eddy, Warren County   Cin? - 3 4 11 +
  *following page 487.

810   1 Apr 1806   A/3/*
Account
Robert Benham, Warren
  County   Cin? - 3 4 8 +
  *following page 487.

811   10 Mar 1806   A/3/*
Account
Jonathan Scott, New
  Jersey   Cin? - 3 4 26 +
  *following page 487.

812   3 Mar 1806   A/3/*
Account
James Kemper, Hamilton
  County   Cin? - 2 3 8 +
  *following page 487.

813   3 Mar 1806   A/3/*
Account
John Wallen   Cin? - 2 3 26 +
  *following page 487.

814   25 Feb 1806   A/3/*
Account
John Eddy, Warren
  County   Cin? - 3 4 11 +
  *following page 487.

815   4 Nov 1805   A/3/*
Account
James Casseday, Virginia   Cin? - 3 4 26 +
  *following page 487.

816   29 Oct 1804   A/3/*
Account
William Harbour, Virginia   Cin? MR 12 4 13 +
  *following page 487.

817   1 Oct 1804   A/3/*
Account
Joseph Van Horne,
  Hamilton County   Cin? MR 2 3 26 -
  *following page 487.

818   1 Feb 1809   A/4/001
[Joseph Wood], Reg Mar
Transmits patents

William Bundy	Mar	-	5	6	36	+
William Bundy	Mar	-	6	7	36	+
Joseph Cox	Mar	-	5	6	29	+
Stephen Bailey	Mar	-	6	7	12	+

819 1 Feb 1809 A/4/001
[Daniel Symmes], Reg Cin
Transmits patents

Name						
Joseph Greene	Cin	EML	3	3	10	+
Samuel Brown	Cin	EML	2	6	7	+
Samuel Brown	Cin	EML	2	6	6	+
Peter Banta	Cin	EML	3	5	9	+
Samuel Beeler	Cin	EML	1	5	25	-
Luther Bruen	Cin	EML	5	7	25	+
Albert Banta	Cin	EML	4	3	31	+
John Bralsford	Cin	EML	3	3	13	+
Samuel Mitchell, Sr.	Cin	EML	3	5	29	+
Daniel Martin	Cin	EML	5	4	5	+
John Morrow	Cin	EML	1	8	8	+
William Barber & Alexander Tilford	Cin	EML	6	5	-	16
William Barber & Alexander Tilford	Cin	EML	6	5	17	-
Susanna Butler	Cin	WML	1	14	17	+
Amos Butler	Cin	WML	2	9	20	+
Benjamin Boone	Cin	WML	2	12	13	+
John Flinn	Cin	Pre	11	2	20	+
William C. Schenck	Cin	Pre	5	2	-	32
William C. Schenck	Cin	Pre?	5	2	-	35
William C. Schenck	Cin	Pre?	5	2	36	+
John Miller	Cin	EML	4	4	27	-

820 2 Feb 1809 A/4/001
David Hoge, Reg Stu
Final certificate

Name						
Mordecai Yarnall	Stu	-	5	9	14	-

821 2 Feb 1809 A/4/002
Peter Mills, Stu
Inventory of vacant Mil and Refugee lots

Vacant	Mil	-	3	2	2	3
Vacant	Mil	-	3	2	2	4
Vacant	Mil	-	3	2	2	11
Vacant	Mil	-	3	2	2	12
Vacant	Mil	-	2	4	7	1
Vacant	Mil	-	2	4	7	2
Vacant	Mil	-	2	4	7	3
Vacant	Mil	-	2	4	7	4
Vacant	Mil	-	2	4	7	5
Vacant	Mil	-	2	4	7	6
Vacant	Mil	-	2	4	7	7
Vacant	Mil	-	2	4	7	8
Vacant	Mil	-	2	4	7	9
Vacant	Mil	-	2	4	7	10
Vacant	Mil	-	2	4	7	11
Vacant	Mil	-	2	4	7	12
Vacant	Mil	-	2	4	7	13
Vacant	Mil	-	2	4	7	14
Vacant	Mil	-	2	4	7	15
Vacant	Mil	-	2	4	7	18
Vacant	Mil	-	2	4	7	19
Vacant	Mil	-	2	4	7	20
Vacant	Mil	-	2	4	7	21
Vacant	Mil	-	2	4	7	22
Vacant	Mil	-	2	4	7	23
Vacant	Mil	-	2	4	7	24
Vacant	Mil	-	2	4	7	25
Vacant	Mil	-	2	4	7	26
Vacant	Mil	-	2	4	7	27
Vacant	Mil	-	2	4	7	28
Vacant	Mil	-	2	4	7	29
Vacant	Mil	-	2	4	7	30
Vacant	Mil	-	2	4	7	31
Vacant	Mil	-	2	4	7	32
Vacant	Mil	-	2	4	7	33
Vacant	Mil	-	2	4	7	34
Vacant	Mil	-	2	4	7	35
Vacant	Mil	-	2	4	7	36
Vacant	Mil	-	2	4	7	37
Vacant	Mil	-	1	2	8	1
Vacant	Mil	-	3	4	8	8
Vacant	Mil	-	3	4	8	13
Vacant	Mil	-	3	4	8	14
Vacant	Mil	-	3	4	8	15
Vacant	Mil	-	3	4	8	16
Vacant	Mil	-	3	4	8	17
Vacant	Mil	-	3	4	8	18
Vacant	Mil	-	3	4	8	23
Vacant	Mil	-	3	4	8	24
Vacant	Mil	-	3	4	8	25
Vacant	Mil	-	3	4	8	26
Vacant	Mil	-	3	4	8	27
Vacant	Mil	-	3	4	8	28
Vacant	Mil	-	3	4	8	33
Vacant	Mil	-	3	4	8	34
Vacant	Mil	-	3	4	8	35
Vacant	Mil	-	3	4	8	36
Vacant	Mil	-	3	4	8	37
Vacant	Mil	-	3	4	8	38
Vacant	Mil	-	1	5	8	18
Vacant	Mil	-	1	5	8	19
Vacant	Mil	-	1	5	8	20
Vacant	Mil	-	1	5	8	30
Vacant	Mil	-	1	5	8	31
Vacant	Mil	-	1	5	8	32
Vacant	Mil	-	1	5	8	33
Vacant	Mil	-	1	5	8	34
Vacant	Mil	-	1	5	8	35
Vacant	Mil	-	3	1	9	4
Vacant	Mil	-	3	1	9	40
Vacant	Mil	-	2	1	10	1
Vacant	Mil	-	2	1	10	2
Vacant	Mil	-	2	1	10	3
Vacant	Mil	-	2	1	10	4
Vacant	Mil	-	2	1	10	5
Vacant	Mil	-	2	1	10	6
Vacant	Mil	-	2	1	10	7
Vacant	Mil	-	2	1	10	8
Vacant	Mil	-	2	1	10	9
Vacant	Mil	-	2	1	10	10
Vacant	Mil	-	2	1	10	11
Vacant	Mil	-	2	1	10	12
Vacant	Mil	-	2	1	10	13
Vacant	Mil	-	2	1	10	14
Vacant	Mil	-	2	1	10	15
Vacant	Mil	-	2	1	10	16
Vacant	Mil	-	2	1	10	17
Vacant	Mil	-	2	1	10	18
Vacant	Mil	-	2	1	10	19
Vacant	Mil	-	2	1	10	20
Vacant	Mil	-	2	1	10	21
Vacant	Mil	-	2	1	10	22
Vacant	Mil	-	2	1	10	23
Vacant	Mil	-	2	1	10	24
Vacant	Mil	-	2	1	10	25
Vacant	Mil	-	2	1	10	26
Vacant	Mil	-	2	1	10	27
Vacant	Mil	-	2	1	10	28
Vacant	Mil	-	2	1	10	29
Vacant	Mil	-	2	1	10	30
Vacant	Mil	-	2	1	10	31
Vacant	Mil	-	2	1	10	32
Vacant	Mil	-	2	1	10	33
Vacant	Mil	-	2	1	10	34
Vacant	Mil	-	2	1	10	35
Vacant	Mil	-	2	1	10	36
Vacant	Mil	-	2	1	10	37

Vacant	Mil	-	2	1	10	38
Vacant	Mil	-	2	1	10	39
Vacant	Mil	-	2	1	10	40
Vacant	Mil	-	4	3	10	2
Vacant	Mil	-	4	3	10	3
Vacant	Mil	-	4	3	10	4
Vacant	Mil	-	4	3	10	5
Vacant	Mil	-	4	3	10	6
Vacant	Mil	-	4	3	10	11
Vacant	Mil	-	4	3	10	12
Vacant	Mil	-	4	3	10	13
Vacant	Mil	-	4	3	10	14
Vacant	Mil	-	4	3	10	15
Vacant	Mil	-	4	3	10	16
Vacant	Mil	-	4	3	10	17
Vacant	Mil	-	4	3	10	18
Vacant	Mil	-	4	3	10	19
Vacant	Mil	-	4	3	10	20
Vacant	Mil	-	4	3	10	30
Vacant	Mil	-	4	3	10	31
Vacant	Mil	-	4	3	10	32
Vacant	Mil	-	1	6	11	1
Vacant	Mil	-	1	6	11	2
Vacant	Mil	-	1	6	11	3
Vacant	Mil	-	1	6	11	4
Vacant	Mil	-	1	6	11	5
Vacant	Mil	-	1	6	11	6
Vacant	Mil	-	1	6	11	7
Vacant	Mil	-	1	6	11	8
Vacant	Mil	-	1	6	11	9
Vacant	Mil	-	1	6	11	10
Vacant	Mil	-	1	6	11	11
Vacant	Mil	-	1	6	11	12
Vacant	Mil	-	1	6	11	13
Vacant	Mil	-	1	6	11	14
Vacant	Mil	-	1	6	11	15
Vacant	Mil	-	1	6	11	16
Vacant	Mil	-	1	6	11	17
Vacant	Mil	-	1	6	11	18
Vacant	Mil	-	1	6	11	19
Vacant	Mil	-	1	6	11	20
Vacant	Mil	-	1	6	11	21
Vacant	Mil	-	1	6	11	22
Vacant	Mil	-	1	6	11	23
Vacant	Mil	-	1	6	11	24
Vacant	Mil	-	1	6	11	25
Vacant	Mil	-	1	6	11	26
Vacant	Mil	-	1	6	11	27
Vacant	Mil	-	1	6	11	28
Vacant	Mil	-	1	6	11	29
Vacant	Mil	-	1	6	11	30
Vacant	Mil	-	1	6	11	31
Vacant	Mil	-	1	6	11	32
Vacant	Mil	-	1	6	11	33
Vacant	Mil	-	1	6	11	34
Vacant	Mil	-	1	6	11	35
Vacant	Mil	-	1	6	11	36
Vacant	Mil	-	1	6	11	37
Vacant	Mil	-	1	6	11	38
Vacant	Mil	-	1	6	11	39
Vacant	Mil	-	1	6	11	40
Vacant	Mil	-	3	1	15	10
Vacant	Mil	-	3	1	15	13
Vacant	Mil	-	3	1	15	21
Vacant	Mil	-	3	1	15	22
Vacant	Mil	-	3	1	15	23
"Located last fall"	*	-	18	17	-	13
"Located last fall"	*	-	18	17	-	14
"Located last fall"	*	-	18	17	-	15

*Refugee tract.

---

822   3 Feb 1809   A/4/002
[Jesse Spencer], Reg Chl
Transmits patents

Henry Haller	Chl	WS	21	10	24	+
Nathaniel Harrington	Chl	-	20	15	32	+
Ebenezer Richards	Chl	MS	21	10	2	+
George Roads	Chl	-	20	11	27	+
John Richstaffer	Chl	-	20	11	27	+
Bazel Meaks?	Chl	MS	21	10	36	+
Charles Steenberger	Chl	-	21	5	-	6
Christian Reim	Chl	-	16	16	17	+
Valentine Reber	Chl	-	20	13	10	-
Henry Strawser	Chl	-	20	10	11	+
Henry Strawser	Chl	-	20	10	12	+

823   3 Feb 1809   A/4/003
[Daniel Symmes], Reg Cin
Transmits patents

Samuel Stitt	Cin	-	4	3	26	+
Henry Ramey	Cin	WML	1	9	28	+
Henry Ramey	Cin	WML	1	8	13	+
George Holeman	Cin	WML	1	13	35	+
James Huston	Cin	WML	1	11	24	+
John & Henry Ramey	Cin	WML	1	9	27	+
Andrew McGarvey &						
David E. Hendricks	Cin	EML	2	6	10	+
Robert Scott	Cin	EML	2	5	27	+
John Richardson	Cin	EML	2	3	29	+
John Simmons	Cin	EML	5	3	12	-
Andrew Zeller & John						
Risinger	Cin	EML	4	3	12	+
Jacob Ruby	Cin	EML	4	4	14	+
Joseph Stubbs	Cin	EML	3	4	34	+
Caspar Shuey	Cin	EML	2	8	27	+
William S. Harderson	Cin	EML	1	9	27	-
Joseph Stubbs	Cin	EML	3	4	33	+
William McCleland	Cin	EML	2	4	25	+

824   4 Feb 1809   A/4/003
[Willys Silliman], Reg Zan
Transmits patents

Joshua W. Satterthwaite	Zan	-	9	8	4	+

825   4 Feb 1809   A/4/003
[David Hoge], Reg Stu
Transmits patents

Alexander McCall	Chl	-	4	8	33	-
Simeon Martin	Chl	-	1	6	31	+
Nathan Heald, Sr.	Chl	-	5	16	10	-
Levi Harris	Chl	-	4	15	32	+
Jacob Hostetler	Chl	-	6	17	24	-
Jacob Schwitzer	Chl	-	3	15	25	+
William Reed	Chl	-	3	14	35	+
John Roller	Chl	-	4	15	24	+
George Hartford	Chl	-	2	6	25	+
John Kiggen	Chl	-	6	10	34	+
Jacob Shoemaker	Chl	-	20	11	18	-
Jacob Spitler	Chl	-	18	15	10	+

826   4 Feb 1809   A/4/004
Isaac Van Horn, Rec Zan
Location of tracts
W. Rhea of Pennsylvania

Error: not military lots	Zan?	-	8	4	2	7
Error: not military lots	Zan?	-	8	4	2	8
Located by others	Zan?	Mil	8	4	3	7
Vacant	Zan?	Mil	8	4	3	8

Isaac Van Horn (as grantee)	Zan?	Mil	6	8	3	15
Isaac Van Horn (as grantee)	Zan?	Mil	6	8	3	16
Isaac Van Horn (as grantee)	Zan?	Mil	6	8	3	5
Vacant	Zan?	Mil	6	8	3	6
Vacant	Zan?	Mil	6	8	3	7
John Gilmer	Zan?	–	7	1	13	–

827   6 Feb 1809   A/4/004
[David Hoge], Reg Stu
Transmits patents

Frederick Sappernick	Stu	–	5	16	12	–
David Smith	Stu	–	5	16	11	–
John Stofer	Stu	–	8	10	28	+
John Sloane	Stu	–	3	15	26	–
John Simmerman	Stu	–	3	16	34	–
Zadok Street	Stu	–	4	17	6	+

828   6 Feb 1809   A/4/005
[Daniel Symmes], Reg Cin
Transmits patents

William Hutchin	Cin	EML	3	3	13	+
Jacob Shively	Cin	EML	5	4	32	+
Daniel Martin	Cin	EML	5	4	5	+
Henry G. Smith	Cin	EML	1	1	4	–
John Sample & Jacob Sample	Cin	EML	4	2	2	–
Daniel Stubbs	Cin	EML	3	4	28	+

829   6 Feb 1809   A/4/005
[Jesse Spencer], Reg Chl
Transmits patents

William Stumps & John Foust	Chl	–	19	12	19	+
Philemon Beecher	Chl	–	20	13	3	+
Nicholas Sidener	Chl	–	20	12	25	+
William Stall	Chl	–	17	18	23	+
John Slough	Chl	–	20	14	35	+
John Shoemaker & George Bowyer	Chl	–	19	15	25	–
John Stephenson	Chl	MS	21	11	10	–
William Smith	Chl	–	19	15	12	+
Joseph Fleming	Chl	MS	21	11	20	+
William Shaw	Chl	–	17	16	8	+
Isaac Shoefer	Chl	–	19	13	4	–

830   7 Feb 1809   A/4/005
Daniel Symmes, Reg Cin
Final certificate
Samuel Gallagher.

831   11 Feb 1809   A/4/006
[David Hoge], Reg Stu

Hugh King	Stu	–	7	18	17	+
John Haun	Stu	–	5	16	8	–
John Hobson	Stu	–	3	10	7	+
George Hartford	Stu	–	4	10	6	+
Michael Hively	Stu	–	7	19	2	–
Thomas Hoey	Stu	–	3	13	13	+
John McCulloch	Stu	–	6	9	10	+
George Mountz	Stu	–	5	17	36	+
James Kelly	Stu	–	4	11	3	–
Michael Miller	Stu	–	6	18	33	+
Michael Miller	Stu	–	6	18	29	+
Michael Miller	Stu	–	6	18	28	+

George Murray	Stu	–	8	10	34	+
Absalom Kent	Stu	–	5	11	31	–
Jacob Kitsmiller	Stu	–	6	18	35	–

832   11 Feb 1809   A/4/006
[Jesse Spencer], Reg Chl
Transmits patents

Philip King	Chl	MS	21	11	12	+
Ezekiel Morris	Chl	MS	21	9	33	+
John McNaghten, Sr.	Chl	–	18	16	35	–
George Honcehhauser?	Chl	–	18	16	32	–
Benjamin Kearns	Chl	–	20	9	19	–
John Moorhead	Chl	–	19	16	35	+

833   11 Feb 1809   A/4/007
[Daniel Symmes], Reg Cin
Transmits patents

Amos Huggins	Cin	EML	4	4	26	–
Jacob Hackleman	Cin	WML	2	8	4	+
William Cunningham	Cin	WML	2	11	33	+
Henry Kinsey	Cin	EML	5	3	1	–
George Kunse	Cin	EML	5	3	9	–
Christian Koch	Cin	EML	4	4	23	+
George Kearn	Cin	EML	4	3	25	+
David Moss	Cin	EML	5	5	24	+
Matthew Hueston	Cin	EML	2	4	1	–
Abner Hallowell	Cin	EML	3	4	17	+
Aaron Montfort	Cin	EML	3	6	31	+
Elnathan Kemper	Cin	WML	1	4	34	+

834   14 Feb 1809   A/4/007
Hon. W. Findley, U.S. Representative
Transmits patents for military land [returned by Findley 3 Mar 1809 because he had forgotten where to forward them].

835   13 Feb 1809   A/4/007
David Hoge, Reg Stu
First certificate
Brooks assigns to Jacob Newman who, in turn, assigns to Henry Eatter

Aaron Brooks	Stu	–	8	10	23	+

836   17 Feb 1809   A/4/008
Goldsmith Chandler, Winchester, Virginia
Assignment of final certificate
General -- Smith; [possible assignment by Thompson to Chandler]

John Thompson	Stu	–	7	9	23	–

837   18 Feb 1809   A/4/008
[Daniel Symmes], Reg Cin
Transmits patents

George Keever	Cin	MR	4	4	29	+
David Hanes?	Cin	MR	7	3	29	+
Mordecai Mendenhall	Cin	MR	9	2	30	+
Henry Keever	Cin	MR	4	4	29	+
Isaac Myers	Cin	MR	6	1	20	+
Josiah Cushman	Cin	Pre	5	2	18	+
Rich & Kirby	Cin	Pre	4	3	2	+
James Wills	Cin	Pre	4	4	28	+
Joseph N. Husted	Cin	Pre	8	4	17	+
Peter Sintz?	Cin	MR	9	4	23	+
John Scott	Cin	EML	2	5	25	–

838   18 Feb 1809   A/4/009
Joseph King, care of Post Master, at the Spread
Eagle, 16 miles from Philadelphia, [in] Dela-
ware County, Pennsylvania
Transmits patent

Joseph King	Zan	-	14	15	18	+

839   18 Feb 1809   A/4/009
[Jesse Spencer], Reg Chl
Transmits patents

Gilbert Stephens	Chl	-	20	9	17	+
John Stevenson	Chl	MS	21	11	11	+
Gilbert Stephens	Chl	-	20	9	18	+

840   18 Feb 1809   A/4/009
[David Hoge], Reg Stu
Transmits patents

Joseph Wright	Stu	-	4	16	12	-
Jacob Christ	Stu	-	8	12	27	-
William Wallace	Stu	-	4	10	11	+
Adam Wolf	Stu	-	5	17	26	+
Thomas Mitchell	Stu	-	3	5	6	-
Abraham Warrington	Stu	-	4	17	24	-
Thomas Wilson	Stu	-	3	9	30	+
Gabriel Walton	Stu	-	4	15	10	-
William Whinney	Stu	-	3	14	19	+
John Crawford	Stu	-	1	6	4	+
James Campbell, Jr.	Stu	-	3	11	4	+
Abner Woolman	Stu	-	5	18	36	+
William Crawford	Stu	-	5	9	29	+
James Caldwell	Stu	-	2	11	5	+
George Clark	Stu	-	5	16	29	+
Henry Woolf	Stu	-	4	16	18	-
Henry Woolf	Stu	-	4	16	30	-
Robert Cummins	Stu	-	4	12	11	+
John Walsh	Stu	-	7	16	31	+
William Scarlet	Stu	-	4	12	8	+
George Starbuck	Stu	-	6	8	1	+
John Edmondson	Stu	-	1	7	4	+
Samuel Clark	Stu	-	3	12	10	+
Enos Ellis	Stu	-	4	15	29	+
Richard Vaughan	Stu	-	6	16	10	+
Theodore Ellis	Stu	-	5	9	33	+
Richard Fawcett	Stu	-	6	19	36	-
Michael Easterday	Stu	-	2	12	5	+
Amos Vernon	Stu	-	5	7	34	+
George Walters	Stu	-	2	6	34	-
James Winder	Stu	-	7	11	12	+
James Wilson	Stu	-	2	6	7	-
Thomas Stanley	Stu	-	5	18	23	+

841   23 Feb 1809   A/4/010
[Daniel Symmes], Reg Cin
Transmits patents

Jacob Miller	Cin	EML	5	3	11	-
John Ward	Cin	EML	3	4	20	+
William Willis	Cin	EML	5	5	8	+
James Harris	Cin	EML	1	7	1	+
David Hanes? [Harris?]	Cin	MR	9	2	13	+
James Wilson	Cin	EML	6	2	8	+
Henry Weaver & Isaac Huff	Cin	EML	4	2	-	27
Henry Weaver & Isaac Huff	Cin	EML	4	2	-	28
Henry Weaver & Isaac Huff	Cin	EML	4	2	29	-
John Compton	Cin	EML	5	6	7	+
William Hixon	Cin	EML	3	4	8	+
Matthew Huston	Cin	EML	1	5	11	+
James Huston	Cin	EML	1	6	31	+
David Wolverton	Cin	EML	2	8	7	+
Marmaduke Coat	Cin	EML	5	7	32	+

Christian Shively, Jr.	Cin	EML	5	4	27	+
Henry Medsker	Cin	EML	5	3	5	+
William Emrick	Cin	EML	5	2	4	-
Christopher Emrick	Cin	EML	4	3	24	+
Henry Capehart	Cin	EML	6	2	18	+
Henry Capehart	Cin	EML	6	2	19	+
Martin Weigbricht	Cin	EML	5	4	18	+
John Brownson	Cin	WML	2	4	13	+
Charles Hunt	Cin	WML	1	13	30	+
John Watts	Cin	WML	1	13	14	+
John Creek	Cin	WML	1	11	31	+
James Hartpence	Cin	WML	1	7	12	+
John Starr	Cin	WML	1	12	19	+
Daniel Conway? [Connery?]	Cin	WML	2	6	11	+
Isaac Willson	Cin	WML	3	10	-	13
Isaac Willson	Cin	WML	3	10	-	24

842   23 Feb 1809   A/4/011
[Willys Silliman], Reg Zan
Transmits patents

Adam Schnider	Zan	-	3	9	20	+
Michael Watermire	Zan	-	14	15	10	+
Elias Wellar	Zan	-	3	10	21	+
John Springer	Zan	-	13	10	5	+
John Springer	Zan	-	14	16	18	+

843   23 Feb 1809   A/4/011
[Jesse Spencer], Reg Chl
Transmits patents

Daniel Hollingshead	Chl	-	17	10	20	+
Jesse Hoff	Chl	-	21	5	27	+
Albright Werlin	Chl	-	20	10	5	+
William Young	Chl	-	19	14	20	+
William Renick	Chl	LS?	21	2	8	+
Peter Walser	Chl	-	16	17	3	+
George Weedman	Chl	-	16	17	3	+
William Wilson, Sr.	Chl	-	17	17	3	+
John Wright	Chl	-	20	11	32	+
John Waggoner	Chl	-	16	16	5	+
William & John Williamson	Chl	MS	21	9	26	+
John Miller	Chl	-	17	17	25	+
Christian Whiteman	Chl	-	20	12	8	+
David Wright	Chl	-	20	15	5	+
Jacob Weaver	Chl	-	18	15	5	+
Isaac Whitsell	Chl	-	20	12	31	+
David Wright	Chl	MS	21	11	13	+
Peter Sain	Chl	-	17	18	12	+
Michael Sturm	Chl	-	17	18	30	+
John Shafer	Chl	-	18	16	5	+
Mary Hays	Chl	-	20	30	12	+
Samuel Harrison	Chl	-	20	9	20	+
James Wells	Chl	-	19	15	28	-
John Courtwright	Chl	-	20	14	28	+
Joseph Cooper	Chl	-	17	18	11	+
Winn Winship	Chl	-	20	11	17	+

844   25 Feb 1809   A/4/012
[David Hoge], Reg Stu
Transmits patents

Levi Jennings	Stu	-	4	17	27	+
Obadiah Jennings	Stu	-	6	9	12	+
Emanuel Dixson	Stu	-	5	18	34	-
Emanuel Dixson	Stu	-	4	16	34	-
Oliver Dunfield	Stu	-	3	5	18	+
Enos Lewis	Stu	-	2	10	14	+

845   25 Feb 1809   A/4/012
[Daniel Symmes], Reg Cin
Transmits patents

Jonathan Jones	Cin	EML	1	4	12	+
Jonathan Jones	Cin	EML	1	4	11	+
Jonathan Jones	Cin	EML	1	4	2	+
John C. Imlay	Cin	EML	3	3	9	+
Charles Dawson	Cin	WML	1	6	23	+
Charles Dawson	Cin	WML	1	6	26	-
James Lamb	Cin	WML	2	13	24	+
James Lamb	Cin	WML	1	13	19	+

846   25 Feb 1809   A/4/012
[Jesse Spencer], Reg Chl
Transmits patents

Adam Lucott	Chl	-	19	14	26	+
John Davidson & Mont- gomery & Lynn	Chl	-	17	1	2	+
William Lancaster	Chl	-	16	17	27	+
David Lasley	Chl	-	16	17	34	+
Joseph Lane	Chl	WS	21	11	30	+
Henry Liphart	Chl	-	20	14	28	+

847   25 Feb 1809   A/4/013
Isaac Smith, care of James Chipley, at Woodstock,
   Shenandoah County, Virginia

Isaac Smith	Chl	MS	21	10	2	+

848   2 Mar 1809   A/4/013
David Hoge, Reg Stu
Assignment of tract
Goldsmith Chandler, assignee of John Thompson.

849   2 Mar 1809   A/4/014
John Roads, Mundellsville, Shenandoah County, Vir-
   ginia
Answers inquiry regarding application for land
General -- Smith.

850   3 Mar 1809   A/4/014
David Hoge, Reg Stu
Final certificate

William Beans	Stu	-	2	12	19	-

851   8 Mar 1809   A/4/014
[Jesse Spencer], Reg Chl
Transmits patents

Winn Winship	Chl	-	20	11	17	+
William Gardner, Sr.	Chl	-	18	15	2	+
Adam Gigar	Chl	-	18	16	34	+
Conrad Pitzer	Chl	-	20	10	18	+
Joseph Dixon	Chl	-	20	8	13	+
Joseph Dixon	Chl	-	19	9	6	+
Peter Zestman?	Chl	-	17	18	25	+
Henry Spangler	Chl	-	20	12	32	+
Henry Spangler	Chl	-	20	12	28	+
Philip Smith	Chl	WS	21	11	17	+
Jacob Yeager, Sr.	Chl	WS	21	11	17	+
George Pontius	Chl	WS	21	11	22	+
John Gay	Chl	WS	21	10	10	+
Luke Decker	Chl	WS	21	10	20	+
John Pickins	Chl	WS	21	10	19	+

852   8 Mar 1809   A/4/015
[Daniel Symmes], Reg Cin
Transmits patents

John Gripe	Cin	EML	4	5	11	+
Alexander Pugh	Cin	EML	3	4	14	+
Alexander Pugh	Cin	EML	2	8	18	+
William Irwin	Cin	EML	1	3	9	+
William Irwin	Cin	EML	1	3	8	+
Michael Fouts	Cin	EML	4	3	4	+
Samuel Stubbs	Cin	EML	3	4	29	+
Philip Slifer	Cin	EML	4	4	23	+
Benjamin Pursel	Cin	WML	2	4	31	+

853   8 Mar 1809   A/4/015
[David Hoge], Reg Stu
Transmits patents

David Gibson	Stu	-	4	10	17	+
Hugh Gilliland	Stu	-	7	10	2	+
Andrew Galbraith	Stu	-	3	11	8	+
James Glenn	Stu	-	2	8	33	+
William Gallagher	Stu	-	4	10	17	+
Richard Gibson	Stu	-	5	17	19	+
Thomas Saint	Stu	-	1	7	33	+
Samuel Goodin	Stu	-	6	9	18	+
Adam Dunlap	Stu	-	5	10	13	+
Charles Porter	Stu	-	2	6	36	+
John Smith, Sr.	Stu	-	1	6	18	+
Jacob Preston	Stu	-	4	12	20	+
Moses Porter	Stu	-	6	16	20	+
Jonah Small	Stu	-	4	17	14	+
Peter Smith	Stu	-	2	10	13	+
William Alman	Stu	-	4	12	10	+
William Alman	Stu	-	4	12	1	+
Morris Albaugh	Stu	-	5	12	12	+
Henry Atterholt	Stu	-	4	15	25	+
Jonathan Sells	Stu	-	6	9	20	+

854   8 Mar 1809   A/4/016
[John Badollet], Reg Vin
Transmits patents

Toussaint Dubois	Vin	-	5W	1S	3	+
Richard Stillwell	Vin	-	4E	6S	15	+

855   8 Mar 1809   A/4/016
George Austine, to be left at Post Office, York,
   Pennsylvania
Transmits patent

George Austine	Stu	-	5	16	18	+

856   9 Mar 1809   A/4/016
David Hoge, Reg Stu
Act of 10 May 1800; withdrawals not permitted
-- Wood; -- Kail.

857   7 Mar 1809   A/4/017
David Hoge, Reg Stu
Transmits patents

Lewis Kinney	Stu	-	3	14	11	-
Joseph Stibbs?	Stu	-	2	11	30	+

858   14 Mar 1809   A/4/017
Post Master, Charleston, Jefferson County, Vir-
   ginia
Transmits patent
J. G. Jackson

G. W. Humphreys	Mil	-	7	4	2	17	

859   14 Mar 1809   A/4/017
John E. Buchanan, Hollidaysburgh, Huntingdon
   County, Pennsylvania

Query regarding patent
Henry Medsker   Cin EML 5 3 5 +

860	14 Mar 1809	A/4/018

Willys Silliman, Reg Zan
Final certificate
Robert Henderson   Zan - 4 15 18 +

861	23 Mar 1809	A/4/018

[David Hoge], Reg Stu
Transmits patents

Jacob Pickering	Stu	-	5	9	34	-
William Patterson	Stu	-	3	9	29	+
John Nichols	Stu	-	5	8	25	+
Henry Dixson, Jr.	Stu	-	3	15	23	+
Joseph Thompson	Stu	-	1	7	5	-
Jacob Nessley	Stu	-	2	10	23	+
Gideon Gaver	Stu	-	3	13	4	+
John Roller	Stu	-	3	14	30	+
John Richards	Stu	-	8	11	8	+
Henry Fox	Stu	-	4	15	23	+
Henry Fox	Stu	-	4	15	24	+
Thomas Furrier	Stu	-	2	11	5	+
John Richards	Stu	-	8	10	33	+
John Richards	Stu	-	8	9	4	+
John Richards	Stu	-	8	11	17	+
Charles Fout	Stu	-	7	20	31	+
Thomas Reeder, Sr.	Stu	-	5	16	9	-
Stephen Ford	Stu	-	3	9	24	+
Josiah Reeves	Stu	-	7	9	12	+
Andrew Dickson	Stu	-	3	10	30	+

862	23 Mar 1809	A/4/018

[Willys Silliman], Reg Zan
Transmits patents

Moses Garman	Zan	-	15	18	9	+
John Nichols	Zan	-	7	5	9	+

863	23 Mar 1809	A/4/019

John Carlisle, Chl
Patent transferred from Cin
Daniel Symmes, Reg Cin
Henry Horn   Cin EML 2 7 35 -

864	23 Mar 1809	A/4/019

William Hoge, Washington, Washington County, Penn-
sylvania
-- Kintner for Vin lands
Joseph Pentecost   Stu - 2 10 24 -

865	23 Mar 1809	A/4/019

[Jesse Spencer], Reg Chl
Transmits patents

George Puncher, Sr.	Chl	MS	21	10	28	+
Nathaniel Teal & Peter Hush?	Chl	-	17	18	8	+
John Pickens	Chl	MS	21	10	17	+
Amos Taylor	Chl	-	20	8	9	+
Jacob Fedder	Chl	MS	21	9	11	+
John Good	Chl	-	17	18	23	+
Jacob Tutewiler	Chl	-	19	16	13	+
Bernhard Poorman	Chl	-	16	17	32	+
William Tallman	Chl	MS	21	9	24	+
William Tallman	Chl	MS	21	9	13	+
Conrad Ready? Jr.	Chl	-	20	11	1	+
Conrad Ready? Jr.	Chl	-	20	9	6	+

Robert Gilson	Chl	WS	21	10	23	+
Valentine Reber	Chl	-	19	11	8	+
Emanuel Ruffman	Chl	-	17	17	7	-

866	23 Mar 1809	A/4/020

[Daniel Symmes], Reg Cin
Transmits patents

John Taylor	Cin	MR	12	5	10	+
John Townsend	Cin	WML	2	13	1	+
Frederick Foutze	Cin	EML	4	3	7	+
Samuel Dick	Cin	EML	1	2	36	+
Andrew Fouts	Cin	WML	2	12	13	+
William Ramey	Cin	WML	1	8	24	+
Joseph Florey	Cin	EML	5	4	20	+
John Fisher	Cin	WML	1	11	25	+
John Templeton	Cin	WML	2	10	4	+
John Titman	Cin	EML	5	4	7	+
Joseph Part	Cin	MR	4	2	8	-

867	23 Mar 1809	A/4/020

David Hoge, Reg Stu
First certificate

Parmenias Sanborn	Stu	-	5	17	7	+
Joseph Matthias	Stu	-	5	17	13	+

868	31 Mar 1809	A/4/020

David Hoge, Reg Stu
First certificates

Peter Walter	Stu	-	5	17	26	+
John Perry	Stu	-	5	10	34	+

869	1 Apr 1809	A/4/021

[Jesse Spencer], Reg Chl
Transmits patents

Philip Hay? [Hoy?]	Chl	-	20	14	29	+
Thomas Hanks	Chl	-	20	9	30	+
Thomas Hanks	Chl	-	21	8	25	+
Jacob Offnere?	Chl	-	21	1	-	14
Isaac Reynolds	Chl	-	16	16	13	+
William Ream	Chl	-	17	18	14	+
Daniel Click	Chl	-	20	14	33	+
Jacob Hinshaw	Chl	-	20	8	1	+
Daniel E. Koy? [Hoy?]	Chl	-	20	14	20	+
Peter Click	Chl	MS	22	3	12	+
John Heslet	Chl	MS	21	9	12	+

870	1 Apr 1809	A/4/021

[Joseph Wood], Reg Mar
Transmits patents

William Outland	Mar	-	6	7	18	+
William Outland	Mar	-	7	7	18	-
Samuel Danford	Mar	-	7	7	36	+

871	1 Apr 1809	A/4/021

[David Hoge], Reg Stu
Transmits patents

Isaac Osburn	Stu	-	5	11	10	+
Henry Dixon	Stu	-	3	15	23	+
William Robinson	Stu	-	4	17	26	-
Horton Howard	Stu	-	6	8	3	+
Edward Carroll	Stu	-	4	15	1	+
George Neff	Stu	-	3	5	18	+

872	1 Apr 1809	A/4/022

[Daniel Symmes], Reg Cin
Transmits patents

[61]

James & Henry Newton?
  [Huston?]   Cin EML   2   6 33   +
Jacob Christman   Cin EML   3   5 36   +
Jacob C. Cook   Cin EML   3   6   8   +
William Neal? [Heal?]   Cin EML   1   8   8   +
John Ozias   Cin EML   2   8 12   +
John Ozias   Cin EML   2   8 13   +
Samuel Dick   Cin EML   2   2   - 30
Samuel Dick   Cin EML   2   2 31   -
Martin Rinehart   Cin EML   2   4 29   +
Nicholas Coble   Cin EML   5   5 13   +
Robert Robison   Cin EML   6   2   8   +
Martin Rice   Cin EML   3   7 27   +
Jacob Cay? [Coy?]   Cin MR   7   2   8   +
James H. Robinson   Cin MR   4   3 26   +
George Cimmerman   Cin MR   8   2 17   +
Jacob Coy   Cin MR   7   2   8   +
  [marginal note: "copied Apl 24, '96"]

873   1 Apr 1809   A/4/022
Willys Silliman, Reg Zan
Transmits patent
Thomas Neftel   Zan   -   9   8   5   +

874   1 Apr 1809   A/4/022
Samuel Gwathmey
Transmits patent
Jesse Henley   Unk 2E   8   3 34   +

875   8 Apr 1809   A/4/022
James Findlay, Rec Cin
Duplicate receipts
John Cook   Cin MR   11   2 19   +
John Cook   Cin MR   11   2 14   +
Elias Brunner   Cin MR   8   4 25   +

876   3 Apr 1809   A/4/023
David Hoge, Reg Stu
First certificates; duplicate receipts
Thompson transfers to Hugh Davison
Thomas Thompson   Stu   -   9   9 14   +
Jesse Slingluff   Stu   -   8 11 20   +
Adam Schaeffer   Stu   -   8 11 23   +
Adam Schaeffer   Stu   -   8 12 33   +
John Dunkin   Stu   -   3 14 18   +

877   8 Apr 1809   A/4/023
Jesse Spencer, Reg Chl
First certificates; duplicate receipts
Will of Michael Baker, deceased; Michael Baker
  transfers to Joseph Baker, "one of the heirs";
  Gore transfers to John Roads
Michael Baker?   Chl Mil 14   8 21   +
Michael Baker?   Chl Mil 14   8 22   +
Jacob Claypool   Chl   -   19 15 21   +
John Gore   Chl   -   18 16 13   +

878   8 Apr 1809   A/4/024
Samuel Finley, Rec Chl
Duplicate receipts
Lawrence Riter   Chl   -   17 18   7   +
Lawrence Riter   Chl   -   17 18 18   +
Lawrence Riter   Chl   -   18 16 12   +
James? Claypool   Chl   -   14   8 22   +
Jacob Claypool   Chl   -   19 15 21   +
Jacob Claypool   Chl   -   14   8 22   +

Jacob Claypool   Chl   -   19 15 21   +
Jacob Claypool   Chl   -   14   8 22   +
Jacob Claypool   Chl   -   14   8 21   +
John Prose?   Chl   -   18 16 13   +

879   8 Apr 1809   A/4/024
Willys Silliman, Reg Zan
First certificate; duplicate receipt
Jacob Newman transfers to Charles Bohn; Samuel
  Smith transfers to Charles Bohn
Samuel Smith   Zan   -   3 10 12   +

880   8 Apr 1809   A/4/025
David Symmes, Reg Cin
First certificate; duplicate receipt
John Cook   Cin MR   2 11 14   +
John Cook   Cin MR   2 11 19   +

881   8 Apr 1809   A/4/025
Peter Wilson
Duplicate receipts
John Dunkin   Stu   -   3 14 18   +
Thomas Ashbaugh   Stu   -   2 13 18   +
Hugh Davison   Stu   -   9   9 14   +
Jesse Slingluff   Stu   -   8 11 20   +
Adam Schaeffer   Stu   -   8 12 33   +
Adam Schaeffer   Stu   -   8 11 23   +

882   8 Apr 1809   A/4/025
[David Hoge], Reg Stu
Transmits patents
Jacob Loutzenheiser   Stu   -   8 11 34   +
Stoffal Miller   Stu   -   5 17 11   +
Joseph Lindesmith   Stu   -   4 15 36   +
Levi Wickersham   Stu   -   6 19 28   +
William Bundy   Stu   -   6   8 27   +
Thomas Wickersham   Stu   -   6 19 28   +
George Waddell   Stu   -   6   9 17   +
Abner Woolman   Stu   -   4 16   5   +
Thomas Latimer   Stu   -   2   8   2   +
Donald McKay   Stu   -   2 10 35   +
Aaron Brooks   Stu   -   1   7 29   +
Benjamin Borton   Stu   -   7   9 12   +
James Leiper   Stu   -   8   9 29   +
Samuel McCune   Stu   -   5   9   8   -
Gawin Lawther   Stu   -   2   6 36   +

883   8 Apr 1809   A/4/026
[Daniel Symmes], Reg Cin
Transmits patents
Robert Burns   Cin MR   5   4   - 26
Thomas John   Cin Pre   7   2 13   +
John Buckhannon &
  William Philips   Cin WML   1   1   -   5
John Buckhannon &
  William Philips   Cin WML   1   1   6   -
Ruth Crane   Cin WML   1 11   8   +
Christly Kingery   Cin WML   1 11 36   +
George Kuns, Sr.   Cin EML   2   4 29   +
Albert Banta   Cin EML   4   3 31   +
John Brownson   Cin EML   6   6 30   +
Daniel Christman   Cin EML   3   6 31   +
John Brotsman   Cin EML   4   4 25   +
Benjamin Coppock   Cin EML   4   7   1   +
John McCormick   Cin EML   1   8 28   +
Charles Burch   Cin EML   2   2   6   +
George Kunse   Cin EML   5   4 28   +

George Kunse	Cin	EML	5	3	6	+
John Buchannon	Cin	EML	3	3	35	+
Abraham Chase	Cin	EML	1	4	6	+
William Wells	Cin	EML	6	7	31	+
John Harper & John Clark	Cin	EML	1	4	29	+

884   11 Apr 1809   A/4/026
William Hoge, Washington, Washington County, Pennsylvania
Transmits patents

Jacob Kintner	Vin	-	3E	4S	2	+
Jacob Kintner	Zan	Mil	3	8	10	+

885   11 Apr 1809   A/4/027
[Jesse Spencer], Reg Chl
Transmits patents

Daniel Harshner	Chl	-	19	11	5	+
Nicholas Ketnar?	Chl	-	18	16	7	+
Conrad Kline	Chl	-	20	11	1	+
Darby Kelly	Chl	-	20	5	3	+
William Wixley	Chl	-	19	15	5	+
David Wright	Chl	-	20	15	30	+
Edmond Ingman	Chl	-	19	14	7	+
John Brooks	Chl	-	17	18	1	+
John Good	Chl	-	18	16	5	+
Stephen Cole	Chl	-	20	13	7	+
Jesse Pugh	Chl	-	18	16	30	+
John McCailey?	Chl	-	16	6	23	+
John Stough	Chl	-	17	17	10	+
Benjamin Daniel	Chl	-	21	5	30	+
James & Henry Johnson	Chl	MS	21	11	19	+
George Kabb	Chl	MS	21	11	14	+
John Kabb	Chl	MS	21	11	13	+
Barnabas Lambert	Chl	MS	22	4	35	+
Henry Ritter	Chl	MS	21	9	25	+
Henry Ritter	Chl	MS	21	9	24	+
Hugh Forsman	Chl	WS	22	3	-	10
Hugh Forsman	Chl	WS	22	3	-	11
Hugh Forsman	Chl	WS	22	3	14	-
Samuel Finley (as grantee)	Chl	WS	21	9	28	-
Jacob Kishler	Chl	WS	21	9	3	+
James Frazier	Chl	WS	21	10	11	+
Samuel Laycock	Chl	WS	21	10	28	+

[Certified copy of this letter sent to Hon. C. Delano Horner, U.S. Representative, 25 Mar 1846.]

886   11 Apr 1809   A/4/027
Philip Smith, care of Post Master, Hanover, York County, Pennsylvania
Transmits patents

Philip Smith	Stu	-	7	18	3	+
Philip Smith	Stu	-	7	18	4	+

887   11 Apr 1809   A/4/028
Hon. John Rea, Chambersburgh, Pennsylvania
Transmits patent
-- Etter

John Gilmer	Zan	Mil	7	1	13	+

888   20 Apr 1809   A/4/028
[David Hoge], Reg Stu
Transmits patents

William Thompson	Stu	-	7	17	13	+
Horton Howard	Stu	-	4	16	6	+
Rudolph Hines	Stu	-	5	10	29	+
John McLaughlin	Stu	-	2	11	30	+
Benjamin Knight	Stu	-	6	13	35	+
Samuel Morris	Stu	-	4	16	5	+
John Ken? [Kerr?]	Stu	-	4	16	7	-
Lydia Morris	Stu	-	4	17	29	+
David Gibny	Stu	-	5	10	14	+
Robert Morrison	Stu	-	5	8	33	+
Donald McKay	Stu	-	2	10	34	+
Malachi Jolley	Stu	-	3	8	9	-

889   19 Apr 1809   A/4/029
[Daniel Symmes], Reg Cin
Transmits patents

Benjamin Horner	Cin	MR	6	2	3	+
Benjamin Horner	Cin	MR	6	2	8	+
Matthew Hueston	Cin	EML	1	6	34	+
William Wells	Cin	EML	5	9	2	+
William Wells	Cin	EML	6	7	31	+
Samuel Jones	Cin	EML	3	3	3	+
Jeremiah Cox	Cin	WML	1	13	5	+
Isaac Cooper	Cin	EML	5	5	36	+
Joseph Cooper	Cin	EML	5	5	36	+
Mahlon Farquhar	Cin	MR	8	3	3	+
Michael Fritz	Cin	EML	3	6	23	+
Joseph Hanna	Cin	EML	2	10	9	+
Christian Grier	Cin	EML	6	4	27	+
David Crissman	Cin	EML	2	8	25	+
Levi Kinman?	Cin	EML	3	3	18	+
George Jones	Cin	EML	3	4	32	+
Adam Garbuck	Cin	MR	7	2	11	+
George Jones	Cin	EML	3	4	33	+
Margaret McCoy	Cin	WML	1	13	18	+
Joseph Trotter	Cin	EML	1	8	29	+
David Halloway	Cin	MR	5	3	8	+
Isaac Cooper	Cin	EML	5	5	36	+
George P. Torrence	Cin	EML	3	2	-	15
George P. Torrence	Cin	EML	3	2	-	22
George P. Torrence	Cin	EML	3	2	10	-
John Fox	Cin	EML	2	8	4	+
David & Jacob Fridge? [Fudge?]	Cin	EML	3	5	35	+

890   1 May 1809   A/4/029
[John Badollet], Reg Vin
Transmits patents

Elliender Warrick	Vin	-	11W	3S	6	+
James Anthony	Vin	-	10W	6S	8	+
Thomas Jones	Vin	-	7W	2N	5	+

891   1 May 1809   A/4/030
[Daniel Symmes], Reg Cin
Transmits patents

William Wills	Cin	EML	6	7	-	32
William Wills	Cin	EML	6	7	33	-
Philip Weaver	Cin	EML	3	3	14	+
Charles Swearingen	Cin	EML	3	4	31	+
Christian Stetler	Cin	EML	6	6	30	+
Andrew Smelzer	Cin	MR	7	3	26	+
John Stonebreaker	Cin	EML	2	4	34	+
David McDill	Cin	EML	1	6	26	+
Daniel Miller	Cin	EML	5	4	11	-

892   1 May 1809   A/4/030
[David Hoge], Reg Stu
Transmits patents

John Spoon	Stu	-	6	18	32	+
Samuel Gibson	Stu	-	5	17	3	+
Ulrey Shively	Stu	-	7	19	29	+

Samuel Dunn	Stu	–	6	8	29	+
Thomas Stanley	Stu	–	4	16	10	+
Hugh Brown	Stu	–	3	9	24	+
Elizabeth Thorn	Stu	–	6	19	34	+
Andrew Smith	Stu	–	2	10	35	+
Jacob Aultman	Stu	–	8	10	12	+

893   1 May 1809   A/4/030
[Jesse Spencer], Reg Chl
Transmits patents
Leonard Neff, assignee of Ben Armsworthy

Leonard Neff	Chl	–	21	8	24	+
John Clarke	Chl	–	20	13	6	+
Jacob Dittoe	Chl	–	17	16	1	+
Abraham Miller	Chl	–	19	16	33	+
Abraham Lorance	Chl	–	21	5	33	+
John Coonrod	Chl	–	20	12	8	+
Abraham Miller	Chl	–	19	16	36	+
William Wilson	Chl	–	16	17	25	+
Isaac Larimer	Chl	–	17	16	18	+
Peter Eversole	Chl	–	19	16	34	+
Jacob Hack	Chl	–	16	16	8	+
Joseph Evans	Chl	MS	21	9	13	+
Jacob Ream	Chl	–	17	18	14	+
John Wright	Chl	MS	21	11	11	+
Barnabas Lambert	Chl	MS	22	4	34	+
Luke Ingman	Chl	–	20	13	12	+
Henry Kunsler	Chl	–	19	16	13	+

894   1 May 1809   A/4/031
Land Office, Jeffersonville
Transmits patents

David Fouts	Jef	–	9E	1N	8	+
Frederick Fisher	Jef	–	9E	2N	29	+
John Ryker	Jef	–	11E	4	30	+

895   1 May 1809   A/4/031
[Joseph Wood], Reg Mar
Transmits patents

Richard Cox	Mar	–	6	7	3	+
Daniel Conard	Mar	–	7	7	6	+
M? Miner [could be William Miner]	Mar	–	7	2	35	+

896   1 May 1809   A/4/031
[Willys Silliman], Reg Zan
Transmits patents

John Adams	Zan	Mil	8	2	14	+
James Leverick	Zan	Mil	1	2	22	+

897   2 May 1809   A/4/032
David Hoge, Reg Stu
Duplicate receipt

John Fisk	Stu	–	8	10	21	+

898   8 May 1809   A/4/032
General T. Worthington
Answers query regarding vacant Mil? lots

Vacant	Mil?	–	16	8	4	3
Vacant	Mil?	–	18	7	1	15
Vacant	Mil?	–	17	7	2	15
Vacant	Mil?	–	17	7	2	16
Vacant	Mil?	–	17	7	2	17

899   9 May 1809   A/4/032
Joseph Vance, Franklinton Ohio

Transmits patents

Benjamin Carpenter	Mil	–	15	1	3	23
James Carpenter	Mil	–	15	1	3	22
Benjamin Carpenter	Mil	–	15	1	3	10
John Parker	Mil	–	15	1	3	40

900   9 May 1809   A/4/033
Isaac Van Horn, Rec Zan
Transmits patents

Isaac Van Horn (as grantee)	Mil	–	8	4	3	8
Isaac Van Horn (as grantee)	Mil	–	6	8	3	6
Isaac Van Horn (as grantee)	Mil	–	6	8	3	7
Isaac Van Horn (as grantee)	Mil	–	6	8	3	15

901   9 May 1809   A/4/033
Hon. John Rea, Chambersburgh, Pennsylvania
Transmits patent

Henry Eatter	Stu	–	8	10	23	+

902   9 May 1809   A/4/033
Gerard Topkin, Baltimore
Transmits patent

Gerard Topkin	Zan	–	5	1	10	+

903   9 May 1809   A/4/033
John Haines, Winchester, Frederick County, Virginia
Transmits patent
Assignment by Samuel Smith to Haines for land not described

John Haines	Stu	–	8	11	18	+

904   9 May 1809   A/4/033
William Bean, Waterford, Loudon County, Virginia
Transmits patent

William Bean	Stu	–	2	12	19	–

905   10 May 1809   A/4/034
J. H. Brinton, 279 Market Street, Philadelphia, Pennsylvania
Duplicate receipts

Brinton & Candy?	Stu	–	7	18	24	+
Brinton & Candy?	Stu	–	8	10	20	+
Brinton & Candy?	Stu	–	6	6	19	+
Brinton & Candy?	Stu	–	7	17	23	+
Brinton & Candy?	Stu	–	7	15	12	+
J. H. Brinton	Stu	–	6	16	12	+

906   10 May 1809   A/4/034
Peter Wilson, Rec Stu
Duplicate receipt
J. H. Brinton.

907   10 May 1809   A/4/035
Daniel Symmes, Reg Cin
First certificate; correction of patents

Achary Berry	Cin	MR	12	3	1	+
Tobias Barkalow	Cin	EML	4	2	2	–
Jonathan Hollingsworth	Cin	WML	2	11	14	+

908   10 May 1809   A/4/035
Willys Silliman, Reg Zan
First certificates

John Self	Zan	-	5	1	6	+
John Self	Zan	-	5	1	15	+

909   10 May 1809   A/4/035
Artemas Sawyer, Athens, Ohio
Proof of service
Thomas Stafford, "late a soldier in the Revolution-
  ary War"; General -- Washington.

910   10 May 1809   A/4/036
James Findlay, Rec Cin
Duplicate receipt
John Cook   Cin MR 11 2 19 +

911   11 May 1809   A/4/036
Samuel Gwathney
Returns of land applications for April and August
  1808 accidentally destroyed.

912   12 May 1809   A/4/037
Daniel Symmes, Reg Cin
First certificate; assignment insufficient;
  final certificate; John Cleves Symmes purchase
Gray assigns to Thomas Wilson

William Gray	Cin	MR	5	3	11	+
John Bigger	Cin	MR	4	3	25	+

913   12 May 1809   A/4/037
Asa Fulkamore, care of Robert Lockhart, Winchester,
  Virginia
Requests transfer to complete patent application
Elias Langham transfers to Asa Fulkamore
Asa Fulkamore   Unk - 22 4 11 -

914   12 May 1809   A/4/038
George Kneapler? to be left at Mrs. Mary Ann
  Bayly's, near Gettysburgh, Adams County, Penn-
  sylvania
Transmits patent
Peter Luk? [Lisk?]   Mil - 8 2 3 1

915   25 May 1809   A/4/038
Gerard Topkin, Baltimore
Duplicate receipt
Gerard Topkin   Zan - 5 1 12 +

916   25 May 1809   A/4/038
Willys Silliman, Reg Zan
First certificate
McKee assigns to Gerard Topkin
Thomas McKee   Zan - 5 1 12 +

917   25 May 1809   A/4/039
David Hoge, Reg Stu
First certificates
Newman assigns to Jacob Hawk

Andrew Newman	Stu	-	9	10	27	+
Robert Thompson	Stu	-	8	10	26	-
Jacob Mishler	Stu	-	8	11	7	+
Jacob Hostetler	Stu	-	5	16	31	+

918   25 May 1809   A/4/039
Daniel Symmes, Reg Cin
First certificate
Foley assigns to Felix Welton; Ramsey assigns to
  Jacob Fenton

John Foley, Jr.	Cin	MR	10	5	9	+
Allen Ramsey	Cin	EML	1	1	9	+
Dennis Boyse?	Cin	EML	2	5	19	+

919   26 May 1809   A/4/040
Thomas Carneal, Frankfort, Kentucky
Application incomplete
Samuel Massey.

920   27 May 1809   A/4/040
David Hoge, Reg Stu
First certificate; duplicate receipts
Laraw transfers to B. Lupton

Jacob Laraw	Stu	-	5	17	33	+
Anthony Wright	Stu	-	6	13	30	+

921   29 May 1809   A/4/041
Willys Silliman, Reg Zan
First certificate; duplicate receipt
Jacob Bentz?   Zan Mil 10 1 20 +

922   29 May 1809   A/4/041
David Hoge, Reg Stu
First certificate
Ferguson transfers to Thomas McNairy
John Ferguson   Stu - 3 9 35 +

923   30 May 1809   A/4/041
Robert? Ralston, Merchant, Philadelphia, Pennsyl-
  vania
Answers query regarding various tracts
William Wells located for Jonas Stanberry;
  Israel Ludlow; Michael Fisher location probably
  in Virginia Military District of Ohio; Richard
  C. Anderson
Plat of   Mil - 19 3 - -

924   2 Jun 1809   A/4/042
Jesse Spencer, Reg Chl
Transmits patent
-- Findlay
Joseph Lane   Chl MS 21 11 30 +

925   2 Jun 1809   A/4/042
John Haines, Winchester, Frederick County, Vir-
  ginia
Transmits patent
John Haines   Stu - 4 16 32 +

926   15 Jun 1809   A/4/042
Valentine Presle, to be left at post office, York,
  Pennsylvania
Transmits patent
Valentine Presle   Stu - 5 16 17 -

927   15 Jun 1809   A/4/042
Goldsmith Chandler, Winchester, Virginia
Transmits patent
Goldsmith Chandler   Stu - 7 9 23 -

928 16 Jun 1809 A/4/043
General T. Worthington
Location of military land warrants

Vacant	Mil	-	11	8	4	3
Vacant	Mil	-	18	7	1	15
Vacant	Mil	-	17	7	2	15
Vacant	Mil	-	17	7	2	16
Vacant	Mil	-	17	7	2	17
Error	Mil	-	16	8	4	3
Error	Mil	-	17	7	1	15
Error	Mil	-	19	7	1	2

929 17 Jun 1809 A/4/043
[Jesse Spencer], Reg Chl
Transmits patents

Daniel McKinney	Chl	-	20	4	29	+
Messrs. Hitchcock	Chl	-	21	1	-	11
Messrs. Hitchcock	Chl	-	21	1	13	-
David Jones	Chl	-	20	10	8	+
David Jones	Chl	-	20	10	5	+
Caspar Walter	Chl	-	18	15	5	+
Meakes & Bixler	Chl	-	19	14	23	+
William McFarland	Chl	-	19	15	19	+
Harman Moore	Chl	-	20	12	35	+
James Smith	Chl	-	19	16	32	+
John Woodruff	Chl	MS	21	10	19	+
William Miller	Chl	MS	21	10	29	+
Ezekiel Bogart	Chl	MS	22	3	-	28
Ezekiel Bogart	Chl	MS	22	3	27	-
Jacob Riley	Chl	WS	21	11	3	+

930 17 Jun 1809 A/4/044
[Daniel Symmes], Reg Cin
Transmits patents

John Millhouse	Cin	MR	11	1	12	+
James Robinson	Cin	MR	4	2	8	+
Jacob Coy	Cin	MR	7	2	8	+
John Whipple	Cin	MR	11	2	35	+
John Whipple	Cin	MR	11	2	28	+
James McCormick	Cin	MR	8	2	8	+
Ichabod Corwin	Cin	MR	4	4	-	11
Samuel McCleery	Cin	EML	2	5	14	-
John Ramey	Cin	WML	2	9	32	+
Hugh Reed	Cin	WML	2	11	24	+
Andrew Brininger	Cin	Pre	4	2	5	+
Nicholas Horner	Cin	Pre	5	2	23	+
Arthur Henrie	Cin	EML	2	1	-	6
Arthur Henrie	Cin	EML	2	1	-	7
Arthur Henrie	Cin	EML	1	1	-	12
Arthur Henrie	Cin	EML	1	1	1	-

931 20 Jun 1809 A/4/044
Daniel Symmes, Reg Cin
Account; first certificate
Achery Berry

John Simpson	Cin	EML	5	6	32	+

932 21 Jun 1809 A/4/045
Hon. N. R. Moore
Transmits patents

Ritter & Self	Unk	-	20	15	13	-

933 21 Jun 1809 A/4/045
General John Smith, U.S. Representative
Transmits patent
John Roads of Shenandoah County, Virginia

John Roads	Unk	-	18	16	13	+

934 21 Jun 1809 A/4/045
Hon. R. I. Meigs, U.S. Senate
Transmits patents

Lockwood & Coleman	Mar	-	3	4	6	+
William Skinner	Mar	-	5	1	-	17
William Skinner	Mar	-	5	1	-	23

935 21 Jun 1809 A/4/045
Joseph Wood, Reg Mar

Richard Hooker	Mar	-	12	13	-	3E?
Richard Hooker	Mar	-	12	13	19	-

936 22 Jun 1809 A/4/046
Hon. James Holland
Military land warrant 1119.

937 22 Jun 1809 A/4/046
Hon. James? Morrow, U.S. Representative
Transmits patent

David Parkhill	Mil	-	3	10	1	7

938 24 Jun 1809 A/4/046
Hon. Philip Reed? [Read?]
Transmits patents

John Kennard	Mil?	-	9	7	3	17
George Scoone, heirs of	Mil?	-	9	7	3	26

939 6 Jul 1809 A/4/046
John Forble? to be left at post office, Baltimore, Maryland
Transmits patent

John Forble?	Chl	MS	21	11	12	+

940 8 Jul 1809 A/4/046
[Willys Silliman], Reg Zan
Transmits patents

Lewis Nips	Zan	-	14	15	9	+
George & Thomas Ritchie	Zan	-	8	8	6	+
John Adams	Zan	Mil	7	4	14	+

941 8 Jul 1809 A/4/047
[Daniel Symmes], Reg Cin
Transmits patents

William McKain	Cin	EML	2	5	27	+
John Vernemman	Cin	EML	5	4	33	+
John Debott	Cin	EML	3	3	11	+
Michael Ingle	Cin	EML	5	8	20	+
Jacob Fouts	Cin	EML	4	3	7	+
Rudolph Flenner	Cin	EML	3	2	-	24
Rudolph Flenner	Cin	EML	3	2	13	-
David & Jacob Fridge? [Fudge?]	Cin	EML	3	5	34	+
Ammi Maltbie	Cin	MR	5	3	11	+
Charles Rector	Cin	MR	10	4	11	-
Alexander Vanpelt	Cin	MR	4	3	8	+
William Wells	Cin	MR	12	1	-	24
John Eddy	Cin	MR	3	4	11	+
Adam Verdier	Cin	MR	10	3	19	+
John Aughe	Cin	MR	5	2	8	+
John Road	Cin	WML	2	13	35	+

942 8 Jul 1809 A/4/047
[David Hoge], Reg Stu
Transmits patents

Patrick McKaig	Stu	–	3	13	5	–
George Venaman	Stu	–	6	12	3	+
Stephen Ford	Stu	–	4	11	12	+
James Glass	Stu	–	2	9	32	+
Jacob Shidler	Stu	–	6	18	19	–
Moses Votaw	Stu	–	4	15	1	+
John Russell	Stu	–	5	7	11	+
Thomas Mansfield	Stu	–	3	9	13	–
John Votaw	Stu	–	3	14	7	+

943   28 Jul 1809   A/4/048
Thomas Carneal, Frankfort, Kentucky
Transmits patents

George Rennick	*	200 acres
Richard C[lough] Anderson	*	2,533 acres
Robert Kendall	*	250 acres

*Land between the Little Miami and the Scioto rivers.

944   29 Jul 1809   A/4/048
David Hoge, Reg Stu
First certificate; duplicate receipts
Abner Gregg transfers to James Eaton; Mrs. Anna Mifflin; Samuel Mifflin, son of Anna Mifflin

George Grove	Stu	–	8	9	11	–
George Grove	Stu	–	8	10	5	+
Jess Hirst	Stu	–	4	15	18	+
Abner Gregg	Stu	–	5	7	4	+
Richard Morrow	Stu	–	8	12	35	+

945   29 Jul 1809   A/4/048
Peter Wilson, Rec Stu
Duplicate receipts

Joshua Wood	Stu	–	6	10	7	+
Jacob McKay	Stu	–	6	10	7	+
Isaac Walker	Stu	–	4	17	10	+
Abner Gregg	Stu	–	5	7	4	+
George Grove	Stu	–	8	9	11	+
George Grove	Stu	–	8	10	5	+
Richard Morrow	Stu	–	8	12	35	+
Jess Hirst	Stu	–	4	15	18	+

946   11 Aug 1809   A/4/049
[David Hoge], Reg Stu
Transmits patents

Stacy Bevan	Stu	–	6	10	2	+
William Morris	Stu	–	4	16	5	+
John McFadon	Stu	–	5	10	13	+
George Mornitz	Stu	–	5	17	36	+
James McBride	Stu	–	4	9	21	+

947   11 Aug 1809   A/4/049
[Daniel Symmes], Reg Cin
Transmits patents

Garner Bobo	Cin	MR	12	1	21	+
Daniel Linn	Cin	WML	2	4	23	+
Thomas Lewis	Cin	WML	2	13	24	+
Jacob Lay	Cin	EML	3	5	2	+

948   11 Aug 1809   A/4/049
[Jesse Spencer], Reg Chl
Transmits patents

John List	Chl	–	20	12	5	+
Messrs. Finley, Worthington, & James	Chl	–	19	15	8	–

Messrs. Miller & Vangundy	Chl	–	20	11	30	+

949   11 Aug 1809   A/4/049
[Willys Silliman], Reg Zan
Transmits patents

Josiah Moore	Zan	Mil	1	9	11	+
John Moore	Zan	–	15	16	12	+
Thomas Lawfarty	Zan	–	9	8	6	+

950   15 Aug 1809   A/4/050
Obadiah Jennings, Stu
Transmits patents

Obadiah Jennings	Stu?	–	8	10	2	+
Aaron Brooks	Stu?	–	1	7	24	+
Aaron Brooks	Stu?	–	1	6	9	+
George Kerns	Stu?	–	1	9	7	–

951   15 Aug 1809   A/4/050
General T. Worthington, Chl
Transmits patents
Heirs of Taylor Webster; -- Baylor's warrant

T. Worthington	Chl	WS	22	2	–	9
T. Worthington	Chl	WS	22	2	–	10

952   19 Aug 1809   A/4/050
Samuel Russell
Application received for land in Stu district.

953   21 Aug 1809   A/4/051
Daniel Symmes, Reg Cin
Final certificate again requested

Not stated	Cin	MR	10	5	9	+

954   21 Aug 1809   A/4/051
David Hoge, Reg Stu
Missing patent

Samuel Kernaghan	Stu	–	5	10	9	–

955   21 Aug 1809   A/4/051
Samuel Kernaghan, Jefferson City, Ohio
States that Reg Stu has been asked to send duplicate final certificate.

956   24 Aug 1809   A/4/052
Oliver Ormsby, Pittsburgh, Pennsylvania
Transmits patents

Oliver Ormsby	Cin	WML	1	4	–	9
Oliver Ormsby	Cin	WML	1	4	–	10
Oliver Ormsby	Cin	WML	1	4	8	–
Adam Rudabaugh	Cin	EML	6	2	7	–
Adam Rudabaugh	Cin	EML	5	4	12	–
Adam Rudabaugh	Cin	EML	5	5	34	–

957   24 Aug 1809   A/4/052
Lewis Cass, Zan
Reports vacant Mil lots

Vacant	Mil	–	1	6	11	1
Vacant	Mil	–	1	6	11	2
Vacant	Mil	–	1	6	11	3
Vacant	Mil	–	1	6	11	4
Vacant	Mil	–	1	6	11	5
Vacant	Mil	–	1	6	11	6

Vacant	Mil	–	1	6	11	7
Vacant	Mil	–	1	6	11	8
Vacant	Mil	–	1	6	11	9
Vacant	Mil	–	1	6	11	10
Vacant	Mil	–	1	6	11	11
Vacant	Mil	–	1	6	11	12
Vacant	Mil	–	1	6	11	13
Vacant	Mil	–	1	6	11	14
Vacant	Mil	–	1	6	11	15
Vacant	Mil	–	1	6	11	16
Vacant	Mil	–	1	6	11	17
Vacant	Mil	–	1	6	11	18
Vacant	Mil	–	1	6	11	19
Vacant	Mil	–	1	6	11	20
Vacant	Mil	–	1	6	11	21
Vacant	Mil	–	1	6	11	22
Vacant	Mil	–	1	6	11	23
Vacant	Mil	–	1	6	11	24
Vacant	Mil	–	1	6	11	25
Vacant	Mil	–	1	6	11	26
Vacant	Mil	–	1	6	11	27
Vacant	Mil	–	1	6	11	28
Vacant	Mil	–	1	6	11	29
Vacant	Mil	–	1	6	11	30
Vacant	Mil	–	1	6	11	31
Vacant	Mil	–	1	6	11	32
Vacant	Mil	–	1	6	11	33
Vacant	Mil	–	1	6	11	34
Vacant	Mil	–	1	6	11	35
Vacant	Mil	–	1	6	11	36
Vacant	Mil	–	1	6	11	37
Vacant	Mil	–	1	6	11	38
Vacant	Mil	–	1	6	11	40
Vacant	Mil	–	1	7	10	1
Vacant	Mil	–	1	7	10	6
Vacant	Mil	–	1	7	10	7
Vacant	Mil	–	1	7	10	8
Vacant	Mil	–	1	7	10	13
Vacant	Mil	–	1	7	10	16
Vacant	Mil	–	1	7	10	17
Vacant	Mil	–	1	7	10	18
Vacant	Mil	–	1	7	10	19
Vacant	Mil	–	1	7	10	20
Vacant	Mil	–	1	7	10	21
Vacant	Mil	–	1	7	10	22
Vacant	Mil	–	1	7	10	27
Vacant	Mil	–	1	7	10	28
Vacant	Mil	–	1	7	10	29
Vacant	Mil	–	1	7	10	30
Vacant	Mil	–	1	7	10	31
Vacant	Mil	–	1	7	10	32
Vacant	Mil	–	1	7	10	33
Vacant	Mil	–	1	7	10	34
Vacant	Mil	–	1	7	10	35
Vacant	Mil	–	1	7	10	36
Vacant	Mil	–	1	7	10	37
Vacant	Mil	–	1	7	10	38
Vacant	Mil	–	3	7	9	2
Vacant	Mil	–	3	7	9	3
Vacant	Mil	–	3	7	9	4
Vacant	Mil	–	3	7	9	5
Vacant	Mil	–	3	7	9	6
Vacant	Mil	–	3	7	9	7
Vacant	Mil	–	3	7	9	8
Vacant	Mil	–	3	7	9	9
Vacant	Mil	–	3	7	9	10
Vacant	Mil	–	3	7	9	11
Vacant	Mil	–	3	7	9	12
Vacant	Mil	–	3	7	9	13
Vacant	Mil	–	3	7	9	14
Vacant	Mil	–	3	7	9	21
Vacant	Mil	–	3	7	9	22

Vacant	Mil	–	3	7	9	23
Vacant	Mil	–	3	7	9	24
Vacant	Mil	–	3	7	9	25
Vacant	Mil	–	3	7	9	27
Vacant	Mil	–	3	7	9	31
Vacant	Mil	–	3	7	9	32
Vacant	Mil	–	3	7	9	33
Vacant	Mil	–	3	7	9	34
Vacant	Mil	–	3	9	11	1
Vacant	Mil	–	3	9	11	2
Vacant	Mil	–	3	9	11	3
Vacant	Mil	–	3	9	11	4
Vacant	Mil	–	3	9	11	5
Vacant	Mil	–	3	9	11	6
Vacant	Mil	–	3	9	11	7
Vacant	Mil	–	3	9	11	8
Vacant	Mil	–	3	9	11	9
Vacant	Mil	–	3	9	11	10
Vacant	Mil	–	3	9	11	11
Vacant	Mil	–	3	9	11	12
Vacant	Mil	–	3	9	11	13
Vacant	Mil	–	3	9	11	14
Vacant	Mil	–	4	9	11	1
Vacant	Mil	–	4	9	11	2
Vacant	Mil	–	4	9	11	6
Vacant	Mil	–	4	9	11	7
Vacant	Mil	–	4	9	11	8
Vacant	Mil	–	4	9	11	9
Vacant	Mil	–	4	9	11	10
Vacant	Mil	–	4	9	11	11
Vacant	Mil	–	4	9	11	12
Vacant	Mil	–	4	9	11	14
Vacant	Mil	–	4	9	11	15
Vacant	Mil	–	4	9	11	16
Vacant	Mil	–	4	9	11	17
Vacant	Mil	–	4	9	11	18
Vacant	Mil	–	4	9	11	19
Vacant	Mil	–	4	9	11	20
Vacant	Mil	–	4	9	11	21
Vacant	Mil	–	4	9	11	22
All lots located	Mil	–	1	8	13	–
Vacant	Mil	–	2	8	13	13
Vacant	Mil	–	1	8	14	2

"The quarter townships are numbered north and south alternately, lot no. 1 being in the SE corner."

958   24 Aug 1809   A/4/053
David Hoge, Reg Stu
First certificates; duplicate receipts
Dickinson & Scott transfer to John Fisk

William R. Dickinson	Stu	–	7	18	18	+
William R. Dickinson	Stu	–	8	11	2	+
Thomas Scott	Stu	–	7	19	14	+

959   24 Aug 1809   A/4/053
Jesse Spencer, Reg Chl
First certificate; duplicate receipt

Daniel Buzard	Chl	–	19	12	3	–

960   24 Aug 1809   A/4/054
William Findley
Transmits patents

Christopher Lenhart	Zan	–	15	17	10	+
Christopher Lenhart	Zan	–	15	17	9	+

961   29 Aug 1809   A/4/054
John H. Brinton, 279 Market Street, Philadelphia,
   Pennsylvania

Duplicate receipts

John H. Brinton?	Unk	- 10	1	-	5
John H. Brinton?	Unk	- 10	1	-	6
John H. Brinton?	Unk	- 9	9	-	26

962   29 Aug 1809   A/4/055
Thomas Carneal, Frankford, Kentucky
Lands in the Virginia Military District [of Ohio]
[Richard Clough] Anderson; John Graham, chief
    clerk, U.S. Department of State.

963   30 Aug 1809   A/4/055
Aaron Lyle, Washington, Pennsylvania
Transmits patent
John Ferguson assigns to McNairy

Thomas McNairy	Stu	-	3	9	35	+

964   30 Aug 1809   A/4/056
Daniel Symmes, Reg Cin
Transmits patent

George Kunze? [Kunse?]	Cin	EML	5	4	9	-

965   30 Aug 1809   A/4/056
John Cook, to the care of the Post Master, Harris-
    burgh, Rockingham County, Virginia
Transmits patents

John Cook	Cin?	MR	11	2	19	+
John Cook	Cin?	MR	11	2	14	+

966   31 Aug 1809   A/4/056
Artemas Sawyer, Athens, Ohio
Military land warrant
Discharge of Thomas Stafford; transfer to Obadiah
    Wells of Stafford's claim.

967   31 Aug 1809   A/4/056
Jesse Spencer, Reg Chl
Final certificate, correct of assignments
John Yost, assignee of George Skinner; Abraham
    Yost; Joseph McCune; -- Nevill; -- Rush;
    Heidler, Reager, Miller, & Bowman.

968   2 Sep 1809   A/4/057
John Bolte, Baltimore, Maryland
Adam Totter transfer to Charles Guildman? [Guildi-
    ner?]

Charles Guildman?	Chl	WS	21	11	12	+

969   5 Sep 1809   A/4/057
John G. Jackson
Answers query

Not stated	Mil?	-	8	2	3	1

970   5 Sep 1809   A/4/058
Jesse Spencer, Reg Chl
First certificates; duplicate receipts

Henry Bowman	Chl	-	17	18	17	+
Job McNamee	Chl	-	18	16	27	+
Christian Wallick	Chl	-	20	12	5	+
Christian Wallick	Chl	-	20	12	18	+
Daniel Bussard	Chl	-	19	12	7	+
James Lambert	Chl	-	20	15	20	+
George Wood	Chl	-	16	15	7	+

Conrad Wallick	Chl	-	20	12	5	+
Conrad Wallick	Chl	-	20	12	18	+
John Kirlen	Chl	-	17	17	21	+
Matthew Woods	Chl	-	16	15	7	+
Nathan Wood	Chl	-	14	8	12	+
John Maysilles	Chl	-	20	15	20	+

971   5 Sep 1809   A/4/059
Thomas Gibson
First certificate; duplicate receipt

David Sleighter	Unk	-	10	12	27	-

972   6 Sep 1809   A/4/059
Willys Silliman, Reg Zan
First certificates; duplcate receipts

John Watermire	Zan	-	14	15	26	+
Taylor & McConnell*	Zan	Mil	6	1	7	+
John Anspach	Zan	Mil	7	1	3	+
John Carlisle, Jr.	Zan	-	13	11	-	7
John Carlisle, Jr.	Zan	-	13	11	8	-
Andrew Thompson**	Zan	-	6	1	10	+
Susanna Fraunce**	Zan	-	6	1	10	+
Jacob Bentz?	Zan	Mil	10	1	20	+

   *Note that John Anspach deposited funds for
      the tract in names of Taylor & McConnell.
   **GLO calls attention to discrepancy wherein
      same tract sold to both parties.

973   6 Sep 1809   A/4/060
James Findlay, Rec Cin
Duplicate receipts

Jacob Blakeminstafer?	Cin	EML	6	4	28	+
Peter Ingleman	Cin	EML	3	4	12	+
John Nusagh	Cin	EML	5	4	20	+
David Rees	Cin	WML	1	5	-	22
David Rees	Cin	WML	1	5	-	23
David Rees	Cin	WML	1	5	21	-
David Rees	Cin	WML	1	5	19	-
David Rees	Cin	WML	1	5	20	+

974   6 Sep 1809   A/4/060
David Hoge, Reg Stu
First certificates; duplicate receipts
Captain John Fisk, Baltimore, Maryland

Isaiah Jenkins	Stu	-	6	10	1	+
Robert Russell	Stu	-	6	10	8	+
Samuel Russell	Stu	-	6	10	2	+
Thomas Gilham	Stu	-	5	8	23	+

975   6 Sep 1809   A/4/061
Daniel Symmes, Reg Cin
First certificate

John Nusagh	Cin	EML	5	4	20	+

976   6 Sep 1809   A/4/061
Captain John Fisk, care of Charles Robinson?
    [Roberson?], 68 Market Space, Baltimore, Mary-
    land
David Hoge, Reg Stu.

977   7 Sep 1809   A/4/061
Daniel Symmes, Reg Cin
Missing power of attorney
Thomas Ewing; -- Rawlins; John Osborne, assignee
    of Samuel Highway & the heirs of Michael Kever,
    deceased; Elizabeth Alexander, an heir.

978   13 Sep 1809   A/4/062
Daniel Symmes, Reg Cin
Discrepancies to be clarified
Peyton Short assigns to Hugh Andrews; John H.
  Crawford transfers to Robert Crawford; Fielding
  Lowry transfers to John Smith

Hugh Andrews	Cin	-	8	2	14	+
Hugh Andrews	Cin	-	8	2	15	+
Robert Crawford	Cin	-	8	2	6	+
John Smith	Cin	-	4	4	14	+
John Smith	Cin	-	10	1	12	+

979   13 Sep 1809   A/4/063
Willys Silliman, Reg Zan
First certificate

Bohn, Slingluff, & Dear-dorff	Zan	Mil	3	8	3	+
Bohn, Slingluff, & Dear-dorff	Zan	Mil	3	8	1	+
Bohn, Slingluff, & Dear-dorff	Zan	Mil	3	8	2	+

980   15 Sep 1809   A/4/063
Stephen R. Price, Lexington, Rockbridge County,
  Virginia
Military land warrants
-- Smith of the War Department

| Already patented | Mil | - | 18 | 7 | 1 | 15 | |
| Vacant | Mil | - | 18 | 7 | 1 | * | |

   *All other lots in section.

981   15 Sep 1809   A/4/063
Daniel Symmes, Reg Cin
Final certificates; discrepancies in payment
Kershner, assignee of John Hole

James Barnet	Cin	Pre	6	2	9	+
Jacob Voorhis	Cin	-	4	4	13	+
Jacob Kershner	Cin	-	6	1	-	31
Jacob Kershner	Cin	-	6	1	25	+

982   16 Sep 1809   A/4/064
David Simmes
Transmits patent

John James Dufour	Unk	-	3W	2N?	-	22
John James Dufour	Unk	-	3W	2N?	-	27
John James Dufour	Unk	-	3W	2N?	15	-

983   16 Sep 1809   A/4/064
Jesse Spencer, Reg Chl
Transmits patents

Joseph McCune	Chl	WS	21	11	31	-
Joseph McCune	Chl	WS	22	4	-	7
Henry Nevill & H. Rush	Chl	WS	21	10	6	+
Thomas Evans	Chl	-	20	13	2	+

984   18 Sep 1809   A/4/064
No addressee
Forfeiture

| John Roth | Unk | - | 3 | 16 | 3 | - |

985   18 Sep 1809   A/4/065
Jesse Spencer, Reg Chl
Final certificate

| Peter Ruffin, heirs | Chl | - | 17 | 17 | 32 | - |

986   26 Sep 1809   A/4/065
Samuel Finley, Rec Chl
Discrepancy in account
Neigh departing for Chl

George Neigh	Chl	-	20	13	28	-
George Neigh	Chl	-	20	13	3	+
George Neigh	Chl	-	20	12	14	+

987   29 Sep 1809   A/4/067
General T. Worthington
Transmits patents [not described]; [military land
  warrant] 114, Walter Baylor
-- Fowler.

988   4 Oct 1809   A/4/067
John Badollet, Reg Cin
Transmits patents
General Washington Johnston.

989   4 Oct 1809   A/4/067
David Hoge, Reg Stu
Final certificate
William Meridoth assigns to Mahlon Smith

| Mahlon Smith | Stu | - | 5 | 8 | 10 | - |

990   9 Oct 1809   A/4/067
Daniel Symmes, Reg Cin
Transmits patent

| John Fossett | Cin | Pre | 4 | 3 | 28 | + |

991   7 Oct 1809   A/4/068
David Hoge, Reg Stu
First certificate; duplicate receipts

| John McDonald | Stu | - | 2 | 10 | 27 | + |
| Lawrence Bower | Stu | - | 4 | 17 | 1 | + |

992   16 Oct 1809   A/4/068
[Jesse Spencer], Reg Chl
Transmits patents

Henry & Reuben Abrams	Chl	-	20	10	1	+
Stephen Cole	Chl	MS	21	9	8	+
John Morris & James Seall	Chl	MS	21	9	33	+
Matthew Ferguson	Chl	WS	21	10	33	+
John Grove	Chl	-	17	18	17	+
Nicholas Raderbach	Chl	-	19	16	28	+
Martin Funk	Chl	-	21	1	9	+

993   17 Oct 1809   A/4/068
David Hoge, Reg Stu
First certificates; duplicate receipts
Bufkin transfers to James Vaughan

William Rupert	Stu	-	2	13	18	+
Joshua Antrim	Stu	-	7	20	23	+
Joshua Antrim	Stu	-	7	20	24	+
Thomas Bufkin	Stu	-	5	17	2	+

994   17 Oct 1809   A/4/069
James Findlay, Rec Cin
Duplicate receipts

Adam Zeller	Cin	EML	3	6	28	+
Adam Schenck	Cin	EML	4	5	13	+
Henry Zeller	Cin	EML	4	2	10	+

| 995 | | | 17 Oct 1809 | | | A/4/069 |
John Sloane
Duplicate receipts
John Hoopes; David Pratt.

| 996 | | | | | 18 Oct 1809 | | | A/4/070 |
[Daniel Symmes], Reg Cin
Transmits patents

Abraham Hosier	Cin	MR	6	2	23	+
James Barret? [Barnet?]	Cin	MR	6	2	9	+
John Campbell	Cin	MR	5	4	–	21
Edward Bernbow	Cin	MR	4	4	–	1
Peyton Short	Cin	MR	8	2	5	+
Ephraim Blackford	Cin	MR	5	3	27	+
John Rippey	Cin	MR	4	4	35	–
John Johnston	Cin	MR	11	2	27	+
Josiah Cushman	Cin	MR	5	2	18	+
John Flinn	Cin	MR	11	2	20	+
Henry Benget?	Cin	EML	1	4	23	+
Jacob Coy	Cin	MR	7	2	8	+
Jacob Huffman	Cin	MR	9	4	27	1*
Thomas Price	Cin	EML	2	5	19	+

*Northwest side of Mad River.

| 997 | | | | 18 Oct 1809 | | | A/4/071 |
[Jesse Spencer], Reg Chl
Transmits patents

George Valentine	Chl	–	20	12	29	+
Christian Van Gundy	Chl	WS	21	9	21	–
John Valentine	Chl	–	20	12	8	+
Martin Dumma	Chl	–	19	16	4	+
Abraham & John Yost	Chl	–	16	16	1	+
Patrick Shanon	Chl	–	17	14	9	+
Jacob Welsh	Chl	–	20	9	17	+
Isaiah Strawn	Chl	–	16	17	5	+

| 998 | | | | 2 Nov 1809 | | | A/4/071 |
Jesse Spencer, Reg Chl
Final certificate; first certificate; duplicate
  receipt

Matthew Woods	Chl	–	16	15	7	+
Enoch Eppart	Chl	–	16	7	17	+
Peter Rode?	Chl	MS	21	11	19	+

| 999 | | | | 2 Nov 1809 | | | A/4/072 |
Elijah Brush, Detroit

Elijah Brush	Cin	EML	4	1	8	+
Elijah Brush	Cin	EML	4	1	18	+
Elijah Brush	Cin	EML	4	1	–	9
Elijah Brush	Cin	EML	4	1	–	19
Elijah Brush	Cin	EML	4	1	–	17
Elijah Brush	Cin	EML	4	1	–	16

| 1000 | | | | 2 Nov 1809 | | | A/4/072 |
Messrs. Gray & Taylor, Merchants, Philadelphia,
  Pennsylvania
Transmits patents
General -- Worthington of Ohio

John Carlisle	Chl	MS	22	4	21	–
John Carlisle	Chl	MS	22	4	–	20

| 1001 | | | | 2 Nov 1809 | | | A/4/072 |
General T. Worthington, Chl
Transmits patent

Taylor Webster, heirs	Chl	WS	21	9	30	–

| 1002 | | | | 6 Nov 1809 | | | A/4/072 |
Daniel Symmes, Reg Cin
Final certificates for correction
Kercheval assigns to Esther Greene; Smith assigns
to Isaac Bear; Wieley transfers to John Miller;
George Kuns paid instalment on Peter Weaver's
land; McDonald assigns to John Taylor, not to
James Taylor, as shown; Lazurus Whitehead as-
signs to John Whitehead, who again assigns to
John Rhode, instead of William Rhode

Charles Hilliar	Cin	MR	11	1	–	36
Peter A. Banta	Cin	EML	3	5	14	+
James Kercheval	Cin	EML	3	4	30	+
William Smith	Cin	EML	4	3	5	+
Joseph Singer	Cin	EML	3	7	34	+
Jacob Miller	Cin	EML	4	1	7	–
Cornelius Wieley	Cin	WML	1	10	1	+
Cornelius Wieley	Cin	EML	1	10	1	+
Joseph McKinney	Cin	MR	9	3	8	+
Henry Stansell*	Cin	Pre	4	3	34	+
Peter Weaver	Cin	EML	5	3	18	+
James McDonald	Cin	MR	6	2	26	+
Lazurus Whitehead	Cin	WML	2	13	6	+

*Error in tract citation.

| 1003 | | | | 7 Nov 1809 | | | A/4/074 |
Levi Barber
Receipt
Isaac Lynn & John Buck.

| 1004 | | | | 8 Nov 1809 | | | A/4/074 |
Jesse Spencer, Reg Chl
First certificate
Totter deeds to Charles Guildener

Adam Totter	Chl	WS	21	11	12	+
Thomas Buck	Chl	MS	21	11	34	+

| 1005 | | | | 8 Nov 1809 | | | A/4/074 |
David Hoge, Reg Stu
Certificates; duplicate receipts

Joseph Reeves	Stu	–	3	15	15	+
Joseph Reeves	Stu	–	3	15	22	+
Robert McCaughey	Stu	–	8	9	9	+

| 1006 | | | | 9 Nov 1809 | | | A/4/075 |
[Jesse Spencer], Reg Chl
Transmits patents

John Morris & James Seall	Chl	MS	21	9	33	+
Philip Clerk? [Cleck?]	Chl	–	20	14	30	+
John Morehart	Chl	–	20	14	28	+
George Crowle	Chl	–	20	15	26	+

| 1007 | | | | 9 Nov 1809 | | | A/4/075 |
[David Hoge], Reg Stu
Transmits patents

William Craig	Stu	–	6	12	27	+
Andrew McGillivray	Stu	–	2	9	29	+
Henry Bough, Jr.	Stu	–	2	10	9	+

| 1008 | | | | 9 Nov 1809 | | | A/4/075 |
[Daniel Symmes], Reg Cin
Transmits patents

Ichabod Corwin	Cin	MR	4	3	8	+
Thomas Chenoweth	Cin	MR	5	3	8	+
Jacob Coy	Cin	MR	6	2	5	+

John Croy	Cin	MR	6	2	35	+
Adam Coblance	Cin	MR	6	1	–	6
Henry Clark	Cin	EML	6	1	–	8
Henry Clark	Cin	EML	6	1	7	–
Charles & Peter Catron? [Catrow?]	Cin	EML	4	3	25	+
George Myers, Elizabeth & John Gephart	Cin	EML	5	2	9	–
George Myers, Elizabeth & John Gephart	Cin	EML	5	2	–	10

1009 9 Nov 1809 A/4/075
Jeffersonville Land Office
Transmits patents

Henry Kime? [Kerne?]	Jef	–	8E	2N	13	+
James Edwards	Jef	–	10E	4–	20	+
Jesse Henley	Jef	–	9E	1N	–	17
Jesse Henley	Jef	–	9E	1N	18	–
Jesse Henley	Jef	–	8E	2N	2	+

1010 9 Nov 1809 A/4/076
[Joseph Wood], Reg Mar
Transmits patents

James Edgerton	Mar	–	5	6	4	+
Susannah Hauson	Mar	–	5	6	10	+

1011 9 Nov 1809 A/4/076
[Willys Silliman], Reg Zan
Transmits patents

Robert Ferson	Zan	–	15	16	18	+
Edy Harris	Zan	Mil	9	6	18	+

1012 25 Nov 1809 A/4/076
Daniel Symmes, Reg Cin
Duplicate receipt; final receipt
[James] Findlay, Rec Cin

Samuel Haines	Cin	EML	5	6	31	–

1013 25 Nov 1809 A/4/076
Peter Mills, [Rec?] Zan
Military land warrant 2046 in favor of Beriah Maybury for 300 acres
Baum & Perry, assignees of Maybury's executors

Beriah Maybury	Zan	Mil	1	1	3	6
Beriah Maybury	Zan	Mil	1	1	3	39
Previously located	Zan	Mil	1	1	3	38
Vacant	Zan	Mil	1	1	3	1
Vacant	Zan	Mil	1	1	3	4
Vacant	Zan	Mil	1	1	3	5
Vacant	Zan	Mil	1	1	3	9
Vacant	Zan	Mil	1	1	3	10
Vacant	Zan	Mil	1	1	3	23
Vacant	Zan	Mil	1	1	3	26
Vacant	Zan	Mil	1	1	3	27
Vacant	Zan	Mil	1	1	3	40

1014 25 Nov 1809 A/4/077
David Hoge, Reg Stu
First certificates; duplicate receipts

Joseph Shields	Stu	–	5	17	11	+
Matthew Mitchell	Stu	–	3	17	5	+
Matthew Mitchell	Stu	–	4	17	5	+
Isak Proctor	Stu	–	6	18	23	+
Price Keith	Stu	–	5	16	24	+
Thomas Sands	Stu	–	5	16	27	+

1015 25 Nov 1809 A/4/078
Jesse Spencer, Reg Chl
Duplicate receipt

Christian Bean	Chl	–	19	16	12	+
John W. Hormeghans	Chl	–	20	14	34	+

1016 25 Nov 1809 A/4/078
J. W. Hormeghans? care of Rev. D. Wagner, Frederick Town, Maryland
Duplicate receipt

J. W. Hormeghans?	Chl	–	20	14	34	+

1017 25 Nov 1809 A/4/079
Willys Silliman, Reg Zan
First certificates; duplicate receipt

Peter Shutt	Zan	–	4	8	4	+
Philip Shutt	Zan	–	4	8	12	+
John Watermire	Zan	–	14	15	26	+

1018 28 Nov 1809 A/4/079
Thomas Gibson
Act of 26 Mar 1804.

1019 28 Nov 1809 A/4/079
Jesse Spencer, Reg Chl
First certificates; duplicate receipts
Member of Congress acting as agent

William Koch	Chl	–	21	11	23	+
William Koch	Chl	–	21	11	24	+

1020 28 Nov 1809 A/4/080
[Daniel Symmes], Reg Cin
Transmits patents

Henry Worman	Cin	MR	6	2	8	+
Peter Sunderland	Cin	MR	6	2	26	+
Andrew Smaleer	Cin	MR	7	3	26	+
Bartholomew Wickard	Cin	EML	2	4	27	+
Samuel Win? [Wise?]	Cin	EML	5	3	5	+
Simeon Vanwinkle	Cin	EML	3	6	28	+
George Davis	Cin	EML	2	6	12	+
Frederick Wolf	Cin	EML	4	3	28	+

1021 28 Nov 1809 A/4/080
[David Hoge], Reg Stu
Transmits patents

William Dunlap	Stu	–	5	10	19	+
Thomas Dunn	Stu	–	5	8	31	–
Joseph Douthell	Stu	–	7	19	23	+
William Duffield	Stu	–	3	10	28	–

1022 28 Nov 1809 A/4/080
Willys Silliman, Reg Zan
Transmits patents [and queries prior receipt of Moore patent]

John Moore	Zan	–	15	16	12	+
Joseph Smith	Zan	Mil	1	1	2	+
Jacob Watz	Zan	Mil	1	9	12	+
Isaac Vanhorne	Zan	–	4	16	11	+
William Wilson	Zan	–	15	17	31	+

1023 28 Nov 1809 A/4/081
[Jesse Spencer], Reg Chl
Transmits patents

John Drum	Chl	–	17	17	10	+

George Dillshaver	Chl	–	20	12	20	+
Thomas Dugan	Chl	LS	22	4	5	+
John Davison & Jacob Hepler	Chl	–	18	1	–	19

1024 30 Nov 1809 A/4/081
Jesse Spencer, Reg Chl
Discrepancies commented upon
John Zane's will on file

John Rush & John Rawles	Chl	WS	22	3	12	–
John Rush & John Rawles	Chl	WS	22	3	–	13
John McMullen	Chl	–	17	18	14	+
John Morris	Chl	MS	21	9	33	+

1025 4 Dec 1809 A/4/082
Affidavit signed by Joseph Nourse, Reg Treas, and
  Albert Gallatin, Sec Treas
Military land warrant 205 in favor of Samuel Bry-
  son, "late a Lieutenant in the Pennsylvania
  line" for 200 acres, was registered [with others]
  on 10 Feb 1800 by John Matthews for Edward D.
  Turner, Oliver Ormsby, and John Matthews
Martin Baum

Matthews, Turner & Ormsby	*	–	12	6	4	–

*4000-acre tract.

1026 4 Dec 1809 A/4/082
John Vance, Franklinton, Ohio
Military land warrants 229 & 449

John Vance	Mil?	–	17	7	2	7
John Vance	Mil?	–	17	7	2	8
Already located	Mil?	–	18	7	1	17

1027 18 Dec 1809 A/4/083
John Henderson, Rec WPR
Duplicate receipt
James Archer, assignee of Robert Moore.

1028 19 Dec 1809 A/4/083
Samuel Finley, Rec Chl
Duplicate receipt
David Neelly.

1029 20 Dec 1809 A/4/083
Jesse Spencer, Reg Chl
First certificate
-- Smilie, U.S. Representative from Pennsylvania.

1030 20 Dec 1809 A/4/083
James? Archer, Hartford County, Maryland
Duplicate receipt
Dr. -- Brownley

James? Archer	WPR	–	–	–	*	–

*"Land on Bayou Pierre."

1031 20 Dec 1809 A/4/084
Felix Welton, Moorsfields, Virginia
Patent application in process

Felix Welton	Cin?	MR	10	5	9	+

1032 20 Dec 1809 A/4/084
David Hoge, Reg Stu
First certificate; duplicate receipts

Michael? Snider	Stu	–	8	12	33	+

David Larkin	Stu	–	6	10	14	+
George Wilson	Stu	–	8	9	8	+
Izak Proctor	Stu	–	6	18	23	+

1033 21 Dec 1809 A/4/085
James Findley, Rec Cin
Duplicate receipt
Lock is assignee [on second tract only]

John Lock	Cin	EML	3	7	26	+
John Lock	Cin	EML	2	7	11	+

1034 21 Dec 1809 A/4/085
Enoch Eppart, to be left at the post office, New
  Market, Shenandoah County, Virginia
Transmits patent

Enoch Eppart	Chl	–	16	7	17	+

1035 21 Dec 1809 A/4/085
Andrew Gregg
Transmits patent

Mathew Woods	Chl	–	16	15	7	+

1036 21 Dec 1809 A/4/085
John Worth, Richmond, Virginia
Transmits patent

James Vaughan	Stu	–	6	17	2	+

1037 21 Dec 1809 A/4/085
Jeremiah Morrow
Transmits patent

Samuel H. Smith	Chl	–	13	7	22	+

1038 21 Dec 1809 A/4/086
Samuel Kernaghan, Stu
Transmits patent

Samuel Kernaghan	Stu?	–	5	10	9	+

1039 21 Dec 1809 A/4/086
[David Hoge], Reg Stu
Transmits patents

George Murray	Stu	–	7	18	26	+
George Murray	Stu	–	7	20	31	+
William Grist & William Philips	Stu	–	6	11	9	+
John Cadwallader, Junior	Stu	–	5	7	10	+
John Cadwallader, Junior	Stu	–	5	7	9	+
Simon Assig?	Stu	–	8	11	35	+
George Tombaugh	Stu	–	7	19	20	–
Nathan Hoopes	Stu	–	4	9	15	+
Daniel Lindesmith	Stu	–	3	14	31	+
George Murray	Stu	–	7	18	27	+
George Foulk	Stu	–	7	19	25	–

1040 22 Dec 1809 A/4/086
[Joseph Wood], Reg Mar
Transmits patents

John Stanley	Mar	–	5	6	10	+
James Edgerton	Mar	–	5	6	35	+
Daniel Thomas	Mar	–	4	5	5	+

1041 22 Dec 1809 A/4/087
[Daniel Symmes], Reg Cin
Transmits patents

Daniel Perry	Cin	EML	2	5	3	–

Samuel Dickey	Cin	EML	4	2	7	-
William Gahagan	Cin	EML	6	5	-	27
Christian Price	Cin	EML	3	5	3	+
Abraham Swartzell	Cin	EML	4	4	28	-
Philip Gunckle	Cin	EML	5	2	7	-
Martin Ruple & Jacob Parker	Cin	EML	3	5	3	+
David Duffield	Cin	EML	3	3	17	+
Michael Wilson	Cin	MR	8	3	8	+
John Williams	Cin	MR	12	5	18	+

1042   21 Dec 1809   A/4/087
Daniel Symmes, Reg Cin
First certificate
Murray transfers to Thomas Marshal; Joseph Nourse
  pays for Humbert's land

Abraham Murray	Cin	EML	1	7	24	+
Jacob Humbert	Cin	EML	5	3	22	+

1043   22 Dec 1809   A/4/087
Jesse Hirst, post office, Waterford, Loudon County,
  Virginia
Lost duplicate receipt

Jesse Hirst	Stu	-	14	15	18	+

1044   23 Dec 1809   A/4/088
John Nusagh, care of Postmaster, Lebanon, Berks
  County, Pennsylvania
Transmits patent

John Nusagh	Cin	EML	5	4	20	+

1045   23 Dec 1809   A/4/088
Hon. Samuel McKee
Transmits patent

Joseph Outman	Unk	-	6E	3S	-	15

1046   23 Dec 1809   A/4/088
No addressee
Transmits patents

Simeon Gard	Cin	EML	1	7	25	+
Samuel Miller	Stu	-	5	18	9	+

1047   23 Dec 1809   A/4/088
Thomas G. Gibson
Transmits patent

David Sleighter	Unk	-	10	12	27	+

1048   23 Dec 1809   A/4/088
William Raynolds, Junior, Canton [Ohio?]
Transmits patent

John Warden? [Worden?]	Unk	-	10	12	15	+

1049   1 Jan 1810   A/4/089
Samuel Finley, Rec Chl
Duplicate receipts

Joel Pusey	Chl	-	14	8	15	+
Joel Pusey	Chl	-	14	8	19	+

1050   30 Dec 1809   A/4/089
John Smith, St. Clairsville, Ohio
Duplicate receipt of Bank of United States at
  Philadelphia, Pennsylvania

John Smith	Stu	-	5	7	11	+

1051   1 Jan 1810   A/4/089
Peter Wilson, Rec Stu
Duplicate receipts

James Walker	Stu	-	3	10	34	+
John Smith	Stu	-	5	7	11	+
Benjamin Knight	Stu	-	6	13	34	+

1052   8 Jan 1810   A/4/090
[David Hoge], Reg Stu
Transmits patents

Daniel Miller, Senior	Stu	-	6	19	27	+
Daniel Miller, Junior	Stu	-	5	17	11	+
Daniel Mathias	Stu	-	7	19	14	+
Daniel Mathias	Stu	-	7	19	3	-

1053   8 Jan 1810   A/4/090
[Daniel Symmes], Reg Cin
Transmits patents

James Porter	Cin	EML	4	3	8	+
Matthias Swartzel	Cin	EML	4	9	13	+
Philip Stoner	Cin	EML	4	3	5	+
Caspar Hendershot	Cin	EML	6	6	-	7
John Miller	Cin	WML	1	10	12	+
John Wolf	Cin	MR	7	3	18	+

1054   8 Jan 1810   A/4/090
Jesse Spencer, Reg Chl
Transmits patents; assignments insufficient

John Rush & John Rawles	Chl	WS	22	3	-	13
John Rush & John Rawles	Chl	WS	22	3	12	-
John McMullen	Chl	-	17	18	14	+

1055   6 Jan 1810   A/4/091
Hon. R. J. Meigs, Jr., U.S. Senate
Transmits patents

Joseph Wood [as grantee]	Chl	-	16	17	13	+
George Nye	Chl	-	16	17	14	+
George Nye	Chl	-	16	17	12	-

1056   9 Jan 1810   A/4/091
David Hoge, Reg Stu
Transmits patents; duplicate receipts

Thomas Fawcett	Stu	-	6	19	35	+
James Walker	Stu	-	3	10	34	+
Nathan Sidwell	Stu	-	6	8	5	-
George Buchanan	Stu	-	5	7	26	+
Robert Vernon	Stu	-	5	7	26	+

1057   9 Jan 1810   A/4/092
Daniel Symmes, Reg Cin
First certificate; duplicate receipts
Martin assigns to Jacob Saum

Henry Martin	Cin	Pre	7	3	20	+
Abraham Holdman	Cin	EML	3	5	17	+

1058   9 Jan 1810   A/4/092
Obadiah Jennings
Comments on patent applications
Jonathan Jennings; Bazaliel Wells assigns to
  Thomas Leatherberry.

1059   9 Jan 1809   A/4/093
Willys Silliman, Reg Zan
Final certificate; final certificate

William Ford	Zan	-	14	15	34	+

1060   10 Jan 1810   A/4/093
Conrad Wallick, Hagerstown, Maryland
Transmits patents

| Conrad Wallick | Ch1 | - | 20 | 12 | 18 | + |
| Conrad Wallick | Ch1 | - | 20 | 12 | 5 | - |

1061   10 Jan 1810   A/4/093
Jacob Binckley, Hagerstown, Maryland
Transmits patents

| Jacob Binckley | Ch1 | - | 17 | 17 | 3 | + |

1062   12 Jan 1810   A/4/094
David Hoge, Reg Stu
Final certificate
Obadiah Jennings; Bazaliel Wells transfers to
   Thomas Leatherberry.

1063   12 Jan 1810   A/4/094
Jesse Spencer, Reg Ch1
Final certificate

John William Henrickhaus?	Ch1	-	20	14	34	+
Benjamin Cox	Ch1	MS	21	9	33	+
Benjamin Cox	Ch1	MS	21	9	31	+

1064   12 Jan 1810   A/4/094
Felix Welton, Morisfields, Virginia
Transmits patent

| Felix Welton | Unk | - | 10 | 5 | 9 | + |

1065   15 Jan 1810   A/4/095
Jesse Spencer, Reg Ch1
Final certificate
Member of Congress acts as agent [not named]

| William Koch | Ch1 | WS | 21 | 11 | 24 | + |
| William Koch | Ch1 | WS | 21 | 11 | 23 | + |

1066   15 Jan 1810   A/4/095
Joseph Wood, Reg Mar
Final certificate returned because of many spell-
   ings of surname
McMeekin, McMeckin, McMeehen, McMahon, Mecmeeken,
   Mec me ken.

1067   15 Jan 1810   A/4/096
Daniel Symmes, Reg Cin
First certificate
Black transfers to Jacob & Roswell Fenton

| William Black | Cin | EML | 1 | 3 | 36 | + |

1068   15 Jan 1810   A/4/096
Willys Silliman, Reg Zan
Final certificate
Ayers assigns to Philip Baker
Jacob Gaddis & Levi

| Springer | Zan | - | 14 | 14 | 9 | + |
| Jacob Ayers | Zan | - | 12 | 12 | - | 8 |

1069   17 Jan 1810   A/4/096
Laurence Bower, care of Postmaster, Emmetsburgh,
   Frederick County, Maryland
Transmits patents

| Laurence Bower | Stu | - | 4 | 17 | 1 | + |

1070   17 Jan 1810   A/4/097
William Rupert, post office, Emmetsburgh, Freder-
   ick County, Maryland
Transmits patent

| William Rupert | Stu | - | 2 | 13 | 18 | + |

1071   17 Jan 1810   A/4/097
Baltzer Hupp, New Market, Shenandoah County, Vir-
   ginia
Transmits patent

| Baltzer Hupp | Ch1 | - | 17 | 18 | 30 | + |

1072   17 Jan 1810   A/4/097
Joseph Strickler, New Market, Shenandoah County,
   Virginia
Transmits patent

| Joseph Strickler | Ch1 | - | 18 | 16 | 13 | + |

1073   17 Jan 1810   A/4/097
Peter Rode, to be left at post office, York, Penn-
   sylvania
Transmits patent

| Peter Rode | Ch1 | MS | 21 | 11 | 19 | + |

1074   17 Jan 1810   A/4/098
Joshua Antrim, to be left at post office, Nineveh,
   Frederick County, Virginia
Transmits patents

| Joshua Antrim | Stu | - | 7 | 20 | 24 | + |
| Joshua Antrim | Stu | - | 7 | 20 | 23 | - |

1075   20 Jan 1810   A/4/098
Hon. John Smilie
Transmits patent

| John P. Finckle | Unk | - | 17 | 14 | 7 | + |

1076   20 Jan 1810   A/4/098
[Daniel Symmes], Reg Cin
Transmits patents

Jonas Hatfield	Cin	EML	4	3	20	+
John Johnston	Cin	EML	6	6	-	6
John Gripe	Cin	EML	5	4	19	+
P. Gunkle, heirs	Cin	EML	4	4	30	+
John Gustin	Cin	MR	4	3	8	+
Adam Garbuck	Cin	MR	7	2	11	+
Stephen Slifer	Cin	MR	6	1	20	+
William Taylor	Cin	MR	10	6	7	+

1077   24 Jan 1810   A/4/099
Willys Silliman, Reg Zan
Final certificate

John Nichols [error?]	Zan	-	7	5	7	+
John Nichols [correct?]	Zan	-	7	5	2	+
James Brown, Junior	Zan	-	10	6	31	+
James Brown, Junior	Zan	-	10	6	32	-

1078   25 Jan 1810   A/4/099
Hon. Alexander Campbell, U.S. Senator
Forwards list of locations made in U.S. Military
   District of Ohio and Refugee Tract [not repro-
   duced on microfilm].

1079   26 Jan 1810 A/4/099
Jesse Spencer, Reg Chl
First certificate; duplicate receipt; tract
 designations MS and WS omitted, causing embarass-
 ment

Henry Orts	Chl	–	18	16	8	+

1080   27 Jan 1810 A/4/100
Hon. R. J. Meigs, Junior
Transmits patent

Joseph Taggert, Alexander McLaughlin, Edward Gray, & Robert Taylor	Mil	–	6	10	3	2
Joseph Taggert, Alexander McLaughlin, Edward Gray, & Robert Taylor	Mil	–	6	10	3	3
Joseph Taggert, Alexander McLaughlin, Edward Gray, & Robert Taylor	Mil	–	6	10	3	4

1081   27 Jan 1810 A/4/100
Andrew Reed, Xenia, Ohio
Transmits patent
Issued to Reed in trust for heirs of Jonathan
 Mercer, deceased

Jonathan Mercer, heirs	Unk	"in lots"	3
Jonathan Mercer, heirs	Unk	"in lots"	20
Jonathan Mercer, heirs	Unk	"in lots"	5
Jonathan Mercer, heirs	Unk	"out lots"	5
Jonathan Mercer, heirs	Unk	"out lots"	52
Jonathan Mercer, heirs	Unk	"out lots"	26

1082   30 Jan 1810 A/4/100
Statement of Account
Three percent allotment arising from the net proceeds of the sales of public lands, 1 Jul 1802
 to 30 Sep 1809, and advances against account
 [state not given, presumably Ohio].

1083   1 Feb 1810 A/4/101
Hon. Matthias Richards, U.S. Representative
Transmits patents

George Owig*	Unk	–	20	12	18	+
George Matz*	Unk	–	20	12	7	+

 *[May be joint owners of both tracts; not clear
  from text.]

1084   1 Feb 1810 A/4/101
Joseph Wood, Reg Mar
Transmits patent

Joseph Patterson	Mar	–	6	7	12	+

1085   1 Feb 1810 A/4/102
David Hoge, Reg Stu
Duplicate receipt
Hawk's agent a member of Congress

Jacob Hawk	Stu	–	9	10	27	+
James Walker	Stu	–	3	10	34	+
Richard Ewars? [Ervan?]	Stu	–	5	7	13	+

1086   2 Feb 1810 A/4/102
-- Homrickhous? Fredericktown, Maryland
Error on final certificate for Chl land.

1087   2 Feb 1810 A/4/103
Willys Silliman, Reg Zan
Duplicate receipt; construction of Act of 11 Feb
 1805

James Larrow (correct)	Zan	–	1	1	8	+
James Larrow (error)	Zan	–	1	1	16	+

1088   5 Feb 1810 A/4/103
John Stine, Reading, Pennsylvania
Answers query regarding failure to issue patents

John Stine	Chl	–	21	11	9	+
John Stine	Chl	–	21	11	8	+

1089   6 Feb 1810 A/4/104
Peter Wilson, Rec Stu
Duplicate receipt

John Hoopes	Stu	–	4	17	21	+
John Hoopes	Stu	–	7	20	9	+

1090   6 Feb 1810 A/4/104
John England, Stu
Duplicate receipt
England acting as agent for Hoopes

John Hoopes	Stu	–	4	17	21	+
John Hoopes	Stu	–	7	20	9	+

1091   6 Feb 1810 A/4/105
Jesse Spencer, Reg Chl
First certificate
Smith aided by member of Congress

Charles Smith	Chl	–	21	9	29	+
Jacob Hancher? [Haucher?]	Chl	–	20	12	19	+

1092   6 Feb 1810 A/4/105
Jared Mansfield, SG
First certificate; duplicate receipt
Spencer transfers to William Stevenson

Jesse Spencer [as grantee]	Chl	–	20	15	18	+

1093   6 Feb 1810 A/4/105
Daniel Symmes, Reg Cin
Final certificate; preferable to issue patent in
 name of "heirs of Elisha Adamson, deceased"
Nathan, Ruth, Loyd, Anna, John, & Elish Adamson;
 attestation of Nancy Adamson; John McClure
 assignee of Robert McClure; Brownlee transfers
 to Levi Jennings; Squire Littell, a magistrate

James Brownlee	Cin	EML	4	2	31	–
James Brownlee	Cin	EML	4	2	–	32
James Brownlee	Cin	EML	4	2	–	33

1094   9 Feb 1810 A/4/106
Joel Elliott, New Market, Frederick County, Mary-
 land
Answers query regarding patent application
Joseph Jackson; Nathan Sidwell; George Buchanan;
 Robert Vernon.

1095   9 Jan 1810 A/4/107
Jesse Spencer, Reg Chl
Transmits patents

Winn Winship, agent for Wisler
Henry Wisler	Chl	-	20	11	31	+
Henry Wisler	Chl	-	20	11	32	+
Henry Wisler	Chl	-	20	11	30	+

1096   9 Feb 1810   A/4/107
[Jesse Spencer], Reg Chl
Transmits patents
Edmund Ingman	Chl	-	19	14	7	+
Peter Miller	Chl	MS	21	9	3	+
Jacob Waggoner	Chl	WS	21	10	31	+
Christian Bearn? [Beam?]	Chl	-	19	16	12	+
John Hepler	Chl	-	20	8	25	+
William Dollarhide, Josias Lambert, James Spring?	Chl	-	18	1	- 18	
William Dollarhide, Josias Lambert, James Spring?	Chl	-	19	1	- 12	
William Dollarhide, Josias Lambert, James Spring?	Chl	-	19	1	13	-

1097   9 Feb 1810   A/4/107
[David Hoge], Reg Stu
Transmits patents
John Gilmore	Stu	-	7	12	13	+
Edward Laferty	Stu	-	6	10	10	+
Andrew Howden	Stu	-	2	6	21	+
John Ault	Stu	-	4	6	6	+
Peter Wise	Stu	-	6	17	4	+
Philip Woolf	Stu	-	5	16	13	+
Valentine Yount?	Stu	-	8	10	23	+
Valentine Yount?	Stu	-	8	10	24	+

1098   9 Feb 1810   A/4/108
[Willys Silliman], Reg Zan
Transmits patents
James Caldwell	Zan	Mil	2	1	3	+
David Findley	Zan	Mil	5	1	1	+
Moses James	Zan	-	14	15	10	+
Joseph James	Zan	-	14	15	10	+
John Johnson	Zan	-	10	8	28	+

1099   10 Feb 1810   A/4/108
Hon. John Rea
Transmits patent
Richard Morrow	Stu	-	8	12	35	+

1100   10 Feb 1810   A/4/108
Daniel Symmes, Reg Cin
Transmits patent
Martha Davis	Cin	EML	1	6	27	+

1101   10 Feb 1810   A/4/109
J. W. Homrickhous, Fredericktown, Maryland
Transmits patent
J. W. Homrickhous	Chl	-	20	14	34	+

1102   12 Feb 1810   A/4/109
Hon. Erastus Root
Transmits list of all unlocated half-sections in
  Canadian & Nova Scotian Refugee Tract [list not
  reproduced on microfilm]
Heirs of Simeon Chester, deceased.

1103   14 Feb 1810   A/4/109
Daniel Symmes, Reg Cin

Duplicate receipt; in case of reversion to
  United States, re-enter it for McCleland
McCleland, assignee of John Stewart
William McCleland	Cin	MR	6	2	11	+

1104   15 Feb 1810   A/4/110
Hon. Matthias Richards
Transmits patents
William Koch	Chl?	WS?	21	11	23	+
William Koch	Chl?	WS?	21	11	24	+

1105   15 Feb 1810   A/4/110
[Daniel Symmes], Reg Cin
Transmits patents
Sylvester Thompson	Cin	EML	4	9	26	+
Valentine Good	Cin	EML	4	3	11	+
James Young	Cin	EML	1	6	6	+

1106   15 Feb 1810   A/4/110
[David Hoge], Reg Stu
Transmits patents
Francis Gilmore	Stu	-	5	11	19	+
Charles Hamlin	Stu	-	6	19	10	+
Charles Hamlin	Stu	-	6	19	9	+
Simon Essig	Stu	-	8	11	35	+
Christopher Mauser?	Stu	-	8	11	23	+
Jonathan Cundiff	Stu	-	4	17	9	+
William Crawford	Stu	-	1	7	35	+

1107   17 Feb 1810   A/4/110
Mrs. Sarah Wood & Mrs. Mary Wood, Morrisville,
  Pennsylvania
Explains procedure for patenting land; duplicate
  receipt
Sarah Wood & Mary Wood	Chl	-	20	11	2	+

1108   20 Feb 1810   A/4/111
Willys Silliman, Reg Zan
Final certificate
Yoho, assignee of Archibald Woods
Jacob Yoho (error)	Zan	-	8	8	13	+
Jacob Yoho (correct)	Zan	-	8	8	12	+

1109   21 Feb 1810   A/4/112
David Hoge, Reg Stu
First certificate; duplicate receipts
Thomas Ashbough	Stu	-	2	13	18	+
John Gardner	Stu	-	5	16	25	+
Izak Proctor	Stu	-	6	18	23	+

1110   22 Feb 1810   A/4/112
Hon. Henry Southard, U.S. Representative
Transmits patent
Daniel Doty & Isaac Southard	Mil	-	15	8	4	1

1111   22 Feb 1810   A/4/112
Hon. Samuel Shaw, U.S. Representative
Transmits patents
All patentees below are assignees of Mathew
  Daviston?
Mathew Daviston?	Mil	-	1	6	2	14
Jacob N. Egbert	Mil	-	2	7	4	15
Jacob N. Egbert	Mil	-	2	7	4	8

Name						
Jacob N. Egbert	Mil	-	2	7	4	9
Richard Platt	Mil	-	2	5	2	25
Richard Platt	Mil	-	2	10	2	15
Samuel Hull? [Hill, Hall?]	Mil	-	3	17	1	7
Samuel Hull? [Hill, Hall?]	Mil	-	3	17	1	10
James Brewster	Mil	-	3	8	4	4
James Brewster	Mil	-	3	8	4	5
James Brewster	Mil	-	3	8	4	6

1112   22 Feb 1810   A/4/113
Samuel Alward, Junior, post office, Morristown,
  New Jersey
Transmits patent

Samuel Alward, Junior	Mil	-	11	6	1	30

1113   28 Feb 1810   A/4/113
Land Office, Jeffersonville, Indiana
Transmits patents

Jacob Fouts	Jef	-	9E	2N	32	+
Jacob Fouts	Jef	-	9E	2N	29	+
Francis Gillmer	Jef	-	9E	1N	-	26

1114   28 Feb 1810   A/4/113
[David Hoge], Reg Stu
Transmits patents

George Macentefer?	Stu	-	8	10	1	+
John Fleming	Stu	-	3	14	31	+
Peter Wise	Stu	-	7	19	19	-
Henry Fox	Stu	-	4	15	27	+
George Kail	Stu	-	7	14	20	+
Stephen Ford [Iford?]	Stu	-	3	9	24	+
John Fife	Stu	-	2	10	17	+
John Fife	Stu	-	2	10	18	+

1115   28 Feb 1810   A/4/113
[Jesse Spencer], Reg Chl
Transmits patents

Jacob & John Marks	Chl	-	20	12	29	+
Joel Strawn	Chl	-	17	18	1	+
John Sharp	Chl	MS	21	11	33	+
Benjamin Cox	Chl	MS	21	9	33	+

1116   28 Feb 1810   A/4/114
[Daniel Symmes], Reg Cin
Transmits patents

Andrew Zeller	Cin	EML	3	7	34	+
Sylvester Thompson	Cin	EML	5	7	17	+
Daniel Fether	Cin	EML	5	5	20	+
Christian Fall? [Fale?]	Cin	EML	3	4	11	+
James Faris	Cin	EML	1	6	25	+
Robert Martin	Cin	EML	1	6	27	+
George Yount	Cin	EML	5	5	1	+
Daniel Miller	Cin	EML	6	2	19	+
Hugh McQueston	Cin	EML	1	7	34	+
Jesse Jay	Cin	MR	5	3	8	+
William Ferguson	Cin	MR	4	3	4	+
William Ferguson	Cin	MR	5	2	11	+
John Ewing	Cin	MR	6	2	26	+
Aaron Street	Cin	MR	5	2	8	+
Daniel McIntosh	Cin	MR	8	4	26	+
Jacob Fouts	Cin	WML	1	13	12	-

1117   28 Feb 1810   A/4/114
Joseph Matthias, to be left at post office, Hanover,
  York County, Pennsylvania
Transmits patent

Joseph Matthias	Stu	-	5	17	13	+

1118   28 Feb 1810   A/4/114
Jacob Misler, York, Pennsylvania
Transmits patent

Jacob Misler	Stu	-	8	11	7	-

1119   1 Mar 1810   A/4/115
Joel Elliot, Newmarket, Frederick County, Maryland
Reports on status of applications at Stu
George Buchanan; Nathan Sidwell; Robert Vernon;
  Israel French, agent for Vernon.

1120   1 Mar 1810   A/4/115
Hon. R. J. Meigs, Junior
Transmits patents

James Warden	Zan	-	12	13	7	+
John Messer	Zan	-	12	13	6	+
Jacob Messer	Zan	-	12	13	7	+

1121   19 Mar 1810   A/4/115
[Willys Silliman], Reg Zan
Transmits patents

George Kollar	Zan	-	15	17	30	+
George Gibbons	Zan	-	12	13	7	+
James Ritter?	Zan	-	15	16	12	+
John Robins	Zan	-	9	8	7	+
William Raynolds	Zan	-	9	7	7	+
William Raynolds	Zan	-	11	13	10	+
John Caldwell	Zan	Mil	2	1	1	+

1122   19 Mar 1810   A/4/116
[David Hoge], Reg Stu
Transmits patents

John Bever	Stu	-	1	6	35	+
John Michael Easterday	Stu	-	3	16	2	+
James Black	Stu	-	4	10	4	+
Jacob Bair	Stu	-	8	11	10	+
John Hammon	Stu	-	8	11	33	+
James Hanna	Stu	-	4	10	29	+

1123   19 Mar 1810   A/4/116
[Jesse Spencer], Reg Chl
Transmits patents

Lawrence Rains	Chl	-	19	9	19	+
Jacob Weaver	Chl	-	19	16	25	+
Leonard Brosius?	Chl	-	16	17	30	+
Jacob Kershner	Chl	-	20	10	1	+
Jacob Kester	Chl	-	20	18	1	+
Daniel Kleck	Chl	-	20	13	7	+
Major Bright	Chl	-	20	14	6	+
Stephen Cole	Chl	-	20	13	7	+
Charles Bennett, Senior	Chl	-	20	4	20	+
Eli Haines	Chl	Mil	14	8	20	+
Eli Haines	Chl	Mil	14	8	19	+
John Crouse	Chl	WS	21	10	26	+
John Crouse	Chl	WS	21	10	27	+
John Comly	Chl	MS	21	9	10	+
John Bishop	Chl	MS	21	10	1	+
John Wilson	Chl	MS	21	11	19	+
William Carson, Senior	Chl	MS	21	11	4	+
Jacob Backard	Chl	MS	21	10	12	+
Joseph Kelly	Chl	MS	21	10	34	+
Thomas Bennett	Chl	LS	22	4	5	+

1124	20 Mar 1810	A/4/117

[Daniel Symmes], Reg Cin
Transmits patents

Frederick Kane? [Hana?]	Cin	EML	2	8	14	+
Frederick Kane? [Hana?]	Cin	EML	2	8	11	+
Thomas Hill	Cin	EML	5	7	20	+
John Bradford	Cin	EML	6	4	-	24
Daniel Hoover	Cin	EML	5	5	11	+
David Hoover	Cin	EML	5	5	11	+
John Brownson	Cin	EML	6	7	-	28
John Boughman	Cin	EML	1	2	-	25
Mathew Hueston	Cin	EML	1	6	34	+
Daniel Bowser	Cin	EML	6	2	19	+
John Sutherland & H. J. Brown	Cin	EML	2	4	11	+
Martin Miley	Cin	EML	2	8	33	+
James Boyse	Cin	EML	1	6	23	+
James Andrew	Cin	MR	7	4	36	+
James Andrew	Cin	MR	7	4	35	+
Robert Benham	Cin	MR	3	4	11	+
David Broadbury	Cin	MR	4	2	11	+
Clark Bates	Cin	MR	2	3	-	26
Samuel Hamilton	Cin	WML	1	9	24	+

1125	22 Mar 1810	A/4/117

[Jesse Spencer], Reg Chl
Transmits patents

Abraham Strickler	Chl	-	17	17	8	+
William Spencer	Chl	-	16	16	1	+
George Stockburger	Chl	-	16	17	7	+
George Stout	Chl	-	20	12	8	+
Nathan Stevenson	Chl	MS	21	11	14	+
Samuel Lander? [Landes?]	Chl	MS	22	3	2	-
Levi Shinn?	Chl	MS	22	4	34	+
James Sappington	Chl	LS	22	4	6	+

1126	22 Mar 1810	A/4/118

Daniel Symmes, Reg Cin
First certificate
Member of Congress intercedes

Joseph Torrence	Cin	EML	3	6	33	+

1127	22 Mar 1810	A/4/118

Christian Eby, to be left at post office, Baltimore, Maryland
Transmits patents
Returned as dead letter, sent again 5 Feb 1813 to
care of John Seely, Innkeeper, Old Town, Baltimore, Maryland

Christian Eby	Chl	-	18	15	10	+
Christian Eby	Chl	-	18	16	17	+
Christian Eby	Chl	-	18	16	8	+

1128	24 Mar 1810	A/4/118

Eli Haines, Rising Sun Post Office, Cecil County,
Maryland
Patent sent to Chl; addressee can pick it up
there, as he is emigrating

Eli Haines	Chl	-	14	8	20	+
Eli Haines	Chl	-	14	8	19	+

1129	24 Mar 1810	A/4/119

Jesse Spencer, Reg Chl
Transmits delayed patent; first certificate; dup-
licate receipts
William Creighton, magistrate; Hall assigns to
James McCleery; Stonebruck assigns to Frederick
Kline; Heistand assigns to Christian Tuss-
ing; -- Scholfield, a magistrate

Ephraim Doolittle	Chl	MS	22	4	23	-
Ephraim Doolittle (error)	Chl	MS	21	4	23	-
Daniel Hall	Chl	-	18	16	11	+
Henry Stonebruck?	Chl	-	18	14	35	+
Joseph Heistand	Chl	-	19	16	8	+
Daniel Hall	Chl	-	18	16	5	+

1130	24 Mar 1810	A/4/120

Mesdames Sarah & Mary Wood, Morrisville, Pennsyl-
vania
Duplicate receipt
Henry Clymer, a magistrate

Sarah & Mary Wood	Chl	-	20	11	2	+

1131	26 Mar 1810	A/4/120

Daniel Symmes, Reg Cin
Correction of patent on pre-emption lands
Conrad Hensberger? assignee of Daniel C. Cooper.

1132	27 Mar 1810	A/4/121

David Hoge, Reg Stu
First certificate; duplicate receipt

Permenas Sanborn? [Lam-born?]	Stu	-	5	17	13	+
Parmenas Sanborn? [Lam-born?]	Stu	-	5	17	7	+

1133	27 Mar 1810	A/4/121

Willys Silliman, Reg Zan
Final certificate

Joseph Evans	Zan	-	12	12	-	17
Joseph Evans	Zan	-	12	12	-	20

1134	30 Mar 1810	A/4/122

Edmund H. Taylor
Duplicate receipts

William Lindlay	Unk	-	4E	2N	3	+
William Lindlay	Unk	-	4E	2N	11	+
Owen Lindlay	Unk	-	1E	1N	20	+
Owen Lindlay	Unk	-	1E	1N	21	+

1135	30 Mar 1810	A/4/122

Willys Silliman, Reg Zan
First certificate; patent to be granted before
adjournment of current session of Congress
Dr. -- Crawford

Samuel Hill	Zan	-	12	13	3	+

1136	30 Mar 1810	A/4/122

Daniel Symmes, Reg Cin
First certificate; duplicate receipts
Handle assigns to Henry Young

Chester Handle	Cin	EML	3	5	33	+
Richard Carr	Cin	Pre	10	1	18	+

1137	30 Mar 1810	A/4/123

David Hoge, Reg Stu
First certificate

John Parry [also Perry]	Stu	-	5	10	34	+
John L. Graves	Stu	-	5	16	24	+
John L. Graves	Stu	-	7	18	24	+

1138	30 Mar 1810	A/4/123				

Hon. Matthias Richards, U.S. Representative
Transmits patent

Charles Smith	Chl	MS	21	9	29	+

1139	30 Mar 1810	A/4/123

Hon. R. J. Meigs, Junior, U.S. Senator
Transmits patent

Lewis Nye	Unk	-	14	15	9	+

1140	31 Mar 1810	A/4/123

Caspar Bottorf, Brownsburgh, Rockbridge County,
  Virginia
Transmits patent

Caspar Bottorf	Cin?	EML	2	7	23	+

  ["East of meridian line drawn from the mouth of
  the great Miami River."]

1141	31 Mar 1810	A/4/124

Michael Snider, to be left at post office, Littles
  Town, Adams County, Pennsylvania
Transmits patent

Michael Snider	Stu	-	8	12	33	+

1142	31 Mar 1810	A/4/124

Elias Hughes, to the care of the postmaster, Lees-
  burg, Virginia

Elias Hughes	Stu	-	5	7	10	+

1143	31 Mar 1810	A/4/124

James Morrison, care of postmaster, Geneva, Fayette
  County, Pennsylvania
Transmits patents

James Morrison	Cin?	EML	3	3	24	+
James Morrison	Cin?	EML	4	2	19	-

1144	31 Mar 1810	A/4/124

Hon. J. G. Jackson
Transmits patents; insufficient assignments
Thomas Baird assigns to Robert Manly; James Baird
  assigns to William Hamilton

William Hamilton	Zan	-	15	18	10	+
William Hamilton	Chl	-	17	18	6	+
William Hamilton	Chl	-	17	18	5	+
Thomas Baird	Zan	-	15	18	15	+
James Baird	Zan	-	15	18	15	+

1145	31 Mar 1810	A/4/125

[Jesse Spencer], Reg Chl
Transmits patents

Barton O'Neal	Chl	-	20	10	10	+
Nicholas Whitsel	Chl	-	20	11	1	+
John Sharp	Chl	-	20	12	19	+
Alexander Frazier	Chl	MS	21	9	5	+
Joseph Hoffhines? & J. G. Reid	Chl	MS	21	10	30	+

1146	31 Mar 1810	A/4/125

Hon. Gurdon S. Mumford
Transmits patents

Evander Childs	Mil	-	11	6	1	22
Evander Childs	Mil	-	11	6	1	23

1147	2 Apr 1810	A/4/125

Jesse Spencer, Reg Chl
First certificate; duplicate receipts
Scofield transfers to John Swier; William Hamil-
  ton, a magistrate; Elias Lovett; Andrew
  Weaver, a magistrate; John Myers; William
  Tomlinson of New Lancaster [state not given]

Elnathan Scofield	Chl	-	19	15	31	+
Conrad Starry?	Chl	MS	22	3	1	+

1148	2 Apr 1810	A/4/126

Daniel Symmes, Reg Cin
Missing final certificate

John R. Mills	Cin	EML	1	1	31	-
John R. Mills	Cin	EML	1	1	-	30*

  *"With island," on Whitewater Creek.

1149	2 Apr 1810	A/4/126

Willys Silliman, Reg Zan
First certificate; duplicate receipts; patent
  to issue before adjournment of Congress; transfer of [U.S.?] stock

Thomas Kelly	Zan	Mil	7	1	9	+

1150	2 Apr 1810	A/4/127

Daniel Symmes, Reg Cin
New final certificate to issue with corrected
  tract citation

Jacob Coy	Cin	Pre	6*	2*	6	+
Jacob Coy	Cin	Pre	6*	2*	12	-

  *Range and township supplied, see serial
  entry 353.

1151	3 Apr 1810	A/4/127

David Hoge, Reg Stu
Transmits patents

Catherine Thorn	Stu	-	6	19	27	+
Sarah Owen	Stu	-	7	9	32	+
James Caldwell	Stu	-	4	7	11	+
Jacob Christ	Stu	-	8	12	34	+
Christian Clinker	Stu	-	8	10	28	+
Francis Levitt? [Lemitt?]	Stu	-	8	9	30	+

1152	3 Apr 1810	A/4/128

[Daniel Symmes], Reg Cin
Transmits patents

Thomas Talbert	Cin	EML	3	4	27	+
John Brower	Cin	EML	4	3	2	+
Abraham McClintock	Cin	EML	5	5	9	+
Robert Rickets	Cin	WML	1	3	17	+
John Reed	Cin	MR	9	5	10	+
Isaac Vannest	Cin	Pre	4	5	17	+

1153	3 Apr 1810	A/4/128

Land Office, Jeffersonville
Transmits patents

John Copple, Senior	Jef	-	9E	2N	29	+
James Anderson	Jef	-	9E	3N	14	+
Levi Borsyer	Jef	-	9E	1N	-	35

1154	3 Apr 1810	A/4/128

[Joseph Wood], Reg Mar
Transmits patents

Jesse Dowson	Mar	–	5	6	4	+
Jesse Dowson	Mar	–	5	6	10	+
William Outland	Mar	–	6	7	12	+

1155   3 Apr 1806   A/4/128
John Johnston, Lancaster, Pennsylvania
Reports on status of land application

A. Winans & John Johnston	Cin	EML	5	8	1	+

1156   4 Apr 1810   A/4/128
Daniel Symmes, Reg Cin
Requests final certificate

[A.] Winans & John Johnston	Cin	EML	5	8	1	+

1157   4 Apr 1810   A/4/129
Hon. John Rea
Transmits patent

Jacob Hawk	Stu	–	9	10	27	+

1158   5 Apr 1810   A/4/129
Jesse Hirst, to care of postmaster, Waterford,
  Loudon County, Virginia
Transmits patent

Jesse Hirst	Unk	–	4	15	18	+

1159   6 Apr 1810   A/4/129
Samuel Finley, Rec Chl
Requests forwarding of duplicate receipt to Jared
  Mansfield, SG

[William Stephenson]	Chl?	–	20	15	18	+

1160   6 Apr 1810   A/4/129
Jared Mansfield, SG
Statement of account
Stephenson, assignee of Jesse Spencer; [Samuel]
  Finley

William Stephenson	Chl?	–	20	15	18	+

1161   6 Apr 1810   A/4/130
Daniel Symmes, Reg Cin
Requests final certificates
John Nicodemus, assignee of Hunt, Cooper, & Baum
  [marginal note: "Westminster, Baltimore County,
  Maryland."]

1162   7 Apr 1810   A/4/130
Joseph Ogle, near Zanesville, Ohio
Transmits patent

Joseph Ogle	Mil	–	7	4	2	18
Previously taken	Mil	–	7	4	2	16

1163   7 Apr 1810   A/4/130
Hon. John Condit
Transmits patent
Bush "late a soldier"

Benjamin Bush, heirs	Mil	–	16	6	1	6

1164   7 Apr 1810   A/4/130
Hon. Gurdon S. Mumford
Transmits patents

Jedediah Waterman	Mil?	–	11	6	1	9
Jedediah Waterman	Mil?	–	17	7	1	24

1165   9 Apr 1810   A/4/131
David Hoge, Reg Stu
Requests final certificates
Thomas Ashbough; John Gardner; member of Con-
  gress interested in receiving patent before
  adjournment of current session.

1166   10 Apr 1810   A/4/131
Matthew Mitchell, Leesburgh, Virginia
Transmits patent

Matthew Mitchell	Unk	–	4	17	5	+

1167   10 Apr 1810   A/4/131
Jesse Spencer, Reg Chl
First certificate; duplicate receipts
Jesse Palmer assigns to Sarah & Mary Wood

Sarah & Mary Wood	Chl	–	20	11	2	+

1168   11 Apr 1810   A/4/131
[Jesse Spencer], Reg Chl
Transmits patents

John Lutz	Chl	–	20	11	19	+
Jonathan Loofbourrow?	Chl	–	16	16	2	+
John Sharp	Chl	–	20	12	20	+

1169   11 Apr 1810   A/4/132
Daniel Symmes, Reg Cin
Nonpayment of instalment incorrect; "he has paid
  in full for the land long ago at the Treasury"

Caleb Gregg	Cin	MR	5	2	8	+

1170   10 Apr 1810   A/4/132
Affidavit
Certifies existence of Military Land Warrant 282
  "granted by James McHenry, late Secretary of
  War, on [21 Jun 1796] for two hundred acres of
  land to Charles Croughton, assignee of John
  Brooke late a Lieutenant"; reassigned 29 Apr
  1797 to Francis Taliaferro Brooke by Croughton
Joseph Nourse, Reg Treas; Albert Gallatin, Sec
  Treas

Jonathan Dayton	*	–	2	10	4	–

*4000-acre tract.

1171   11 Apr 1810   A/4/133
Hon. Gurdon S. Mumford
Transmits patent

Samuel Decker	Mil	–	16	7	4	26

1172   13 Apr 1810   A/4/133
William Raynolds, Junior
Final certificate

-- Waxler	Unk	–	13	15	12	+

1173   14 Apr 1810   A/4/133
Daniel Symmes, Reg Cin
First certificate; duplicate receipt

James Creegan	Cin	MR	12	1	21	+

1174   14 Apr 1810   A/4/133
Joseph Wood, Reg Mar
Transmits patents

James McMehin	Mar	-	3	2	36	+
James McMehin	Mar	-	4	3	6	+
George Goetz	Mar	-	3	3	-	9
George Goetz	Mar	-	3	3	-	10

1175   19 Apr 1810   A/4/134
Richard Forrest, Department of State
Transmits five certificates for lands granted to
  Major General La Fayette
-- Madison, attorney in fact.

1176   4 May 1810   A/4/134
Willys Silliman, Reg Zan
Duplicate receipt
Young, assignee of Thomas Kelly

Moses Young	Zan	-	7	1	9	+

1177   8 May 1810   A/4/134
David Hoge, Reg Stu
Duplicate receipts
Magruder, assignee of Daniel Thompson

John Gardner	Stu	-	5	16	25	+
-- Magruder	Stu	-	4	15	14	+

1178   15 May 1810   A/4/134
Daniel Symmes, Reg Cin
Reports tract sold on 1 Sep 1799 to Byers, patent
  issued Dec 1801

James Byers	Cin	Pre	5	2	17	-

1179   15 May 1810   A/4/135
Israel French, Junior, Newmarket, Frederick County,
  Maryland
Transmits patents

Robert Vernon	Stu	-	5	7	26	+
William Anderson	Stu	-	6	8	29	+

1180   16 May 1810   A/4/135
Thomas Gibson
Transmits patent

David Smith	Unk	-	13	15	6	+

1181   16 May 1810   A/4/135
[Jesse Spencer], Reg Chl
Transmits patent

John Good	Chl	-	17	18	8	+
Jacob Hough	Chl	-	20	9	5	+
Daniel Lieby	Chl	-	16	16	30	+
Henry Hosher	Chl	-	20	8	5	+
Zebulon Lee	Chl	-	20	15	35	+
Peter Hedrick	Chl	-	16	17	18	+
James Henderson	Chl	-	17	18	27	+
John Greave	Chl	-	20	8	35	+
Jonathan Holmes	Chl	MS	22	3	22	+
John Lyle	Chl	MS	22	4	12	+
Isaac Hoffer	Chl	MS	21	9	24	+
William Lucas, Senior	Chl	LS	21	3	-	31
William Lucas, Senior	Chl	LS	21	3	32	-
Samuel Lytle	Chl	WS	21	9	35	+

1182   16 May 1810   A/4/136
[Willys Silliman], Reg Zan
Transmits patents

Thomas Davis	Zan	-	15	17	27	+
Jacob Smith	Zan	-	14	15	2	+
Samuel Parker & William						
Launder? [Saunder?]	Zan	-	13	12	9	+

1183   16 May 1810   A/4/136
[David Hoge], Reg Stu
Transmits patent

John Ruse	Stu	-	5	16	19	+
Caleb Gregg	Stu	-	5	7	4	+
George Vaneman	Stu	-	5	11	13	+
George Vaneman	Stu	-	5	11	33	+
John Votaw	Stu	-	3	14	7	+
Isaac Votaw	Stu	-	4	17	19	+
Alexander Greene	Stu	-	5	7	4	+
Joseph Fisher	Stu	-	5	18	28	+
Thomas Leatherberry	Stu	-	2	8	17	+
James Gaff, Senior	Stu	-	8	11	34	+
Samuel Lucas	Stu	-	4	6	28	+

1184   21 May 1810   A/4/136
[Jesse Spencer], Reg Chl
Transmits patents
Edward Sherlock, assignee [certificate missing, or
  it "would have been forwarded with Mr. Doo-
  little's."]

Ephraim Doolittle	Chl	MS	22	4	23	-
Jacob Green	Chl	WS	21	11	23	+
John Hite	Chl	-	18	16	27	+

1185   21 May 1810   A/4/137
Mesdames Sarah & Mary Woods, Morrisville, Pennsylvania

Sarah Woods & Mary Woods	Chl	-	20	11	2	+

1186   22 May 1810   A/4/137
[David Hoge], Reg Stu
Transmits patents

Thomas Stanley	Stu	-	5	17	12	+
Abraham Snider	Stu	-	3	15	20	-
Adam Schaeffer	Stu	-	8	12	33	+
Thomas Saint	Stu	-	1	7	33	+
Alexander McCoy	Stu	-	3	11	29	+
Benjamin Hough	Stu	-	2	6	28	-
Thomas Fawcett	Stu	-	6	19	35	-

1187   22 May 1810   A/4/137
James McCleery, to be left at post office, New
  Holland, Lancaster County, Pennsylvania
Transmits patent

James McCleery	Chl	-	18	16	11	+

1188   22 May 1810   A/4/137
Christian Tussing, to be left at post office, New
  Market, Shenandoah County, Virginia
Transmits patent

Christian Tussing	Chl	-	19	16	8	+

1189   22 May 1810   A/4/138
Frederick Kline, to be left at post office, New
  Market, Shenandoah County, Virginia
Transmits patent

Frederick Kline	Chl	-	18	14	35	+

1190   23 May 1810   A/4/138
Daniel Symmes, Reg Cin
Duplicate receipts; first certificates
Brunner, assignee of -- Whiteman
David Osborne, assignee   Cin MR 12   5   9   +
Philip Corner? [Comer?]   Cin MR 12   3   8   +
Elias Brunner   Cin MR* 8   4 25   -
David Reese [Rees]   Cin WML 1   5 19   +
David Reese [Rees]   Cin WML 1   5   - 22
David Reese [Rees]   Cin WML 1   5   - 23
David Reese [Rees]   Cin WML 1   5 21   -
David Reese [Rees]   Cin WML 1   5 20   +
Christian Bleakenstaff   Cin EML 6   4 27   +
Dennis Boyse, assignee   Cin EML 2   5 19   +
    *Pre-emption.

1191   23 May 1810   A/4/139
David Hoge, Reg Stu
Duplicate receipts; first certificate
Hugh Davidson   Stu -   9   9 14   +
Joseph Spencer   Stu -   4   7 26   +
William Craig   Stu -   4 15 30   +
Daniel Thompson   Stu -   4 15 14   +

1192   26 May 1810   A/4/139
J. W. Condy, Philadelphia
Duplicate receipts [mentions another "party con-
    cerned"]
J. W. Condy   Stu -   6 16   1   +
J. W. Condy   Stu -   6 16   2   +
J. W. Condy   Stu -   6 14 30   +
J. W. Condy   Stu -   6 15 13   +
J. W. Condy   Stu -   7 17 14   +
J. W. Condy   Stu -   8 10 20   +

1193   26 May 1810   A/4/140
Peter Wilson, Rec Stu
Duplicate receipts
Jonathan W. Condy? [Coudy?].

1194   26 May 1810   A/4/140
Hon. Richard Stanford, Clover Garden, North Caro-
    lina
Replies regarding forfeiture feared
Jonathan Lindlay   Jef - 1E 1N   8   +

1195   26 May 1810   A/4/141
Edmond H. Taylor, Rec Jef
Duplicate receipt
Member of Congress [Richard Stanford] concerned
Jonathan Lindley   Jef - 1E 1N   8   +

1196   28 May 1810   A/4/141
Thomas Gibson
First certificate; duplicate receipt
Frederick Stump   Unk - 10 12 33   +

1197   29 May 1810   A/4/141
John Self, Front Royal, Frederick County, Virginia
Patents apparently forwarded to Zan
John Self   Zan -   5   1   6   +
John Self   Zan -   5   1 15   +

1198   31 May 1810   A/4/142
Jesse Hirst, Waterford, Loudon County, Virginia
Transmits patents
Jesse Hirst   Stu -   4 15 18   +

1199   1 Jun 1810   A/4/142
John Ward, Stu
Transmits patents
John Ward   Stu -   2   7 26   +

1200   1 Jun 1810   A/4/142
Daniel Symmes, Reg Cin
Transmits corrected patent
Jacob Coy   Cin MR   7   2   8   +

(End of part 1 of source A, rolls 3 and 4)

1201   15 Jul 1796 A/1/001
John Nevill
Appointment as Receiver at Pittsburgh; "An Act
 providing for the sale of the lands of the United
 States in the territory northwest of the River
 Ohio and above the mouth of the Kentucky River";
 bond requirement; compensation.

1202   15 Jul 1796 A/1/001
George Wallace
Appointment [as Superintendent of Land Sales,
 Pittsburgh] under §6 of "An Act providing for
 the sale of land of the United States in the
 territory northwest of the River Ohio and above
 the mouth of the Kentucky River"; concurrence
 of Governor, or Secretary, of Northwest Territory required.

1203   12 Aug 1796 A/1/002
Winthrop Sergeant, Secretary of Northwest Territory
Public sale of land in Seven Ranges to take place
 at Pittsburgh, 24 Oct 1796; public notice required; George Wallace nominated by U.S. President to organize the sale
George Wallace of Pittsburgh.

1204   12 Aug 1796 A/1/002
John Nevill
Bond requirement; map showing lots already sold
 in Seven Ranges, lots reserved to United States,
 residue for sale
George Wallace appointed Superintendent of Land
 Sales.

1205   12 Aug 1796 A/1/003
George Wallace
Public notice regarding land sale in Seven Ranges.

1206   12 Aug 1796 A/1/003
Arthur St. Clair, Governor of Northwest Territory
Previous sales of land in Seven Ranges termed im-
 perfectly accounted for; advertisement of 24
 Oct 1796 sale at Pittsburgh to be placed in Fort
 Washington newspaper
George Wallace; John Nevill.

1207   5 Oct 1796 A/1/004
John Nevill
Seven Ranges survey made in accordance with Congressional Ordinance of 20 May 1785; sales procedure; cash instalment of five percent down;
 certificates of deposit to be issued; ten percent discount to be given for payment in full
 within thirty days; patent procedure to be followed by U.S. Secretary of State
James Frazier [fictitious name?].

1208   5 Oct 1796 A/1/007
George Wallace; Governor of Northwest Territory;
 Secretary of Northwest Territory
Instructions sent to John Nevill; Seven Ranges
 survey made under Ordinance of 20 May 1785 only
 delineated the exterior lines of the townships;
 sections were not surveyed; public to be told
 that fractional sections occur.

1209   5 Oct 1796 A/1/008
John Nevill
List of lots in Seven Ranges, printed forms, and
 registers forwarded.

1210   12 Oct 1796 A/1/009
John Nevill, Pittsburgh
Accounting forms forwarded for Seven Ranges sale.

1211   11 Nov 1796 A/1/010
Arthur St. Clair, Governor of Northwest Territory,
 Pittsburgh
Sales prospects for Seven Ranges lands reported
 by St. Clair to be poor; previous sales records
 in disorder; difficulty regarding internal
 divisions of townships foreseen; -- Kemberly's
 small grant.

1212   25 Nov 1796 A/1/010
Governor Arthur St. Clair; John Nevill; George
 Wallace
Seven Ranges survey error noted; -- Kemberly's
 patent omitted; land payments also to be
 accepted in Washington with duplicate receipts
 to be sent to Nevill in Pittsburgh.

1213   25 Nov 1796 A/1/011
John Nevill, Pittsburgh
Weekly returns should distinguish between specie
 and bank notes; payments also being accepted
 in Washington with duplicate receipts forwarded
 to Nevill.

1214   26 Jan 1797 A/1/011
John Nevill, Inspector
Instruction to note on weekly return all the forfeitures due to nonpayment of first instalments; Nevill should not make advance payments
 to contractors without prior authorization from
 Washington; receipt form detailed.

1215   7 Apr 1797 A/1/012
John Nevill
Payments to be made to Colonel Thomas Butler and
 George Wallace; compensation for damages done
 by insurgents in four western counties of Penn-
 sylvania.

1216   25 Oct 1797 A/1/013
John Nevill
Statement of land sales requested.

1217   11 Sep 1798 A/1/014
John Nevill
Delinquency of Collector -- Mielkiske to be ascertained; -- Johnson mentioned; bill drawn;
 balance on hand; Samuel Hogden to provide names
 of Quartermaster's agents authorized to draw on
 Nevill.

1218   14 Mar 1799 A/1/015
Winthrop Sargent, Governor of Mississippi Terri-
 tory
Transmits notices regarding "An Act regulating the

grants of land appropriated for military service and for the Society of United Brethren for Propagating the Gospel Among the Heathen," and a supplementary act passed 2 Mar 1799.

1219   14 Mar 1799   A/1/015
John Nevill, Pittsburgh
Same as serial entry 1218 above; notice to be published in *Pittsburgh Gazette*.

1220   23 May 1800   A/1/015
Peregrine Foster
Appointment as Register of LO Mar; oath and bond required; further instructions not presently possible due to removal of U.S. Treasury from Trenton to Washington.

1221   23 May 1800   A/1/016
Israel Ludlow
Appointment as Register of LO Cin; same requirements as in serial entry 1220 above.

1222   23 May 1800   A/1/016
Thomas Worthington
Appointment as Register of LO Chl; same requirements as in serial entry 1220 above.

1223   23 May 1800   A/1/017
David Hoge
Appointment as Register of LO Stu; same requirements as in serial entry 1220 above.

1224   23 May 1800   A/1/017
Elijah Backus
Appointment as Receiver of LO Mar; same requirements as in serial entry 1220 above.

1225   23 May 1800   A/1/018
James Findlay
Appointment as Receiver of LO Cin; same requirements as in serial entry 1220 above.

1226   23 May 1800   A/1/018
Samuel Finley
Appointment as Receiver of LO Chl; same requirements as in serial entry 1220 above.

1227   23 May 1800   A/1/019
Zaccheus Biggs
Appointment as Receiver of LO Stu; same requirements as in serial entry 1220 above.

1228   21 Aug 1800   A/1/020
Thomas Worthington, Reg Chl
Sureties being investigated; right of pre-emption under law; occupancy by a sawmill or gristmill, or intent to erect such mill, sufficient to give pre-emptive right at $2 per acre; mills erected on fractional sections give right of pre-emption to whole section.

1229   26 Sep 1800   A/1/021
Zaccheus Biggs, Rec Stu
Act of 10 May 1800, entitled "An Act to amend the Act providing for sale of lands . . . in the territory northwest of the Ohio and above the mouth of the Kentucky River"; forms transmitted; stock payments; quarterly report required and described; account of deposit, including surveyor's expenses; sales of public lands account; forfeiture account; interest account; cash & stock account; discount account; commission account; inadequacy of personal compensation to be remedied by Congress.

1230   26 Sep 1800   A/1/024
David Hoge, Reg Stu; Peregrine Foster, Reg Mar; Thomas Worthington, Reg Chl; Israel Ludlow, Reg Cin
Act of 10 May 1800 entitled, "An Act to amend the Act entitled an Act providing for the sale of public land . . . in the territory northwest of the Ohio and above the mouth of the Kentucky River"; right to purchase land possible by following three modes: (a) by erecting, or beginning to erect, a gristmill or sawmill prior to 10 May 1800, (b) by being the first applicant for lands authorized to be disposed of by private sale, (c) by being highest bidder at any public sale; fractional sections sold with, and considered part of, adjacent whole sections; deposits for surveying expenses; five percent down payment on land; forms required.

1231   29 Sep 1800   A/1/026
Peregrine Foster, Reg Mar
Investigating sureties
Elijah Backus.

1232   29 Sep 1800   A/1/027
James Ross, Pittsburgh
Opinion regarding the following sureties: for David Hoge, John Hoge & Joseph Pentecost; for Zaccheus Biggs, Benjamin Biggs, Zachariah Sprigg, and Absalom Ridgely; for Thomas Worthington, Henry Massie & William Creighton; for Samuel Finley, Thomas Worthington, William Patton, & James Dunlop; for James Findlay, James Smith, William McMillan, & Arthur St. Clair, Jr.; for Peregrine Foster, Jonathan Stone & William Browning.

1233   29 Sep 1800   A/1/028
David Hoge, Reg Stu; Peregrine Foster, Reg Mar; Thomas Worthington, Reg Chl; Israel Ludlow, Reg Cin
Transmits forms.

1234   2 Oct 1800   A/1/028
Peregrine Foster, Reg Mar
Transmits forms for Elijah Backus whose acceptance of appointment is still unknown.

1235   17 Nov 1800   A/1/029
David Hoge, Reg Stu

General plat for Seven Ranges; sales of land in
Seven Ranges made at New York & Pittsburgh,
lists enclosed.

1236   21 Nov 1800   A/1/029
Thomas Worthington, Reg Chl
Lands sold at public sale to be entered on books
exactly as those privately applied for.

1237   21 Nov 1800   A/1/030
Samuel Finley, Rec Chl
Explains forms.

1238   30 Dec 1800   A/1/031
Zaccheus Biggs, Rec Stu
Requests statement of funds collected.

1239   25 Feb 1801   A/1/031
Zaccheus Biggs, Rec Stu
Authorizes purchase of safe.

1240   21 Mar 1801   A/1/032
Elijah Backus, Rec Mar; James Findlay, Rec Cin;
Samuel Finley, Rec Chl; Zaccheus Biggs, Rec Stu
Act of 10 May 1800; eight-percent discount.

1241   17 Mar 1801   A/1/032
Thomas Worthington, Reg Chl
Canadian & Nova Scotian refugee lands set aside;
land auction at Chl.

1242   16 May 1801   A/1/033
Zaccheus Biggs, Rec Stu
Transfer of funds to Secretary of War from Stu ac-
count; procedure to be followed.

1243   29 May 1801   A/1/034
Israel Ludlow, Reg Cin
Land auction at Cin.

1244   29 May 1801   A/1/034
Arthur St. Clair, Governor, Northwest Territory
Same as serial entry 43 above.

1245   3 Jun 1801   A/1/035
James Findlay, Rec Cin
Expenditures made were not in accordance with law
and Rec is liable for difference.

1246   15 Jun 1801   A/1/037
Elijah Backus, Rec Mar
Endorsement required.

1247   9 Jun 1801   A/1/037
Israel Ludlow, Reg Cin
Fractional sections.

1248   9 Jun 1801   A/1/037
Israel Ludlow, Reg Cin; Peregrine Foster, Reg Mar;

Thomas Worthington, Reg Chl; David Hoge, Reg
Stu
Procedure in case of errors discovered.

1249   10 Jun 1801   A/1/038
Thomas Worthington, Reg Chl
Right to receive fee at public sales of land;
pre-emption rights; fees not a part of government revenue.

1250   10 Jun 1801   A/1/040
All Receivers
Instructions regarding accounting for funds re-
ceived; forms.

1251   10 Jun 1801   A/1/042
Arthur St. Clair
Fees for entry of land
Thomas Worthington, Reg Chl.

1252   11 Jun 1801   A/1/042
Zaccheus Biggs, Rec Stu
Six-percent U.S. stock.

1253   19 Jun 1801   A/1/045
Thomas Worthington, Reg Chl; Israel Ludlow, Reg
Cin; Peregrine Foster, Reg Mar; David Hoge,
Reg, Stu
Instructions for accounting reports.

1254   26 Jun 1801   A/1/047
Thomas Worthington, Reg Chl
Construction of §§5,7 of the Act of 16 May 1800.

1255   27 Jun 1801   A/1/048
All Receivers
Acceptance of U.S. stock; repayments for land
purchases; state loan offices.

1256   30 Jun 1801   A/1/052
Samuel Finley, Rec Chl
Public sale of land at Chl.

1257   30 Jun 1801   A/1/053
Arthur St. Clair
Public sale of land at Chl.

1258   9 Jul 1801   A/1/054
Arthur St. Clair
Query regarding promise to grant land to Captains
White-eyes and Killbuck of Delaware Tribe of
Indians
Zaccheus Biggs.

1259   9 Jul 1801   A/1/054
Zaccheus Biggs, Rec Stu
Fractional sections adjacent to Moravian reserva-
tions; grant to Captains White-eyes and Killbuck.

1260   10 Jul 1801   A/1/055
Israel Ludlow, Reg Cin
Public sale of land at Cin.

1261   16 Jul 1801   A/1/056
Thomas Worthington, Reg Chl
Fees on sale of public land; intruders upon pub-
lic land.

1262   24 Jul 1801   A/1/057
Elijah Backus, Rec Mar
Directed to accept bills of SG.

1263   31 Jul 1801   A/1/057
Thomas Worthington, Reg Chl
Forfeiture of lands for nonpayment.

1264   31 Jul 1801   A/1/059
Elijah Backus, Rec Mar
Prevents repayments to land applicants.

1265   5 Aug 1801   A/1/060
Israel Ludlow, Reg Cin
Forfeiture of lands; sales of fractional sections
John Fulton; John Hamilton.

1266   5 Aug 1801   A/1/061
David Hoge, Reg Stu
Forfeiture of land; assignments of land.

1267   5 Aug 1801   A/1/063
James Findlay, Rec Cin
Symmes grant
Samuel Meredith; William Cuane? [Creane?]; John
Burnett; Judge [John Cleves]Symmes.

1268   7 Aug 1801   A/1/065
Thomas Worthington, Reg Chl
Canadian & Nova Scotian Refugee lands; "application bears . . . strong marks of speculation
unwarranted by law."

1269   7 Aug 1801   A/1/065
Thomas Worthington, Reg Chl
Fees for sales of land; Attorney General's opin-
ion.

1270   11 Aug 1801   A/1/066
Israel Ludlow, Reg Chl
Sales of fractional sections.

1271   13 Aug 1801   A/1/066
Zaccheus Biggs, Rec Stu
Transfers of U.S. stock; repayments to land appli-
cants
Robert Johnston; Bazaliel Wells; -- McConnell.

1272   15 Aug 1801   A/1/068
Samuel Finley, Rec Chl
Submission of accounts.

1273   15 Aug 1801   A/1/069
No addressee
Forfeitures of land; fees for land sold at public
sale.

1274   17 Aug 1801   A/1/070
David Hoge, Reg Stu
Calculation of discount
Charles Long, Frederickstown, Maryland
Charles Long   Stu -   1   8 13   -

1275   21 Aug 1801   A/1/071
Israel Ludlow, Reg Cin
Forfeitures of land for nonpayment.

1276   28 Aug 1801   A/1/073
James Findlay, Rec Cin; Samuel Finley, Rec Chl
Directs payment of bills of SG.

1277   28 Aug 1801   A/1/073
Peregrine Foster, Reg Mar
Repayment of purchase money
-- McIntire; -- Putnam; -- Dusenberry.

1278   7 Sep 1801   A/1/074
Thomas Worthington, Reg Chl
Pre-emption rights; mill rights
-- Derush   Chl - 22   5   7   -
Not stated   Chl - 28   1   -   -

1279   9 Sep 1801   A/1/075
All Rec
Transfers of U.S. stock.

1280   9 Sep 1801   A/1/075
William Wells, Zanesville, Northwest Territory
Land between two Miami Rivers; Symmes grant;
Pittsburgh sale; Act of 2 Mar 1799; six per-
cent stock; pre-emption right.

1281   15 Sep 1801   A/1/077
Thomas Worthington, Reg Chl
Repayments of purchase price; forfeitures of
land.

1282   18 Sep 1801   A/1/078
Thomas Worthington, Reg Chl
Forfeitures of land.

1283   30 Sep 1801   A/1/078
James Findlay, Rec Cin
Public sale of land, Cin, 6-25 Apr 1801.

1284   8 Oct 1801   A/1/079
James Findlay, Rec Cin
Act of 3 Mar 1801, appointments under §4; pre-
emption rights; John Cleves Symmes' lands
between the two Miami Rivers; Act of 2 Mar
1799 [see commissions which follow this serial
number]
William Goforth of Columbia; John Riley of Cin;
-- Poyers? [Byers?]; -- Wells.

1285   20 Oct 1801   A/1/081
David Hoge, Reg Stu
Act of 18 May 1796

Zenas Kimberly   Stu - 1 3 - 26
Zenas Kimberly   Stu - 2 3 -   2

1286   26 Oct 1801   A/1/082
James Findlay, Rec Cin
Judge [John Cleves] Symmes
James Byers   Cin Pre 5 2 17 -

1287   5 Nov 1801   A/1/083
Colonel E. Langham, Chl
"Malconduct" of Reg Chl [Thomas Worthington].

1288   1 Dec 1801   A/1/084
David Hoge, Reg Stu
Sale at New York; salt springs
Samuel Dannel
Not stated   Stu - 1 3 - -
Not stated   Stu - 2 2 - -

1289   4 Dec 1801   A/1/085
James Findlay, Rec Cin
Pre-emptive right of purchasers under John Cleves
   Symmes.

1290   19 Dec 1801   A/1/088
Israel Ludlow, Reg Cin
Forfeitures
Samuel Vance; Caleb Swann.

1291   12 Jan 1802   A/1/089
Samuel Finley, Rec Chl
Draft
Elnathan Schofield.

1292   23 Jan 1802   A/1/089
All Receivers
Transfers of funds to SG
Rufus Putnam, SG.

1293   26 Jan 1802   A/1/091
James Findlay, Rec Cin
Pre-emption rights of certain persons under devise
   from John Cleves Symmes.

1294   29 Jan 1802   A/1/091
David Hoge, Reg Stu
Refund of payments after forfeiture.

1295   5 Apr 1802   A/1/092
All Registers
Act of 10 May 1800, §7; prevention of reversion
   of lands upon which first payments have been
   made; forfeitures.

1296   5 Apr 1802   A/1/093
David Hoge, Reg Stu
Congressional report in case of Arthur Morrison.

1297   5 Apr 1802   A/1/094
All Receivers
Accounting reports.

1298   5 Apr 1802   A/1/095
Zaccheus Biggs, Rec Stu
Refund on land purchased
Arthur Morrison   Stu - 5 8 4 -

1299   27 Apr 1802   A/1/096
David Hoge, Reg Stu
Refund of land payment
Henry McGanah of Jefferson County [state not
   given].

1300   28 Apr 1802   A/1/096
Zaccheus Biggs, Rec Stu
Refund for miscalculation of discount.

1301   5 May 1802   A/1/097
[Rufus Putnam], SG; [Zaccheus Biggs], Rec Stu;
   [David Hoge], Reg Stu
Act of 1 May 1802; surveying of township bound-
   aries.

1302   5 May 1802   A/1/098
All Registers
Annual commissions to Registers on land sales
   [separate individual letters to all Receivers
   follow on microfilm].

1303   6 May 1802   A/1/101
Zaccheus Biggs, Rec Stu; David Hoge, Reg Stu
Establishment of roads in Stu district; Seven
   Ranges; Zanesville; Muskingum River; Ohio
   Company; Whelen [Wheeling?]; Hockhocking;
   U.S. Military District of Ohio.

1304   8 Jun 1802   A/1/102
Zaccheus Biggs, Rec Stu
Refund of land payments
Henry McGanah; Zenas Kimberly.

1305   11 Jun 1802   A/1/103
James Findlay, Rec Cin
Relinquishments of land mistakenly applied for
Jacob White

1306   15 Jun 1802   A/1/104
Thomas Worthington, Reg Chl
Canadian & Nova Scotian refugee lands; mill-
   right pre-emption
-- Derush
Previously sold   Chl - 22 5 6 -
Previously sold   Chl - 22 5 7 -
Previously sold   Chl - 22 5 - 2
Previously sold   Chl - 22 5 - 3
Previously sold   Chl - 22 5 - 4
Previously sold   Chl - 22 5 - 8
Previously sold   Chl - 22 5 - 1
Previously sold   Chl - 22 5 - 5

1307   18 Jun 1802   A/1/104
Zaccheus Biggs, Rec Stu
Disputed land to be determined by lot; refund of
   land deposit
Stuart McClave; Abraham Naffsher.

1308   28 Jun 1802   A/1/105
Israel Ludlow, Reg Cin; James Findlay, Rec Cin
Roads in Hamilton County, [Ohio]; Fort Hamilton;
   Fort Recovery; Fort Wayne & Detroit; Lancaster
   in Fairfield [County?]; Great Miami River.

1309   28 Jun 1802   A/1/107
David Hoge, Reg Stu
Roads to be opened: Stu to Chl, Grave Creek or
   Pultney to Lancaster in Fairfield County &
   Scioto River, Mar to St. Clairsville, Stu to
   Seven Ranges; Scioto Salt Spring to Ohio Com-
   pany.
Not stated   Stu - 5 10 5 -

1310   6 Aug 1802   A/1/110
Thomas Worthington, Reg Chl
Fractional sections.

1311   7 Aug 1802   A/1/110
Samuel Finley, Rec Chl
Official misconduct charges to be investigated by
   Court of Common Pleas [letters to Thomas Worth-
   ington, defendant, and -- Langham, complainant,
   follow].
Thomas Worthington; E. Langham.

1312   9 Aug 1802   A/1/113
Edwin Putnam, Attorney at Law, Mar
Requests that Edwin Putnam take care of land office business in the event that Peregrine Foster,
   who resigns, leaves before new appointment of
   replacement.

1313   13 Aug 1802   A/1/113
James Findlay, Rec Cin
Refunds overpayment
David Ziegler.

1314   16 Aug 1802   A/1/114
John Selman, Cin
Appointment as Commissioner "under the laws giving
   a right of pre-emption to purchasers under Judge
   [John Cleves] Symmes."

1315   8 Sep 1802   A/1/115
David Hoge, Reg Stu
Roads; finances [letter of instruction to Rec fol-
   lows].

1316   6 Oct 1802   A/1/117
Israel Ludlow, Reg Cin
Discussion of law regarding claimants under John
   Cleves Symmes.

1317   25 Oct 1802   A/1/118
[James Findlay], Rec Cin; [Samuel Finley], Rec
   Chl; [Zaccheus Biggs], Rec Stu
Payment of bills of SG.

1318   27 Oct 1802   A/1/118
Israel Ludlow, Reg Cin
Deposits for land; pre-emptive rights of purchasers

under John Cleves Symmes
William Crane; Montgomery & Newbold; John
   Bennett

1319   27 Oct 1802   A/1/119
Thomas Worthington, Reg Chl
Mill-right pre-emption
-- Derush.

1320   6 Nov 1802   A/1/120
Zaccheus Biggs, Rec Stu; James Findlay, Rec Cin;
   Samuel Finley, Rec Chl
Method of transferring funds to U.S. Treasury.

1321   22 Dec 1802   A/1/122
James Findlay, Rec Cin
Large discrepancies in accounts noted.

1322   5 Jan 1803   A/1/123
Zaccheus A. Beatty, Stu
Accounting adjustment; U.S. stock.

1323   5 Jan 1803   A/1/124
David Hoge, Reg Stu
Instruction regarding accounting for U.S. stock
Zaccheus A. Beatty.

1324   10 Jan 1803   A/1/125
Thomas Worthington, "late" Reg Chl
Worthington's resignation as Reg Chl and as Super-
   visor of Internal Revenue.

1325   27 Jan 1803   A/1/126
Samuel Finley, Rec Chl
Remittances.

1326   21 Feb 1803   A/1/127
Elijah Backus, Rec Mar
Continuance of Mar land office and salary.

1327   23 Feb 1803   A/1/127
John Selman, Cin
Transmits commission appointing him Commissioner
   "under the law giving a right of pre-emption to
   purchasers under Judge [John Cleves] Symmes."

1328   28 Mar 1803   A/1/131
James Findlay, Rec Cin
Transfer of funds to George Dearborn for payment
   of troops at Natchez.

1329   28 Mar 1803   A/1/133
Zaccheus Biggs, Rec Stu
Transfer of funds to George Dearborn; not to be
   paid in notes of the Bank of the United States
   or its branches, or of the Bank of Columbia,
   or of the Bank of Alexandria.

1330   31 Mar 1803   A/1/133
James Findlay, Rec Cin

Remittance to U.S. Treasury; "no bank notes, except those of the Bank of the United States to be remitted."

1331   12 Apr 1803   A/1/134
Jesse Spencer, Reg Chl
Acknowledges receipt of official bond and oath of office.

1332   16 Apr 1803   A/1/134
Zaccheus Biggs, Rec Stu
Financing of roads.

1333   16 Apr 1803   A/1/134
David Hoge, Reg Stu
Financing of roads.

1334   25 Apr 1803   A/1/136
Israel Ludlow, Reg Cin
Act of 3 Mar 1803, §7; U.S. Military District of Ohio; Moravian Brethren; pre-emption purchases [similar letter to James Findlay, Rec Cin follows].

1335   27 Apr 1803   A/1/137
James Findlay, Rec Cin
Forfeiture
Daniel Miller.

1336   4 Jun 1803   A/1/138
David Hoge, Reg Stu
Road to Hockhocking approved.

1337   14 Jun 1803   A/1/138
Zaccheus Biggs, Rec Stu
Repayment on purchase of fractional sections
Noah Linsley.

1338   16 Jun 1803   A/1/138
Jesse Spencer, Reg Chl
Fees permitted to Registers; destruction of purchaser's certificate; assignments & conveyances
-- Stewart; -- Miller; -- Evans.

1339   24 Jun 1803   A/1/141
Jesse Spencer, Reg Chl
Authorization to open road; Will's Creek; Salt Creek of Muskingum River; Hockhocking.

3140   24 Jun 1803   A/1/142
David Hoge, Reg Stu
Financing of road; Seven Ranges; Will's Creek; Hockhocking
-- Gray.

1341   29 Jun 1803   A/1/143
Israel Ludlow, Reg Cin
Methods of adjusting over- and underpayments when land surveyed discloses major differences in acreage from that shown in plats.
David Ziegler.

1342   23 Jul 1803   A/1/145
Zaccheus Biggs, Rec Stu; Elijah Backus, Rec Mar
Transfer of funds to SG.

1343   26 Jul 1803   A/1/145
Isaac Briggs, Surveyor, Mississippi Territory, Natchez
Instructions for the surveying & numbering of ranges & townships; private surveys; British grants; grants under the United States.

1344   27 Jul 1803   A/1/148
Samuel Finley, Rec Chl
Transfer of funds to David Ziegler, Marshal of District of Ohio.

1345   27 Jul 1803   A/1/148
David Hoge, Reg Stu
Surveying of roads; Grave Creek; New Lancaster
John Badollet of Greene County [state not mentioned].

1346   27 Jul 1803   A/1/149
E. Turner, Reg Natchez, & Joseph Chambers, Reg Mobile
Confirmation of land titles to residents settled thereon by 27 Oct 1795; Bourbon Act; agreement with State of George; pre-emption rights; Spanish grants; British patents & warrants; public auction sales; private sales; records to be kept; Indian lands east of Tombigbee River.

1347   9 Aug 1803   A/1/157
David Hoge, Reg Stu; Joseph Wood, Reg Mar
Act of 10 May 1800; Act of 1 May 1802; surveying of Seven Ranges; fractional sections; Pittsburgh sale; reserved sections.

1348   9 Aug 1803   A/1/159
Thomas Rodney, Mississippi Commissioner, Dover, Delaware
Method of payment for services.

1349   19 Aug 1803   A/1/160
Samuel Finley, Rec Chl
Investigation of Worthington's "malconduct" in office
-- Abrams; -- Langham.

1350   25 Aug 1803   A/1/161
David Hoge, Reg Stu; Zaccheus Biggs, Rec Stu
Financing of roads.

1351   12 Sep 1803   A/1/161
Robert Williams
Appointment as land commissioner; lands south of Tennessee
-- Turner, Reg Natchez.

1352   12 Oct 1803   A/1/162
Israel Ludlow, Reg Cin
Special act for J. J. Dufour & associates.

1353   18 Oct 1803   A/1/162
David Hoge, Reg Stu
Transfer of funds.

1354   18 Oct 1803   A/1/163
Zaccheus Biggs, Rec Stu
Transfers of funds.

1355   2 Nov 1804   A/1/163
David Hoge, Reg Stu; Zaccheus Biggs, Rec Stu
Transfers of funds.

1356   9 Nov 1803   A/1/164
Isaac Briggs, Surveyor, Mississippi Territory
Accounting procedures; ". . . thanks for the information respecting the Louisiana speculations,
  which will meet with due attention. . . ."

1357   18 Nov 1803   A/1/165
Robert C. Nicholas, Commissioner, Mississippi
  Territory
Transfers of funds
John A. Seits.

1358   28 Nov 1803   A/1/165
Edward Turner, Reg Mississippi Territory
Act of 3 Mar 1803, §5; Articles of Agreement with
  State of Georgia; evidence required for Commis-
  sioners to issue certificates.

1359   30 Nov 1803   A/1/166
Samuel Finley, Rec Chl
Transfer of funds
Jared Mansfield, SG.

1360   29 Nov 1803   A/1/166
Zaccheus Biggs, Rec Stu
Bank of Pennsylvania, Pittsburgh branch; transfers
  of funds
Thomas Wilson, cashier.

1361   30 Nov 1803   A/1/168
James Findlay, Rec Cin
Transfer of funds
Jared Mansfield, SG.

1362   15 Dec 1803   A/1/168
Edward Turner, Reg Mississippi Territory
Forwards commission (appointment).

1363   9 Jan 1804   A/1/168
Joseph Wood, Reg Mar
"Fractional sections may not be sold unless con-
  nected with some entire section."

1364   9 Jan 1804   A/1/169
Thomas Rodney, Robert Williams, and Edward Turner,
  Commissioners, Washington, Mississippi Territory
Articles of Agreement and Cession with Georgia;
  Indian boundary line (Choctaws); Bourbon Act
General -- Wilkinson.

1365   10 Jan 1804   A/1/169
Samuel Finley, Rec Chl
Transfer of funds
Jared Mansfield, SG.

1366   10 Jan 1804   A/1/170
James Findlay, Rec Cin
Transfer of funds
Jared Mansfield, SG.

1367   10 Jan 1804   A/1/170
Elijah Backus, Rec Mar
Transfer of funds
Jared Mansfield, SG.

1368   11 Jan 1804   A/1/171
Israel Ludlow, Reg Cin
Locations of Isaac Zane.

1369   16 Jan 1804   A/1/171
Thomas Rodney, Robert Williams, & Edward Turner,
  Commissioners, Mississippi Territory
Articles of Agreement & Cession with Georgia;
  Indian boundary line (Choctaw); Bourbon Act.

1370   18 Jan 1804   A/1/172
Richard Claiborne, Clerk, Board of Commissioners
Bill
Major Ferdinand Lee Claiborne; Dr. -- Lattimore.

1371   25 Jan 1804   A/1/172
Edward Turner, Reg Mississippi Territory
Spanish titles; status of present occupants.

1372   2 Feb 1804   A/1/174
Israel Ludlow, Reg Cin
Resignation from post of Reg Cin; survey of Indi-
  ana Territory
Jared Mansfield, SG.

1373   17 Feb 1804   A/1/174
Thomas Rodney, Robert Williams, & Edward Turner,
  Commissioners, Mississippi Territory
Bourbon Act of State of Georgia.

1374   10 Mar 1804   A/1/175
Charles Killgore, Reg Cin
Transmits commission (appointment) as Reg Cin;
  oath & bond required.

1375   16 Mar 1804   A/1/175
Samuel Finley, Rec Chl
Transfer of funds to U.S. Army [money to be shipped
  to New Orleans]
Lt. -- Armistead, U.S. Army; -- Alline, U.S.
  Navy.

1376   30 Mar 1804   A/1/176
[David Hoge], Reg Stu; [Jesse Spencer], Reg Chl;
[Charles Killgore], Reg Cin; [Joseph Wood],
  Reg Mar
Computation of interest, discounts, instalments;
  fee system to be replaced by salaries for Regs.

1377   2 Apr 1804   A/1/178
Edward Turner, Reg Mississippi Territory
Transmits Congressional enactment.

1378   5 Apr 1804   A/1/178
Benjamin Tupper, Rec Mar
Transmits commission (appointment); oath & bond
  required.

1379   6 Apr 1804   A/1/178
Samuel Finley, Rec Chl
Transfer of funds to U.S. Army.

1380   9 Apr 1804   A/1/179
Willys Silliman, Reg Zan; Thomas Van Swearingen,
  Rec Zan
Transmits commissions (appointments); oaths &
  bonds required; public sale at Zan to be held
  in May 1804
Jared Mansfield, SG.

1381   10 Apr 1804   A/1/179
David Hoge, Reg Stu; Zaccheus Biggs, Rec Stu;
  Willys Silliman, Reg Zan; Thomas Van Swearingen,
  Rec Zan; Joseph Wood, Reg Mar; Benjamin Tupper,
  Rec Mar; Jesse Spencer, Reg Chl; Samuel Finley,
  Rec Chl; Charles Killgore, Reg Cin; James
  Findlay, Rec Cin
Act of 26 Mar 1804 . . . for disposal of public
  lands in the Indiana Territory; sales in sec-
  tions, half-sections, & quarter-sections; frac-
  tional sections may be sold separately; auction
  of lands remaining in U.S. Military District of
  Ohio; interest; issuance of final certificates;
  reserved sections in Ludlow's Survey; Act of
  3 Mar 1801, §10; public sale of lands in U.S.
  Military District of Ohio to be held at Chl &
  Zan.

1382   11 Apr 1804   A/1/182
Charles Killgore, Reg Cin; James Findlay, Rec Cin
Act of 26 Mar 1804, §§7,8; Cin public sale;
  instalment payments; Ludlow Survey.

1383   13 Apr 1804   A/1/183
Michael Jones of Cin, Reg Kaskaskia; John Badollet
  of New Geneva, Pennsylvania, Reg Vincennes
Transmits commissions (appointments); oaths &
  bonds required; ". . . for the present your
  duties will be confined to those arising from
  receiving, filing, & recording evidences of
  claims"; after 1 Jan 1805 to act also as Land
  Commissioners.

1384   24 Apr 1804   A/1/184
Thomas Rodney, Commissioner, Mississippi Territory
Expenses of Board of Commissioners.

1385   25 Apr 1804   A/1/185
Elijah Backus, late Rec Mar
Transfer of funds; accounts to be submitted
Rufus Putnam; Benjamin Tupper, Rec Mar.

1386   25 Apr 1804   A/1/185
Benjamin Tupper, Rec Mar
Transfer of funds
Elijah Backus; Jared Mansfield; Rufus Putnam.

1387   27 Apr 1804   A/1/186
[David Hoge], Reg Stu; [Joseph Wood], Reg Mar;
  [Willys Silliman], Reg Zan; [Jesse Spencer],
  Reg Chl; [Charles Killgore], Reg Cin
Division of LO districts.

1388   3 May 1804   A/1/188
John Badollet, near New Geneva, Pennsylvania
Instructions for opening road to Vincennes.

1389   11 May 1804   A/1/189
Jesse Spencer, Reg Chl
Letter acknowledged
-- Carpenter;   -- Denny.

1390   26 May 1804   A/1/189
Jacob Ayers, Zan
Fractional sections.

1391   28 May 1804   A/1/189
Joseph Wood, Reg Mar
Zan lands cannot be sold at Mar.

1392   29 May 1804   A/1/190
Benjamin Tupper, Rec Mar
Fractional section
Bazaliel Wells.

1393   31 May 1804   A/1/190
Edward Turner, Reg Mississippi Territory
British grants; conflicting or adverse claims;
  Spanish grants; Act of 10 May 1800, §12.

1394   26 May 1804   A/1/191
Charles Killgore, Reg Cin
Reserved sections
Isaac Zane.

1395   1 Jun 1804   A/1/191
Samuel Finley, Rec Chl
Payment of surveying expenses.

1396   1 Jun 1804   A/1/191
Joseph Chambers, Reg EPR, St. Stephens
Transmits commission (appointment); oath & bond
  required; instructions.

1397   2 Jun 1804   A/1/192
William B. Shields, Agent for Investigating
  Claims, care of Thomas Rodney, Commissioner,
  Washington, Mississippi Territory
Appointment to office; Bourbon Act; Spanish
  grants.

1398   5 Jun 1804   A/1/193
Willys Silliman, Reg Zan
Voided sales at Mar; fractional sections; collu-
  sion suspected in sale of certain fractional
  section
John Matthews; John Zane.

1399   5 Jun 1804   A/1/194
Samuel Finley, Rec Chl

Bond of Thomas Van Swearingen
Benjamin Kerns;   Duncan McArthur.

1400   6 Jun 1804   A/1/194
George Hoffman, Reg Det
Transmits commission (appointment);   oath & bond
   required;   " . . . your duties will be confined
   to those arising from receiving, filing, & recording evidences of claims."

1401   7 Jun 1804   A/1/195
Zaccheus Biggs, Rec Stu
Transfer of funds to Pittsburgh.

1402   8 Jun 1804   A/1/196
Zaccheus Biggs, Rec Stu
Transfer of funds
John Badollet, Reg Vin.

1403   8 Jun 1804   A/1/196
John Badollet, Reg Vin
Transfer of funds
Zaccheus Biggs, Rec Stu.

1404   8 Jun 1804   A/1/197
Jesse Spencer, Reg Chl
Road from Chl to Hockhocking.

1405   8 Jun 1806   A/1/197
Jesse Spencer, Reg Chl
Merging of survey districts 3 & 4
James Kilburn;   Elnathan Scofield;   James Denny.

1406   8 Jun 1804   A/1/198
Charles Killgore, Reg Cin
Merging of survey districts 1, 4, & 5.
William Ludlow;   Maxwell Ludlow;   Benjamin Chambers.

1407   8 Jun 1804   A/1/198
David Hoge, Reg Stu
Division of survey districts
W. Heald;   B[enjamin] Hough;   A. Holmes.

1408   27 Jun 1804   A/1/199
Michael Jones, Reg Kas
Receipt of bond & oath.

1409   9 Jul 1804   A/1/199
John Badollet, Reg Vin;   Michael Jones, Reg Kas
Congressional resolutions of 20 Jun & 29 Aug 1788;
   Act of 3 Mar 1791;   claims derived under French
   & British grants;   confirmation of claims made
   by Governor [St. Clair & Harrison];   survey of
   township lines.

1410   10 Jul 1804   A/1/202
Zaccheus Biggs, Rec Stu;   Samuel Finley, Rec Chl;
   Benjamin Tupper, Rec Mar;   James Findlay, Rec Cin
Conflicts between surveys of SG & district sur-
   veyors;   Act of 26 Mar 1804;   Act of 10 May 1800;
   payments for variances in actual acreage sold.

1411   17 Jul 1804   A/1/203
Samuel Finley, Rec Chl
Transfer of funds
George Hoffman, Reg Det.

1412   18 Jul 1804   A/1/204
John Badollet, "now at New Geneva, Pennsylvania,"
   Reg Vin
Opening road between Grave Creek & New Lancaster;
   transfers of funds
Joseph Tomlinson;   David Hoge, Reg Stu;   -- Nourse.

1413   19 Jul 1804   A/1/205
David Hoge, Reg Stu
Transfer of funds
John Badollet, Reg Vin;   Zaccheus Biggs, Rec Stu.

1414   24 Jul 1804   A/1/205
Willys Silliman, Reg Zan
Adequacy of notice of public sale
-- Matthews.

1415   25 Jul 1804   A/1/206
Jesse Spencer, Reg Chl
Act of 10 May 1800;   alleged breach of contract
   due to regulation for ascertaining boundaries;
   expenses for running interior lines;   Act of
   26 Mar 1804.

1416   25 Jul 1804   A/1/207
Benjamin Tupper, Rec Mar
Conflict of jurisdiction between Mar & Zan land
   offices.

1417   1 Aug 1804   A/1/208
Charles Killgore, Reg Cin
Act of 26 Mar 1804, §12.

1418   2 Aug 1804   A/1/208
Samuel Finley, Rec Chl
Expenses of public sales.

1419   2 Aug 1804   A/1/208
Benjamin Tupper, Rec Mar
Expenses of public sales.

1420   6 Aug 1804   A/1/209
Thomas Van Swearingen, Rec Zan
Expenses of public sales.

1421   6 Aug 1804   A/1/209
Samuel Finley, Rec Chl
Correction of errors in accounts.

1422   17 Aug 1804   A/1/210
Charles Killgore, Reg Cin
Act of 1 May 1802;   fractional sections

John James Dufour	Cin	-	3	2	12	-
John James Dufour	Cin	-	3	2	14	-
John James Dufour	Cin	-	3	2	-	13
John James Dufour	Cin	-	3	2	-	23

| John James Dufour | Cin | - | 3 | 2 | - | 7 |
| John James Dufour | Cin | - | 3 | 2 | - | 18 |

1423   19 Sep 1804   A/1/210
Samuel Finley, Rec Chl
Act of 3 Mar 1803; three-percent apportionment to
  State of Ohio
William McFarland, Treasurer of State of Ohio.

1424   20 Sep 1804   A/1/211
Benjamin Tupper, Rec Mar
Accounting matters
Elijah Backus.

1425   21 Sep 1804   A/1/211
Willys Silliman, Reg Zan
Land sold at Mar alleged to have been resold at
  Zan

| W. McCluney & -- Holker | Mar | - | 12 | 13 | 19 | - |
| W. McCluney & -- Holker | Mar | - | 12 | 13 | - | 30 |

1426   21 Sep 1804   A/1/212
James Findlay, Rec Cin
Transfer of funds
Jared Mansfield, SG.

1427   25 Sep 1804   A/1/212
Benjamin Tupper, Rec Mar
Conflict of jurisdiction between Mar & Zan land
  offices
John Matthews; Isaac Zane.

1428   25 Sep 1804   A/1/213
David Hoge, Reg Stu
Opening of road to New Lancaster; transfer of
  funds.

1429   26 Sep 1804   A/1/213
George Hoffman, Reg Det
Instructions.

1430   26 Sep 1804   A/1/213
Michael Jones, Reg Kas
French & British grants; grants of State of Vir-
  ginia in Illinois Territory; Act of 20 Jun 1788;
  Act of 3 Mar 1791, §2; Resolution of 20 Jun
  1788.

1431   27 Sep 1804   A/1/214
Samuel Finley, Rec Chl
Statement of accounts; public sales of land
-- Winship.

1432   3 Oct 1804   A/1/215
Zaccheus Biggs, Rec Stu
Transfer of funds to Office of Discount & Deposit,
  Pittsburgh.

1433   8 Oct 1804   A/1/215
Samuel Finley, Rec Chl
Three-percent apportionment to State of Ohio;
  transfer of funds.

1434   12 Oct 1804   A/1/216
Joseph Chambers, Reg Mississippi Territory
Claims east of Tensaw; survey of former Indian
  lands on Mobile [River]; commission (appointment) enclosed.

1435   13 Oct 1804   A/1/217
Frederick Bates, Rec Det
Commission (appointment) enclosed; oath & bond
  required; instructions.

1436   15 Oct 1804   A/1/217
Elijah Backus, Rec Kas
Commission (appointment) enclosed;. oath & bond
  required.

1437   15 Oct 1804   A/1/218
Nathaniel Ewing, Rec Vin
Commission (appointment) enclosed; oath & bond
  required.

1438   15 Oct 1804   A/1/219
Samuel Finley, Rec Chl; James Findlay, Rec Cin;
  Benjamin Tupper, Rec Mar; Elijah Backus, Rec
  Kas; Frederick Bates, Rec Det
Order transferring funds from named Collectors of
  Revenue to Receivers
John G. Macan, Chl; James Smith, Cin; Griffin
  Green, Mar; Robert Morrison, Kas; Peter
  Audrain, Det.

1439   16 Oct 1804   A/1/219
David Hoge, Reg Stu
Opening of roads in Stu district; opening of
  road from Graves Creek to Lancaster
Thomas Gray.

1440   16 Oct 1804   A/1/220
Jesse Spencer, Reg Chl
Opening of roads.

1441   16 Oct 1804   A/1/220
Richard Claiborne, Clerk, Board of Commissioners
  [Mississippi Territory]
Instructions; transfer of funds
-- Rodney; -- Voss.

1442   16 Oct 1804   A/1/221
Willys Silliman, Reg Zan
Act of 10 May 1800, §7; instructions as to dut-
  ies, etc.

1443   16 Oct 1804   A/1/223
Thomas Van Swearingen, Rec Zan
Instructions regarding accounting entries, etc.
  [this statement important as explanation of
  accounting details required by GLO].

1444   17 Oct 1804   A/1/228
Willys Silliman, Reg Zan
Sales accounting required.

1445   18 Oct 1804 A/1/229
Charles Killgore, Reg Cin
Sales accounting required.

1446   18 Oct 1804 A/1/229
Charles Killgore, Reg Cin
Discounting of first instalments; Act of -- May
 1800; pre-emptions under Symmes' Grant.

1447   19 Oct 1804 A/1/230
Willys Silliman, Reg Zan
Act of -- May 1800; purchasers of whole, half, &
 quarter sections; division of whole sections.

1448   23 Oct 1804 A/1/230
William B. Shields, Agent for Investigating Claims,
 Washington, Mississippi Territory
Payment of witnesses.

1449   2 Nov 1804 A/1/231
Samuel Finley, Rec Chl
Transfer of funds
David Ziegler, Marshal of District of Ohio.

1450   5 Nov 1804 A/1/231
William B. Shields, Agent for Investigating Claims,
 Washington, Mississippi Territory
Transmits letter from U.S. President
Governor -- Claiborne.

1451   5 Nov 1804 A/1/231
Benjamin Tupper, Rec Mar
Refund of monies
-- Matthew; -- Zane.

1452   5 Nov 1804 A/1/232
Thomas Fitzpatrick, Reg WPR, Adams County, Mississippi Territory
Transmits commission (appointment); oath & bond
 required [letter mentions a predecessor].

1453   7 Nov 1804 A/1/232
David Hoge, Reg Stu
Land application suspended
David Vance "of Ohio" Stu - 3 7 31 -

1454   16 Nov 1804 A/1/233
Thomas Fitzpatrick, Reg WPR, Adams County, Mississippi Territory
Transmits copy of instructions previously sent to
 predecessor on 27 Jul 1803.

1455   16 Nov 1804 A/1/233
Samuel Finley, Rec Chl
Transfer of funds
Jared Mansfield, SG.

1456   16 Nov 1804 A/1/233
Benjamin Tupper, Rec Mar
Transfer of funds
Jared Mansfield, SG

1457   16 Nov 1804 A/1/234
Charles Killgore, Reg Cin; James Findlay, Rec
 Cin; Jesse Spencer, Reg Chl; Samuel Finley,
 Rec Chl
Instructions.

1458   16 Nov 1804 A/1/234
James Findlay, Rec Cin
Transfer of funds
Jared Mansfield, SG.

1459   19 Nov 1804 A/1/235
David Hoge, Reg Stu
Opening of road from Grave Creek to Lancaster
John Badollet, Reg Vin.

1460   24 Nov 1804 A/1/235
Jesse Spencer, Reg Chl
Transfer of funds; opening of road to Hockhock-
 ing.

1461   24 Nov 1804 A/1/236
Samuel Finley, Rec Chl
Transfer of funds
Jared Mansfield, SG.

1462   24 Nov 1804 A/1/237
Benjamin Tupper, Rec Mar
Transfer of funds
Jared Mansfield, SG.

1463   28 Nov 1804 A/1/237
Joseph Wood, Reg Mar; Benjamin Tupper, Rec Mar;
 David Hoge, Reg Stu; Zaccheus Biggs, Rec Stu
Instructions.

1464   6 Dec 1804 A/1/238
David Hoge, Reg Stu
Conflicting claims
John Connell; David Vance.

1465   10 Dec 1804 A/1/238
Joseph Chambers, Reg EPR, Hobukintoopa, [Missis-
 sippi Territory?]
Death of -- Kirby; failure to sign certificates;
 failure of Board of Commissioners to complete
 its assigned business
-- Nicholas.

1466   13 Dec 1804 A/1/240
Charles Killgore, Reg Cin
Pre-emption right under contracts with Judge John
 Cleves Symmes.

1467   17 Dec 1804 A/1/241
Willys Silliman, Reg Zan
Contested sale; fractional sections.

1468   28 Dec 1804 A/1/242
Frederick Bates, Rec Det
Transmits commission (appointment); oath & bond
 required.

1469   28 Dec 1804 A/1/243
Elijah Backus, Rec Kas
Transmits commission (appointment); oath & bond
 required.

1470   28 Dec 1804 A/1/243
Joseph Chambers, Reg EPR, Washington, Mississippi
 Territory
Transmits commission (appointment); oath & bond
 required; completion of work by Board of Commis-
 sioners; claims east of Tensaw; Choctaw claim
 considered frivolous
-- Nicholas.

1471   28 Dec 1804 A/1/244
John Badollet, Reg Vin; Michael Jones, Reg Kas;
 George Hoffman, Reg Det; Nathaniel Ewing, Rec
 Vin
Transmits commissions (appointments); oath & bond
 required.

1472   10 Dec 1804 A/1/245
Robert C. Nicholas, Commissioner, Lexington, Ken-
 tucky
British grants; request that Nicholas return to
 Mississippi Territory due to Kirby's death
-- Kirby; Joseph Chambers, Reg EPR.

1473   20 Dec 1804 A/1/246
Robert C. Nicholas, Commissioner, Lexington, Ken-
 tucky
Return to Mississippi Territory; land claims east
 of Tombigbee & island called Nannee-Hubla
-- Morrison.

1474   3 Jan 1805 A/1/247
Robert Williams, Commissioner, Washington, Missis-
 ippi Territory
Continuance on Board of Commissioners.

1475   5 Jan 1805 A/1/248
David Parmalee, Clerk of Board of Commissioners,
 EPR, Mississippi Territory
Continuance of Board's deliberations
Robert C. Nicholas; Joseph Chambers, Reg EPR.

1476   7 Jan 1805 A/1/248
Jesse Spencer, Reg Chl
First certificate
Gissel, Smith, & Miessa.

1477   21 Jan 1805 A/1/250
Circular letter to Ohio Registers & Receivers
Appointment of auditors to examine LO records
Philip Greene, Mar; William Creighton, Chl;
 Daniel Symmes, Cin; James Pritchard, Stu.

1478   2 Feb 1805 A/1/251
Joseph Wood, Reg Mar
Withdrawal of location
Matthias Noffinger.

1479   8 Mar 1805 A/1/252
James Findlay, Rec Cin
Transfer of funds to Pittsburgh, Office of Dis-
 count & Deposit of the Bank of Pennsylvania.

1480   8 Mar 1805 A/1/254
Samuel Finley, Rec Chl
Transfer of funds to Pittsburgh, Office of Discount
 & Deposit of the Bank of Pennsylvania.

1481   11 Mar 1805 A/1/255
Thomas Rodney, Robert Williams, & Thomas Hill Williams, Commissioners, EPR
Act to dispose of lands south of State of Tennessee; Act of 27 Mar 1804, §§1, 12; British
 grants; complaints of inhabitants of Washington
 County [Mississippi Territory].

1482   11 Mar 1805 A/1/256
David Parmalee, Clerk of Board of Commissioners,
 EPR
Act amending Act to dispose of lands south of
 State of Tennessee; transfer of funds.

1483   11 Mar 1805 A/1/258
Robert C. Nicholas & Joseph Chambers, Commission-
 ers, EPR
Settlement of claims EPR district.

1484   12 Mar 1805 A/1/258
Isaac Van Horn, Rec Zan
Transmits commission (appointment); oath & bond
 required.

1485   13 Mar 1805 A/1/258
George Hoffman, Reg Det; Michael Jones, Reg Kas;
 John Badollet, Reg Vin
Act supplementing an Act to dispose of lands in
 Indiana Territory.

1486   13 Mar 1805 A/1/260
Joseph Wood, Reg Mar; Willys Silliman, Reg Zan;
 Jesse Spencer, Reg Chl; Charles Killgore, Reg
 Cin; David Hoge, Reg Stu
Act concerning mode of surveying public lands;
 Act supplementing an Act to dispose of lands
 in Indiana Territory [see also explanatory let-
 ter of 15 Mar 1805 which follows on same page].

1487   16 Mar 1805 A/1/262
David Hoge, Reg Stu
Act of 1 May 1802, §7; withdrawal of application
James Lattimore   Stu - 3 8 2 -

1488   16 Mar 1805 A/1/262
Willys Silliman, Reg Zan
Land forfeiture.

1489   18 Mar 1805 A/1/263
Thomas Hill Williams, Reg, Washington, Mississippi
 Territory
Transmits commission (appointment); oath & bond
 required.

1490   18 Mar 1805   A/1/263
Thomas Hill Williams, Reg, Washington, Mississippi
  Territory
President requests him to accept office of Reg,
  previously declined
-- Turner; Robert Williams, Governor of Mississ-
  ippi Territory.

1491   25 Mar 1805   A/1/264
James Findlay, Rec Cin
Money deposited in branch Bank of Norfolk by Gov-
  ernor Harrison of Indiana Territory for purchase
  of lands; pre-emption lands
Daniel Symmes.

1492   30 Mar 1805   A/1/265
John Thompson, Reg WOr
Transmits commission (appointment); oath & bond
  required; boundary between EOr & WOr still undecided.

1493   30 Mar 1805   A/1/266
John W. Gurley, Reg EOr
Transmits commission (appointment); oath & bond
  required; boundary between EOr & WOr still undecided; French & Spanish grants; fraudulent
  grants in Upper Louisiana.

1494   3 Apr 1805   A/1/269
David Hoge, Reg Stu
Requires that books be posted currently [comment
  based upon auditing report].

1495   3 Apr 1805   A/1/269
Zaccheus Biggs, Rec Stu
Requires books to be posted currently [comment
  based upon auditing report].

1496   4 Apr 1805   A/1/270
James Findlay, Rec Cin
Comment on auditing report; accumulation of paper
  of the Kentucky Bank; transfer of funds to U.S.
  Army
Daniel Symmes; Major -- Swan; Capt. James Ster-
  rett.

1497   4 Apr 1805   A/1/270
Circular letter to all Receivers
Construction of Act of 26 Mar 1804, §11; instal-
  ment payments.

1498   17 Apr 1805   A/1/272
Zaccheus Biggs, Rec Stu; David Hoge, Reg Stu; SG
Act of 1 May 1802, §7
William Bell, purchaser at New York
Alteration of boundary line affecting following
  sections:

Stu	-	3	6 22	-
Stu	-	3	6 23	-
Stu	-	3	6 17	-
Stu	-	3	6 29	-

1499   23 Apr 1805   A/1/272
Thomas Rodney & other Commissioners, WPR, Washington, Mississippi Territory

Act of 27 Mar 1804, §5; Commissioners pre-
  sence, or absence, to be reported
-- Turner.

1500   25 Apr 1805   A/1/273
Thomas Van Swearingen, Rec Zan
Correction of accounting statement.

1501   25 Apr 1805   A/1/273
Samuel Finley, Rec Chl
Comments on tardiness of reporting; legal suit
  against Governor [Arthur] St. Clair.

1502   27 Apr 1805   A/1/274
James Findlay, Rec Cin "now at Pittsburgh"
Leave of absence granted
Major -- Swan.

1503   6 May 1805   A/1/274
Samuel Finley, Rec Chl
Transmits transcript of account with Governor
  [Arthur] St. Clair as Superintendent of Public
  Sales [see serial entry 1501].

1504   7 May 1805   A/1/275
Joseph Wood, Reg Mar
Ohio Company.

1505   8 May 1805   A/1/275
James L. Donaldson, Baltimore, Maryland
Transmits commission (appointment) as Recorder,
  Louisiana Territory; oath & bond required.

1506   9 May 1805   A/1/276
David Hoge, Reg Stu
Sale of forfeited lands; *The Scioto Gazette*; the
  Pittsburgh *Tree of Liberty*; rules for sale of
  forfeited lands.

1507   10 May 1805   A/1/279
James Tremble, Francis Vacher, Commissioners, WOr;
  Benjamin Sebastian, John Coburn, Commissioners,
  EOr; John B. C. Lucas, Clement C. Penrose,
  Commissioners for Louisiana Territory
Transmits commissions (appointments) as commis-
  sioners to investigate land claims; board for
  EOr to sit at New Orleans; board for WOr to
  sit either at Opelousas or on the Red River.

1508   13 May 1805   A/1/280
James L. Donaldson, Recorder, Louisiana Territory,
  [addressed to Baltimore, Maryland]
Bond approved.

1509   13 May 1805   A/1/281
James Findlay, Rec Cin
Transfer of funds
James Lowry Donaldson, Recorder of Land Titles,
  Louisiana Territory.

1510   13 May 1805   A/1/281
James Lowry Donaldson, Baltimore, Maryland
Instructions to be transmitted to Louisiana when
  sales of land are authorized.

1511   25 May 1805   A/1/282
James Findlay, Rec Cin
Complaint
John Smith   Cin - 10   1 11   -

1512   25 May 1805   A/1/282
Benjamin Tupper, Rec Mar
Repayment authorized because township not in Mar
    district [presumed to be in Zan district]
Archibald Woods & David
    Lockwood   Zan? -   3   5 11   +
Archibald Woods & David
    Lockwood   Zan? -   3   5   -   5

1513   27 May 1805   A/1/282
Francis Vacher, Commissioner, care of Dr. John F.
    Vacher, New York
Forwards information regarding appointment to
    Board of Commissioners, WOr, & his trip to that
    place.

1514   4 Jun 1805   A/1/283
Samuel Finley, Rec Chl
Transfer of funds
[Jared Mansfield] SG.

1515   4 Jun 1805   A/1/283
James Findlay, Rec Cin; Zaccheus Biggs, Rec Stu
Transfer of funds
[Jared Mansfield] SG.

1516   14 Jun 1805   A/1/284
W. B. Shields, Agent, Washington, Mississippi
    Territory
Confirmation of land titles under British or Span-
    ish grants by Articles of Agreement & Cession
    with State of Georgia.

1517   14 Jun 1805   A/1/285
James Findlay, Rec Cin
Pre-emption rights in reserved sections
[John] Smith.

1518   17 Jun 1805   A/1/287
George Hoffman, Reg Det
Bond approved.

1519   17 Jun 1805   A/1/287
Samuel Finley, Rec Chl
Reprimands failure to ship money to Pittsburgh as
    instructed.

1520   17 Jun 1805   A/1/287
Joseph Wood, Reg Mar
Final certificate
William Dusinberry.

1521   25 Jun 1805   A/1/288
Richard Claiborne, Clerk of Board of Commissioners,
    Washington, Mississippi Territory
Account
Andrew Marshalk.

1522   26 Jun 1805   A/1/288
Joseph Chambers, Reg, Washington County, Mississ-
    ippi Territory
Bond approved.

1523   26 Jun 1805   A/1/289
Samuel Finley, Rec Chl
Transfer of funds
Michael Baldwin, Marshal of Ohio District.

1524   2 Jul 1805   A/1/289
Zaccheus Biggs, Rec Chl
Transfer of funds to Office of Discount & Deposit,
    Pittsburgh, Pennsylvania
[Jared Mansfield] SG.

1525   2 Jul 1805   A/1/290
John Thompson, Louisville, Kentucky, Reg WOr
Bond approved; boundaries between EOr & WOr
    established by U.S. President; transfer of
    funds; French & Spanish grants; fraudulent
    grants in Upper Louisiana.

1526   5 Jul 1805   A/1/292
James Findlay, Rec Cin
Overpayment
William Barkalow   Cin WML   5   2 33   -

1527   5 Jul 1805   A/1/293
Willys Silliman, Reg Zan; Charles Killgore, Reg
    Cin; Jesse Spencer, Reg Chl; Joseph Wood, Reg
    Mar; David Hoge, Reg Stu; John Badollet, Reg
    Vin; Michael Jones, Reg Kas; George Hoffman,
    Reg Det
Circular letter regarding final certificates to
    assignees of purchasers.

1528   5 Jul 1805   A/1/294
David Hoge, Reg Stu
Revised survey of Seven Ranges.

1529   6 Jul 1805   A/1/295
Frederick Bates, Rec Det
No conflict seen between his position as judge &
    his position as Rec.

1530   8 Jul 1805   A/1/295
Francis Vacher, New York
Transfer of funds; boundaries between EOr & WOr
James Trimble of Tennessee; John Thompson of Ken-
    tucky.

1531   8 Jul 1805   A/1/296
Samuel Finley, Rec Chl; James Findlay, Rec Cin;
    Benjamin Tupper, Rec Mar
Act of 26 Mar 1804; instalment payments.

1532   8 Jul 1805   A/1/297
James Trimble, Knoxville, Tennessee
Transfer of funds; boundaries between EOr & WOr.

1533   8 Jul 1805   A/1/298
Allan B. Magruder of Kentucky, Agent WOr; James
Brown, District Attorney of New Orleans, Agent
EOr; Felix Grundy of Kentucky, Agent, Louisiana
District
Instructions & appointments as agents of United
  States for investigating land claims; large
  grant on Washita River of Baron Bapstrop [Bas-
  trop]; large grant of Marquis Grandmaison, now
  claimed by Daniel Clark
John W. Gurley, Reg EOr; John Thompson, Reg WOr.

1534   9 Jul 1805   A/1/300
John W. Gurley, Reg EOr
Transcripts of existing land records
James Brown, U.S. District Attorney.

1535   9 Jul 1805   A/1/301
Thomas H. Williams, Reg, Washington, Mississippi
  Territory
Notice accompanying evidence of claim.

1536   9 Jul 1805   A/1/302
[Felix Grundy], Agent, Louisiana Territory
Fraudulent grants in Louisiana Territory "said to
  be granted by the last two governors"
Ant[oine] Soulard, former surveyor of Louisiana.

1537   9 Jul 1805   A/1/303
W. B. Shields, Agent, Washington, Mississippi
  Territory
Settling of account
James Brown, Agent EOr;   -- Ybanez.

1538   10 Jul 1805   A/1/304
Jesse Spencer, Reg Chl
Final certificate correction
Mathew's Survey; Worthington's Survey
James Martin   Chl MS? 21 9 28 +
Winn Winship   Chl WS? 21 10 12 +

1539   11 Jul 1805   A/1/304
David Hoge, Reg Stu; Joseph Wood, Reg Mar; Jesse
  Spencer, Reg Chl; Charles Killgore, Reg Cin
Act of 18 May 1796, §3; Act of 30 Apr 1802, §7;
  reserved sections (no. 16) for schools.

1540   12 Jul 1805   A/1/306
David Hoge, Reg Stu; Joseph Wood, Reg Mar; Jesse
  Spencer, Reg Chl; Willys Silliman, Reg Zan;
  Charles Killgore, Reg Cin
Presidential proclamation regarding public sales
  of reserved sections.

1541   13 Jul 1805   A/1/307
Willys Silliman, Reg Zan
Reserved sections in lieu of section 16 of each
  township.

1542   13 Jul 1805   A/1/308
Charles Killgore, Reg Cin
Reserved sections in Symmes grant.

1543   13 Jul 1805   A/1/308
Joseph Wood, Reg Mar
Reserved sections in lieu of sections 16 [in each
  township] already sold; Ohio Company
-- Tallmadge, U.S. Representative

Section already sold	Mar	-	8	3	16	-
Section already sold	Mar	-	9	3	16	-
Section already sold	Mar	-	10	4	16	-
Section already sold	Mar	-	11	8	16	-
Section already sold	Mar	-	8	4	-	16
Section already sold	Mar	-	9	4	-	16
Section already sold	Mar	-	10	5	-	16
Replacement reserve section	Mar	-	8	3	8	-
Replacement reserve section	Mar	-	9	3	8	-
Replacement reserve section	Mar	-	10	4	8	-
Replacement reserve section	Mar	-	11	8	8	-
Replacement reserve section	Mar	-	8	4	-	+
Replacement reserve section	Mar	-	11	9	-	+
Section already sold	Mar	-	12	8	16	-
Section already sold	Mar	-	13	7	16	-
Section already sold	Mar	-	14	11	16	-
Section already sold	Mar	-	15	13	16	-
Section already sold	Mar	-	16	8	16	-
Section already sold	Mar	-	16	9	16	-
Section already sold	Mar	-	16	10	16	-
Section already sold	Mar	-	16	11	16	-
Section already sold	Mar	-	16	12	16	-
Section already sold	Mar	-	16	13	16	-
Replacement reserve section	Mar	-	12	8	8	-
Replacement reserve section	Mar	-	13	7	8	-
Replacement reserve section	Mar	-	14	11	8	-
Replacement reserve section	Mar	-	15	13	8	-
Replacement reserve section	Mar	-	15	8	26	-
Replacement reserve section	Mar	-	15	9	26	-
Replacement reserve section	Mar	-	15	10	26	-
Replacement reserve section	Mar	-	15	11	26	-
Replacement reserve section	Mar	-	15	12	26	-
Replacement reserve section	Mar	-	15	13	26	-

1544   15 Jul 1805   A/1/310
John W. Gurley, Reg EOr;   John Thompson, Reg WOr
Grant to Major General La Fayette
-- Briggs.

1545   24 Jul 1805   A/1/312
John W. Gurley, Reg WOr
Transcript of Spanish land records.

1546   2 Aug 1805   A/1/313
Samuel Finley, Rec Chl
Jurisdiction of U.S. Government in State of Ohio;
  prosecution for trespass [on federal lands]
-- Waller; -- Gallagher.

1547   2 Aug 1805   A/1/314
Joseph Wood, Reg Mar
Act of 26 Mar 1804; fractional sections; reserved
    sections.

1548   5 Aug 1805   A/1/314
Benedict Van Pradelles, "now at New Orleans," Com-
    missioner to investigate land claims in EOr
Transmits commission (appointment): oath & bond
    required
John W. Gurley.

1549   20 Aug 1805   A/1/316
David Hoge, Reg Stu
School [or reserved] sections number 16.

1550   27 Aug 1805   A/1/316
John Thompson, Louisville, Kentucky, Reg WOr
Opelousas selected as office site.

1551   20 Aug 1805   A/1/317
Charles Killgore, Reg Cin
Pre-emption rights under John Cleves Symmes
Peyton Short.

1552   3 Oct 1805   A/1/318
Samuel Finley, Rec Chl
Payment of three-percent allowance to State of
    Ohio
William McFarland, Treasurer, State of Ohio.

1553   3 Oct 1805   A/1/319
Samuel Finley, Rec Chl
Transfer of funds
Michael Baldwin, Marshal of Ohio [District].

1554   4 Oct 1805   A/1/319
Jesse Spencer, Reg Chl
Method of computing payments on certain final
    certificates.

1555   5 Oct 1805   A/1/323
David Hoge, Reg Stu
Substitution of reserved sections
Reserved section already
    sold   Stu - 3 7 - 16
Substituted reserve sec-
    tion   Stu - 3 7 15 +

1556   5 Oct 1805   A/1/323
James Findlay, Rec Cin
Error in account
Joseph Dodds, assignee
John Haggin   Cin Pre 6 1 15 -

1557   5 Oct 1805   A/1/324
Willys Silliman, Reg Zan
Application
Gilbert Seaman

1558   7 Oct 1805   A/1/325
David Hoge, Reg Stu
Act of 1 May 1802, §7; Act of 10 May 1800; chang-
    ing of boundaries to effect following sections:
                      Stu - 2 8 - -
                      Stu - 2 8 9 -
                      Stu - 2 8 10 -
                      Stu - 2 8 15 -
                      Stu - 2 8 16 -
                      Stu - 2 8 3 -
                      Stu - 2 8 4 -
                      Stu - 2 8 9 -
                      Stu - 2 8 10 -

1559   10 Oct 1805   A/1/325
James Brown, Agent, New Orleans
Division between EOr & WOr; quiet possession;
    fraudulent claims
John W. Gurley.

1560   10 Oct 1805   A/1/326
John W. Gurley, Reg EOr
Robbery of U.S. mails.

1561   21 Oct 1805   A/1/326
Charles Killgore, Reg Cin
Approves sections selected in lieu of reserved
    sections.

1562   21 Oct 1805   A/1/327
James Findlay, Rec Cin
Transfer of funds
Jared Mansfield, SG.

1563   23 Oct 1805   A/1/328
John Badollet, Reg Vin; Michael Jones, Reg Kas
Act of 3 Mar 1791; militia grants; Congressional
    Resolution of 20 Jun 1788; Congressional Resolu-
    tion of 29 Aug 1788; donation tracts at Vin &
    in Illinois Territory; Illinois & Wabash Com-
    panies have no valid title; Indian titles in-
    valid without a treaty; Proclamation of 1763
    by the King of Great Britain.

1564   31 Oct 1805   A/1/329
Joseph Chambers, Reg EPR, Fort St. Stephens, Miss-
    issippi Territory
Forms for record-keeping; pre-emption certificates;
    rights of transferees.

1565   4 Nov 1805   A/1/330
James Findlay, Rec Cin
Draft payable to drowned man [Vacher] was cashed
    by an impersonator
Francis Vacher of New York.

1566   5 Nov 1805   A/1/331
James Brown, Agent at New Orleans, [by] Natchez
    mail
Claim of -- Ibanez; post road via Mobile &
    Georgia too uncertain for use.

1567   5 Nov 1805   A/1/331
Thomas H. Williams, Reg WPR, Washington, Mississippi Territory
Act of 10 May 1804; pre-emption rights of certificate holders in Mississippi Territory; forfeitures; donation lands only to actual settlers; holders of British & Spanish complete grants not considered settlers; Act of 3 Mar 1803; *National Intelligencer*
S. H. Smith.

1568   5 Nov 1805   A/1/333
Thomas H. Williams, Reg WPR, Washington, Mississippi Territory
Act of 27 Mar 1804; proof of attendance of Board of Commissioners
-- Rodney.

1569   8 Nov 1805   A/1/334
Jesse Spencer, Reg Chl
First & final certificates in joint names causing problems of inheritance; Act of 26 Mar 1804
Joseph Stewart & Henry Abrams; Samuel Spurgeon & Henry Doane?; Samuel Kratzer & Ludowick Bonsey; -- Loveland & -- Smith, assign to Henry Abrams.

1570   11 Nov 1805   A/1/335
Jesse Spencer, Reg Chl
Authorization to substitute other sections for section number 16 as reserved sections.

1571   18 Nov 1805   A/1/335
Zaccheus Biggs, Rec Stu; Benjamin Tupper, Rec Mar; Isaac Van Horn, Rec Zan; Samuel Finley, Rec Chl; James Findlay, Rec Cin
Circular letter regarding shortages in payments
John R. Mills of Cin township.

1572   23 Nov 1805   A/1/336
John Thompson, Reg WOr, Opelousas
Transfer of funds.

1573   26 Nov 1805   A/1/336
Thomas Walker Maury, Rec EPR, Lindsey's store, Virginia
Appointment as Rec EPR; oath & bond required.

1574   29 Nov 1805   A/1/337
Thomas Walker Maury, Rec EPR, Lindsey's store, Albemarle County, Virginia
Instructions.

1575   10 Dec 1805   A/1/337
Joseph Chambers, Reg EPR
Instructions.

1576   10 Dec 1805   A/1/338
David Hoge, Reg Stu
Complications in a particular case of assignment
John Connell; -- Barr; -- Vance.

1577   13 Dec 1805   A/1/339
Thomas Walker Maury, Rec EPR

Packet to be delivered to Joseph Chambers, Reg EPR, Fort St. Stephens, Mississippi Territory.

1578   19 Dec 1805   A/1/339
James Findlay, Rec Cin
Instructions regarding endorsements to drafts.

1579   19 Dec 1805   A/1/340
Charles Killgore, Reg Cin
No land location to be changed, excepting by special act of Congress.

1580   23 Dec 1805   A/1/340
John Badollet, Reg Vin
"Sugar-camp rights"; grants made by the Governor; militia donation tracts.

1581   27 Dec 1805   A/1/341
Joseph Wood, Reg Mar
Newly-discovered fractional sections
Smith was assignee of Elijah Hunt, assignee of James Ross who was purchaser at Pittsburgh; public sale [at Mar?] of May 1804

Henry Smith	Mar	-	5	1 24	-
Henry Smith	Mar	-	5	1	- 18
William Shinner? [Skinner]	Mar	-	5	1	- 17

1582   30 Dec 1805   A/1/342
David Hoge, Reg Stu
Isaac Thorn, deceased, executors William & Thomas Thorn

Isaac Thorn	Stu	-	2 12	3	-

1583   4 Jan 1806   A/1/342
Isaac Van Horn, Rec Zan
Instructions regarding monthly report.

1584   9 Jan 1806   A/1/343
Zaccheus Biggs, Rec Stu
Complaint filed at Washington against clerks employed by Biggs alleged to deal in stock & delay receipt of specie payment; bribery implied.

1585   10 Jan 1806   A/1/343
James Findlay, Rec Cin
Petition before Congress.

1586   5 Feb 1806   A/1/344
Joshua Lewis, Benedict van Pradelles, & John W. Gurley, Commissioners, EOr
Appointment of translator for French & Spanish languages; method of transferring funds.

1587   26 Feb 1806   A/1/344
Thomas W. Maury, Rec EPR, now at Lindsey's store, [Albemarle County], Virginia
"Congress has not yet acted upon the subject of payments for lands in Mississippi Territory."

1588   27 Feb 1806   A/1/345
Samuel Finley, Rec Chl
Transfer of funds.

1589   27 Feb 1806   A/1/345
Willys Silliman, Reg Zan
Settlement of conflict in case of two applications
  for the same tract.

1590   6 Mar 1806   A/1/345
John W. Gurley, Reg EOr
Contingency fund inadmissible.

1591   7 Mar 1806   A/1/345
Charles Killgore, Reg Cin
Final certificate underpayment; Act of 26 Mar
  1804.
John Rippey   Cin Pre 4   4 35   -

1592   6 Mar 1806   A/1/347
Willys Silliman, Reg Zan
Instructions regarding re-entry.

1593   13 Mar 1806   A/1/347
Jesse Spencer, Reg Chl
Final certificates for correction
Christopher Cagy   Chl - 18 15 13   +
Major Bright   Chl - 20 14 12   +
Elizabeth Taylor & Ben-
  jamin Kepner   Chl - 20 11   6   -
Jacob Pebler   Chl - 18 15 35   +

1594   17 Mar 1806   A/1/347
Isaac Van Horn, Rec Zan
Transfer of funds to bank at Pittsburgh.

1595   20 Mar 1806   A/1/348
James L. Donaldson, Recorder of Land Titles for
  Territory of Louisiana
Commission (appointment); bond required.

1596   30 Mar 1806   A/1/348
Nicholas Perkins, Reg EPR, Washington County, Miss-
  issippi Territory
Commission (appointment); oath & bond required.

1597   25 Mar 1806   A/1/349
John B. C. Lucas, James L. Donaldson, Clement B.
  Penrose, Commissioners of Land Claims, Louisiana
  Territory
Act extending powers of SG to Territory of Louisi-
  ana . . .; deputy SG to be appointed by Jared
  Mansfield, SG; plats to be submitted by claim-
  ants; abstract of New Orleans land records;
  contrary to treaty, part of Spanish Intendant's
  records removed to Pensacola
-- Soulard.

1598   26 Mar 1806   A/1/350
John B. C. Lucas, James L. Donaldson, Clement B.
  Penrose, Commissioners of Land Claims, Louisiana
  Territory
"Two of your decisions which appeared injurious to
  the United States & contrary to the true intents
  . . . of law" have been examined by the U.S.
  Attorney General & laid before the President of
  the United States; quantity of land allowable

to actual settlers; permission to settle
lands.

1599   31 Mar 1806   A/1/351
Thomas W. Maury, Rec EPR, now at Lindsey's store,
  [Albemarle County], Virginia
Transmits commission (appointment); new bond re-
quired.

1600   31 Mar 1806   A/1/352
John W. Gurley, Reg EOr
Transmits commission (appointment); new bond re-
quired.

1601   31 Mar 1806   A/1/352
John Thompson, Reg WOr
Transmits commission (appointment); bond re-
quired.

1602   3 Mar 1806   A/1/353
Isaac Van Horn, Rec Zan
Transmits new commission (appointment); bond re-
quired.

1603   4 Apr 1806   A/1/353
James Findlay, Rec Cin
Error in discount calculation
John Ozias   Cin EML 3   6 10   -

1604   19 Apr 1806   A/1/353
Jesse Spencer, Reg Chl
Road from Lancaster to Dayton to pass through
  Xenia; extension to Kas
-- Worthington.

1605   22 Apr 1806   A/1/354
[Zaccheus Biggs], Rec Stu; [Samuel Finley], Rec
  Stu; [Benjamin Tupper], Rec Mar; [Isaac Van
  Horn], Rec Zan
Act of 16 Apr 1806, §1; U.S. stock.

1606   22 Apr 1806   A/1/355
[Jesse Spencer], Reg Chl; [Charles Killgore],
  Reg Cin; [Joseph Wood], Reg Mar; [Willys
  Silliman], Reg Zan
Regulations for sale of lands on failure of orig-
  inal purchaser to pay purchase price [forfeit-
  ure]; encloses act to suspend sale of certain
  lands temporarily.

1607   22 Apr 1806   A/1/356
David Hoge, Reg Stu
Encloses act to suspend sales of certain lands
  temporarily.

1608   23 Apr 1806   A/1/356
David Parmelee, Commissioner of Land Titles, Or-
  leans Territory, care of D. Gallston, Collector,
  New York
Appointment of deputy registers; Board of Commis-
  sioners at WOr to be reduced to two members
[John W.] Gurley; [John] Thompson.

1609   24 Apr 1806 A/1/356
Thomas W. Maury, Rec EPR, Lindsey's store, [Albe-
 marle County], Virginia
Pre-emption rights; bond required.

1610   24 Apr 1806 A/1/357
Thomas Rodney, Robert Williams, & Thomas H. Wil-
 liams, Commissioners, WPR
Adverse British grants
Governor -- Williams.

1611   24 Apr 1806 A/1/358
W. B. Shields, Agent, Washington, Mississippi Territory
Transmits additional act [not described] of interest.

1612   24 Apr 1806 A/1/359
Nicholas Perkins, Reg EPR
Surveying of British grants
Thomas H. Williams.

1613   25 Apr 1806 A/1/359
Jesse Spencer, Reg Chl
Final certificate
Transfer to Winship & Baylor by Noah Zane; Joseph
 Ruffner
Winn Winship & Jacob Baylor Chl - 19 15 27 -

1614   30 Apr 1806 A/1/360
Samuel Finley, Rec Chl; James Findlay, Rec Cin
Transportation of accumulated funds to Pittsburgh
 for deposit in the Office of Discount & Deposit.

1615   2 May 1806 A/1/360
All Rec & Reg, Mar, Chl, Cin, Stu, Zan
Audit of funds & accounts
Philip Greene, Mar; William Creighton, Chl; Dan-
 iel Symmes, Cin; James Pritchard, Stu; William
 Wells, Zan.

1616   2 May 1806 A/1/361
Daniel Symmes, Cin; William Creighton, Chl;
 Philip Greene, Mar; James Pritchard, Stu; Wil-
 liam Wells, Zan
Instructions regarding audits of accounts & books
 of Reg & Rec.

1617   2 May 1806 A/1/363
Peter Audrain, Reg Det
Transmits commission (appointment); oath & bond
 required.

1618   2 May 1806 A/1/364
John Badollet, Reg Vin
Laying out of new tracts of land, as required under
 §1 of Act respecting claims of land in Indiana
 Territory; location of college township.

1619   5 May 1806 A/1/365
James Findlay, Rec Cin
Transfer of funds to SG.

1620   5 May 1806 A/1/365
Michael Jones, Elijah Bacchus, Commissioners, Kas
Requests precise statement of lands claimed under
 French & British grants; survey of townships
 east of Mississippi River; many fraudulent
 claims in Kas district; donations to heads of
 family & militia; authority of local French
 commandants to grant title to land considered
 doubtful; New Orleans records.

1621   5 May 1806 A/1/367
Allan B. Magruder, Agent, Opelousas [WOr]
Discontinuance of office of agent in WOr.

1622   5 May 1806 A/1/367
Francis Vacher, Commissioner, Opelousas [WOr]
Removal from office.

1623   5 May 1806 A/1/367
John W. Gurley, Reg EOr; John Thompson, Reg WOr
Act supplementary to an act entitled "An Act for
 ascertaining & adjusting the titles & claims
 within the territory of Orleans . . ."; lib-
 eralizing intent of Congress; appointment of
 deputy registers; grant to General La Fayette;
 "Mr. Vacher's conduct has induced the President
 to remove him. . . ."
-- Parmelye, "late clerk of Mobile board"; --
 Magruder discontinued because of intemperance.

1624   6 May 1806 A/1/369
Charles Killgore, Reg Cin
Final certificate
John Vance   Cin - 5 4 - 18
John Vance   Cin - 5 4 - 24
John Vannuys & Isaac
 Paxton   Cin Pre 5 4 - 21

1625   6 May 1806 A/1/369
John Thompson, Reg WOr
Access to records; incomplete titles; transfer
 of funds
James Brown, agent, New Orleans.

1626   7 May 1806 A/1/370
William C. Carr, agent, St. Louis
Act of 2 Mar 1805, §6; lead mines; Act supplementary to an act entitled "An Act for ascertaining & adjusting the titles & claims to land
 within the territory of Orleans & the District
 of Louisiana."

1627   7 May 1806 A/1/371
John B. C. Lucas, Clement B. Penrose, James L.
 Donaldson, Commissioners, St. Louis
Conditions under which permission to settle shall
 be presumed; claims of minors; New Madrid
 representation; strict conformity to law en-
 joined; time for presenting claims not extended.

1628   8 May 1806 A/1/372
James Stille, Clerk, Land Commissioners, New Orleans
Compensation.

1629   9 May 1806   A/1/372
Thomas Rodney, Commissioner, Washington, Mississippi Territory
Query regarding expenditure
Garret, Wood & Co. of Natchez.

1630   9 May 1806   A/1/373
James L. Donaldson, Record of Land Titles, St. Louis
Authorization for expenditure.

1631   10 May 1806   A/1/373
John Henderson, Rec WPR
Transmits commission (appointment); oath & bond required; payment in stock for public lands sold in Mississippi Territory has not been authorized.

1632   12 May 1806   A/1/374
David Hoge, Reg Stu
Transmits patent "in the name of 'David Barr in trust for such person or persons to whom he has assigned his right.' Had David Vance . . . completed the payments, I would have directed the patent to issue in his name . . ."
John Connell

David Barr		Stu	–	3	7 30	–

1633   14 May 1806   A/1/374
James Findlay, Rec Cin
Discrepancy in account

Benjamin Maltbie	Cin	Pre	5	2 4	+

1634   14 May 1806   A/1/374
John Badollet, Reg Vin
Road from Mississippi River to Ohio River (St. Louis, Vin, Dayton); road from Kas to Vin & other branches
Governor -- Harrison.

1635   16 May 1806   A/1/375
Charles Gratiot, Clerk of Board of Commissioners, St. Louis
Authorization for expenditure.

1636   23 Jun 1806   A/1/376
[Zaccheus Biggs], Rec Stu; [Samuel Finley], Rec Chl; [James Findlay], Rec Cin; [Benjamin Tupper], Rec Mar; [Isaac Van Horn], Rec Zan
Act of 18 Apr 1806, §1; market price of six per cent [U.S.] stock.

1637   24 Jun 1806   A/1/376
Benjamin Tupper, Rec Mar
Authorized to bring public monies to Washington.

1638   1 Jul 1806   A/1/377
James Pritchard, Stu; Philip Greene, Mar
Acknowledges receipt of audit report.

1639   3 Jul 1806   A/1/377
Zaccheus Biggs, Rec Stu; Samuel Finley, Rec Chl;
Isaac Van Horn, Rec Zan
Transfer of funds to SG.

1640   7 Jul 1806   A/1/378
Thomas H. Williams, Reg WPR, Washington, Mississippi Territory
Importance of an early sale of public lands noted -- Briggs.

1641   10 Jul 1806   A/1/378
Charles Killgore, Reg Cin
Survey book needed, per audit report
Daniel Symmes.

1642   11 Jul 1806   A/1/379
Charles Killgore, Reg Cin
Final certificate (pre-emption) suspended
Edward Dearth.

1643   16 Jul 1806   A/1/379
Daniel Symmes, Cin; William Wells, Zan
Acknowledges receipt of audit report.

1644   6 Aug 1806   A/1/380
John Thompson, Reg WOr
"So far as I can judge, your conduct has been perfectly correct. . . ."

1645   15 Aug 1806   A/1/380
Samuel Finley, Rec Chl
Three percent allowance to State of Ohio covering period 1 Jul 1804 to 30 Jun 1806
William McFarland, Treasurer of the State of Ohio.

1646   16 Aug 1806   A/1/380
John Badollet & Nathaniel Ewing, Commissioners for Land Claims, Vin
Tracts set aside to satisfy former claims; college township; French & British grants; Act of 21 Apr 1806, §2.

1647   19 Aug 1806   A/1/382
Charles Killgore, Reg Cin
-- Cadbury's application.

1648   21 Aug 1806   A/1/383
David Hoge, Reg Stu
Public auction sale at New York; "a patent will I presume issue on his applying to the Department of State for the same"

Arnold H. Dohrman	Stu?	–	2	5	2	–

1649   22 Aug 1806   A/1/383
William Creighton, Chl
Acknowledges receipt of audit report & asks for recount of cash on hand.

1650   26 Aug 1806   A/1/383
Peter Audrain, Reg Det
Bond found inadmissible.

1651   14 Aug 1806   A/1/384
John Badollet, Reg Vin
Roads in Indiana Territory [important discussion
  of various routes]; transfer of funds
Governor [William H.] Harrison.

1652   25 Aug 1806   A/1/387
M. P. Leduc, Interpreter, Board of Land Commission-
  ers, St. Louis
Payment of bills.

1653   8 Sep 1806   A/1/387
William C. Carr, Agent, St. Louis
Acknowledges receipt of letter, but U.S. President
  in Bedford County, Virginia, & decision must
  wait.

1654   8 Sep 1806   A/1/387
J. B. C. Lucas, C. B. Penrose, J. L. Donaldson,
  Commissioners of Land Claims, St. Louis
Act supplementary to "An Act for ascertaining &
  adjusting the titles & claims to land within
  the Territory of Orleans & the District of
  Louisiana" [see important instructions which
  were enclosed with this letter at A/1/392:
  claims incomplete on 1 Oct 1800 to be rejected;
  French & Spanish titles; land must have been
  occupied; Act of 2 Mar 1805, §1; U.S. Attorney
  General's opinion of 12 Mar 1806].

1655   11 Sep 1806   A/1/388
John Badollet & Nathaniel Ewing, Vin
Act of 21 Apr 1806; " . . . tracts which you pro-
  pose to reserve contain much more land than is
  necessary to satisfy unlocated claims"
Discussed in letter   Vin - 10 1S - -
Discussed in letter   Vin - 10 1N - -
Discussed in letter   Vin - 9 1N - -
Discussed in letter   Vin - 7 3N - -
Discussed in letter   Vin - 7 4N - -
Discussed in letter   Vin - 7 5N - -

1656   12 Sep 1806   A/1/389
J. N. Gurley & B. van Pradelles, Land Commissioners
  at New Orleans
Suspension of transcript of proceedings approved;
  appointment of one of the Commissioners to the
  office of clerk disapproved.

1657   12 Sep 1806   A/1/389
John Thompson, Reg WOr, Opelousas
Act of 2 Mar 1805, §§3, 4, 5, 6; Act of 21 Apr
  1806, §6; compensation to Registers [important
  summary of compensation policies]; compensation to Interpreters & Commissioners of Land
  Claims; claims to land should be received liber-
  ally but investigated strictly according to law.

1658   12 Sep 1806   A/1/390
Thomas H. Williams, Reg WPR [addressed herein as
  Reg, Mississippi Territory]
Compensation of Registers.

1659   13 Sep 1806   A/1/391
Samuel Finley, Rec Chl

Receipt
Thomas Worthington.

1660   7 Oct 1806   A/1/394
Charles Killgore, Reg Cin
"It has been stated to this department that in
  some instances you have prevented persons from
  entering land which they had intended to purchase by giving them erroneous information that
  the land had been previously entered"; ". . .
  it is also generally mentioned that fees have
  been demanded for a mere & accidental sight of
  the office map"
Abraham Rall
Alexander Kirkpatrick vs
  James McLellan   Cin EML 2 4 20 +

1661   10 Oct 1806   A/1/394
John Badollet, Reg Vin
Designates township for "seminary of learning"
Seminary of learning Vin - 11W 2S - -

1662   11 Oct 1806   A/1/394
John Badollet, Nathaniel Ewing, Vin
Presidential proclamation fixing time of sale of
  public land at Vin; private claims; college
  township; salt springs; school sections (number 16 of each township); Act of 26 Mar 1804,
  §6; Wabash River coal deposit
Governor [William H.] Harrison.

1663   14 Oct 1806   A/1/395
Jesse Spencer, Reg Chl
Discrepancy in final certificate
Jesse Spencer (as grantee)
Winn Winship   Chl - 20 12 31 +

1664   15 Oct 1806   A/1/396
Isaac Briggs, Surveyor General, Washington, Miss-
  issippi Territory
Advances of funds to deputy surveyors in Orleans
  Territory.

1665   15 Oct 1806   A/1/396
[Samuel Finley], Rec Chl; [Benjamin Tupper], Rec
  Mar; [Zaccheus Biggs], Rec Stu
Transport of funds to Office of Discount & Deposit,
  Pittsburgh.

1666   15 Oct 1806   A/1/397
Jesse Spencer, Reg Chl
Discrepancy in computation of discount on final
  certificate 208 [name not given].

1667   1 Nov 1806   A/1/397
David Hoge, Reg Stu
"It has been stated . . . that persons wishing to
  purchase [tract described below] are prevented
  from so doing by reason of some affidavit lodged
  by a former purchaser stating there was a salt
  spring on the land. The assertion is now denied . . ."
Benjamin Hough
Not stated   Stu - 3 11 33 -

1668   6 Nov 1806   A/1/398
William C. Carr, Agent, St. Louis
Requests return of previous instructions for ascer-
taining title to lands in Louisiana Territory.

1669   14 Nov 1806   A/1/398
John B. C. Lucas, Clement B. Penrose, James L.
Donaldson, Commissioners, St. Louis
Act of 21 Apr 1806, §8; rules prescribed in rela-
tion to forms of the transcript of decisions in
favor of land claimants; French & Spanish titles;
warrants of survey under Act of 2 Mar 1805, §1;
claims derived from actual settlement on land;
[important basic instructions for Commission
deliberations].

1670   17 Nov 1806   A/1/400
William C. Carr, Agent, St. Louis
Calls attention to instructions sent to Commissioners [see entry 1669]; calls "particular
attention to the strong presumptions of fraud,
arising from the appearance of the records of
surveys lately disclosed to Mr. Bent."

1671   18 Nov 1806   A/1/401
Thomas H. Williams, Reg WPR
Pre-emption right to purchase land; Spanish
grants.

1672   19 Nov 1806   A/1/401
David Parmelee, Commissioner, Northern District of
Orleans Territory
Act of 3 Apr 1806.

1673   21 Nov 1806   A/1/402
James Findlay, Rec Cin
Duplicate receipt
John James Dufour (now in Europe).

1674   22 Nov 1806   A/1/402
Benjamin Tupper, Rec Mar
Liability for purchase of personal drafts.

1675   22 Nov 1806   A/1/402
Jesse Spencer, Reg Chl
Issues preliminary instructions regarding legality
of certain sales [not otherwise described].

1676   28 Nov 1806   A/1/403
Circular letter to all Registers, Supervisor of
Kentucky, & U.S. Agent at St. Louis
Presidential proclamation forwarded; "you are
also required to communicate . . . any information respecting the projected illegal expedition
or enterprize of which you may be possessed."

1677   12 Dec 1806   A/1/403
Charles Killgore, Reg Cin
Requires personal statement of facts, not deposi-
tions, regarding application of McLellan & Rall
[apparently an investigation of official conduct; see entry 1660]

McLellan *vs* Rall   Cin EML 2 4 28 +

1678   8 Dec 1806   A/1/404
John Badollet, Reg Vin
Authorizes expenditure for roadbuilding.

1679   12 Dec 1806   A/1/404
James Findlay, Rec Cin
Interest on instalment purchase of pre-emption
land.

1680   12 Dec 1806   A/1/404
Thomas H. Williams, Reg WPR
Orders an investigation of official conduct
George Davis, late assistant SG; -- Briggs; Wil-
liam Dunbar.

1681   19 Dec 1806   A/1/405
Charles Killgore, Reg Cin
Transmits patent; "I must also ask, whether in
cases where more land is surveyed than was ex-
pressed in the Commissioners' certificates, the
surplus is regularly charged to the parties"
Edmund Richardson   Cin Pre 4 4 27 +

1682   1 Jan 1807   A/1/405
John Thompson, Reg WOr
Calls attention to erroneous charge & payments.

1683   13 Jan 1807   A/1/405
Joshua Lewis, Benedict van Pradelles, & John W.
Gurley, Land Commissioners, District of Orleans
Directs inquiry into claim of the City of New
Orleans to certain commons extending from the
City to Bayou St. John.

1684   19 Jan 1807   A/1/406
John Badollet, Reg Vin
Construction of law [not described] would require
action by Congress "and not to the mere executive officers. . . ."

1685   19 Jan 1807   A/1/406
Charles Killgore, Reg Cin
Acknowledges receipt of letter & accepts explana-
tion given therein.

1686   19 Jan 1807   A/1/406
Nathaniel Ewing, Rec Vin; John Badollet, Reg Vin
Fractional sections adjoining Indian boundary not
to be sold in forthcoming public sale.

1687   19 Jan 1807   A/1/407
James Findlay, Rec Cin
Transfer of funds
Jared Mansfield, SG.

1688   24 Jan 1807   A/1/407
Thomas H. Williams, Reg WPR
Act of 26 Mar 1804; surveying expenses for pre-
emption tracts.

1689   6 Feb 1807   A/1/407
Michael Jones, Reg Kas
Authorizes transmittal to the Governor of Indiana
   Territory of a list of land claims filed [which
   Jones had previously refused to give the Gover-
   nor]; prohibited from indicating to Governor
   which claims rejected or confirmed; reasons
   for rejections must be filed with the Department
   of Treasury; "I embrace this opportunity to
   state that information has been received from
   several quarters of gross attempts being made to
   impose unfounded & fraudulent claims. . . ."

1690   6 Feb 1807   A/1/408
Thomas Walker Maury, Rec EPR, Fort St. Stephens
Act of 26 Mar 1804, §13; surveying expenses on
   pre-emption lands; Act of 11 Mar 1805, §3.

1691   10 Feb 1807   A/1/409
Benedict van Pradelles & John W. Gurley, Land Com-
   missioners, New Orleans
Compensation for Commissioners and translator.

1692   11 Feb 1807   A/1/409
Peter Audrain, Reg Det
Directs late claims to be made to Congress
-- Bates; -- Killburn.

1693   11 Feb 1807   A/1/409
John W. Gurley, Reg EOr
Land grant to General La Fayette; definition of
   improved lands; fortifications & surrounding
   lands come within meaning of act.

1694   13 Feb 1807   A/1/410
Jesse Spencer, Reg Chl
Late instalment
-- Forster.

1695   13 Feb 1807   A/1/410
Land Commissioners for Louisiana, St. Louis [John
   B. C. Lucas, Clement B. Penrose, James L. Donald-
   son]
Approves suggested suspension of activities pend-
   ing Congressional action; compensation.

1696   20 Feb 1807   A/1/411
[Michael Jones], Reg Kas; [Thomas H. Williams],
   Reg WPR; [Nicholas Perkins], Reg EPR; [Peter
   Audrain], Reg Det
Act of 26 Mar 1804, §9; fractional sections to be
   sold, singly or with others, at public auction.

1697   24 Feb 1807   A/1/411
Samuel Finley, Rec Chl
Transfer of funds to Treasurer of State of Ohio on
   account of three percent allowance, covering per-
   iod 30 Jun 1802 to 1 Jan 1807
William McFarland, Treasurer of State of Ohio

1698   24 Feb 1807   A/1/412
Peter Audrain, Reg Det
Compensation & repayment of debt incurred while
   Collector of Revenue at Detroit.

1699   25 Feb 1807   A/1/412
Nicholas Perkins, Reg EPR, Fort St. Stephens
Conversion of pre-emption claims into donations;
   compensation.

1700   25 Feb 1807   A/1/413
Thomas Walker Maury, Rec EPR, Fort St. Stephens
Compensation of Reg EPR
Nicholas Perkins, Reg EPR from 1 Jun 1806; Joseph
   Chambers, Reg EPR to 31 May 1806.

1701   3 Mar 1807   A/1/414
Ferdinand Ybanez, Translator to the Land Commis-
   sioners, New Orleans
Transfer of funds for salary.

1702   9 Mar 1807   A/1/413
John Badollet, Reg Vin
Notes new law regarding disposal of Vin lands;
   public sale at Vin; method of offering for
   sale; salt springs; coal mines.

1703   9 Mar 1807   A/1/415
John Henderson, Rec WPR
Public funds not to be used to purchase bills for
   remittance.

1704   18 Mar 1807   A/1/416
Levi Barber, Rec Mar
Transmits commission (appointment); oath & bond
   required.

1705   21 Mar 1807   A/1/416
Thomas M. Maury, Rec EPR, Fort St. Stephens
Extension of payment period on pre-emption claims.

1706   21 Mar 1807   A/1/417
John Henderson, Rec WPR
Extension of payment period on pre-emption claims;
   surveying fees; transfer of funds
Seth Pease, Surveyor of Public Lands South of
   Tennessee.

1706   23 Mar 1807   A/1/417
Benjamin Tupper, late Rec Mar
Closing of accounts; transfer of all funds to
   Office of Discount & Deposit, Pittsburgh
Levi Barber, Rec Mar.

1708   23 Mar 1807   A/1/418
James Findlay, Rec Cin; Samuel Finley, Rec Chl
Transfer of funds to Office of Discount & Deposit,
   Pittsburgh.

1709   25 Mar 1807   A/1/418
Stanley Griswold, Secretary of Michigan, Det
Act regulating the grants of land in the territory
   of Michigan; compensation as member of Board of
   Commissioners.

1710   25 Mar 1807   A/1/418
Peter Audrain, Reg Det
An Act regulating the grants of land in the

territory of Michigan; Board of Commissioners to consider claims under the act; transcript of decisions to be forwarded quarterly; instructions regarding recordkeeping; requests report on all claims disallowed under restrictive present law
[Frederick] Bates, Rec Det, accepting appointment in Louisiana; -- Taylor of Kentucky, formerly surveyor, accepts appointment in Indiana.

1711   26 Mar 1807 A/1/420
James Findlay, Rec Cin
Transfer of funds
John Badollet, Reg Vin.

1712   26 Mar 1807 A/1/420
John Badollet, Reg Vin
Act confirming claims to land in Vin & Det; Governor's grants; "continuation" tract on upper prairie; recordkeeping & accounting reports.

1713   28 Mar 1807 A/1/421
David Hoge, Reg Stu; Willys Silliman, Reg Zan; Jesse Spencer, Reg Chl; Joseph Wood, Reg Mar; Charles Killgore, Reg Cin; John Badollet, Reg Vin; LO Jef [no Reg named]
Act of 3 Mar 1807 to prevent settlements being made on lands ceded to the United States until authorized by law; permits to remain on land, if occupied before passage of Act; appointment of deputies to facilitate registration of squatters; estimate of number of intruders on public land requested; application for lead mines or salt springs.

1714   28 Mar 1807 A/1/423
Peter Audrain, Reg Det
Act of 3 Mar 1807 to prevent settlements being made on lands ceded to the United States until authorized by law; appointment of deputies to facilitate registration of squatters; recordkeeping; removal of intruders contemplated; lead mines & salt springs.

1715   28 Mar 1807 A/1/425
Michael Jones, Reg Kas
Act of 3 Mar 1807 to prevent settlements being made on lands ceded to the United States until authorized by law; appointment of deputies to facilitate registration of squatters; recordkeeping; lead mines & salt springs; ". . . it is particularly desirable to know whether any persons claiming under the Wabash & Illinois companies, under certain large court deeds not recognized by any law, or any other unfounded or fraudulent claims, have attempted or will attempt settlements. As there will be no hesitation in removing persons of that description, it is necessary that the information should reach the Executive without delay."

1716   28 Mar 1807 A/1/427
Thomas H. Williams, Reg WPR; Nicholas Perkins, Reg EPR
Act of 3 Mar 1807 to prevent settlement on lands ceded to the United States, until authorized by law; permission to remain on such lands; appointment of deputy registers; claimants of pre-emption rights; British grants; Spanish land titles; removal of intruders; lead mines or salt springs.

1717   2 Apr 1807 A/1/430
John Thompson, Reg WOr; John N. Gurley, Reg EOr
Act respecting claims to lands in the Territory of Orleans; appointment of deputy registers; compensation; fraudulent & doubtful claims.

1718   2 Apr 1807 A/1/432
Frederick Bates, Recorder, St. Louis
Act respecting claims to lands in the Territory of Orleans & Louisiana; Attorney General's opinion; Spanish laws & established usages; compensation
-- Lucas; -- Penrose.

1719   3 Apr 1807 A/1/434
James Brown, Agent, New Orleans
Act respecting claims to land in the Territories of Orleans & Louisiana; claim of the City of New Orleans.

1720   3 Apr 1807 A/1/434
Charles Killgore, Reg Cin
Sections 8, 11, 26, & 29 [township & range not stated] were to have been sold at public sale for not less than $8 per acre; requests explanation as to why now being offered at lower price
[This letter appended to regular letterbook and seems to be a copy of a letter also in another file].

1721   7 Apr 1807 A/1/435
James Brown, Agent, New Orleans
Asks for recommendation of attorney to act as agent in WPR
-- Magruder (resigned).

1722   9 Apr 1807 A/1/435
William C. Carr, Agent, St. Louis
An Act respecting claims to land in the Territories of Orleans & Louisiana; fraudulent claims.

1723   10 Apr 1807 A/1/435
James Abbott, Rec Det
Transmits commission (appointment); oath & bond required.

1724   11 Apr 1807 A/1/436
William Sprigg & Richard Cocke, Commissioners, EOr
Transmits commissions (appointments); compensation.

1725   11 Apr 1807 A/1/436
John Thompson, Reg WOr
Encloses letter for David Parmelye.

1726   11 Apr 1807   A/1/437
David Parmelye, Commissioner, WOr
Dismissal; superseded by Richard Cocke.

1727   11 Apr 1807   A/1/437
Benjamin Tupper, late Rec Mar
Ordered to turn over all records to his successor,
  Levi Barber.

1728   11 Apr 1807   A/1/437
Levi Barber, Rec Mar
Comments on bond submitted; mentions letter to
  Benjamin Tupper [see entry 1727].

1729   15 Apr 1807   A/1/437
John Thompson, Reg WOr
Deputy registers to be discontinued when no longer
  required.

1730   16 Apr 1807   A/1/438
William H. Harrison, Governor of Indiana, & the
  Land Officers at Vin [John Badollet, Reg Vin;
  Nathaniel Ewing, Rec Vin]
Prospective judicial interference with public sale
  of land; expulsion of intruders on public land
-- Handley.

1731   17 Apr 1807   A/1/438
R[ichard] C[lough] Anderson, Surveyor of the Lands
  in the Virginia Reservation, Clarksville, Indiana Territory
Act of 2 Mar 1807 respecting the location & surveys of Virginia military warrants; copies of
  surveys needed.

1732   18 Apr 1807   A/1/439
John Henderson, Rec WPR
Decides against suggestions to move office to Nat-
  chez from Washington, Mississippi Territory.

1733   21 Apr 1807   A/1/439
David Parmelye, late Land Commissioner, WOr
Compensation authorized.

1734   22 Apr 1807   A/1/440
Michael Jones & Elijah Backus, Commissioners, Kas
French & British grants; Governor's confirmation
  of claims; criteria for determining validity of
  claims; fraudulent claims and forgery.

1735   30 Apr 1807   A/1/440
William H. Harrison, Governor, Indiana Territory
Lease for United States Salt Works on Saline Creek;
  removal of intruders on government land
-- Taylor & -- Bringman; Mrs. -- Bell; -- White
  [agent at salt works].

1736   20 Apr 1807   A/1/442
John Badollet, Reg Vin; Michael Jones, Reg Kas
No permissions to be granted for settlement on Sa-
  line Creek as tenants at will.

1737   5 May 1807   A/1/442
Thomas Hill Williams, Reg WPR
Final certificate gives no tract designation;
  pre-emption rights
James Smith.

1738   16 May 1807   A/1/443
Levi Barber, Rec Mar
Bond approved.

1739   16 May 1807   A/1/443
William Sprigg, New Orleans, & Richard Cocke, Kentucky
Original commissions forwarded erroneously designated appointees as Commissioners EOr, correctly
  stated should have been WOr.

1740   16 May 1807   A/1/443
James Morrison, Supervisor of Kentucky
Transmits letter to Richard Cocke of Kentucky.

1741   25 May 1807   A/1/443
William H. Harrison, Governor of Indiana, Vin
Lease of salt springs to -- Taylor & -- Bringman
  not to exceed three years in duration.

1742   25 May 1807   A/1/444
James Findlay, Rec Cin
Transfer of funds
[Jared Mansfield], SG.

1743   27 May 1807   A/1/444
Joseph Chambers, U.S. Agent, Fort Stoddert, Miss-
  issippi Territory
Appointment as Rec at Fort St. Stephens of Lemuel
  Henry, "with whose particular place of residence
  I am unacquainted."

1744   27 Mar 1807   A/1/444
Thomas W. Maury, late Rec, Fort St. Stephens
Records to be turned over to successor, Lemuel
  Henry.

1745   27 May 1807   A/1/444
Lemuel Henry, Rec EPR
Transmits commission (appointment); oath & bond
  required.

1746   26 May 1807   A/1/445
Daniel Symmes, Cin; William Creighton, Chl;
  Joseph Buell, Mar; James Pritchard, Stu; Wil--
  liam Wells, Zan
Authorization to audit the books & records of Reg
  & Rec in offices designated above; Act of 10
  May 1800; instructions.

1747   26 Mar 1807   A/1/446
Circular letter to Registers & Receivers, Mar,
  Chl, Cin, Stu, Zan
Notification that certain persons will audit books
  & records

Joseph Buell, Mar; William Creighton, Chl; Daniel Symmes, Cin; James Pritchard, Stu; William Wells, Zan.

1748   3 Jul 1807   A/1/447
Gideon Fitz, Washington, Mississippi Territory
-- Pease, new SG, will answer surveying questions.

1749   3 Jul 1807   A/1/448
Stanley Griswold
Inquires whether sureties offered by James Abbott, Rec Det, are sufficient
Richard Smythe; J. Lasselle; Jacques Campeau; Charles Goin.

1750   9 Jul 1807   A/1/448
Levi Barber, Rec Mar
Surveying portion of fractional section.

1751   11 Jul 1807   A/1/448
Charles Killgore, Reg Cin
Final certificate on disputed tract; Attorney General's opinion is that -- Dufour's ownership of below-mentioned tract is valid; patent not to issue to Jared Mansfield

| Jared Mansfield (as grantee) | Cin | WML | 2 | 1 | - | 1 |
| Jared Mansfield (as grantee) | Cin | WML | 2 | 1 | - | 2 |

1752   11 Jul 1807   A/1/449
James Findlay, Rec Cin
[Charles Killgore], Reg Cin to hand you a copy of letter in which he was instructed not to issue patent to Jared Mansfield [see entry 1751]
-- Dufour.

1753   13 Jul 1807   A/1/449
John Thompson, Reg WOr
Compensation
-- Sprigg; -- Cocke.

1754   12 Jul 1807   A/1/449
John W. Gurley, Reg EOr
Compensation.

1755   14 Jul 1807   A/1/450
Joshua Lewis, Commissioner of Land Claims, New Orleans
Error in appointments for Judge -- Sprigg; should have been appointed to WOr, instead of EOr.

1756   15 Jul 1807   A/1/450
John McLean, Danbury, Fairfield County, Connecticut
Sale of United States lands south of Connecticut Reserve [in Ohio] to take place next spring.
-- Badger.

1757   18 Jul 1807   A/1/450
General Joseph Buell, Mar
Acknowledges receipt of audit report.

1758   18 Jul 1807   A/1/451
Stanley Griswold, Peter Audrain, James Abbott, Land Commissioners, Det
Expenses allowable.

1759   22 Jul 1807   A/1/451
Richard Cocke, Land Commissioner, WOr, now at Springfield, Washington County, Kentucky
Delay permissible; to arrive at Opelousas in December.

1760   22 Jul 1807   A/1/451
John B. C. Lucas, Clement B. Penrose, Commissioners, St. Louis
Comments on payment to Messrs. Hunt & Haskinson; -- Donaldson will not return to St. Louis.

1761   22 Jul 1807   A/1/452
Jesse Spencer, Reg Chl
Expenditures for opening road to Dayton
Joseph Nourse, Reg Treas.

1762   22 Jul 1807   A/1/452
Samuel Finley, Rec Chl
Transfer of funds for Dayton road
Jesse Spencer, Reg Chl; Joseph Nourse, Reg Treas.

1763   27 Jul 1807   A/1/452
Willys Silliman, Reg Zan
Appointment of agents to register intruders on public lands may be suspended.

1764   28 Jul 1807   A/1/453
William Wells, Zan
Acknowledges receipt of audit report.

1765   28 Jul 1807   A/1/453
James Pritchard, Stu
Acknowledges receipt of audit report.

1766   29 Jul 1807   A/1/453
James Brown, U.S. Land Agent, New Orleans
Survey of New Orleans commons.

1767   30 Jul 1807   A/1/453
William Creighton, Chl
Acknowledges receipt of audit report.

1768   15 Aug 1807   A/1/453
John Badollet, Reg Vin
Appropriation of funds for Indiana roads [This letter is a loose insert after page 453 of letterbook].

1769   13 Aug 1807   A/1/454
William H. Harrison, Governor; John Gibson, Secretary, Indiana Territory
Transmits accusatory letter & asks for an investigation of charges against [Nathaniel] Ewing, as directed by U.S. President.

1770   18 Aug 1807   A/1/454
William C. Carr, Agent, St. Louis
Attendance at meetings of Board of Commissioners.

1771   20 Aug 1807   A/1/454
Nathaniel Ewing, Rec Vin
Transfer of funds to John Badollet, Reg Vin, for
    road expenditures.

1772   22 Aug 1807   A/1/455
John Badollet, Reg Vin
Act of 26 Mar 1804, §13 repealed; Act of 26 Mar
    1804, §15; proofs required for a valid assign-
    ment of land claim.

1773   22 Aug 1807   A/1/456
Stanley Griswold, Commissioner, Det
Grants of land greater that those previously
    claimed are precluded by law.

1774   27 Aug 1807   A/1/456
Frederick Bates, Recorder, St. Louis
Contingent expenses; Act of 2 Mar 1805; Act of
    3 Mar 1807; compensation
-- Donaldson; -- Lucas; -- Penrose.

1775   28 Aug 1807   A/1/457
Nathaniel Ewing, Rec Vin
Acknowledges receipt of accounting report; pay-
    ments to territorial governor & judges
Judge -- Davis.

1776   1 Sep 1807   A/1/457
Ethan A. Brown, Cin
Acknowledges receipt of audit report.

1777   5 Oct 1807   A/1/457
John Williams, Stu
Refund of money, or application to another tract,
    not authorized by Congress.

1778   9 Oct 1807   A/1/458
Charles Killgore, Reg Cin; James Findlay, Rec Cin
Authorization to auction town lots in Cin; Act of
    28 Feb 1806.

1779   13 Oct 1807   A/1/458
James Brown, U.S. Agent for Land Claims, New Or-
    leans
Common lands of City of New Orleans; Act of 3 Mar
    1807.

1780   15 Oct 1807   A/1/459
David Hoge, Reg Stu
Audit report discloses Stu LO books to be eleven &
    eighteen months in arrears in posting.

1781   15 Oct 1807   A/1/460
Zaccheus Biggs, Rec Stu
Audit report discloses books to be considerably in
    arrears in posting; informed that quarterly

reports have not been submitted since end of
1800 [!]; ". . . I will be under the neces-
sity of stating the delay to the President,
if the accounts to the last of 1806 are not
shortly received."

1782   15 Oct 1807   A/1/460
John Henderson, Rec WPR
Transfer of funds
Seth Pease, Surveyor of Public Lands South of
    Tennessee.

1783   17 Oct 1807   A/1/460
Jesse Spencer, Reg Chl
Suspension of projected road to Dayton.

1784   17 Oct 1807   A/1/461
Levi Barber, Rec Mar
Requests information on capitalization of Bank of
    Mar & its ability to transfer funds to East
    Coast.

1785   17 Oct 1807   A/1/461
Governor [William H.] Harrison, Vin
Discusses route for road from salt springs.
-- White.

1786   22 Oct 1807   A/1/461
William C. Carr, U.S. Land Agent, St. Louis
Conflicts between American laws & Spanish laws &
    usages will be resolved in favor of American
    enactments.

1787   31 Oct 1807   A/1/462
James Morrison or William Wilkins, Lexington, Ken-
    tucky
Permit to transport to Louisville or Lexington
    one-sixth part of the salt produced at the
    Wabash saline
-- White, U.S. Agent at the saline.

1788   31 Oct 1807   A/1/462
William H. Harrison, Governor, Indiana Territory
Transmits copy of authorization to transport salt
    to Kentucky; Harrison to fix price of salt;
    ". . . you are authorized to revoke the permis-
    sion whenever you shall think it injurious to
    the public or productive of monopoly, or giving
    any undue advantage to one part of the country
    over another. . . ."

1789   31 Oct 1807   A/1/463
Isaac White, U.S. Agent, Wabash Saline
Notifies of authorization to Morrison & Wilkins
    to transport salt to Kentucky [see entry 1787];
    instructions.

1790   13 Nov 1807   A/1/463
Clement B. Penrose, Commissioner, St. Louis
Comments on accounts submitted.

1791   15 Nov 1807   A/1/464
Frederick Bates, Recorder, St. Louis
Lease of lead mines; royalties to federal government should be in metal & not in mineral &
should probably be one-fifth or one-eighth of
total production.

1792   18 Nov 1809   A/1/464
John Thompson, Reg WOr
Bill drawn by Thompson in favor of Messrs. Louail-
lers & Brothers has been refused.

1793   18 Nov 1807   A/1/465
B. J. Bradford, Printer, Nashville, Tennessee
Bil should be sent to Governor [William H.] Harri-
son; advertisement regarding saline.

1794   21 Nov 1807   A/1/465
John Henderson, Rec WPR
Drafts of surveyor returned for endorsement.

1795   24 Nov 1807   A/1/466
David Parmelee, late Land Commissioner, care of
postmaster, New Orleans
Compensation.
Ozias Lewis, Litchfield, Connecticut.

1796   28 Nov 1807   A/1/466
Henry Champion, Colchester, Connecticut
Southern boundary of Connecticut Reserve.

1797   2 Dec 1807   A/1/466
Thomas Moore, Commissioner for laying out the
western road, Union Town, Pennsylvania
Draft of section of road to Brownsville, Pennsylvania, requested.

1798   5 Dec 1807   A/1/467
Nathaniel Ewing, Rec Vin
Returns bill for proper endorsement
John Badollet [Reg Vin]; Benjamin Chambers;
Governor [William H.] Harrison.

1799   8 Dec 1807   A/1/467
Lemuel Henry, Rec EPR; James Abbott, Rec Det
Transmits new commission (appointment).

1800   12 Dec 1807   A/1/467
The President of the United States
Survey of southern & western boundaries of Connec-
ticut Reserve
Seth Pease, surveyor then employed by Connecticut
owners.

1801   17 Dec 1807   A/1/468
Isaac Humphreys, Mar
Lease of reserved section; special act of Congress
possibly required.

1802   17 Dec 1807   A/1/468
Thomas G. Gibson, Reg Can

Transmits commission (appointment; oath & bond
required; Presidential proclamation of sale
at Can in May 1808
John Sloan[e] of New Lisbon, Rec Can.

1803   17 Dec 1807   A/1/469
John Sloan[e], Rec Can
Transmits commission (appointment); oath & bond
required; public sale at Can in May 1808
Thomas G. Gibson, Reg Can.

1804   17 Dec 1807   A/1/470
Samuel Gwathney, Reg Jef
Transmits commission (appointment); oath & bond
required; public sale at Jef in April 1808
Edmund H. Taylor, Rec Jef.

1805   17 Dec 1807   A/1/470
Edmund H. Taylor, Rec Jef
Transmits commission (appointment); oath & bond
required; public sale at Jef in April 1808
Samuel Gwathney, Reg Jef.

1806   18 Dec 1807   A/1/471
David Hoge, Reg Stu
Presidential proclamation to be published in
various western Pennsylvania & Virginia news-
papers.

1807   19 Dec 1807   A/1/471
Governor [William H.] Harrison, Vin
President authorizes lease of lead mine to John
Brown, John Shouse, & Isaac E. Gano, "all of
Kentucky"; [terms of lease specified in appen-
dix to this letter].

1808   21 Dec 1807   A/1/472
Nathaniel Ewing, Rec Vin
Transfer of funds
Jared Mansfield, SG.

1809   23 Dec 1807   A/1/472
Augustine Prevost, Greenfield, Green County, New
York (Albany mail)
Disputes between Spanish & British conflicting
claims to be left to courts of law; other con-
ditions still undecided by Congress.

1810   25 Dec 1807   A/1/472
Augustine Prevost
Returns of Reg WPR, just received, discloses that
"4,400 acres of the land claimed in your name,
being also claimed by actual settlers either
with or without Spanish grants, the Land Commissioners have granted certificates to those
settlers . . .;" remedy at law will be required.

1811   28 Dec 1807   A/1/473
Zaccheus Biggs, Rec Stu
Balance on hand must be transported to Branch
Bank in Pittsburgh.

1812   4 Jan 1808   A/1/473
Epaphias W. Bull, Danbury, Connecticut
Forwards letter from SG [subject not stated].

1813   9 Jan 1808   A/1/473
John Henderson, Rec WPR
Discount to pre-emption holders; prepayments of
   instalments.

1814   9 Jan 1808   A/1/475
Lemuel Henry, Rec EPR
Discount to be paid on prepaid instalments.

1815   13 Jan 1808   A/1/475
Jacob Kline or William Marshall, Columbia, Pennsylvania
The question whether U.S. President can lease Ohio
   salt springs to anyone other than settlers is
   being considered by Attorney General.

1816   13 Jan 1808   A/1/475
Circular letter addressed to the following:

Receivers	LO	Registers
Levi Barber	Mar	Joseph Wood
Isaac Van Horn	Zan	Willys Silliman
Zaccheus Biggs	Stu	David Hoge
Samuel Finley	Chl	Jesse Spencer
James Findlay	Cin	Daniel Symmes
James Abbott	Det	Peter Audrain
Nathaniel Ewing	Vin	John Badollet
Elijah Bacchus	Kas	Michael Jones
John Sloan[e]	Can	Thomas G. Gibson
Edmund H. Taylor	Jef	Samuel Gwathney (Chl)
(New Lisbon)		
John Henderson	WPR	Thomas H. Williams
Lemuel Henry	EPR	Nicholas Perkins
--	WOr	John Thompson
--	EOr	John W. Gurley

In order to prevent fraud at public sales, highest bidders must deposit one-twentieth down
   payment immediately.

1817   1 Feb 1808   A/1/476
Samuel Finley, Rec Chl
Transfer of funds to Pittsburgh faulty & must be
   corrected.

1818   1 Feb 1808   A/1/477
Zaccheus Biggs, Rec Stu
Complains of locking up large sum of money, rather
   than depositing it in Pittsburgh, as directed
-- Jenkinson; Albert Gallatin.

1819   10 Feb 1808   A/1/477
Isaac Humphreys, Mar
Question of sale of reserved section while under a
   prior lease submitted to Congress.

1820   11 Feb 1808   A/1/477
Daniel Symmes, Reg Cin
Questions whether section 29, listed hereinafter,
   is a reserved section

Reserved section	Cin	MR	-	- 1	-
Reserved section	Cin	MR	-	- 11	-
Reserved section	Cin	MR	-	- 16	-
Reserved section	Cin	MR	-	- 26	-
Reserved section?	Cin	MR	-	- 29	-

1821   15 Feb 1808   A/1/478
Governor of Ohio
Transmits list of eighteen quarter townships &
   three sections of land selected by lot for the
   use of schools; Act to extend the time for locating Virginia military warrants . . . & appropriating lands for the use of schools in the
   Virginia Military Reservation."

1822   15 Feb 1808   A/1/478
Thomas G. Gibson, Reg Can
Transmits list of thirteen sections reserved for
   the Indians & eighteen quarter townships &
   three sections selected for the use of schools
   in the Virginia Military Reservation.

1823   23 Feb 1808   A/1/478
Daniel Symmes, Reg Cin
Power to remove intruders is discretionary &
   there is no present plan to move against settlers in Cin district.

1824   4 Mar 1808   A/1/479
John Badollet, Reg Vin
Act of 3 Mar 1807; patents may issue in favor of
   present claimants unless Governor's patents
   have actually issued.

1825   4 Mar 1808   A/1/479
John Badollet, Reg Vin
Conflict between SG & Reg Vin regarding surveying
   of private claims to be resolved amicably with-
   out recourse to Sec Treas
Jared Mansfield, SG.

1826   5 Mar 1808   A/1/480
Richard Cocke, Commissioner, WOr, Opelousas
Compensation.

1827   7 Mar 1808   A/1/481
James Findlay, Rec Cin
Ordered to transport all funds in his possession
   to Pittsburgh.

1828   7 Mar 1808   A/1/481
Samuel Finley, Rec Chl
Ordered to transport all funds in his possession
   to Pittsburgh, Office of Discount & Deposit
William Creighton, U.S. Attorney for District of
   Ohio.

1829   7 Mar 1808   A/1/481
Bartlett Collins, Point Coupee, Orleans Territory
Act of 3 Mar 1807; removal of intruders; Collins
   claims to be prior occupant of lands located for
   General La Fayette.

1830   8 Mar 1808   A/1/482
Thomas B. Steele, 6 Bridge Street, Baltimore,

Maryland
Steele's claim to land presumed to be in Kas
district, as Vin report does not show the
claim in Vin district.

1831   9 Mar 1808   A/1/483
John Henderson, Rec WPR
Accounting details.

1832   11 Mar 1808   A/1/483
David Hoge, Reg Stu
Lease of salt spring
-- Hardenbrook (lessee)   Stu - 3 11 34 -

1833   12 Mar 1808   A/1/484
Jacob Kline & William Marshall, Columbia, Lancas-
ter County, Pennsylvania
Notification of lease of salt spring in Jefferson
County, Ohio
Lodowick Hardenbrook (lessee) [see entry 1832].

1834   12 Mar 1808   A/1/484
Henry Champion, Hartford, Connecticut
Transmits correspondence with [Jared?] Mansfield
[subject not stated].

1835   18 Mar 1808   A/1/484
John Brown, Frankfort, Kentucky
Immediate possession of land permitted if lead-
mine lease is consummated.

1836   19 Mar 1808   A/1/484
Jesse Spencer, Reg Chl
Disposition of land offered at public sale for
which there was no bidder.

1837   19 Mar 1808   A/1/485
John Andrews, Cin
Clerks of Registers must look to their employers
for payment of wages.

1838   19 Mar 1808   A/1/485
William Garrard, Commissioner, WOr, Opelousas, now
at Middletown, Jefferson County, Kentucky
Transmits commission (appointment).

1839   21 Mar 1808   A/1/485
David Hoge, Reg Stu; William Creighton, U.S. Attor-
ney for Ohio District
Requests opinion on sureties offered by John
Sloane, Rec Can
Reazin Beale; Joseph Stibbs.

1840   24 Mar 1808   A/1/486
Zaccheus Biggs, Rec Stu, now at Washington, [D.C.]
"I learnt with equal surprise & regret from your
conversation & note of yesterday that there was
a deficiency in the public monies entrusted to
your care. The letters from John Smith, a Senator from the State of Ohio, . . . only show that
you advanced him [$11,300] . . . but do not ex-
plain what could be your motives for such

transaction. It may however be inferred that
you borrowed money afterwards, in order that,
at the time when it was being counted, the
deficiency might not be discovered. . . ."

1841   26 Mar 1808   A/1/487
Isaac Van Horn, Rec Zan
Rescinds authorization to transfer funds
[Jared Mansfield], SG.

1842   26 Mar 1808   A/1/487
James Findlay, Rec Cin
Transfer of funds
[Jared Mansfield], SG.

1843   1 Apr 1808   A/1/487
[Thomas G. Gibson], Reg Can; [John Sloane], Rec
Can
Instructed to notify bidders at public sale that
section boundary markers have been removed by
speculators & will be replaced by SG.

1844   7 Apr 1808   A/1/487
Nicholas Perkins, Reg EPR
Requests explanation of transaction in which
donee of 640 acres of donation land only given
pre-emption certificate for 160 acres
Francis Stringer.

1845   13 Apr 1808   A/1/488
Levi Barber, Rec Mar
Authorized to deposit federal funds in Bank of Mar.

1846   13 Apr 1808   A/1/488
Isaac Van Horn, Rec Zan
Authorized to deposit federal funds in Bank of Mar.

1847   14 Apr 1806   A/1/488
Land Commissioners, Det
Jurisdiction over land claims limited to lands in
which the Indian title had been previously ex-
tinguished; Act of 3 Mar 1807.

1848   15 Apr 1808   A/1/489
Benedict van Pradelles, Reg EOr
Transmits commission (appointment); oath & bond
required.

1849   15 Apr 1808   A/1/489
Thomas B. Robertson, Commissioner, EOr
Transmits commission (appointment).

1850   30 Apr 1808   A/1/489
Report of persons charged with investigating ac-
cusations has been laid before President, who
directs me to state that "it is deemed improper
that any Officer superintending . . . sales of
public lands should be concerned in any companies . . . the tendency of which is by lessening
competition to prevent the highest prices being
obtained for the lands."
-- Hunt? [Hurst?].

1851   30 Apr 1808   A/1/490
Circular letter to the following officials: Governors of Indiana, Michigan, Orleans, & Mississippi; Recorder of Land Titles in Louisiana; Surveyor General; Surveyor of Public Lands South of Tennessee; all Registers & Receivers
"It has commonly happened at the public sales of public lands that Companies have been formed for the purpose either of purchasing on speculation or of dividing the land purchased amongst themselves . . .;" U.S. President states that such associations should be discountenanced "as far as possible."

1852   11 May 1808   A/1/490
Peter Audrain, Reg Det
Transmits act supplementing "An Act regulating the grants of land in the Territory of Michigan;" pre-emption rights.

1853   12 May 1808   A/1/491
Samuel Finley, Rec Chl
Transfer of funds; three-percent allowance to the State of Ohio
William McFarland, Treasurer of State of Ohio.

1854   17 May 1808   A/1/492
Isaac Van Horn, Rec Zan
Transfer of funds
[Jared Mansfield], SG.

1855   20 May 1808   A/1/492
James Findlay, Rec Cin
Accounting report missing.

1856   21 May 1808   A/1/492
Joseph Wood, Reg Mar
Final certificate to be refused, pending proof that tract had previously been offered at public sale
John McIntire   Mar - 14 16 - 1*
  *Portion east of Muskingum River.

1857   30 May 1808   A/1/493
John McIntire, Zan
Acknowledges deposition of Daniel Converse that Reg Mar refused to issue final certificate
John McIntire   Mar - 14 16 - 1E
John McIntire   Mar - 14 16 16 -

1858   30 May 1808   A/1/493
Joseph Wood, Reg Mar
Requests forwarding of duplicate receipt
John McIntire   Mar - 14 16 16 -

1859   1 Jun 1808   A/1/493
[Nicholas Perkins], Reg EPR; [Thomas H. Williams], Reg WPR
Transmits act supplementing "An Act regulating the grants of land & providing for the disposal of the lands . . . south of the State of Tennessee. . . ."

1860   1 Jun 1808   A/1/494
Joshua Lewis & Benedict van Pradelles, Commissioners EOr, New Orleans
Incorrect compensation drawn.

1861   2 Jun 1808   A/1/494
Thomas H. Williams, Reg WPR
Report of British grants not received; claimants of pre-emption rights; public sale of land scheduled for Jan 1809
[Seth] Pease, Surveyor.

1862   3 Jun 1808   A/1/495
Ethan A. Brown, Cin; William Creighton, Chl; Joseph Buell, Mar; William Wells, Zan; Alexander McLean, Stu; Benjamin Parke, Vin; William Dunbar, Washington, Mississippi Territory [for LO WPR]; Edmund P. Gaines, Fort St. Stephens, Mississippi Territory [for LO EPR]; all Receivers; all Registers
Form letter empowering named persons to audit books of all Registers & Receivers.

1863   3 Jun 1808   A/1/496
Ethan A. Brown, Cin; William Creighton, Chl; Joseph Buell, Mar; William Wells, Zan; Alexander McLean, Stu; Benjamin Parke, Vin; William Dunbar, Washington, Mississippi Territory [for LO WPR]; Edmund P. Gaines [at Fort Stoddert], Fort St. Stephens, Mississippi Territory [for LO EPR]
Instructions regarding audit.

1864   3 Jun 1808   A/1/498
Samuel Finley, Rec Chl
Error in accounting report noted.

1865   6 Jun 1808   A/1/498
William Robertson, care of Ethan A. Brown, Cin
Issuance of patent suspended
William Robertson   Cin WML 3 1 - 5
William Robertson   Cin WML 3 1 - 6

1866   30 Jun 1808   A/1/498
William Garrard, Commissioner WOr, now at Middletown, Kentucky
Instructions; compensation
[John] Thompson, Reg WOr.

1867   30 Jun 1808   A/1/499
Thomas Gibson, Reg Can
Expenses allowed.

1868   1 Jul 1808   A/1/499
Elijah Bacchus [so spelled] & Michael Jones, Commissioners, Kas
Tracts of land selected appear to be too large for land to be located.

1869   1 Jul 1808   A/1/499
Daniel Symmes, Reg Cin
Claim of Joel Williams to land within City of Cin WML appear not to prevail over that of the United States.

1870   1 Jul 1808   A/1/500
Samuel Gwathney, Reg Jef; Edmund H. Taylor, Rec
  Jef
Compensation for public sales clerks.

1871   2 Jul 1808   A/1/500
William H. Harrison, Governor, Indiana Territory
Modification of terms of salt spring lease per-
  mitted, if not due to lessee's mismanagement
  -- Morrison.

1872   5 Jul 1808   A/1/501
Edmund H. Taylor, Rec Jef
Expenses allowed; accounting instructions.

1873   9 Jul 1808   A/1/501
Samuel Finley, Rec Chl
Requests explanation of failure to transport all
  funds to Branch Bank at Pittsburgh [discrepancy
  in the order of $35,000].

1874   12 Jul 1808   A/1/501
Isaac Van Horn, Rec Zan
Expense authorization.

1875   12 Jul 1808   A/1/501
[Daniel Symmes], Reg Cin; [Jesse Spencer], Reg
  Chl; [David Hoge], Reg Stu; [Willys Silliman],
  Reg Zan; [Joseph Wood], Reg Mar
Transmits Presidential proclamation announcing
  sales of reserved sections.

1876   29 Jul 1808   A/1/502
James Findlay, Rec Cin
Transfer of funds
[Jared Mansfield], SG.

1877   30 Jul 1808   A/1/502
Thomas Gibson, Reg Can; John Sloane, Rec Can
Forfeitures.

1878   2 Aug 1808   A/1/503
Peter Audrain, Reg Det
Authorization to hire temporary clerk.

1879   5 Aug 1808   A/1/503
David Hoge, Reg Stu
Final certificate suspended
Obadiah Jennings
William Thompson   Stu -   7 17 13   +

1880   9 Aug 1808   A/1/503
Samuel Finley, Rec Chl
Acknowledges receipt of explanatory letter "and
  regret that it is my duty to say that it is unsatisfactory."

1881   26 Aug 1808   A/1/504
Edmund H. Taylor, Rec Jef
Accounting reports & expense authorization.

1882   29 Aug 1808   A/1/504
David Hoge, Reg Stu
Discrepancy noted
Peter Kail vs Isaac Wood Stu -   5 11 18   +

1883   5 Sep 1808   A/1/505
Samuel Finley, Rec Chl
Transfer of funds
[William] Creighton; Lewis Cass, Marshal of Ohio;
  Samuel C. Vano? late a paymaster in the Army.

1884   4 Oct 1808   A/1/505
Lemuel Henry, Rec EPR, Fort St. Stephens
Transfer of funds
Henry Toulmin, Judge of Mississippi Territory.

1885   4 Oct 1808   A/1/506
William Wells, Zan
Acknowledges receipt of audit report.

1886   4 Oct 1808   A/1/506
William Creighton, Chl
Acknowledges receipt of audit report.

1887   4 Oct 1808   A/1/506
Benjamin Parke, Vin
Acknowledges receipt of audit report.

1888   4 Oct 1808   A/1/506
Edmund P. Gaines, Rec, Fort Stoddert
Acknowledges receipt of audit report.

1889   4 Oct 1808   A/1/507
Edmund H. Taylor, Rec Jef
Office rent not for government account.

1890   10 Oct 1808   A/1/507
John Badollet, Reg Vin
Commissioners certificate for land in fork of
  White River
Eli Hawkins.

1891   11 Oct 1808   A/1/507
John Smith, Cin
Answers query regarding forfeiture of specific
  tract
Not stated   Cin Pre   5   3 28   +

1892   12 Oct 1808   A/1/507
Richard Cocke, Commissioner, WOr, Opelousas
Compensation incorrectly computed.

1893   12 Oct 1808   A/1/508
Benedict van Pradelles, Reg EOr
Compensation incorrectly computed.

1894   18 Oct 1808   A/1/507
Peter Wilson, Rec Stu
Transmits commission (appointment); oath & bond
  required.

1895   30 Oct 1808   A/1/509
Thomas H. Williams, Reg WPR, Washington, Mississippi Territory
Public sale of land in Jan 1809; British & Spanish grants; Act of 2 Mar 1803; Act of 21 Apr
  1806, §1; Act of 31 Mar 1808; Presidential
  exception on application of British minister [in
  Washington, D.C.?]; pre-emption rights
H. J. Harris; Hon. J. Davis.

1896   20 Oct 1808   A/1/510
Thomas H. Williams, Reg WPR, Washington, Mississippi Territory
Act of 2 Mar 1805, §5; Act of 21 Apr 1806, §1;
  Act of 31 Mar 1808, §4; pre-emption claims
  cannot be located either on British grants or
  on Spanish or British warrants or orders of
  survey; Act of 19 Jan 1808; Act of 31 Mar
  1808, §§4, 6.

1897   20 Oct 1808   A/1/511
Nicholas Perkins, Reg EPR
Act of 19 Jan 1808, §1; pre-emption claims;
  right of pre-emption extended to cover quarter
  section adjacent to quarter section upon which
  habitation is situated; Act of 31 Aug 1808.

1898   21 Oct 1808   A/1/511
Richard Cocke, Commissioner WOr, Opelousas
Transmits new commission superseding erroneous one.

1899   24 Oct 1808   A/1/512
Jacob Ayers, Zan
Five-percent deduction not allowed when payment is
  tendered in six-percent stock.

1900   25 Oct 1808   A/1/512
John Badollet, Reg Vin
Revised rules of assignment; Act of 3 Mar 1807
  [important statement of procedure].

1901   25 Oct 1808   A/1/513
Benedict van Pradelles, Reg EOr
Six thousand-acre tracts surveyed for General La
  Fayette rejected due to faulty certificate de-
  scriptions
-- Duplantier, agent of General La Fayette; --
  Madison, attorney in fact of General La Fayette.

1902   25 Oct 1808   A/1/513
Postmaster, Nashville, Tennessee
Requests letter to Freeman be forwarded to new
  purchase at bend of Tennessee River
[Thomas] Freeman, U.S. surveyor.

1903   27 Oct 1808   A/1/514
John Sloane, Rec Cin
Directs funds to be transported to Office of Dis-
  count & Deposit, Pittsburgh.

1904   27 Oct 1808   A/1/514
Marie Philippe Leduc, Translator to Land Board,
  St. Louis
No present law permitting compensation for services
  outside St. Louis.

1905   27 Oct 1808   A/1/514
Benedict van Pradelles, Reg EOr; James Brown,
  Agent for Land Claims, New Orleans
Transmits information regarding a claim "corrobor-
  ated from a respectable source" [no names men-
  tioned; very circumspectly phrased letter].

1906   28 Oct 1808   A/1/515
William Robertson, care of Major William Ruffin,
  Cin
Addressee directed patent to be made out in his
  own name but, on same day, gave an assignment
  to another party*
Samuel Martin of New York, assignee
William Robertson   Cin WML 3 1 - 5
William Robertson   Cin WML 3 1 - 6
  *[Assignment may have predated letter request-
  ing patent in own name].

1907   28 Oct 1808   A/1/515
Samuel Martin, 63 William Street, New York
Notifies addressee, the assignee of William Robert-
  son, that the latter had directed patent to issue
  in his own name, rather than that of assignee
William Robertson   Cin WML 3 1 - 5
William Robertson   Cin WML 3 1 - 6

1908   25 Oct 1808   A/1/516
Thomas Freeman, Deputy Surveyor, U.S. New Purchase,
  Mississippi Territory
Act of 3 Mar 1807 to prevent settlements being
  made on lands ceded to United States until
  authorized by law; President directs addressee
  to register settlers & grant permission to remain; to discriminate between actual settlers
  & "those who under pretence of pretended Georgia titles intend either forcibly to occupy the
  lands or to extort money from ignorant settlers;" public sale expected to take place in
  Apr 1809 [text of proclamation to settlers fol-
  lows].

1909   5 Nov 1808   A/1/517
William H. Harrison, Governor of Indiana, Vin
Inability of Messrs. -- Brown, -- Gano, -- Schultz
  [see serial entry 1807] to find lead mine in
  Indiana Territory; Messrs. Henry C. Gist & J.
  Bledsoe of Kentucky think they know its loca-
  tion, & U.S. President authorizes grant of lease
  to them; President denies permission to trans-
  port salt from Wabash Saline to West Tennessee
  & Knox County on same terms previously granted.

1910   5 Nov 1808   A/1/518
James Morrison, Lexington, Kentucky
Forwards letter granting permission to -- Gist &
  -- Bledsoe to negotiate with Governor [William
  H. Harrison] for lead-mine lease

1911   5 Nov 1808   A/1/518
John Brown, Frankfort, Kentucky
Transmits copy of letter to Governor of Indiana.

1912   5 Nov 1808   A/1/518
Robert Williams, Governor, Mississippi Territory,
  Washington [Mississippi Territory?]

Informs regarding instructions given Thomas Freeman, Deputy Surveyor, regarding settlers in New Purchase [see entry 1908]; pretended Yazoo [Land Company] settlers to be removed by force in Apr 1809; appointment of civil officers in area; intrusions in Orleans Territory requires further legislation.

1913   11 Nov 1808 A/1/519
John B. C. Lucas, Commissioner, St. Louis
Protest of two bills.

1914   19 Nov 1808 A/1/519
David Hoge, Reg Stu
Requests information regarding James Johnson, Bez-[aliel] Wells, James Pritchard, sureties of Peter Wilson, Rec Stu.

1915   23 Nov 1808 A/1/519
Nicholas Perkins, Reg EPR
Claim of Francis Stringer; Act of 21 Apr 1806.

1916   30 Nov 1808 A/1/519
John Badollet, Reg Vin
Case of Moses Hopper [not otherwise described].

1917   30 Nov 1808 A/1/520
Edmund H. Taylor, Rec Jef
Accounting voucher required.

1918   16 Dec 1808 A/1/520
Peter Wilson, Rec Stu
Transmits new commission (appointment); bond required.

1919   21 Dec 1808 A/1/520
John Badollet, Reg Vin
Comments & instructions regarding disputed road contract
-- Chambers; [Nathaniel] Ewing, Rec Vin.

1920   21 Dec 1808 A/1/521
B. Chambers, Lawrenceburgh, Indiana Territory
Disputed road contract to be decided upon by [Nathaniel] Ewing, Rec Vin
[John Badollet], Reg Vin.

1921   21 Dec 1808 A/1/521
Nathaniel Ewing, Rec Vin
Instructions regarding the handling of disputed road contract
B. Chambers; John Badollet, Reg Vin.

1922   30 Dec 1808 A/1/522
Nathaniel Ewing, Rec Vin; Edmund H. Taylor, Rec Jef
Instructed to make frequent deposit of accumulating funds in Bank of Kentucky.

1923   30 Dec 1808 A/1/522
John Thompson, Reg WOr, Opelousas
Transfer of funds.

1924   2 Jan 1809 A/1/522
Thomas H. Williams, Reg WPR, Washington, Mississippi Territory
Missing schedule of disallowed claims of minors.

1925   4 Jan 1809 A/1/523
John Girault, Washington, Mississippi Territory
Acknowledges receipt of audit report on LO WPR.

1926   6 Jan 1809 A/1/523
Samuel Gwathney, Reg Jef
Instruction on method of correcting an error
Peter Covert (correct) Jef - ? 1N 3 +
Peter Covert (error) Jef - ? 4N 3 +

1927   10 Jan 1809 A/1/523
David Parmelee, Litchfield, Connecticut
Again rejects claim for compensation.

1928   24 Jan 1809 A/1/523
David Hoge, Reg Stu
Instruction regarding loss of first certificate.

1929   4 Feb 1809 A/1/524
John Badollet, Reg Vin
Impossible to rectify error in location
Jacob Garrett.

1930   9 Feb 1809 A/1/524
Nathaniel Ewing, Rec Vin
Surveying expenses on private claims.

1931   9 Feb 1809 A/1/524
John Badollet, Reg Vin
Survey of private claims
[Jared Mansfield], SG.

1932   13 Feb 1809 A/1/525
Jesse Spencer, Reg Chl
Impossibility of rectifying error in location
Not stated   Chl MS 22 3 24 +

1933   16 Feb 1809 A/1/525
Daniel Symmes, Reg Cin
Pre-emption right of Peyton Short to lands between Great Miami River, Mad River, & northern boundary of Ludlow's Survey; Act of 1 Mar 1801, §5.

1934   17 Feb 1809 A/1/526
Peter Audrain, Reg Det
Act of 21 Apr 1806 to provide for the adjustment of titles of land in the town of Detroit & Territory of Michigan; Act of 3 Mar 1807 prohibits Board of Commissioners from deciding on Det land claims
Matthew Elliott.

1935   21 Feb 1809 A/1/526
Thomas Hill Williams, Reg WPR, Washington, Mississippi Territory
Act of 19 Jan 1808, §§1, 3; due date for first payment on land claimed under pre-emption
-- Poindexter; Governor [Robert] Williams.

1936   22 Feb 1809   A/1/527
Frederick Bates, Recorder, St. Louis
Act of 3 Mar 1807; Morales' regulations; has con-
   fidence in the judgment of Board of Commissioners.

1937   24 Feb 1809   A/1/527
Levi Barber, Rec Mar
Authorization for expenditure.

1938   24 Feb 1809   A/1/527
Michael Jones & Elijah Backus, Commissioners, Kas
Continuance of Board of Commissioners; ". . .
   governor of the New Territory will be authorized to investigate the complaints to which you
   allude."

1939   2 Mar 1809   A/1/527
Nathaniel Ewing, Rec Vin
Instructions regarding Rec entries when payments
   are made at the Treasury [Washington, D.C.].

1940   3 Mar 1809   A/1/528
Philip Grymes, Reg EOr
Transmits commission (appointment); oath & bond
   required.

1941   6 Mar 1809   A/1/529
John Henderson, Rec WPR, Washington, Mississippi
   Territory
Compensation to Reg WPR to include one-percent com-
   mission on all land sales
[Thomas H.] Williams, Reg WPR.

1942   6 Mar 1809   A/1/529
Thomas H. Williams, Reg WPR
Compensation.

1943   16 Mar 1809   A/1/529
Peter Wilson, Rec Stu
Requests explanation of refusal of Wilson's former
   sureties to remain responsible
-- Jenkinson.

1944   16 Mar 1809   A/1/529
Edmund H. Taylor, Rec Jef
Transfers of funds required by law before receiv-
   ing compensation.

1945   18 Mar 1809   A/1/530
James Findlay, Rec Cin
Acknowledges receipt of accounting reports.

1946   20 Mar 1809   A/1/530
Daniel Symmes, Reg Cin
Delayed payments of first instalments; forfeit-
   ures of initial down payments
Piatt & Carter; John James.

1947   20 Mar 1809   A/1/530
Joshua Lewis, Commissioner, New Orleans
Compensation.

1948   20 Mar 1809   A/1/531
David Hoge, Reg Stu; Joseph Wood, Reg Mar;
   Willys Silliman, Reg Zan; Jesse Spencer, Reg
   Chl; Daniel Symmes, Reg Cin
Act to extend the time for making payment for the
   public lands of the United States; instructions
   regarding extension of credit to purchasers.

1949   21 Mar 1809   A/1/531
L. Geo[rge] Coussier, Indiana Territory, by Port
   William, Kentucky
L. Geo[rge] Coussier?*   Cin   WML   3   2   15   -
L. Geo[rge] Coussier?*   Cin   WML   3   2   -   22
L. Geo[rge] Coussier?*   Cin   WML   3   2   -   27
   *But see serial entry 1950.

1950   21 Mar 1809   A/1/532
Daniel Symmes, Reg Cin
John James Dufour   Cin   WML   3   2   15   -
John James Dufour   Cin   WML   3   2   -   22
John James Dufour   Cin   WML   3   2   -   27

1951   22 Mar 1809   A/1/532
Nathaniel Ewing, Rec Vin
Personal endorsement of draft required.

1952   30 Mar 1809   A/1/532
Frederick Bates, Recorder, St. Louis
Authorization for expenditure.

1953   31 Mar 1809   A/1/532
William H. Harrison, Governor of Indiana Territory, Vin
President directs revocation of permit to transport salt to Kentucky formerly given to lessees
   [of Wabash Saline].

1954   5 Apr 1809   A/1/533
James Findlay, Rec Cin
Directs transport of funds to Pittsburgh.

1955   5 Apr 1809   A/1/533
Samuel Finley, Rec Chl
Directs transport of all funds to Pittsburgh, Off-
   ice of Discount & Deposit.

1956   5 Apr 1809   A/1/533
W. C. C. Claiborne, Governor, New Orleans Terri-
   tory
Act for the relief of certain Alabama & Wyandot
   Indians; location of Alabama Indian reserva-
   tion
[Seth Pease], Surveyor of Lands South of Tennes-
   see.

1957   5 Apr 1809   A/1/534
Thomas H. Williams, Reg WPR; John Henderson, Rec
   WPR; Nicholas Perkins, Reg EPR; Lemuel Henry,
   Rec EPR
Act for the disposal of certain tracts of land in
   the Mississippi Territory claimed under Spanish
   grants . . . & to confirm the claims of Alexander
   Ellis & Daniel Harrogal; instructions.

1958   10 Apr 1809   A/1/534
John Brahan, Rec Nas [for Madison County, Miss-
    issippi Territory]; William Dickson, Reg Nas
    [for Madison County, Mississippi Territory]
Transmits commissions (appointments); oath &
    bond required.

1959   24 Apr 1809   A/1/535
Nathaniel Ewing, Rec Vin
Duplicate receipts
Jacob Kintner.

1960   30 Apr 1809   A/1/535
Ninian Edwards, Governor, Illinois Territory
Salt springs on Saline Creek to be placed under
    Edwards' supervision [important statement of
    governmental policy, marketing tactics, & mar-
    kets for salt].

1961   1 May 1809   A/1/536
William H. Harrison, Governor, Indiana Territory
Salt springs of Saline Creek, now being within
    newly-established Illinois Territory, will be-
    come the administrative responsibility of the
    Governor of Illinois Territory
Governor [Ninian] Edwards.

1962   2 May 1809   A/1/537
Thomas H. Williams, Reg WPR, Washington, Mississ-
    ippi Territory
Restatement of forfeiture rules.

1963   5 May 1809   A/1/537
Nicholas Perkins, Reg EPR, Fort St. Stephens, Miss-
    issippi Territory
Restatement of discount rules.

1964   5 May 1809   A/1/537
James Abbott, Rec Det
Duties of office
[Frederick] Bates, former Rec Det; [Peter] Audrain,
    Reg Det.

1965   8 May 1809   A/1/537
Thomas H. Williams, Reg WPR, Washington, Mississ-
    ippi Territory
Designates lands in substitution for sections 16
    already located upon

Reserved section	WPR	-	1E	1	30	-
Reserved section	WPR	-	1W	1	36	-
Reserved section	WPR	-	1E	2	18	-
Reserved section	WPR	-	2E	3	19	-
Reserved section	WPR	-	2E	6	30	-
Reserved section	WPR	-	3E	1	32	-

1966   8 May 1809   A/1/538
Peter Wilson, Rec Stu
Accepts explanation for discrepancy previously
    noted; misapplication & defalcation of funds
[Zaccheus] Biggs, former Rec Stu.

1967   8 May 1809   A/1/538
Isaac Van Horn, Rec Zan

Inquires regarding receipts of Bank of the
    United States, Philadelphia
Richard Flowers; Jonathan Carlisle.

1968   9 May 1809   A/1/538
Reuben Attwater, Peter Audrain, & James Abbott,
    Land Commissioners, Det
Conflicting claims of -- Mayett [Maillet?] & --
    Forsyth.

1969   9 May 1809   A/1/539
John Thompson, Reg WOr, Opelousas
Settling of accounts
George King, clerk.

1970   13 May 1809   A/1/539
Joseph.Wood, Reg Mar
Sale of Zan district land at Mar LO; U.S. Supreme
    Court decision in Matthews case
Trueman Peet & Peleg Mason; -- McCluney & --
    Hooker.

1971   31 May 1809   A/1/540
Ninian Edwards, Governor, Illinois Territory
Copies of accounts of Isaac White, U.S. Agent "at
    the saline near the mouth of the Wabash"
-- Taylor & -- Bringman.

1972   1 Jun 1809   A/1/540
Joseph Wood, Reg Mar
Act of 2 Mar 1809; extension of credit
Trueman Peet.

1973   6 Jun 1809   A/1/541
James Windus? Franklin Township, Bergen County,
    Jersey City Post Office, New Jersey
Explains procedure for purchasing land.

1974   7 Jun 1809   A/1/541
Benjamin Tupper, late Rec Mar, Springfield, Ohio
Balance due the government must be paid forthwith
    to "preclude the necessity of resorting [to]
    compulsory measures against yourself & sureties
    for its recovery."

1975   10 Jun 1809   A/1/541
Thomas B. Robertson, Commissioner, New Orleans
Philip Grymes to succeed [Benedict van] Pradelles
    as Reg EOr; Houmas claim by -- Conway et al is
    futile.

1976   13 Jun 1809   A/1/541
Parke Walton, Washington, Mississippi Territory
Approves expense account for public sale.

1977   15 June 1809   A/1/542
John Henderson, Rec WPR, Washington, Mississippi
    Territory
Case of Daniel Harrogel.

1978   16 Jun 1809   A/1/542
Thomas Gibson, Reg Can
Preservation of entry book.

1979   19 Jun 1809 A/1/542
Richard Cocke, Commissioner, WOr, Opelousas
Compensation dispute discussed.

1980   21 Jun 1809 A/1/542
Philip Grymes, Reg EOr, New Orleans
Approves sureties.

1981   23 Jun 1809 A/1/542
William Dixon [Dickson], Reg Nas [for Madison
 County, Mississippi Territory]
Act of 10 May 1800; instructions
[Jared Mansfield], SG; John Brahan of Natchez,
 Rec Nas [for Madison County, Mississippi Terri-
 tory].

1982   26 Jun 1809 A/1/542
William Dickson, Reg Na; John Brahan, Rec Nas
Transmits new commissions (appointments).

1983   28 Jun 1809 A/1/542
Philip Grymes, Reg EOr, New Orleans
Report on Board of Commissioners [EOr] submitted
 to Land Committee of U.S. House of Representatives.

1984   30 Jun 1809 A/1/542
Nicholas Perkins, Reg EPR, St. Stephens, Mississippi Territory
"The Secretary of War . . . informs me that no
 part of your claim on account of your services
 in conducting A[aron] Burr to this place is
 chargeable to the War Department. . . . It would
 be best for you to apply by letter to the President himself. . . ."

1985   30 Jun 1809 A/1/544
Michael Jones & E. Backus, Commissioners, Kas
[Robert] Robinson "your present clerk" appointed
 Agent for LO Kas.

1986   30 Jun 1809 A/1/544
Robert Robinson, Clerk of Board of Land Commissioners, Kas
Appointment as Agent; admonishes particular vigil-
 ance against fraud; ". . . To large speculative
 claims your attention is specially called."

1987   1 Jul 1809 A/1/544
John Badollet, Reg Vin
Accepts vouchers for road contract
[Nathaniel] Ewing, Rec Vin.

1988   11 Jul 1809 A/1/544
John Brahan, Rec Nas; William Dickson, Reg Nas
Transmits instructions as to duties.

1989   12 Jul 1809 A/1/544
William H. Harrison, Governor, Indiana Territory
Time for negotiating lead-mine lease with -- Bledsoe & -- Gist extended, as they have not found
 the location yet.

1990   20 Jul 1809 A/1/544
Ethan A. Brown, Cin; William Creighton, Chl;
 James Pritchard, Stu; Joseph Buell, Mar; Wil-
 liam Wells, Zan; Benjamin Parke, Vin; John
 Girault, Washington, Mississippi Territory [for
 WPR]; Edmund P. Gaines, St. Stephens, Mississ-
 ippi Territory [for EPR]; Zaccheus A. Beatty,
 Can; Richard Ferguson, Jef
Certificate of appointment authorizing audit of
 corresponding land offices.

1991   20 Jul 1809 A/1/545
Ethan A. Brown, Cin; William Creighton, Chl;
 James Pritchard, Stu; Joseph Buell, Mar; Wil-
 liam Wells, Zan; Benjamin Parke, Vin; John
 Girault near Natchez, Washington, Mississippi
 Territory [for WPR]; Edmund P. Gaines at Fort
 Stod[dert], St. Stephens, Mississippi Territory
 [for EPR]; Zaccheus A. Beatty, Can; Richard
 Ferguson of Louisville, Kentucky, Jef.
Instructions for LO audits.

1992   21 Jul 1809 A/1/546
Thomas H. Williams, Reg WPR, Washington, Mississippi Territory
Claims of -- Ellis & -- Harregal; Act of 21 Apr
 1806, §1; Act of 3 Mar 1803, §6.

1993   22 Jul 1809 A/1/546
Samuel Finley, Rec Chl
Acceptance of bank or state paper not convertible
 into specie was inadmissible & against long-
 standing instructions; directed to deposit all
 negotiable funds in Branch Bank, Pittsburgh, or
 in Bank of Kentucky, Frankfort.

1994   29 Jul 1809 A/1/546
Nathaniel Ewing, Rec Vin
Authorization for expenditure.

1995   31 Jul 1809 A/1/547
Philip Grymes, Reg EOr, New Orleans
Compensation for William Wikoff, deputy register
Administratrix of estate of [Benedict van] Prad-
 elles.

1996   31 Jul 1809 A/1/547
Joseph Saul, Administrator of estate of John W.
 Gurley, late Reg EOr, New Orleans
Asserts possible claim of United States against
 estate.

1997   31 Jul 1809 A/1/547
Mrs. Cassandra van Pradelles, Administratrix of
 the Estate of [Benedict van] Pradelles, deceased,
 New Orleans
Act of 3 Mar 1807; asserts claim of United States
 against estate
[Philip] Grymes, Reg EOr.

1998   3 Aug 1809 A/1/548
Samuel Gwathney, Reg Jef
Asks opinion regarding Richard Taylor, Junior, &
 Thomas N. Thruston, sureties of Edmund H. Taylor,
 Rec Jef.

1999   3 Aug 1809   A/1/548
William Dickson, Reg Nas
Requests return of plats
[Jared Mansfield], SG.

2000   3 Aug 1809   A/1/548
John Henderson, Rec WPR, Washington, Mississippi
    Territory
Transfer of funds
Seth Pease, Surveyor of Public Lands South of Ten-
    nessee.

2001   7 Aug 1809   A/1/548
Nathaniel Ewing, Rec Vin
In response to B. Chamber's complaint to U.S.
    President regarding disposition of disputed road
    contract, directs submission of complete state-
    ment of facts to Judge -- Parke.

2002   7 Aug 1809   A/1/548
Colonel B. Chambers, Laurenceburgh, Indiana Terri-
    tory
Directs statement of facts to be submitted to
    Judge -- Parke; "I will only add that I have
    given no particular instructions to Mr. Ewing,
    as you seem to suppose in your Letter [to the
    President]. . . ."

2003   7 Aug 1809   A/1/549
Judge -- Parke of Indiana Territory
Notification that instructions have been given to
    B. Chambers & [Nathaniel] Ewing, [Rec Vin] to
    lay the facts before addressee.

2004   12 Aug 1809   A/1/549
Thomas F. Riddick, St. Louis
Compensation for year 1808 refused; Act of 3 Mar
    1807.

2005   2 Sep 1809   A/1/549
Peter Audrain, Reg Det
Grants permission to leave post for visit to Wash-
    ington, D.C.

2006   4 Sep 1809   A/1/549
John F. Mansfield, Cin
Case of William Hiatt has no remedy in present law;
    withdrawing or shifting land entry not permitted;
    Act of 10 May 1800, §10.

2007   6 Sep 1809   A/1/549
James Findlay, Rec Cin
Transfer of funds
[Jared Mansfield], SG.

2008   6 Sep 1809   A/1/549
John Thompson, Reg WOr, Opelousas
Information regarding a claim in Lower Louisiana
    [not otherwise described]; "'I was also in-
    formed that the interpreter to the Board was to
    receive one half of a valuable Island for using
    his influence with the Board, in case Claimants
    succeeded.'"

2009   9 Sep 1809   A/1/550
Jesse Spencer, Reg Chl
Final certificate unsatisfactory
Joseph Loveland & Joseph Stewart [also referred
    to in text as Smith]
Henry Abrams* (assignee) Chl - 19 15 34 -
    *Also called Henry Adams in text.

2010   9 Sep 1809   A/1/550
Michael Jones & Elijah Backus, Commissioners, Kas
Report of investigation made by Governor [Ninian]
    Edwards to be laid before President; urges
    prompt decisions in order to quiet the public
    "& that it is absolutely necessary in order to
    reconcile the Mass of the inhabitants to the
    General Government"; ". . . in the present dis-
    tracted state of the territory, I am of the
    opinion that you or the agents interfering in
    its local politics will be injurious to your-
    selves & to the General Government."

2011   18 Sep 1809   A/1/550
William Wells, Zan
Acknowledges receipt of audit report.

2012   27 Sep 1809   A/1/551
William H. Harrison, Governor, Indiana Territory
Discusses compensation for superintending Saline;
    "Governor [Ninian] Edwards was requested to en-
    quire generally into the situation of that
    establishment. . . . He has done so accordingly
    but has not intimated any thing in the nature of
    a charge against you, . . . although he has
    stated some complaints which had been made
    against the Agent. . . ."

2013   29 Sep 1809   A/1/551
Jesse Spencer, Reg Chl
Computation of interest; drawing lots for right
    of entry in case of simultaneous application by
    two parties for same quarter section.

2014   2 Oct 1809   A/1/551
Philip Grymes, Reg EOr, New Orleans
". . . [C]onsidering the length of time during
    which the Commissioners have been allowed com-
    pensation without any efficient services having
    been rendered, I think that their refusal to
    continue to act until they had ascertained
    whether that additional compensation would be
    allowed would give offence. . . ."

2015   2 Oct 1809   A/1/552
Samuel Finley, Rec Chl
Audit report appears to reveal large shortage of
    funds; Rec refused also to allow examination
    of books [Original letter sent by Col. Worthing-
    ton, duplicate thereof by mail].

2016   16 Oct 1809   A/1/552
Robert Robinson, Clerk of Land Commissioners, Kas
Compensation.

2017   18 Oct 1809   A/1/553
John J. Worth, Richmond, Virginia
First certificate, James Vaughan, Stu district.

2018   20 Oct 1809   A/1/553
Samuel Gwathney, Reg Jef
Sale of tracts containing salt springs forbidden &
sales declared null *ab initio* "whenever such
springs were known to exist at the time of purchase, . . . although they may not have been reported in the book of surveys."

2019   20 Oct 1809   A/1/553
John Henderson, Rec WPR, Washington, Mississippi
   Territory
Bills returned for endorsement
Seth Pease, Surveyor.

2020   4 Nov 1809   A/1/553
Philip Grymes, Reg EOr, New Orleans
Requests answer to letter of 25 Oct 1808 to pred-
ecessor regarding locations made by the agent of
General La Fayette.

2021   9 Nov 1809   A/1/553
John Sloane, Rec Can
Directs transportation of funds to Pittsburgh.

2022   10 Nov 1809   A/1/554
James Findlay, Rec Cin
Draft returned for endorsement
[Jared Mansfield], SG.

2023   16 Nov 1809   A/1/554
George Simpson, Cashier, Bank of United States
   [place not stated]
Correction of erroneous deposit
Isaac Van Horn, Rec Zan; Joseph Carver.

2024   18 Nov 1809   A/1/554
Reverend Joseph Anderson, St. Clairsville, Ohio
Refuses "partial indulgence" on instalment payment
   for land.

2025   24 Nov 1809   A/1/554
John Brahan, Rec Nas
Compensation & expenses allowable.

2026   25 Nov 1809   A/1/554
[Ninian] Edwards, Governor, Illinois Territory
Acknowledges report regarding Edwards' report on
   Saline; terms for new lease [important discus-
   sion of governmental considerations and require-
   ments].

2027   8 Dec 1809   A/1/557
John Brahan, Rec Nas
Expense account.

2028   9 Dec 1809   A/1/557
James Findlay, Rec Cin
Transfer of funds
[Jared Mansfield], SG.

2029   28 Dec 1809   A/1/557
John Henderson, Rec WPR, Washington, Mississippi
   Territory
Transfer of funds
John H. Williams, Secretary of Mississippi Terri-
   tory.

2030   18 Jan 1810   A/1/558
John Henderson, Rec WPR, Washington, Mississippi
   Territory
Transfer of funds
Jonathan Burrall, Cashier, Office of Discount &
   Deposit, New York.

2031   26 Jan 1810   A/1/558
Hon. Jeremiah? Morrow, Chairman
Transmits report on activities of Land Commissions
   in Orleans & Mississippi territories & projected
   time of completing adjustments of private claims;
   Act of 3 Mar 1807
[John Thompson], Reg WOr.

2032   27 Jan 1810   A/1/558
John Sloane, Rec Can
Payments made by John Hoopes & David Pratt; ac-
   counting instructions.

2033   13 Feb 1810   A/1/558
Lemuel Henry, Rec EPR, St. Stephens, Mississippi
   Territory
Comments on irregular [emergency?] payment made
   to -- Dinsmoor, Agent to the Choctaws.

2034   15 Feb 1810   A/1/559
James Findlay, Rec Cin
"I enclose a copy of an affidavit made by William
   Bridges of Mason County, Virginia, before Judge
   Coulter of that State, & also an extract of a
   Letter from Judge Coulter to Mr. Swoope a
   representative in Congress, relating to a plan
   formed by several persons for robbing the Boat,
   in which you annually transport the monies collected by you to Pittsburgh"; directed to send
   money to Bank of Kentucky, Frankfort; "I request you . . . to inform me particularly of
   the situation of Valtiers? [Valliers?] business
   & what prospect there is of a speedy recovery
   of the money purloined by him."

2035   15 Feb 1810   A/1/559
Philip Grymes, Reg EOr, New Orleans
Compensation due -- Wikoff, deputy register, &
   one other; claims against estate of Benedict
   van Pradelles
[Cassandra] van Pradelles.

2036   19 Feb 1810   A/1/560
Samuel Finley, Rec Chl
Points out large error in accounting report; "I
   cannot help observing that there must be some
   inattention or inaccuracy in the mode of keep-
   ing your accounts, when an error of this Magni-
   tude is not noticed for two months successively."

2037   20 Feb 1810   A/1/560
Isaac Van Horn, Rec Zan
Accounting discrepancy, Charles Henderson account.

2038   24 Feb 1810   A/1/560
Nathaniel Ewing, Rec Vin
Transfer of funds
[Jared Mansfield] SG.

2039   14 Mar 1810   A/1/560
[Ninian] Edwards, Governor, Illinois Territory, Kas
Lease of Saline to Jonathan Taylor, Charles Wilkins
   & James Morrison approved by President
-- White.

2040   15 Mar 1810   A/1/561
Edmund H. Taylor, Rec Jef; Nathaniel Ewing, Rec
   Vin
Transfer of funds to Lieutenant Ambrose Whitlock,
   District Paymaster [U.S. Army]
Robert Alexander, President, Bank of Kentucky.

2041   20 Mar 1810   A/1/561
Lemuel Henry, Rec EPR; Nicholas Perkins, Reg EPR,
   St. Stephens, Mississippi Territory
Requests explanation of claim made by Josias Bul-
   lock.

2042   21 Mar 1810   A/1/561
James Findlay, Rec Cin; John Brahan, Rec Nas
Transfer of funds to Lieutenant Alpha Kingsley,
   District Paymaster [U.S. Army, to pay troops
   "in his district comprizing Kentucky & Tennes-
   see."

2043   22 Mar 1810   A/1/562
Samuel Finley, Rec Chl
Transfer of funds; three-percent allowance to
   State of Ohio; road fund; transfer of remain-
   ing LO funds to Pittsburgh; warns of recent at-
   tempt to rob Rec Cin during transport of funds
William McFarland, Treasurer of State of Ohio.

2044   23 Mar 1810   A/1/562
John Brahan, Rec Nas
Transfer of funds to U.S. Army
Col. -- Meigs, Agent for War Department.

2045   26 Mar 1810   A/1/562
John Brahan, Rec Nas
Complains of irregular accounting procedures.

2046   13 Mar 1810   A/1/563
Thomas H. Williams, Reg WPR, Washington, Mississippi Territory
Acknowledges receipt of surveys; pre-emption
   claims.

2047   30 Mar 1810   A/1/563
Samuel Finley, Rec Chl
Statement of 1807 land transactions

Andrew Forster	Chl	-	17	18	33	+
Andrew Forster	Chl	-	17	18	29	+
Andrew Forster	Chl	-	17	18	19	+
Andrew Forster	Chl	-	17	18	18	+
William Forster	Chl	-	17	18	20	+
William Forster	Chl	-	17	18	28	+
William Forster	Chl	-	17	18	18	+
William Forster	Chl	-	17	18	29	+

2048   3 Apr 1810   A/1/563
Isaac Van Horn, Rec Zan
Credit denial
Samuel Clarkson.

2049   4 Apr 1810   A/1/564
Lemuel Henry, Rec EPR, St. Stephens, Mississippi
   Territory
New sureties required, because one formerly given
   is deceased & another has left the district.

2050   16 Apr 1810   A/1/564
Nathaniel Ewing, Rec Vin
Transfer of funds
[Jared Mansfield] SG.

2051   10 Apr 1810   A/1/564
Lemuel Henry, Rec EPR, St. Stephens, Mississippi
   Territory
Act regulating grants of land . . . south of Ten-
   nessee, §3 construction; pre-emption rights;
   interest due on instalments; Spanish warrants
   of survey
-- Gaines.

2052   20 Apr 1810   A/1/564
James Findlay, Rec Cin
Transfer of funds
Jared Mansfield, SG.

2053   28 Apr 1810   A/1/564
Philip Grymes, Reg EOr, New Orleans
Act of 21 Apr 1806; Act of 3 Mar 1807; compensa-
   tion of deputy registers; claim against estate
   of [Benedict] van Pradelles
B. Hubbard; -- Wikoff; -- Cantrell.

2054   1 Dec 1809*   A/1/565
William Dickson [Reg Nas]; Daniel Symmes [Reg
   Cin]; John Badollet [Reg Vin]; Richard Fergu-
   son, Louisville; Joseph Crockett, Lexington,
   Frankfort, & Bairdstown
Directed to advertise prospective lease of U.S.
   Saline, near Wabash River in Illinois Territory.
   *Letter out of sequence; no explanation given.

2055   4 May 1810   A/1/565
John Badollet, Reg Vin
Act to prescribe the mode in which application
   shall be made for the purchase of land at the
   several land offices; clause pertaining to
   Joab Garret.

2056   4 May 1810   A/1/566
Levin Wailes, Reg WOr
Transmits commission (appointment); oath & bond
   required.

2057   4 May 1810   A/1/566
Lewis Sewall, Reg EPR

Transmits commission (appointment); oath & bond
required [transmitted via Lemuel Henry, Rec
EPR].

2058   5 May 1810   A/1/566
David Hoge, Reg Stu; Joseph Wood, Reg Mar; Willys
Silliman, Reg Zan; Daniel Symmes, Reg Cin
Act of 30 Apr 1810 to extend the time for making
payment for the public lands . . .; Act of 3 Mar
1809.

2059   5 May 1810   A/1/567
Philip Grymes, Reg EOr, New Orleans; Levin Wailes,
Reg WOr, Opelousas; Frederick Bates, Recorder,
St. Louis
Informs of failure of bill for compensation of Com-
missioners to pass both Houses of Congress.

2060   7 May 1810   A/1/567
Daniel Symmes, Reg Cin
Act providing for sale of certain lands in the
Indiana Territory
[Jared Mansfield] SG.

2061   7 May 1810   A/1/567
Joseph Saul, Administrator of Estate of John W.
Burley
Claim of United States against estate
[Philip] Grymes, Reg EOr; B. Hubbard, deputy
register.

2062   7 May 1810   A/1/568
John Badollet, Reg Vin
Act providing for the sale of certain lands in the
Indiana Territory, §3; sale of tracts in Jef
district.

2063   7 May 1810   A/1/568
Samuel Gwathney, Reg Jef
Boundaries between Jef & Vin districts.

2064   7 May 1810   A/1/569
Willys Silliman, Reg Zan
Down payment required at public sales; full pay-
ment required on forfeited lands.

2065   11 May 1810   A/1/569
Gideon Fitz, Principal Deputy Surveyor, WOr, Opel-
ousas
Transmits commission (appointment).

2066   11 May 1810   A/1/569
Gideon Fitz, Opelousas (private)
Acknowledges receipt of report to Mr. Jefferson on
state of land claims; "Both from your letter &
from other information it seems that there can
be very little difficulty in deciding on those
claims not exceeding one league square. . . .
For it is generally understood that there are
but few, if any, fraudulent or doubtful claims
of that size in the district, those which are
considered as of a doubtful nature being the
large provisional grants to Bapstrop, Maison

Rouge, the parish of Atakapas, etc., & perhaps
some purchases of Indian Villages & vacheries.
. . ."

2067   12 May 1810   A/1/570
Parke Walton, Rec WPR, Washington, Mississippi
Territory
Transmits commision (appointment); oath & bond
required
[John] Henderson.

2068   12 May 1810   A/1/570
John Henderson
"The President having thought himself obliged as
a result of the enquiry into your conduct to
appoint another person to succeed you . . .
[has appointed] Parke Walton."

2069   7 May 1810   A/1/571
Michael Jones, Reg Kas
Decisions of Land Commissioners now confirmed by
enclosed Congressional act; further legisla-
tion needed regarding Donation & Militia claims;
Act of 3 Mar 1807; Act of 21 Apr 1806, §§1, 2;
Governors' confirmations.

2070   14 May 1810   A/1/572
Michael Jones, Reg Kas
Discussion of approved claims upon which Congress
has enacted legislation; British grants; com-
mons & lots within named settlements in Illinois
Territory [Kas, Grand Prairie, Prairie du Rocher,
Fort Chartres, St. Philip, Prairie Dupont, Caho-
kia]
David Robinson; William & Elias Rector; -- But-
chet & E. Langlois; -- Boisbrient; -- Chapin;
-- Delisle; Philip Renault.

2071   18 May 1810   A/1/573
Seth Pease, Surveyor, Washington, Mississippi
Territory
Approves appointment of William Brown as deputy
surveyor.

2072   18 May 1810   A/1/573
Michael Jones, Reg Kas
"I hear with great pleasure the result of the
wicked attempt which has been made against you
& hope that the parties may be brought to pun-
ishment"
-- Shaw; [Elijah] Backus.

2073   23 May 1810   A/1/574
Michael Jones, Reg Kas; Elijah Backus, Rec Kas
Governors' confirmations; powers of the governors
to give or confirm titles enumerated; Congressional Resolution of 20 Jun 1788; Congressional
Resolution of 28 Aug 1788; Act of 3 Mar 1791,
§4; ancient grants defined in §2 of Act of 3
Mar 1791; Proclamation [of British King] of
1763; Act of 7 May 1800; Governor St. Clair's
patent to -- St. Clair & -- Edgar of question-
able validity [important historical statement].

2074   28 May 1810   A/1/576
Lemuel Henry, Rec EPR
Case of Samuel Mims as assignee of John Turnbull's
  1600 acres on the Tombigbee River by virtue of a
  Spanish warrant or order of survey, dated 31 Jul
  1787; Act of 31 Mar 1808; Act of 28 Feb 1809
William Rogers; John P. Hainsworth, representa-
  tive of Matthew Shaw.

2075   27 Jun 1810   A/1/577
Henry Houtz, Dauphin County, Pennsylvania
Acknowledges receipt of remittance for land in Cin
  district [notation states patent issued on 28
  Sep 1810].

2076   27 Jun 1810   A/1/577
William Dickson [Dixon], Reg Nas
Removal of intruders not having permits to remain
  issued by Thomas Freeman; list of permitted
  residents to be given to officer in charge of
  troops.

2077   27 Jun 1810   A/1/577
Ethan A. Brown, Cin; Edward Tiffin, Chl; James
  Pritchard, Stu; Joseph Buell, Mar; William
  Wells, Zan; Benjamin Parke, Vin; John Girault,
  Washington, Mississippi Territory [for WPR];
  George L. Gaines, St. Stephens, Mississippi
  Territory [for EPR]; Zaccheus A. Beatty, Can;
  Richard Ferguson, Jef; John Childress, Junior,
  Nas
Certificate of appointment to audit books of Rec
  & Reg in corresponding districts.

2078   27 Jun 1810   A/1/578
Ethan A. Brown, Cin; Edward Tiffin, Chl; James
  Pritchard, Stu; Joseph Buell, Mar; William
  Wells, Zan; Benjamin Parke, Vin; John Girault,
  (near Natchez), Washington, Mississippi Terri-
  tory [for WPR]; George L. Gaines, St. Stephens,
  Mississippi Territory [for EPR]; Zaccheus A.
  Beatty (Cambridge, Ohio), Can; Richard Ferguson
  (Louisville), Jef; John Childress, Junior, Nas
Instructions for audit of books of Reg & Rec in
  corresponding districts.

2079   27 Jun 1810   A/1/579
Michael Jones, Reg Kas
Transmits claims approved by Commissioners & con-
  firmed by Act of 1 May 1810.

2080   29 Jun 1810   A/1/579
[Ninian] Edwards, Governor, Illinois Territory
Alleged oversupply of salt in western country occa-
  sions request by lessees of U.S. Saline for
  reduction in prices; calculation of royalty
  ["rent"] under reduced price authorized by U.S.
  President.

2081   29 Jun 1810   A/1/580
Messrs. Taylor, Wilkins, & Morrison, Lessees of
  U.S. Saline, Lexington, Kentucky
Reduction in salt price authorized by U.S. Presi-
  dent [followed by letter to James Morrison to
  same effect].

2082   30 Jun 1810   A/1/580
Parke Walton, Rec WPR, Washington, Mississippi
  Territory
Transfer of funds
Seth Pease, Surveyor of Lands South of Tennessee.

2083   30 Jun 1810   A/1/580
Lemuel Henry, Rec EPR, St. Stephens, Mississippi
  Territory
Transfer of funds
Judge -- Toulmin.

2084   5 Jul 1810   A/1/581
[Ninian] Edwards, Governor, Illinois Territory
Authorization to negotiate new lease of U.S. Sa-
  line.

2085   6 Jul 1810   A/1/581
Nehemiah Tilton, Reg WPR, Wilmington, Delaware
Transmits commission (appointment); oath & bond
  required.

2086   7 Jul 1810   A/1/581
Nathaniel Ewing, Rec Vin
Account of Dr. Samuel McKee.

2087   9 Jul 1810   A/1/581
George Doup, care of [Samuel Gwathney], Reg Jef
Final certificated erased & Doup's name inserted
Frederick Geiger   Jef* - 3E 6S - 4
Frederick Geiger   Jef* - 3E 6S - 5
  *Probably entered in Vin LO.

2088   9 Jul 1810   A/1/582
Samuel Gwathney, Reg Jef
Requests explanation of irregular erasure [see
  preceding entry].

2089   9 Jul 1810   A/1/582
John Sloan[e], Rec Can
Permission to accept partial payments.

2090   9 Jul 1810   A/1/582
John Badollet, Reg Vin
Irregular erasure of final certificate must be
  explained
George Doup
Frederick Geiger   Vin - 3E 6S - 4
Frederick Geiger   Vin - 3E 6S - 5

2091   10 Jul 1810   A/1/583
Samuel Gwathney, Reg Jef
Presidential proclamation of public sale; --
  Clarke's grant.

2092   11 Jul 1810   A/1/583
[Ninian] Edwards, Governor, Illinois Territory
Power to negotiate new lease of U.S. Saline.

2093   12 Jul 1810   A/1/583
John Brahan, Rec Nas

Transfer of funds to U.S. Army; troops to be sent
   into Madison County [Mississippi Territory] to
   eject intruders
R. J. Meigs; Lieutenant Alpha Kingsley.

2094   13 Jul 1810   A/1/583
Samuel Finley, Rec Chl
Acknowledges receipt of funds for Finley's account.

2095   16 Jul 1810   A/1/584
Edmund H. Taylor, Rec Jef
Transfer of funds to U.S. Army to pay troops in
   Louisiana Territory
Lieutenant Ambrose Whitlock; [Nathaniel] Ewing,
   Rec Vin.

2096   19 Jul 1810   A/1/584
Parke Walton, Rec WPR, Washington, Mississippi
   Territory
Act of 3 Mar 1803, §3; interest on pre-emption
   land payments
Lemuel Henry, Rec EPR.

2097   20 Jul 1810   A/1/584
John Badollet, Reg Vin
Confirmation of accounts
Thomas Aikman; Spencer Wood.

2098   27 Jul 1810   A/1/585
Tully Robinson, U.S. Attorney, New Orleans
Claim against late Collector's estate [name not
   given]; common lands of City of New Orleans.

2099   16 Jul 1810   A/1/585
Charles Randle
Presidential appointment to inspect proposed road
   from Cumberland by Union Town to Brownsville
   [Pennsylvania].

2100   1 Aug 1810   A/1/586
[Ninian] Edwards, Governor, Illinois Territory
Discusses leasing of U.S. Saline & improvements to
   navigation on Saline Creek.

2101   3 Aug 1810   A/1/586
William Ruffin, Cin
"There is no evidence . . . that would justify
   issuing a patent in the name of Craig & Bledsoe

as assignees of William Robertson. [On] the
   contrary an assignment from him to a certain
   Martin has long ago been transmitted. . . ."

2102   3 Aug 1810   A/1/587
Richard Cocke, now at Philadelphia
Settlement of compensation to be remitted to him
   in Kentucky.

2103   9 Aug 1810   A/1/587
Parke Walton, Rec WPR, Washington, Mississippi
   Territory
Commissioners "were a court without appeal for the
   purpose for which they were instituted"; writ
   of mandamus to be treated with respect but a
   plea against court's jurisdiction is to be entered; Reg & Rec have no power to rectify their
   own mistakes when acting as Commissioners;
   ejectment remedy available
Peter Little.

2104   9 Aug 1810   A/1/587
William Garrard, Land Commissioner, WOr, Opelousas,
   Orleans Territory
Compensation.

2105   15 Aug 1810   A/1/587
Lewis Sewall, Reg EPR
Office rent for own account.

2106   17 Aug 1810   A/1/588
William Wells, Zan
Acknowledges receipt of audit report.

2107   17 Aug 1810   A/1/588
Charles Randle
Cost estimate for Cumberland Road.

2108   21 Aug 1810   A/1/588
James Findlay, Rec Cin
Transfer of funds
[Jared Mansfield] SG.

2109   A/1/589
End papers bear notation: "For a letter to Buck-
   ner Thruston dated 22 Aug 1810 see next Book
   page 4."

(End of part 2 of source A, roll 1)

2110   21 Oct 1796 B/1/001
Rufus Putnam, SG
Israel Ludlow recommended as surveyor.

2111   25 Jan 1797 B/1/001
To: Sec Treas
From: Rufus Putnam, SG, Mar
Requests instructions.

2112   14 Mar 1797 B/1/003
Rufus Putnam, SG
Instructions; method of payment; accounting;
 priority to military lands survey under Act of
 1 Jun 1796; Moravian settlements; Seven Ranges;
 Ohio Company; Ordinance of Congress under the
 Confederation, passed 20 May 1785; method of
 numbering sections [plat].

2113   17 Mar 1797 B/1/006
Rufus Putnam, SG
Transfer of funds from Israel Ludlow to -- Dayton.

2114   8 Apr 1797 B/1/007
To: Sec Treas
From: Rufus Putnam, SG, Mar
Indian boundary between Muskingum [River] & Lora-
 mie's store; Moravian agents; military lands
William Skinner; Israel Ludlow.

2115   6 May 1797 B/1/008
To: Sec Treas
From: Rufus Putnam, SG, Mar
Greenville Treaty; boundary from Fort Recovery to
 Loramie's store
Dudley Woodbridge; General -- Wilkinson; Israel
 Ludlow.

2116   18 May 1797 B/1/009
To: Sec Treas
From: Rufus Putnam, SG, Mar
Boundary from Fort Recovery to Loramie's store &
 Muskingum River; Fort Laurence crossing; Seven
 Ranges; Moravian agents; [U.S.] Military Tract
 divided into five districts [Putnam's oath of
 office follows]
Judge Dudley Woodbridge; Judge [John Cleves]
 Symmes; Israel Ludlow; Absalom Martin; Zac-
 cheus Biggs of Ohio County, Virginia; -- Mat-
 thews of Hamilton County [state not given];
 -- Jackson of Harrison County, Virginia; John
 Otis; Tekd? Nye.

2117   5 Jun 1797 B/1/013
To: Sec Treas
From: Rufus Putnam, SG
Oath signed by William Rufus Putnam, Deputy Sur-
 veyor; Moravian lands; Tuscarawas Ford
Israel Ludlow.

2118   22 Jul 1797 B/1/014
To: Sec Treas
From: Rufus Putnam, Mar
Moravian grants [plats]; U.S. Military District;
 Fort Laurence crossing; Loramie's store

Israel Ludlow; -- Heckewelder; Absalom Martin;
 Zaccheus Biggs; -- Matthews; -- Jackson;
 William Rufus Putnam.

2119   15 Jun 1797 B/1/015
To: Rufus Putnam, SG
From: Israel Ludlow [at] "Fork of a creek near
 Loramie's"
Indian escorts [Ludlow's oath of office follows]
Thomas Gibson.

2120   29 Jul 1797 B/1/020
To: Sec Treas
From: Rufus Putnam, SG
Moravian surveys; contract with John Matthews &
 John G. Jackson [enclosed]; Act of 1 Jun 1796
 regulating the grants of land appropriated for
 military service
William Rufus Putnam; Levi Whipple; George Jack-
 son, father of John G. Jackson, a minor; David
 Davison.

2121   1 Sep 1797 B/1/021
To: Sec Treas
From: Rufus Putnam, SG
Transfer of funds
-- Ludlow; -- Dayton.

2122   2 Sep 1797 B/1/023
To: Sec Treas
From: Rufus Putnam, SG
Accounts submitted; Moravian lands; boundary
 line between Tuscarawas crossing [Fort Laurence]
 & Lorimie's store
William Rufus Putnam; -- Ludlow; Isaac Zane.

2123   13 Aug 1797 B/1/025
To: Rufus Putnam, SG
From: Captain Israel Ludlow
Indian boundary line from Fort Laurence crossing
 to Loramie's store; Wyandot Indians; Chippewas
 & Iowa Indians
Isaac Zane; Isaac Williams, a Wyandot chief;
 Billy Zane; Harronnyo, chief at Upper Sandusky
 [Indian] towns.

2124   19 Jul 1797 B/1/025
To: Isaac Williams, Wyandot Chief
From: Israel Ludlow
Requests meeting at Lorimie's store to discuss
 boundary line survey; Shawnee & Delaware Indian
 representatives not satisfied.

2125   16 Sep 1797 B/1/026
Rufus Putnam, SG
Indian boundary line; relations with U.S. Army
William Rufus Putnam; Israel Ludlow; General
 -- Wilkinson.

2126   9 Sep 1797 B/1/027
To: Sec Treas
From: Rufus Putnam, SG
Transfer of funds
Dudley Woodbridge.

2127   2 Dec 1797   B/1/027
To: Sec Treas
From: Rufus Putnam, SG
Zane grant [plats]; McCullock's ferry; Muskingum
River crossing; road opened
Ebenezer Zane; Isaac Zane; Joel Zane; Joseph
Wood; Solomon McCullock; Marquis Combs.

2128   12 Feb 1798   B/1/032
Rufus Putnam, SG
Zane's grant
Ebenezer Zane.

2129   27 Jan 1798   B/1/032
To: Sec Treas
From: Rufus Putnam, SG
Transfer of funds
Earl Sproat; John Matthews; Dudley Woodbridge;
Absalom Martin; Zaccheus Biggs.

2130   18 Jan 1798   B/1/033
To: Sec Treas
From: Rufus Putnam, SG
Quarterly accounts; land sales at Pittsburgh &
Cin
William Rufus Putnam; John Nourse [Reg Treas];
John Matthews; John G. Jackson; Israel Ludlow;
Absalom Martin; Zaccheus Biggs.

2131   26 Aug 1797*   B/1/035
To: Sec Treas
From: Rufus Putnam, SG
Transfer of funds
Dudley Woodbridge
   *Appears to be similar to entry 2126.

2132   9 Mar 1798   B/1/035
To: Sec Treas
From: Rufus Putnam
Ludlow's survey completed; Martin's survey 2/3
in arrears; Biggs' survey 1/2 in arrears; Seven
Ranges; survey plans for year 1798; re-survey
of Indian boundary
Israel Ludlow; Absalom Martin; Zaccheus Biggs.

2133   31 Mar 1798   B/1/037
Rufus Putnam, SG
Expresses regret at delays in surveying.

2134   7 Oct 1797   B/1/037
To: Sec Treas
From: Rufus Putnam, SG
Transfer of funds; survey of military lands
William Skinner; Dudley Woodbridge; Israel Lud-
low.

2135   21 Apr 1798   B/1/038
To: Sec Treas
From: Rufus Putnam, SG
Delayed surveys; accounts
Absalom Martin; Zaccheus Biggs; Israel Ludlow;
John Matthews; John G. Jackson.

2136   1 Jun 1798   B/1/039
Rufus Putnam, SG
Delayed surveys; [U.S.] Military District; ac-
counts.

2137   31 May 1798   B/1/040
To: Sec Treas
From: Rufus Putnam, SG
Accounts
Israel Ludlow; Zaccheus Biggs; Charles Green;
Benjamin Ives Gilman; Absalom Martin.

2138   8 Jun 1798   B/1/041
To: Sec Treas
From: Rufus Putnam, SG
Contracts & oaths of office [copies of contracts
& oaths follow]
Israel Ludlow; Benjamin Ives Gilman; Thomas
Worthington of Berkeley County, Virginia; Wil-
liam Rufus Putnam; Levi Whipple; Jeffery
Matthewson; Is[rael?] Pierce; Jonathan Stone;
Elias Langham of Berkeley County, Virginia;
Nehemiah Davis; Ichabod? Nye; John Bever of
Georgetown, Allegheny County, Pennsylvania;
R. I. Meigs; Daniel Wells; William C. Schenck.

2139   30 Jun 1798   B/1/053
Rufus Putnam, SG
Recommendation of Secretary of War for Ephraim B.
Ellis to be Deputy Surveyor.

2140   3 Aug 1798   B/1/054
To: Sec Treas
From: Rufus Putnam, SG
Accounts; [U.S.] Military District; transfer of
funds
Absalom Martin; William Skinner; Elias Lanham;
Zaccheus Biggs.

2141   6 Aug 1798   B/1/054
Rufus Putnam, SG
Act authorizing the grant & conveyance of a cer-
tain lot of ground to Elis? Williams.

2142   24 Sep 1798   B/1/055
Rufus Putnam, SG
Intruders from Kentucky in Ohio; [U.S.] Military
District
Jacob Barnet [Burnet?]; Elias Boudinot.

2143   13 Oct 1798   B/1/055
To: Sec Treas
From: Rufus Putnam, SG
[U.S.] Military District; survey delayed; ac-
counts
Absalom Martin; Dudley Woodbridge; Francis De
La Court; Paul Sproat.

2144   30 Oct 1798   B/1/057
To: Sec Treas
From: Rufus Putnam, SG
Intruders from Kentucky in Ohio; intent to take
possession without purchase from United States
government.

2145   30 Oct 1798   B/1/057
To: Sec Treas
From: Rufus Putnam, SG
Accounts
William Skinner; Dudley Woodbridge; Charles
  Greene; Absalom Martin.

2146   13 Nov 1798   B/1/058
To: Sec Treas
From: Rufus Putnam, SG
Act authorizing the grant & conveyance of a cer-
  tain lot of ground to Elie Williams [plat];
  accounts; [U.S.] Military District
William Skinner; Absalom Martin; Robert Elliott;
  Thomas Kennedy; Israel Ludlow; John S. Gano;
  James Findlay; James Smith; Robert Benham;
  George Gordon.

2147   9 Jan 1799   B/1/060
To: Sec Treas
From: Rufus Putnam, SG
Accounts [contracts follow]; [U.S.] Military Dis-
  trict
Zaccheus Biggs of Ohio County, Virginia; William
  Rufus Putnam; Stephen Frost; John Matthews;
  Ebenezer Buckingham; Increase Matthews; Ben-
  jamin Ives Gilman; France D'Herbercourt?;
  Dudley Woodbridge; Absalom Martin.

2148   5 Mar 1799   B/1/064
To: Sec Treas
From: Rufus Putnam, SG
Accounts
-- Harrison.

2149   14 Mar 1799   B/1/067
Rufus Putnam, SG
Letter enclosing copy of public notice regarding
  "An Act regulating the grants of land appropri-
  ated for military service & for the Society of
  United Brethren for propagating the Gospel
  among the Heathens [Moravians]"; [public not-
  ice precedes this entry].

2150   15 Mar 1799   B/1/068
To: Sec Treas
From: Rufus Putnam, SG
Indian boundary line survey; Indians request a
  road
Israel Ludlow; General -- Wilkinson.

2151   20 Mar 1799   B/1/069
Rufus Putnam, SG
Indian boundary line survey
Governor [Arthur] St. Clair.

2152   2 Feb 1799   B/1/069
To: Sec Treas
From: Rufus Putnam, SG
[U.S.] Military District survey; accounts
Dudley Woodbridge; Charles Greene; Francis D'Her-
  bercourt?; Josiah Munroe; John Matthews; Earl
  Sproat; Ebenezer Buckingham; Levi Whipple.

2153   19 Apr 1799   B/1/070
Rufus Putnam, SG
Indian boundary line survey
Major General -- Hamilton.

2154   1 May 1799   B/1/071
Rufus Putnam, SG
"An Act to authorize the sale of certain lands between the Great & Little Miami Rivers . . . and
  for giving pre-emption to certain purchasers &
  settlers"
John C[leve] Symmes; George Turner; J. Dunlap.

2155   9 May 1799   B/1/072
To: Sec Treas
From: Rufus Putnam, SG
Indian boundary line survey
Israel Ludlow; Governor [Arthur] St. Clair.

2156   24 May 1799   B/1/072
Rufus Putnam, SG
Indian boundary line survey to have military es-
  cort.

2157   8 Aug 1799   B/1/073
To: Sec Treas
From: Rufus Putnam, SG
Accounts; public notice of pre-emption law; In-
  dian boundary line survey military escort
J. Nourse [Reg Treas]; -- Simpson; Absalom Mar-
  tin; John C. Symmes; Israel Ludlow; Col. --
  Hamtramck.

2158   27 Jul 1799   B/1/074
Contract for survey [form without addressee]
Ebenezer Buckingham; Stephen Pierce; Levi Whip-
  ple.

2159   16 Jul 1799   B/1/076
Contract for survey [form without addressee]
Zaccheus Biggs; Levi Whipple; Ebenezer Bucking-
  ham.

2160   27 Jul 1799   B/1/077
Contract for survey [form without addressee]
John Bever of George Town, Allegheny County, Penn-
  sylvania; Levi Whipple; Ebenezer Buckingham.

2161   15 Aug 1799   B/1/078
To: Sec Treas
From: Rufus Putnam, SG
Indian boundary line survey
Israel Ludlow; Col. -- Hamtramck.

2162   20 Jul 1799   B/1/080
Rufus Putnam, SG
Letter from Israel Ludlow, at Fort Loramie, trans-
  mitting letter from Indian; Indian boundary line
  survey; Indian relations
Niamineseea; Selipego [both chiefs of Shawness In-
  dians].

2163   2 Sep 1799   B/1/081
Rufus Putnam, SG
Indian boundary line survey; Indian relations
Israel Ludlow.

2164   28 Apr 1796   B/1/081
Contract between John C. Symmes & William Wells
Claim of pre-emption right
Robert Morris; John Dinsmore; Christian Newcomer;
  Susan A. Ridley; William Wells of Glastonbury,
  Hartford County, Connecticut; Talcott Camp; J.
  Pierce; S. Hillegas; William Crean; James
  Byers
William Wells   Sym MR 5 3   5   -
William Wells   Sym MR 5 3 17   -
William Wells   Sym MR 5 3 23   -
William Wells   Sym MR 5 3 35   -
William Wells   Sym MR 5 3 36   -
William Wells   Sym MR 5 4 35   -
William Wells   Sym MR 5 4 23   -
William Wells   Sym MR 5 4   - 17

2165   18 Sep 1799   B/1/084
To: Sec Treas
From: Rufus Putnam, SG
Indian boundary line survey; Indian relations
Israel Ludlow; Captain -- Hamilton; Lieutenant
  -- Stall.

2166   24 Oct 1799   B/1/086
To: Sec Treas
From: Rufus Putnam, SG
Transfer of funds; road survey; Seven Ranges;
  Connecticut grant
Thomas Worthington; John Brown, U.S. Senator
  from Kentucky; Israel Ludlow.

2167   15 Jan 1800   B/1/086
To: Sec Treas
From: Rufus Putnam, SG
Accounts
Thomas Worthington; Zaccheus Biggs; John Beaver
  [also Bever]; Dudley Woodbridge; Earl Sproat;
  William Ludlow; Benjamin Chambers; Ebenezer
  Sproat; Danciel C. Cooper; Israel Ludlow;
  -- Harrison [auditor].

2168   5 Feb 1800   B/1/087
To: Sec Treas
From: Rufus Putnam, SG
Zane's Trace; Zane grant
Ebenezer Zane; Josiah Munroe; Benjamin Ives Gil-
  man.

2169   2 Apr 1800   B/1/087
To: Sec Treas
From: Rufus Putnam, SG
Transfer of funds
Elias Langham.

2170   23 May 1800   B/1/087
Rufus Putnam, SG
Act of 10 May 1800 to amend the Act entitled "An
  Act providing for the sale of lands of the
  United States in the Territory northwest of the

River Ohio . . ."; Presidential appointments
Peregrine Foster, Reg Mar; Israel Ludlow, Reg Cin;
  Thomas Worthington, Reg Chl; David Hoge, Reg
  Stu; Elijah Backus, Rec Mar; James Findlay,
  Rec Cin; Samuel Finley, Rec Chl; Zaccheus
  Biggs, Rec Stu.

2171   5 Jun 1800   B/1/088
To: Joseph Nourse, Reg Treas
From: Rufus Putnam, SG
Acknowledges letter
Israel Ludlow.

2172   12 Jul 1800   B/1/088
To: Sec Treas
From: Rufus Putnam, SG
Transfer of records to new registers; need for
  clerical assistance; Seven Ranges; surveying
  of townships & sections
David Hoge, Reg Stu; Israel Ludlow.

2173   8 Oct 1800   B/1/092
Rufus Putnam, SG
Survey of Seven Ranges; Act of 18 May 1796; surveying of townships & sections; Act of 10 May
  1800, §10.

2174   12 Feb 1801   B/1/093
To: Sec Treas
From: Rufus Putnam, SG
Transfer of funds
Jonathan Dayton; Israel Ludlow.

2175   17 Mar 1801   B/1/093
Rufus Putnam, SG
Act regulating the grants of land appropriated
  for the Refugees from the British Provinces of
  Canada & Nova Scotia.

2176   10 Jan 1801   B/1/093
To: Sec Treas
From: Rufus Putnam, SG
Accounts; Act of 10 May 1800 [contracts with
  Thomas Worthington, Zaccheus Biggs, Alexander
  Holmes, John Bever, Ebenezer Buckingham, Levi
  Barber]
Alexander Holmes; Thomas Worthington; Charles
  Greene; William Rufus Putnam; Levi Whipple;
  Philip Greene; Ichabod Nye; Elnathan Sco-
  field.

2177   2 Apr 1801   B/1/104
To: Sec Treas
From: Rufus Putnam, SG
Transfer of funds
Elnathan Scofield; Jacob Bowman; Dudley Wood-
  bridge; William Cleveland.

2178   20 May 1801   B/1/105
To: Sec Treas
From: Rufus Putnam, SG
Act of 10 May 1800; comments upon various devia-
  tions in surveys.

2179   12 Jun 1801   B/1/107
Rufus Putnam, SG
New policy for transfers of funds; Canadian &
   Nova Scotian refugees.

2180   22 Jun 1801   B/1/108
Rufus Putnam, SG
Indian boundary line survey.

2181   6 Jul 1801   B/1/108
To: Sec Treas
From: Rufus Putnam, SG
Indian boundary line survey; Canadian & Nova Sco-
   tian refugee lands; accounts [contracts with
   Israel Ludlow, Elnathan Scofield, John G. Macan,
   Elias Langham, Benjamin Franklin Stone, Levi
   Barber]
Elnathan Scofield; Elijah Backus; William Skin-
   ner; Dudley Woodbridge; Joseph Nourse; Sproat
   & Matthews; William Rufus Putnam; Levi Whipple;
   D. C. Cooper; Ichabod Nye.

2182   9 Jul 1801   B/1/118
To: Sec Treas
From: Rufus Putnam, SG
Indian boundary line survey
Elijah Backus; James Findlay.

2183   24 Jul 1810   B/1/119
Rufus Putnam, SG
Transfer of funds; township surveys; Indian
   boundary line survey
Elijah Backus.

2184   10 Aug 1801   B/1/119
To: Sec Treas
From: Rufus Putnam, SG
Transfers of funds; township surveys; Act of 10
   May 1800; duties of Surveyor General; total
   miles surveyed to date [valuable summary of work
   accomplished]
Elijah Backus; Israel Ludlow.

2185   12 Aug 1801   B/1/123
To: Sec Treas
From: Rufus Putnam, SG
Transfer of funds; plats forwarded; Indian
   boundary line survey
Elijah Backus.

2186   28 Aug 1801   B/1/124
Rufus Putnam, SG
Transfer of funds; Act of 2 Mar 1799, §3; Symmes
   contract
-- Byers.

2187   25 Sep 1801   B/1/124
Rufus Putnam, SG
Purchasers at New York & Pittsburgh of land in
   Seven Ranges; Act of 10 May 1800, §3; settle-
   ment of conflicting claims.

2188   12 Nov 1801   B/1/127
Rufus Putnam, SG
Act of 10 May 1801; suspension of township sub-
   divisions.

2189   6 Oct 1801   B/1/127
To: Sec Treas
From: Rufus Putnam, SG
Leases to settlers in Jefferson County, Ohio; Act
   of 2 Mar 1799
John Cleves Symmes
James Byars   Unk Pre   5   2 17   -

2190   7 Oct 1801   B/1/129
To: Sec Treas
From: Rufus Putnam, SG
Indian boundary line survey; transfer of funds
Samuel Finley; Elijah Backus; James Findlay.

2191   15 Oct 1801   B/1/130
To: Sec Treas
From: Rufus Putnam, SG
Subdivision of Seven Ranges suspended; Act of 10
   May 1800; Dohrman grant; Act of 18 May 1796;
   original surveys made for sales at New York &
   Pittsburgh of land in Seven Ranges; Act of 10
   May 1800
Alexander Wolcott; Zaccheus Biggs
Not stated   Mar   -   2   6   -   *
Arnold H. Dohrman   Mar   -   17 13   -   -
Not stated   Mar   -   2   7   -   -
   *Northeast quarter section.

2192   4 Nov 1801   B/1/136
To: Sec Treas
From: Rufus Putnam, SG
Transfer of funds; Canadian & Nova Scotian refu-
   gee lands
James Findlay; Samuel Finley.

2193   19 Nov 1801   B/1/137
To: Sec Treas
From: Rufus Putnam, SG
Canadian & Nova Scotian refugee lands surveyed.

2194   4 Jan 1802   B/1/137
To: Sec Treas
From: Rufus Putnam, SG
Transfer of funds; estimate of expenditures for
   period July through December 1801
Israel Ludlow, Cin; Zaccheus Biggs, Stu; John
   Bever, Stu; Alexander Holmes, Stu; James
   Findlay; Elijah Backus; Levi Barber, Mar;
   Thomas Worthington, Chl; Elias Langham, Chl;
   John Macan, Chl; Benjamin Franklin Stone, Chl;
   Elnathan Scofield, Chl.

2195   7 Jan 1802   B/1/139
To: Sec Treas
From: Rufus Putnam, SG
Symmes grant; Virginia Military District of Ohio;
Thomas Worthington.

2196   23 Jan 1802   B/1/141
Rufus Putnam, SG
Transfer of funds.

2197   26 Jan 1802   B/1/141
Rufus Putnam, SG
Purchasers under Symmes grant; boundary of Vir-
  ginia Military District of Ohio.

2198   11 Mar 1802   B/1/142
To: Sec Treas
From: Rufus Putnam, SG
Boundaries of Symmes grant; U.S. Military District
Israel Ludlow.

2199   29 Mar 1802   B/1/143
Rufus Putnam, SG
Survey of the land between the two Miami rivers
Israel Ludlow.

2200   5 May 1802   B/1/144
Rufus Putnam, SG
Act of 1 May 1802; Act of 10 May 1800.

2201   24 May 1802   B/1/145
To: Sec Treas
From: Rufus Putnam, SG
Survey of land between two Miami rivers; survey
  of Virginia Military District; survey of Symmes
  grant; Seven Ranges; pre-emption rights
Israel Ludlow.

2202   3 May 1802   B/1/146
Contract for survey [form without addressee]
Survey of land between two Miami rivers
Israel Ludlow of Hamilton County [Ohio]; Levi
  Whipple & Levi Barber of Washington County [Ohio];
  C. Chillgore [Killgore]; Griffin Yeatman.

2203   12 Jun 1802   B/1/147
Rufus Putnam, SG
Purchasers under Symmes grant; survey of lands
  between two Miami rivers; pre-emption claims.

2204   2 Jul 1802   B/1/147
Rufus Putnam, SG
Division of Seven Ranges; purchasers at New York
  & Pittsburgh of lands in Seven Ranges; Act of
  10 May 1800 [important set of rules].

2205   10 Jun 1802   B/1/148
To: Sec Treas
From: Rufus Putnam, SG
Act of 10 May 1800; purchasers at New York &
  Pittsburgh of lands in Seven Ranges; sale at
  Stu [plat]; conflicting claims in Seven Ranges

Not stated	Mar	-	3	6	-	-
Not stated	Mar	-	3	9	-	-
Not stated	Mar	-	3	8	-	-
Not stated	Mar	-	2	5	-	-

2206   25 Jun 1802   B/1/151
Rufus Putnam, SG

Conflicting claims in Seven Ranges; Act of 10
  May 1800; instructions for survey of subdivi-
  sions within Seven Ranges; purchasers at New
  York & Pittsburgh of lands in Seven Ranges.

2207   26 Jun 1802   B/1/154
Rufus Putnam, SG
Roads in Northwest Territory.

2208   8 Jul 1802   B/1/155
To: Sec Treas
From: Rufus Putnam, SG
Survey of land between two Miami rivers; transfer
  of funds
Zaccheus Biggs; Elijah Backus.

2209   17 Jul 1802   B/1/156
To: Sec Treas
From: Rufus Putnam, SG
Subdivisions of Seven Ranges; roads.

2210   19 Jul 1802   B/1/157
To: Sec Treas
From: Rufus Putnam, SG
Subdivision of Seven Ranges; sales at New York
  & Pittsburgh of land in Seven Ranges; Act of
  10 May 1800.

2211   9 Aug 1802   B/1/158
Rufus Putnam, SG
Resignation of P[eregrine] Foster, Reg Mar.

2212   23 Aug 1802   B/1/158
To: Sec Treas
From: Rufus Putnam, SG
Recommendation of Edwin Putnam, son of Surveyor
  General Rufus Putnam, for Reg Mar; Mar "land
  office is not worth any man's attention on
  account of the profit"
[Peregrine] Foster; Hon. -- Lincoln, Attorney
  General; Charles Greene; Matthew Backus.

2213   6 Oct 1802   B/1/159
Rufus Putnam, SG
[Joseph] Wood appointed Reg Mar
Edwin Putnam.

2214   9 Oct 1802   B/1/159
To: Sec Treas
From: Rufus Putnam, SG
Transfer of funds
Samuel Finley; Zaccheus Biggs.

2215   25 Oct 1802   B/1/160
Rufus Putnam, SG
Transfer of funds.

2216   3 Mar 1803   B/1/160
Rufus Putnam, SG
Transfer of funds.

2217   8 Apr 1803   B/1/160
Isaac Briggs, Surveyor of Lands South of Tennessee
Instructions regarding duties; Act of 18 May 1796;
  Act of 10 May 1800; Articles of Agreement with
  Georgia; claims under British grants.

2218   16 Apr 1803   B/1/165
Rufus Putnam, SG
Roads in Northwest Territory.

2219   22 Apr 1803   B/1/166
Rufus Putnam, SG
Subdivision of U.S. Military District; boundary
  survey of Virginia Military District of Ohio.

2220   7 May 1803   B/1/167
To: Sec Treas
From: Rufus Putnam, SG
Land between the two Miami rivers; settlers under
  Virginia military warrants
Israel Ludlow.

2221   4 Jun 1803   B/1/167
Rufus Putnam, SG
Land between the two Miami rivers.

2222   23 Jul 1803   B/1/167
Rufus Putnam, SG
Transfers of funds
Moses Hook, assistant military agent at Pittsburgh;
  General -- Irvine, superintendent of military
  stores, Philadelphia.

2223   19 Sep 1803   B/1/168
Jared Mansfield, New Haven, Connecticut
Commission as Surveyor General with headquarters
  at Mar; instructions & duties; Virginia Mili-
  tary District of Ohio; Connecticut Reserve;
  Symmes grant; Ohio Company; U.S. Military Dis-
  trict
Rufus Putnam.

2224   21 Sep 1803   B/1/170
Rufus Putnam, SG
Replacement of Rufus Putnam by Jared Mansfield;
  roads in Northwest Territory.

2225   26 Jul 1803   B/1/171
Isaac Briggs, Surveyor, Mississippi Territory
Surveying instructions; British grants.

2226   23 Aug 1803   B/1/173
Jared Mansfield, SG
Instructions; Act of 18 May 1796; Act of 10 May
  1800; Act of 1 Jun 1796; Act of 1 Mar 1800;
  Act of 26 Apr 1802; Act of 3 Mar 1803; Act of
  21 Apr 1792 [Ohio Company]; Act of 12 Apr 1792
  [Symmes grant]; Act of 2 Mar 1799; Act of 3 Mar
  1801; Act of 1 May 1802; Act of 17 May 1796
  [Zane grant]; Act of 3 Mar 1795 [Gallipolis];
  Act of 3 Apr 1802 [Isaac Zane]; Act of 30 Apr
  1802 [formation of Ohio Territory]
Stephen Monot, Gallipolis.

2227   9 Nov 1803   B/1/176
Isaac Briggs, Surveyor General, Mississippi Territory
Instructions; Louisiana speculation; Ohio survey.

2228   30 Nov 1803   B/1/177
Jared Mansfield, SG
Transfers of funds; instructions.

2229   15 Dec 1803   B/1/178
Isaac Briggs, Surveyor General, Mississippi Terri-
tory
Commission issued.

2230   10 Jan 1804   B/1/178
[Jared Mansfield], SG
Transfer of funds
James Findlay, Rec Cin; Samuel Finley, Rec Chl;
  Elijah Backus, Rec Mar.

2231   25 Jan 1804   B/1/179
Isaac Briggs, SG, Mississippi Territory
Ellicot's line of demarcation; Louisiana speculation "considered sufficiently important to be
  communicated to Congress without, however, mentioning your name."

2232   9 Mar 1804   B/1/179
[Jared Mansfield] SG
Instructions; transfers of funds.

2233   6 Apr 1804   B/1/180
[Jared Mansfield] SG
Act for disposal of Indiana lands; Zanesville
  land office organized; U.S. Military District;
  Ohio Company; Seven Ranges; Virginia Military
  District; method of survey of Indiana Terri-
  tory; survey of Vincennes Tract; survey of
  Detroit district; surveying instruments im-
  ported from England
Willis Silliman, Reg Zan; Israel Ludlow.

2234   25 Apr 1804   B/1/182
Jared Mansfield, SG
Transfer of funds
Elijah Backus "late Rec Mar"; -- Tupper.

2235   25 Apr 1804   B/1/183
Rufus Putnam, "late" SG
Settling of accounts; road from Wheeling to Lime-
  stone
Elijah Backus; -- Tupper.

2236   27 Apr 1804   B/1/183
Jared Mansfield, SG
Nominations for deputy surveyors.

2237   30 Apr 1804   B/1/183
Jared Mansfield, SG
Survey of Indiana Territory; Vincennes Tract;
  Act of 10 May 1800; public sale Spring 1805;
  Indian boundary line [in Indiana]
-- Freeman.

2238   9 Jun 1804   B/1/184
Jared Mansfield, SG
Surveys of Stu, Zan, Chl, & Cin districts; ap-
  pointments of deputy surveyors [listed herein-
  after]; headquarters for SG to be moved
-- Brownson; -- Sunck; -- Franklin
Deputy surveyors:

William Heald	Stu District No. 1
Benjamin Hough	Stu District No. 2
Alexander Holmes	Stu District No. 3
Levi Barber	Mar District No. 1
Joseph Wood	Mar District No. 2
Levi Whipple	Zan District No. 1
Abel Lewis	Zan District No. 2 & 3
James Kilburn	Chl District No. 1
Elnathan Scofield	Chl District No. 2
James Denny	Chl District No. 3 & 4
William Ludlow	Cin District No. 1, 4, 5
Maxwell Ludlow	Cin District No. 2
Benjamin Chambers	Cin District No. 3

2239   10 Jul 1804   B/1/186
Jared Mansfield, SG
Vincennes district lands; Kaskaskia district land.

2240   17 Jul 1804   B/1/187
Jared Mansfield, SG
Appointments to deputy surveyorship
Alexander Holmes; Benjamin Hough.

2241   26 Jul 1804   B/1/188
Jared Mansfield, SG
Surveys of interior lines; effect on prior pur-
  chasers & surveys; surveying fees.

2242   21 Sep 1804   B/1/189
Jared Mansfield, SG
Instructions to deputy surveyors; surveying fees;
  headquarters of SG.

2243   18 Oct 1804   B/1/191
Jared Mansfield, SG, "now at Vincennes"
Instructions to deputy surveyors.

2244   16 Nov 1804   B/1/191
Surveyor General
Transfers of funds; survey of Vincennes Tract.

2245   24 Nov 1804   B/1/192
Jared Mansfield, SG
Transfers of funds; survey of Vincennes Tract
Samuel Finley, Rec Chl; Benjamin Tupper, Rec Mar.

2246   5 Nov 1804   B/1/192
William Ludlow, District Surveyor, Cin
Instructions to deputy surveyors.

2247   13 Nov 1804   B/1/193
Alexander Holmes, District Surveyor, Stu
Complaint regarding survey

William Bell	Stu	-	3	6	23	-
William Bell	Stu	-	3	6	22	-

2248   20 Feb 1805   B/1/194
Isaac Briggs, SG, Mississippi Territory
Political pressure from Mississippi Congressional
  representative regarding surveying delays.

2249   13 Mar 1805   B/1/194
Isaac Briggs, SG, Mississippi Territory
Surveying of internal lines; remonstrates regard-
  ing delays.

2250   13 Mar 1805   B/1/195
Jared Mansfield, SG
Act regarding mode of surveying; Act of 26 Mar
  1804; survey of Vincennes district; Treaty of
  Greenville; Detroit survey; Sandusky survey;
  Chicago survey; Connecticut Reserve; Act of
  28 Apr 1800; surveying instruments from Eng-
  land; purchase from Sac & Fox Indians; survey
  of Illinois Territory boundaries & Kas district
-- Jouett, Indian Agent

2251   15 Mar 1805   B/1/200
Jared Mansfield, SG
Survey of Fort Defiance area.

2252   4 Apr 1805   B/1/200
Jared Mansfield, SG
Boundary survey for Connecticut Reserve; purchase of lands north of U.S. Military District
  from Indians.

2253   17 Apr 1805   B/1/201
Jared Mansfield, SG
Act of 1 May 1802, §7; sale at New York of lands
  in Seven Ranges

William Bell	Mar	-	3	6	23	-
Not stated	Mar	-	3	6	22	-
Not stated	Mar	-	3	6	17	-
Not stated	Mar	-	3	6	29	-

2254   20 Apr 1805   B/1/202
Jared Mansfield, SG
Laws concerning fractional sections; Act of 26
  Mar 1804, §§9, 10, 12; Act of 11 Feb 1805, §2;
  extent of Connecticut Reserve; surveying instru-
  ments from England; surveying fees
-- Jouett, Indian Agent; Benjamin Hough.

2255   27 May 1805   B/1/205
Isaac Briggs, SG, Mississippi Territory
Act for adjusting titles in territory of Orleans
  & district of Louisiana; surveying sequence;
  survey of alluvial lands; special survey for
  grant to General La Fayette
Joseph M. White, New Orleans; [John W.] Gurley,
  Reg EOr.

2256   3 Jun 1805   B/1/207
Jared Mansfield, SG
Estimate of cost of surveying Ohio lands and Vin-
  cennes Tract; transfer of funds; U.S. Military
  District.

2257   5 Jun 1805   B/1/208
Jared Mansfield, SG
Recommends appointment of -- Freeman as assistant
   surveyor.

2258   12 Jun 1805   B/1/209
Isaac Briggs, SG, Mississippi Territory
Survey of private claims in Mississippi Territory;
   transfer of funds
Robert Williams.

2259   1 Jul 1805   B/1/209
Jared Mansfield, SG
Survey of Indiana Territory; Vincennes Tract
-- Ellicot.

2260   2 Jul 1805   B/1/210
Isaac Briggs, SG, Mississippi Territory
Private claims in Territory of Orleans; [private]
   claims in Louisiana District; survey of grant
   to General La Fayette; duties of Orleans &
   Mississippi Land Commissioners; surveys of pri-
   vate claims; conversion of French *arpent* to
   English land measurements; survey of alluvial
   lands; transfer of funds
Joseph White, New Orleans; -- Ellicot.

2261   26 Aug 1805   B/1/216
Isaac Briggs, SG, Mississippi Territory
Transfer of funds
-- McGrew.

2262   8 Oct 1805   B/1/216
Jared Mansfield, SG
Surveying instruments from England; malignant
   fever at New York & Philadelphia
-- Froughton.

2263   21 Oct 1805   B/1/217
Jared Mansfield, SG
Transfer of funds.

2264   21 Oct 1805   B/1/217
Jared Mansfield, SG
Act of 11 Feb 1805, §2(3); Connecticut Reserve;
   legal suit against lessees of reserved section.

2265   5 Nov 1805   B/1/218
Isaac Briggs, SG, Mississippi Territory
Expense account.

2266   19 Dec 1805   B/1/218
Jared Mansfield, SG
Authorizes commencement of survey.

2267   25 Mar 1806   B/1/219
Isaac Briggs, SG, Mississippi Territory
Act extending powers of SG to Louisiana Territory;
   selection of principal deputy; Spanish land
   grants
-- Soulard of St. Louis, surveyor under Spanish
   government.

2268   24 Apr 1806   B/1/220
Isaac Briggs, SG, Mississippi Territory
British grants; survey of district west of Pearl
   River.

2269   1 May 1806   B/1/220
Jared Mansfield, SG
Survey appropriation; survey of Vincennes Tract;
   land grants [confirmations] made by governors;
   Greenville Treaty boundary; Connecticut Re-
   serve; purchase of Indian lands in northern
   Ohio; Virginia Military District of Ohio; U.S.
   Military District; Chicago survey; transfer of
   funds.

2270   6 May 1806   B/1/223
Jared Mansfield, SG
Act authorizing sale of Cincinnati lands; land
   leased to Elie Williams in 1798
Elie Williams; Jeremiah Hunt, assignee.

2271   6 May 1806   B/1/224
Jared Mansfield, SG
Recommendation of Seth Pease to survey public
   land west of Connecticut Reserve.

2272   8 May 1806   B/1/224
Isaac Briggs, SG, Mississippi Territory
Act adjusting titles & claims within territory of
   Orleans & district of Louisiana; appointment of
   principal deputy; survey fees; settlement of
   an American population in western district of
   Orleans Territory "considered as intimately con-
   nected with the welfare & even the safety of that
   newly acquired territory"; General La Fayette's
   land grant.

2273   20 Jun 1806   B/1/225
William Ludlow, Cin
Surveyors cannot be compelled to survey quarter
   sections.

2274   26 Jun 1806   B/1/226
Jared Mansfield, SG
Cincinnati survey; tract adjoining Connecticut
   Reserve considered very "saleable"; numbering
   of ranges in State of Ohio
Elie Williams; Jeremiah Hunt.

2275   3 Jul 1806   B/1/226
Jared Mansfield, SG
Appointment of Silas Bent as principal deputy sur-
   veyor of Louisiana; transfer of funds
-- Messenger; -- Soulard, former surveyor for
   Spanish government; Governor -- Wilkinson;
   Jeremiah Hunt.

2276   8 Jul 1806   B/1/227
Jared Mansfield, SG
Patent of Jeremiah Hunt to land in Cincinnati.

2277   10 Jul 1806   B/1/227
Jared Mansfield, SG

Public sale of land in Vin district; appointment of principal deputy surveyor for Louisiana.

2278   21 Jul 1806   B/1/228
Jared Mansfield, SG
Fort Washington survey
General -- Harman; Judge [John C.] Symmes; Jeremiah Hunt.

2279   10 Aug 1806   B/1/228
Jared Mansfield, SG
Expense account.

2280   14 Aug 1806   B/1/229
Jared Mansfield, SG
Expense accounts; proclamation for sale of land in Vin district.

2281   10 Aug 1806   B/1/229
Jared Mansfield, SG
Sale of lands in Vin district; Act of 26 Mar 1804.

2282   7 Oct 1806   B/1/230
Jared Mansfield, SG
Concerning Bazaliel Wells, Stu.

2283   7 Oct 1806   B/1/230
Benjamin Hough, Stu
Act of 1 May 1802, §7; case of Latimore; Act of 10 May 1800
James Crawford; -- Latimore.

2284   10 Oct 1806   B/1/231
Jared Mansfield, SG
Fort Washington tract; Cincinnati survey
[John C.] Symmes.

2285   11 Oct 1806   B/1/231
Jared Mansfield, SG
Transmission of survey books
Lieutenant James Swearingen, military agent at Pittsburgh.

2286   14 Oct 1806   B/1/232
Jared Mansfield, SG
Requests surveying information regarding below-cited tract
Not stated   Chl - 20 12 31 +

2287   27 Oct 1806   B/1/232
Jared Mansfield, SG
Private claims in Kas district.

2288   3 Nov 1806   B/1/232
Jared Mansfield, SG
Survey of lands adjacent to Connecticut Reserve.

2289   3 Nov 1806   B/1/233
Isaac Briggs, SG, Mississippi Territory
Public sale of lands west of Pearl River
George Davis.

2290   12 Dec 1806   B/1/233
Isaac Briggs, SG, Mississippi Territory
Charges made by George Davis, formerly assistant surveyor, against Isaac Briggs alleging fraud
Thomas H. Williams, Reg WPR; William Dunbar.

2291   22 Dec 1806   B/1/233
Cincinnati survey; Symmes patent.

2292   31 Dec 1806   B/1/234
Jared Mansfield, SG
Public sale of lands in Vin district.

2293   19 Jan 1807   B/1/234
Jared Mansfield, SG
Transfers of funds.

2294   21 Mar 1807   B/1/235
Seth Pease, SG, Mississippi Territory
Transfers of funds; survey of private claims in Mississippi Territory; instructions; public sale of lands in WPR district; contravention of Presidential orders not to survey west of Natchitoches in order not to disturb negotiations with Spanish government
John Henderson, Rec WPR; Isaac Briggs.

2295   27 Mar 1807   B/1/237
Jared Mansfield, SG
Transmits various Congressional acts; private claims at Vin; appointment of assistant surveyor for Michigan Territory; surveying of Michigan Territory; surveying instruments from England; public lands adjacent to Connecticut Reserve; lower town of Delaware Indians -- Bent; George Ash; Senator -- Smith.

2296   28 Mar 1807   B/1/238
Jared Mansfield, SG
Leasing of reserved sections.

2297   30 Mar 1807   B/1/238
Seth Pease, SG, Mississippi Territory
Treaty with Chickasaw Indians; survey of Mississippi Territory.

2298   16 Apr 1807   B/1/239
Jared Mansfield, SG
Survey of internal lines of U.S. Military District.

2299   20 Apr 1807   B/1/240
Jared Mansfield, SG
Internal lines of Seven Ranges
Not stated   Mar - 2 7 - -

2300   22 Apr 1807   B/1/240
Jared Mansfield, SG
Survey of Connecticut Reserve.

2301   25 May 1807   B/1/241
Jared Mansfield, SG
Lands not purchased from Indians in Michigan

Territory; appointment of deputy surveyor for
Michigan Territory; transfer of funds.

2302   25 May 1807   B/1/241
Jared Mansfield, SG
Survey of Town of Cincinnati; public sale of land
    at Cin.

2303   3 Jun 1809   B/1/241
Jared Mansfield, SG
Decision regarding mode of dividing public grounds
    suspended at request of Griffin Yeatman of the
    Select Council of Cincinnati.

2304   20 Jun 1807   B/1/242
Seth Pease, Surveyor of Lands South of Tennessee
Repayment of Governor Williams' personal advance
Gideon Fitz, deputy surveyor; Governor [Robert]
    Williams; [Isaac] Briggs.

2305   3 Jul 1807   B/1/242
Jared Mansfield, SG
Appointment of deputy surveyor for Michigan Terri-
    tory; fixing of first meridian in Michigan
    Territory; no land yet purchased from Indians
    since Greenville Treaty.

2306   8 Jul 1807   B/1/242
Jared Mansfield, SG
Quarter townships in U.S. Military District only
    partially located by holders of 50- & 100-acre
    bounty land warrants.

2307   14 Jul 1807   B/1/243
Seth Pease, Surveyor, Washington, Mississippi
    Territory
Correction of surveys previously made; compensa-
    tion; "Mr. [Gideon] Fitz may be informed that
    there is no immediate prospect of surveying lands
    north of the Red River in the territory of Or-
    leans."

2308   31 Aug 1807   B/1/243
Jared Mansfield, SG
Quarter townships in U.S. Military District only
    partially located by holders of 50- & 100-acre
    bounty land warrants; subdivision of townships
    in northern part of Cin district cannot be re-
    surveyed without legal provision for that pur-
    pose.

2309   8 Sep 1807   B/1/244
Jared Mansfield, SG
Case of Henry Whittinger; Act of 10 May 1800, $10,
    prohibits withdrawal or change of otherwise valid
    land application.

2310   11 Sep 1807   B/1/244
Jared Mansfield, SG
Need for additional deputy surveyor at Det.

2311   21 Sep 1807   B/1/244
Isaac Briggs, late Surveyor of Lands South of
    Tennessee, Brookville, Maryland

Compensation; accounting for payments to deputy
    surveyors.

2312   16 Oct 1807   B/1/245
Seth Pease, Surveyor, Washington, Mississippi
    Territory
Transfer of funds
John Henderson, Rec WPR, Washington, Mississippi
    Territory.

2313   22 Oct 1807   B/1/245
Jared Mansfield, SG
Boundaries of Connecticut Land Company lands
Henry Champion.

2314   23 Oct 1807   B/1/245
Seth Pease, Surveyor, Washington, Mississippi
    Territory
Mode of surveying Orleans Territory was improper;
    residence of deputy surveyor for Orleans Terri-
    tory
-- Lafon; -- Gilbert, deputy surveyor.

2315   4 Nov 1807   B/1/246
Jared Mansfield, SG
Patent for reserved section purchased by Jared
    Mansfield [as grantee] forwarded to Cin LO.

2316   16 Nov 1807   B/1/246
Jared Jansfield, SG
Surveying Det private claims; ". . . for tran-
    quilizing that District it is desirable that
    the claims should be surveyed as soon as poss-
    ible, & for that as well as for other reasons
    connected with the relative situations of the
    officers of the United States there"
-- Hult, deputy surveyor, Det.

2317   17 Nov 1807   B/1/246
Jared Mansfield, SG
Boundary between Jef & Vin districts; Act of 2
    Mar 1807 to extend the time for locating Vir-
    ginia military warrants; reserved sections in
    area between U.S. Military District & Connecti-
    cut Reserve; public sale at Jef in Apr 1808;
    public sale at Vin in May 1808.

2318   17 Nov 1807   B/1/247
Seth Pease, Surveyor
Office furnishings for own account.

2319   5 Dec 1807   B/1/247
Jared Mansfield, SG
Final certificate correction; Act of 10 May 1800,
    $10
Henry Shook, assignee of Jesse Spencer [as grantee]
Jesse Spencer [as grantee] Chl WS 21 11 35   +

2320   16 Dec 1807   B/1/247
Jared Mansfield, SG
President accepts southern boundary of Connecticut
    Reserve as surveyed by Seth Pease; western
    boundary to be resurveyed.

2321   19 Dec 1807   B/1/248
Jared Mansfield, SG
Controversies in Det district require appointment
   of additional surveyor.

2322   21 Dec 1807   B/1/248
Jared Mansfield, SG
Boundary line between Vin & Kas districts.

2323   21 Dec 1807   B/1/248
Jared Mansfield, SG
Transfer of funds
[Nathaniel Ewing], Rec Vin.

2324   2 Feb 1808   B/1/249
Jared Mansfield, SG
Requests opinion regarding Isaac Bates & Hugh Moore
   as sureties of Daniel Symmes, Reg Cin.

2325   11 Mar 1808   B/1/249
Seth Pease, Surveyor
Compensation.

2326   12 Mar 1808   B/1/249
Jared Mansfield, SG
Re-measuring of southern boundary of Connecticut
   Reserve; establishment of western boundary of
   Connecticut Reserve.

2327   26 Mar 1808   B/1/250
Jared Mansfield, SG
Transfer of funds at Zan & Cin.

2328   1 Apr 1808   B/1/250
Jared Mansfield, SG
Replacement of markers at corners of sections just
   south of Connecticut Reserve "lately destroyed
   . . . for nefarious purposes."

2329   30 Apr 1808   B/1/250
Jared Mansfield, SG, & [Seth Pease] Surveyor of
   Lands South of Tennessee
President directs that all associations [land companies, etc., formed to speculate in land]
   "ought as far as practicable to be discountenanced, & that it is at all events deemed improper
   that any of the said Superintendents [of public
   sales] should be concerned in any such Company
   or in any operations the tendency of which is to
   lessen competition. . . ."

2330   14 May 1808   B/1/251
Jared Mansfield, SG
Act supplementary to an Act regulating the grants
   of land in the Territory of Michigan; running
   boundary lines of new purchase [under protection
   of troops]
Governor -- Hull, Michigan Territory.

2331   9 Jul 1808   B/1/251
Jared Mansfield, SG
"It is not intended to progress much this year with
   the survey of the new Michigan survey;" leases.

2332   9 Jul 1808   B/1/251
Jared Mansfield, SG
Claim of William Rector for running survey lines
   in Kas district.

2333   12 Jul 1808   B/1/252
Seth Pease, Surveyor
Transfer of funds
[John Henderson], Rec WPR.

2334   29 Jul 1808   B/1/252
Jared Mansfield, SG
Transfer of funds
[James Findlay] Rec Cin.

2335   10 Aug 1808   B/1/252
Jared Mansfield, SG
Apprehensions that Arthur Orr will obtain patent
   in own name
Arthur Orr, assignee of Daniel Ingersoll.

2336   31 Aug 1808   B/1/253
Seth Pease, Surveyor
Channel of Mississippi River is boundary between
   Orleans & Mississippi territories; islands to
   be surveyed as fractional sections; River sur-
   vey; -- William's & -- Dunbar's inquiry
G. Davis; [Isaac] Briggs; -- Freeman.

2337   1 Sep 1808   B/1/254
Jared Mansfield, SG
Survey of Connecticut Reserve boundary; leased
   reserve sections
Israel Ludlow.

2338   20 Oct 1808   B/1/254
Jared Mansfield, SG
Resurvey of private claims
William Rector.

2339   20 Oct 1808   B/1/254
Seth Pease, Surveyor
Townships ready for sale in WPR district.

2340   25 Oct 1808   B/1/255
Seth Pease, Surveyor
Faulty descriptions on six certificates to General
   La Fayette [marginal notation: "Certified copy
   J. M. White at . . .? New Orleans, March 16,
   1839"]
-- Desplantier; -- Madison, attorney in fact for
   General La Fayette.

2341   25 Oct 1808   B/1/255
Seth Pease, Surveyor
Transmits letter to be forwarded to -- Freeman.

2342   7 Nov 1808   B/1/255
Seth Pease, Surveyor
Transmits letter from [Isaac] Briggs, former Sur-
   veyor of Lands South of Tennessee.

2343   9 Nov 1808   B/1/255
Seth Pease, Surveyor
Compensation.

2344   15 Nov 1808   B/1/256
Seth Pease, Surveyor
Report to President states that number of intruders
    in the fork of the Tombigbee & Alabama rivers is
    increasing rapidly, thus making a survey urgent.

2345   25 Nov 1808   B/1/256
Seth Pease, Surveyor
Requests early survey of boundary between United
    States lands & those of Choctaw Indians.

2346   9 Feb 1809   B/1/256
Jared Mansfield, SG
Resurvey of private claims in Indiana Territory.

2347   22 Mar 1809   B/1/257
Seth Pease, Surveyor
Authorizes additional clerk.

2348   5 Apr 1809   B/1/257
Seth Pease, Surveyor
Act for relief of certain Alabama & Wyandot Indians;
    survey of Alabama Indian reservation.

2349   5 Apr 1809   B/1/257
Jared Mansfield, SG
Act for relief of certain Alabama & Wyandot Indians;
    survey of Wyandot Indian reservations.

2350   10 Apr 1809   B/1/258
Jared Mansfield, SG
Resignation of -- Heald, district surveyor of
    Columbia County [Ohio] & appointment of Joseph
    Laswell.

2351   13 Jun 1809   B/1/258
Seth Pease, Surveyor
Requests estimate of expenses for rest of year.

2352   23 Jun 1809   B/1/258
Seth Pease, Surveyor
Missing accounts; Act of 10 May 1800; Act of 11
    Feb 1805.

2353   21 Jul 1809   B/1/258
Jared Mansfield, SG
Claim of [William?] Rector can be granted only by
    Congress.

2354   21 Jul 1809   B/1/259
Seth Pease, Surveyor
Transmits Comptroller's opinion regarding cost of
    surveying private claims
-- Davis.

2355   3 Aug 1809   B/1/259
Seth Pease, Surveyor
Transfer of funds
[John Henderson] Rec WPR.

2356   3 Aug 1809   B/1/259
Jared Mansfield, SG, "now at New Haven, Connecti-
    cut"
"I cannot until after the arrival of the President,
    who is daily expected, decide how long I will
    continue here, nor where I may go afterwards."

2357   5 Sep 1809   B/1/260
Jared Mansfield, SG
Apparent surveying error in fixing corner of town-
    ship: Mil - 3   2   -   -
Zaccheus Biggs; Zaccheus A. Beatty; William
    McCluney.

2358   6 Sep 1809   B/1/260
Jared Mansfield, SG, New Haven, Connecticut
Transfer of funds
[James Findlay] Rec Cin.

2359   9 Sep 1809   B/1/261
Jared Mansfield, SG
Subdivision of U.S. Military District into 100-
    acre lots.

2360   27 Sep 1809   B/1/261
Seth Pease, Surveyor
Compensation for Mississippi River survey by --
    Davis
[Isaac] Briggs.

2361   4 Nov 1809   B/1/262
Seth Pease, Surveyor
Requests answer to letter regarding grants to
    General La Fayette.

2362   9 Dec 1809   B/1/262
Jared Mansfield, SG
Transfer of funds for surveying private claims in
    Kas district.

2363   15 Dec 1809   B/1/262
Seth Pease, Surveyor
Approves appointment of Alexander Donelson as
    deputy surveyor for Madison County [Mississippi
    Territory].

2364   2 Jan 1810   B/1/262
Jared Mansfield, SG
Act for the relief of W. Rector & E. Rector.

2365   4 Jan 1810   B/1/263
Seth Pease, Surveyor
"It does not appear necessary to progress with the
    public surveys faster than there is a probabil-
    ity of sales. . . . I should think that at this
    time the prospect of selling in [EPR district]
    cannot be very great."

2366   3 Feb 1810 B/1/263
Seth Pease, Surveyor
Compensation.

2367   10 Feb 1810 B/1/264
Seth Pease, Surveyor
Funds for surveying new purchase from the Choctaw
 Indians west of Pearl River
[John] Henderson, Rec WPR.

2368   17 Feb 1810 B/1/264
Seth Pease, Surveyor
Numbering of sections in townships containing pri-
 vate claims.

2369   24 Feb 1810 B/1/264
Jared Mansfield, SG
Transfer of funds
[Nathaniel Ewing] Rec Vin.

2370   30 Mar 1810 B/1/265
Seth Pease, Surveyor
Statement of account.

2371   6 Apr 1810 B/1/266
Jared Mansfield, SG
Transfer of funds
[Nathaniel Ewing] Rec Vin.

2372   20 Apr 1810 B/1/266
Jared Mansfield, SG
Transfer of funds
[James Findlay] Rec Cin.

2373   24 Apr 1810 B/1/266
Jared Mansfield, SG
Compensation; -- Fulton's "business."

2374   7 May 1810 B/1/267
Jared Mansfield, SG
Act for sale of certain lands in Indiana Territory; boundary between Jef & Vin districts;
 laying out town of Shawneetown; tract purchased from Piankashaw Indians not attached to
 any land district [marginal note mentions Reg
 at Shawneetown, Apr 1813].

2375   18 May 1810 B/1/268
Jared Mansfield, SG
Law required for sale of islands in Great Miami
 River.

2376   18 May 1810 B/1/268
Jared Mansfield, SG
Survey of new purchase by Governor [William H.]
 Harrison.

2377   18 May 1810 B/1/268
Seth Pease, Surveyor
Approves appointment of William Brown as district
 surveyor.

2378   19 May 1810 B/1/269
Jared Mansfield, SG
Locations made in U.S. Military District.

2379   30 Jun 1810 B/1/269
Jared Mansfield, SG
Laying out town of Shawneetown; erroneous survey
 made by -- Fulton.

2380   30 Jun 1810 B/1/269
Seth Pease, Surveyor
Payment of refused draft
[Gideon] Fitz; -- Walton, Rec.

(End of source B)

2381   -- Mar 1801   C/1/001
James Findlay, Rec Cin
Transmits opinion of U.S. Attorney General regard-
ing mode of computing discounts under Act of 10
May 1800 [see following entry]
Samuel Dexter.

2382   no date   C/1/001
To: Samuel Dexter, U.S. Treasury Department
From: L. Lincoln, U.S. Attorney General
Act of 10 May 1800, §5(3), (4); mode of computing
discount on land purchases.

2383   29 May 1801   C/1/002
Israel Ludlow, Reg Cin
Public sale at Cin; document lost in mail
Governor [Arthur] St. Clair.

2384   3 Jun 1801   C/1/002
James Findlay, Rec Cin
Not patents to issue, excepting upon payment in
full.

2385   9 Jun 1801   C/1/004
Israel Ludlow, Reg Cin
Instruction regarding partial payments.

2386   9 Jun 1801   C/1/005
Israel Ludlow, Reg Cin
Fractional sections.

2387   10 Jun 1801   C/1/006
James Findlay, Rec Cin
Instruction regarding accounting statement & trans-
fers of funds.

2388   19 Jun 1801   C/1/007
Israel Ludlow, Reg Cin [circular letter]
Instructions regarding monthly reports to be sub-
mitted; reversions.

2389   5 Aug 1801   C/1/009
Israel Ludlow, Reg Cin
Applications for forfeited land; instructions re-
garding monthly accounting reports
John Fulton; John Hamilton.

2390   5 Aug 1801   C/1/009
Israel Ludlow, Reg Cin
Application for forfeited land; correction of
errors
John Fulton; John Hamilton.

2391   5 Aug 1801   C/1/010
James Findlay, Rec Cin
Various errors noted
S. Meredith; W. Crane; John Burnett; John C.
Symmes; A. Shane; E. Vautress; E. Vanmallers.

2392   11 Aug 1801   C/1/012
Israel Ludlow, Reg Cin
Fractional sections.

2393   21 Aug 1801   C/1/013
Israel Ludlow, Reg Cin
Forfeitures.

2394   5 Sep 1801   C/1/013
James Findlay, Rec Cin [Marshal for District of
Ohio]
Instructions regarding payments to jurors & wit-
nesses [strictly speaking, this letter does not
deal with land matters].

2395   8 Oct 1801   C/1/016
James Findlay, Rec Cin
Appointments of Commissioners to grant pre-emptions
under John Cleves Symmes; Act of 3 Mar 1801, §4;
Act of 2 Mar 1799
William Goforth of Columbia [Northwest Territory?];
John Reily of Cin; -- Byers; [Bazaliel?] Wells.

2396   26 Oct 1801   C/1/017
James Findlay, Rec Cin
Pre-emption right under John Cleves Symmes
James Byers   Cin - 5 2 17 -

2397   4 Dec 1801   C/1/018
James Findlay, Rec Cin
Pre-emption right under John Cleves Symmes.

2398   19 Dec 1801   C/1/019
Israel Ludlow, Reg Cin
Forfeitures [encloses copy of letter, see serial
2399]
Samuel Vance; Caleb Swan.

2399   26 Jun 1801   C/1/020
Thomas Worthington, Reg Chl
Act of 16 May 1800, §§5, 7; instalment payments;
forfeitures.

2400   23 Jan 1802   C/1/021
James Findlay, Rec Cin
Transfer of funds
Rufus Putnam, SG.

2401   26 Jun 1802   C/1/022
James Findlay, Rec Cin
Pre-emption rights under John Cleves Symmes.

2402   5 Apr 1802   C/1/023
James Findlay, Rec Cin
Instructions regarding monthly accounting reports.

2403   5 Apr 1802   C/1/024
Israel Ludlow, Reg Cin
Act of 10 May 1800, §7; prevention of reversions.

2404   11 Jun 1802   C/1/026
James Findlay, Rec Cin
Correction of error
Jacob White.

2405   28 Jun 1802   C/1/027
James Findlay, Rec Cin
Queries regarding laying-out of roads.

2406   13 Aug 1802   C/1/028
James Findlay, Rec Cin
Overpayment
David Ziegler.

2407   5 Oct 1802   C/1/029
Israel Ludlow, Reg Cin
Pre-emption rights under John Cleves Symmes.

2408   25 Oct 1802   C/1/030
James Findlay, Rec Cin
Transfer of funds
Rufus Putnam, SG.

2409   27 Oct 1802   C/1/031
Israel Ludlow, Reg Cin
Pre-emption rights under John Cleves Symmes
William Crane; -- Montgomery & -- Newbold.

2410   6 Nov 1802   C/1/032
James Findlay, Rec Cin
Questionnaire regarding accumulation of funds in
   specie & in bank notes.

2411   22 Dec 1802   C/1/033
James Findlay, Rec Cin
Discrepancies noted in accounting reports.

2412   3 Mar 1802   C/1/034
James Findlay, Rec Cin
Transfer of funds
Rufus Putnam, SG.

2413   28 Mar 1803   C/1/036
James Findlay, Rec Cin
Transfer of funds to U.S. Army
George Dearborn.

2414   26 Apr 1803   C/1/038
Israel Ludlow, Reg Cin; James Findlay, Rec Cin
Act of 3 Mar 1803, §7; prolongation of payment
   period allowed to pre-emption purchasers.

2415   27 Apr 1803   C/1/040
James Findlay, Rec Cin
Forfeitures
Daniel Miller.

2416   29 Jun 1803   C/1/041
Israel Ludlow, Reg Cin
Policy to be followed for sale of sections contain-
   ing more, or less, than the standard 640 acres
David Ziegler.

2417   12 Oct 1803   C/1/043
Israel Ludlow, Reg Cin

Mode of purchase
J. J. Dufour & associates.

2418   2 Feb 1804   C/1/043
Israel Ludlow, Reg Cin
Ludlow's resignation laid before President; sur-
   vey of the Indiana Territory.

2419   11 Feb 1804   C/1/044
Israel Ludlow, Reg Cin
Ordered to delay sales pending instructions
Israel Zane; Isaac Zane.

2420   10 Mar 1804   C/1/045
Charles Killgore, Reg Cin
Transmits commission (appointment); oath & bond
   required.

2421   30 Mar 1804   C/1/046
Charles Killgore, Reg Cin
Instructions regarding interest on instalments;
   Registers to be paid fixed annual salary,
   rather than fee on sales.

2422   10 Apr 1804   C/1/050
Charles Killgore, Reg Cin; James Findlay, Rec Cin
New instructions issued; half & quarter sections;
   fractional sections; U.S. Military District
   lands; Virginia Military District [of Ohio]
   lands; interest on instalments; patent fees;
   reserved lands between two Miami rivers, in
   Ludlow's Survey, & north of Symmes' patent;
   Act of 3 Mar 1801, §10; establishment of surveying districts; public sale of land at Cin.

2423   11 Apr 1804   C/1/055
James Findlay, Rec Cin; Charles Killgore, Reg Cin
Public sale at Cin; forfeitures; instalment pay-
   ments; Ludlow's Survey.

2424   27 Apr 1804   C/1/059
Charles Killgore, Reg Cin
Erection of surveying districts.

2425   28 Apr 1804   C/1/062
James Findlay, Rec Cin
Transfer of funds.

2426   26 May 1804   C/1/062
Charles Killgore, Reg Cin
Purchases of Isaac Zane.

2427   8 Jun 1804   C/1/063
Charles Killgore, Reg Cin
Erection of surveying districts
William Ludlow; Maxfield Ludlow; Benjamin Cham-
   bers.

2428   10 Jul 1804   C/1/064
James Findlay, Rec Cin
Act of 26 Mar 1804; Act of 10 May 1800, §3; sur-
   veying differences.

2429   30 Jul 1804   C/1/065
No addressee
Act of 26 Mar 1804, §11; interest on instalments;
   [similar letter, addressed to Joseph Nourse, Reg
   Treas, follows].

2430   1 Aug 1804   C/1/069
Charles Killgore, Reg Cin
Act of 26 Mar 1804, §12.

2431   17 Aug 1804   C/1/070
Charles Killgore, Reg Cin
Act of L May 1802; definition of adjoining frac-
   tional sections

John James Dufour	Cin	-	3	2	12	-
John James Dufour	Cin	-	3	2	14	-
John James Dufour	Cin	-	3	2	-	13
John James Dufour	Cin	-	3	2	-	23
John James Dufour	Cin	-	3	2	-	7
John James Dufour	Cin	-	3	2	-	18

2432   21 Sep 1804   C/1/071
James Findlay, Rec Cin
Transfer of funds
Jared Mansfield, SG.

2433   18 Oct 1804   C/1/072
Charles Killgore, Reg Cin
Pre-emption rights under John Cleves Symmes; dis-
   counts.

2434   18 Nov 1804   C/1/073
James Findlay, Rec Cin
Transfer of funds
Jared Mansfield, SG.

2435   13 Dec 1804   C/1/074
Charles Killgore, Reg Cin
Pre-emption rights under John Cleves Symmes.

2436   21 Jan 1805   C/1/076
Charles Killgore, Reg Cin; James Findlay, Rec Cin
Appointment of Daniel Symmes as auditor for Cin
   district.

2437   8 Mar 1805   C/1/078
James Findlay, Rec Cin
Transfer of funds to Office of Discount & Deposit,
   Bank of Pennsylvania, Pittsburgh.

2438   13 Mar 1805   C/1/080
Charles Killgore, Reg Cin
Sale of reserved sections; Act concerning mode of
   surveying public lands; Act disposing of lands
   in Indiana Territory, §7.

2439   15 Mar 1805   C/1/082
Charles Killgore, Reg Cin
Act concerning mode of surveying public lands, §2
   (3).

2440   25 Mar 1805   C/1/083
James Findlay, Rec Cin
Payment by Governor William H. Harrison at branch
   bank at Norfolk, Virginia [comments upon audit
   report]
Daniel Symmes.

2441   29 Mar 1805   C/1/084
Charles Killgore, Reg Cin
Issuance of final certificates
Charles Wilkins of Kentucky

Charles Wilkins	Cin	WML	1	5	21	-
Charles Wilkins	Cin	WML	1	5	-	22
Charles Wilkins	Cin	WML	1	5	-	23
Charles Wilkins	Cin	EML	1	1	6	-
Charles Wilkins	Cin	EML	1	1	-	5
Charles Wilkins	Cin	EML	1	1	-	7
Charles Wilkins	Cin	EML	1	1	-	8

2442   4 Apr 1805   C/1/085
James Findlay, Rec Cin
Act of 26 Mar 1804, §11; partial payments.

2443   4 Apr 1805   C/1/086
James Findlay, Rec Cin
Comments upon audit report; accumulation of Ken-
   tucky paper; transfer of funds to U.S. Army
Daniel Symmes; Major -- Swan; Captain James
   Sterrett.

2444   13 May 1805   C/1/087
No addressee
Transfer of funds to James Lowry Donaldson, ap-
   pointed Register of Louisiana district.

2445   25 May 1805   C/1/088
James Findlay, Rec Cin
Refusal of application queried

| John Smith | Cin | - | 10 | 1 | 11 | - |

2446   4 Jun 1805   C/1/088
James Findlay, Rec Cin
Transfer of funds.

2447   14 Jun 1805   C/1/089
James Findlay, Rec Cin
Pre-emption right to reserved section
[John] Smith [see entry 2445].

2448   5 Jul 1805   C/1/090
James Findlay, Rec Cin
Overpayment

| William Barkalow | Cin | EML | 5 | 2 | 33 | - |

2449   5 Jul 1805   C/1/091
Charles Killgore, Reg Cin
Instructions regarding assignment of land.

2450   11 Jul 1805   C/1/092
Charles Killgore, Reg Cin
Act of 18 May 1796, §3; Act of 30 Apr 1802, §7;
   school land (sections 16). ·

2451   12 Jul 1805   C/1/094
Charles Killgore, Reg Cin
Proclamation of U.S. President regarding sales of
   reserved sections.

2452   13 Jul 1805   C/1/095
Charles Killgore, Reg Cin
Sections 16 & 29 in Symmes grant [section 29 re-
   served for religious purposes].

2453   20 Aug 1805   C/1/095
Charles Killgore, Reg Cin
Pre-emption right under John Cleves Symmes [enclo-
   sure: Short's letter, mentioning Act of 3 Mar
   1801]
Peyton Short; estate of Sharp Delany.

2454   5 Oct 1805   C/1/100
James Findlay, Rec Cin
Act of 26 Mar 1804, §8; error in discount allowed
Joseph Dodds, assignee
John Haggin   Cin Pre 6 1 15 -

2455   21 Oct 1805   C/1/101
Charles Killgore, Reg Cin
Reserved sections.

2456   4 Nov 1805   C/1/101
James Findlay, Rec Cin
Payment of draft to Vacher presumed to bear fraudulent endorsement
Francis Vacher, "a young gentleman of New York,"
   appointed Commissioner of Land Claims in Louisiana, was drowned between Pittsburgh & Marietta.

2457   19 Dec 1805   C/1/102
James Findlay, Rec Cin
Instructions regarding draft endorsements.

2458   19 Dec 1805   C/1/103
Charles Killgore, Reg Cin
Land locations changed only by special Congressional
   acts.

2459   15 Jan 1806   C/1/104
James Findlay, Rec Cin
Petition to Congress by would-be purchasers.

2460   29 Mar 1806   C/1/104
James Findlay, Rec Cin
Overpayment
John Osias   Cin WML 3 6 10 -

2461   30 Apr 1806   C/1/105
James Findlay, Rec Cin
Transfer of funds to Office of Discount & Deposit,
   Bank of Pennsylvania, Pittsburgh.

2462   22 Apr 1806   C/1/106
James Findlay, Rec Cin
Act of 18 Apr 1806; payments in U.S. stock.

2463   2 May 1806   C/1/107
James Findlay, Rec Cin; Charles Killgore, Reg Cin
Appointment of auditor for records of Cin LO
Daniel Symmes.

2464   5 May 1806   C/1/108
James Findlay, Rec Cin
Transfer of funds
[Jared Mansfield] SG.

2465   6 May 1806   C/1/110
Charles Killgore, Reg Cin
Final certificate
John Vance   Cin - 5 4 - 18
John Vance   Cin - 5 4 - 24
John Vannuys & Isaac
   Paxton   Cin Pre 5 4 - 21

2466   7 May 1806   C/1/111
John B. C. Lucas, Clement C. Penrose, & James L.
   Donaldson, Commissioners for Louisiana, St.
   Louis
Act for ascertaining & adjusting titles & claims
   to land within Orleans Territory & Louisiana
   District, §§1, 2, 7; New Madrid representation
F. R. Conway, Recorder of Land Titles, St. Louis.

2467   14 May 1806   C/1/112
James Findlay, Rec Cin
Deficiency in payment
Benjamin Maltbie   Cin Pre ? 2 4 +

2468   23 Jun 1806   C/1/113
James Findlay, Rec Cin
Act of 18 Apr 1806, §1; U.S. stock.

2469   10 Jun 1806   C/1/114
Charles Killgore, Reg Cin
Comments on auditor's report
Daniel Symmes.

2470   11 Jul 1806   C/1/115
Charles Killgore, Reg Cin
Improper patent
Edward Dearth.

2471   19 Aug 1806   C/1/115
Charles Killgore, Reg Cin
Fractional sections
-- Cadbury.

2472   8 Sep 1806   C/1/116
No addressee
Instructions for Land Commissioners appointed for
   Louisiana Territory; Act of 2 Mar 1805, §2;
   French & Spanish grants; fraudulent claims
John B. C. Lucas; C[lement] B. Penrose; [James
   L.] Donaldson.

2473   7 Oct 1806   C/1/119
Charles Killgore, Reg Cin
"It has been stated . . . that in some instances
   you have prevented persons from entering land

. . . by giving them the erroneous information
that the land had been previously entered"
Abraham Roll
Alexander Kirkpatrick &
  James McLellan   Cin - 2E 4 28 +

2474   18 Nov 1806   C/1/120
James Findlay, Rec Cin
U.S. stock
John R. Mills of Cincinnati township; William
Feno, New York Commissioner of Loans.

2475   28 Nov 1806   C/1/121
James Findlay, Rec Cin; Charles Killgore, Reg Cin
Presidential proclamation of 28 Nov 1806; ". . .
the extent of the combination [plot] & some of
its particular objectives are not yet ascertained. It will be proper that you should pay
particular attention to the public monies in
your possession & guard against any attempt upon
them. You are also requested to communicate
without delay . . . any information . . . obtained respecting the projected illegal enter-
prise."

2476   8 Dec 1806   C/1/122
Charles Killgore, Reg Cin
Again requests explanation for erroneous informa-
tion given to would-be purchasers [see entry
2473]
Abraham Roll
Alexander Kirkpatrick &
  James McLellan   Cin - 2E 4 28 -

2477   12 Dec 1806   C/1/123
James Findlay, Rec Cin
Computation of interest on instalment payments for
pre-emption lands.

2478   19 Dec 1806   C/1/123
Charles Killgore, Reg Cin
Patent transmitted [with comment]
Edmund Richardson   Cin Pre 4 4 27 +

2479   19 Jan 1807   C/1/124
Charles Killgore, Reg Cin
Accepts explanation [refers to entries 2473 &
2476?].

2480   19 Jan 1807   C/1/125
James Findlay, Rec Cin
Transfer of funds.

2481   11 Feb 1807   C/1/125
Charles Killgore, Reg Cin; James Findlay, Rec Cin
Abolishment of surveying fees; Act of 26 Mar 1804,
§13.

2482   13 Feb 1807   C/1/126
Charles Killgore, Reg Cin
Authentication of officials witnessing assignments.

2483   13 Feb 1807   C/1/126
Commissioners for Land Claims, Louisiana Terri-
tory, St. Louis
Suspension of further decisions until Congressional
action is taken; compensation
-- Bates appointed Commissioner, in lieu of [James]
L. Donaldson; [John B. C.]Lucas; [Clement C.]
Penrose; F. R. Conway, Recorder of Land Titles.

2484   23 Mar 1807   C/1/127
James Findlay, Rec Cin
Transport of funds to Office of Discount & Deposit,
Pittsburgh.

2485   26 Mar 1807   C/1/128
James Findlay, Rec Cin
Transfer of funds
John Badollet, Reg Vin.

2486   28 Mar 1807   C/1/128
Charles Killgore, Reg Cin
Intruders on public lands; Act of 3 Mar 1807;
appointment of deputy registers to grant settlement permits in specified areas; applications
for lead mines or salt springs [forms follow].

2487   2 Apr 1807   C/1/133
Frederick Bates, Recorder, St. Louis
An Act respecting claims to land in the Territory
of Orleans & Louisiana District, §4; Spanish
laws & usage; decisions of Board of Commissioners
to be revised; compensation
[John B. C.] Lucas; [Clement C.] Penrose; F. R.
Conway, Recorder of Land Titles.

2488   3 Apr 1807   C/1/137
Charles Killgore, Reg Cin
Reserved sections 8, 11, & 26; query regarding
section 29.

2489   25 May 1807   C/1/138
James Findlay, Rec Cin
Transfer of funds
[Jared Mansfield] SG.

2490   26 May 1807   C/1/138
James Findlay, Rec Cin; Charles Killgore, Reg Cin
Daniel Symmes appointed to audit books of Cin LO.

2491   26 May 1807   C/1/140
Daniel Symmes, Cin
Instructions for audit of Cin LO.

2492   11 Jul 1807   C/1/143
Charles Killgore, Reg Cin
Returns final certificate, resale; opinion of
U.S. Attorney General
[John James] Dufour
Jared Mansfield [as gran-
  tee]   Cin WML 2 1 - 1
Jared Mansfield [as gran-
  tee]   Cin WML 2 1 - 2

2493   no date   C/1/144
Opinion of U.S. Attorney General
Upon payment of first instalment, inchoate title
   vested in purchaser subject to divesting for
   non-compliance with other requirements; Act of
   15 Apr 1806
[John James] Dufour; C. A. Rodney.

2494   11 Jul 1807   C/1/148
James Findlay, Rec Cin
Repayment to party abandoning claim [John James
   Dufour or Jared Mansfield (as grantee)].

2495   9 Oct 1807   C/1/149
[Charles Killgore] Reg Cin
Survey of Town of Cincinnati; public sale of Cin-
   cinnati lots; Act of 28 Feb 1806.

2496   9 Oct 1807   C/1/149
James Findlay, Rec Cin
Public sale of Cincinnati lots.

2497   17 Dec 1807   C/1/150
Daniel Symmes, Reg Cin
Transmits commission (appointment); oath & bond
   required.

2498   11 Feb 1808   C/1/150
Daniel Symmes, Reg Cin
Question of whether section 29 in tract of land between the two Miami rivers to be considered a
   reserved section.

2499   7 Mar 1808   C/1/151
James Findlay, Rec Cin
Transport of funds to Pittsburgh.

2500   20 May 1808   C/1/151
James Findlay, Rec Cin
Missing accounting reports.

2501   23 Feb 1808   C/1/152
Daniel Symmes, Reg Cin
Intruders on public land; removal power is discretionary & "there is not at present any intention
   to exercise that power . . . in your District."

2502   23 Jun 1808   C/1/152
Daniel Symmes, Reg Cin
Appointment of Ethan Allen Brown to audit books of
   Cin LO.

2503   1 Jul 1808   C/1/153
Daniel Symmes, Reg Cin
Title of Joel Williams to lands in Town of Cincin-
   nati WML
[John Cleves] Symmes.

2504   12 Jul 1808   C/1/154
Daniel Symmes, Reg Cin
Presidential Proclamation announcing sales of re-
   served sections.

2505   29 Jul 1808   C/1/154
James Findlay, Rec Cin
Transfer of funds
[Jared Mansfield] SG.

2506   16 Feb 1809   C/1/155
Daniel Symmes, Reg Cin
Pre-emptive right of Peyton Short to lands between
   Great Miami River, Mad River, & northern boundary
   of Ludlow's Survey; Act of 1 Mar 1801, §8.

2507   20 Mar 1809   C/1/157
Daniel Symmes, Reg Cin
Case of Piatt & Carter *versus* John James; late
   payment of first instalment accepted only where
   no intervening purchaser has appeared.

2508   20 Mar 1809   C/1/158
Daniel Symmes, Reg Cin
An Act to extend the time for making payment for
   the public lands of the United States; pre-
   emption rights; interest; instalments; extension of credit.

2509   21 Mar 1809   C/1/159
Daniel Symmes, Reg Cin
Sufficient payments received in U.S. Treasury to
   suspend prospective sale [of forfeited land];
   Act of 2 Mar 1809

John James Dufour	Cin	WML	3	2	15	–
John James Dufour	Cin	WML	3	2	–	22
John James Dufour	Cin	WML	3	2	–	27

2510   5 Apr 1809   C/1/160
James Findlay, Rec Cin
Transport of funds to Pittsburgh.

2511   5 Jul 1809   C/1/161
James Findlay, Rec Cin
Acknowledges receipt from brother Nathan Findlay
   of $114,000 "deposited on your account."

2512   20 Jul 1809   C/1/161
Daniel Symmes, Reg Cin
Appointment of Ethan A. Brown to audit books of
   Cin LO.

2513   6 Sep 1809   C/1/162
James Findlay, Rec Cin
Transfer of funds
[Jared] Mansfield, SG.

2514   29 Oct 1809   C/1/162
President of the United States
Intruders settling on public lands of Madison
   County (Bend of Tennessee [River]), Mississippi
   Territory; heads of 300-400 families have
   signed declarations to remain as tenants of
   United States; queries whether Michael Freeman,
   only Yazoo [Company] claimant, to be removed by
   force; additional [?] 300 families expected to
   resist government & keep forcible possession
Thomas Freeman; [William] Dickson, Reg Madison
   County, Mississippi Territory.

2515   9 Dec 1809   C/1/163
James Findlay, Rec Cin
Transfer of funds
[Jared Mansfield] SG.

2516   1 Dec 1809   C/1/163
Daniel Symmes, Reg Cin
Advertisement for lease of U.S. Saline near
  Wabash River, Illinois Territory.

2517   15 Feb 1810   C/1/164
James Findlay, Rec Cin
Affidavit of William Bridger of Mason County, Virginia, before Judge -- Coulter of that state &
  extract of letter to -- Swoope, U.S. Representative, relating to a plan to rob the boat in
  which Rec Cin annually transports funds to Pittsburgh; directs transport of money to Bank of
  Kentucky, Frankfort; inquires regarding
  Vatter's "business & what prospect there is of

a speedy recovery of the money purloined by
him."

2518   21 Mar 1810   C/1/165
James Findlay, Rec Cin
Transfer of funds to U.S. Army
Lieutenant Alpha Kingsley, district postmaster
  [in error: should read quartermaster].

2519   20 Apr 1810   C/1/166
James Findlay, Rec Cin
Transfer of funds
Jared Mansfield, SG.

2520   4 May 1810   C/1/166
Daniel Symmes, Reg Cin
Act to prescribe the mode in which application
  shall be made for the purchase of land at the
  several land offices, §1.

(End of source C)

2521   20 Jul 1781 D/89/226
Petition to the Continental Congress from William
 Trent of New Jersey, in behalf of himself & other
 proprietors of a tract of land called Indiana
Protests an act of the Virginia Legislature depriv-
 ing the proprietors of their property "westward
 of the Alleg[h]eny Mountain. . . ."

2522   13 Oct 1780 D/89/230
Letter from William Trent [at Philadelphia] in behalf of the proprietors of the Vandalia & Indiana
 companies
Requests that a date be established for oral argu-
 ment to hear their claims to territory contested
 by Virginia.

2523   11 Sep 1779 D/89/234
Memorial of George Morgan, agent of the proprietors
 of a "tract of land called Indiana"
Indian treaties with Shawanese, Delaware, & Huron
 tribes [Six Nation, Fort Stanwix, 1768]; boundaries delineated; Vandalia Tract; protest proposed sale of these lands by State of Virginia.

2524   30 Nov 1785 D/164/161
Report of the houses situated between Yellow Creek
 & the mouth of the Muskingum [River] on the Ohio
 destroyed by a detachment under the command of
 Captain John Dougherty
James Fry   "little below Yellow Creek"
Isaac Edgington "Hart's Rock"
Joseph Edgington ditto
Joseph Casey   "along the shore below Cross
         Creek"
Walter Cain   ditto
Francis Riley   ditto
George Ackinson ditto
John Carpenter ditto
George Nashan
 [Nation]   ditto
Aaron Delong   ditto
William Huff   ditto
John Castleman "Mingo Bottom"
Joseph Ross   ditto
Alceignos Baily ditto
William Sparks ditto
Jacob Laight   ditto
John McDaniel "a compact village 8 miles above
        W[h]eeling consisting of 8 houses
        & one block house within compass
        of one Quarter of a Mile"
John Tilton   ditto
Abraham Davis ditto
Thomas Johnson ditto
John Nickson   ditto
Joseph Munster ditto
William Hagland ditto
"The house of John Carpenter with a sick family in
 it of George Norriss' left standing near the
 houses of his which were destroyed." There were
 other unidentified houses destroyed--five between
 Wheeling & Muskingum.

2525   27 Apr 1786 D/164/293
List of houses destroyed
Abraham Croxen
 [Croghan?] "25 miles from Ft. McIntosh"
Jeremiah Stanbury ditto

James Fry   ditto "Fry's house has been sold
        3 times"
John Castleman "10 miles above Mingo Town"
John Boley   ditto
David Waddle   ditto
James Light
 [Laight]   Grass Creek; "Light house was
        sold for £125"
Henry Long   Grass Creek
Walkter Kenney ditto
James Jolliff   "Noriss Town"
John Carpenter ditto; "Carpenter place was sold
        for £270"
George Nation   Noriss Town
David Kingerland ditto
Peter Flynn   "4 miles from Noriss Town"
Jacob Keller   ditto
Solomon Delong ditto
William Huff   "between Noriss Town & Wheeling
        Creek"
John McDonald ditto
John Davis   ditto
Peter Street   ditto
Jonas Mauser   ditto
James Dorothy
 [Daugherty?] ditto
John Litton   ditto
Robert Putney "at Wheeling"
James Fleming ditto
Jacob Judah   ditto
James Sylvester ditto
Samuel Delong ditto
Archibald Frame "from 3 miles to 7 miles on
        Wheeling Creek"
John Coleman   ditto
Adam House   ditto
". . . and six other houses--I could not procure
 their names."

2526   D/73/135
Schedule of Sales of Land in the Western Territory
 of the United States, at Public Auction [held at
 New York] from the 21st September to the 9th
 October 1787

Arnold H. Dohrman	7Rg -	2	3 -	17
Arnold H. Dohrman	7Rg -	2	5 -	2
Absalom Martin	7RG -	2	3 -	18
Absalom Martin	7Rg -	2	3 -	23
Abijah Hammond	7Rg -	2	3 -	19
Abijah Hammond	7Rg -	2	3 -	20
Abijah Hammond	7Rg -	3	3 -	21
Abijah Hammond	7Rg -	3	5 -	1
Abijah Hammond	7Rg -	3	5 -	3
Robert Kirkwood	7Rg -	2	3 -	27
Robert Kirkwood	7Rg -	2	5 -	9
Robert Kirkwood	7Rg -	2	5 -	15
Robert Kirkwood	7Rg -	2	5 -	18
John Couvenhoven	7Rg -	2	5 -	4
John Couvenhoven	7Rg -	2	7 -	7
William McKennan	7Rg -	2	5 -	10
William McKennan	7Rg -	2	5 -	17
William Manning	7Rg -	2	5 -	13
John Foulks	7Rg -	2	5 -	12
John Foulks	7Rg -	2	9 -	1
John Foulks	7Rg -	2	9 -	9
John Foulks	7Rg -	3	2 -	10
Benjamin Manning	7Rg -	2	5 -	14
Jacob Martin	7Rg -	2	5 -	19
John Learmonth? [Leaven-worth?]	7Rg -	2	5 -	20
John Learmonth?	7Rg -	2	5 -	21

Name						
John Lyon	7Rg	–	2	5	–	22
Hon. Arthur Lee	7Rg	–	2	5	–	30
Hon. Arthur Lee	7Rg	–	2	3	–	30
Hon. Arthur Lee	7Rg	–	2	3	–	34
Hon. Arthur Lee	7Rg	–	2	3	–	35
Hon. Arthur Lee	7Rg	–	2	3	–	36
James Gray	7Rg	–	2	7	–	1
James Gray	7Rg	–	2	7	–	2
James Gray	7Rg	–	2	7	–	4
James Gray	7Rg	–	2	7	–	6
James Gray	7Rg	–	2	7	–	27
James Gray	7Rg	–	2	7	–	31
James Gray	7Rg	–	2	7	–	32
James Gray	7Rg	–	2	9	–	7
James Gray	7Rg	–	3	2	–	17
Daniel Turner	7Rg	–	2	7	–	5
Dr. Robert Johnston	7Rg	–	2	5	–	31
Dr. Robert Johnston	7Rg	–	2	7	–	10
Dr. Robert Johnston	7Rg	–	2	7	–	17
Dr. Robert Johnston	7Rg	–	2	7	–	18
Dr. Robert Johnston	7Rg	–	2	7	–	13
Dr. Robert Johnston	7Rg	–	2	7	–	19
Dr. Robert Johnston	7Rg	–	2	7	–	21
Dr. Robert Johnston	7Rg	–	2	7	–	22
Dr. Robert Johnston	7Rg	–	2	7	–	23
Dr. Robert Johnston	7Rg	–	2	7	–	24
Dr. Robert Johnston	7Rg	–	2	9	–	4
Dr. Robert Johnston	7Rg	–	2	7	–	34
Dr. Robert Johnston	7Rg	–	2	9	–	5
Dr. Robert Johnston	7Rg	–	3	6	–	13
Dr. Robert Johnston	7Rg	–	3	6	–	23
Dr. Robert Johnston	7Rg	–	3	6	–	24
Dr. Robert Johnston	7Rg	–	3	8	–	1
Dr. Robert Johnston	7Rg	–	3	10	–	3
Dr. Robert Johnston	7Rg	–	4	1	–	35
John D. Mercier	7Rg	–	2	7	–	12
Joshua Mercereau	7Rg	–	2	7	–	28
Joshua Mercereau	7Rg	–	2	9	–	10
Joshua Mercereau	7Rg	–	2	9	–	17
George Douglass	7Rg	–	3	2	–	9
Henry? H. Livingston	7Rg	–	3	1	–	all[1]
Cornelius Ray	7Rg	–	3	2	–	19
James Burnside	7Rg	–	3	2	–	24
Henry Kuhl	7Rg	–	3	6	–	3
Henry Kuhl	7Rg	–	4	7	–	3
Henry Kuhl	7Rg	–	4	7	–	17
Rev. William Linn	7Rg	–	3	10	–	4
Jacob Blackwell	7Rg	–	4	7	–	10
John Martin	7Rg	–	4	7	–	20
Alexander McComb &	7Rg	–	2	3	–	24
John Edgar	7Rg	–	2	3	–	26
Alexander McComb & / John Edgar	7Rg	–	2	3	–	29
Alexander McComb & / John Edgar	7Rg	–	2	3	–	31
Alexander McComb & / John Edgar	7Rg	–	2	3	–	32
Alexander McComb & / John Edgar	7Rg	–	2	5	–	5
Alexander McComb & / John Edgar	7Rg	–	2	5	–	6
Alexander McComb & / John Edgar	7Rg	–	2	5	–	7
Alexander McComb & / John Edgar	7Rg	–	2	5	–	23
Alexander McComb & / John Edgar	7Rg	–	2	5	–	24
Alexander McComb & / John Edgar	7Rg	–	2	5	–	25
Alexander McComb & / John Edgar	7Rg	–	2	5	–	27
Alexander McComb &						
John Edgar	7Rg	–	2	5	–	28
Alexander McComb & / John Edgar	7Rg	–	2	5	–	32
Alexander McComb & / John Edgar	7Rg	–	2	5	–	33
Alexander McComb & / John Edgar	7Rg	–	2	5	–	34
Alexander McComb & / John Edgar	7Rg	–	2	5	–	35
Alexander McComb & / John Edgar	7Rg	–	2	5	–	36
Alexander McComb & / John Edgar	7Rg	–	2	6	–	all[2]
Alexander McComb & / John Edgar	7Rg	–	2	7	–	3
Alexander McComb & / John Edgar	7Rg	–	2	8	–	all[3]
Alexander McComb & / John Edgar	7Rg	–	2	9	–	13
Alexander McComb & / John Edgar	7Rg	–	2	9	–	14
Alexander McComb & / John Edgar	7Rg	–	2	9	–	19
Alexander McComb & / John Edgar	7Rg	–	2	9	–	20
Alexander McComb & / John Edgar	7Rg	–	3	6	–	18
Alexander McComb & / John Edgar	7Rg	–	3	6	–	30
Alexander McComb & / John Edgar	7Rg	–	3	6	–	36
Alexander McComb & / John Edgar	7Rg	–	3	8	–	6
Alexander McComb & / John Edgar	7Rg	–	4	1	–	24
Alexander McComb & / John Edgar	7Rg	–	4	1	–	34
Alexander McComb & / John Edgar	7Rg	–	3	7	–	all[4]
Nathaniel McFarland	7Rg	–	2	7	–	9
Nathaniel McFarland	7Rg	–	2	7	–	15
Nathaniel McFarland	7Rg	–	2	7	–	14
Nathaniel McFarland	7Rg	–	2	7	–	20
Nathaniel McFarland	7Rg	–	2	7	–	25
Nathaniel McFarland	7Rg	–	2	7	–	30
Nathaniel McFarland	7Rg	–	2	7	–	35
Nathaniel McFarland	7Rg	–	2	7	–	36
Nathaniel McFarland	7Rg	–	2	9	–	12
Nathaniel McFarland	7Rg	–	2	9	–	18
Nathaniel McFarland	7Rg	–	3	2	–	14
Nathaniel McFarland	7Rg	–	3	6	–	1
Nathaniel McFarland	7Rg	–	3	6	–	2
Nathaniel McFarland	7Rg	–	3	6	–	4
Nathaniel McFarland	7Rg	–	3	6	–	5
Nathaniel McFarland	7Rg	–	3	6	–	7
Nathaniel McFarland	7Rg	–	3	8	–	24
Nathaniel McFarland	7Rg	–	4	1	–	23
Nathaniel McFarland	7Rg	–	4	1	–	28
John Hopkins	7Rg	–	1	3	–	all
John Hopkins	7Rg	–	2	1	–	29
John Hopkins	7Rg	–	2	1	–	30
John Hopkins	7Rg	–	2	1	–	35
John Hopkins	7Rg	–	2	2	–	all
John Hopkins	7Rg	–	4	7	–	15
John Hopkins	7Rg	–	4	7	–	21
John Hopkins	7Rg	–	4	7	–	22
John Hopkins	7Rg	–	4	7	–	23
John Hopkins	7Rg	–	4	7	–	24
John Hopkins	7Rg	–	4	7	–	27
John Hopkins	7Rg	–	4	7	–	28
William Duer	7Rg	–	2	1	–	36
William Duer	7Rg	–	2	7	–	33

William Duer	7Rg	–	3	8	–	31
William Duer	7Rg	–	4	7	–	4
William Duer	7Rg	–	4	7	–	9
William Duer	7Rg	–	4	7	–	14
Joseph Hardy	7Rg	–	3	6	–	6
Joseph Hardy	7Rg	–	3	8	–	32
Joseph Hardy	7Rg	–	4	1	–	18

[1] Apparently all lots in township; 5316 acres.

[2] A total of 19,840 acres.

[3] A total of 19,686 acres.

[4] A total of 19,840 acres.

(End of source D)

[151]

2527   24 Oct - 3 Dec 1796   E/-/--

Account of Sales of Lands at Pittsburgh [Pennsylvania] under the direction of Arthur St. Clair, Governor of the North Western Territory, & George Wallace, Esq. [& General John Neville] pursuant to the 8th Section of the Act of Congress passed on the 18th of May 1796, entitled "An Act providing for the sale of the Lands of the United States in the Territory North West of the River Ohio & above the mouth of Kentucky River."

Name						
James Ross, Pittsburgh	7Rg	-	1	1	-	28
James Ross, Pittsburgh	7Rg	-	1	1	-	29
James Ross, Pittsburgh	7Rg	-	1	1	-	34
James Ross, Pittsburgh	7Rg	-	1	1	-	35
Benjamin Miller, North West Territory	7Rg	-	1	2	-	19
Benjamin Miller, North West Territory	7Rg	-	1	2	-	25
Benjamin Miller, North West Territory	7Rg	-	1	2	-	31
Isaac Craig, Pittsburgh	7Rg	-	1	2	-	20
Isaac Craig, Pittsburgh	7Rg	-	1	2	-	26
Joseph Dorsey, Washington County, Pennsylvania	7Rg	-	1	2	-	21[1]
Joseph Dorsey, Washington County, Pennsylvania	7Rg	-	1	2	-	27[1]
Bazill Wells, Washington County, Pennsylvania	7Rg	-	1	2	-	29
Bazill Wells, Washington County, Pennsylvania	7Rg	-	1	2	-	35
Bazill Wells, Washington County, Pennsylvania	7Rg	-	1	2	-	36
John Wilkins, Jr., Pittsburgh	7Rg	-	1	4	-	19
John Wilkins, Jr., Pittsburgh	7Rg	-	1	4	-	25
Bazill Wells, Washington County, Pennsylvania	7Rg	-	1	4	-	34
Bazill Wells, Washington County, Pennsylvania	7Rg	-	1	4	-	35
Bazill Wells, Washington County, Pennsylvania	7Rg	-	1	4	-	36
Isaac Craig, Pittsburgh	7Rg	-	1	5	-	6
Isaac Craig, Pittsburgh	7Rg	-	1	5	-	12
Archibald Woods, Ohio County, Virginia	7Rg	-	2	3	-	24
Robert Woods, Ohio County, Virginia	7Rg	-	2	4	-	13
Robert Woods, Ohio County, Virginia	7Rg	-	2	4	-	19
Bazill Wells, Washington County, Pennsylvania	7Rg	-	2	4	-	26
Bazill Wells, Washington County, Pennsylvania	7Rg	-	2	4	-	20
Absalom Martin, Washington County, North West Territory	7Rg	-	2	4	-	15
Absalom Martin, Washington County, North West Territory	7Rg	-	2	4	-	21
Absalom Martin, Washington County, North West Territory	7Rg	-	2	4	-	27
John Tilton, Washington County, North West Territory	7Rg	-	2	4	-	22
John Tilton, Washington County, North West Territory	7Rg	-	2	4	-	16
Joseph Dorsey, Washington County, Pennsylvania	7Rg	-	2	4	-	11[2]
Joseph Dorsey, Washington County, Pennsylvania	7Rg	-	2	4	-	17[2]
Joseph Dorsey, Washington County, Pennsylvania	7Rg	-	2	4	-	23[2]
David Robertson, Westmoreland County [Pennsylvania]	7Rg	-	2	4	-	35
George Humphreys, Ohio County, Virginia	7Rg	-	2	4	-	36
Stephen Abraham, Ohio County, Virginia	7Rg	-	2	5	-	7[3]
Bazill Wells, Washington County, Pennsylvania	7Rg	-	2	7	-	3
Bazill Wells, Washington County, Pennsylvania	7Rg	-	2	8	-	7
Bazill Wells, Washington County, Pennsylvania	7Rg	-	2	8	-	8
Alexander Addison, Washington County, Pennsylvania	7Rg	-	2	8	-	14
Bazill Wells, Washington County, Pennsylvania	7Rg	-	2	8	-	3
Bazill Wells, Washington County, Pennsylvania	7Rg	-	2	8	-	9
Bazill Wells, Washington County, Pennsylvania	7Rg	-	3	2	-	15
John Woods, Pittsburgh	7Rg	-	3	3	-	19[4]
John Woods, Pittsburgh	7Rg	-	3	3	-	25[4]
John Woods & Thomas Butler, Pittsburgh	7Rg	-	3	3	-	20
John Woods & Thomas Butler, Pittsburgh	7Rg	-	3	3	-	14
Archibald Woods, Ohio County, Virginia	7Rg	-	3	4	-	1
Archibald Woods, Ohio County, Virginia	7Rg	-	3	4	-	7
Abijah Hunt, Cincinnati, North West Territory & Elias Langham, Berkley County, Virginia	7Rg	-	3	4	-	2[5]
Abijah Hunt, Cincinnati, North West Territory & Elias Langham, Berkley County, Virginia	7Rg	-	3	4	-	8[5]
Abner Barker, Pittsburgh	7Rg	-	2	4	-	31
James Alexander & James Clark, Hartford County, Maryland	7Rg	-	2	4	-	32
William Skinner, Ohio County, Virginia	7Rg	-	2	4	-	34
Moses Chapline, Ohio County, Virginia	7Rg	-	2	4	-	29
Benjamin Biggs, Ohio County, Virginia	7Rg	-	2	4	-	24
Archibald Woods, Ohio County, Virginia	7Rg	-	2	4	-	33
Moses Chapline & Andrew Woods, Ohio County, Virginia	7Rg	-	2	3	-	33
Jacob Croes & A. Ridgely, Ohio County, Virginia	7Rg	-	2	4	-	28
Isaac Craig, Pittsburgh	7Rg	-	1	5	-	23
Isaac Craig, Pittsburgh	7Rg	-	1	5	-	24
Bazill Wells, Washington County, Pennsylvania	7Rg	-	4	7	-	5
Bazill Wells, Washington County, Pennsylvania	7Rg	-	4	7	-	6[6]
Bazill Wells, Washington County, Pennsylvania	7Rg	-	4	9	-	8[6]
Bazill Wells, Washington County, Pennsylvania	7Rg	-	4	9	-	9[7]
James Ross, Pittsburgh	7Rg	-	5	1	-	18

James Ross, Pittsburgh	7Rg	- 5	1	-	24
James Ross, Pittsburgh	7Rg	- 5	1	-	26
James Ross, Pittsburgh	7Rg	- 5	1	-	31
James Ross, Pittsburgh	7Rg	- 5	1	-	32
James Ross, Pittsburgh	7Rg	- 6	1	-	27
James Ross, Pittsburgh	7Rg	- 6	1	-	21
James Ross, Pittsburgh	7Rg	- 6	1	-	22
James Ross, Pittsburgh	7Rg	- 6	1	-	28
Abijah Hunt, Cincinnati, & Dudley Woodbridge, Marietta	7Rg	- 6	1	-	33
Abijah Hunt, Cincinnati, & Dudley Woodbridge, Marietta	7Rg	- 6	1	-	34
Dudley Woodbridge, Marietta	7Rg	- 7	1&2	-	30
Dudley Woodbridge, Marietta	7Rg	- 7	1&2	-	36
Dudley Woodbridge, Marietta	7Rg	- 7	1&2	-	31
John Wilkins, Jr., Pittsburgh	7Rg	- 7	2	-	14
John Wilkins, Jr., Pittsburgh	7Rg	- 7	2	-	20
John Wilkins, Jr., Pittsburgh	7Rg	- 7	2	-	19
John Wilkins, Jr., Pittsburgh	7Rg	- 7	2	-	25
John Wilkins, Jr., Pittsburgh	7Rg	- 7	2	-	26
John Wilkins, Jr., Pittsburgh, & Dudley Woodbridge, Marietta	7Rg	- 7	2	-	9
John Wilkins, Jr., Pittsburgh, & Dudley Woodbridge, Marietta	7Rg	- 7	2	-	10
John Wilkins, Jr., Pittsburgh, & Dudley Woodbridge, Marietta	7Rg	- 7	2	-	3
John Wilkins, Jr., Pittsburgh, & Dudley Woodbridge, Marietta	7Rg	- 7	2	-	4[8]
James Ross, Pittsburgh	7Rg	- 6	2	-	1
James Ross, Pittsburgh	7Rg	- 6	2	-	2
Joseph Dorsey, Washington County, Pennsylvania	7Rg	- 1	2	-	33
John McCulloch, Ohio County, Virginia	7Rg	- 3	6	-	10
Isaac Craig, Pittsburgh	7Rg	- 5	2	-	7
Isaac Craig, Pittsburgh	7Rg	- 5	2	-	13

Absalom Martin, Ohio County, Virginia	7Rg	- 6	9	-	1[9]
John Carpenter, North West Territory	7Rg	- 2	5	-	7
Robert Caldwell, Ohio County, Virginia	7Rg	- 2	5	-	24
Samuel Mahon, Pittsburgh	7Rg	- 2	5	-	23
Thomas Butler, Pittsburgh	7Rg	- 2	8	-	13
John Beaver, Allegheny County, Pennsylvania	7Rg	- 2	8	-	19
Robert Caldwell, Ohio County, Pennsylvania	7Rg	- 3	8	-	13
Bazill Wells, Washington County, Pennsylvania	7Rg	- 3	10	-	10
Robert Caldwell, Ohio County, Virginia	7Rg	- 4	9	-	7

Other names mentioned [in summary account of expenses which follows the Account of Sales]: Hon. James Ross; James O'Hara, contractor; Major -- Kirkpatrick; General -- Wilkinson; James Chambers; Samuel Peoples; William Morrow; Major Isaac Craig, Deputy Quartermaster, [U.S. Army]; Colonel -- Butler; Judge -- Wallace.

[1] Paid by Judge -- Addison.

[2] Moiety to be paid in Philadelphia by Alexander Addison.

[3] Forfeited to the United States, 26 Nov 1796.

[4] Relinquished by the purchaser in consequence of error in the map which places [tract] at Captenas [Creek] but in fact it is at the mouth of Sunfish [Creek].

[5] Moiety to be paid by Abijah Hunt at Philadelphia.

[6] Deposit paid by David Vance.

[7] Forfeited & deposit paid by B.W. [Bazill Wells].

[8] Advertised for 625 acres, but supposed to contain 640 acres & sold as such.

[9] Deposit paid by A. Tannehill.

(End of source E)

2528 10 May 1792 F/-/082
Town of Greenwich, Connecticut

Sufferer	£
John Addington	10
Samuel Ask	12
Abigail Armour	6
Mary Austin	3
Isaac Anderson	44
Obadiah Banks	42
Jeremiah Chapman	3
Odel Close, Jr.	15
H. N. Church	25
Jonathan Connery	63
Peter Cyphas	23
James Cunningham	12
Laurau Brumall	4
James Brown	15
William Bush	41
John Bush	11
James Barns	51
Samuel Banks	3
Roger Brown	148
Isaac Bush	5
Nehemiah Brown	95
William Blake	3
Bazaleel Brown	68
Charity Banks	8
Silas Betts	217
David Bush	159
James Brundage	30
James Brush	0
Samuel Brush	13
Deborah Brush	31
Walter Butler	2
Charles Brundage	4
Elisha Belcher	39
William Brundage	50
Peter Brown	5
John Clapp, Jr.	129
Thomas Clapp	333
Odel Close	257
Jacob Conklin	63
Newell Conklin	3
Odel Close, Admr.	49
Reuben Coe	34
Abraham Close	17
Joseph Close	145
Jonathan Coe	41
Joseph Chambers	9
Deborah Close	12
Daniel Carter	5
Hannah Close	39
Thomas Davis	8
Stephen Davis	113
Daniel Darrow	19
Humphrey Denton	74
John Dunn	15
Isaac Davis	16
James Ferris	43
Uriah Field	213
Oliver Fairchild	9
Jabez Ferris	28
Jonathan Finch	0
Nathuel Finch	28
Timothy Ferris	17
Solomon Finney	17
Joshua Franklin	27
Sylvanus Ferris	43
Jabez Fitch	41
Josiah Ferris	20
Timothy Finch	60
Joseph Ferris	11
Moses Ferris	6
Ezra Finch	86
Joseph Ferris	7
Park Ferris	7
John Gregg	213
Charles Green	198
Anne Griggs	44
Jabez Holmes	1
Reuben Holmes	33
Mills Hobby	6
Isaac Howe	84
Mindwell Hitchcock	18
Abraham Hayes	24
Thomas Hobby, Jr.	19
Hannah Hayes	2
Joseph Hobby, Jr.	26
John Hobby	146
Isaac Holmes	64
David Hallcock	1
Isaac Holmes, Jr.	96
William Hubbard	16
Nathaniel Hibbard	3
Thomas Hitchcock	33
Nathaniel Heusted	41
Ebenezer Howe	14
Jona[than] Hibbard, Jr.	31
Benjamin Hubby	35
Ebenezer Hubby	39
Peter Heusted	86
Abraham Heusted	0
Moses Heusted, Jr.	2
Ebenezer Holmes	3
James Hounam	204
Meeting House	20
Thomas Hobby	70
Benjamin Heusted	6
Nathaniel Hubby	12
Sarah Hait	4
Joseph Hubby, Jr.	31
Elizabeth Ingersoll	69
Nathaniel Ingersoll	60
William Jacobs	60
Anne Ingersoll	15
Job Ireland	1
Amos Jessup	20
Thomas Johnson	42
William Johnson	8
James Johnstone	9
Israel Knapp, Jr.	5
Ebenezer Knapp	148
Jonah Knapp	44
Nathaniel Knapp	16
Eunice Knapp	15
Joshua Knapp	125
John Knapp	23
Charles Knapp	11
William Kinch	6
Jonathan Knapp	26
Ezekiel Knapp	25
Abraham Knapp	2
Widow Kinch	9
Samuel Lockwood	108
Israel Lockwood	51
Philip Lockwood	0
Enos Lockwood	14
Thaddeus Lockwood	55
John Loudin	8
Caleb Lyon	9
Joseph Lockwood	31
William Lee	8
Timothy Lockwood	10
Hannah Lockwood	29
William Lockwood	19
Gilbert Lyon	17
Abraham Lockwood	0
Amos Lyon	19
James Lyon	58
Ezekiel Lockwood	10
James Lyon, Jr.	8
Caleb Lyon, Jr.	29
Theophilus Lockwood	2
Jonas Mead	20
Andrew Marshall	27
Peter Mead, Jr.	41
Caleb Mead	34
Reuben Merrit	25
John Mead, Jr.	55
Nathaniel Mead, 3d	18
Jared Mead	68
Daniel Marshall	22
Elizabeth Moore	7
Martin McDonald	5
Ezra Marshall	0
Benjamin Mead	111
Rachael Marshall	10
Peter Mead, esq.	139
John Mead	162
Hannah Mead	3
Sarah Mead	71
Ebenezer Mead	6
Charles Mead	1
Eliphalet Mead, Jr.	96
Jehiel Mead	6
Abraham Mead	18
Eliphalet Mead	5
Nehemiah Mead	55
Mathew Mead	61
Titus Mead	95
Nehemiah Mead, Jr.	9
Daniel Merritt	36
Silas Mead	62
Thomas Mesnard	6
William Marshall	15
Deliverance Mead	39
Jemima Mead	18
Rev. Jona[than] Murdock	79
Jesse Mead	22
Henry Mead	105
Elizabeth Mead	14
Dr. Amos Mead	180
Joshua Mead	11
Jerusha Mead	7
John Mesnard, Jr.	6
James Moe	32
Nathan Merritt	47
Edmond Mead	11
Jeremiah Mead, Jr.	93
Gilbert Marshall	0
Deliverance & Jared Mead	200
Henry Marshall	35
Joseph Mead	40
Shadrach Mead	42
Caleb Mead, 2d	77
Abigail Mead	6
Jonah Mead	24
Enos Mead	13
Sybil Mead	87
Angus McCall	13
Zacheus Mead	10
Ezra Marshall	56
Elkanah Mead	8
John Mesnard	14
Andrew Mead	36
Jotham Mead	27
Eliphalet & Jehiel Mead	85
Robert Nutt	15
Francis Nash	646
Daniel Ogden	116
Joseph Palmer	100
Stephen Palmer	7
Sarah Parsons	6
Theophilus Peck Jr.	50
Solomon Purdy	84
James Phillips	20
Denham Palmer	2
John Palmer	4
Mary Peck	8
Catharine Peck	16
Heth Peck	9
John Purdy	10
Winans Palmer	7
Daniel Palmer	36
Benjamin Peck	24
Samuel Palmer	77
Titus Palmer	3
Jere[miah] & Jona[than] W. Palmer	9
Horton Reynolds	66
William Rundall	81
Susannah Reynolds	19
Anne Reynolds	22
Nathaniel Reynolds, Jr.	11
John Rich	21
Hannah Rundall	45
Hannah Rich	9
Mary Rich	44
Reuben Rundall	44
Amy Rundall	5
Joanna Reynolds	12
Solomon Rundall	40
Thomas Rich	46
Timothy Rundall	8
Jonathan Reynolds	18
Abigail Rundall	3
Samuel Rundall	4
Ambrose & Jona[than] Reynolds	18
Nathaniel Reynolds	48
Shubael Rundall	10
Joseph Sacket	14
Samuel Seymour	196
Joshua Smith	149
Jonah Smith	70
Justus Sacket	224
Daniel Smith	76
Oliver Sherwood	10
Drake Seymour	124
Jabez Sherwood	47
Henry Studwell	86
Thomas Studwell	2
Gilbert Sherwood	8
Rev. William Seward	25
Benjamin Sutton	6
Jesse Sutton	6

Sufferer	£	Sufferer	£	Sufferer	£	Sufferer	£
Daniel & Joshua Smith	219	William Waters	12	Jedediah Brown	162	Mary Lockwood	2
Gold John Sellick	14	Ebenezer Whelpley	1	Sarah Johnson	34	James Smith	22
Roger Southerland	15	Israel Wood	182	Joseph Whitney	183	Betsey Hale	22
John Town	15	John Willis	48	Susannah Butler	7	Mary Brown	10
William Town	3	John Weeks	10	Abraham Gregory	50	Silas Bessey	13
Oliver Tomkins	8	Francis Wilmot	6	Lydia Comstock	9	Abraham Lockwood	3
Michael C. Timpany	77	Jeffery Wilmeten	10	Nathaniel Benedict, 2d	152	Abner Booth	40
Mary Town	5	Isaac Wholpley	21	Josiah Raymond	239	Charles Pope	8
Zebediah Taylor	10			Col. Stephen St. John	713	Gershom Hyatt	32

2529   10 May 1792   F/-/085
Town of Norwalk, Connecticut

Sufferer	£	Sufferer	£	Sufferer	£	Sufferer	£
Thomas Benedict	779	Lemuel Brooks	288	Daniel McAuley	248	Pomp Leaming	15
Josiah Thatcher	400	Richard Camp	242	Daniel Seymour	12	Bewley Arnold	12
James Fitch, Jr.	320	Asa Hayt	382	Deborah Dickenson	17	Sarah Eversley	27
Thomas Fitch	388	Catharine Boughton	23	Jame Hitchcock	19	Mary Smith	17
James Fitch	219	Elizabeth Ketchum	46	Elizabeth Rogers, 2d	1	Thomas Darrow	17
John Lockwood, Jr.	249	John Kellogg	76	Hannah Hanford	60	Nathan Hendrick	20
Abraham Camp's heirs	143	John Seymour	345	Deborah Pickett	22	William Garner	41
Seth Seymour's heirs	157	Josiah Wentworth	152	Mary Resco	3	Stephen G. Thatcher	13
Nathaniel Raymond, Jr.	144	Daniel Hanford	304	Rebecca Smith	3	Stephen & Hooker St. John	30
Fountain Smith	159	Jesse Benedict	114	Obadiah Siscat	3	Nathaniel Raymond	4
John Seymour, Jr.	162	Samuel Fairchild	131	Abigail Weeks	4	Susanna Fitch	24
Abraham Benedict	73	Simeon Raymond	428	Anne Seymour	3	Thomas Hayes	13
Thomas Betts	168	Jedediah Hanford	39	Platt Townsend	3	Auley McAuley	31
John & Daniel Eversley	154	Enoch Benedict	84	John Platt	1	Joseph A. Wright	96
John Benedict	173	David Hanford's heirs	42	Stephen Lockwood	19	Dr. Uriah Roger's heirs	225
Daniel Hyatt	85	Matthew Keeler	166	Nathan Hyatt, Jr.	30	Jesse Raymond	147
Peter Betts	180	Mary Benedict	40	John Rogers	41	John Richards	7
Ebenezer Whiting	108	David Comstock	314	Stephen Whitney	19	Joseph Waring	15
Gold Hayt	195	Thomas Fitch's heirs	415	Jesse Brown	44	Isaac Richards	45
Uriah Raymond	125	John Rich	72	Hannah Fitch's heirs	141	Eli Read	59
Abigail Raymond	144	Ebenezer Hyatt	77	Jacob Arnold	25	Jesse Read	4
Jabez Sanders	32	Nathan Mallory	157	Daniel Hyatt	9	John Bigsby	7
John Cannon	1933	Daniel Thatch's heirs	216	John Eversley	11	Benjamin Read	43
Lois Whitney	89	Samuel Grummond	30	Syphax Negro	1	Daniel Richards	42
Stephen Smith	48	Ebenezer Lockwood	82	David Whitney	1	Solomon Whitman	18
Ezra Picket	83	Isaiah Marvin	159	Anne Seymour	7	David Read	126
John Saunders	242	Eliakim Smith	204	John Lockwood	10	Nathan Waring	33
William Seymour	93	Daniel Seymour, Jr.	88	David Judah	10	Richard Youngs	31
Nathaniel Benedict	360	Dan Finch	120	Timothy Whitney	1	Mary Read	48
Eliphalet Lockwood	721	Hezekiah Raymond	153	Thomas Betts, Jr.	14	Gershom Richards	32
Hannah Hooker	212	John Betts	304	Haynes Fitch	42	Clapp Raymond	34
Hezekiah Lockwood	176	Edward Wentworth	81	Michael Judah	13	John Birchard	35
John Gregory, Jr.	222	Isaac Scudder	662	Uriah Smith	35	Sith Abbot	55
Ebenezer Gregory	57	John Lockwood, 3d	218	Samuel Burrall	31	Capt. Eliakim Raymond	81
Daniel Smith	99	Nathan Jarvis	279	Hannah Brown	6	Simeon Stewart	70
Peter Quintard	401	Jabez Raymond	294	James Hayt's heirs	26	Capt. Phineas Hanford	43
Noal Smith	90	Nehemiah St. John	89	Stephen Keeler	25	Azor Mead	36
John Darrow	193	Hezekiah Hanford	269	David Both	6	Phineas Hanford, Jr.	26
Thaddeus Betts	254	Jona[than] Fitch's heirs	195	Eleazer Scott	16	Richard Dunning	27
Matthew Mallory	87	Nathan Hayt	180	James Crowley	4	Matthew Marvin	49
John St. John	52	Daniel Fitch's heirs	259	Stephen St. John	20	Elizabeth Whelpley	18
William St. John	318	John Belden	304	Nathaniel Street	33	Lydia Fitch	20
John Hayt	72	Nathan Beers	195	Moses St. John	3	Elijah Fitch	10
Daniel Jackson	53	Benjamin Isaac's heirs	406	Isaac Waring	4	Samuel Keeler	31
Josiah Thatcher, Jr.	194	Samuel Marvin	319	Giles Mallory	12	Samuel Middlebrook	14
Elizabeth Rogers	229	Thomas Grummond	206	David Seymour	4	Ezra Waterbury	11
Eliakim Raymond	297	Jacob Jennings	22	Mary Harvey	15	Hannah Gregory	13
				Rebecca Warson	4	Ebenezer Bennet, Jr.	14
				Jarvis Kellogg	2	Nathan Adams	14
				William Mott	11	James Betts	17
				Mary Avery	11	Benjamin Keeler	11
				Peter Hitchcock	12	Nathan Keeler	3
				Joshua Rogers	15	James Whelpley	4
				Desire Siscat	8	Capt. Samuel Comstock	2
				Robert Waters	12	Benjamin Betts	3
				Jedediah Raymond	11		
				Nehemiah St. John, 2d	7		
				Esther St. John	2		

Rev. Isaac Lewis	5
Daniel Sturges	2
Peter Sturges	1
Esther Wasson	5
Capt. Josiah Thatcher	16
Ephraim Steward	5
Silas Hicok	4
Jesse Birchard	8
Simeon Steward, Jr.	8
Benjamin Steward	15
John Fillco	2
Col. Mathew Mead	5
David Webb	2
John Rockwell	6
Elizabeth Gaylord	5
Nathan Hicok	2
James S. Olmsted	3
Samuel Stewart	42
Michael Morehouse, Jr.	7
Andrew Morehouse	2
Michael Morehouse	4
James Keeler	8
Josiah Taylor, Jr.	4
Thaddeus Keeler	2
Sarah Morehouse	6
Ebenezer Fitch	3
Nathan Burrall	3
Jeremiah Webb	7
Elizabeth Dunning	7
Solomon Morehouse	6
Rebecca Deforest	8
Mary Fleet	16
Benjamin Betts, Jr.	4

2530
Town of Fairfield

Sufferers	£
Abraham Andrus	430
Sarah Andrus	192
Col. Elijah Abel	720
John Allen	545
David Allen	476
George Allen	231
Anthony Annibal	155
Peter Burr	282
Reuben Beers	510
David Beers	164
Samuel Beers	96
Ebenezer Bartram	144
Joseph Beers	91
David Burr	388
Wakeman Burr	364
Samuel Burr	481
Job Bartram	963
Gershom Burr	301
Thaddeus Burr	1374
Simon Couch, 3d	227
John Davis	63
Ann Dimon	318
William Dimon	625
N. Thompson Nichols	68
Elizabeth Gold	247
Nathan Godfredy	310
David Jennings, 2d	255
Rebecca Jennings	127
Moses Jennings	600
Isaac Jennings	281

James Olmsted	7
William St. John	35
Daniel Gregory	19
Thaddeus Morehouse	2
Joseph Olmsted	2
Thaddeus Betts	18
Eliphalet Lockwood	24
Jabez Raymond	39
Charles Pope	6
Haynes Fitch	48
Hezekiah Hanford	60
Daniel Hanford	20
James Fitch, Jr.	24
Rebecca Fitch	63
Robert Waters	6
Dan[iel] Finch	3
Uriah Smith	4
Simeon Raymond	14
William Raymond	5
Moses Raymond	5
Timothy Hayt	6
Benjamin Merril	5
Jedediah Raymond	15
Hannah Dickinson	24
Moses Dickinson's heirs	260
Silas Bartow	49
Samuel Ketchum	4
Evert Ellerson	14
Michael Judah	1
John Read	10
Betty Jarvis	2

10 May 1792   F/-/088

Sufferers	£
Peter Hendrick	399
Abigail Hubbell	177
Stephen Jennings	195
Jeremy Jennings	197
Ebenezer Jessup	283
Moso Kent	185
Lathrop Lewis	27
Sturges Lewis	53
Jonathan Lewis	922
Widow Eunice Morehouse	68
Gideon Morehouse	67
Ebenezer Morehouse	83
Grummon Morehouse	7
John Morehouse	234
Hezekiah Nichols	395
Daniel Osborn	135
Eleazer Osborn, Jr.	181
Widow Mary Penfield	140
Solomon Sturges	319
Mabel Osborn	605
Samuel Penfield	1065
John Parrott	86
Nathaniel Parsons	86
John Raymond & E. Cooley	56
Samuel Rowland	477
Andrew Rowland	1569
Samuel Squire	413
John Smedley	764

Seth Sturges	431
Joseph Squier	65
Thomas Staples	247
Joseph Sturges's heirs	340
Jonathan Sturges	748
Hezekiah Sturges	532
Samuel Sturges	235
Samuel Smedley	416
Eliphalet Thorp	401
Jabez Thorp	148
John Turney	527
Stephen Thorp	515
Ansel Traby	97
John Wasson	161
Andrew Wakeman	208
Ebenezer Wakeman	69
Joseph Wakeman	167
Thomas H. Wakeman	239
Mary Cutler	44
David Annible	44
Nehemiah Buddington	15
Andrew Bulkley	34
James Bulkley	1
Walter Buddington	21
Widow Abigail Burr	59
William Buddington	37
Walter Carson	27
Jonathan Darrow	254
Isaac Jarvis	24
Abigail Jennings	50
Justin Jennings	31
Levi Mallery	22
Abigail Osborn	106
John Parsons	22
Ephraim Robbins	107
John Robinson	36
Ebenezer Sturges	89
John Squier, Jr.	16
Judson Sturges	129
Isaac Tucker	69
Samuel Smith	20
Isaac Turney	20
John Williams, Jr.	14
John Williams	116
Ruth Wakeman	22
Wright White	46
Mary Alvord	20
Isaac Burr	23
Amelia Burr	10
Ruth Burr	4
Charles Burr	25
Luce Burr	5
George Batterson	56
Dudley Baldwin	8
William Batterson	16
Samuel Burr, Jr.	3
Samuel Burr, 3d	15
David Burr	11
Abigail Burr, Jr.	50
Nathan Bulkley	12
Widow Abigail Bulkley & Jonathan Bulkley	55
Olive Bulkley	30
Ebenezer Bulkley	1
Nehemiah Banks	5
David Barlow	375
Priscilla Burr	282
Nathaniel Burr	23
Nathan Burr	4

William Carter	16
Ann Caldwell	8
Thomas & Simon Couch	10
Abigail Chapman	3
John Coke	1
Caleb Desbrow	18
Rev. Andrew Elliot	550
Francis Forgue	152
Abigail Thompson	8
Nathan T. Nichols	82
Hannah McKinsey	1
Jemima Gould	6
Abel Gold	114
Abel Gold, Jr.	4
Daniel Gorham	20
Joseph Gold, deceased	17
Martha Fairchild	44
Justin Hobart	16
Jabez Hubbell	33
Isaac Hubbell	19
Isaac Hayes	87
Anne Hull	65
John Thickling	20
Sarah Hews	15
Peter Jennings	7
Lyman Jennings	6
Hezekiah Jennings	1
Daniel Jennings	32
David Jennings	28
Martha Jennings	28
Ephraim Jennings	28
Margaret Keeler	13
Esther Lord	7
Jonathan Maltby	47
Jonathan Middlebrook	4
Jesse Morehouse	16
Hannah Morehouse	34
David Osborn	21
Free negro Ned	7
Samuel Osborn	37
Nehemiah Phippeny	13
James Penfield	7
Jabez Perry	3
John Perry	7
Abraham Parrott	5
Sarah Penfield	16
Benjamin Rumsey	1
Lucretia Redfield	28
Widow Sarah Redfield	29
Robert Ross	3
Rev. Hezekiah Ripley	369
Joseph Sprague	2
Grace Spalding	90
Francis D. Sword	3
Benjamin Squier	1
Samuel Squier, 2d	83
Seth Smith	56
Zachariah Sanford	2
Mary Smith	17
Ebenezer Squier	15
Stephen Turney	88
Samuel Taylor	10
William Thorp	25
Ruel Thorp	6
Widow Hannah Taylor	40

Sufferer	£	Sufferer	£
Jehiel Whitehead	7	House of Peter Bulkley & Joseph Sturges	91
Richard Wane	5	Edward Buddington	81
Abigail Whitear	112	Andrew Jennings	210
Samuel King	5	Aaron Jennings	100
Gideon Wells	29	William Livesay	152
John Wilson	5	Heirs of Benjamin Osborn	152
Nathaniel Wilson	11		
John Whitehead	17		
Abigail Wyncoop	60		
Joseph Wakeman	4		
Increase Bradley	180		

2531   10 May 1792   F/-/090

Losses sustained by Fairfield, Connecticut, inhabitants in the British expedition to Danbury

Sufferers	£	Sufferers	£
Benjamin Allen	5	Ebenezer Sherwood	2
Ephraim Burr	96	Joseph Sherwood	10
Gilbert Bryan	50	Jehiel Sherwood	5
Ebenezer Baker	22	Joshua Squires & Samuel Burr	36
Gershom Banks	15	Andrew Sturges	14
George Burr	16	Gershom Thorp	9
John Banks	23	William Thorp	3
Ephraim Burr, Jr.	5	Jessup Wakeman	12
Nathan Bennett	15	Samuel Whitney, Jr.	27
Joseph Bennett	56	Peter Whitney	7
Francis Bradley, 3d	3	Widow Elizabeth Sturges	150
Pinckney Burr	14	Moses Bulkley	50
Elias Bennett	20	Josiah Bulkley	10
Job Bartram	14	Nathan Burns	2
Thomas Bennett	3	Ebenezer Munro	2
Sarah Bryant	18	Add to Nehemiah Buddington	1
James Bennett	26	Mary Alvord	8
Abigail Desbrow	10	Jonah Bulkley	1
Jason Desbrow	16	Deduct from Isaac Jarvis	0
Hezekiah Cooley	3	George Cable	400
John Crossman	6	County-House	0
Caleb Desbrow	9	Jail & Jailer's house	0
Jabez Desbrow	5	Schoolhouse on the green	0
John Desbrow	16	Old Schoolhouse	0
Shubael Gorham	5	Meetinghouse	0
Solomon Gray	1	Church-house	0
Ann Godfrey	4	Meetinghouse at Green's farm	0
Hezekiah Hull	10	Church glebe, house & barn	0
Isaac Hayes	28		
John Hyde	48		
John Hyde, Jr.	7		
Joseph Hyde	35		
Ebenezer Jessup	3		
Joseph Lyon	32		
Seth Meeker	22		
John Morehouse	16		
Benjamin Meeker	16		
Rebecca Nash	6		
Sarah Ogden	20		
Daniel Osborn	1		
Cornelius Stratton	1		
John Stratton	1		

2532   10 May 1792   F/-/091

Town of Danbury

Sufferers	£	Sufferers	£
Daniel Taylor, Esq.	656	Mathew Benedict, Jr.	218
Major Taylor	463	David Wood	289
John McLean	523	Abigail Wood	18
Zadock Benedict	68	Jonah Benedict	206
Joseph Wildman	278	Rev. Ebenezer White	218
John Wood	263		

Sufferer	£	Sufferer	£
Joseph P. Cook, Esq.	53	Ezra Stevens	3
Ezra Starr	1214	Bethiah Judd	1
Matthew Benedict	177	John Peck	2
Benjamin Sperry	113	Joseph Benedict	8
Jabez Rockwell	159	Anne Northrop	3
Thaddeus Benedict, Esq.	349	Benjamin Hicock	9
Eli Mygatt, Esq.	542	Benjamin Cartis	4
James Clark	524	Samuel Benedict	4
Comfort Hoyt	50	William Griffin	4
Confort Hoyt, Jr.	479	Elisha Dibble	4
Sarah Benedict	41	Patience Guthrie	4
Daniel Church	40	Benjamin Boughton	2
Eliphalet Barnum	42	Andrew Comstock	5
Mary Barnum	23	Nathaniel Stevens	3
Elnathan Gregory	31	Joseph Bebee	13
Rev. Noah Wetmore	28	Jonathan Hayes	12
Elizabeth Henries	18	Nathaniel Gregory	19
Christiana Rose	1	Daniel Millson	1
Matthew Barnum	3	Stephen Trowbridge	7
Comfort Barnum	2	Justus Hoyt	2
Joshua Benedict	13	Matthew Gregory	12
Matthew Crowfeet	4	Jacob Finch	3
Anne Shepard	8	James Fielding	3
David Judd	10	Matthew Wilkes	3
Charles Peck	6	John Barnum	6
Joseph Benedict, Jr.	8	John Porter	2
Preserve Wood	3	Nathan Taylor, Jr.	4
Joseph Gregory	8	Timothy Northum	2
Hannah Lockwood	3	Timothy Benedict	2
Isaac Coller	5	Timothy Wildman	3
Christiana Starr	6	Alexander Stewart	6
Nathan Taylor, 3d	15	Stephen Scofield	6
Samuel Taylor, Esq.	22	Thomas Benedict	14
John Taylor	11	Roger Negro	1
Rachel Gregory	4	Ebenezer Benedict, Jr.	5
Samuel Lambert	4	Joseph Broadbrooks	4
Horace Knapp	3	Oliver Benedict	5
Nathaniel Lockwood	8	Ebenezer Benedict	6
Seth Crowfeet	4	David Northrop	4
Samuel Andrus	8	Enos Camp	4
Wait Desbrow	10	Ephraim Barnum	4
Isaac Davis	2	Daniel Stevens	3
Hannah Andrus	15	Elijah Wood	2
Timothy Ketchum	23	Thaddeus Barnum	17
Caleb Baldwin	2	Philip Corbin	11
John Knapp	7	Nathaniel Benedict	4
Abijah Benedict	5	Thomas Taylor	12
Thomas Wildman	4	Thomas Taylor, Jr.	10
Samuel Wood	1	James Trowbridge	7
Hannah Wood	5	Daniel Wildman	32
Thomas Starr	9	Benjamin Taylor	3
Jonas Benedict	2	John Elliot	2
Seth Shove	6	Matthew Starr	3
Elias Taylor	4	Thomas H. Benedict	9
Rebecca Crowfeet	2	William Stone	7
Phineas Peck	1	John Stone	5
Eliphalet Peck	1	Lemuel Benedict	3
Benjamin Shove	3	Nathaniel Starr	4
William Wille	1	Ebenezer Munson, Jr.	21
Comfort Wildman	12	John Gregory	4
Aaron Stone	3	Jeremiah Dunning	2
Sarah Peck	1	James Crary	5
Jonathan Taylor	6	Amos Northrop	2
Abijah Barnum	7	David Northrop	4
Oliver Taylor	5	Obial Picket	4
Abial Phillips	7	John Sturdevant	5
Daniel Hicock	6	Salle Pill	7
Benjamin Wood	1	Eleazer Hoyt	2
		Caleb Church	4
		Thomas Benedict, Jr.	10

Sufferer	£	Sufferer	£
Josiah Starr	9	Thomas Taylor	32
Joshua Knapp	43	Benjamin Daily	2
Moses Knapp	4	Shadrach Morris	10
Ebenezer Munson	23	Noah Hoyt	3
Hannah Robertson	2	Samuel Gregory	62
Josiah Starr	13	Daniel Pierce	4
Isaac Benedict	4	Richard Smith	6
Thomas Benedict	2	Henry Peck	2
Robert Benedict	2	Daniel Comstock	9
Samuel Benedict, Jr.	8	John Shepard	1
Mary Greenslate	10	Joseph Birchard	2
Anthony Angwene	3	Judith Taylor	1
Samuel Brown	1	Sarah Bassett	1
John Couch	6	Amos Collins	5
Stephen Jarvis	43	Joshua Starr	5
Ezra Dibble, Jr.	17	Matthew Taylor	24
Joseph M. White	31	William B. Alger	19
Aaron Knapp	5	Caleb Hoyt	5
Joseph Gunn	4		

2533   10 May 1792   F/-/093

New Haven and East Haven, Connecticut, losses

Sufferers	£	Sufferers	£		£		£
Abraham Augur	60	Jonathan Fitch	173	Jeremiah McCumber	20	Samuel Wilmot	63
Hezekiah Augur	29	Jehiel Forbes	174	Amos Morris	1236	William Ward	23
Eldad Atwater	52	Levi Forbes	6	William Mansfield	48	John Wise	32
David Austin, Esq.	276	Samuel Green	54	Jonah Mix	16	Daniel Wilmot	43
Timothy Atwater	8	Samuel Griswold	22	Stephen Munson	23	John White, Jr.	24
Phineas Andrus	19	Caleb Gilbert	49	Joseph Mix	12	Rev. Chauncey	
Joseph Adams	14	James Gilbert	12	William Miles	6	Whittlesey	326
John Allen	16	Stephen Gorham	28	Joseph Munson	11	Thomas Wooster	591
Christopher Allen	7	Hezekiah Gorham	21	John Miles	48	John Whiting, Esq.	159
Samuel Austin	70	William Grenough	28	William Munson	73	Titus Beecher	5
Abner Austin	57	Samuel Gills	53	Samuel Munson	42	Hannah Bingly	10
Abiah Allen	14	Timothy Gilbert	4	Israel Munson	27	Isaac Beecher	4
Oliver Allen	41	Samuel Gorham	9	Alless Miles	5	Sarah Brown	13
Samuel Bird	42	Richard Hood	37	Edward Maley	266	Peter Buckley	3
Abraham Bradley	101	Nathan Howell	10	Amos Munson	19	Joseph Bishop	8
Joseph Bradley	403	Samuel Huggins	92	Paul Noyes	3	Elias Beech	4
Benjamin Brown	30	Ezekiel Hays	73	David Osborn	31	Archibald Blakely	11
Israel Bishop	32	Josiah Holly	53	Nathan Oakes	19	Tilley Blakely	14
Isaac Bishop	37	Abiah Hall	4	Mehitabel Osborn	4	Abraham Barns	4
Abel Barrett	28	Amos Hotchkis	34	William Plimmaist	33	Atkins Broughton	8
John Bradley, Jr.	31	Samuel Horton	77	Jacob & Abijah		George Cook	46
Stephen Ball	36	Jonah Hotchkis	19	Pardy	402	Cornelius Cunn-	
Francis Brown	13	Ebenezer Huggins	48	Mary Pardy	135	ingham	21
Peter Benheir	71	Mary Hubbard	6	Hezekiah Parmele	109	John Catlin	8
Phineas Bradley,		Joseph Howell	76	Martin Parrett	28	Nathan Catlin	9
Jr.	20	Samuel Howell	39	William Punchard	20	Zachariah Candee	8
Daniel Bishop	79	Susanna Hotchkis	14	Jacob Pinto	23	Levi Clinton	6
John Beecher, Jr.	23	Obadiah Hotchkis	69	Ichabod Page	59	David Cook	30
Gurdon Bradley	66	Caleb Hotchkis	9	Sarah Parmele	9	Russell Clark	2
Azariah Bradley	19	Henry F. Hughes	38	James Plant	95	Samuel Clark	8
Samuel Barnes	14	Elijah Hill	17	Jeremiah Parmele	19	Samuel Cook	19
Stephen Bradley	4	Stephen Herrick	15	Charles Prindle	47	Samuel Chatterton	33
Thomas Burrall	17	Jabez Johnson	13	John Pease	19	John Clause	3
Timothy Bontique	23	Timothy Jones, Jr.	38	Benjamin Pardy	89	John Carew	9
James Bradley	48	Timothy & William		Jehu Robertson	27	Sarah Davenport	
Buckminster		Jones	168	John Richards	13	Isaac Doolittle	27
Brentnall	51	Isaac Jones	149	Philemon Smith	53	Samuel Deenwell	34
Eleazer Brown	9	Levi Ives	46	Benjamin Sanford	32	Henry Daggett	38
Nanda Cambridge	15	Peter Johnson	21	William Sherman	37	Rhoda Denison	10
Charles Chauncey	48	Silas Kimberly	10	Francis Sage	34	Hamlin Dwight	3
Samuel Candy	51	Azael Kimberly	53	Jonathan Sabin	65	Dr. Napthali Dag-	
John Chandler	108	Mary Kimberly	19	Timothy Sperry	31	gett	33
Timothy Dwight	11	Elam Luddington	408	Charles Sabin	29	Isaac Dickerman	32
Samuel Dwight	9	Daniel Lyman, Esq.	143	Jesse Stephens	19	William Doak	15
Thomas Davis	21	Jesse Levenworth	143	Elias Shipman	11	Rev. Jona[than]	
Jacob Daggett	50	William Lyon	92	Caleb Trowbridge	126	Edwards	58
Amos Doolittle	11	Ebenezer Lines	21	Jeremiah Townsend,		William Eyers	5
Nathan Drummon	6	John Lathrop	72	Jr.	7	Robert Fairchild	15
				Daniel Tuttle	13	Ezra Ford	17
				Isaac Townsend	12	Abel Frisbie	26
				Benajah Thomas	7	Samuel Goodwin	14
				Robert Townsend	16	John Goodrich	141
				Hezekiah Tuttle	54	Timothy Gorham	11
				Richard Tuttle	13	Ruth Gordon	8
				Michael Todd	74	Henry Gibbs	4
				Jeremiah Townsend	36	Amos Gilbert	13
				Jacob Thompson	61	Sarah Goldsmith	53
				Timothy Townsend	11	Joel Gilbert	2
				Abraham Tuttle,		Daniel Goodsell	12
				Jr.	27	David Gilbert	8
				John Townsend	3	Martin Gotter,	
				Stephen Trowbridge	8	deceased	19
				Samuel Tuttle	271	John Goodsell	9
				Joseph Tuttle	93	Stephen Hotchkiss	4
				Timothy Tuttle	79	Christian Hanson	21
				Noah Tucker	100	Ebenezer Hull	5
				Jesse Upson	48	Hannah Hotchkiss	5
				Jotham Williams	3	Sarah Hunt	3
				John Woodward	839	Frederick Harding	12
				John Woodward,		Eleanora Hogg	2
				Jr.	741	Joseph Hutts	1
				Moses Wells	256	Jared Henningway	5

Hannah How	13	Lamberton Painter	12	Samuel Alling	16	Lemuel Benham	13
Sarah Howe	14	Martin Patchen	31	Ebenezer Alling	16	Thomas Bill	10
William Helins	43	Levi Pardy	4	Lorrain Alling	4	Hanover Barney	12
David Hull	20	Jonas Prentice	28	Hezekiah Alling	15	Lucy Barker	2
James Hull	9	Sarah Pomeroy	28	David Atwater	4	Israel Burnell	10
Silas Hotchkis	3	James Prescott	26	David Austin, Jr.	11	Nathan Beers	13
Nehemiah Hotchkis	15	Philip Rexford	16	Abigail Andrus	2	William Brentnall	17
Nehemiah Higgins	2	Samuel Robinson	10	Jedediah Andrus	10	David Bacher	19
Enos Hotchkis	4	Rachel Russell	4	Jeremiah Atwater	228	Daniel Brown	6
Mary Horton	6	Zachariah Reed	3	Jonah Atwater	17	Timothy P. Bonticou	4
Stephen Honeywell	2	James Rice	64	Archibald Austin	72	Lamberton Painter	24
Abigail Hughes	38	Hannah Russell	18	William Ally	9	Silas Kimberly	194
Stephen Johnson	14	Martin Ray	71	John Austin	10	Mary Kimberly	20
Simeon Jocelyn	11	Hannah Sackett	5	Stephen Austin	13	John Beecher	26
Amaziah Jocelyn	26	Adonijah Sherman	30	Joel Atwater	1	Thomas Benham	11
Abraham Johnson	6	John Scott	7	Samuel Bishop, Esq.	14	Jotham Williams	6
Mabel Johnson	6	James Sherman	7	Phebe Brown	7	Andrew Smith	14
Enos Johnson	2	Leveret Stevens	3	Timothy Bonticou,		William Trowbridge	7
Tack and wife	18	Sarah Stephens	5	Jr.	13	Anna Clinton	4
Jared Ingersoll	2	Elizabeth Stillman	27	Eleanor Bonticou	33	Rev. Noah Williston	27
Richard Johnson	11	Widow Scovill	7	Stephen Brown	19	Azel Kimberly	33
Lydia Johnson	5	William Sherman	23	Jona[than] Bridglin	4	John Mix	38
Elijah King	12	Moses Strong	10	Abraham Bradley,			
Sarah Kimberly	28	Abigail Starr	14	Jr.	6		
Marak Kilby	1	Benjamin Smith	3	Willard Brentnal	36		
Lydia Kimberly	21	Nehemiah Smith	10				
Nathaniel Kimberly	2	George Smith	20				
James Lyndes	5	Nathan Smith	10				
Edward Larkin	21	Mary Stillwell	14	**2534**		10 May 1792	F/-/097
Samuel Little	11	Hezekiah Sabin	79	Town of New London			
Major Lines	14	Hezekiah Sabin,		Sufferers	£	Sufferers	£
James Lane	9	Jr.	22	Philip Allen	10	John McCurdy	1128
Mark Levenworth	7	Edmond Smith	5	James Angel	169	Samuel Coit	19
Gad Luke	28	Amos Sherman	35	Lydia Beebe	24	John Clark & sons	135
Susanna Mahon	1	Joseph Smith, 3d	12	Abigail Bell	7	John Deshon	1177
John Mix, Jr.	10	John Storer	56	William Brooks	66	Deshon & Co.	557
Daniel Mansfield	12	Hannah Storer	5	John Barr	72	Henry Deshon	900
Elisha Mix	25	James Thompson	1	Ann Bulkley	494	Joseph Deshon	100
Mary Miles	3	John B. Troop	7	Samuel Brown	493	Richard Deshon	267
Amos Monson	1	Joseph Thompson	13	Stephen Babcock	34	Mons. Dumont	264
Robert Matthews	8	John Townsend	17	Joanna Beebe	236	Jonathan Douglas	1447
Esther Mansfield	299	Thankful Thompson	23	David Byrne	336	Sarah Davis	8
Kirsted Mansfield	10	Isaac Thompson	3	John Barna	84	Richard Douglass	263
James Murray	10	Abraham Tuttle	4	Jeremiah Brown	124	Robert Douglass	200
Nathan Mansfield	4	Abraham Thompson	5	Hannah Beebe	7	Ebenezer Douglass	17
Silas Merriman	2	Stephen Tuttle	1	Hannah Bolten	32	Peter Darrow	10
David Mulford	8	Timothy Tallmadge	38	Walter Beebe	9	Nathan Douglass	942
Hannah Mansfield	9	Joseph Trowbridge	10	Percy Beer	7	Nicholas Darrow	10
Patuna Mix	21	Ebenezer Townsend	9	Nathan Bailey	20	James Darrow	2
Phebe Miller	15	William Trowbridge	13	Cornelius Cunning-		Nathaniel Dicken-	
David Munson	2	John Trowbridge	18	ham	63	son	15
Hannah Mix	36	Cornelius Thayer	4	Joanna Culver	11	Timothy Durfey	21
Dr. Timothy Mix	17	Moses Thompson	6	Richard Chapman	73	Isaac Champlin	142
Moses Mansfield	6	William Van Deur-		Esther Cutler	7	Clark Elliot	297
Nathaniel Mix	11	son	62	Joseph Chals	76	John Champlin	104
William Noyes	12	Moses Venturet	31	Joseph Collins	41	Sarah Edmonds	20
Anne Platt	11	Michael Vaun	4	John Critchet	6	John Crocker	85
Mary & Lydia		Thomas Wilson	51	Joseph Coit	1299	Abigail Elliot	497
Pardy	10	Lois Walls	9	William Coit	45	John Irwin	800
William Punchard	27	Thomas Wilmot	3	James Culver	8	Jacob Finch	130
Ebenezer Peck	23	Allice Wise	9	Joseph Cocks	1	Ann Fosdick &	
Thomas Punderson	3	John Ward	25	Lodwick Champlin	11	sons	1046
Thomas Punderson,		Rev. -- Williston	21	Elizabeth Chris-		Ebenezer Goddard	7
Jr.	15	Samuel White	3	tophers	49	Mary Goodfaith	15
Mary Pease	2	Samuel White	3	Rebecca Church	53	Elizabeth Griffin	5
David Phipps	7	John Warner	4	William Comstock	4	Thomas Gardner	22
John Pierpont	18	Newton Whittlesey	33	Thomas Coit	24	Roger Gibson	885
Abigail Potter	25	Henry York	4	Nathaniel Coit,		Mary Gardner	124
Moses Pardy	16	Daniel Abbot	4	Jr.	16	David Gardner	11
Solomon Phipps	44	Joseph Alling	4	Joshua Coit	40	John Gordon	2
Elijah Painter	14	James Alling	12	Joseph Champlin	73	George Gibbs	21
				Jonathan Colfax	16	Matthew Griswold	10

Russell Hubbard	1012	James Miller	93
Joseph Hurlbut	965	John Morris	30
Thomas Hopkins	199	Giles Mumford	44
Ruth Harris	63	Jabez Miner	8
Elizabeth Holes-worth	46	Lawrence Marting	56
Thomas Hancock	148	Ephraim Miner	344
Mary Hurlbut	213	Lydia Creen	13
Joseph Harris, Jr.	5	Anthony Mitchell	24
Stephen Holt	229	David Mumford	318
Nathaniel Harris	3	Isaac Moseley	500
Edward & John Hallum	310	David Manwarring	51
Edward & George Hallum	215	Lewis Minor	71
		Thomas Jones	40
Edward Hallum	11	Elizabeth Newcomb	12
William Higgins	5	George Newcomb	238
Daniel Hurlburt	127	Widow Nelson	64
Sarah Harris	177	Mary Newberry	14
John Harris, 2d	33	Nathaniel Overton	27
John Hempsted & others	31	Isaac Oliver	40
John Hallam	418	Owen Neil	92
Benjamin Harris	19	Joseph Owen	76
Abigail Holt	19	Richard Potter	382
Nathaniel Hempsted	7	Christopher Prince	512
John Hartle	45	Abigail Potter	573
Joseph Holt	3	Zuriah Preston	22
Lydia Harris	60	Joseph Plumb	25
Thomas Holt	5	Green Plumb	44
Bridget Harris	25	Ichabod Powers, Jr.	189
James Holt	22	Andrew Palmer	106
John Harris, 1st	1	Widow Palmer	43
Walter Harris	18	Simeon Peck	20
Grace Harris	29	James Parteer	22
Ebenezer Holt	15	Sarah Poole	5
Daniel Harris	5	Joshua Powers	5
Eliphalet Harris	21	William Packwood	12
Daniel Holt	32	Ichabod Powers	620
Jonathan Holt	26	John Pennwert	223
Ann Hancock	140	John Potter	84
Titus Hurlburt	1961	Joseph Packwood	817
Stephen Hempsted	70	Joshua Potter	9
Moses Jeffrey	36	John Prentice	4
Lydia Jonston	22	Eliza Plumb	198
Robert Kennedy	350	James Pitman	146
Mary Lewis	6	Stephen Rougett	37
Christopher Lef-fingwell	25	Mary Rogers	9
James Lamphier	233	Patrick Robinson	3
Lydia Lattimer	27	Ann Richards	225
James Lamphier, Jr.	42	James Rogers	456
Picket Lattimer	565	Guy Richards & sons	811
Samuel Lattimer	911	Mary Richards	259
Ambs Lester	13	Benjamin Rogers	10
Ebenezer Lester	9	Jabez Richards	4
John Lester	36	Solomon Rogers	101
Edgcomb Lee	43	Amos Rogers	31
Deodat Little	207	Samuel Roberts	94
Samuel Lattimer	24	George Rogers	15
Michael Love	23	David Richards	1
Richard Lattimer	27	James Rogers	2
Rosman Lawrence	54	Harris Rogers	129
Peter Lattimer	317	Peter Rogers	16
John Lathrop	2	William Rogers	18
Amasa Learnid	18	Peter Rogers, Jr.	2
Jeremiah Miller	2536	Peter Robinson	82
James McEvers' heirs	600	John Rogers	21
		David Roberts	18
James Matthews	30	William Rogers	5
Robert Manwaring	21	James Penniman	138
		Daniel Stole	28
		Gurdon Salton-stall, Esq.	1440

Thomas Smith	11
William Skinner	15
Seth Seers	14
Jona[than] & J. Starr	53
Bathsheba Skinner	130
Bathsheba Smith	466
Eliza Shapley	382
Adam Shapley	21
Lydia Spinch	10
Ann Squier	8
Nathaniel & Thomas Shaw	2834
John Shepard	77
Robert Smith	25
Starr & Tallman	150
John Springer	18
Ann Simmonds	14
Peter Perry	10
John Coster	14
Judas P. Spooner	22
Widow Dorsett	2
Richard Stroud	24
James Smith	4
James Stewart	14
Lucy Starr	5
William Stark	17
Sarah Setchell	57
John Spencer	58
Joshua Starr	1251
Roswell Salton-stall	1800
Winthrop Salton-stall	1182
Nathaniel Thorp	3
Bethiah Tallman	68
Daniel Tinker	23
James Tilley	1587

John Tilley	7
Mary Taylor	27
Daniel Truman	6
Edward Tucker	26
John Welch	47
Walter Welch	60
Ebenezer Way	16
John Ward	17
Lucretia Wolfe	5
Anthony Wolfe	5
Simon Wolcott	1083
Eliza Wescott	87
James Young	13
Temperance Moore	24
Samuel Belden	1772
Joanna Short	277
James Thompson	350
Michael Melally	94
John Way	590
Thomas Bowhay	50
Joshua Hempsted	63
Nathaniel Salton-stall	146
John Thompson	60
Spere Douglass	9
Chapman Simmons	23
Elizabeth Beebe	16
John Hallum & Benjamin Harris	300
Mary Ward	23
Stelphen Culver	4
Mehitabel Leet	124

2535

Town of Ridgefield

10 May 1792   F/-/099

Sufferer	£	Sufferer	£
Samuel Olmsted	75	Hope Rhodes	8
Ebenezer Olmsted	5	Stephen Smith	8
Thaddeus Rockwell	27	Martha Keeler	2
Samuel Olmsted, 3d	24	John Watrous	4
Philip B. Bradley, Esq.	20	David Perry	3
Lydia Gilbert	35	James Scott	3
Timothy Keeler, 2d	54	Philip Dauchey	3
Gamaliel Northrop	88	Matthew Keeler	7
Benjamin Northrop	159	John Smith	13
Daniel Smith	183	Samuel Smith	19
John Northrop	143	Benjamin Smith	5
Thomas Seymour	66	Jeremiah Birchard	1
Hannah Seymour	18	Samuel Camp	39
Sarah Morehouse	189	Isaac Keeler	194
David Olmsted	36	Lemuel Abbot	6
Joseph Stebbins	20	James Northrop	54
Daniel Smith, 3d	31	Abraham Rockwell	10
James Sturges	11	John Keeler	23
John Dauchey	11	Timothy Benedict	7
George Talcott	13	Ichabod Doolittle	6
Daniel Smith, 2d	3	Jemima Keeler	1
Ebenezer Jones	5	David Rockwell	8
Bartlett Talcott	6	Samuel Keeler	5
Ebenezer Stebbins	2	Ebenezer Sherwood	6
Jesse Benedict	12	Stephen Norris	3
John Abbott	4	Daniel Cooley	2
Bartholomew Weed	4	Mary Hayes	4
		Abijah Rockwell	3
		Abijah Smith	17

Jonah Foster	10	Mary Gray	1
Sarah Silsbe	3	David Rockwell, 2d	3
Elihu Deforest	2	Abner Wilson	9
Prue Northrop	4	Samuel Keeler, 2d	1
Nathan Foster	1		

"N.B. The sums advanced to the town of Ridge-field, by grants of the General Assembly, are deducted from each man's respective sum and the net balances ascertained."

2536   10 May 1792   F/-/100

Town of Groton

Sufferers	£	Sufferers	£		£		£
Amos Avery	12	Benjamin Chester	442	Jona[than] Havens	11	Lydia Latham	92
Prudence Avery	271	Benjamin Chester, as executor	301	Ruth Holliday	44	Mary Latham	4
Thankful Avery	264	Charles Chester	7	Edward Jeffrey	158	Jonathan Latham	3
Rufus Avery	133	Thomas Chester	1	Alexander Kidd	9	Elizabeth Latham	16
Lydia Avery	158	Daniel Chester	20	Thomas Mumford, Esq.	604	Amos Prentice, Esq.	566
Latham Avery	108	Jason Chester	21	Elizabeth Moore	63	Elisha Prior	35
Ebenezer Avery	30	Esther Conklin	39	Henry Mason	28	Abigail Palmer	7
Phebe Avery	2	Simeon Chester	9	Nancy Moore	31	Alexander Reed	61
Peter Avery	5	Nathan Darrow	9	Prudence Minor	18	Thomas Shaw	1
George Avery	8	Mary Dodge	14	Rebecca Minor	1	Nathaniel Seabury	4
Hannah Avery	15	Charles Eldridge, Jr.	755	Elisha Morgan	8	Thankful Stanton	1
Elizabeth Avery	2	Daniel Eldridge	5	Joshua & Isaac Morgan	5	Jabez Sholes	1
Benjamin Avery	4	Sergeant Daniel Eldridge	1	Mary Moore	11	Nathan Sholes	1
Caleb Avery	7	Thomas Griffin	3	Frederick Moore	269	John Starr	1
Ezekiel Bailey	3	Robert Gallup	11	Shoram Negro	6	Sarah Stedman	1
Stephen Billings	74	Andrew Gallup	14	Ebenezer Ledyard, Esq.	1151	Lucretia Sholes	4
James Bailey	3	John Hicks	7	John Latham	95	James Smith	6
Samuel Chester	11			Bridget Ledyard	398	Experience Ward	3
Eldridge Chester	7			Youngs Ledyard, deceased	75	Eunice Williams	15
Jedediah Chester	22			Benjamin & Caleb Ledyard	200	Samuel Walsworth	11
				Anne Ledyard	142	Christopher Woodbridge	1
				Anne Leeds	58	Peter Williams	27
				Benajah Lester	1	Benjamin Vose	6
				Capt. Edward Latham	4	Ezekiel Yerington	2
				Thomas D. Lewis	1	Elizabeth Seabury	178
				Widow A. Latham	37	John Brown	29
				Capt. William Latham	45	Daniel Williams	8
						Elisha Avery	11

(End of source F)

2537

	Location			Acres	Located by	G/-/-- When
Ref	16	18	1	367	John Paskell	21 Apr 1802
Ref	16	18	2	361	Samuel Rogers	
Ref	16	18	3	337		
Ref	16	18	4	355		
Ref	16	18	5	352		
Ref	16	18	6	350	Charlotte Hazen	1812
Ref	16	18	7	322	Martha Bogart	12 Jan 1802
Ref	16	18	8	321	Jacob Vander- hyden	12 Jan 1802
Ref	16	18	9	321	David Gay	12 Jan 1802
Ref	16	18	10	321	William How	12 Jan 1802
Ref	16	18	11	320	David Gay	12 Jan 1802
Ref	16	18	12	321	Samuel Fales	21 Apr 1802
Ref	16	18	13	322	Jacob Vander- hyden	12 Jan 1802
Ref	16	18	14	320	Martha Bogart	12 Jan 1802
Ref	16	18	15	321	Bartholomew Van Heer	12 Jan 1802
Ref	16	18	16	322	Bartholomew Van Heer	12 Jan 1802
Ref	16	18	17	323	John Edgar	12 Jan 1802
Ref	16	18	18	323	John Allen	12 Jan 1802
Ref	16	18	19	326	Samuel Rogers	
Ref	16	18	20	323	Samuel Rogers	
Ref	16	18	21	323	Col. James Livingston	12 Jan 1802
Ref	16	18	22	322	David Jenks	12 Jan 1802
Ref	16	18	23	322	John Allen	12 Jan 1802
Ref	16	18	24	321	John Livingston	12 Jan 1802
Ref	16	18	25	321	Atwood Fales	21 Apr 1802
Ref	16	18	26	320	David Gay	12 Jan 1802
Ref	16	18	27	322	William How	12 Jan 1802
Ref	16	18	28	324	Atwood Fales	21 Apr 1802
Ref	16	18	29	321	Atwood Fales	21 Apr 1802
Ref	16	18	30	321	Edward Chinn	12 Jan 1802

2538

	Location			Acres	Located by	G/-/-- When
Ref	17	19	1	350		
Ref	17	19	2	346		
Ref	17	19	3	338	Samuel Rogers	
Ref	17	19	4	355	Lewis F. Deles- dernier	12 Jan 1802
Ref	17	19	5	343	John Allen	12 Jan 1802
Ref	17	19	6	348	Seth Harding	12 Jan 1802
Ref	17	19	7	315	John Morrison	1812
Ref	17	19	8	313		
Ref	17	19	9	313	John Edgar	12 Jan 1802
Ref	17	19	10	317	John Edgar	12 Jan 1802
Ref	17	19	11	334	Cloe Shannon	1812
Ref	17	19	12	322		
Ref	17	19	13	319		
Ref	17	19	14	318	Israel Ruland, Heirs of	1812*
Ref	17	19	15	319		
Ref	17	19	16	321		
Ref	17	19	17	320	Ebenezer Gard- ner	22 Nov 1808
Ref	17	19	18	321		
Ref	17	19	19	322	Ebenezer Gard- ner	22 Nov 1808
Ref	17	19	20	323	Simeon Chester	11 Jan 1811
Ref	17	19	21	323		
Ref	17	19	22	320		
Ref	17	19	23	320	Samuel Rogers	
Ref	17	19	24	323	Noah Miller	12 Jan 1802
Ref	17	19	25	324		
Ref	17	19	26	326		

	Location			Acres	Located by	
Ref	17	19	27	319		
Ref	17	19	28	316		
Ref	17	19	29	316		
Ref	17	19	30	316		

*In Remarks column: "double entry."

2539

	Location			Acres	Located by	G/-/-- When
Ref	18	17	1	341	Seth Harding	12 Jan 1802
Ref	18	17	2	339		
Ref	18	17	3	337	John Edgar	12 Jan 1802
Ref	18	17	4	335	Noah Miller	12 Jan 1802
Ref	18	17	5	333	Ambrose Cole	12 Jan 1802
Ref	18	17	6	330	John Edgar	12 Jan 1802
Ref	18	17	7	319	Joseph Bindon	12 Jan 1802
Ref	18	17	8	327		
Ref	18	17	9	330		
Ref	18	17	10	334		
Ref	18	17	11	331	John Allen	12 Jan 1802
Ref	18	17	12	329	James Cole	
Ref	18	17	13	328	Parker Clarke	
Ref	18	17	14	326	Parker Clarke	
Ref	18	17	15	331	Parker Clarke	
Ref	18	17	16	339	James Boyd, Heirs of*	
Ref	18	17	17	337		
Ref	18	17	18	335	Simeon Chester	11 Jan 1811
Ref	18	17	19	332		
Ref	18	17	20	335		
Ref	18	17	21	335		
Ref	18	17	22	335		
Ref	18	17	23	335		
Ref	18	17	24	326		
Ref	18	17	25	328	Seth Harding	12 Jan 1802
Ref	18	17	26	328	Charlotte Hazen	1812*
Ref	18	17	27	327		
Ref	18	17	28	324		
Ref	18	17	29	324	Nathaniel Rey- nolds, Heirs of	1812*
Ref	18	17	30	325	Cloe Shannon	1812*
Ref	18	17	31	325		
Ref	18	17	32	330		
Ref	18	17	33	330		
Ref	18	17	34	332		
Ref	18	17	35	328		
Ref	18	17	36	331	Cloe Shannon	1812
Ref	18	17	37	329		
Ref	18	17	38	324		
Ref	18	17	39	324		
Ref	18	17	40	334		
Ref	18	17	41	334		
Ref	18	17	42	334		
Ref	18	17	43	334	Samuel Rogers	
Ref	18	17	44	334	Samuel Rogers	
Ref	18	17	45	335		
Ref	18	17	46	334		
Ref	18	17	47	334		
Ref	18	17	48	325		
Ref	18	17	49	330		
Ref	18	17	50	338	Parker Clarke	
Ref	18	17	51	332	Ebenezer Gard- ner	22 Nov 1808
Ref	18	17	52	326		
Ref	18	17	53	327		
Ref	18	17	54	326		
Ref	18	17	55	324		

*In Remarks column: "double entry."
**In Remarks column: "3 times entered."

2540

	Location			Acres	Located by	G/-/-- When
Ref	19	17	1	372	Seth Harding	12 Jan 1802
Ref	19	17	2	369	John Allen	12 Jan 1802
Ref	19	17	3	369	John D. Mercier	12 Jan 1802
Ref	19	17	4	369	P. F. Cazeau	12 Jan 1802
Ref	19	17	5	370	Isaac Danks	30 Apr 1802
Ref	19	17	6	352	Isaac Danks	30 Apr 1802
Ref	19	17	7	310		
Ref	19	17	8	311		
Ref	19	17	9	318		
Ref	19	17	10	315		
Ref	19	17	11	314		
Ref	19	17	12	316		
Ref	19	17	13	315	Martha Walker	12 Jan 1802
Ref	19	17	14	317	Jeremiah Duggan, Heirs of	12 Jan 1802
Ref	19	17	15	314	Lewis F. Delesdernier	12 Jan 1802
Ref	19	17	16	316	John McGown	12 Jan 1802
Ref	19	17	17	318	Joshua Lamb	20 Apr 1802
Ref	19	17	18	313		
Ref	19	17	19	322		
Ref	19	17	20	318		
Ref	19	17	21	314		
Ref	19	17	22	314		
Ref	19	17	23	317		
Ref	19	17	24	319	John Fulton	1812
Ref	19	17	25	319	John Fulton	1812
Ref	19	17	26	324	James Boyd, Heirs of	1812
Ref	19	17	27	320		
Ref	19	17	28	321		
Ref	19	17	29	319	James Boyd, Heirs of	1812
Ref	19	17	30	312	Elijah Ayer, Heirs of	1812
Ref	19	17	31	318		
Ref	19	17	32	316		
Ref	19	17	33	319		
Ref	19	17	34	319		
Ref	19	17	35	323		
Ref	19	17	36	322		
Ref	19	17	37	323		
Ref	19	17	38	319		
Ref	19	17	39	316		
Ref	19	17	40	320		
Ref	19	17	41	324		
Ref	19	17	42	323		
Ref	19	17	43	324		
Ref	19	17	44	323		
Ref	19	17	45	322		
Ref	19	17	46	317		
Ref	19	17	47	321		
Ref	19	17	48	329		
Ref	19	17	49	329		
Ref	19	17	50	327		
Ref	19	17	51	322		
Ref	19	17	52	320		
Ref	19	17	53	320		
Ref	19	17	54	321		

2541

	Location			Acres	Located by	G/-/-- When
Ref	20	16	1	353		
Ref	20	16	2	301		
Ref	20	16	3	348		
Ref	20	16	4	333		
Ref	20	16	5	331	William How	12 Jan 1802
Ref	20	16	6	334	John Livingston	12 Jan 1802
Ref	20	16	7	316	Lt. Col. Bradford	12 Jan 1802
Ref	20	16	8	315	Col. James Livingston	12 Jan 1802
Ref	20	16	9	319		
Ref	20	16	10	318		
Ref	20	16	11	312		
Ref	20	16	12	310		
Ref	20	16	13	318		
Ref	20	16	14	316		
Ref	20	16	15	316		
Ref	20	16	16	317		
Ref	20	16	17	314		
Ref	20	16	18	311		
Ref	20	16	19	312		
Ref	20	16	20	312	Joshua Lamb	20 Apr 1802
Ref	20	16	21	316		
Ref	20	16	22	317		
Ref	20	16	23	319		
Ref	20	16	24	319		
Ref	20	16	25	314		
Ref	20	16	26	312		
Ref	20	16	27	318		
Ref	20	16	28	319		
Ref	20	16	29	314	Daniel Earll	11 Feb 1802
Ref	20	16	30	314	Adam Johnston	5 Apr 1802
Ref	20	16	31	320	Jonathan Eddy	12 Jan 1802
Ref	20	16	32	320	Jonas C. Minot	12 Jan 1802
Ref	20	16	33	324	James Crawford	26 Feb 1802
Ref	20	16	34	326	James Crawford	26 Feb 1802
Ref	20	16	35	322		
Ref	20	16	36	322		
Ref	20	16	37	325		
Ref	20	16	38	325		
Ref	20	16	39	329		
Ref	20	16	40	326	John Dodge, Heirs of	25 May 1802
Ref	20	16	41	323		
Ref	20	16	42	321		
Ref	20	16	43	323		
Ref	20	16	44	324	John Dodge, Heirs of	25 May 1802
Ref	20	16	45	326	John Dodge, Heirs of	25 May 1802
Ref	20	16	46	323		
Ref	20	16	47	321		
Ref	20	16	48	318		
Ref	20	16	49	317		
Ref	20	16	50	320		
Ref	20	16	51	322	P. F. Cazeau	12 Jan 1802
Ref	20	16	52	321	P. F. Cazeau	12 Jan 1802
Ref	20	16	53	319		
Ref	20	16	54	320	John Torrey	21 Jan 1802

2542

	Location			Acres	Located by	G/-/-- When
Ref	21	12	1	322	Martha Walker	12 Jan 1802
Ref	21	12	2	333	Gilbert Seaman, Heirs of	1812
Ref	21	12	3	330	Lt. William Maxwell	12 Jan 1802
Ref	21	12	4	329	James Boyd, Heirs of	1812
Ref	21	12	5	329	Simeon Chester	11 Jan 1811
Ref	21	12	6	327		
Ref	21	12	7	315	Charlotte Hazen	1812
Ref	21	12	8	316	Robert Sharp	1812*
Ref	21	12	9	314		

Ref	21	12	10	313				
Ref	21	12	11	316	Elijah Ayre,			
					Heirs of		1812	
Ref	21	12	12	317				
Ref	21	12	13	316	Benjamin			
					Thompson	12 Jan 1802		
Ref	21	12	14	314	Martha Walker	12 Jan 1802		
Ref	21	12	15	319				
Ref	21	12	16	322				
Ref	21	12	17	316	Joseph Levetre	12 Jan 1802		
Ref	21	12	18	316	Edward Faulkner	12 Jan 1802		
Ref	21	12	19	318				
Ref	21	12	20	319	David Dickey		1812	
Ref	21	12	21	324				
Ref	21	12	22	321	Joshua Lamb	20 Apr 1802		
Ref	21	12	23	315	John Allen	12 Jan 1802		
Ref	21	12	24	318	John Holstead	12 Jan 1802		
Ref	21	12	25	317	Edward Autell,			
					Heirs of		1812	
Ref	21	12	26	313	John Morrison		1812	
Ref	21	12	27	311				
Ref	21	12	28	313	Edward Autell,			
					Heirs of		1812	
Ref	21	12	29	315				
Ref	21	12	30	313				
Ref	21	12	31	317	Jonathan Eddy	12 Jan 1802		
Ref	21	12	32	319				
Ref	21	12	33	320				
Ref	21	12	34	318				
Ref	21	12	35	318				
Ref	21	12	36	321	Martin Brooks	20 Apr 1802		
Ref	21	12	37	323	Lewis F. Deles-			
					dernier	12 Jan 1802		
Ref	21	12	38	319	John D. Mercier	12 Jan 1802		
Ref	21	12	39	327				
Ref	21	12	40	328				
Ref	21	12	41	324				
Ref	21	12	42	327				
Ref	21	12	43	329	John Starr	12 Jan 1802		
Ref	21	12	44	328				
Ref	21	12	45	330				
Ref	21	12	46	326				
Ref	21	12	47	320	Martin Brooks	20 Apr 1802		
Ref	21	12	48	322	Seth Harding	12 Jan 1802		
Ref	21	12	49	327	Martin Brooks	20 Apr 1802		
Ref	21	12	50	318				
Ref	21	12	51	318	D. Shelden, Jr.,			
					for Heirs of			
					S. Chester	9 Mar 1811		
Ref	21	12	52	322				
Ref	21	12	53	320				
Ref	21	12	54	319	Jonathan Eddy	12 Jan 1802		

*In Remarks column: "warrant."

2543   G/–/––

				Location	Acres	Located by	When
Ref	22	5	1	323	Edward Faulkner	12 Jan 1802
Ref	22	5	2	318	Martha Walker	12 Jan 1802
Ref	22	5	3	320	Martha Walker	12 Jan 1802
Ref	22	5	4	306	John Starr	12 Jan 1802
Ref	22	5	5	304	John Starr	12 Jan 1802
Ref	22	5	6	293	Lt. Col. Brad-	
					ford	12 Jan 1802
Ref	22	5	7	303	John D. Rush	12 Jan 1802
Ref	22	5	8	320	John D. Rush	12 Jan 1802
Ref	22	5	9	328	John Holstead	12 Jan 1802
Ref	22	5	10	328	Martha Walker	12 Jan 1802
Ref	22	5	11	308	James Price	12 Jan 1802
Ref	22	5	12	314	Seth Harding	12 Jan 1802
Ref	22	5	13	324	Seth Noble	12 Jan 1802
Ref	22	5	14	320	Thomas Faulkner	12 Jan 1802
Ref	22	5	15	316	Lt. Col. Liv-	
					ingston	12 Jan 1802
Ref	22	5	16	317	Lt. Col. Brad-	
					ford	12 Jan 1802
Ref	22	5	17	316	P. F. Cazeau	12 Jan 1802
Ref	22	5	18	312	Lt. William	
					Maxwell	12 Jan 1802
Ref	22	5	19	313	P. F. Cazeau	12 Jan 1802
Ref	22	5	20	314	P. F. Cazeau	12 Jan 1802
Ref	22	5	21	316	Noah Miller	12 Jan 1802
Ref	22	5	22	311	John Edgar	12 Jan 1802
Ref	22	5	23	318	Joseph Lievetre	12 Jan 1802
Ref	22	5	24	315	Jonas C. Minot	12 Jan 1802
Ref	22	5	25	326	John Allen	12 Jan 1802
Ref	22	5	26	327	Benjamin	
					Thompson	12 Jan 1802
Ref	22	5	27	329	John McGown	12 Jan 1802
Ref	22	5	28	321	Jonathan Eddy	12 Jan 1802
Ref	22	5	29	307	Joseph Bindon	12 Jan 1802
Ref	22	5	30	326	John Edgar	12 Jan 1802
Ref	22	5	31	325	Seth Harding	12 Jan 1802
Ref	22	5	32	321	Seth Noble	12 Jan 1802
Ref	22	5	33	318	P. F. Cazeau	12 Jan 1802
Ref	22	5	34	319	Col. James	
					Livingston	12 Jan 1802
Ref	22	5	35	319	Seth Harding	12 Jan 1802
Ref	22	5	36	320	James Price	12 Jan 1802
Ref	22	5	37	321	John McGown	12 Jan 1802
Ref	22	5	38	321	Jonas C. Minot	12 Jan 1802
Ref	22	5	39	317	Edward Faulkner	12 Jan 1802
Ref	22	5	40	320	Thomas Faulkner	12 Jan 1802
Ref	22	5	41	322	Jonathan Eddy	12 Jan 1802
Ref	22	5	42	315	Thomas Faulkner	12 Jan 1802
Ref	22	5	43	320	Martha Walker*	12 Jan 1802

*Spelled "Walkner."

(End of source G)

2544   2 Sep 1789   H/-/119
An act to establish the treasury department [First Congress, first session, chapter 12].

2545   2 Apr 1790   H/-/119
An act to accept a cession of the claims of the state of North Carolina, to a certain district of Western territory [First Congress, second session, chapter 6].

2546   4 Aug 1790   H/-/119
An act making provision for the debt of the United States [First Congress, second session, chapter 34].

2547   10 Aug 1790   H/-/119
An act to enable the officers and soldiers of the Virginia line, on continental establishment, to obtain titles to certain lands, lying north-west of the river Ohio, between the Little Miami and Sciota [First Congress, second session, chapter 40].

2548   3 Mar 1791   H/-/119
An act for granting lands to the inhabitants and settlers at Vincennes and the Illinois country, in the territory northwest of the Ohio, and for confirming them in their possessions [First Congress, third session, chapter 27].

2549   3 Jan 1792   H/-/119
An act for carrying into effect a contract between the United States and the state of Pennsylvania [Second Congress, first session, chapter 4].

2550   27 Mar 1792   H/-/120
An act for the relief of certain widows, orphans, invalids and other persons [Second Congress, first session, chapter 13].

2551   12 Apr 1792   H/-/120
An act for ascertaining the bounds of a tract of land, purchased by John Cleves Symmes [Second Congress, first session, chapter 19].

2552   21 Apr 1792   H/-/120
An act authorising the grant and conveyance of certain lands to the Ohio Company of Associates [Second Congress, first session, chapter 25].

2553   5 May 1792   H/-/120
An act authorising the grant and conveyance of certain lands to John Cleves Symmes and his associates [Second Congress, first session, chapter 30].

2554   21 Feb 1793   H/-/120
An act to repeal part of a resolution of Congress, of the twenty-ninth of August, one thousand seven hundred and eighty-eight, respecting the inhabitants of Post Saint Vincents

2555   18 Apr 1794   H/-/120
An act to authorise Ephraim Kimberly to locate the land warrant, issued to him for services in the late American army [Third Congress, chapter 20].

2556   9 Jun 1794   H/-/120
An act to amend the act, entitled "An act to enable the officers and soldiers of the Virginia line, on continental establishment, to obtain titles to certain lands, lying north-west of the river Ohio, between the Little Miami and Sciota" [Third Congress, chapter 62].

2557   3 Mar 1795   H/-/120
An act making further provision for the support of public credit, and for the redemption of the public debt [Third Congress, chapter 110].

2558   3 Mar 1795   H/-/120
An act to authorise a grant of lands to the French inhabitants of Galliopolis, and for other purposes therein mentioned [Third Congress, chapter 114].

2559   17 May 1796   H/-/120
An act to authorise Ebenezer Zane to locate certain lands, in the territory of the United States, north-west of the river Ohio [Fourth Congress, chapter 28].

2560   18 May 1796   H/-/120
An act providing for the sale of the lands of the United States, in the territory north-west of the river Ohio, and above the mouth of Kentucky river [Fourth Congress, chapter 29].

2561   19 May 1796   H/-/120
An act to regulate trade and intercourse with the Indian tribes, and to preserve peace on the frontiers [Fourth Congress, chapter 30].

2562   1 Jun 1796   H/-/121
An act regulating the grants of land appropriated for military services, and for the society of the United Brethren, for propagating the gospel among the heathen [Fourth Congress, chapter 46].

2563   3 Mar 1797   H/-/121
An act to authorise the receipt of evidences of the public debt, in payment for the lands of the United States [Fourth Congress, chapter 68].

2564   7 Apr 1798   H/-/121
An act for the relief of the refugees from the British provinces of Canada and Nova Scotia [Fifth Congress, chapter 43].

2565   7 Apr 1798   H/-/121
An act for an amicable settlement of limits with the state of Georgia, and authorising the

establishment of a government in the Mississippi territory [Fifth Congress, chapter 45].

2566   25 Jun 1798   H/-/121
An act to authorise a grant of lands to Stephen Monot and others, inhabitants of Galliopolis, therein named [Fifth Congress, chapter 76].

2567   16 Jul 1798   H/-/121
An act authorising the grant and conveyance of a certain lot of ground to Elie Williams [Fifth Congress, chapter 104].

2568   2 Mar 1799   H/-/121
An act to amend the act, entitled, "An act regulating the grants of land appropriated for military services, and for the society of the United Brethren, for propagating the gospel among the heathen" [Fifth Congress, chapter 135].

2569   2 Mar 1799   H/-/121
An act to authorise the sale of certain lands, between the Great and Little Miami rivers, in the territory of the United States, north-west of the Ohio; and for giving a pre-emption to certain purchasers and settlers [Fifth Congress, chapter 140].

2570   11 Feb 1800   H/-/121
An act giving further time to the holders of military warrants to register and locate the same [Sixth Congress, chapter 8].

2571   1 Mar 1800   H/-/121
An act in addition to an act, entitled, "An act regulating the grants of land appropriated for military services, and for the society of the United Brethren for propagating the gospel among the heathen" [Sixth Congress, chapter 13].

2572   28 Apr 1800   H/-/121
An act to authorise the President of the United States to accept, for the United States, a cession of jurisdiction of the territory west of Pennsylvania, commonly called the Western Reserve of Connecticut [Sixth Congress, chapter 38].

2573   7 May 1800   H/-/121
An act to divide the territory of the United States, northwest of the Ohio, into two separate governments [Sixth Congress, chapter 41].

2574   10 May 1800   H/-/122
An act supplemental to the act, entitled "An act for an amicable settlement of limits, with the state of Georgia; and authorising the establishment of a government in the Mississippi Territory" [Sixth Congress, chapter 50].

2575   10 May 1800   H/-/122
An act for the relief of Ithamar Canfield [Sixth Congress, chapter 52].

2576   10 May 1800   H/-/122
An act to amend the act, entitled, "An act providing for the sale of the lands of the United States, in the territory north-west of the Ohio, and above the mouth of Kentucky river" [Sixth Congress, chapter 55].

2577   13 May 1800   H/-/122
An act to authorise the issuing [of] certain patents [Sixth Congress, chapter 59].

2578   18 Feb 1801   H/-/122
An act regulating the grants of land appropriated for the refugees from the British provinces of Canada and Nova Scotia [Sixth Congress, chapter 76].

2579   27 Feb 1801   H/-/122
An act for the relief of Arnold Henry Dohrman, or his legal representatives [Sixth Congress, chapter 85].

2580   3 Mar 1801   H/-/122
An act giving a right of pre-emption to certain persons, who have contracted with John Cleves Symmes, or his associates, for lands lying between the Miami rivers, in the territory of the United States, north-west of the Ohio [Sixth Congress, chapter 94].

2581   30 Mar 1802   H/-/122
An act to regulate trade and intercourse with the Indian tribes, and to preserve peace on the frontiers [Seventh Congress, chapter 13].

2582   3 Apr 1802   H/-/122
An act for the relief of Isaac Zane [Seventh Congress, chapter 18].

2583   26 Apr 1802   H/-/122
An act in addition to an act, entitled, "An act in addition to an act, regulating the grants of land, appropriated for military services, and for the society of the United Brethren, for propagating the gospel among the heathen" [Seventh Congress, chapter 30].

2584   30 Apr 1802   H/-/122
An act to enable the people of the eastern division of the territory north-west of the river Ohio, to form a constitution and state government, and for the admission of such state into the Union, on an equal footing with the original states, and for other purposes [Seventh Congress, chapter 40].

2585   1 May 1802   H/-/122
An act to empower John James Dufour, and his associates, to purchase certain lands [Seventh Congress, chapter 42].

2586   1 May 1802   H/-/122
An act to extend and continue in force the provi-
sions of an act, entitled, "An act giving a right
of pre-emption to certain persons, who have contracted with John Cleves Symmes, or his associates, for lands lying between the Miami rivers,
in the territory north-west of the Ohio; and for
other purposes" [Seventh Congress, chapter 44].

2587   3 Mar 1803   H/-/123
An act in addition to, and in modification of, the
propositions contained in the act, entitled, "An
act to enable the people of the eastern division
of the territory north-west of the river Ohio,
to form a constitution and state government, and
for the admission of such state into the Union,
on an equal footing with the original states;
and for other purposes" [Seventh Congress, chapter 74].

2588   3 Mar 1803   H/-/123
An act regulating the grants of land, and provid-
ing for the disposal of the lands of the United
States, south of the state of Tennessee [Seventh
Congress, chapter 80].

2589   3 Mar 1803   H/-/123
An act concerning the salt springs, on the waters
of the Wabash river [Seventh Congress, chapter
81].

2590   3 Mar 1803   H/-/123
An act to revive and continue in force an act in
addition to an act, entitled, "An act in addition to an act, regulating the grants of land,
appropriated for military services, and for the
society of the United Brethren, for propagating
the gospel among the heathen;" and for other
purposes [Seventh Congress, chapter 83].

2591   3 Mar 1803   H/-/123
An act in addition to the act, entitled, "An act
regulating the grants of land, appropriated for
the refugees from the British provinces of Canada
and Nova Scotia" [Seventh Congress, chapter 88].

2592   16 Mar 1804   H/-/123
An act to revive and continue in force an act, entitled, "An act for the relief of the refugees
from the British provinces of Canada and Nova
Scotia" [Eighth Congress, chapter 23].

2593   19 Mar 1804   H/-/123
An act granting further time for locating military
land-warrants; and for other purposes [Eighth
Congress, chapter 26].

2594   23 Mar 1804   H/-/123
An act to ascertain the boundary of the lands, reserved by the state of Virginia, north-west of
the river Ohio, for the satisfaction of her officers and soldiers on continental establishment,
and to limit the period for locating the said
lands [Eighth Congress, chapter 33].

2595   26 Mar 1804   H/-/123
An act making provision for the disposal of the
public lands in the Indiana territory; and for
other purposes [Eighth Congress, chapter 35].

2596   16 Mar 1804   H/-/123
An act erecting Louisiana into two territories,
and providing for the temporary government
thereof [Eighth Congress, chapter 38].

2597   27 Mar 1804   H/-/123
An act supplementary to the act, entitled, "An act
regulating the grants of land, and providing for
the disposal of the lands of the United States,
south of the state of Tennessee" [Eighth Congress, chapter 61].

2598   11 Feb 1805   H/-/124
An act concerning the mode of surveying the public
lands of the United States [Eighth Congress,
chapter 74].

2599   2 Mar 1805   H/-/124
An act further to amend an act, entitled, "An act
regulating the grants of land, and providing
for the disposal of the lands of the United
States, south of the state of Tennessee" [Eighth
Congress, chapter 84].

2600   2 Mar 1805   H/-/124
An act for ascertaining and adjusting the titles
and claims to land, within the territory of Orleans and the district of Louisiana [Eighth
Congress, chapter 86].

2601   2 Mar 1805   H/-/124
An act to authorise the secretary of war to issue
military land warrants; and for other purposes
[Eighth Congress, chapter 87].

2602   3 Mar 1805   H/-/124
An act supplementary to the act, entitled, "An
act making provision for the disposal of the
public lands, in the Indiana territory; and
for other purposes" [Eighth Congress, chapter
102].

2603   21 Feb 1806   H/-/124
An act to repeal in part, the fourth section of
an act, entitled "An act to authorise a grant
of lands to the French inhabitants of Galliopolis; and for other purposes therein mentioned" [Ninth Congress, chapter 7].

2604   28 Feb 1806   H/-/124
An act authorising the sale of a tract of land,
in the town of Cincinnati, and state of Ohio
[Ninth Congress, chapter 10].

2605   28 Feb 1806   H/-/124
An act extending the powers of the surveyor general
to the territory of Louisiana; and for other
purposes [Ninth Congress, chapter 11].

2606   15 Apr 1806   H/-/124
An act to authorise the secretary of war to issue
   land warrants; and for other purposes [Ninth
   Congress, chapter 26].

2607   15 Apr 1806   H/-/124
An act to suspend the sale of certain lands in the
   state of Ohio, and the Indiana territory [Ninth
   Congress, chapter 28].

2608   18 Apr 1806   H/-/124
An act to authorise the state of Tennessee to issue
   grants and perfect titles to certain lands therein
   described; and to settle the claims to the vacant
   and unappropriated lands within the same [Ninth
   Congress, chapter 31].

2609   21 Apr 1806   H/-/124
An act supplementary to an act, entitled "An act
   for ascertaining and adjusting the titles, and
   claims to land, within the territory of Orleans,
   and the district of Louisiana" [Ninth Congress,
   chapter 39].

2610   21 Apr 1806   H/-/124
An act respecting the claims to land in the Indiana
   territory and state of Ohio [Ninth Congress, chapter 40].

2611   21 Apr 1806   H/-/124
An act to provide for the adjustment of titles of
   land in the town of Detroit and territory of
   Michigan, and for other purposes [Ninth Congress,
   chapter 43].

2612   21 Apr 1806   H/-/125
An act in addition to an act, intitled "An act regulating the grants of land and providing for the
   disposal of the lands of the United States, south
   of the state of Tennessee" [Ninth Congress, chapter 46].

2613   18 Apr 1806   H/-/125
An act to repeal so much of any act or acts as
   authorise the receipt of evidences of the public
   debt, in payment for the lands of the United
   States; and for other purposes, relative to the
   public debt [Ninth Congress, chapter 50].

2614   2 Mar 1807   H/-/125
An act to extend the time for locating Virginia
   military warrants, for returning surveys thereon
   to the office of the secretary of the department
   of war and appropriating lands for the use of
   schools, in the Virginia military reservation,
   in lieu of those heretofore appropriated [Ninth
   Congress, chapter 66].

2615   3 Mar 1807   H/-/125
An act authorising patents to issue for lands located and surveyed by virtue of certain Virginia
   resolution warrants [Ninth Congress, chapter 76].

2616   3 Mar 1807   H/-/125
An act making compensation to Messrs. Lewis and
   Clarke, and their companions [Ninth Congress,
   chapter 77].

2617   3 Mar 1807   H/-/125
An act regulating the grants of land in the territory of Michigan [Ninth Congress, chapter 79].

2618   3 Mar 1807   H/-/125
An act making appropriations for carrying into
   effect a treaty between the United States and
   the Chickasaw tribe of Indians; and to establish a land office in the Mississippi territory
   [Ninth Congress, chapter 80].

2619   3 Mar 1807   H/-/125
An act respecting claims to land in the territories of Orleans and Louisiana [Ninth Congress,
   chapter 81].

2620   3 Mar 1807   H/-/125
An act to prevent settlements being made on lands
   ceded to the United States, until authorised
   by law [Ninth Congress, chapter 91].

2621   3 Mar 1807   H/-/125
An act confirming claims to land in the district
   of Vincennes; and for other purposes [Ninth
   Congress, chapter 92].

2622   3 Mar 1807   H/-/125
An act making provision for the disposal of the
   public lands, situated between the United States
   military tract and the Connecticut reserve, and
   for other purposes [Ninth Congress, chapter 94].

2623   19 Jan 1808   H/-/125
An act supplemental to an act, intitled "An act
   regulating the grants of land and providing for
   the disposal of the lands of the United States,
   south of the State of Tennessee" [Tenth Congress,
   chapter 10].

2624   29 Feb 1808   H/-/126
An act making farther provision for the disposal
   of the sections of land heretofore reserved for
   the future disposition of Congress [Tenth Congress, chapter 26].

2625   18 Mar 1808   H/-/126
An act granting William Wells the right of pre-
   emption [Tenth Congress, chapter 36].

2626   21 Mar 1808   H/-/126
An act extending the time for issuing and locating
   military land warrants [Tenth Congress, chapter
   37].

2627   31 Mar 1808   H/-/126
An act concerning the sale of·the lands of the

U[nited] States, and for other purposes [Tenth Congress, chapter 40].

2628   25 Apr 1808   H/-/126
An act supplemental to "An act regulating the grants of land in the territory of Michigan" [Tenth Congress, chapter 67].

2629   15 Feb 1809   H/-/126
An act to revive and continue for a further time the authority of the commissioners of Kaskaskia [Tenth Congress, chapter 83].

2630   28 Feb 1809   H/-/126
An act for the disposal of certain tracts of land in the Mississippi territory, claimed under Spanish grants, reported by the land commissioners as antedated, and to confirm the claims of Abraham Ellis and Daniel Harregal [Tenth Congress, chapter 89].

2631   28 Feb 1809   H/-/126
An act for the relief of certain Alibama and Wyandott Indians [Tenth Congress, chapter 90].

2632   2 Mar 1809   H/-/126
An act to extend the time for making payment for the public lands of the United States [Tenth Congress, chapter 93].

2633   15 Jun 1809   H/-/126
An act authorising the appointment of an agent for the land office at Kaskaskia, and allowing compensation to the commissioners and clerk [Eleventh Congress, chapter 3].

2634   15 Jun 1809   H/-/126
An act supplementary to an act, entitled "An act making appropriations for carrying into effect a treaty between the United States and the Chickasaw tribe of Indians; and to establish a land office in the Mississippi territory" [Eleventh Congress, chapter 4].

2635   19 Dec 1809   H/-/126
An act extending the time for issuing and locating military land warrants [Eleventh Congress, chapter 20].

2636   28 Dec 1809   H/-/126
An act for the relief of William and Elias Rector [Eleventh Congress, chapter 21].

2637   24 Feb 1810   H/-/126
An act to prescribe the mode in which application shall be made for the purchase of land at the several land offices; and for the relief of Joab Garret [Eleventh Congress, chapter 28].

2638   24 Feb 1810   H/-/126
An act further to prov-de for the refugees from the British provinces of Canada and Nova Scotia, and for other purposes [Eleventh Congress, chapter 29].

2639   16 Mar 1810   H/-/127
An act to extend the time for locating Virginia military land warrants, and for returning the surveys thereon to the secretary of the department of war [Eleventh Congress, chapter 34].

2640   30 Apr 1810   H/-/127
An act providing for the sale of certain lands in the Indiana territory, and for other purposes [Eleventh Congress, chapter 52].

2641   30 Apr 1810   H/-/127
An act to extend the time for making payment for the public lands of the United States in certain cases [Eleventh Congress, chapter 53].

2642   1 May 1810   H/-/127
An act confirming the decisions of the commissioners in favour of the claimants of land in the district of Kaskaskia [Eleventh Congress, chapter 57].

2643   1 May 1810   H/-/127
An act allowing compensation to Robert Robinson [Eleventh Congress, chapter 59].

(End of source H)

NAME INDEX

Altvater, *see* Oldfather

Alvord, Mary, 2530, 2531

Alward, Samuel, Junior, 1112

Anderson, Archibald, 750

Anderson, Isaac, 541

Anderson, Isaac, 2528

Anderson, James, 1153

Anderson, John, 243, 775

Anderson, Joseph (Reverend), 2024

Anderson, Richard Clough (Surveyor, Virginia
      Military District of Ohio), 17,
      923, 943, 962, 1731

Anderson, William, 358, 1179

Andrew, James, 1124

Andrews, Hugh, 290, 705, 978

Andrews, John (Clerk, Cin LO), 1837

Andrus, Abigail, 2533

Andrus, Abraham, 2530

Andrus, Hannah, 2532

Andrus, Jedediah, 2533

Andrus, Phineas, 2533

Andrus, Samuel, 2532

Andrus, Sarah, 2530

Angel, James, 2534

Angwene, Anthony, 2532

Annesley, Robert, 703, 704

Annesley, --, 689

Annesley & Tunis, 603

Anniball, Anthony, 2530

Annible, David, 2530

Ansbaugh, Adam, 225, 540

Anspach, John, 972

Anthony, James, 890

Antill (Antell), Edward, 2542

Antrim, Caleb, 542

Antrim, Daniel, 367

Antrim, Joshua, 993, 1074

Applegate, Joseph, 192

Appleton, Abel, 657

Archer, James, 1027, 1030

Archer, John, 172, 452

Armistead, -- (Lieutenant, U.S. Army), 1375

Armour, Abigail, 2528

Armstrong, Archibald, 593

Armstrong, Edward, 91, 133, 154

Armstrong, James, 535, 756

Armstrong & Carothers, 273

Armstrong, -- (Colonel), 82, 92

Armsworthy, Ben, 893

Arnett, Samuel, 685

Arnett, William, 657

Arnold, Bewley, 2529

Arnold, Frederick, 448

Arnold, George, 116, 374, 483, 600

Arnold, Henry, 378

Arnold, Jacob, 190, 374

Arnold, Jacob, 2529

Arrowsmith, Samuel, 417, 460, 540

Artherton, Peter, 500

Ash, George, 2295

Ashbaugh, Henry, 775

Ashbaugh, Thomas, 881

Ashbough, Thomas, 1109, 1165

Ashby, Bayless, 541

Ashley, Moses, 189

Ask, Samuel, 2528

Assig, Simon, 1039

Assig, *see also* Essig

Aten, Henry, 129, 698

Atkinson, George, 114

Atterholt, George, 219

Atterholt, Henry, 853

Attwater, Reuben (Commissioner, Det), 1968

Barricklaw, Henry, 807

Barrington, John, 645

Barron, Robert, 600

Barth, Stephen, 180

Bartholomew, Moses, 774

Barton, Benjamin, 807

Barton, David, 780

Barton, see also Borton

Bartow, Silas, 2529

Bartram, Ebenezer, 2530

Bartram, Job, 2530, 2531

Bashear, John, 344

Bashore, John, 381, 806

Bassett, Sarah, 2532

Bastrop, -- (Baron), 1533

Bates, Clark, 1124

Bates, Frederick (Rec Det; Recorder of Land Titles,
        St. Louis), 1435, 1438, 1468, 1529,
        1692, 1710, 1718, 1774, 1791, 1851,
        1936, 1952, 1964, 2059, 2483, 2487

Bates, Isaac, 577, 2324

Bates, William, 607

Batterson, George, 2530

Batterson, William, 2530

Baucher, Anthony, 173

Bauder, Nicholas, 203

Bauer, see Bower

Baum, Martin, 229, 1025

Baum & Perry, 1013

Baum, Hunt, & Cooper, 1161

Bauman, Christopher, 293

Bayard, J. A., 164

Baye, William, 513

Baylor, Jacob, 383, 629, 1613

Baylor, Walker, 783, 787

Baylor, Walter, 987

Baylor, --, 951

Bayly, Mary Ann, 914

Beal, Robert, 807

Beall, Reasin, 334, 759, 1839

Beam, Christian, 1096

Bean, Christian, 1015

Bean, Paul, 249

Bean, William, 904

Beans, William, 850

Bear, Isaac, 1002

Bearey, Jacob, 781

Bearn, Christian, 1096

Beatley, Isaac, 26

Beatty, David, 159

Beatty, Jeremiah, 577

Beatty, Zaccheus A., 3, 19, 1322, 1323, 1990,
        1991, 2077, 2078, 2357

Beaty, David, 577

Beaver, John, 2527

Bebb, Edward, 271

Bebee, Joseph, 2532

Beck, Samuel, 190

Beckler, John, 775

Bedle, Joseph, 190, 577

Beebe, Elizabeth, 2534

Beebe, Hannah, 2534

Beebe, Joanna, 2534

Beebe, Lydia, 2534

Beebe, Walter, 2534

Beech, Elias, 2533

Beech, Jacob, 629

Beech, John, 629

Beecher, Isaac, 2533

Beecher, John, 2533

Beecher, John, Junior, 2533

Beecher, Philemon, 829

Beecher, Titus, 2533

Beeler, Samuel, 819

Beemer, George, 63, 70, 73, .94, 187, 300

Bentley, Harin, 613

Bentz, Jacob, 921, 972

Bernbow, Edward, 996

Berry, Achary, 638, 907, 931

Berry, Edward, 701

Berry, Jacob, 103, 193

Berry, John, 320

Berry, *see also* Bearey

Berryhill, Samuel, 68

Bessey, Silas, 2529

Betts, Benjamin, 2529

Betts, Benjamin, Junior, 2529

Betts, James, 2529

Betts, John, 2529

Betts, Peter, 2529

Betts, Silas, 2528

Betts, Thaddeus, 2529

Betts, Thomas, 2529

Betts, Thomas, Junior, 2529

Betz, Abraham, 807

Bevan, Stacy, 946

Bever, John, 192, 1122, 2138, 2160, 2167, 2176, 2194

Beymer, George, 63, 187, 419

Beymer, *see also* Beemer

Bibler, Susannah, 615

Bierce, William, 181

Biere, *see* Beery

Bigger, Abigail, 734

Bigger, James, 734

Bigger, John, 159, 912

Bigger, Joseph, 734

Biggs, Benjamin, 1232, 2527

Biggs, Zaccheus (Rec Stu), 3, 13, 43, 48, 52, 62, 79, 104, 124, 132, 135, 161, 262, 266, 278, 279, 286, 294, 311, 317, 326, 349, 351, 371, 395, 401, 406, 414, 465, 475, 561, 589, 624, 639, 655, 703, 707, 722, 727, 1227, 1229, 1232, 1238, 1239, 1240, 1242, 1250, 1252, 1255, 1258, 1259, 1271, 1279, 1292, 1297, 1298, 1300, 1301, 1303, 1304, 1307, 1317, 1320, 1329, 1332, 1337, 1342, 1350, 1354, 1355, 1360, 1376, 1381, 1401, 1402, 1403, 1410, 1413, 1432, 1463, 1495, 1497, 1498, 1515, 1524, 1571, 1584, 1605, 1615, 1636, 1639, 1665, 1747, 1781, 1811, 1816, 1818, 1840, 1851, 1862, 1966, 2116, 2118, 2129, 2130, 2132, 2135, 2137, 2140, 2147, 2159, 2167, 2170, 2176, 2191, 2194, 2208, 2214, 2357

Biggs, Zaccheus (as grantee), 302

Bigsby, John, 2529

Bill, Thomas, 2533

Billings, Stephen, 2536

Binckley, Christian, 225, 249, 272

Binckley, Jacob, 623, 1061

Bindon, Joseph, 2539, 2543

Bingly, Hannah, 2533

Birchard, Jeremiah, 2535

Birchard, Jesse, 2529

Birchard, John, 2529

Birchard, Joseph, 2532

Bird, Samuel, 2533

Bishop, Daniel, 2533

Bishop, Henry, 355

Bishop, Isaac, 2533

Bishop, Israel, 2533

Bishop, John, 1123

Bishop, Joseph, 2533

Bishop, Phanuel, 235, 244

Bishop, Samuel, 2533

Black, Andrew, 614

Black, Jacob, Senior, 613

Black, James, 1122

Black, Samuel, 786

Black, William, 1067

Blackburn, Moses, 358

Blackford, Ephraim, 996

Blackford, John, 544

Blackledge, Abraham, 613

Boyer, Henry, 806

Boyer, Lewis, 179

Boyer, Michael, 469, 491

Boyse, Dennis, 918, 1190

Boyse, James, 1124

Bradfield, John, 358, 779

Bradford, B. J., 1793

Bradford, John, 367, 779, 1124

Bradford, -- (Lieutenant Colonel), 7, 2541, 2543

Bradford, *see also* Bralsford

Bradley, Abraham, 715

Bradley, Abraham, 2533

Bradley, Abraham, Junior, 2533

Bradley, Azariah, 2533

Bradley, Francis 3d, 2531

Bradley, Gurdon, 2533

Bradley, Increase, 2530

Bradley, James, 2533

Bradley, John, Junior, 2533

Bradley, Joseph, 2533

Bradley, Philip B., 2535

Bradley, Phineas, Junior, 2533

Bradley, Stephen, 2533

Brahan, John (Rec Nas), 1958, 1981, 1982, 1988, 2025, 2027, 2042, 2044, 2045, 2093

Bralsford, John, 819

Brandenburgh, Jacob, 807

Brandt, Adam, 272

Branson, Lyonel, 7, 8, 22

Branson & Claypoole, 602

Braucher, *see* Broucher

Brauer, *see* Brougher

Breckenridge, Samuel, 448

Brentnal, Willard, 2533

Brentnal, William, 2533

Brentnall, Buckminster, 2533

Brewster, James, 1111

Brewster, Samuel, 367

Bridger, William, 2034, 2517

Bridges, William, 2034, 2517

Bridglin, Jonathan, 2533

Briggs, Isaac (Surveyor of Public Lands South of Tennessee), 1343, 1356, 1640, 1644, 2217, 2225, 2227, 2229, 2231, 2248, 2249, 2255, 2258, 2260, 2261, 2265, 2267, 2268, 2272, 2289, 2290, 2294, 2304, 2305, 2306, 2308, 2309, 2311, 2336, 2342, 2360

Briggs, --, 1544, 1680

Bright, George, 799

Bright, -- (Major), 397, 1123, 1593

Bringman, --, 1735, 1741

Bringman & Taylor, 1971

Brininger, Andrew, 930

Brink, Isaac, 432

Brinker, Andrew, 219, 613

Brinton, John H., 689, 703, 704, 905, 906, 961

Brinton & Candy, 905

Broadbrooks, Joseph, 2532

Broadbury, David, 1124

Brook, Aaron, 698

Brooke, Francis Taliaferro, 1170

Brooke, John, 1170

Brooks, Aaron, 835, 882, 950

Brooks, John, 885

Brooks, Lemuel, 2529

Brooks, Martin, 2542

Brooks, Thomas, 283

Brooks, William, 2534

Broom(e), James M., 245, 252, 291

Brosius, Leonard, 1123

Brotsman, John, 883

Broucher, Conrad, 255

Brougher, Conrad, 499

Broughton, Atkins, 2533

Brower, John, 1152

Brown, Aaron,   241

Brown, Adam,   500

Brown, Bazaleel,   2528

Brown, Benjamin,   234, 327

Brown, Benjamin,   2533

Brown, Daniel,   2533

Brown, Eleazar,   2533

Brown, Ephraim,   614

Brown, Ethan Allen,   1776, 1862, 1863, 1865, 1990,
        1991, 2077, 2078, 2502, 2512

Brown, Francis,   2533

Brown, Hannah,   2529

Brown, Henry,   586

Brown, Hugh,   892

Brown, H. J.,   1124

Brown, James (District Attorney at New Orleans &
        U.S. Agent for Land Claims),   1533,
        1534, 1537, 1559, 1566, 1625, 1719,
        1721, 1766, 1779

Brown, James,   523, 614

Brown, James,   2528

Brown, James, Junior,   614, 1077

Brown, Jedediah,   2529

Brown, Jeremiah,   2534

Brown, Jesse,   2529

Brown, John,   386, 577, 614, 1807, 1835, 1911,
        2536

Brown, John (U.S. Senator),   2166

Brown, Joseph,   614

Brown, Mary,   2529

Brown, Mathew,   555

Brown, Nehemiah,   2528

Brown, Peter,   2528

Brown, Phebe,   2533

Brown, Roger,   389

Brown, Roger,   2528

Brown, Samuel,   236, 250, 819

Brown, Samuel,   2532, 2534

Brown, Sarah,   2533

Brown, Stephen,   2533

Brown, William, Senior,   448

Brown, William,   219

Brown, William (Deputy Surveyor),   2071, 2377

Brown, Zephaniah,   430

Brown & Sutherland,   511

Brown, Gano, & Schultz,   1909

Browning, William,   1232

Brownlee, James,   387, 653, 1093

Brownley, -- (Doctor),   1030

Brownson, John,   544, 658, 883, 1124

Brownson, --,   2238

Bruen, Luther,   819

Brumall, Laurau,   2528

Brummage, John,   616

Brundage, Charles,   2528

Brundage, James,   2528

Brundage, William,   2528

Brundige, Nathaniel,   629

Brunner, Elias,   875, 1190

Brunner, Jacob,   781

Brush, Deborah,   2528

Brush, Elijah,   579, 999

Brush, James,   2528

Brush, Samuel,   2528

Bryan, Conrad,   775

Bryan, Gilbert,   2531

Bryan, Stephen,   807

Bryan, William,   295

Bryant, Sarah,   2531

Bryson, Hugh,   319

Bryson, Samuel,   1025

Buchanan, George,   1056, 1094, 1119

Buchanan, James,   410

Buchanan, John E.,   859

Buchannon, John,   883

Buck, Daniel, 550, 606

Buck, John, 1003

Buck, Thomas, 523, 1004

Buckhannon, Andrew, 435

Buckhannon, James, 552

Buckhannon, John, 883

Buckingham, Ebenezer, 2147, 2152, 2158, 2159, 2160, 2176

Buckles, John, 267

Buckley, Michael, 325

Buckley, Peter, 2533

Bucknall, John, 386

Budd, Joseph, 307

Budd, Joshua, 79, 643

Buddington, Edward, 2530

Buddington, Nehemiah, 2530

Buddington, Walter, 2530

Buddington, William, 2530

Buell, Joseph, 1746, 1747, 1757, 1862, 1863, 1990, 1991, 2077, 2078

Buffington, Thomas, 381, 806

Bufkin, Thomas, 993

Bugh, Peter, 600

Bulkley, Abigail, 2530

Bulkley, Andrew, 2530

Bulkley, Ann, 2534

Bulkley, Ebenezer, 2530

Bulkley, James, 2530

Bulkley, Jonah, 2531

Bulkley, Jonathan, 2530

Bulkley, Josiah, 2531

Bulkley, Moses, 2531

Bulkley, Nathan, 2530, 2531

Bulkley, Olive, 2530

Bulkley, Peter, 2530

Bull, Epaphias W., 1812

Bullock, Josias, 2041

Bumgarner, Jacob, 665

Bundy, William, 818, 882

Burch, Charles, 883

Burditt, Nathan, 807

Burnell, Israel, 2533

Burnet, Jacob, 1, 480

Burnett, John, 1267, 2391

Burnett, see also Barnet

Burns, George, 248

Burns, Robert, 883

Burnside, James, 2526

Burr, Aaron, 1984

Burr, Abigail, 2530

Burr, Abigail, Junior, 2530

Burr, Amelia, 2530

Burr, Charles, 2530

Burr, David, 2530

Burr, Ephraim, 2531

Burr, Ephraim, Junior, 2531

Burr, George, 2531

Burr, Gershom, 2530

Burr, Isaac, 2530

Burr, Luce, 2530

Burr, Nathan, 2530

Burr, Nathaniel, 2530

Burr, Peter, 2530

Burr, Pinckney, 2531

Burr, Priscilla, 2530

Burr, Ruth, 2530

Burr, Samuel, 2530

Burr, Samuel, 2531

Burr, Samuel, Junior, 2530

Burr, Samuel 3d, 2530

Burr, Thaddeus, 2530

Burr, Wakeman, 2530

Burrall, Jonathan (Cashier, Office of Discount & Deposit, New York), 2030

Cox, Benjamin, 1063, 1115

Cox, Christopher, 248

Cox, Emmer, 435

Cox, Jeremiah, 889

Cox, John, 594

Cox, Joseph, 249, 818

Cox, Nicholas, 355

Cox, Richard, 895

Cox, Samuel, 435

Cox, Solomon, 2, 14

Cox, Walter, 379

Cox, see Cocks

Coy, Jacob, 312, 353, 367, 372, 544, 779, 872, 930, 996, 1008, 1150, 1200

Crabs, Philip, 358

Crague, John, 248

Craig, Isaac, 2527

Craig, John, 345

Craig, William, 1007, 1191

Craig, William, Senior, 249

Craig & Bledsoe, 2101

Craighead, William, 726

Crain, James, 580

Crane, Jonas, 310

Crane, Jonathan, 159

Crane, Moses, 372

Crane, Ruth, 883

Crane, William, 1318, 2391, 2409

Crary, James, 2532

Crawford, Daniel, 334

Crawford, James, 2283, 2541

Crawford, John, 840

Crawford, John H., 978

Crawford, Robert, 978

Crawford, William, 129, 840, 1106

Crawford, -- (Doctor), 1135

Creane, William, 1267, 2164

Creegan, James, 1173

Creek, John, 841

Creen, Lydia, 2534

Creighton, William, 1129, 1232, 1477, 1615, 1616, 1649, 1746, 1747, 1767, 1828, 1839, 1862, 1863, 1883, 1886, 1990, 1991, 2015

Crissman, David, 889

Crissman, Jacob, 389

Crissman, see also Christman

Critchet, John, 2534

Crocker, John, 2534

Crockett, Joseph, 2054

Croes, Jacob, 2527

Croghan, see Croxen

Crooks, Henry, 680

Crossman, John, 2531

Crouch & Radcliff, 402

Croughton, Charles, 1170

Crouse, John, 225, 1123

Crowfeet, Matthew, 2532

Crowfeet, Rebecca, 2532

Crowfeet, Seth, 2532

Crowle, George, 1006

Crowley, James, 2529

Croxen, Abraham, 2525

Croy, John, 1008

Crumbacher, Jacob, 376

Crumbacher, John, 15, 726

Cruse, Henry, 373

Cryder, Michael, 405, 408

Cuane, William, 1267

Culbertson, Robert, 21, 225, 259

Culver, James, 2534

Culver, Joanna, 2534

Culver, Stephen, 2534

Cummins, Robert, 840

Cundiff, Jonathan, 1106

Dawson, Charles, 845

Dawson, John, 431

Dawson, *see also* Dowson

Dayton, Jonathan, 59, 60, 1170, 2174

Dayton, --, 2113, 2121

Dean, Walter, 189

Dearborn, George, 1328, 1329, 2413

Dearborn, H. (Secretary of War), 514

Deardorff, Bohn, & Slingluff, 697, 979

Dearman, King, 711

Dearth, Edward, 367, 1642, 2470

Debott, John, 941

Decker, Elisha, 806

Decker, Luke, 851

Decker, Samuel, 1171

Deenwell, Samuel, 2533

Deffenbaugh, Abram, 775

Deffenbaugh, Adam, 243

Deforest, Elihu, 2535

Deforest, Rebecca, 2529

De la Court, Francis, 2143, 2147, 2152

Delader, Jacob, 716

Delanter, David, 700

Delanter, Jacob, 700

Delany, Sharp, 2453

Delaplaine, Joshua, 191

De Lashmutt, *see* Lashmutt

Deleny, Philip, 343

Delesdernier, Lewis F., 2538, 2540, 2542

Delisle, --, 2070

Delong, Aaron, 2524

Delong, John, 2524

Delong, Nicholas, 289

Delong, Samuel, 2525

Delong, Solomon, 2525

Demott, Abraham, 507

Denison, Rhoda, 2533

Denman, Samuel, 558

Denniston, James, 779

Denny, David, 499

Denny, James, 173, 1405, 2238

Denny, Samuel, 492, 499

Denny, William, 492

Denny, --, 1389

Denton, Humphrey, 2528

Derush, John, 7, 10, 21, 24, 216, 1278, 1306, 1319

Derwater, John, 357, 388

Desbrow, Abigail, 2531

Desbrow, Caleb, 2530, 2531

Desbrow, Jabez, 2531

Desbrow, Jason, 2531

Desbrow, John, 2531

Desbrow, Wait, 2532

Deshon, Henry, 2534

Deshon, John, 2534

Deshon, Joseph, 2534

Deshon, Richard, 2534

Deshon & Company, 2534

Desplantier, *see* Duplantier

Dever, John, 502

Deverbaugh, George, 513

Dewitt, Zachariah P., 711

Dexter, Samuel, 2381, 2382

D'Herbercourt, *see* De la Court

D'Hibicourt, *see* De la Court

Dibble, Elisha, 2532

Dibble, Ezra, Junior, 2532

Dice, John, 558

Dick, Samuel, 44, 400, 534, 694, 866

Dickenson, Deborah, 2529

Dickenson, Nathaniel, 2534

Dickerman, Isaac, 2533

Dickerson, Thomas, 343

Dickey, David, 2542

Dickey, Samuel, 531, 1041

Dickinson, Hannah, 2529

Dickinson, Moses, 2529

Dickinson, William R., 958

Dickson, Andrew, 861

Dickson, William, 84, 85

Dickson, William (Reg Nas), 1958, 1981, 1982, 1988, 1999, 2054, 2076, 2514

Dieffenbach, *see* Deffenbaugh

Dildine, Richard, 321

Dill, John, 435

Dille, Caleb, 792

Dillshaver, George, 1023

Dilworth, Benjamin, 207

Dimon, Ann, 2530

Dimon, William, 2530

Dindore, John, 629

Dinsmoor, -- (Agent to Choctaw Indians), 2033

Dinsmore, John, 2164

Dittoe, Anthony, 799

Dittoe, Jacob, 374, 629, 635, 791, 799, 806, 893

Dixon, Emanuel, 136

Dixon, Henry, 871

Dixon, Henry, Junior, 334

Dixon, Joseph, 435, 851

Dixon, Samuel, 635

Dixson, Emanuel, 844

Dixson, Henry, Junior, 861

Dixson, Joshua, 321

Doak, William, 2533

Doane, Henry, 1569

Dobrow, Thomas, 711

Dodds, Joseph, 217, 1556, 2454

Dodge, John, 2541

Dodge, Mary, 2536

Dohrman, Andrew H., 2526

Dohrman, Arnold Henry, 1648, 2191, 2579

Dollarhide, William, 1096

Donaldson, James Lowry (Recorder of Land Titles, Louisiana Territory), 1505, 1508, 1509, 1510, 1595, 1597, 1598, 1627, 1630, 1654, 1669, 1695, 1760, 1774, 2444, 2466, 2472, 2483

Donelson, Alexander (Deputy Surveyor), 2363

Doolittle, Amos, 2533

Doolittle, Ephraim, 1129, 1184

Doolittle, Ichabod, 2535

Doolittle, Isaac, 2533

Doran, Patrick, 452

Dorner, Frederick, 798

Dorner, George, 798

Dorner, Jacob, 798

Dorothy, James, 2525

Dorsett, --, 2534

Dorsey, Joseph, 242, 256, 2527

Doty, Daniel, 367, 1110

Doudna, John, 334, 461

Doudna, Knowis, 461

Dougherty, John (Captain), 2524

Douglass, Ebenezer, 2534

Douglass, George, 38, 75, 2526

Douglass, James, 807

Douglass, John, 747

Douglass, Jonathan, 2534

Douglass, Nathan, 2534

Douglass, Richard, 2534

Douglass, Robert, 2534

Douglass, Spere, 2534

Doup, George, 2087, 2090

Dow, Lorenzow, 743

Dowden, Thomas, 617, 618

Dowson, Jesse, 1154

Doyle, Mary, 295

Drake, David, 358

Drake, Pritchard, & Drake, 547

Drum, John, 1023

Drummon, Nathan, 2533

Drybread, George, 590

Dubois, Alexander, 511

Dubois, Isaac, 511

Dubois, Toussaint, 854

Dubois, William, 523

Dudderer, Conrad, 331, 774

Dudderer, John, 744

Duer, William, 2526

Duffield, David, 1041

Duffield, William, 1021

Dufour, John James, 982, 1422, 1673, 1751, 1752, 1950, 2585

Dufour, John James, & Associates, 1352, 2417, 2431, 2492, 2493, 2494, 2509

Dugan, Thomas, 1023

Duggan, Jeremiah (Colonel), 2540

Dumma, Martin, 997

Dumont, --, 2534

Dunbar, William, 1680, 1862, 1863, 2290

Dunbar, --, 2336

Duncan, Benjamin, 432, 435

Duncan & Ewings, 320

Duncan, see also Dunkin

Dundas & Hepburn, 182

Dunfield, Oliver, 844

Dunkil, John, 468

Dunkin, John, 876, 881

Dunlap, Adam, 853

Dunlap, J., 2154

Dunlap, Samuel, 361, 759

Dunlap, William, 1021

Dunlevy, Daniel, 309

Dunlop, James, 1232

Dunn, John, 2528

Dunn, Samuel, 892

Dunn, Thomas, 345, 1021

Dunning, Elizabeth, 2529

Dunning, Jeremiah, 2532

Dunning, Richard, 2529

Duplantier, --, 1901, 2020, 2340

Durfey, Timothy, 2534

Dusenberry, --, 1277

Dusinberry, William, 186, 196, 1520

Dwight, Hamlin, 2533

Dwight, Samuel, 2533

Dwight, Timothy, 2533

Dyer, Anthony, 66

Eaker, William, 713

Eakin, William (U.S. Representative), 740

Earhart, Nicholas, 448

Earll, Daniel, 2541

Easterday, John Michael, 1122

Easterday, Michael, 840

Easterley, Michael, 302, 361

Easton, Moses, 92

Eaton, Elizabeth, 338

Eaton, James, 944

Eaton, John, 335, 336, 337, 338, 339, 340, 352

Eaton, Joseph, 516, 605

Eaton, Origen, 67

Eatter, Henry, 835, 901

Eby, Christian, 729, 1127

Eckey, John, 731

Eddy, John, 809, 814, 941

Eddy, Jonathan, 2541, 2542, 2543

Edgar, John, 2537, 2538, 2539, 2543

Edgar, Robert, 472, 544

Fife, William, 699

Filbert, *see* Gilbert

Fillco, John, 2529

Finch, Dan, 2529

Finch, Ezra, 2528

Finch, Jacob, 2532, 2534

Finch, Jonathan, 2528

Finch, Nathuel, 2528

Finch, Timothy, 2528

Finck, John, 272

Finckle, John P., 1075

Findlay, James (Rec Cin), 51, 61, 78, 97, 106, 159,
166, 214, 229, 232, 265, 278, 288, 290,
299, 370, 377, 451, 463, 472, 478, 482,
488, 497, 528, 549, 551, 553, 556, 560,
571, 572, 576, 577, 583, 586, 590, 593,
598, 638, 671, 688, 713, 740, 745, 804,
875, 910, 973, 994, 1012, 1033, 1225,
1229, 1232, 1240, 1245, 1250, 1255,
1267, 1276, 1279, 1283, 1284, 1286,
1289, 1292, 1293, 1297, 1305, 1308,
1313, 1317, 1320, 1321, 1328, 1330,
1334, 1335, 1361, 1366, 1381, 1382,
1410, 1426, 1438, 1457, 1458, 1479,
1491, 1496, 1502, 1509, 1511, 1515,
1517, 1526, 1531, 1556, 1562, 1565,
1571, 1578, 1585, 1603, 1605, 1614,
1615, 1619, 1633, 1636, 1673, 1679,
1687, 1708, 1711, 1742, 1747, 1752,
1778, 1816, 1827, 1842, 1851, 1855,
1862, 1876, 1945, 1954, 2007, 2022,
2028, 2034, 2042, 2052, 2108, 2146,
2170, 2182, 2190, 2192, 2194, 2230,
2245, 2334, 2358, 2372, 2381, 2384,
2387, 2391, 2394, 2395, 2396, 2397,
2400, 2401, 2402, 2404, 2405, 2406,
2408, 2410, 2411, 2412, 2413, 2414,
2415, 2422, 2423, 2425, 2428, 2432,
2434, 2436, 2437, 2440, 2442, 2443,
2445, 2446, 2447, 2448, 2454, 2456,
2457, 2459, 2460, 2461, 2462, 2463,
2464, 2467, 2468, 2474, 2475, 2477,
2480, 2481, 2484, 2485, 2489, 2490,
2494, 2496, 2499, 2500, 2505, 2510,
2511, 2513, 2515, 2517, 2518, 2519

Findlay, James (as grantee), 565

Findlay, Nathan, 2511

Findlay, William, 141

Findlay, --, 924

Findley, David, 1098

Findley, William (U.S. Representative), 295, 296,
304, 505, 631, 648, 834, 960

Fink, Abraham, 483

Fink, George, 699

Fink, *see also* Finck

Finley, Robert, 87

Finley, Samuel (Rec Ch1), 105, 119, 174, 176, 221,
230, 233, 237, 247, 263, 275, 278, 280
282, 284, 287, 289, 315, 348, 410, 415,
417, 468, 479, 490, 529, 546, 563, 602,
623, 641, 649, 654, 878, 986, 1028,
1049, 1159, 1160, 1226, 1229, 1232,
1237, 1240, 1250, 1255, 1256, 1272,
1276, 1279, 1291, 1292, 1297, 1311,
1317, 1320, 1325, 1344, 1349, 1359,
1365, 1375, 1376, 1379, 1381, 1395,
1399, 1410, 1411, 1418, 1421, 1423,
1431, 1433, 1438, 1449, 1455, 1457,
1461, 1480, 1497, 1501, 1503, 1514,
1519, 1523, 1531, 1546, 1552, 1553,
1571, 1588, 1605, 1614, 1615, 1636,
1639, 1645, 1659, 1665, 1697, 1708,
1747, 1762, 1816, 1817, 1828, 1851,
1853, 1862, 1864, 1873, 1880, 1883,
1955, 1993, 2015, 2036, 3043, 2047,
2094, 2170, 2190, 2192, 2214, 2230,
2245

Finley, Samuel (as grantee), 885

Finley, Worthington, & James, 948

Finney, James, 345

Finney, Solomon, 2528

Firestone, John, 334

Fisher, Frederick, 894

Fisher, John, 448, 866

Fisher, Joseph, 1183

Fisher, Michael, 923

Fisher, Nathan, 699

Fisher, Solomon, 260

Fisk, John, 897, 958, 974, 976

Fitch, Daniel, 2529

Fitch, Ebenezer, 2529

Fitch, Elijah, 2529

Fitch, Hannah, 2529

Fitch, Haynes, 2529

Fitch, Jabez, 2528

Fitch, James, 2529

Fitch, James, Junior, 2529

Fitch, Jonathan, 2533

Fitch, Lydia, 2529

Handle, Chester, 1136

Handley, --, 1730

Hanes, David, 837, 841

Hanes, Leonard, 389

Hanes, *see also* Haines

Hanford, Daniel, 2529

Hanford, David, 2529

Hanford, Hannah, 2529

Hanford, Hezekiah, 2529

Hanford, Jedediah, 2529

Hanford, Phineas (Captain), 2529

Hanford, Phineas, Junior, 2529

Hanks, Thomas, 869

Hanna, Benjamin, 756

Hanna, James, 1122

Hanna, John, 68, 197, 208, 223, 260, 404, 560, 663, 763

Hanna, Joseph, 889

Hanna, Robert, 361

Hanna, Samuel, 219, 345

Hanna, *see also* Hana

Hannam, John, 639

Hansel, David, 779

Hansell, Christian, 758

Hanson, Christian, 2533

Hanson, Susannah, 1010

Harah, James Gilcreast, 223

Harah, William, 241

Harborn, Abner, 507

Harborn, Noah, 758, 790

Harborn, William, 507

Harbour, William, 379, 816

Hardenbrook, Lodowick, 1832, 1833

Harderson, William S., 823

Hardin, Henry, 379

Hardin, James, 541

Harding, Frederick, 2533

Harding, Seth, 2538, 2539, 2540, 2542, 2543

Hardy, Joseph, 2526

Hardy, --, 466

Hare, Henry, 129

Harlin, George, 372

Harlin, John, 555

Harman, Frederick, 469, 499

Harman, John, 361

Harman, -- (General), 2278

Harmer, George, 544

Harmer, *see also* Harman

Harner, George, 489, 555

Harness, George, 348

Harness, Joseph, 255

Harper, John, 883

Harper, Nathan, 390

Harper, Samuel, 449

Harr, John, Junior, 220

Harregal, *see* Harrogal

Harrington, Nathaniel, 822

Harris, Benjamin, 2534

Harris, Bridget, 2534

Harris, Daniel, 2534

Harris, David, 841

Harris, Edy, 1011

Harris, Eliphalet, 2534

Harris, Enoch, 522, 661

Harris, Grace, 2534

Harris, H. J., 1895

Harris, Israel, 217

Harris, James, 841

Harris, John, 1st, 2534

Harris, John, 2nd, 2534

Harris, Joseph, Junior, 2534

Harris, Levi, 825

Harris, Lydia, 2534

Hicock, Daniel, 2532

Hicok, Nathan, 2529

Hicok, Silas, 2529

Hiester, Joseph, 180

Higgins, Nehemiah, 2533

Higgins, William, 2534

Highway, Samuel, 604, 977

Hilger, Andrew, 113

Hilger, Henry, 113, 155, 277, 308

Hill, Elijah, 2533

Hill, George, 784

Hill, Samuel, 415, 1111, 1135

Hill, Thomas, 1124

Hill, William, 268

Hilliar, Charles, 1002

Hillegas, S., 2164

Himbaugh, Henry, 344

Hinchman, Henry, 782

Hines, Rudolph, 888

Hinshaw, Jacob, 869

Hinton, Thomas, 424

Hirley, Michael, 256

Hirst, Jess, 944, 945, 1043, 1158, 1198

Hitchcock, Jane, 2529

Hitchcock, Mindwell, 2528

Hitchcock, Peter, 2529

Hitchcock, Thomas, 2528

Hitchcock, --, 929

Hite, Abraham, 225

Hite, Andrew, 193, 225, 320, 662

Hite, Christopher, 628

Hite, Isaac, 80

Hite, John, 381, 1184

Hively, Michael, 831

Hixon, William, 379, 841

Hobart, Justin, 2530

Hobaugh, Philip, 313

Hobby, John, 2528

Hobby, Joseph, Junior, 2528

Hobby, Mills, 2528

Hobby, Thomas, 2528

Hobby, Thomas, Junior, 2528

Hobson, John, 831

Hocker, Andrew, 367

Hodgin, Stephen, 756

Hodgin, William, 223

Hoerauf, *see* Hairrauf

Hoesch, *see* Hush

Hoey, Thomas, 661, 831

Hoff, Jesse, 843

Hoffer, Isaac, 1181

Hoffhines, Joseph, 1145

Hoffman, George (Reg Det), 1400, 1411, 1429, 1471, 1485, 1518, 1527

Hoffman, George, 120, 511

Hofheinz, *see* Hoffhines

Hogden, Samuel, 1217

Hoge, David (Reg Stu), 15, 20, 32, 41, 46, 47, 55, 99, 104, 112, 114, 126, 129, 134, 136, 160, 192, 198, 207, 218, 219, 223, 231, 234, 236, 241, 242, 248, 256, 260, 273, 278, 302, 309, 318, 321, 323, 333, 334, 343, 345, 354, 358, 360, 361, 366, 376, 394, 396, 433, 447, 456, 461, 469, 476, 486, 493, 502, 512, 516, 519, 520, 522, 535, 542, 545, 548, 554, 566, 567, 569, 574, 578, 582, 587, 591, 594, 599, 603, 613, 620, 634, 640, 642, 643, 661, 670, 683, 686, 691, 696, 699, 718, 721, 724, 726, 731, 744, 749, 753, 755, 756, 759, 774, 780, 782, 788, 792, 807, 820, 825, 831, 835, 840, 844, 848, 850, 853, 856, 857, 861, 867, 868, 871, 876, 882, 888, 892, 897, 917, 920, 922, 942, 944, 946, 954, 958, 974, 976, 989, 991, 993, 1005, 1007, 1014, 1021, 1032, 1039, 1052, 1056, 1062, 1085, 1097, 1106, 1109, 1114, 1122, 1132, 1137, 1151, 1165, 1177, 1183, 1186, 1191, 1223, 1230, 1232, 1233, 1235, 1248, 1253, 1266, 1274, 1285, 1288, 1294, 1295, 1296, 1299, 1301, 1302, 1303, 1315, 1323, 1333, 1336, 1340, 1345, 1347, 1350, 1353, 1355, 1376, 1381, 1387, 1412, 1413, 1428, 1439, 1453,

Jennings, Daniel, 2530

Jennings, David, 2530

Jennings, Ephraim, 2530

Jennings, Gideon, 616

Jennings, Hezekiah, 2530

Jennings, Isaac, 2530

Jennings, Jacob, 2529

Jennings, Jeremy, 2530

Jennings, Jonathan, 1058

Jennings, Justin, 2530

Jenning(s), Levi, 653, 844, 1093

Jennings, Lyman, 2530

Jennings, Martha, 2530

Jennings, Moses, 2530

Jennings, Obadiah, 129, 215, 476, 510, 660, 698,
        759, 844, 950, 1058, 1062, 1879

Jennings, Peter, 2530

Jennings, Rebecca, 2530

Jennings, Stephen, 2530

Jessop, Amos, 2528

Jessop, Jonathan, 236, 261

Jessup, Ebenezer, 2530, 2531

Jewett, David, 189

Job, Samuel, 758

Jocelyn, Amaziah, 2533

Jocelyn, Simeon, 2533

John, Griffith, 594

John, John, 367

John, Thomas, 367, 883

Johns, George, 320

Johns, Henry, 320, 610, 636

Johns, John, 636

Johnson, Abraham, 2533

Johnson, Enos, 2533

Johnson, Francis, 456

Johnson, Henry, 885

Johnson, Jabez, 2533

Johnson, James, 885, 1914

Johnson, John, 260, 520, 1098

Johnson, Josiah, 157

Johnson, Lydia, 2533, 2534

Johnson, Mabel, 2533

Johnson, Nathaniel, 320, 405

Johnson, Peter, 2533

Johnson, Richard, 2533

Johnson, Sarah, 2529

Johnson, Stephen, 2533

Johnson, Thomas, 2524, 2528

Johnson, William, 2528

Johnson, William, 223

Johnson, --, 1217

Johnston, Adam, 2541

Johnston, Andrew, 223, 741

Johnston, Cave, 507, 590

Johnston, George, 696

Johnston, James, 13, 15, 19, 223, 491

Johnston, John, 755, 793, 996, 1076, 1155, 1156

Johnston, Mahalah, 593

Johnston, Robert (Doctor), 2526

Johnston, Robert, 1271

Johnston, Thomas, 2525

Johnston, Washington (General), 988

Johnstone, James, 2528

Jolliff, James, 2525

Jolly, Malachi, 260, 888

Jones, Abraham, 635

Jones, Churchill, 431

Jones, David (Reverend), 127, 140, 151, 177, 178

Jones, David, 929

Jones, Ebenezer, 2535

Jones, George, 889

Jones, Henry, 593

Jones, Isaac, 2533

Jones, Jonathan, 845

Jones, Mauries, 601

Jones, Michael (Reg Kas), 1383, 1408, 1409, 1430,
   1471, 1485, 1527, 1563, 1620, 1676,
   1689, 1696, 1715, 1734, 1736, 1816,
   1851, 1868, 1938, 1985, 2010, 2069,
   2070, 2072, 2073, 2079

Jones, Newton, 547

Jones, Peter, 760

Jones, Samuel, 889

Jones, Thomas, 2534

Jones, Thomas, 505, 675, 778, 890

Jones, Thomas, Junior, 675

Jones, Timothy, 2533

Jones, Timothy, Junior, 2533

Jones, William, 2533

Jouett, -- (Indian Agent), 2250, 2254

Judah, David, 2529

Judah, Jacob, 2525

Judah, Michael, 2529

Judd, Bethiah, 2532

Judd, David, 2532

Justice, John, 355

Kabb, George, 885

Kabb, John, 885

Kagy, *see* Cagy

Kaher, Henry, 700

Kail, George, 1114

Kail, Peter, 753, 1882

Kail, --, 856

Kail, *see also* Kell

Kalback, Henry, 647, 687

Kalback & Shaffer, 344

Kammerer, Philip, 243

Kampf, David, 502

Kandle, *see* Randle

Kane, Frederick, 1124

Kane, James M., 511

Kane, *see* Cain

Kearn, George, 833

Kearns, Benjamin, 832

Keeder, *see* Reeder

Keeler, Benjamin, 2529

Keeler, Isaac, 2535

Keeler, James, 2529

Keeler, Jemima, 2535

Keeler, John, 2535

Keeler, Margaret, 2530

Keeler, Martha, 2535

Keeler, Matthew, 2529, 2535

Keeler, Nathan, 2529

Keeler, Samuel, 2529, 2535

Keeler, Samuel 2nd, 2535

Keeler, Stephen, 2529

Keeler, Timothy 2nd, 2535

Keeler, Thaddeus, 2529

Keene, Samuel Y., 621

Keever, George, 837

Keever, Henry, 837

Keever, Martin, 367

Keever, Peter, 367

Keffer, Valentine, 320

Kehl, *see* Kail

Keim, *see* Kime

Keith, Price, 1014

Kell, Benjamin, 637

Keller, Henry, 32, 48, 284

Keller, Jacob, 2525

Keller, Peter, 219

Kelley, A., 175

Kellogg, Jervis, 2529

Kellogg, John, 2529

Kellog, Seth, 267, 353

Kelly, Darby, 885

Kelly, James, 831

Kelly, Joseph, 583, 590, 1123

Kelly, Thomas, 1149, 1176

Kelsey, John, 367

Kemp. Kudwick, 444, 544

Kemper, Elnathan, 833

Kemper, James, 812

Ken, John, 888

Kendall, Robert, 943

Kennard, John, 938

Kennedy, Robert, 2534

Kennedy, Thomas, 2146

Kennedy, William, 66, 93

Kenney, Lewis, 219

Kenney, Walter, 2525

Kent, Abraham, 780

Kent, Absalom, 207, 219, 831

Kent, Jacob, 190

Kent, Moso, 2530

Kentner, Jacob, 739

Kentner, *see* Kintner

Kepler, John, 365

Kepley, Michael, 219

Kepner, Benjamin, 1593

Kercheval, James, 1002

Kerlin, John, 660

Kernaghan, Samuel, 345, 954, 955, 1038

Kerne, Henry, 1009

Kerns, Benjamin, 36, 225, 1399

Kerns, George, 950

Kerns, Godfroy, 296

Kerr, John, 313, 346, 888

Kershner, Jacob, 580, 981, 1123

Kesler, Martin, 378

Kester, Jacob, 1123

Kester, Mathias, 460

Ketchum, Elizabeth, 2529

Ketchum, Samuel, 2529

Ketchum, Timothy, 2532

Ketnar, Nicholas, 885

Kever, Martin, Junior, 495

Kever, Michael, 604, 977

Kidd, Alexander, 2536

Kiefer, *see* Keever

Kiefer, *see* Keffer

Kiggen, John, 825

Kilburn, Charles, 189

Kilburn, James, 1405, 2238

Kilby, Marak, 2533

Kilgore, James, 225

Killbuck (Delaware Indian), 1258, 1259

Killburn, --, 1692

Killgore, Charles (Reg Cin), 58, 97, 102, 107, 111, 115, 117, 122, 130, 131, 137, 139, 143, 144, 159, 162, 165, 168, 185, 190, 191, 204, 211, 213, 217, 224, 257, 267, 271, 278, 310, 312, 341, 350, 353, 356, 367, 372, 373, 379, 384, 386, 387, 389, 400, 409, 423, 439, 442, 444, 446, 470, 471, 473, 477, 480, 485, 489, 494, 495, 498, 500, 503, 507, 511, 517, 521, 523, 526, 530, 531, 534, 538, 541, 544, 547, 555, 565, 570, 705, 1374, 1376, 1381, 1382, 1387, 1394, 1406, 1417, 1422, 1445, 1446, 1457, 1466, 1477, 1486, 1527, 1539, 1540, 1542, 1551, 1561, 1579, 1591, 1606, 1615, 1624, 1641, 1642, 1647, 1660, 1676, 1677, 1681, 1685, 1713, 1720, 1747, 1751, 1752, 1778, 2202, 2420, 2421, 2422, 2423, 2424, 2426, 2427, 2430, 2431, 2433, 2435, 2436, 2438, 2439, 2441, 2449, 2450, 2451, 2452, 2453, 2455, 2458, 2463, 2465, 2469, 2470, 2471, 2473, 2475, 2476, 2478, 2479, 2481, 2482, 2486, 2488, 2490, 2492, 2495

Kimberley, Azael, 2533

Kimberly, Ephraim, 2555

Kimberly, Lydia, 2533

Kimberly, Mary, 2533

Kimberly, Nathaniel, 2533

Kimberly, Sarah, 2533

Kimberly, Silas, 2533

Kimberly, Zenas, 1212, 1285, 1304

Kime, Henry, 1009

Kinch, William, 2528

Kinch, --, 2528

King, Elijah, 2533

King, George (Clerk, WOr LO), 1969

King, Hugh, 831

King, Joseph, 838

King, Philip, 378, 832

King, Robert, 645

King, Samuel, 2530

King, Thomas, 380

King, William, 511

Kingerland, David, 2525

Kingery, Christly, 883

Kingsley, Alpha (Lieutenant, U.S. Army Paymaster), 2042, 2093, 2518

Kinman, Levi, 889

Kinney, Lewis, 219, 857

Kinney, Richard, 273

Kinser, George, 435

Kinsey, Henry, 833

Kintner, Jacob, 772, 884, 1959

Kintner, --, 864

Kirby, -- (Land Commissioner, EPR), 1465, 1472

Kirby & Rich, 837

Kirk, William, 219

Kirkpatrick, Alexander, 1660, 2473, 2476

Kirkpatrick, William, 312

Kirkpatrick, -- (Major), 2527

Kirkwood, Robert, 2526

Kirlen, John, 970

Kishler, Jacob, 885

Kitchell, Asa, 191

Kitsmiller, Jacob, 831

Kitt, Jacob, 248

Kleck, Daniel, 1123

Klein, *see* Cline

Kline, Conrad, 885

Kline, Frederick, 1129, 1189

Kline, Jacob, 1815, 1833

Knagy, Christian, 469

Knagy, Jacob, 469

Knapp, Aaron, 2532

Knapp, Abraham, 2528

Knapp, Charles, 2528

Knapp, Ebenezer, 2528

Knapp, Eunice, 2528

Knapp, Ezekiel, 2528

Knapp, Horace, 2532

Knapp, Israel, Junior, 2528

Knapp, John, 2528, 2532

Knapp, Jonah, 2528

Knapp, Jonathan, 2528

Knapp, Joshua, 2528, 2532

Knapp, Moses, 2532

Knapp, Nathaniel, 2528

Kneapler, George, 914

Knight, Benjamin, 888, 1051

Knight, Samuel, 774

Knipper, Jacob, 259, 449

Knotts, Nathaniel, 111, 139

Knowland, *see* Nolind

Koch, Christian, 833

Koch, William, 1019, 1065, 1104

Koffle, Peter, 371

Kollar, George, 1121

Koop, John, 578

Kore, Christian, 369, 419, 462

Kore, Michael, 369, 419, 462

Kore & Thomas, 419

Koy, Daniel E., 869

Kraner, Henry, 378

Kraner, Michael, 378

Kratzer, Samuel, 464, 1569

Krebs, *see* Crabs

Kreider, *see* Cryder

Krumbacher, *see* Crumbacher

Kuhl, Henry, 2526

Kuhn, Jacob, 207

Kuns, George, Senior, 883

Kuns, George, 159, 1002

Kuns, Jacob, 130

Kunse, George, 833, 883

Kunsler, Henry, 893

Kuntz, Emanuel, 433

Kunze, George, 964

Kupplens, Jacob, 433

Kupplins, John, 634

Lacey, William, 433

Lackett, *see* Lockett

La Fayette, -- (Major General), 1175

Laferty, Edward, 1097

Laffarty, *see* Lawfarty

Lafon, -- (Deputy Surveyor), 2314

Laight, Jacob, 2524

Laight, *see also* Light

Laitner, Chris[topher], 361, 469

Lamb, Jacob, 747

Lamb, James, 748, 845

Lamb, John, 343

Lamb, Joshua, 2540, 2541

Lambert, Barnabas, 885, 893

Lambert, B., 629

Lambert, James, 970

Lambert, Josias, 1096

Lambert, Samuel, 2532

Lamborn (Lambourn), Parmenas, 589, 1132

Lamme, John, 752

Lamme, Nathan, 353, 367

Lamphier, James, 2534

Lamphier, James, Junior, 2534

Lancaster, William, 846

Land, James, 597

Lander, Samuel, 1125

Landis, David, 647, 687

Landis, Henry, 687

Lane, James, 2533

Lane, Joseph, 846, 924

Lane, William, 747

Langham, Elias (Colonel), 913, 1287, 1311, 2138, 2140, 2169, 2181, 2194, 2527

Langham, --, 1349

Langlois, E., & Butchet, 2070

Laraw, Jacob, 920

Laraw, *see also* Larrow

Larimer, Isaac, 420, 893

Larkin, David, 1032

Larkin, Edward, 2533

Larrison, John, 365

Larrow, James, 1087

Larrow, *see also* Laraw

Lashmutt, Elias N. de, 292

Lasley, David, 846

Lasselle, J., 1749

Laswell, Joseph, 2350

Latham, A., 2536

Latham, Edward (Captain), 2536

Latham, Elizabeth, 2536

Latham, John, 2536

Latham, Jonathan, 2536

Latham, Lydia, 2536

McMillan, William, 1232

McMullin, Hugh, 158

McMullin, John, 305, 1024, 1054

McMullin, Thomas, 167

McNaghten, John, Senior, 832

McNaghten, John, 435

McNair, John (soldier), 187

McNairy, Thomas, 922, 963

McNamee, Job, 404, 641, 644, 649, 684, 970

McNeal, John, 806

McPherrin, Thomas, 456

McPherrin, W., 456

McPherson, Andrew, 566

McPike, Hugh, 223

McQueston, Hugh, 786, 1116

McQuilkin, James, 461

McQuisten, Andrew, 517, 779

McTeer, Robert, 629

McVickers, Duncan, 470

McWhirter, James, 239

McWhorter, John, 440, 453

McWilliams, Samuel, 469

Macy, Micajah, 469

Maddens, William, 367

Maddin, --, 154

Madding, Thomas, 91, 154

Maddock, Samuel, 730, 779

Madison, James, 80, 1175, 1901

Madison, --, 2340

Magruder, Allan B. (U.S. Land Agent, WOr), 1533,
      1621, 1623, 1721

Magruder, --, 1177

Mahon, Samuel, 2527

Mahon, Susanna, 2533

Maillet, --, 1968

Majors, William, 779

Malcom, William (Colonel), 91

Maley, Edward, 2533

Mallery, Levi, 2530

Mallory, Giles, 2529

Mallory, Matthew, 2529

Mallory, Nathan, 2529

Maltbie, Ammi, 941

Maltbie, Benjamin, 353, 1633, 2467

Maltby, Jonathan, 2530

Manly, Robert, 1144

Manning, Benjamin, 2526

Manning, William, 2526

Mansfield, Daniel, 2533

Mansfield, Esther, 2533

Mansfield, Hannah, 2533

Mansfield, Jared (Surveyor General), 238, 382, 742,
      1092, 1160, 1359, 1361, 1365, 1366,
      1367, 1372, 1380, 1386, 1426, 1455,
      1456, 1458, 1461, 1462, 1498, 1514,
      1515, 1524, 1562, 1597, 1619, 1639,
      1687, 1742, 1808, 1825, 1834, 1841,
      1843, 1851, 1854, 1876, 1931, 1981,
      1999, 2007, 2022, 2028, 2038, 2050,
      2052, 2060, 2108, 2223, 2224, 2226,
      2227, 2230, 2232, 2233, 2234, 2236,
      2237, 2238, 2239, 2240, 2241, 2242,
      2243, 2244, 2245, 2250, 2251, 2252,
      2253, 2254, 2256, 2257, 2259, 2262,
      2263, 2264, 2266, 2269, 2270, 2271,
      2274, 2275, 2276, 2277, 2278, 2279,
      2280, 2281, 2282, 2284, 2285, 2286,
      2287, 2288, 2292, 2293, 2294, 2296,
      2298, 2299, 2300, 2301, 2302, 2303,
      2310, 2313, 2315, 2316, 2317, 2319,
      2320, 2321, 2322, 2323, 2324, 2326,
      2327, 2328, 2329, 2330, 2331, 2332,
      2334, 2335, 2337, 2338, 2346, 2349,
      2350, 2353, 2356, 2357, 2358, 2359,
      2362, 2364, 2369, 2371, 2372, 2373,
      2374, 2375, 2376, 2378, 2379, 2432,
      2434, 2464, 2505, 2513, 2515, 2519

Mansfield, Jared (as grantee), 386, 530, 568, 1751,
      1752, 2315, 2492, 2494

Mansfield, John F., 2006

Mansfield, Kirsted, 2533

Mansfield, Moses, 2533

Mansfield, Nathan, 2533

Mansfield, Thomas, 334, 942

Mansfield, William, 2533

Mansfield, --, 322

Mayer, Daniel, 449

Mayer(s), Henry, 774, 780

Mayett, --, 1968

Maynard, Peter, 189

Maysilles, John, 970

Mead, Abigail, 2528

Mead, Abraham, 2528

Mead, Amos (Doctor), 2528

Mead, Andrew, 2528

Mead, Azor, 2529

Mead, Benjamin, 2528

Mead, Caleb, 2528

Mead, Caleb 2nd, 2528

Mead, Charles, 2528

Mead, Deliverance, 2528

Mead, Ebenezer, 2528

Mead, Edmond, 2528

Mead, Eliphalet, 2528

Mead, Eliphalet, Junior, 2528

Mead, Elizabeth, 2528

Mead, Elkanah, 2528

Mead, Enos, 2528

Mead, Hannah, 2528

Mead, Henry, 2528

Mead, Jared, 2528

Mead, Jehiel, 2528

Mead, Jemima, 2528

Mead, Jeremiah, Junior, 2528

Mead, Jerusha, 2528

Mead, Jesse, 2528

Mead, John, 2528

Mead, John, Junior, 2528

Mead, Jonas, 2528

Mead, Joseph, 2528

Mead, Joshua, 2528

Mead, Jotham, 2528

Mead, Mathew, 2528

Mead, Mathew (Colonel), 2529

Mead, Nathaniel 3rd, 2528

Mead, Nehemiah, 2528

Mead, Nehemiah, Junior, 2528

Mead, Peter, 2528

Mead, Peter, Junior, 2528

Mead, Sarah, 2528

Mead, Shadrach, 2528

Mead, Silas, 2528

Mead, Sybil, 2528

Mead, Titus, 2528

Mead, Zac[c]heus, 2528

Meakes & Bixler, 929

Meaks, Bazel, 822

Means, Robert, 677

Medsker, Henry, 370, 553, 841, 859

Meek, Samuel, 358

Meeker, Benjamin, 2531

Meeker, Seth, 2531

Megrew, James B., 248

Meigs, R. I., 2138

Meigs, R. J. (Colonel), 2044, 2093

Meigs, R. J., Junior (U.S. Senator), 934, 1055, 1080, 1120, 1139

Meissa, Jacob, 193

Melally, Michael, 2534

Melandore, Jacob, 565

Mendenhall, Elijah, 786

Mendenhall, Mordecai, 837

Mercer, Jonathan, 1081

Mercereau, Joshua, 2526

Mercier, John D., 2526, 2540, 2542

Meredith, S., 2391

Meredith, Samuel, 1267

Meridith, William, 475, 989

Merit, Jesse, 776

Shoemaker & Geehr, 272

Sholes, Jabez, 2536

Sholes, Lucretia, 2536

Sholes, Nathan, 2536

Shook, Henry, 2319

Shoram (Negro), 2536

Short, James, 225

Short, Joanna, 2534

Short, Peyton, 290, 705, 978, 996, 1551, 1933,
     2453, 2506

Shotte, Richard, 752

Shouse, John, 1807

Shove, Benjamin, 2532

Shove, Seth, 2532

Showley, Jacob, 203

Shriver, Peter, 207, 219

Shuey, Caspar, 823

Shull, Peter, 583

Shungletaker, Jacob, 544

Shutt, Peter, 1017

Shutt, Philip, 1017

Siddall, Isaac, 334, 396, 569

Siddall, John, 345

Sidener, Nicholas, 829

Sidwell, David, 500, 538

Sidwell, Nathan, 1094

Sidwell, Henry, 769

Sidwell, Nathan, 1056, 1119

Siebert, see Seebert

Sieger, see Saygar

Siler, Jacob, 544

Siler, Philip, 367

Sill, Henry, 587

Silliman, Willys (Wyllys) (Reg Zan), 142, 199, 281,
     298, 357, 365, 380, 388, 496, 525,
     537, 539, 562, 596, 616, 618, 674,
     709, 717, 765, 768, 777, 785, 795,
     798, 824, 842, 860, 862, 873, 879,
     896, 908, 916, 921, 940, 949, 972,
     979, 1011, 1017, 1022, 1059, 1068,

1077, 1087, 1098, 1108, 1121, 1133,
1135, 1149, 1176, 1182, 1380, 1381,
1387, 1398, 1414, 1425, 1442, 1444,
1447, 1467, 1486, 1488, 1527, 1540,
1541, 1557, 1589, 1592, 1606, 1615,
1676, 1713, 1747, 1763, 1816, 1851,
1862, 1875, 1948, 2058, 2064, 2233

Silsbe, Sarah, 2535

Simison, Robert, 469

Simley, see Lemley

Simmerman, John, 827

Simmerman, see also Cimmerman

Simmes, David, 982

Simmons, John, 823

Simmonds, Ann, 2534

Simmons, Chapman, 2534

Simons, Andrew, 469

Simpson, George (Cashier, Bank of the United States),
     2023

Simpson, John, 931

Simpson, --, 2157

Sinclair, James, 309, 321

Singer, Joseph, 1002

Sinks, George, 131

Sintz, Peter, 837

Siscat, Desire, 2529

Siscat, Obadiah, 2529

Sites, Lewis, 259

Sites, see also Lites

Skinner, Bathsheba, 2534

Skinner, George, 967

Skinner, William, 934, 2114, 2134, 2135, 2140, 2145,
     2146, 2181, 2527, 2534

Skinner & Barber, 249, 253

Skinner, see also Shinner

Slagle, Daniel, 207, 219

Slauter, John, 673

Sleighter, David, 971, 1047

Slifer, Philip, 852

Slifer, Stephen, 1076

Smith, Stephen, 2529, 2535

Smith, S., 514

Smith, Thomas, 421

Smith, Thomas, 2534

Smith, Uriah, 2529

Smith, William, 535, 587, 829, 1002

Smith, William A., 617, 618

Smith, -- (U.S. Senator), 2295

Smith, -- (of U.S. War Department), 980

Smith, --, 1569

Smith, Gissel, & Miessa, 1476

Smythe, Richard, 1749

Snedeker, Garret, 343

Snider, Abraham, 1186

Snider, Michael, 561, 744, 1032, 1141

Snodgrass, James, 190

Snowden, James, 372

Snyder, Adam, Junior, 662

Snyder, Isaac, 174

Soulard, Ant[oine](Surveyor of Louisiana Territory
        for Spanish Government), 1536, 1597,
        2267, 2275

Southard, Henry (U.S. Representative), 1110

Southard, Isaac, 1110

Southerland, Roger, 2528

Spalding, Grace, 2530

Spangler, Henry, 851

Sparks, William, 2524

Speace, Philip, 435

Spencer (Spenser), Jesse (Reg Ch1), 34, 35, 36, 98,
        103, 116, 120, 121, 125, 175, 193, 194,
        202, 203, 210, 216, 220, 222, 225, 226,
        243, 249, 255, 259, 264, 272, 278, 316,
        320, 344, 355, 362, 374, 378, 381, 383,
        385, 397, 402, 405, 408, 418, 420, 424,
        448, 460, 467, 474, 483, 492, 499, 513,
        524, 533, 536, 540, 550, 573, 575, 580,
        597, 600, 606, 610, 615, 629, 633, 635,
        644, 647, 649, 652, 660, 662, 665, 669,
        681, 693, 701, 708, 712, 720, 725, 728,
        729, 738, 747, 760, 770, 775, 781, 784,
        789, 791, 799, 805, 806, 829, 832, 839,
        843, 846, 851, 865, 869, 877, 885, 893,
        924, 929, 948, 959, 967, 970, 983, 985,
        992, 997, 998, 1004, 1106, 1015, 1019,

1023, 1024, 1029, 1054, 1063, 1065,
1079, 1091, 1095, 1096, 1115, 1123,
1125, 1129, 1145, 1147, 1167, 1168,
1181, 1184, 1331, 1338, 1339, 1381,
1387, 1389, 1404, 1405, 1415, 1440,
1457, 1460, 1476, 1477, 1486, 1527,
1538, 1539, 1540, 1554, 1569, 1570,
1593, 1604, 1606, 1613, 1615, 1663,
1666, 1675, 1676, 1694, 1713, 1747,
1761, 1762, 1783, 1816, 1836, 1851,
1862, 1875, 1932, 1948, 2009, 2013

Spencer, Jesse (as grantee), 382, 407, 418, 524,
        595, 708, 1092, 1160, 1663, 2319

Spencer, John, 2534

Spencer, Joseph, 503, 1191

Spencer, J., & H. Abrams, 193

Spencer, William, 343, 1125

Sperry, Benjamin, 2532

Sperry, Timothy, 2533

Spicer, Jacob, 146

Spiess, see Speace

Spinch, Lydia, 2534

Spinning, Isaac, 544

Spitler, Jacob, 825

Spoon, John, 892

Spooner, Judas P., 2534

Sprague, Joseph, 2530

Spring, James, 1096

Springer, Jacob, 302

Springer, John, 842

Springer, John, 2534

Springer, Levi, 1068

Springer, William, 405

Sprigg, William (Land Commissioner, WOr), 1724,
        1739, 1753, 1755

Sprigg, Zachariah, 1232

Sproat, Ebenezer, 2167

Sproat, Earl, 2129, 2152, 2167

Sproat, E. (Major), 253

Sproat, Joseph, 361

Sproat, Paul, 2143

Sproat & Mathews, 2181

Talbert, Thomas, 1152

Tlabot, William, 73, 96

Talcott, Bartlett, 2535

Talcott, George, 2535

Tallmadge, Timothy, 2533

Tallmadge, -- (U.S. Representative), 1543

Tallman, Bethiah, 2534

Tallman, William, 865

Tallman & Starr, 2534

Tayler, Oliver, 2532

Taylor, Amos, 865

Taylor, Benjamin, 2532

Taylor, Daniel, 2532

Taylor, Edmund H. (Rec Jef), 757, 1134, 1195, 1710,
        1735, 1745, 1804, 1805, 1806, 1816,
        1851, 1870, 1872, 1881, 1889, 1917,
        1922, 1944, 1998, 2040, 2095

Taylor, Edward, 599

Taylor, Elias, 2532

Taylor, Elizabeth, 1593

Taylor, Hannah, 2530

Taylor, James, 343, 503, 539, 555, 1002

Taylor, John, 866, 1002

Taylor, John, 2532

Taylor, Jonathan, 161, 256, 512, 2039, 2081

Taylor, Jonathan, 2532

Taylor, Josiah, Junior, 2529

Taylor, Judith, 2532

Taylor, Major, 2532

Taylor, Mary, 2534

Taylor, Matthew, 2532

Taylor, Nathan, Junior, 2532

Taylor, Nathan 3d, 2532

Taylor, Richard, Junior, 1998

Taylor, Robert, 1080

Taylor, Samuel, 2530, 2532

Taylor, Thomas, 2532

Taylor, Thomas, Junior, 2532

Taylor, Walter, 797

Taylor, William, 1076

Taylor, Zebadiah, 2528

Taylor & Bringman, 1971

Taylor & Gray, 1000

Taylor & McConnell, 972

Teal, Arthur, 378

Teal, Edward, 237, 247

Teal, Edward, Junior, 272

Teal, Nathaniel, 600, 865

Teal, Walter, 378

Tease, Hugh, 248

Teitors, Elisha, 192

Templeton, John, 866

Tenney, Samuel, 150

Terrell, Lemuel, 718

Test, Zaccheus, 223

Thatch, Daniel, 2529

Thatcher, Josiah (Captain), 2529

Thatcher, Josiah, 2529

Thatcher, Josiah, Junior, 2529

Thatcher, Stephen G., 2529

Thayer, Cornelius, 2533

Thickling, John, 2530

Thomas, Absalom, 367

Thomas, Benajah, 2533

Thomas, Camm, 366

Thomas, Daniel, 1040

Thomas, David, 65, 146

Thomas, Henry, 369, 419, 462

Thomas, Jacob, 562, 618

Thomas, John, Senior, 469

Thomas, William, 353, 388

Thomas & Kore, 419

Thomas & Liston, 565

Thompson, Abigail, 2530

SUBJECT INDEX

WPR district, establishment of LO in, 2618, 2634
    LO, suggestion to move from Washington, Mississippi Territory, to Natchez, disapproved, 1732
    New Purchase, survey of, 2367
    survey of, 2268, 2294

Wyandot Indians, 2123, 2348, 2349, 2631

Yazoo company, claimant under, 2514
    settlers under, 1908, 1912

Zan district. *See also* Conflict between Mar & Zan land offices
    establishment of, 2233
    military lands annexed to, 496
    survey of, 2238

Zane grants, 30, 140, 2127, 2128, 2168, 2226, 2426, 2559, 2582

TRACT INDEX

CHILLICOTHE LAND OFFICE DISTRICT

Chl LO, in general,   2, 7, 10, 11, 12, 14, 21, 22, 24

Chl	-	1	6	31	+	825
Chl	-	2	6	25	+	825
Chl	-	3	14	35	+	825
Chl	-	3	15	25	+	825
Chl	-	3	16	6	+	362
Chl	-	4	8	33	-	825
Chl	-	4	15	24	+	825
Chl	-	4	15	32	+	825
Chl	-	5	3	3 13		621
Chl	-	5	3	3 16		621
Chl	-	5	3	3 33		621
Chl	-	5	6	10	-	825
Chl	-	6	10	34	+	825
Chl	-	6	17	24	-	825
Chl	-	13	7	22	+	1037
Chl	-	14	8	12	+	970
Chl	-	14	8	15	+	1049
Chl	-	14	8	19	+	725, 1049
Chl Mil	14	8	19	+		1123, 1128
Chl	-	14	8	20	+	725
Chl Mil	14	8	20	+		1123, 1128
Chl	-	14	8	21	+	878
Chl Mil	14	8	21	+		602, 877
Chl	-	14	8	22	+	878
Chl Mil	14	8	22	+		602, 651, 877
Chl Mil	14	8	23	+		651
Chl	-	16	1	23	+	806
Chl	-	16	1	24	-	381
Chl	-	16	1	- 25		381
Chl	-	16	5	11	-	249
Chl	-	16	6	13	+	243
Chl	-	16	6	23	+	885
Chl	-	16	6	26	+	513
Chl	-	16	7	17	+	998, 1034
Chl	-	16	7	35	+	806
Chl	-	16	15	7	+	747, 970, 998, 1035
Chl	-	16	16	1	+	997, 1125
Chl	-	16	16	2	+	1168
Chl	-	16	16	3	+	662
Chl	-	16	16	5	+	843
Chl	-	16	16	6	+	225, 600
Chl	-	16	16	7	+	435, 647, 687
Chl	-	16	16	8	+	432, 647, 687, 893
Chl	-	16	16	9	+	424, 629
Chl	-	16	16	10	+	435
Chl	-	16	16	13	+	806, 869
Chl	-	16	16	14	+	791
Chl	-	16	16	17	+	536, 822
Chl	-	16	16	18	+	378, 806
Chl	-	16	16	19	+	435, 806
Chl	-	16	16	20	+	635
Chl	-	16	16	23	+	799
Chl	-	16	16	30	+	1181
Chl	-	16	16	32	+	662
Chl	-	16	17	3	+	843
Chl	-	16	17	4	+	378
Chl	-	16	17	5	-	573
Chl	-	16	17	5	+	997
Chl	-	16	17	6	-	540, 633, 648
Chl	-	16	17	7	-	631
Chl	-	16	17	7	+	1125
Chl	-	16	17	8	-	631
Chl	-	16	17	12	-	1055
Chl	-	16	17	13	+	1055
Chl	-	16	17	14	+	1055
Chl	-	16	17	18	+	1181
Chl	-	16	17	19	+	249
Chl	-	16	17	20	+	249
Chl	-	16	17	25	+	893
Chl	-	16	17	27	+	846

Ch1	-	16	17	28	+	381, 806	Ch1	-	17	17	12	-	378
Ch1	-	16	17	29	+	344	Ch1	-	17	17	13	-	249, 647, 687
Ch1	-	16	17	30	+	1123	Ch1	-	17	17	14	-	513
Ch1	-	16	17	31	+	249	Ch1	-	17	17	17	-	116
Ch1	-	16	17	32	+	635, 865	Ch1	-	17	17	18	-	536
Ch1	-	16	17	34	+	846	Ch1	-	17	17	19	-	397
Ch1	-	17	1	1	+	432	Ch1	-	17	17	20	-	225
Ch1	-	17	1	2	+	846	Ch1	-	17	17	21	+	660, 970
Ch1	-	17	10	20	+	843	Ch1	-	17	17	25	+	775, 843
Ch1	-	17	14	5	-	1339	Ch1	-	17	17	26	-	405
Ch1	-	17	14	6	+	243	Ch1	-	17	17	30	-	320
Ch1	-	17	14	9	+	997	Ch1	-	17	17	31	-	435
Ch1	-	17	14	12	+	775	Ch1	-	17	17	32	-	597, 985
Ch1	-	17	14	13	+	405, 448	Ch1	-	17	18	1	+	885, 1115
Ch1	-	17	14	14	+	505	Ch1	-	17	18	2	+	378
Ch1	-	17	15	7	+	435	Ch1	-	17	18	5	+	600, 1144
Ch1	-	17	16	1	+	791, 893	Ch1	-	17	18	6	+	1144
Ch1	-	17	16	2	-	799	Ch1	-	17	18	7	+	878
Ch1	-	17	16	4	+	378	Ch1	-	17	18	8	+	865, 1181
Ch1	-	17	16	5	+	378, 693	Ch1	-	17	18	10	+	410, 552
Ch1	-	17	16	6	+	405	Ch1	-	17	18	11	+	435, 843
Ch1	-	17	16	7	+	499, 652	Ch1	-	17	18	12	+	843
Ch1	-	17	16	8	+	829	Ch1	-	17	18	14	+	869, 893, 1024, 1054
Ch1	-	17	16	10	+	98, 125, 272	Ch1	-	17	18	17	+	407, 970, 992
Ch1	-	17	16	13	+	747	Ch1	-	17	18	18	-	2047
Ch1	-	17	16	17	+	799	Ch1	-	17	18	18	+	878
Ch1	-	17	16	18	+	420, 893	Ch1	-	17	18	19	-	2047
Ch1	-	17	16	19	+	103, 193	Ch1	-	17	18	20	-	2047
Ch1	-	17	16	20	+	225, 320	Ch1	-	17	18	20	+	225, 662
Ch1	-	17	16	28	+	806	Ch1	-	17	18	23	+	806, 829, 865
Ch1	-	17	17	1	+	225	Ch1	-	17	18	25	+	540, 851
Ch1	-	17	17	3	+	225, 623, 843, 1061	Ch1	-	17	18	27	+	1181
Ch1	-	17	17	6	-	225	Ch1	-	17	18	28	-	2047
Ch1	-	17	17	7	-	865	Ch1	-	17	18	29	-	2047
Ch1	-	17	17	8	+	1125	Ch1	-	17	18	30	+	175, 615, 843, 1071
Ch1	-	17	17	10	+	272, 885, 1023	Ch1	-	17	18	33	+	2047

Ch1	–	17	18	34	+	355
Ch1	–	17	18	35	+	320
Ch1	–	17	18	36	–	448
Ch1	–	17	19	18	–	2047
Ch1	–	18	1	–	3	230
Ch1	–	18	1	3	+	378
Ch1	–	18	1	–	18	1096
Ch1	–	18	1	–	19	1023
Ch1	–	18	1	26	–	230, 378
Ch1	–	18	1	–	27	230, 378
Ch1	–	18	1	–	28	230, 378
Ch1	–	18	1	–	29	230, 378
Ch1	–	18	1	–	30	230, 378
Ch1	–	18	7	–	3	230
Ch1	–	18	7	26	–	230
Ch1	–	18	7	–	27	230
Ch1	–	18	7	–	28	230
Ch1	–	18	7	–	29	230
Ch1	–	18	7	–	30	230
Ch1	–	18	9	7	+	435
Ch1	–	18	13	3	+	103, 193
Ch1	–	18	13	6	–	781
Ch1	–	18	13	10	+	320
Ch1	–	18	14	1	–	435
Ch1	–	18	14	2	–	259
Ch1	–	18	14	3	–	355
Ch1	–	18	14	4	–	435
Ch1	–	18	14	5	–	282
Ch1	–	18	14	–	6	282
Ch1	–	18	14	11	–	424
Ch1	–	18	14	12	–	408
Ch1	–	18	14	14	+	449
Ch1	–	18	14	17	–	499
Ch1	–	18	14	21	+	635
Ch1	–	18	14	24	+	378
Ch1	–	18	14	27	–	381
Ch1	–	18	14	28	–	448
Ch1	–	18	14	33	–	355
Ch1	–	18	14	34	–	397
Ch1	–	18	14	35	+	1129, 1189
Ch1	–	18	14	36	+	435
Ch1	–	18	15	1	+	272, 397
Ch1	–	18	15	2	+	247, 378, 851
Ch1	–	18	15	3	+	255, 747
Ch1	–	18	15	4	–	381
Ch1	–	18	15	4	+	432
Ch1	–	18	15	5	+	843, 929
Ch1	–	18	15	6	+	435
Ch1	–	18	15	8	+	799
Ch1	–	18	15	9	+	272
Ch1	–	18	15	10	+	448, 729, 825, 1127
Ch1	–	18	15	11	–	259, 662
Ch1	–	18	15	12	+	259, 344
Ch1	–	18	15	13	+	600, 629, 1593
Ch1	–	18	15	14	+	193, 225
Ch1	–	18	15	15	–	284
Ch1	–	18	15	17	+	355
Ch1	–	18	15	18	+	243
Ch1	–	18	15	19	+	116
Ch1	–	18	15	20	+	116, 320
Ch1	–	18	15	24	+	320, 448
Ch1	–	18	15	25	+	513, 629
Ch1	–	18	15	26	–	225
Ch1	–	18	15	27	+	499
Ch1	–	18	15	30	–	483
Ch1	–	18	15	30	+	600
Ch1	–	18	15	32	+	378, 405
Ch1	–	18	15	33	+	225, 272
Ch1	–	18	15	34	+	225
Ch1	–	18	15	35	–	499
Ch1	–	18	15	35	+	225, 1593
Ch1	–	18	15	36	+	249, 344

Ch1	-	18	16	5	+	843, 885, 1129	Ch1	-	19	13	8	+		378
Ch1	-	18	16	7	+	885	Ch1	-	19	13	10	-		225
Ch1	-	18	16	8	+	729, 1079, 1127	Ch1	-	19	13	17	-		499
Ch1	MS	18	16	8	+	805	Ch1	-	19	13	18	-		435
Ch1	-	18	16	11	+	1129, 1187	Ch1	-	19	13	19	-		474, 708
Ch1	-	18	16	12	+	878	Ch1	-	19	13	20	-		355
Ch1	-	18	16	13	+	701, 877, 878, 1072	Ch1	-	19	14	-	1		225
Ch1	-	18	16	17	+	284, 729, 1127	Ch1	-	19	14	2	-		499
Ch1	-	18	16	23	+	784	Ch1	-	19	14	3	+		344, 449
Ch1	-	18	16	24	-	728	Ch1	-	19	14	4	+		259
Ch1	-	18	16	27	+	404, 641, 970, 1184	Ch1	-	19	14	5	+		515, 784
Ch1	-	18	16	29	-	641, 644, 684	Ch1	-	19	14	6	+		407
Ch1	-	18	16	30	+	885	Ch1	-	19	14	7	+		885, 1096
Ch1	-	18	16	31	+	378	Ch1	-	19	14	8	+		225
Ch1	-	18	16	32	-	832	Ch1	-	19	14	9	+		355
Ch1	-	18	16	34	+	851	Ch1	-	19	14	10	+		225
Ch1	-	18	16	35	-	832	Ch1	-	19	14	14	+		378, 524
Ch1	-	18	16	36	-	435	Ch1	-	19	14	19	+		225, 455
Ch1	-	19	1	-	12	1096	Ch1	-	19	14	20	+		843
Ch1	-	19	1	13	-	1096	Ch1	-	19	14	23	+		929
Ch1	-	19	3	5	-	255	Ch1	-	19	14	26	+		846
Ch1	-	19	6	27	+	629	Ch1	-	19	14	31	+		225
Ch1	-	19	7	23	+	629	Ch1	-	19	14	32	+		225, 344
Ch1	-	19	9	6	+	435, 851	Ch1	-	19	15	1	+		378, 448
Ch1	-	19	9	19	+	1123	Ch1	-	19	15	2	+		799
Ch1	-	19	11	5	+	885	Ch1	-	19	15	3	+		405, 435
Ch1	-	19	11	8	+	865	Ch1	-	19	15	4	-		197, 208
Ch1	-	19	12	3	-	959	Ch1	-	19	15	5	+		320, 885
Ch1	-	19	12	6	+	378	Ch1	-	19	15	7	-		225
Ch1	-	19	12	7	+	970	Ch1	-	19	15	8	-		948
Ch1	-	19	12	9	+	435	Ch1	-	19	15	10	-		272
Ch1	-	19	12	19	+	513, 829	Ch1	-	19	15	11	+		378, 799
Ch1	-	19	12	27	+	550, 606	Ch1	-	19	15	12	+		249, 474, 829
Ch1	-	19	12	31	+	243	Ch1	-	19	15	13	-		193
Ch1	-	19	13	2	+	405	Ch1	-	19	15	14	-		448
Ch1	-	19	13	4	-	829	Ch1	-	19	15	18	-		385, 513

Ch1	–	19	15	19	+	929
Ch1	–	19	15	21	+	654, 877, 878
Ch1	–	19	15	25	–	829
Ch1	–	19	15	26	+	193
Ch1	–	19	15	27	–	383, 483, 629, 1613
Ch1	–	19	15	28	–	843
Ch1	–	19	15	30	+	407
Ch1	–	19	15	31	+	662, 1147
Ch1	–	19	15	33	+	225
Ch1	–	19	15	34	–	2009
Ch1	–	19	15	36	–	225
Ch1	–	19	16	1	+	284
Ch1	–	19	16	2	+	259
Ch1	–	19	16	4	+	997
Ch1	–	19	16	5	+	226, 251, 284
Ch1	–	19	16	8	+	1129, 1188
Ch1	–	19	16	12	+	1015, 1096
Ch1	–	19	16	13	+	865, 893
Ch1	–	19	16	14	+	203
Ch1	–	19	16	17	–	320
Ch1	–	19	16	23	+	203
Ch1	–	19	16	25	+	1123
Ch1	–	19	16	27	+	378
Ch1	–	19	16	28	+	992
Ch1	–	19	16	29	+	249
Ch1	–	19	16	31	+	449
Ch1	–	19	16	32	+	929
Ch1	–	19	16	33	+	893
Ch1	–	19	16	34	+	893
Ch1	–	19	16	35	+	284, 832
Ch1	–	19	16	36	+	893
Ch1	–	20	4	20	+	1123
Ch1	–	20	4	29	+	929
Ch1	–	20	5	3	+	885
Ch1	–	20	7	–	+	448
Ch1	–	20	7	–	5	193, 201
Ch1	–	20	7	–	6	193, 201
Ch1	–	20	8	1	+	320, 869
Ch1	–	20	8	5	+	1181
Ch1	–	20	8	6	+	479, 662
Ch1	–	20	8	9	+	175, 865
Ch1	–	20	8	10	–	355
Ch1	–	20	8	13	+	851
Ch1	–	20	8	14	–	249
Ch1	–	20	8	17	–	225
Ch1	–	20	8	18	–	272
Ch1	–	20	8	19	–	225
Ch1	–	20	8	24	–	635
Ch1	–	20	8	25	+	1096
Ch1	–	20	8	26	–	513
Ch1	–	20	8	–	31	193, 201
Ch1	–	20	8	–	32	193
Ch1	–	20	8	32	–	201
Ch1	–	20	8	33	–	448
Ch1	–	20	8	35	+	1181
Ch1	–	20	9	5	+	1181
Ch1	–	20	9	6	+	865
Ch1	–	20	9	17	+	839, 997
Ch1	–	20	9	18	+	839
Ch1	–	20	9	19	–	479, 832
Ch1	–	20	9	20	+	843
Ch1	–	20	9	30	+	869
Ch1	–	20	10	1	+	580, 992, 1123
Ch1	–	20	10	3	+	513
Ch1	–	20	10	4	+	499
Ch1	–	20	10	5	+	843, 929
Ch1	–	20	10	6	+	320
Ch1	–	20	10	7	+	760
Ch1	–	20	10	8	+	929
Ch1	–	20	10	10	+	424, 1145
Ch1	–	20	10	11	+	822
Ch1	MS	20	10	11	+	775

Ch1	-	20	10	12	+	822	Ch1	-	20	12	19	+	1095, 1145
Ch1	-	20	10	17	+	432	Ch1	-	20	12	20	+	1023, 1168
Ch1	-	20	10	18	+	272, 851	Ch1	-	20	12	22	+	280
Ch1	-	20	10	20	+	243, 448	Ch1	-	20	12	23	+	344
Ch1	-	20	11	1	+	865, 885, 1145	Ch1	-	20	12	24	+	615
Ch1	-	20	11	2	+	1107, 1130, 1167, 1185	Ch1	-	20	12	25	+	272, 435, 770, 829
Ch1	-	20	11	4	+	203	Ch1	-	20	12	26	+	424, 720
Ch1	-	20	11	6	-	1593	Ch1	-	20	12	28	+	635, 851
Ch1	-	20	11	8	-	255	Ch1	-	20	12	29	+	681, 997, 1115
Ch1	-	20	11	12	+	499	Ch1	-	20	12	31	+	843, 1663, 2286
Ch1	-	20	11	13	-	448	Ch1	-	20	12	32	+	851
Ch1	-	20	11	17	+	843, 851	Ch1	-	20	12	34	+	378
Ch1	-	20	11	18	-	825	Ch1	-	20	12	35	+	770, 929
Ch1	-	20	11	19	+	1168	Ch1	-	20	12	36	+	720
Ch1	-	20	11	20	-	435	Ch1	-	20	13	2	+	789, 806, 983
Ch1	-	20	11	22	+	221	Ch1	-	20	13	3	+	829, 986
Ch1	-	20	11	23	-	564	Ch1	-	20	13	5	-	662
Ch1	-	20	11	27	+	822	Ch1	-	20	13	6	+	893
Ch1	-	20	11	30	+	499, 948, 1095	Ch1	-	20	13	7	+	885, 1123
Ch1	-	20	11	31	+	499, 1095	Ch1	-	20	13	8	+	225
Ch1	-	20	11	32	+	499, 513, 843, 1095	Ch1	-	20	13	10	-	822
Ch1	-	20	11	33	+	550, 606	Ch1	-	20	13	12	+	893
Ch1	-	20	11	34	-	781	Ch1	-	20	13	13	+	378
Ch1	-	20	11	35	-	255	Ch1	-	20	13	14	-	408
Ch1	-	20	11	36	-	775	Ch1	-	20	13	17	-	513
Ch1	-	20	12	1	+	225, 513	Ch1	-	20	13	18	-	315
Ch1	-	20	12	3	+	197, 208	Ch1	-	20	13	23	-	635
Ch1	-	20	12	4	+	197, 208	Ch1	-	20	13	25	+	408
Ch1	-	20	12	5	+	225, 654, 948, 970, 1060	Ch1	-	20	13	27	+	408
Ch1	-	20	12	8	+	280, 681, 843 893, 997, 1125	Ch1	-	20	13	28	-	986
							Ch1	-	20	13	29	-	784
Ch1	-	20	12	11	+	348, 435	Ch1	-	20	13	30	+	760
Ch1	-	20	12	12	-	35	Ch1	-	20	13	32	-	479
Ch1	-	20	12	13	+	378, 448	Ch1	-	20	13	32	+	460, 784
Ch1	-	20	12	14	+	208, 209, 348 529, 712, 986	Ch1	-	20	13	33	-	467, 490, 806
Ch1	-	20	12	18	+	654, 781, 970, 1060	Ch1	-	20	13	34	-	210

Ch1	-	20	13	35	+	460		
Ch1	-	20	13	36	-	747		
Ch1	-	20	14	2	+	378, 789		
Ch1	-	20	14	3	+	432		
Ch1	-	20	14	4	+	775		
Ch1	-	20	14	6	+	1123		
Ch1	-	20	14	7	+	320		
Ch1	-	20	14	8	-	287		
Ch1	-	20	14	10	+	435		
Ch1	-	20	14	11	+	255, 448		
Ch1	-	20	14	12	+	193, 397, 1593		
Ch1	-	20	14	13	+	378		
Ch1	-	20	14	20	+	869		
Ch1	-	20	14	26	+	381		
Ch1	-	20	14	28	+	843, 846, 1006		
Ch1	-	20	14	29	+	662, 869		
Ch1	-	20	14	30	+	1006		
Ch1	-	20	14	32	+	747		
Ch1	-	20	14	33	+	869		
Ch1	-	20	14	34	+	1015, 1016, 1063, 1101		
Ch1	WS	20	14	34	+	784		
Ch1	-	20	14	35	+	829		
Ch1	-	20	14	36	+	449		
Ch1	-	20	15	4	+	789		
Ch1	-	20	15	5	+	287, 843		
Ch1	-	20	15	6	+	287		
Ch1	-	20	15	7	+	264		
Ch1	-	20	15	8	+	264		
Ch1	-	20	15	10	+	615		
Ch1	-	20	15	13	-	712		
Ch1	-	20	15	18	+	1092, 1159, 1160		
Ch1	-	20	15	20	+	970		
Ch1	-	20	15	24	+	378		
Ch1	-	20	15	26	+	1006		
Ch1	-	20	15	27	+	610		
Ch1	-	20	15	30	+	885		

Ch1	-	20	15	32	+			822
Ch1	-	20	15	33	+			424
Ch1	-	20	15	34	-			243
Ch1	-	20	15	35	+		344, 1181	
Ch1	-	20	18	1	+			1123
Ch1	-	20	30	12	+			843
Ch1	-	21	all	-	-		11, 12	
Ch1	-	21	1	9	+			992
Ch1	-	21	1	-	11			929
Ch1	-	21	1	13	-			929
Ch1	-	21	1	-	14			869
Ch1	LS	21	2	8	+			843
Ch1	-	21	2	-	19			378
Ch1	-	21	2	-	20			378
Ch1	-	21	3	17	+			635
Ch1	-	21	3	19	-		263, 275, 280	
Ch1	LS	21	3	31	19			280
Ch1	MS	21	3	-	31			1181
Ch1	LS	21	3	32	-		280, 1181	
Ch1	MS	21	4	23	-			1129
Ch1	-	21	5	-	6			822
Ch1	-	21	5	23	+			665
Ch1	-	21	5	26	+			513
Ch1	-	21	5	27	+			843
Ch1	-	21	5	30	+			885
Ch1	-	21	5	31	+			806
Ch1	-	21	5	33	+		665, 893	
Ch1	-	21	7	2	-			225
Ch1	-	21	7	-	3			225
Ch1	-	21	7	-	4			225
Ch1	-	21	7	5	-			36
Ch1	-	21	7	6	-			36
Ch1	-	21	7	7	-			36
Ch1	-	21	7	9	-			255
Ch1	-	21	7	10	-			255
Ch1	-	21	7	-	11			255

Ch1	–	21	7	–	12	255
Ch1	–	21	7	–	17	193, 201
Ch1	–	21	8	5	–	405
Ch1	WS	21	8	6	–	408
Ch1	WS	21	8	7	–	225
Ch1	–	21	8	21	+	233
Ch1	–	21	8	24	+	893
Ch1	–	21	8	25	+	615, 869
Ch1	–	21	8	26	+	378
Ch1	–	21	8	27	–	708
Ch1	–	21	8	–	28	708
Ch1	–	21	8	–	29	708
Ch1	–	21	8	–	30	424
Ch1	–	21	8	–	31	424
Ch1	MS	21	9	1	–	781
Ch1	MS	21	9	3	+	1096
Ch1	WS	21	9	3	+	885
Ch1	MS	21	9	5	+	1145
Ch1	WS	21	9	5	–	635
Ch1	WS	21	9	6	+	378
Ch1	MS	21	9	8	–	259
Ch1	MS	21	9	8	+	992
Ch1	WS	21	9	8	–	225
Ch1	MS	21	9	10	+	1123
Ch1	MS	21	9	11	+	865
Ch1	MS	21	9	12	+	344, 869
Ch1	WS	21	9	12	–	272
Ch1	MS	21	9	13	+	865, 893
Ch1	MS	21	9	14	–	662
Ch1	WS	21	9	14	–	629
Ch1	WS	21	9	17	–	600
Ch1	–	21	9	19	–	24
Ch1	WS	21	9	20	–	225
Ch1	WS	21	9	21	–	997
Ch1	MS	21	9	24	+	865, 885, 1181
Ch1	–	21	9	25	+	255
Ch1	MS	21	9	25	+	885
Ch1	WS	21	9	25	+	629
Ch1	MS	21	9	26	+	843
Ch1	WS	21	9	27	–	540
Ch1	–	21	9	28	+	1538
Ch1	MS	21	9	28	+	243, 435
Ch1	WS	21	9	28	–	885
Ch1	–	21	9	29	+	1091
Ch1	MS	21	9	29	+	738, 1138
Ch1	WS	21	9	30	–	1001
Ch1	MS	21	9	31	+	775, 1063
Ch1	–	21	9	32	+	320
Ch1	MS	21	9	32	+	405
Ch1	–	21	9	33	+	103
Ch1	MS	21	9	33	+	832, 992, 1006 1024, 1063, 1115
Ch1	WS	21	9	33	+	225
Ch1	WS	21	9	34	+	424
Ch1	WS	21	9	35	+	1181
Ch1	MS	21	10	1	+	806, 1123
Ch1	MS	21	10	2	+	355, 669, 822, 847
Ch1	WS	21	10	3	+	316, 448, 513
Ch1	–	21	10	4	+	116, 193
Ch1	MS	21	10	5	+	378
Ch1	WS	21	10	5	+	701
Ch1	WS	21	10	6	+	784, 983
Ch1	WS	21	10	7	+	435
Ch1	WS	21	10	8	+	225, 272
Ch1	WS	21	10	9	+	355, 424
Ch1	–	21	10	10	+	851
Ch1	–	21	10	11	+	249
Ch1	MS	21	10	11	+	806
Ch1	WS	21	10	11	+	533, 885
Ch1	–	21	10	12	+	1538
Ch1	MS	21	10	12	+	1123
Ch1	MS	21	10	17	+	865
Ch1	MS	21	10	18	–	448

Ch1	WS	21	10	18	+		432	Ch1	–	21	11	12	+	222, 738
Ch1	–	21	10	19	+		851	Ch1	MS	21	11	12	+	264, 832, 939
Ch1	MS	21	10	19	+		929	Ch1	WS	21	11	12	+	968, 1004
Ch1	WS	21	10	19	+		806	Ch1	MS	21	11	13	+	843, 885
Ch1	–	21	10	20	+	249, 851	Ch1	MS	21	11	14	+	885, 1125
Ch1	WS	21	10	23	+	435, 865	Ch1	WS	21	11	14	+	405
Ch1	WS	21	10	24	+		822	Ch1	WS	21	11	17	–	448
Ch1	MS	21	10	26	–		259	Ch1	WS	21	11	17	+	851
Ch1	WS	21	10	26	+		1123	Ch1	–	21	11	18	+	193
Ch1	WS	21	10	27	+		1123	Ch1	MS	21	11	19	+	885, 998, 1073, 1123
Ch1	MS	21	10	28	+		865	Ch1	WS	21	11	–	19	225
Ch1	WS	21	10	28	+		885	Ch1	MS	21	11	20	+	829
Ch1	MS	21	10	29	+	805, 929	Ch1	WS	21	11	20	–	225
Ch1	WS	21	10	29	+	243, 492	Ch1	WS	21	11	22	+	851
Ch1	MS	21	10	30	+		1145	Ch1	–	21	11	23	+	1019
Ch1	WS	21	10	31	+		1096	Ch1	WS	21	11	23	+	499, 1065, 1104, 1184
Ch1	MS	21	10	32	–		407	Ch1	–	21	11	24	+	1019
Ch1	WS	21	10	32	+	408, 499	Ch1	WS	21	11	24	+	1065, 1104
Ch1	WS	21	10	33	+		992	Ch1	WS	21	11	25	+	635
Ch1	MS	21	10	34	+		1123	Ch1	WS	21	11	26	+	243
Ch1	MS	21	10	36	+	781, 822	Ch1	WS	21	11	29	–	415
Ch1	MS	21	11	3	+		513	Ch1	MS	21	11	30	+	924
Ch1	WS	21	11	3	+	775, 929	Ch1	WS	21	11	30	+	846
Ch1	MS	21	11	4	+		1123	Ch1	WS	21	11	31	–	983
Ch1	WS	21	11	5	+		355	Ch1	MS	21	11	33	+	1115
Ch1	–	21	11	6	+		220	Ch1	MS	21	11	34	+	289, 1004
Ch1	MS	21	11	6	+		407	Ch1	WS	21	11	35	+	784, 2319
ChJ	MS	21	11	7	–		382	Ch1	MS	21	11	36	+	448
Ch1	MS	21	11	7	+	418, 524	Ch1	WS	21	19	25	+	629
Ch1	–	21	11	8	+	681, 1088	Ch1	–	22	all	–	–	11, 12
Ch1	WS	21	11	8	+		468	Ch1	WS	22	1	–	1	408
Ch1	–	21	11	9	+	681, 1088	Ch1	WS	22	1	–	2	408
Ch1	WS	21	11	9	+	467, 468	Ch1	WS	22	1	–	3	225
Ch1	MS	21	11	10	–		829	Ch1	WS	22	1	–	4	225
Ch1	WS	21	11	10	–		243	Ch1	–	22	2	–	–	24
Ch1	MS	21	11	11	+	839, 893	Ch1	WS	22	2	1	+	432

Ch1	MS	22	2	3	–		275, 405
Ch1	MS	22	2	–	4		275, 405
Ch1	MS	22	2	–	9		499
Ch1	WS	22	2	–	9		951
Ch1	MS	22	2	10	–		499
Ch1	WS	22	2	–	10		951
Ch1	MS	22	2	15	–		225
Ch1	MS	22	2	–	16		225
Ch1	MS	22	2	–	21		405
Ch1	MS	22	2	23	–		405
Ch1	MS	22	2	24	–		708
Ch1	MS	22	2	26	–		499
Ch1	MS	22	2	–	27		499
Ch1	MS	22	2	34	–		120
Ch1	–	22	2	35	–		120
Ch1	MS	22	2	36	+		407
Ch1	LS	22	3	1	–		781
Ch1	MS	22	3	1	+		1147
Ch1	WS	22	3	1	–		435
Ch1	WS	22	3	–	1		806
Ch1	LS	22	3	–	2		781
Ch1	MS	22	3	2	–		1125
Ch1	WS	22	3	–	2		479
Ch1	–	22	3	3	–		315
Ch1	WS	22	3	–	3		479
Ch1	–	22	3	–	4		315
Ch1	WS	22	3	–	4		479
Ch1	–	22	3	–	5		315
Ch1	WS	22	3	5	–		479
Ch1	WS	22	3	6	–		806
Ch1	–	22	3	–	7		263, 275
Ch1	–	22	3	7	+		280
Ch1	WS	22	3	8	–		760
Ch1	WS	22	3	–	9		760
Ch1	WS	22	3	–	10		885
Ch1	WS	22	3	–	11		885

Ch1	MS	22	3	12	+		784, 869
Ch1	WS	22	3	–	13		1024, 1054
Ch1	–	22	3	14	–		629
Ch1	WS	22	3	14	–		885
Ch1	MS	22	3	15	–		424
Ch1	MS	22	3	16	+		424
Ch1	MS	22	3	22	+		499, 784, 1181
Ch1	MS	22	3	24	+		1932
Ch1	MS	22	3	27	–		929
Ch1	MS	22	3	–	28		929
Ch1	MS	22	4	1	+		424
Ch1	–	22	4	2	–		22
Ch1	MS	22	4	3	+		448
Ch1	WS	22	4	–	3		806
Ch1	–	22	4	4	–		176, 220
Ch1	WS	22	4	–	4		806
Ch1	–	22	4	–	5		220
Ch1	LS	22	4	5	+		1023, 1123
Ch1	WS	22	4	–	5		225
Ch1	LS	22	4	6	+		1125
Ch1	WS	22	4	–	7		983
Ch1	MS	22	4	–	8		435
Ch1	MS	22	4	–	9		435
Ch1	MS	22	4	10	–		435
Ch1	–	22	4	11	+		784
Ch1	MS	22	4	12	+		1181
Ch1	MS	22	4	15	–		259
Ch1	MS	22	4	16	–		259
Ch1	MS	22	4	17	–		259
Ch1	MS	22	4	–	20		1000
Ch1	MS	22	4	21	–		1000
Ch1	MS	22	4	22	–		225
Ch1	MS	22	4	23	–		1129, 1184
Ch1	–	22	4	24	+		320
Ch1	MS	22	4	24	+		635, 747
Ch1	MS	22	4	26	–		448

Ch1	MS	22	4	27	–	225
Ch1	MS	22	4	34	+	893, 1125
Ch1	MS	22	4	35	+	885
Ch1	–	22	5	1	–	7
Ch1	–	22	5	–	1	1306
Ch1	–	22	5	2	–	7
Ch1	–	22	5	–	2	1306
Ch1	–	22	5	3	–	7
Ch1	–	22	5	–	3	1306
Ch1	–	22	5	4	–	7
Ch1	–	22	5	–	4	1306
Ch1	–	22	5	5	–	7
Ch1	–	22	5	–	5	1306
Ch1	–	22	5	6	–	7, 9, 1306
Ch1	–	22	5	7	–	7, 8, 10, 21, 22, 1278, 1306
Ch1	–	22	5	7	+	216
Ch1	–	22	5	–	8	1306
Ch1	–	22	5	9	–	7
Ch1	–	22	5	10	–	7
Ch1	–	22	5	15	–	7
Ch1	–	23	15	23	–	36
Ch1	–	28	1	–	–	1278

CINCINNATI LAND OFFICE DISTRICT

Cin LO, in general,						5
Cin	MR	all	all	1	–	1820
Cin	MR	all	all	11	–	1820
Cin	MR	all	all	16	–	1820
Cin	MR	all	all	26	–	1820
Cin	MR	all	all	29	–	1820
Cin	MR	?	?	35	+	477
Cin	MR	?	?	36	+	477
Cin	–	–	2	8	–	102
Cin	–	–	2	9	+	102
Cin	–	–	2	14	+	102

Cin	–	–	2	23	+	102
Cin	–	–	3	26	+	102
Cin	–	–	3	27	–	102
Cin	–	–	3	35	+	102
Cin	–	–	3	36	+	102
Cin	EML	1	1	1	–	480, 742, 930
Cin	EML	1	1	2	–	495
Cin	EML	1	1	–	2	742
Cin	EML	1	1	4	–	828
Cin	EML	1	1	5	–	191
Cin	EML	1	1	–	5	2441
Cin	WML	1	1	–	5	883
Cin	EML	1	1	6	–	2441
Cin	WML	1	1	6	–	883
Cin	EML	1	1	–	7	2441
Cin	EML	1	1	–	8	2441
Cin	EML	1	1	9	+	918
Cin	EML	1	1	–	11	495
Cin	EML	1	1	–	12	480, 930
Cin	EML	1	1	15	+	130
Cin	EML	1	1	16	–	130
Cin	EML	1	1	17	–	614
Cin	EML	1	1	19	–	299
Cin	EML	1	1	20	–	507
Cin	EML	1	1	21	–	386
Cin	EML	1	1	–	22	386
Cin	EML	1	1	–	27	386
Cin	EML	1	1	–	28	386
Cin	EML	1	1	–	29	507
Cin	EML	1	1	–	30	1148
Cin	EML	1	1	31	–	1148
Cin	EML	1	1	–	31	555
Cin	EML	1	2	2	–	500
Cin	EML	1	2	4	+	485
Cin	EML	1	2	5	–	758
Cin	EML	1	2	10	–	507

Cin EML	1	2	11	-		500	Cin EML	1	4	6	+		593
Cin EML	1	2	17	-		555	Cin EML	1	4	13	+		517
Cin EML	1	2	19	-		310	Cin EML	1	4	25	-		115
Cin EML	1	2	24	-		389	Cin EML	1	4	26	-		523
Cin EML	1	2	-	25		1124	Cin WML	1	4	26	-		500
Cin EML	1	2	28	-		776	Cin WML	1	4	35	-		389
Cin EML	1	2	32	-		191	Cin WML	1	5	-	1		367
Cin EML	1	2	33	+		583	Cin WML	1	5	2	-		379
Cin EML	1	2	36	+		866	Cin EML	1	5	11	+		841
Cin WML	1	2	36	+		503	Cin WML	1	5	13	-		521
Cin WML	1	3	-	1		547	Cin WML	1	5	-	13		451, 489
Cin WML	1	3	-	2		547	Cin EML	1	5	14	+		657
Cin WML	1	3	3	-		547	Cin WML	1	5	14	-		521
Cin EML	1	3	8	+		852	Cin WML	1	5	-	14		451, 489
Cin EML	1	3	9	+		852	Cin WML	1	5	15	-		451, 489, 521
Cin WML	1	3	17	+		1152	Cin WML	1	5	19	-		973
Cin EML	1	3	25	+		538	Cin WML	1	5	19	+		1190
Cin EML	1	3	26	+	560, 657, 711		Cin WML	1	5	20	+		973, 1190
Cin EML	1	3	27	+	271, 590		Cin WML	1	5	21	-		973, 1190, 2441
Cin EML	1	3	34	+		637	Cin WML	1	5	-	22		973, 1190, 2441
Cin EML	1	3	36	+		1067	Cin WML	1	5	-	23		973, 1190, 2441
Cin EML	1	4	2	-		790	Cin EML	1	5	24	+		560, 711
Cin EML	1	4	2	+		845	Cin EML	1	5	25	-		819
Cin EML	1	4	6	+		883	Cin WML	1	5	-	27		560, 748
Cin WML	1	4	8	-		956	Cin WML	1	5	-	28		560, 748
Cin WML	1	4	-	9		956	Cin WML	1	5	29	-		560, 748
Cin WML	1	4	-	10		956	Cin EML	1	6	6	+		1105
Cin EML	1	4	11	+		845	Cin EML	1	6	8	+		614
Cin EML	1	4	12	+		845	Cin EML	1	6	14	+		779
Cin EML	1	4	23	+		996	Cin EML	1	6	17	+		614
Cin WML	1	4	-	25		500	Cin EML	1	6	23	+		523, 779, 1124
Cin EML	1	4	29	+		883	Cin WML	1	6	23	+		845
Cin WML	1	4	34	+		833	Cin EML	1	6	24	+		786
Cin EML	1	4	35	+		685	Cin EML	1	6	25	+		1116
Cin WML	1	4	-	36		389	Cin EML	1	6	26	+		637, 891
Cin EML	1	4	5	+		523	Cin WML	1	6	26	-		845

Cin EML	1	6	27	+		1100, 1116
Cin WML	1	6	27	+		442, 583, 590
Cin EML	1	6	31	+		841
Cin EML	1	6	34	+		565, 889, 1124
Cin EML	1	6	36	+		517, 786
Cin WML	1	6	36	−		367
Cin EML	1	7	1	+		841
Cin WML	1	7	9	+		614
Cin WML	1	7	10	−		389, 758
Cin WML	1	7	11	+		387, 530
Cin WML	1	7	12	+		779, 841
Cin WML	1	7	13	+		498, 590
Cin WML	1	7	14	+		541
Cin EML	1	7	24	+		1042
Cin WML	1	7	24	+		224
Cin EML	1	7	25	+		1046
Cin EML	1	7	29	+		776
Cin EML	1	7	30	+		776
Cin EML	1	7	34	+		1116
Cin EML	1	7	36	+		399
Cin WML	1	8	2	+		442
Cin WML	1	8	4	+		650
Cin EML	1	8	8	+		538, 819, 872
Cin WML	1	8	13	+		823
Cin WML	1	8	18	+		526
Cin WML	1	8	24	+		866
Cin EML	1	8	28	+		883
Cin EML	1	8	29	+		889
Cin WML	1	8	32	−		779
Cin EML	1	8	33	+		800
Cin WML	1	9	24	+		1124
Cin EML	1	9	27	−		823
Cin WML	1	9	27	+		823
Cin WML	1	9	28	+		823
Cin EML	1	10	1	+		1002
Cin WML	1	10	1	+		1002
Cin WML	1	10	7	+		511
Cin WML	1	10	8	+		511
Cin WML	1	10	12	+		1053
Cin WML	1	10	18	+		577
Cin WML	1	10	24	+		511, 779
Cin WML	1	10	25	+		758
Cin WML	1	11	8	+		883
Cin WML	1	11	24	+		823
Cin WML	1	11	25	+		866
Cin WML	1	11	31	+		841
Cin −	1	11	36	+		883
Cin WML	1	12	6	+		748
Cin WML	1	12	8	+		541
Cin WML	1	12	17	+		758
Cin WML	1	12	18	+		786
Cin WML	1	12	19	+		526, 841
Cin WML	1	12	36	+		601
Cin WML	1	13	5	+		889
Cin WML	1	13	12	+		1116
Cin WML	1	13	14	+		841
Cin WML	1	13	17	+		786
Cin EML	1	13	18	+		786
Cin WML	1	13	18	+		503, 889
Cin WML	1	13	19	+		845
Cin WML	1	13	30	+		653, 841
Cin WML	1	13	35	+		823
Cin WML	1	14	17	+		819
Cin WML	1	14	34	+		763
Cin WML	2	1		−	1	1751, 2492
Cin WML	2	1		−	2	1751, 2492
Cin WML	2	1	3	+		503
Cin EML	2	1		−	6	480, 930
Cin.EML	2	1		−	7	480, 930
Cin EML	2	2		−	3	310
Cin EML	2	2		−	4	310
Cin EML	2	2	5	−		310

Cin	EML	2	2	6	+		883
Cin	EML	2	2	7	−		570
Cin	EML	2	2	8	+		190
Cin	EML	2	2	−	16		446
Cin	EML	2	2	−	17		446
Cin	EML	2	2	−	18		570
Cin	EML	2	2	−	19		389
Cin	EML	2	2	−	30		534, 872
Cin	EML	2	2	31	−		872
Cin	EML	2	2	−	31		534
Cin	EML	2	3	4	−		191
Cin	−	2	3	8	+		812
Cin	EML	2	3	8	+		694
Cin	MR	2	3	11	+		400
Cin	−	2*	3	11	+	(*fractional range)	386, 530
Cin	EML	2	3	−	13		711
Cin	EML	2	3	20	−		115
Cin	EML	2	3	23	+		541
Cin	EML	2	3	24	−		711
Cin	−	2	3	26	+		813
Cin	MR	2	3	26	−		817
Cin	MR	2	3	−	26		1124
Cin	EML	2	3	27	25		191
Cin	EML	2	3	27	26		191
Cin	EML	2	3	27	35		191
Cin	EML	2	3	27	36		191
Cin	EML	2	3	28	−		190
Cin	EML	2	3	29	+		823
Cin	EML	2	3	30	−		601
Cin	EML	2	3	31	−		271
Cin	EML	2	3	32	+		577
Cin	EML	2	4	1	−		480, 650, 833
Cin	EML	2	4	2	+		271, 511
Cin	EML	2	4	3	+		470
Cin	EML	2	4	4	+		711
Cin	EML	2	4	11	+		1124
Cin	EML	2	4	13	+		614
Cin	WML	2	4	13	+		841
Cin	EML	2	4	20	+		1660
Cin	EML	2	4	23	+		159
Cin	WML	2	4	23	+		947
Cin	EML	2	4	24	+		577
Cin	EML	2	4	25	+		191, 823
Cin	EML	2	4	27	+		1020
Cin	EML	2	4	28	+		507, 1677, 2473, 2476
Cin	EML	2	4	29	+		872, 883
Cin	WML	2	4	31	+		852
Cin	EML	2	4	32	−		190
Cin	EML	2	4	33	−		577
Cin	EML	2	4	33	+		159
Cin	EML	2	4	34	+		891
Cin	EML	2	4	35	+		694
Cin	EML	2	4	36	−		586
Cin	EML	2	5	2	+		719, 763
Cin	EML	2	5	3	−		650, 1041
Cin	EML	2	5	4	−		356
Cin	EML	2	5	5	+		719
Cin	EML	2	5	9	−		593
Cin	EML	2	5	10	−		517
Cin	EML	2	5	13	+		541
Cin	EML	2	5	14	−		930
Cin	EML	2	5	19	+		918, 996, 1190
Cin	EML	2	5	23	−		593
Cin	EML	2	5	24	−		748
Cin	EML	2	5	25	−		489, 837
Cin	WML	2	5	26	−		576
Cin	EML	2	5	27	+		823, 941
Cin	EML	2	5	28	−		517
Cin	EML	2	5	29	−		748
Cin	EML	2	5	32	−		470
Cin	EML	2	5	33	−		590
Cin	EML	2	6	6	+		819

Cin	EML	2	6	7	+		819	Cin	WML	2	11	11	+	786, 800
Cin	EML	2	6	10	+		823	Cin	EML	2	11	14	+	685
Cin	WML	2	6	11	+		841	Cin	MR	2	11	14	+	880
Cin	EML	2	6	12	+		748, 1020	Cin	WML	2	11	14	+	907
Cin	EML	2	6	33	+	107, 498, 790, 872		Cin	WML	2	11	16	+	663
Cin	EML	2	6	34	+		790	Cin	WML	2	11	- 16		560
Cin	EML	2	7	11	+		1033	Cin	MR	2	11	19	+	880
Cin	EML	2	7	23	+	507, 556, 1140		Cin	WML	2	11	24	+	779, 930
Cin	EML	2	7	26	+		614	Cin	WML	2	11	25	+	758
Cin	EML	2	7	27	-		614	Cin	WML	2	11	27	+	763
Cin	EML	2	7	35	-		863	Cin	WML	2	11	33	+	833
Cin	WML	2	8	3	+	526, 657		Cin	WML	2	12	13	+	819, 866
Cin	EML	2	8	4	+		889	Cin	WML	2	13	1	+	866
Cin	WML	2	8	4	+	657, 833		Cin	WML	2	13	6	+	1002
Cin	EML	2	8	7	+	473, 841		Cin	WML	2	13	13	+	786
Cin	EML	2	8	9	+		565	Cin	WML	2	13	24	+	845, 947
Cin	EML	2	8	11	+		1124	Cin	WML	2	13	25	+	748, 941
Cin	EML	2	8	12	+		872	Cin	EML	2	15	11	-	730
Cin	EML	2	8	13	+		872	Cin	EML	2	15	- 12		730
Cin	EML	2	8	14	+		1124	Cin	EML	2	15	- 13		730
Cin	EML	2	8	18	+		852	Cin	EML	2	15	- 14		730
Cin	EML	2	8	25	+		889	Cin	WML	3	1	- 5		1865, 1906, 1907
Cin	EML	2	8	27	+		823	Cin	WML	3	1	- 6		1865, 1906, 1907
Cin	EML	2	8	28	+	576, 711		Cin	EML	3	1	- 7		373
Cin	EML	2	8	33	+		1124	Cin	EML	3	1	- 8		373
Cin	WML	2	9	9	+		748	Cin	EML	3	1	- 18		373
Cin	WML	2	9	20	+		819	Cin	Pre	3	1	18	-	425
Cin	WML	2	9	29	+		779	Cin	EML	3	2	1	-	565
Cin	WML	2	9	32	+	685, 930		Cin	EML	3	2	2	-	482, 511
Cin	WML	2	9	33	+	577, 685		Cin	EML	3	2	4	-	444
Cin	WML	2	9	34	+		763	Cin	EML	3	2	5	-	586
Cin	WML	2	10	4	+		866	Cin	EML	3	2	6	-	485
Cin	EML	2	10	9	+		889	Cin	-	3	2	- 7		1422, 2431
Cin	WML	2	10	11	+		523	Cin	EML	3	2	9	-	555, 695
Cin	WML	2	10	12	+		511	Cin	EML	3	2	10	-	889
Cin	WML	2	10	28	+		748	Cin	-	3	2	12	-	1422, 2431

Cin EML	3	2	12	-		800	Cin EML	3	3	14	+	891
Cin -	3	2	-	13	1422, 2431		Cin EML	3	3	17	+	1041
Cin EML	3	2	13	-		941	Cin EML	3	3	18	+	159, 694, 889
Cin -	3	2	14	-	1422, 2431		Cin EML	3	3	19	+	224, 500
Cin EML	3	2	14	-		137	Cin EML	3	3	20	+	257, 511
Cin EML	3	2	-	15		889	Cin EML	3	3	23	+	786
Cin WML	3	2	15	-	1949, 1950, 2509		Cin EML	3	3	24	+	685, 1143
Cin EML	3	2	16	-		470	Cin EML	3	3	25	+	547
Cin -	3	2	-	18	1422, 2431		Cin EML	3	3	27	+	224
Cin EML	3	2	18	+		614	Cin Pre	3	3	27	+	389
Cin EML	3	2	19	-		389	Cin EML	3	3	28	+	257, 446
Cin EML	3	2	20	-		265	Cin EML	3	3	30	+	115, 503
Cin EML	3	2	-	21		470	Cin EML	3	3	31	+	257
Cin EML	3	2	-	22		889	Cin EML	3	3	32	-	507
Cin WML	3	2	-	22	1949, 1950, 2509		Cin EML	3	3	33	-	507
Cin -	3	2	-	23	1422, 2431		Cin EML	3	3	34	+	444
Cin EML	3	2	23	+		137	Cin Pre	3	3	34	+	389
Cin EML	3	2	-	24		941	Cin EML	3	3	35	+	583, 883
Cin EML	3	2	-	27		470	Cin EML	3	3	36	-	204
Cin WML	3	2	-	27	1949, 1950, 2509		Cin EML	3	4	4	+	793
Cin EML	3	2	-	28		470	Cin -	3	4	8	+	810, 841
Cin EML	3	2	-	29		265	Cin EML	3	4	9	+	379
Cin EML	3	2	30	-		265	Cin -	3	4	11	+	809, 814
Cin EML	3	2	-	31		586	Cin EML	3	4	11	+	1116
Cin EML	3	2	32	-		586	Cin MR	3	4	11	+	941, 1124
Cin EML	3	3	1	+	400, 590		Cin EML	3	4	12	+	671, 973
Cin EML	3	3	3	+	530, 889		Cin EML	3	4	13	+	576
Cin EML	3	3	4	+	685, 763, 786		Cin EML	3	4	14	+	852
Cin EML	3	3	5	+	719, 758, 763		Cin EML	3	4	17	+	833
Cin EML	3	3	6	+		663	Cin EML	3	4	20	+	841
Cin EML	3	3	7	+		503	Cin EML	3	4	24	+	583
Cin EML	3	3	8	+	663, 763		Cin -	3	4	26	+	811, 815
Cin EML	3	3	9	+	530, 845		Cin EML	3	4	27	+	1152
Cin EML	3	3	10	+		819	Cin EML	3	4	28	+	538, 828
Cin EML	3	3	11	+	477, 941		Cin EML	3	4	29	+	730, 852
Cin EML	3	3	13	+	819, 828		Cin EML	3	4	30	+	1002

Cin	EML	3	4	31		+	577, 891	Cin	WML	3	10	-	13	841
Cin	EML	3	4	32		+	763, 779, 889	Cin	WML	3	10	-	24	841
Cin	EML	3	4	33		+	593, 823, 889	Cin	EML	4	1	-	4	530
Cin	EML	3	4	34		+	547, 786, 823	Cin	EML	4	1	-	5	530
Cin	-	3	4	35		-	190	Cin	EML	4	1	6	-	530
Cin	EML	3	4	35		+	470, 583	Cin	EML	4	1	7	-	1002
Cin	EML	3	5	2		+	947	Cin	EML	4	1	8	-	480
Cin	EML	3	5	3		+	1041	Cin	EML	4	1	8	+	999
Cin	EML	3	5	9		+	819	Cin	EML	4	1	-	9	480, 999
Cin	EML	3	5	10		+	776	Cin	EML	4	1	-	16	480, 999
Cin	-	3	5	12		+	168	Cin	EML	4	1	-	17	480, 999
Cin	EML	3	5	14		+	1002	Cin	EML	4	1	18	-	480
Cin	EML	3	5	15		+	804	Cin	EML	4	1	18	+	999
Cin	EML	3	5	17		+	773, 1057	Cin	EML	4	1	-	19	480, 999
Cin	EML	3	5	18		+	565	Cin	EML	4	2	1	-	341, 353
Cin	EML	3	5	22		-	804	Cin	Pre	4	2	1	+	423
Cin	EML	3	5	27		+	779	Cin	EML	4	2	2	-	828, 907
Cin	EML	3	5	29		+	819	Cin	Pre	4	2	2	+	367, 544
Cin	EML	3	5	33		+	1136	Cin	Pre	4	2	5	+	930
Cin	EML	3	5	34		+	941	Cin	EML	4	2	6	-	507
Cin	EML	3	5	35		+	511, 889	Cin	EML	4	2	7	-	531, 1041
Cin	EML	3	5	36		+	872	Cin	Pre	4	2	7	+	389
Cin	EML	3	6	3		-	190	Cin	MR	4	2	8	-	866
Cin	EML	3	6	8		+	872	Cin	MR	4	2	8	+	614, 930
Cin	EML	3	6	10		-	271, 1603	Cin	Pre	4	2	9	+	372
Cin	WML	3	6	10		-	2460	Cin	-	4	2	10	+	143
Cin	EML	3	6	23		+	889	Cin	EML	4	2	10	+	994
Cin	EML	3	6	27		-	790	Cin	Pre	4	2	10	+	367, 372
Cin	EML	3	6	28		+	994, 1020	Cin	EML	4	2	11	-	224
Cin	EML	3	6	31		+	500, 833, 883	Cin	MR	4	2	11	+	1124
Cin	EML	3	6	33		+	1126	Cin	EML	4	2	-	12	341, 353
Cin	EML	3	6	34		-	650	Cin	EML	4	2	-	13	341, 353
Cin	EML	3	7	26		+	1033	Cin	EML	4	2	-	14	224
Cin	EML	3	7	27		+	872	Cin	Pre	4	2	14	+	372
Cin	EML	3	7	28		+	500	Cin	Pre	4	2	15	+	372
Cin	EML	3	7	34		+	1002, 1116	Cin	Pre	4	2	17	+	754

Cin	Pre	4	2	18		+	367	Cin	Pre	4	3	23		+	367
Cin	EML	4	2	19		−	1143	Cin	EML	4	3	24		+	538, 841
Cin	EML	4	2	21		−	356	Cin	−	4	3	25		+	159
Cin	EML	4	2	−	22		356	Cin	EML	4	3	25		+	833, 1008
Cin	Pre	4	2	22		+	444	Cin	MR	4	3	25		+	912
Cin	EML	4	2	−	27		841	Cin	−	4	3	26		+	823
Cin	EML	4	2	−	28		841	Cin	MR	4	3	26		+	400, 872
Cin	Pre	4	2	28		+	367	Cin	Pre	4	3	27		+	544
Cin	EML	4	2	29		−	841	Cin	EML	4	3	28		+	1020
Cin	EML	4	2	31		−	653, 1093	Cin	Pre	4	3	28		−	288
Cin	EML	4	2	−	32		653, 1093	Cin	Pre	4	3	28		+	990
Cin	EML	4	2	−	33		653, 1093	Cin	EML	4	3	29		+	442
Cin	EML	4	3	1		+	446	Cin	Pre	4	3	30		−	386, 544
Cin	EML	4	3	2		+	1152	Cin	EML	4	3	31		+	819, 883
Cin	Pre	4	3	2		+	837	Cin	Pre	4	3	33		+	793
Cin	EML	4	3	4		+	852	Cin	Pre	4	3	34		+	544, 1002
Cin	MR	4	3	4		+	1116	Cin	−	4	3	35		−	190
Cin	Pre	4	3	4		+	793	Cin	−	4	3	35		+	168
Cin	EML	4	3	5		+	1002, 1053	Cin	Pre	4	3	35		+	409
Cin	Pre	4	3	6		+	389, 793	Cin	EML	4	3	36		+	379
Cin	EML	4	3	7		+	866, 941	Cin	EML	4	4	1		−	650
Cin	Pre	4	3	7		+	367, 740	Cin	MR	4	4	−	1		996
Cin	EML	4	3	8		+	1053	Cin	MR	4	4	2		−	379
Cin	MR	4	3	8		+	159, 941, 1008, 1076	Cin	EML	4	4	5		−	804
Cin	Pre	4	3	10		+	793	Cin	Pre	4	4	−	6		191, 409
Cin	EML	4	3	11		+	446, 1105	Cin	Pre	4	4	6		+	409
Cin	MR	4	3	11		+	637	Cin	MR	4	4	−	8		379
Cin	EML	4	3	12		+	586, 823	Cin	MR	4	4	−	11		930
Cin	Pre	4	3	12		+	590	Cin	−	4	4	13		+	981
Cin	EML	4	3	13		+	130, 379	Cin	−	4	4	14		+	978
Cin	EML	4	3	14		+	547	Cin	EML	4	4	14		+	823
Cin	Pre	4	3	15		+	372	Cin	Pre	4	4	15		+	367
Cin	EML	4	3	17		+	694, 758	Cin	Pre	4	4	17		−	544
Cin	EML	4	3	18		+	800	Cin	Pre	4	4	18		−	544
Cin	EML	4	3	20		+	576, 1076	Cin	Pre	4	4	21		+	544
Cin	−	4	3	22		−	58	Cin	Pre	4	4	22		+	367

Cin EML	4	4	23	+	833, 852	
Cin Pre	4	4	23	-	604	
Cin Pre	4	4	23	+	367	
Cin Pre	4	4	24	+	353, 495	
Cin EML	4	4	25	+	883	
Cin Pre	4	4	25	+	544	
Cin EML	4	4	26	-	833	
Cin EML	4	4	27	-	819	
Cin Pre	4	4	27	+	191, 367, 423, 1681, 2478	
Cin -	4	4	28	+	290	
Cin EML	4	4	28	-	1041	
Cin Pre	4	4	28	+	353, 837	
Cin EML	4	4	29	+	776	
Cin MR	4	4	29	+	837	
Cin EML	4	4	30	+	1076	
Cin Pre	4	4	30	+	353, 367	
Cin Pre	4	4	31	+	353	
Cin -	4	4	32	-	97, 117	
Cin -	4	4	33	-	97, 117	
Cin EML	4	4	33	-	503	
Cin EML	4	4	34	-	716	
Cin Pre	4	4	34	+	367	
Cin -	4	4	35	+	168	
Cin MR	4	4	35	-	996	
Cin Pre	4	4	35	-	1591	
Cin EML	4	4	36	-	523	
Cin EML	4	5	11	+	852	
Cin EML	4	5	13	+	994	
Cin Pre	4	5	17	+	1152	
Cin EML	4	5	26	+	763	
Cin EML	4	5	36	+	657	
Cin EML	4	6	33	+	748	
Cin EML	4	7	1	+	883	
Cin EML	4	9	13	+	1053	
Cin EML	4	9	26	+	1105	
Cin -	5	1	-	-	58	

Cin EML	5	1	-	3	191
Cin EML	5	1	-	4	191
Cin EML	5	1	5	-	131
Cin EML	5	1	6	-	565
Cin EML	5	1	-	7	565
Cin EML	5	1	8	+	131
Cin EML	5	2	-	2	590
Cin EML	5	2	-	10	1008
Cin EML	5	2	-	22	446
Cin EML	5	2	-	23	446
Cin Pre	5	2	-	23	409
Cin Pre	5	2	-	31	191
Cin Pre	5	2	-	32	819
Cin EML	5	2	-	33	191
Cin EML	5	2	-	34	191
Cin Pre	5	2	-	35	819
Cin -	5	2	1	-	53
Cin Pre	5	2	1	+	551, 609
Cin EML	5	2	3	-	590
Cin -	5	2	4	+	217
Cin EML	5	2	4	-	841
Cin Pre	5	2	4	+	353, 1633, 2467
Cin -	5	2	5	+	217
Cin EML	5	2	5	-	776
Cin EML	5	2	6	-	497, 790
Cin EML	5	2	7	-	1041
Cin Pre	5	2	7	+	372
Cin EML	5	2	8	-	446
Cin MR	5	2	8	+	159, 941, 1116, 1169
Cin EML	5	2	9	-	1008
Cin -	5	2	10	+	144
Cin -	5	2	11	+	162
Cin MR	5	2	11	+	1116
Cin Pre	5	2	12	+	734
Cin Pre	5	2	13	-	409
Cin Pre	5	2	14	+	409

Cin EML	5	2	15	+		130	Cin EML	5	3	9	-			833
Cin Pre	5	2	15	+		353	Cin Pre	5	3	9	+		353, 367	
Cin EML	5	2	16	-		130	Cin EML	5	3	10	-			694
Cin -	5	2	17	-		2396	Cin Pre	5	3	10	-			367
Cin Pre	5	2	17	-	1178, 1286		Cin EML	5	3	11	-			841
Cin EML	5	2	18	-		477	Cin MR	5	3	11	+		912, 941	
Cin MR	5	2	18	+		996	Cin EML	5	3	12	-			823
Cin Pre	5	2	18	+		837	Cin EML	5	3	14	-			446
Cin EML	5	2	19	-		446	Cin EML	5	3	14	+			162
Cin EML	5	2	20	-	165, 166, 185		Cin Pre	5	3	15	+			544
Cin EML	5	2	21	-		446	Cin EML	5	3	17	-			271
Cin Pre	5	2	23	+		930	Cin MR*	5	3	17	-	(*Symmes Grant)	2164	
Cin Pre	5	2	25	+		544	Cin EML	5	3	18	+			1002
Cin Pre	5	2	27	+		409	Cin EML	5	3	19	-			257
Cin EML	5	2	28	+		190	Cin -	5	3	19	+			544
Cin EML	5	2	29	-		446	Cin Pre	5	3	19	+			389
Cin MR	5	2	30	-		379	Cin -	5	3	20	+			544
Cin Pre	5	2	31	+		409	Cin EML	5	3	20	-			523
Cin EML	5	2	32	-		130	Cin Pre	5	3	20	+			372
Cin EML	5	2	33	-		2448	Cin -	5	3	22	+			217
Cin WML	5	2	33	-		1526	Cin EML	5	3	22	+			1042
Cin Pre	5	2	36	-		819	Cin MR*	5	3	23	-	(*Symmes Grant)	2164	
Cin Pre	5	2	36	+		353	Cin Pre	5	3	24	+		191, 367	
Cin EML	5	3	1	-		833	Cin EML	5	3	-	25			257
Cin Pre	5	3	1	+	191, 353, 409		Cin Pre	5	3	25	+		367, 480	
Cin EML	5	3	4	-		570	Cin EML	5	3	26	-			257
Cin Pre	5	3	4	+		367	Cin EML	5	3	27	-			565
Cin -	5	3	5	+		553	Cin MR	5	3	27	+			996
Cin EML	5	3	5	+	570, 841, 859, 1020		Cin EML	5	3	28	-			523
Cin MR*	5	3	5	-	(*Symmes Grant) 2164		Cin Pre	5	3	28	+		367, 688, 1891	
Cin EML	5	3	6	+		883	Cin EML	5	3	29	-			609
Cin Pre	5	3	6	-		367	Cin MR	5	3	29	+			159
Cin Pre	5	3	6	+	257, 409		Cin -	5	3	30	-			111
Cin EML	5	3	7	-		541	Cin -	5	3	30	+			217
Cin EML	5	3	8	-		446	Cin EML	5	3	30	-			614
Cin MR	5	3	8	+	889, 1108, 1116		Cin EML	5	3	30	+			463

Cin EML	5	3	31	+		730
Cin EML	5	3	32	-		442
Cin Pre	5	3	32	+		191
Cin EML	5	3	33	-		583
Cin Pre	5	3	33	+		367
Cin EML	5	3	34	-		485
Cin Pre	5	3	34	+		353
Cin EML	5	3	- 35			485
Cin MR*	5	3	35	-	(*Symmes Grant)	2164
Cin EML	5	3	- 36			485
Cin MR*	5	3	36	-	(*Symmes Grant)	2164
Cin EML	5	4	5	+		819, 828
Cin EML	5	4	7	+		866
Cin EML	5	4	9	-		964
Cin EML	5	4	11	-		891
Cin EML	5	4	12	-		956
Cin EML	5	4	13	+		614
Cin EML	5	4	15	+		804
Cin EML	5	4	17	-		130
Cin MR*	5	4	- 17		(*Symmes Grant)	2164
Cin EML	5	4	18	+		159, 841
Cin -	5	4	- 18			1624, 2465
Cin EML	5	4	19	+		159, 1076
Cin EML	5	4	20	+	577, 866, 973, 975, 1044	
Cin MR	5	4	- 21			996
Cin Pre	5	4	- 21			1624, 2465
Cin EML	5	4	23	-		511
Cin MR*	5	4	23	-	(*Symmes Grant)	2164
Cin -	5	4	- 24			1624, 2465
Cin EML	5	4	24	-		590
Cin Pre	5	4	24	+		367
Cin EML	5	4	25	-		793
Cin MR	5	4	- 26			883
Cin EML	5	4	27	+	570, 590, 841	
Cin EML	5	4	28	+		883
Cin Pre	5	4	- 31			191

Cin -	5	4	32	+		556
Cin EML	5	4	32	+		828
Cin EML	5	4	33	-		534, 941
Cin EML	5	4	34	-		601
Cin MR*	5	4	35	-	(*Symmes Grant)	2164
Cin Pre	5	4	36	+		312, 367
Cin EML	5	5	1	+		1116
Cin EML	5	5	2	+		131, 488
Cin EML	5	5	3	+		500, 541
Cin EML	5	5	4	+		379, 446
Cin EML	5	5	5	+		500, 541
Cin EML	5	5	8	+		841
Cin EML	5	5	9	+		480, 1152
Cin EML	5	5	10	+		763
Cin EML	5	5	11	+		1124
Cin EML	5	5	13	+		872
Cin EML	5	5	20	+		1116
Cin EML	5	5	23	+		500
Cin EML	5	5	24	+		500, 833
Cin EML	5	5	25	+		271
Cin EML	5	5	28	+	350, 471, 508	
Cin EML	5	5	30	-		350
Cin EML	5	5	30	+		471
Cin EML	5	5	33	-		565
Cin EML	5	5	34	-		956
Cin EML	5	5	36	+		889
Cin EML	5	6	7	+		841
Cin EML	5	6	17	-		224
Cin EML	5	6	31	-	377, 560, 1012	
Cin EML	5	6	32	+		931
Cin EML	5	6	33	-		271
Cin EML	5	7	1	+		507
Cin EML	5	7	17	+		1116
Cin EML	5	7	19	+		224
Cin EML	5	7	20	+		1124
Cin EML	5	7	25	+		819

Cin EML	5	7	31	+	565	Cin MR	6	2	8	+		889, 1020
Cin EML	5	7	32	+	758, 841	Cin MR	6	2	9	+		996
Cin EML	5	8	1	+	1155, 1156	Cin Pre	6	2	9	+		981
Cin EML	5	8	20	+	941	Cin EML	6	2	11	−		528
Cin EML	5	8	31	+	657	Cin MR	6	2	11	+		1103
Cin EML	5	8	36	+	507	Cin EML	6	2	−	12	528
Cin EML	5	9	2	+	889	Cin Pre	6	2	12	−		1150
Cin EML	5	9	3	+	565	Cin Pre	6	2	12	+		353
Cin Pre	6	1	3	+	372	Cin EML	6	2	−	13	528
Cin Pre	6	1	4	−	372	Cin EML	6	2	−	14	528
Cin MR	6	1	6	−	478	Cin Pre	6	2	14	−		409
Cin MR	6	1	−	6	1008	Cin EML	6	2	15	−		528
Cin EML	6	1	7	−	1008	Cin EML	6	2	18	+		841
Cin EML	6	1	−	8	1008	Cin Pre	6	2	18	+		372
Cin Pre	6	1	9	+	372	Cin EML	6	2	19	+		841, 1116, 1124
Cin −	6	1	14	+	217	Cin MR	6	2	23	+		996
Cin −	6	1	15	−	217	Cin Pre	6	2	23	+		577
Cin Pre	6	1	15	−	1556, 2454	Cin Pre	6	2	25	+		191
Cin MR	6	1	20	+	837, 1076	Cin MR	6	2	26	+		1002, 1020, 1116
Cin −	6	1	25	+	981	Cin MR	6	2	29	+		442
Cin −	6	1	−	31	981	Cin −	6	2	30	−		50
Cin Pre	6	1	31	+	556	Cin Pre	6	2	30	+		367
Cin Pre	6	1	35	+	556	Cin EML	6	2	31	−		498
Cin Pre	6	2	1	+	353, 367	Cin EML	6	2	32	−		482, 511
Cin Pre	6	2	2	+	372	Cin EML	6	2	−	33	482, 511
Cin MR	6	2	3	+	889	Cin MR	6	2	35	+		1008
Cin EML	6	2	5	−	779	Cin EML	6	3	−	1	423
Cin MR	6	2	5	+	779, 1008	Cin EML	6	3	−	2	423
Cin Pre	6	2	6	+	353, 1150	Cin EML	6	3	10	+		500
Cin −	6	2	7	+	190	Cin EML	6	3	18	+		786
Cin −	6	2	7	1	190	Cin Pre	6	3	−	27	367
Cin −	6	2	7	2	190	Cin Pre	6	3	−	28	367
Cin −	6	2	7	3	190	Cin EML	6	3	30	+		779
Cin −	6	2	7	4	190	Cin EML	6	3	31	−		568
Cin EML	6	2	7	−	956	Cin Pre	6	3	31	+		544
Cin EML	6	2	8	+	841, 872	Cin Pre	6	3	33	−		367

Cin EML	6	3	34	+		609	Cin Pre	7	2	22	+	544
Cin Pre	6	3	34	–		353	Cin MR	7	2	26	+	779
Cin Pre	6	3	36	+		353, 544	Cin Pre	7	2	27	+	409
Cin EML	6	4	–	24		1124	Cin Pre	7	2	28	+	409
Cin EML	6	4	27	+		889, 1190	Cin MR	7	2	29	+	159
Cin EML	6	4	28	+		973	Cin Pre	7	2	32	+	367
Cin EML	6	5	–	4		577	Cin Pre	7	2	33	+	472, 544
Cin EML	6	5	5	–		577	Cin Pre	7	3	5	+	577
Cin EML	6	5	–	16		819	Cin Pre	7	3	17	+	489, 544
Cin EML	6	5	17	–		819	Cin MR	7	3	18	+	1053
Cin EML	6	5	–	27		1041	Cin Pre	7	3	19	+	793
Cin EML	6	5	29	+		713	Cin Pre	7	3	20	+	477, 1057
Cin EML	6	6	–	6		1076	Cin Pre	7	3	21	+	477
Cin EML	6	6	–	7		1053	Cin –	7	3	22	+	190
Cin EML	6	6	–	18		719	Cin –	7	3	24	–	229
Cin EML	6	6	19	+		590, 658, 719	Cin MR	7	3	26	+	891, 1020
Cin EML	6	6	20	+		719	Cin Pre	7	3	27	+	544
Cin EML	6	6	29	+		190	Cin MR	7	3	29	+	837
Cin EML	6	6	30	+		763, 883, 891	Cin Pre	7	3	30	+	372
Cin EML	6	6	32	+		190	Cin Pre	7	3	31	+	312, 367, 372
Cin EML	6	7	18	+		790	Cin –	7	3	35	–	229
Cin EML	6	7	–	28		1124	Cin Pre	7	3	35	–	232
Cin EML	6	7	31	+		883, 889	Cin Pre	7	4	–	28	577
Cin EML	6	7	–	32		891	Cin Pre	7	4	34	+	544, 577
Cin EML	6	7	33	–		891	Cin MR	7	4	35	+	609, 1124
Cin Pre	7	2	1	–		367	Cin MR	7	4	36	+	1124
Cin Pre	7	2	2	+		191, 353	Cin MR	8	2	5	+	996
Cin Pre	7	2	7	+		353	Cin –	8	2	6	+	978
Cin MR	7	2	8	+		872, 930, 996, 1200	Cin MR	8	2	8	+	930
Cin Pre	7	2	9	+		367, 372	Cin –	8	2	14	+	978
Cin MR	7	2	11	+		159, 889, 1076	Cin –	8	2	15	+	978
Cin Pre	7	2	12	+		191, 544	Cin MR	8	2	17	+	872
Cin Pre	7	2	13	+		883	Cin MR	8	2	30	+	746
Cin Pre	7	2	14	+		191	Cin MR	8	3	3	+	889
Cin Pre	7	2	19	+		367	Cin –	8	3	7	–	229
Cin –	7	2	22	+		444	Cin MR	8	3	8	+	555, 1041

Cin	MR	8	3	9	+		590		
Cin	MR	8	3	10	+		590		
Cin	MR	8	3	26	−		715		
Cin	−	8	4	5	−		229		
Cin	−	8	4	17	−		229		
Cin	Pre	8	4	17	+		837		
Cin	−	8	4	23	−		229		
Cin	MR	8	4	25	−		1190		
Cin	MR	8	4	25	+		875		
Cin	Pre	8	4	25	−		598		
Cin	MR	8	4	26	+		1116		
Cin	Pre	8	4	36	+		353		
Cin	MR	8	5	9	+		657		
Cin	Pre	8	15	14	+		705		
Cin	MR	9	2	13	+		841		
Cin	Pre	9	2	18	+		367, 544		
Cin	MR	9	2	20	+		779		
Cin	MR	9	2	30	+		837		
Cin	Pre	9	3	1	+		367		
Cin	Pre	9	3	2	+		367		
Cin	MR	9	3	8	+		1002		
Cin	Pre	9	3	31	+		389		
Cin	MR	9	4	4	+		583		
Cin	Pre	9	4	6	−		353		
Cin	−	9	4	7	−		229		
Cin	Pre	9	4	21	+		723		
Cin	MR	9	4	23	+		837		
Cin	MR	9	4	27	1 (NW side, Mad River)	996				
Cin	MR	9	5	10	+		1152		
Cin	MR	9	5	13	+		694		
Cin	MR	9	5	19	−		800		
Cin	MR	9	5	30	+		494, 549		
Cin	MR	9	6	18	+		758		
Cin	Pre	9	14	21	+		723		
Cin	Pre	10	1	4	+		444, 544		
Cin	−	10	1	11	−		1511, 2445		

Cin	MR	10	1	−	11		650		
Cin	−	10	1	12	+		978		
Cin	Pre	10	1	18	+		1136		
Cin	Pre	10	2	9	+		793		
Cin	MR	10	2	13	+		577		
Cin	Pre	10	2	25	+		367		
Cin	Pre	10	2	30	+		544		
Cin	Pre	10	2	36	+		544		
Cin	MR	10	3	19	+		941		
Cin	MR	10	3	25	+		614, 786		
Cin	Pre	10	4	4	+		353		
Cin	Pre	10	4	7	+		544		
Cin	Pre	10	4	10	−		353		
Cin	MR	10	4	11	−		941		
Cin	MR	10	5	9	+		918, 953, 1031		
Cin	MR	10	5	25	+		494		
Cin	MR	10	6	7	+		1076		
Cin	MR	11	1	3	+		507		
Cin	MR	11	1	12	+		930		
Cin	Pre	11	1	21	+		793		
Cin	Pre	11	1	−	27		793		
Cin	MR	11	1	−	36		1002		
Cin	MR	11	2	13	+		446		
Cin	MR	11	2	14	−		572		
Cin	MR	11	2	14	+		875, 965		
Cin	MR	11	2	19	+		875, 910, 965		
Cin	MR	11	2	20	+		996		
Cin	Pre	11	2	20	+		544, 819		
Cin	Pre	11	2	21	+		544, 793		
Cin	MR	11	2	27	+		996		
Cin	Pre	11	2	27	+		793		
Cin	MR	11	2	28	+		930		
Cin	MR	11	2	35	+		930		
Cin	MR	11	3	2	+		577		
Cin	MR	11	3	9	+		444		
Cin	MR	11	3	15	+		577		

Cin	MR	11	4	2	+	779
Cin	MR	11	4	8	−	678
Cin	Pre	11	4	8	−	678
Cin	MR	11	4	18	+	507
Cin	MR	11	4	30	+	793
Cin	−	11	10	24	+	482
Cin	MR	12	1	21	+	947, 1173
Cin	MR	12	1	− 24		941
Cin	MR	12	1	− 32		214
Cin	MR	12	3	1	−	638
Cin	MR	12	3	1	+	907
Cin	MR	12	3	8	+	1190
Cin	EML	12	3	36	+	473
Cin	MR	12	3	36	+	473, 637
Cin	EML	12	4	1	−	384
Cin	MR	12	4	1	+	590
Cin	MR	12	4	9	+	694
Cin	MR	12	4	13	−	507
Cin	MR	12	4	13	+	379, 816
Cin	MR	12	4	19	−	790
Cin	MR	12	5	9	+	1190
Cin	MR	12	5	10	+	866
Cin	MR	12	5	18	+	1041
Cin	MR	13	4	7	+	494
Cin	−	15	8	4	−	92
Cin	−	17	16	18	+	571
Cin	−	19	6	12	+	745
Cin	−	21	2	32	+	571

TOWN OF CINCINNATI

Cin	Square 1, lot 10	702
Cin	Square 1, lot 11	702
Cin	Square 1, lot 12	702
Cin	Square 1, lot 16	702
Cin	Square 1, lot 17	702

TOWN OF DAYTON

Cin	Dayton, fraction 8	217
Cin	Dayton, fraction 14	217
Cin	Dayton, fraction 46	217
Cin	Dayton, fraction 51	217
Cin	Dayton, fraction 52	217

EAST PEARL RIVER LAND OFFICE DISTRICT

EPR	[Pre]	−	−	*	−	(*on Tensaw Lake)	743

JEFFERSONVILLE LAND OFFICE DISTRICT

Jef	−	?	1N	3	+	1926
Jef	−	?	4N	3	+	1926
Jef	−	1E	1N	8	+	1194, 1195
Jef	−	3E	6S	− 4		2087, 2090
Jef	−	3E	6S	− 5		2087, 2090
Jef	−	8E	2N	2	+	1009
Jef	−	8E	2N	13	+	1009
Jef	−	9E	1N	3	+	736
Jef	−	9E	1N	8	+	894
Jef	−	9E	1N	− 17		1009
Jef	−	9E	1N	18	−	1009
Jef	−	9E	1N	− 26		1113
Jef	−	9E	1N	− 35		1153
Jef	−	9E	2N	29	+	894, 1113, 1153
Jef	−	9E	2N	32	+	1113
Jef·	−	9E	3N	14	+	1153
Jef	−	9E	4N	3	+	736
Jef	−	10E	4	20	+	1009
Jef	−	11E	4	30	+	894

MARIETTA LAND OFFICE DISTRICT						
Mar LO, in general						6
Mar	-	?	?	19	30	735
Mar	-	2	6	-	+	2191
Mar	-	2	7	-	-	2191, 2299
Mar	-	3	1	-	26	306
Mar	-	3	2	8	-	74
Mar	-	3	2	8	+	118
Mar	-	3	2	9	-	75
Mar	-	3	2	14	-	75
Mar	-	3	2	15	-	75
Mar	-	3	2	36	+	1174
Mar	-	3	3	-	9	1174
Mar	-	3	3	-	10	1174
Mar	-	3	4	-	5	559
Mar	-	3	4	6	+	934
Mar	-	3	4	-	11	559
Mar	-	3	4	14	-	441
Mar	-	3	4	14	+	274
Mar	-	3	4	20	-	592
Mar	-	3	4	27	-	319
Mar	-	3	4	33	-	319
Mar	-	3	6	17	-	2253
Mar	-	3	6	22	-	2253
Mar	-	3	6	23	-	2253
Mar	-	3	6	29	-	2253
Mar	-	4	3	6	+	1174
Mar	-	4	5	4	-	506
Mar	-	4	5	5	+	1040
Mar	-	4	5	23	+	592
Mar	-	4	5	34	+	592
Mar	-	5	1	-	17	934, 1581
Mar	-	5	1	-	18	1581
Mar	-	5	1	-	23	934
Mar	-	5	1	24	-	1581
Mar	-	5	6	4	+	1010, 1154
Mar	-	5	6	10	+	1010, 1040, 1154
Mar	-	5	6	17	+	592
Mar	-	5	6	29	+	818
Mar	-	5	6	33	+	527
Mar	-	5	6	35	+	1040
Mar	-	5	6	36	+	818
Mar	-	6	1	29	-	592
Mar	-	6	7	3	+	895
Mar	-	6	7	12	+	818, 1084, 1154
Mar	-	6	7	18	+	870
Mar	-	6	7	36	+	818
Mar	-	7	2	35	+	895
Mar	-	7	2	36	-	268
Mar	-	7	7	6	+	895
Mar	-	7	7	18	+	592, 870
Mar	-	7	7	36	+	870
Mar	-	8	3	8	-	1543
Mar	-	8	3	16	-	1543
Mar	-	8	4	-	+	1543
Mar	-	8	4	-	16	1543
Mar	-	9	3	8	-	1543
Mar	-	9	3	16	-	1543
Mar	-	9	4	-	16	1543
Mar	-	10	4	8	-	1543
Mar	-	10	4	16	-	1543
Mar	-	10	5	-	16	1543
Mar	-	11	8	8	-	1543
Mar	-	11	8	16	-	1543
Mar	-	11	9	-	+	1543
Mar	-	12	8	8	-	1543
Mar	-	12	8	16	-	1543
Mar	-	12	13	-	3E	935
Mar	-	12	13	14	-	364
Mar	-	12	13	19	-	935, 1425
Mar	-	12	13	30	-	100
Mar	-	12	13	-	30	1425

Mar	–	13	7	8	–		1543		UNITED STATES MILITARY DISTRICT OF OHIO				
Mar	–	13	7	16	–		1543	Mil	–	1	1	3	7	677
Mar	–	13	12	–	–		6	Mil	–	1	1	3	37	677
Mar	–	13	12	4	–		142, 765	Mil	–	1	2	8	1	821
Mar	–	13	12	5	+		142	Mil	–	1	2	22	+	298
Mar	–	13	12	–	5E		765	Mil	–	1	5	8	18	821
Mar	–	13	12	–	5W		765	Mil	–	1	5	8	19	821
Mar	–	13	12	6	+		142	Mil	–	1	5	8	20	821
Mar	–	13	12	–	6W		765	Mil	–	1	5	8	30	821
Mar	–	14	11	8	–		1543	Mil	–	1	5	8	31	821
Mar	–	14	11	16	–		1543	Mil	–	1	5	8	32	821
Mar	–	14	12	12	–		6	Mil	–	1	5	8	33	821
Mar	–	14	16	1	–		31	Mil	–	1	5	8	34	821
Mar	–	14	16	1	+		142	Mil	–	1	5	8	35	821
Mar	–	14	16	–	1		765	Mil	–	1	6	2	5	677
Mar	–	14	16	–	1E	765, 1856, 1857		Mil	–	1	6	2	14	1111
Mar	–	14	16	12	–	6, 142, 765		Mil	–	1	6	11	1	821, 957
Mar	–	14	16	16	–	680, 1857, 1858		Mil	–	1	6	11	2	821, 957
Mar	–	15	8	26	–		1543	Mil	–	1	6	11	3	821, 957
Mar	–	15	9	26	–		1543	Mil	–	1	6	11	4	821, 957
Mar	–	15	10	26	–		1543	Mil	–	1	6	11	5	821, 957
Mar	–	15	11	26	–		1543	Mil	–	1	6	11	6	821, 957
Mar	–	15	12	26	–		1543	Mil	–	1	6	11	7	821, 957
Mar	–	15	13	8	–		1543	Mil	–	1	6	11	8	821, 957
Mar	–	15	13	16	–		1543	Mil	–	1	6	11	9	821, 957
Mar	–	15	13	26	–		1543	Mil	–	1	6	11	10	821, 957
Mar	–	15	14	all	–		227	Mil	–	1	6	11	11	821, 957
Mar	–	15	14	19	–		227	Mil	–	1	6	11	12	821, 957
Mar	–	15	17	29	–		196	Mil	–	1	6	11	13	821, 957
Mar	–	16	8	16	–		1543	Mil	–	1	6	11	14	821, 957
Mar	–	16	9	16	–		1543	Mil	–	1	6	11	15	821, 957
Mar	–	16	10	16	–		1543	Mil	–	1	6	11	16	821, 957
Mar	–	16	11	16	–		1543	Mil	–	1	6	11	17	821, 957
Mar	–	16	12	16	–		1543	Mil	–	1	6	11	18	821, 957
Mar	–	16	13	16	–		1543	Mil	–	1	6	11	19	821, 957
Mar	–	17	13	–	1		2191	Mil	–	1	6	11	20	821, 957

Mil	–	1	6	11	21	821, 957	Mil	–	1	7	10	31		957
Mil	–	1	6	11	22	821, 957	Mil	–	1	7	10	32		957
Mil	–	1	6	11	23	821, 957	Mil	–	1	7	10	33		957
Mil	–	1	6	11	24	821, 957	Mil	–	1	7	10	34		957
Mil	–	1	6	11	25	821, 957	Mil	–	1	7	10	35		957
Mil	–	1	6	11	26	821, 957	Mil	–	1	7	10	36		957
Mil	–	1	6	11	27	821, 957	Mil	–	1	7	10	37		957
Mil	–	1	6	11	28	821, 957	Mil	–	1	7	10	38		957
Mil	–	1	6	11	29	821, 957	Mil	–	1	8	3	–		156
Mil	–	1	6	11	30	821, 957	Mil	–	1	8	3	23		154
Mil	–	1	6	11	31	821, 957	Mil	–	1	8	3	24		154
Mil	–	1	6	11	32	821, 957	Mil	–	1	8	4	16		398
Mil	–	1	6	11	33	821, 957	Mil	–	1	8	4	17		416
Mil	–	1	6	11	34	821, 957	Mil	–	1	8	13	1		957
Mil	–	1	6	11	35	821, 957	Mil	–	1	8	13	2		957
Mil	–	1	6	11	36	821, 957	Mil	–	1	8	13	3		957
Mil	–	1	6	11	37	821, 957	Mil	–	1	8	13	4		957
Mil	–	1	6	11	38	821, 957	Mil	–	1	8	13	5		957
Mil	–	1	6	11	39	821	Mil	–	1	8	13	6		957
Mil	–	1	6	11	40	821, 957	Mil	–	1	8	13	7		957
Mil	–	1	7	10	1	957	Mil	–	1	8	13	8		957
Mil	–	1	7	10	6	957	Mil	–	1	8	13	9		957
Mil	–	1	7	10	7	957	Mil	–	1	8	13	10		957
Mil	–	1	7	10	8	957	Mil	–	1	8	13	11		957
Mil	–	1	7	10	13	957	Mil	–	1	8	13	12		957
Mil	–	1	7	10	16	957	Mil	–	1	8	13	13		957
Mil	–	1	7	10	17	957	Mil	–	1	8	13	14		957
Mil	–	1	7	10	18	957	Mil	–	1	8	13	15		957
Mil	–	1	7	10	19	957	Mil	–	1	8	13	16		957
Mil	–	1	7	10	20	957	Mil	–	1	8	13	17		957
Mil	–	1	7	10	21	957	Mil	–	1	8	13	18		957
Mil	–	1	7	10	22	957	Mil	–	1	8	13	19		957
Mil	–	1	7	10	27	957	Mil	–	1	8	13	20		957
Mil	–	1	7	10	28	957	Mil	–	1	8	13	21		957
Mil	–	1	7	10	29	957	Mil	–	1	8	13	22		957
Mil	–	1	7	10	30	957	Mil	–	1	8	13	23		957

Mil	–	1	8	13	24		957	Mil	–	2	1	10	19	821
Mil	–	1	8	13	25		957	Mil	–	2	1	10	20	821
Mil	–	1	8	13	26		957	Mil	–	2	1	10	21	821
Mil	–	1	8	13	27		957	Mil	–	2	1	10	22	821
Mil	–	1	8	13	28		957	Mil	–	2	1	10	23	821
Mil	–	1	8	13	29		957	Mil	–	2	1	10	24	821
Mil	–	1	8	13	30		957	Mil	–	2	1	10	25	821
Mil	–	1	8	13	31		957	Mil	–	2	1	10	26	821
Mil	–	1	8	13	32		957	Mil	–	2	1	10	27	821
Mil	–	1	8	13	33		957	Mil	–	2	1	10	28	821
Mil	–	1	8	13	34		957	Mil	–	2	1	10	29	821
Mil	–	1	8	13	35		957	Mil	–	2	1	10	30	821
Mil	–	1	8	13	36		957	Mil	–	2	1	10	31	821
Mil	–	1	8	13	37		957	Mil	–	2	1	10	32	821
Mil	–	1	8	13	38		957	Mil	–	2	1	10	33	821
Mil	–	1	8	13	39		957	Mil	–	2	1	10	34	821
Mil	–	1	8	13	40		957	Mil	–	2	1	10	35	821
Mil	–	1	8	14	2		957	Mil	–	2	1	10	36	821
Mil	–	2	1	10	1		821	Mil	–	2	1	10	37	821
Mil	–	2	1	10	2		821	Mil	–	2	1	10	38	821
Mil	–	2	1	10	3		821	Mil	–	2	1	10	39	821
Mil	–	2	1	10	4		821	Mil	–	2	1	10	40	821
Mil	–	2	1	10	5		821	Mil	–	2	2	3	–	73, 96
Mil	–	2	1	10	6		821	Mil	–	2	2	3	2	308, 330
Mil	–	2	1	10	7		821	Mil	–	2	2	3	10	330
Mil	–	2	1	10	8		821	Mil	–	2	3	4	–	70, 73, 93, 94
Mil	–	2	1	10	9		821	Mil	–	2	3	4	3	145
Mil	–	2	1	10	10		821	Mil	–	2	3	4	19	145
Mil	–	2	1	10	11		821	Mil	–	2	3	4	20	145
Mil	–	2	1	10	12		821	Mil	–	2	3	4	21	145
Mil	–	2	1	10	13		821	Mil	–	2	3	4	22	300, 330
Mil	–	2	1	10	14		821	Mil	–	2	3	4	27	300, 330
Mil	–	2	1	10	15		821	Mil	–	2	3	4	28	145
Mil	–	2	1	10	16		821	Mil	–	2	4	7	1	821
Mil	–	2	1	10	17		821	Mil	–	2	4	7	2	821
Mil	–	2	1	10	18		821	Mil	–	2	4	7	3	821

Mil	–	2	4	7	4	821	Mil	–	2	7	4	8	1111
Mil	–	2	4	7	5	821	Mil	–	2	7	4	9	1111
Mil	–	2	4	7	6	821	Mil	–	2	7	4	15	1111
Mil	–	2	4	7	7	821	Mil	–	2	7	4	25	330
Mil	–	2	4	7	8	821	Mil	–	2	7	4	26	330
Mil	–	2	4	7	9	821	Mil	–	2	7	4	27	677
Mil	–	2	4	7	10	821	Mil	–	2	8	4	11	677
Mil	–	2	4	7	11	821	Mil	–	2	8	4	12	677
Mil	–	2	4	7	12	821	Mil	–	2	8	13	13	957
Mil	–	2	4	7	13	821	Mil	–	2	10	2	2	677
Mil	–	2	4	7	14	821	Mil	–	2	10	2	3	677
Mil	–	2	4	7	15	821	Mil	–	2	10	2	4	330
Mil	–	2	4	7	18	821	Mil	–	2	10	2	14	737
Mil	–	2	4	7	19	821	Mil	–	2	10	2	15	1111
Mil	–	2	4	7	20	821	Mil	–	2	10	2	17	677
Mil	–	2	4	7	21	821	Mil	*	2	10	4	–	(*4000-acre tract) 1170
Mil	–	2	4	7	22	821	Mil	–	3	1	1	18	181
Mil	–	2	4	7	23	821	Mil	–	3	1	2	3	145
Mil	–	2	4	7	24	821	Mil	–	3	1	9	4	821
Mil	–	2	4	7	25	821	Mil	–	3	1	9	40	821
Mil	–	2	4	7	26	821	Mil	–	3	1	15	10	821
Mil	–	2	4	7	27	821	Mil	–	3	1	15	13	821
Mil	–	2	4	7	28	821	Mil	–	3	1	15	21	821
Mil	–	2	4	7	29	821	Mil	–	3	1	15	22	821
Mil	–	2	4	7	30	821	Mil	–	3	1	15	23	821
Mil	–	2	4	7	31	821	Mil	–	3	2	–	–	2357
Mil	–	2	4	7	32	821	Mil	–	3	2	2	3	821
Mil	–	2	4	7	33	821	Mil	–	3	2	2	4	821
Mil	–	2	4	7	34	821	Mil	–	3	2	2	11	821
Mil	–	2	4	7	35	821	Mil	–	3	2	2	12	821
Mil	–	2	4	7	36	821	Mil	–	3	4	8	8	821
Mil	–	2	4	7	37	821	Mil	–	3	4	8	13	821
Mil	–	2	5	2	25	1111	Mil	–	3	4	8	14	821
Mil	–	2	6	1	3	149	Mil	–	3	4	8	15	821
Mil	–	2	6	1	4	149	Mil	–	3	4	8	16	821
Mil	–	2	6	1	6	149	Mil	–	3	4	8	17	821

Mil	–	3	4	8	18		821
Mil	–	3	4	8	23		821
Mil	–	3	4	8	24		821
Mil	–	3	4	8	25		821
Mil	–	3	4	8	26		821
Mil	–	3	4	8	27		821
Mil	–	3	4	8	28		821
Mil	–	3	4	8	33		821
Mil	–	3	4	8	34		821
Mil	–	3	4	8	35		821
Mil	–	3	4	8	36		821
Mil	–	3	4	8	37		821
Mil	–	3	4	8	38		821
Mil	–	3	5	1	6		677
Mil	*	3	7	1	–	(*4000-acre tract)	108, 127
Mil	–	3	7	9	2		957
Mil	–	3	7	9	3		957
Mil	–	3	7	9	4		957
Mil	–	3	7	9	5		957
Mil	–	3	7	9	6		957
Mil	–	3	7	9	7		957
Mil	–	3	7	9	8		957
Mil	–	3	7	9	9		957
Mil	–	3	7	9	10		957
Mil	–	3	7	9	11		957
Mil	–	3	7	9	12		957
Mil	–	3	7	9	13		957
Mil	–	3	7	9	14		957
Mil	–	3	7	9	21		957
Mil	–	3	7	9	22		957
Mil	–	3	7	9	23		957
Mil	–	3	7	9	24		957
Mil	–	3	7	9	25		957
Mil	–	3	7	9	27		957
Mil	–	3	7	9	31		957
Mil	–	3	7	9	32		957

Mil	–	3	7	9	33		957
Mil	–	3	7	9	34		957
Mil	*	3	8	4	–	(*4000-acre tract)	108, 127
Mil	–	3	8	4	4		1111
Mil	–	3	8	4	5		1111
Mil	–	3	8	4	6		1111
Mil	–	3	9	11	1		957
Mil	–	3	9	11	2		957
Mil	–	3	9	11	3		957
Mil	–	3	9	11	4		957
Mil	–	3	9	11	5		957
Mil	–	3	9	11	6		957
Mil	–	3	9	11	7		957
Mil	–	3	9	11	8		957
Mil	–	3	9	11	9		957
Mil	–	3	9	11	10		957
Mil	–	3	9	11	11		957
Mil	–	3	9	11	12		957
Mil	–	3	9	11	13		957
Mil	–	3	9	11	14		957
Mil	–	3	10	1	7		937
Mil	–	3	10	1	9		677
Mil	–	3	10	1	12		677
Mil	–	3	10	1	14		677
Mil	–	3	10	1	15		677
Mil	–	3	10	1	16		677
Mil	–	3	10	1	17		677
Mil	–	3	10	1	18		677
Mil	–	3	10	1	19		677
Mil	–	3	10	1	22		677
Mil	–	3	10	1	23		677
Mil	–	3	10	1	24		677
Mil	–	3	10	2	3		677
Mil	–	3	10	2	4		330
Mil	–	3	10	2	5		330
Mil	–	3	10	2	6		532, 677

Mil	–	3	10	2	7			677
Mil	–	3	10	2	8			677
Mil	–	3	10	2	9			677
Mil	–	3	17	1	7			1111
Mil	–	3	17	1	10			1111
Mil	–	4	3	10	2			821
Mil	–	4	3	10	3			821
Mil	–	4	3	10	4			821
Mil	–	4	3	10	5			821
Mil	–	4	3	10	6			821
Mil	–	4	3	10	11			821
Mil	–	4	3	10	12			821
Mil	–	4	3	10	13			821
Mil	–	4	3	10	14			821
Mil	–	4	3	10	15			821
Mil	–	4	3	10	16			821
Mil	–	4	3	10	17			821
Mil	–	4	3	10	18			821
Mil	–	4	3	10	19			821
Mil	–	4	3	10	20			821
Mil	–	4	3	10	30			821
Mil	–	4	3	10	31			821
Mil	–	4	3	10	32			821
Mil	*	4	4	3	–	(*4000-acre tract)		108, 127
Mil	–	4	4	3	6			677
Mil	–	4	4	3	7			677
Mil	–	4	4	3	9			677
Mil	–	4	4	3	10			677
Mil	–	4	4	3	11			677
Mil	–	4	4	3	12			677
Mil	–	4	4	3	21			677
Mil	–	4	4	3	22			677
Mil	–	4	4	3	23			677
Mil	–	4	4	3	24			677
Mil	–	4	4	3	25			677
Mil	–	4	9	11	1			957
Mil	–	4	9	11	2			957
Mil	–	4	9	11	6			957
Mil	–	4	9	11	7			957
Mil	–	4	9	11	8			957
Mil	–	4	9	11	9			957
Mil	–	4	9	11	10			957
Mil	–	4	9	11	11			957
Mil	–	4	9	11	12			957
Mil	–	4	9	11	14			957
Mil	–	4	9	11	15			957
Mil	–	4	9	11	16			957
Mil	–	4	9	11	17			957
Mil	–	4	9	11	18			957
Mil	–	4	9	11	19			957
Mil	–	4	9	11	20			957
Mil	–	4	9	11	21			957
Mil	–	4	9	11	22			957
Mil	*	5	3	3	–	(*4000-acre tract)		108, 127
Mil	–	5	3	3	34			431
Mil	–	5	3	3	35			431
Mil	–	5	3	3	36			431
Mil	*	5	7	1	–	(*4000-acre tract)		108, 127
Mil	*	5	9	3	–	(*4000-acre tract)		108, 127
Mil	*	6	2	1	–	(*4000-acre tract)		108, 127
Mil	–	6	6	2	6			677
Mil	–	6	6	2	7			677
Mil	–	6	6	2	22			751
Mil	–	6	8	3	6			900
Mil	–	6	8	3	7			900
Mil	–	6	8	3	15			900
Mil	–	6	10	3	2			1080
Mil	–	6	10	3	3			1080
Mil	–	6	10	3	4			1080
Mil	*	7	4	2	–	(*4000-acre tract)		108, 127

Mil	–	7	4	2	7	501
Mil	–	7	4	2	8	501
Mil	–	7	4	2	13	501
Mil	–	7	4	2	14	501
Mil	–	7	4	2	15	501
Mil	–	7	4	2	16	501, 677, 1162
Mil	–	7	4	2	17	501, 677, 858
Mil	–	7	4	2	18	501, 1162
Mil	–	7	4	2	23	501
Mil	–	7	4	2	24	501
Mil	–	7	4	2	25	501
Mil	–	7	4	2	26	501
Mil	–	7	4	2	27	501
Mil	–	7	4	2	28	501
Mil	–	7	4	2	33	501
Mil	–	7	4	2	34	501
Mil	–	7	4	2	35	501
Mil	–	7	4	2	36	501
Mil	–	7	4	2	37	501
Mil	–	7	4	2	38	501, 677
Mil	–	7	4	2	39	677
Mil	–	7	4	2	40	677
Mil	–	7	6	1	29	330
Mil	–	7	6	1	30	330
Mil	–	7	6	1	31	330
Mil	–	7	6	1	32	330
Mil	–	7	6	1	33	330
Mil	–	7	6	1	34	330
Mil	–	7	6	1	35	330
Mil	–	7	6	1	36	330
Mil	–	7	7	2	–	737
Mil	–	7	7	2	2	677
Mil	–	7	9	2	25	677
Mil	–	7	9	2	37	677
Mil	–	7	9	2	38	677
Mil	–	7	9	2	39	677

Mil	–	8	2	1	1	501
Mil	–	8	2	1	15	429
Mil	–	8	2	1	17	291
Mil	–	8	2	1	24	330
Mil	–	8	2	1	25	179
Mil	–	8	2	3	1	914, 969
Mil	–	8	2	3	22	677
Mil	–	8	2	3	37	677
Mil	–	8	4	3	3	332, 347
Mil	–	8	4	3	4	332, 347
Mil	–	8	4	3	5	332, 347
Mil	–	8	4	3	6	332, 347
Mil	–	8	4	3	7	677
Mil	–	8	4	3	8	900
Mil	–	8	5	1	21	677, 679
Mil	–	8	5	1	22	677, 679
Mil	*	8	7	3	– (*4000-acre tract)	108, 127
Mil	–	8	9	1	2	677
Mil	–	8	9	1	11	677
Mil	–	8	9	1	12	677
Mil	–	8	9	1	13	677
Mil	–	8	9	1	14	677
Mil	–	8	9	1	15	677
Mil	–	8	9	1	16	677
Mil	–	8	9	1	17	677
Mil	–	8	9	1	18	677
Mil	–	8	9	1	30	761
Mil	–	8	9	1	31	761
Mil	*	8	9	3	– (*4000-acre tract)	108, 127
Mil	–	9	1	–	–	64
Mil	–	9	1	3	23	431
Mil	–	9	1	3	24	431
Mil	–	9	1	3	39	431
Mil	–	9	7	3	16	673, 677
Mil	–	9	7	3	17	938

Mil	–	9	7	3	26		938
Mil	–	9	7	3	28		673, 677
Mil	–	9	7	3	38		673, 677
Mil	–	9	7	3	39		673, 677
Mil	–	9	7	3	40		673, 677
Mil	*	10	1	2	–	(*4000-acre tract)	108, 127
Mil	–	10	3	4	1		677
Mil	–	10	3	4	7		677
Mil	–	10	3	4	8		677
Mil	–	10	3	4	9		677
Mil	–	10	3	4	19		677
Mil	–	10	3	4	21		677
Mil	–	10	3	4	22		677
Mil	–	10	3	4	23		677
Mil	–	10	3	4	27		677
Mil	–	10	3	4	29		677
Mil	–	10	3	4	36		428
Mil	–	10	7	1	2		673, 677
Mil	–	10	7	1	3		673, 677
Mil	–	10	7	1	4		677
Mil	–	10	7	1	14		673, 677
Mil	–	10	7	1	15		673, 677
Mil	–	10	7	1	23		677
Mil	–	10	7	1	25	677 [twice listed as claimed], 677 [shown vacant]	
Mil	–	10	7	1	26	677 [apparently vacant], 677 [claimed]	
Mil	–	10	7	1	39		677
Mil	–	10	7	1	40	677 [twice listed]	
Mil	*	11	6	1	–	(*4000-acre tract)	108, 127
Mil	–	11	6	1	9		1164
Mil	–	11	6	1	22		1146
Mil	–	11	6	1	23		1146
Mil	–	11	6	1	30		1112
Mil	*	11	8	1	–	(*4000-acre tract)	108, 127, 244
Mil	–	11	8	1	6		149
Mil	–	11	8	1	7		149
Mil	–	11	8	1	8		149
Mil	–	11	8	1	9		149
Mil	–	11	8	1	10		149
Mil	–	11	8	1	11		149
Mil	–	11	8	1	22		149
Mil	–	11	8	1	23		149
Mil	–	11	8	1	24		149
Mil	–	11	8	1	25		149
Mil	–	11	8	4	3		928
Mil	–	11	9	4	24		183
Mil	–	11	9	4	25		750
Mil	–	11	9	4	26		750
Mil	–	11	9	4	27		750
Mil	–	11	9	4	28		750
Mil	–	12	2	3	–		239
Mil	*	12	6	4	–	(*4000-acre tract)	1025
Mil	–	13	8	2	10		677
Mil	–	13	8	4	1		276
Mil	–	13	8	4	2		276
Mil	–	13	8	4	3		276
Mil	–	13	8	4	4		276
Mil	–	13	8	4	5		276
Mil	–	13	8	4	26		677
Mil	–	14	2	1	–		491
Mil	–	15	1	–	–		440
Mil	–	15	1	3	1		295
Mil	–	15	1	3	2		295
Mil	–	15	1	3	5		677
Mil	–	15	1	3	6		677
Mil	–	15	1	3	7		303, 330
Mil	–	15	1	3	8		677
Mil	–	15	1	3	9		677
Mil	–	15	1	3	10		899
Mil	–	15	1	3	11		677

Mil	-	15	1	3	12		677
Mil	-	15	1	3	15		295
Mil	-	15	1	3	16		295
Mil	-	15	1	3	17		295
Mil	-	15	1	3	18		295
Mil	-	15	1	3	19		296
Mil	-	15	1	3	20		304, 330
Mil	-	15	1	3	22		899
Mil	-	15	1	3	23		899
Mil	-	15	1	3	24		454
Mil	-	15	1	3	25		453
Mil	-	15	1	3	26		330
Mil	-	15	1	3	31		182
Mil	-	15	1	3	32		182
Mil	-	15	1	3	39		292, 330
Mil	-	15	1	3	40		899
Mil	-	15	2	2	1		677
Mil	-	15	2	2	2		677
Mil	-	15	2	2	11		677
Mil	-	15	2	2	12		677
Mil	-	15	2	2	15		677
Mil	-	15	2	2	16		677
Mil	-	15	2	2	17		677
Mil	-	15	2	2	18		677
Mil	-	15	2	2	20		801
Mil	-	15	7	2	22		677
Mil	-	15	7	2	23		677
Mil	-	15	7	2	30		677
Mil	-	15	7	2	31		677
Mil	*	15	7	3	-	(*4000-acre tract)	108, 127, 177, 178
Mil	-	15	7	4	-		95
Mil	-	15	7	4	5		180
Mil	-	15	7	4	7		252
Mil	-	15	7	4	11		430
Mil	-	15	7	4	12		452
Mil	-	15	7	4	21		430
Mil	-	15	7	4	22		430
Mil	-	15	7	4	28		314, 330
Mil	-	15	7	4	33		314, 330
Mil	-	15	7	4	34		314, 330
Mil	-	15	7	4	35		314, 330
Mil	-	15	7	4	36		314, 330
Mil	-	15	7	4	37		314, 330
Mil	-	15	8	3	9		677
Mil	-	15	8	3	10		677
Mil	-	15	8	3	11		677
Mil	-	15	8	3	12		677
Mil	-	15	8	3	17		677
Mil	-	15	8	3	18		677
Mil	-	15	8	3	19		677
Mil	-	15	8	3	20		677
Mil	-	15	8	4	1		1110
Mil	-	15	8	4	2		677
Mil	-	15	8	4	11		677
Mil	-	15	8	4	12		677
Mil	-	15	8	4	15		677
Mil	-	15	8	4	16		677
Mil	-	15	8	4	22		677
Mil	-	15	8	4	23		677
Mil	-	15	8	4	24		677
Mil	-	15	8	4	25		677
Mil	-	15	8	4	27		677
Mil	-	16	6	1	6		1163
Mil	*	16	7	2	-	(*4000-acre tract)	108, 127
Mil	-	16	7	2	25		677
Mil	-	16	7	2	40		677
Mil	*	16	7	4	-	(*4000-acre tract)	108, 127
Mil	-	16	7	4	1		677
Mil	-	16	7	4	2		677
Mil	-	16	7	4	3		677
Mil	-	16	7	4	4		677

Mil	–	16	7	4	5		677	Mil	–	17	7	2	15	898, 928
Mil	–	16	7	4	6		677	Mil	–	17	7	2	16	898, 928
Mil	–	16	7	4	7		677	Mil	–	17	7	2	17	898, 928
Mil	–	16	7	4	8		677	Mil	–	17	7	2	18	677
Mil	–	16	7	4	16		677	Mil	–	17	7	2	19	677
Mil	–	16	7	4	17		677	Mil	–	17	7	2	20	305, 330
Mil	–	16	7	4	26		1171	Mil	–	17	7	2	21	305, 330
Mil	–	16	7	4	30		677	Mil	–	17	7	2	23	330
Mil	–	16	7	4	31		677	Mil	–	17	7	2	24	330
Mil	–	16	7	4	32		677	Mil	–	17	7	4	19	293
Mil	–	16	7	4	33		459	Mil	–	17	7	4	23	297
Mil	–	16	7	4	34		459	Mil	–	17	7	4	24	297
Mil	–	16	7	4	35		459	Mil	–	17	7	4	39	293
Mil	–	16	7	4	36		677	Mil	–	18	2	2	11	628
Mil	–	16	7	4	37		677	Mil	–	18	2	2	12	628
Mil	–	16	7	4	38		677	Mil	–	18	4	1	–	188
Mil	–	16	7	4	39		677	Mil	–	18	7	1	1	980
Mil	–	16	8	4	1		677	Mil	–	18	7	1	2	980
Mil	–	16	8	4	2		677	Mil	–	18	7	1	3	980
Mil	–	16	8	4	3		898, 928	Mil	–	18	7	1	4	980
Mil	–	16	8	4	5		677	Mil	–	18	7	1	5	980
Mil	–	16	8	4	7		752	Mil	–	18	7	1	6	980
Mil	–	17	4	2	–		189	Mil	–	18	7	1	7	980
Mil	*	17	6	3	–	(*4000-acre tract) 558	Mil	–	18	7	1	8	980
Mil	–	17	7	1	1		303	Mil	–	18	7	1	9	980
Mil	–	17	7	1	15		928	Mil	–	18	7	1	10	588, 627, 677, 980
Mil	–	17	7	1	24		1164	Mil	–	18	7	1	11	588, 627, 677, 980
Mil	–	17	7	2	3		677	Mil	–	18	7	1	12	980
Mil	–	17	7	2	4		677	Mil	–	18	7	1	13	980
Mil	–	17	7	2	5		677	Mil	–	18	7	1	14	980
Mil	–	17	7	2	6		677	Mil	–	18	7	1	15	898, 928, 980
Mil	–	17	7	2	7		1026	Mil	–	18	7	1	16	677, 980
Mil	–	17	7	2	8		1026	Mil	–	18	7	1	17	980, 1026
Mil	–	17	7	2	9		305, 330	Mil	–	18	7	1	18	980
Mil	–	17	7	2	10		677	Mil	–	18	7	1	19	980
Mil	–	17	7	2	11		677	Mil	–	18	7	1	20	301, 313, 980

Mil	–	18	7	1	21	301, 313, 980
Mil	–	18	7	1	22	980
Mil	–	18	7	1	23	980
Mil	–	18	7	1	24	980
Mil	–	18	7	1	25	980
Mil	–	18	7	1	26	980
Mil	–	18	7	1	27	980
Mil	–	18	7	1	28	980
Mil	–	18	7	1	29	980
Mil	–	18	7	1	30	980
Mil	–	18	7	1	31	980
Mil	–	18	7	1	32	980
Mil	–	18	7	1	33	980
Mil	–	18	7	1	34	980
Mil	–	18	7	1	35	980
Mil	–	18	7	1	36	980
Mil	–	18	7	1	37	980
Mil	–	18	7	1	38	980
Mil	–	18	7	1	39	980
Mil	–	18	7	1	40	980
Mil	–	18	7	2	1	292
Mil	–	18	7	2	2	292
Mil	–	18	7	2	7	330
Mil	–	18	7	2	8	330
Mil	–	18	7	2	10	330
Mil	–	19	2	3	1	339, 352
Mil	–	19	2	3	2	339, 352
Mil	–	19	2	3	11	339, 352
Mil	–	19	2	3	12	339, 352
Mil	–	19	3	–	–	923
Mil	–	19	6	3	1	338, 352
Mil	–	19	6	3	2	338, 352
Mil	–	19	6	3	11	338, 352
Mil	–	19	6	3	12	338, 352
Mil	–	19	7	1	1	677
Mil	–	19	7	1	2	928

Mil	–	19	7	1	3	677
Mil	–	19	7	1	4	677
Mil	–	19	7	1	5	363, 677
Mil	–	19	7	1	6	363, 677
Mil	–	19	7	1	7	346, 363

CANADIAN AND NOVA SCOTIAN REFUGEE TRACT

Ref	–	16	18	1	–	2537
Ref	–	16	18	2	–	2537
Ref	–	16	18	3	–	2537
Ref	–	16	18	4	–	2537
Ref	–	16	18	5	–	2537
Ref	–	16	18	6	–	2537
Ref	–	16	18	7	–	2537
Ref	–	16	18	8	–	2537
Ref	–	16	18	9	–	2537
Ref	–	16	18	10	–	2537
Ref	–	16	18	11	–	2537
Ref	–	16	18	12	–	2537
Ref	–	16	18	13	–	2537
Ref	–	16	18	14	–	2537
Ref	–	16	18	15	–	2537
Ref	–	16	18	16	–	2537
Ref	–	16	18	17	–	2537
Ref	–	16	18	18	–	2537
Ref	–	16	18	–	18	509
Ref	–	16	18	19	–	2537
Ref	–	16	18	20	–	2537
Ref	–	16	18	21	–	2537
Ref	–	16	18	22	–	2537
Ref	–	16	18	23	–	2537
Ref	–	16	18	24	–	2537

Ref	–	16	18	25	–	2537	Ref	–	18	17	1	–	2539
Ref	–	16	18	26	–	2537	Ref	–	18	17	2	–	2539
Ref	–	16	18	27	–	2537	Ref	–	18	17	3	–	2539
Ref	–	16	18	28	–	2537	Ref	–	18	17	4	–	2539
Ref	–	16	18	29	–	2537	Ref	–	18	17	5	–	412, 2539
Ref	–	16	18	30	–	2537	Ref	–	18	17	6	–	2539
Ref	–	17	19	1	–	2538	Ref	–	18	17	7	–	2539
Ref	–	17	19	2	–	2538	Ref	–	18	17	8	–	2539
Ref	–	17	19	3	–	2538	Ref	–	18	17	9	–	2539
Ref	–	17	19	4	–	2538	Ref	–	18	17	10	–	2539
Ref	–	17	19	5	–	2538	Ref	–	18	17	11	–	2539
Ref	–	17	19	6	–	2538	Ref	–	18	17	12	–	2539
Ref	–	17	19	7	–	2538	Ref	–	18	17	13	–	821, 2539
Ref	–	17	19	8	–	2538	Ref	–	18	17	14	–	821, 2539
Ref	–	17	19	9	–	2538	Ref	–	18	17	15	–	821, 2539
Ref	–	17	19	10	–	2538	Ref	–	18	17	16	–	2539
Ref	–	17	19	11	–	2538	Ref	–	18	17	17	–	2539
Ref	–	17	19	12	–	2538	Ref	–	18	17	18	–	2539
Ref	–	17	19	13	–	2538	Ref	–	18	17	19	–	2539
Ref	–	17	19	14	–	2538	Ref	–	18	17	20	–	2539
Ref	–	17	19	15	–	2538	Ref	–	18	17	21	–	2539
Ref	–	17	19	16	–	2538	Ref	–	18	17	22	–	2539
Ref	–	17	19	17	–	2538	Ref	–	18	17	23	–	2539
Ref	–	17	19	18	–	2538	Ref	–	18	17	24	–	2539
Ref	–	17	19	19	–	2538	Ref	–	18	17	25	–	2539
Ref	–	17	19	20	–	2538	Ref	–	18	17	26	–	2539
Ref	–	17	19	21	–	2538	Ref	–	18	17	27	–	2539
Ref	–	17	19	22	–	2538	Ref	–	18	17	28	–	2539
Ref	–	17	19	23	–	2538	Ref	–	18	17	29	–	2539
Ref	–	17	19	24	–	2538	Ref	–	18	17	30	–	2539
Ref	–	17	19	25	–	2538	Ref	–	18	17	31	–	2539
Ref	–	17	19	26	–	2538	Ref	–	18	17	32	–	2539
Ref	–	17	19	27	–	2538	Ref	–	18	17	33	–	2539
Ref	–	17	19	28	–	2538	Ref	–	18	17	34	–	2539
Ref	–	17	19	29	–	2538	Ref	–	18	17	35	–	2539
Ref	–	17	19	30	–	2538	Ref	–	18	17	36	–	2539

Ref	–	18	17	37	–	2539	Ref	–	19	17	18	–	2540
Ref	–	18	17	38	–	2539	Ref	–	19	17	19	–	2540
Ref	–	18	17	39	–	2539	Ref	–	19	17	20	–	2540
Ref	–	18	17	40	–	2539	Ref	–	19	17	21	–	2540
Ref	–	18	17	41	–	2539	Ref	–	19	17	22	–	2540
Ref	–	18	17	42	–	2539	Ref	–	19	17	23	–	2540
Ref	–	18	17	43	–	2539	Ref	–	19	17	24	–	2540
Ref	–	18	17	44	–	2539	Ref	–	19	17	25	–	2540
Ref	–	18	17	45	–	2539	Ref	–	19	17	26	–	2540
Ref	–	18	17	46	–	2539	Ref	–	19	17	27	–	2540
Ref	–	18	17	47	–	2539	Ref	–	19	17	28	–	2540
Ref	–	18	17	48	–	2539	Ref	–	19	17	29	–	2540
Ref	–	18	17	49	–	2539	Ref	–	19	17	30	–	2540
Ref	–	18	17	50	–	2539	Ref	–	19	17	31	–	2540
Ref	–	18	17	51	–	2539	Ref	–	19	17	32	–	2540
Ref	–	18	17	52	–	2539	Ref	–	19	17	33	–	2540
Ref	–	18	17	53	–	2539	Ref	–	19	17	34	–	2540
Ref	–	18	17	54	–	2539	Ref	–	19	17	35	–	2540
Ref	–	18	17	55	–	2539	Ref	–	19	17	36	–	2540
Ref	–	19	17	1	–	2540	Ref	–	19	17	37	–	2540
Ref	–	19	17	2	–	2540	Ref	–	19	17	38	–	2540
Ref	–	19	17	3	–	2540	Ref	–	19	17	39	–	2540
Ref	–	19	17	4	–	2540	Ref	–	19	17	40	–	2540
Ref	–	19	17	5	–	2540	Ref	–	19	17	41	–	2540
Ref	–	19	17	6	–	2540	Ref	–	19	17	42	–	2540
Ref	–	19	17	7	–	2540	Ref	–	19	17	43	–	2540
Ref	–	19	17	8	–	2540	Ref	–	19	17	44	–	2540
Ref	–	19	17	9	–	2540	Ref	–	19	17	45	–	2540
Ref	–	19	17	10	–	2540	Ref	–	19	17	46	–	2540
Ref	–	19	17	11	–	2540	Ref	–	19	17	47	–	2540
Ref	–	19	17	12	–	2540	Ref	–	19	17	48	–	2540
Ref	–	19	17	13	–	2540	Ref	–	19	17	49	–	2540
Ref	–	19	17	14	–	2540	Ref	–	19	17	50	–	2540
Ref	–	19	17	15	–	2540	Ref	–	19	17	51	–	2540
Ref	–	19	17	16	–	2540	Ref	–	19	17	52	–	2540
Ref	–	19	17	17	–	2540	Ref	–	19	17	53	–	2540

Ref	–	19	17	54	–	2540	Ref	–	20	16	36	–	2541
Ref	–	20	16	1	–	2541	Ref	–	20	16	37	–	2541
Ref	–	20	16	2	–	2541	Ref	–	20	16	38	–	2541
Ref	–	20	16	3	–	2541	Ref	–	20	16	39	–	2541
Ref	–	20	16	4	–	2541	Ref	–	20	16	40	–	2541
Ref	–	20	16	5	–	2541	Ref	–	20	16	41	–	2541
Ref	–	20	16	6	–	2541	Ref	–	20	16	42	–	2541
Ref	–	20	16	7	–	2541	Ref	–	20	16	43	–	2541
Ref	–	20	16	8	–	2541	Ref	–	20	16	44	–	2541
Ref	–	20	16	9	–	2541	Ref	–	20	16	45	–	2541
Ref	–	20	16	10	–	2541	Ref	–	20	16	46	–	2541
Ref	–	20	16	11	–	2541	Ref	–	20	16	47	–	2541
Ref	–	20	16	12	–	2541	Ref	–	20	16	48	–	2541
Ref	–	20	16	13	–	2541	Ref	–	20	16	49	–	2541
Ref	–	20	16	14	–	2541	Ref	–	20	16	50	–	2541
Ref	–	20	16	15	–	2541	Ref	–	20	16	51	–	2541
Ref	–	20	16	16	–	2541	Ref	–	20	16	52	–	2541
Ref	–	20	16	17	–	2541	Ref	–	20	16	53	–	2541
Ref	–	20	16	18	–	2541	Ref	–	20	16	54	–	2541
Ref	–	20	16	19	–	2541	Ref	–	21	12	1	–	2542
Ref	–	20	16	20	–	2541	Ref	–	21	12	2	–	2542
Ref	–	20	16	21	–	2541	Ref	–	21	12	3	–	2542
Ref	–	20	16	22	–	2541	Ref	–	21	12	4	–	2542
Ref	–	20	16	23	–	2541	Ref	–	21	12	5	–	2542
Ref	–	20	16	24	–	2541	Ref	–	21	12	6	–	2542
Ref	–	20	16	25	–	2541	Ref	–	21	12	7	–	2542
Ref	–	20	16	26	–	2541	Ref	–	21	12	8	–	2542
Ref	–	20	16	27	–	2541	Ref	–	21	12	9	–	2542
Ref	–	20	16	28	–	2541	Ref	–	21	12	10	–	2542
Ref	–	20	16	29	–	2541	Ref	–	21	12	11	–	2542
Ref	–	20	16	30	–	2541	Ref	–	21	12	12	–	2542
Ref	–	20	16	31	–	2541	Ref	–	21	12	13	–	2542
Ref	–	20	16	32	–	2541	Ref	–	21	12	14	–	2542
Ref	–	20	16	33	–	2541	Ref	–	21	12	15	–	2542
Ref	–	20	16	34	–	2541	Ref	–	21	12	16	–	2542
Ref	–	20	16	35	–	2541	Ref	–	21	12	17	–	2542

Ref	–	21	12	18	–	2542	Ref	–	21	12	54	–	2542
Ref	–	21	12	19	–	2542	Ref	–	22	5	1	–	2543
Ref	–	21	12	20	–	2542	Ref	–	22	5	2	–	2543
Ref	–	21	12	21	–	2542	Ref	–	22	5	3	–	2543
Ref	–	21	12	22	–	2542	Ref	–	22	5	4	–	2543
Ref	–	21	12	23	–	2542	Ref	–	22	5	5	–	2543
Ref	–	21	12	24	–	2542	Ref	–	22	5	6	–	2543
Ref	–	21	12	25	–	2542	Ref	–	22	5	7	–	2543
Ref	–	21	12	26	–	2542	Ref	–	22	5	8	–	2543
Ref	–	21	12	27	–	2542	Ref	–	22	5	9	–	2543
Ref	–	21	12	28	–	2542	Ref	–	22	5	10	–	2543
Ref	–	21	12	29	–	2542	Ref	–	22	5	11	–	2543
Ref	–	21	12	30	–	2542	Ref	–	22	5	12	–	2543
Ref	–	21	12	31	–	2542	Ref	–	22	5	13	–	2543
Ref	–	21	12	32	–	2542	Ref	–	22	5	14	–	2543
Ref	–	21	12	33	–	2542	Ref	–	22	5	15	–	2543
Ref	–	21	12	34	–	2542	Ref	–	22	5	16	–	2543
Ref	–	21	12	35	–	2542	Ref	–	22	5	17	–	2543
Ref	–	21	12	36	–	2542	Ref	–	22	5	18	–	2543
Ref	–	21	12	37	–	2542	Ref	–	22	5	19	–	2543
Ref	–	21	12	38	–	2542	Ref	–	22	5	20	–	2543
Ref	–	21	12	39	–	2542	Ref	–	22	5	21	–	2543
Ref	–	21	12	40	–	2542	Ref	–	22	5	22	–	2543
Ref	–	21	12	41	–	2542	Ref	–	22	5	23	–	2543
Ref	–	21	12	42	–	2542	Ref	–	22	5	24	–	2543
Ref	–	21	12	43	–	2542	Ref	–	22	5	25	–	2543
Ref	–	21	12	44	–	2542	Ref	–	22	5	26	–	2543
Ref	–	21	12	45	–	2542	Ref	–	22	5	27	–	2543
Ref	–	21	12	46	–	2542	Ref	–	22	5	28	–	2543
Ref	–	21	12	47	–	2542	Ref	–	22	5	29	–	2543
Ref	–	21	12	48	–	2542	Ref	–	22	5	30	–	2543
Ref	–	21	12	49	–	2542	Ref	–	22	5	31	–	2543
Ref	–	21	12	50	–	2542	Ref	–	22	5	32	–	2543
Ref	–	21	12	51	–	2542	Ref	–	22	5	33	–	2543
Ref	–	21	12	52	–	2542	Ref	–	22	5	34	–	2543
Ref	–	21	12	53	–	2542	Ref	–	22	5	35	–	2543

Ref	–	22	5	36	–	2543	
Ref	–	22	5	37	–	2543	
Ref	–	22	5	38	–	2543	
Ref	–	22	5	39	–	2543	
Ref	–	22	5	40	–	2543	
Ref	–	22	5	41	–	2543	
Ref	–	22	5	42	–	2543	
Ref	–	22	5	43	–	2543	

SEVEN RANGES

7Rg	–	1	1	–	28	2527	
7Rg	–	1	1	–	29	2527	
7Rg	–	1	1	–	34	2527	
7Rg	–	1	1	–	35	2527	
7Rg	–	1	2	–	19	2527	
7Rg	–	1	2	–	20	2527	
7Rg	–	1	2	–	21	2527	
7Rg	–	1	2	–	25	2527	
7Rg	–	1	2	–	26	2527	
7Rg	–	1	2	–	27	2527	
7Rg	–	1	2	–	29	2527	
7Rg	–	1	2	–	30	2527	
7Rg	–	1	2	–	31	2527	
7Rg	–	1	2	–	33	2527	
7Rg	–	1	2	–	35	2527	
7Rg	–	1	2	–	36	2527	
7Rg	–	1	3	–	all	2526	
7Rg	–	1	4	–	19	2527	
7Rg	–	1	4	–	25	2527	
7Rg	–	1	4	–	34	[152], 2527	
7Rg	–	1	4	–	35	[152], 2527	
7Rg	–	1	4	–	36	[152], 2527	
7Rg	–	1	5	–	6	2527	

7Rg	–	1	5	–	12	2527
7Rg	–	1	5	–	23	2527
7Rg	–	1	5	–	24	2527
7Rg	–	2	1	–	29	2526
7Rg	–	2	1	–	30	2526
7Rg	–	2	1	–	35	2526
7Rg	–	2	1	–	36	2526
7Rg	–	2	2	–	all	2526
7Rg	–	2	3	–	17	2526
7Rg	–	2	3	–	18	2526
7Rg	–	2	3	–	19	2526
7Rg	–	2	3	–	20	2526
7Rg	–	2	3	–	23	2526
7Rg	–	2	3	–	24	2526, 2527
7Rg	–	2	3	–	26	2526
7Rg	–	2	3	–	27	2526
7Rg	–	2	3	–	29	2526
7Rg	–	2	3	–	30	2526
7Rg	–	2	3	–	31	2526
7Rg	–	2	3	–	32	2526
7Rg	–	2	3	–	33	2527
7Rg	–	2	3	–	34	2526
7Rg	–	2	3	–	35	2526
7Rg	–	2	3	–	36	2526
7Rg	–	2	4	–	11	2527
7Rg	–	2	4	–	13	2527
7Rg	–	2	4	–	15	2527
7Rg	–	2	4	–	16	2527
7Rg	–	2	4	–	17	2527
7Rg	–	2	4	–	19	2527
7Rg	–	2	4	–	20	2527
7Rg	–	2	4	–	21	2527
7Rg	–	2	4	–	22	2527
7Rg	–	2	4	–	23	2527
7Rg	–	2	4	–	24	2527
7Rg	–	2	4	–	26	2527

7Rg	–	2	4	–	27	2527	7Rg	–	2	5	–	36	2526
7Rg	–	2	4	–	28	2527	7Rg	–	2	6	–	all	2526
7Rg	–	2	4	–	29	2527	7Rg	–	2	7	–	1	2526
7Rg	–	2	4	–	32	2527	7Rg	–	2	7	–	2	2526
7Rg	–	2	4	–	33	2527	7Rg	–	2	7	–	3	2526, 2527
7Rg	–	2	4	–	34	2527	7Rg	–	2	7	–	4	2526
7Rg	–	2	4	–	35	2527	7Rg	–	2	7	–	5	2526
7Rg	–	2	4	–	36	2527	7Rg	–	2	7	–	6	2526
7Rg	–	2	5	–	2	1648, 2526	7Rg	–	2	7	–	7	2526
7Rg	–	2	5	–	4	2526	7Rg	–	2	7	–	9	2526
7Rg	–	2	5	–	5	2526	7Rg	–	2	7	–	10	2526
7Rg	–	2	5	–	6	2526	7Rg	–	2	7	–	12	2526
7Rg	–	2	5	–	7	2526, 2527	7Rg	–	2	7	–	13	2526
7Rg	–	2	5	–	9	2526	7Rg	–	2	7	–	14	2526
7Rg	–	2	5	–	10	2526	7Rg	–	2	7	–	15	2526
7Rg	–	2	5	–	12	2526	7Rg	–	2	7	–	17	2526
7Rg	–	2	5	–	13	2526	7Rg	–	2	7	–	18	2526
7Rg	–	2	5	–	14	2526	7Rg	–	2	7	–	19	2526
7Rg	–	2	5	–	15	2526	7Rg	–	2	7	–	20	2526
7Rg	–	2	5	–	17	2526	7Rg	–	2	7	–	21	2526
7Rg	–	2	5	–	18	2526	7Rg	–	2	7	–	22	2526
7Rg	–	2	5	–	19	2526	7Rg	–	2	7	–	23	2526
7Rg	–	2	5	–	20	2526	7Rg	–	2	7	–	24	2526
7Rg	–	2	5	–	21	2526	7Rg	–	2	7	–	25	2526
7Rg	–	2	5	–	22	2526	7Rg	–	2	7	–	27	2526
7Rg	–	2	5	–	23	2526, 2527	7Rg	–	2	7	–	28	2526
7Rg	–	2	5	–	24	2526, 2527	7Rg	–	2	7	–	30	2526
7Rg	–	2	5	–	25	2526	7Rg	–	2	7	–	31	2526
7Rg	–	2	5	–	27	2526	7Rg	–	2	7	–	32	2526
7Rg	–	2	5	–	28	2526	7Rg	–	2	7	–	33	2526
7Rg	–	2	5	–	30	2526	7Rg	–	2	7	–	34	2526
7Rg	–	2	5	–	31	2526	7Rg	–	2	7	–	35	2526
7Rg	–	2	5	–	32	2526	7Rg	–	2	7	–	36	2526
7Rg	–	2	5	–	33	2526	7Rg	–	2	8	–	all	2526
7Rg	–	2	5	–	34	2526	7Rg	–	2	8	–	3	2527
7Rg	–	2	5	–	35	2526	7Rg	–	2	8	–	7	2527

7Rg	–	2	8	–	8		2527	7Rg	–	3	5	–	1	2526
7Rg	–	2	8	–	9		2527	7Rg	–	3	5	–	3	2526
7Rg	–	2	8	–	13		2527	7Rg	–	3	6	–	1	2526
7Rg	–	2	8	–	14		2527	7Rg	–	3	6	–	2	2526
7Rg	–	2	8	–	19		2527	7Rg	–	3	6	–	3	2526
7Rg	–	2	9	–	1	[152],	2526	7Rg	–	3	6	–	4	2526
7Rg	–	2	9	–	4		2526	7Rg	–	3	6	–	5	2526
7Rg	–	2	9	–	5		2526	7Rg	–	3	6	–	6	2526
7Rg	–	2	9	–	7	[152],	2526	7Rg	–	3	6	–	7	2526
7Rg	–	2	9	–	10		2526	7Rg	–	3	6	–	10	2527
7Rg	–	2	9	–	12		2526	7Rg	–	3	6	–	13	2526
7Rg	–	2	9	–	13		2526	7Rg	–	3	6	–	18	2526
7Rg	–	2	9	–	14		2526	7Rg	–	3	6	–	23	2526
7Rg	–	2	9	–	17		2526	7Rg	–	3	6	–	24	2526
7Rg	–	2	9	–	18		2526	7Rg	–	3	6	–	30	2526
7Rg	–	2	9	–	19		2526	7Rg	–	3	6	–	36	2526
7Rg	–	2	9	–	20		2526	7Rg	–	3	7	–	all	2526
7Rg	–	3	1	–	all	306,	2526	7Rg	–	3	8	–	1	2526
7Rg	–	3	2	–	8		[38]	7Rg	–	3	8	–	2	2526
7Rg	–	3	2	–	9	[38],	2526	7Rg	–	3	8	–	6	2526
7Rg	–	3	2	–	10		2526	7Rg	–	3	8	–	13	2527
7Rg	–	3	2	–	14	[38],	2526	7Rg	–	3	8	–	24	2526
7Rg	–	3	2	–	15	[38],	2527	7Rg	–	3	8	–	31	2526
7Rg	–	3	2	–	17		2526	7Rg	–	3	8	–	32	2526
7Rg	–	3	2	–	19		2526	7Rg	–	3	10	–	3	2526
7Rg	–	3	2	–	24		2526	7Rg	–	3	10	–	4	2526
7Rg	–	3	3	–	14		2527	7Rg	–	3	10	–	10	2527
7Rg	–	3	3	–	19		2527	7Rg	–	4	1	–	18	2526
7Rg	–	3	3	–	20		2527	7Rg	–	4	1	–	23	2526
7Rg	–	3	3	–	21		2526	7Rg	–	4	1	–	24	2526
7Rg	–	3	3	–	25		2527	7Rg	–	4	1	–	28	2526
7Rg	–	3	4	–	1		2527	7Rg	–	4	1	–	34	2526
7Rg	–	3	4	–	2		2527	7Rg	–	4	1	–	35	2526
7Rg	–	3	4	–	7		2527	7Rg	–	4	7	–	3	2526
7Rg	–	3	4	–	8		2527	7Rg	–	4	7	–	4	2526
7Rg	–	3	4	–	31		2527	7Rg	–	4	7	–	5	2527

7Rg	–	4	7	–	6	2527
7Rg	–	4	7	–	9	2526
7Rg	–	4	7	–	10	2526
7Rg	–	4	7	–	14	2526
7Rg	–	4	7	–	15	2526
7Rg	–	4	7	–	17	2526
7Rg	–	4	7	–	20	2526
7Rg	–	4	7	–	21	2526
7Rg	–	4	7	–	22	2526
7Rg	–	4	7	–	23	2526
7Rg	–	4	7	–	24	2526
7Rg	–	4	7	–	27	2526
7Rg	–	4	7	–	28	2526
7Rg	–	4	9	–	7	2527
7Rg	–	4	9	–	8	2527
7Rg	–	4	9	–	9	2527
7Rg	–	5	1	–	18	2527
7Rg	–	5	1	–	24	2527
7Rg	–	5	1	–	26	2527
7Rg	–	5	1	–	31	2527
7Rg	–	5	1	–	32	2527
7Rg	–	5	2	–	7	2527
7Rg	–	5	2	–	13	2527
7Rg	–	6	1	–	21	2527
7Rg	–	6	1	–	22	2527
7Rg	–	6	1	–	27	2527
7Rg	–	6	1	–	28	2527
7Rg	–	6	1	–	33	2527
7Rg	–	6	1	–	34	2527
7Rg	–	6	2	–	1	2527
7Rg	–	6	2	–	2	2527
7Rg	–	6	9	–	1	2527
7Rg	–	7	1&2	–	30	2527
7Rg	–	7	1&2	–	31	2527
7Rg	–	7	1&2	–	36	2527
7Rg	–	7	2	–	3	2527

7Rg	–	7	2	–	4	2527
7Rg	–	7	2	–	9	2527
7Rg	–	7	2	–	10	2527
7Rg	–	7	2	–	14	2527
7Rg	–	7	2	–	19	2527
7Rg	–	7	2	–	20	2527
7Rg	–	7	2	–	25	2527
7Rg	–	7	2	–	26	2527

STEUBENVILLE LAND OFFICE DISTRICT

Stu LO, in general							4, 13, 15
Stu	–	1	2	5	–		46
Stu	–	1	2	32	–		114
Stu	–	1	2	33	–		45, 46
Stu	–	1	2	34	–		248
Stu	–	1	3	–	–		1288
Stu	–	1	3	–	36		1285
Stu	–	1	4	17	–		218
Stu	–	1	4	–	26		520
Stu	–	1	4	–	27		755
Stu	–	1	4	31	+		129
Stu	–	1	4	32	–		520
Stu	–	1	4	–	33		755
Stu	–	1	5	–	29		731
Stu	–	1	5	30	–		731
Stu	–	1	5	–	35		718, 802
Stu	–	1	5	36	–		718, 802
Stu	–	1	6	2	–		634
Stu	–	1	6	4	+		840
Stu	–	1	6	5	+		807
Stu	–	1	6	6	–		433
Stu	–	1	6	7	+		129
Stu	–	1	6	9	+		950

Stu	–	1	6	10	–	698	Stu	–	1	8	11	–	219
Stu	–	1	6	11	–	273	Stu	–	1	8	12	–	219
Stu	–	1	6	13	–	522	Stu	–	1	8	13	–	1274
Stu	–	1	6	18	+	853	Stu	–	1	8	14	–	192
Stu	–	1	6	25	–	192	Stu	–	1	8	17	–	248
Stu	–	1	6	26	–	192, 248	Stu	–	1	8	19	–	136
Stu	–	1	6	28	–	522	Stu	–	1	8	20	–	321
Stu	–	1	6	29	–	548	Stu	–	1	8	23	–	219
Stu	–	1	6	30	–	206	Stu	–	1	8	24	–	248
Stu	–	1	6	31	+	486	Stu	–	1	8	25	–	135, 136
Stu	–	1	6	32	–	749	Stu	–	1	8	26	–	248
Stu	–	1	6	35	+	1122	Stu	–	1	8	27	–	358
Stu	–	1	7	2	+	741	Stu	–	1	8	28	–	686
Stu	–	1	7	4	+	840	Stu	–	1	8	30	–	223
Stu	–	1	7	5	–	655, 670, 861	Stu	–	1	8	31	–	557
Stu	–	1	7	6	+	395	Stu	–	1	8	32	–	302
Stu	–	1	7	8	+	782	Stu	–	1	8	33	–	32
Stu	–	1	7	9	+	782	Stu	–	1	8	34	+	807
Stu	–	1	7	11	–	302	Stu	–	1	8	35	+	223, 309
Stu	–	1	7	12	–	219	Stu	–	1	9	1	–	780
Stu	–	1	7	13	–	433	Stu	–	1	9	2	–	699
Stu	–	1	7	18	+	569	Stu	–	1	9	3	–	79, 643
Stu	–	1	7	20	+	554	Stu	–	1	9	4	–	241
Stu	–	1	7	23	–	62	Stu	–	1	9	5	–	361
Stu	–	1	7	24	+	950	Stu	–	1	9	6	–	376
Stu	–	1	7	25	+	223	Stu	–	1	9	7	–	950
Stu	–	1	7	28	+	756, 807	Stu	–	1	9	8	–	294, 585
Stu	–	1	7	29	+	882	Stu	–	1	9	9	–	433
Stu	–	1	7	33	+	853, 1186	Stu	–	1	9	11	–	661
Stu	–	1	7	35	+	1106	Stu	–	1	9	12	–	774
Stu	–	1	8	1	–	241	Stu	–	1	9	13	–	241
Stu	–	1	8	2	–	207	Stu	–	1	9	14	–	343
Stu	–	1	8	3	–	358	Stu	–	1	9	18	–	207
Stu	–	1	8	5	–	334	Stu	–	1	9	25	–	241
Stu	–	1	8	7	–	112	Stu	–	1	9	26	–	248
Stu	–	1	8	8	–	219	Stu	–	1	9	27	–	248

Stu	–	3	6	17		–		1498	Stu	–	3	8	8	–	241
Stu	–	3	6	20		+		302, 594	Stu	–	3	8	9	–	888
Stu	–	3	6	22		–		1498, 2247	Stu	–	3	8	10	–	260
Stu	–	3	6	23		–		1498, 2247	Stu	–	3	8	12	–	223
Stu	–	3	6	28		–		241	Stu	–	3	8	14	–	358
Stu	–	3	6	29		–		642, 1498	Stu	–	3	8	17	–	241
Stu	–	3	6	30		–		279, 328	Stu	–	3	8	18	–	219
Stu	–	3	6	34		–		248	Stu	–	3	8	19	–	248
Stu	–	3	7	1		–		766, 771	Stu	–	3	8	20	–	522
Stu	–	3	7	2		–		223	Stu	–	3	8	23	–	256
Stu	–	3	7	3		–		248	Stu	≐	3	8	25	–	354
Stu	–	3	7	5		–		248, 266	Stu	–	3	8	29	–	223
Stu	–	3	7	6		–		343	Stu	–	3	8	30	–	394
Stu	–	3	7	7		–		219	Stu	–	3	8	33	–	343
Stu	–	3	7	8		–		343	Stu	–	3	8	34	–	522
Stu	–	3	7	9		–		241	Stu	–	3	8	35	–	309
Stu	–	3	7	13		–		19	Stu	–	3	8	36	–	132, 248
Stu	–	3	7	15		+		1555	Stu	–	3	9	5	–	334
Stu	–	3	7	–	16			1555	Stu	–	3	9	8	–	242
Stu	–	3	7	17		–		241	Stu	–	3	9	9	–	192
Stu	–	3	7	20		–		47	Stu	–	3	9	10	–	242
Stu	–	3	7	23		–		241	Stu	–	3	9	12	–	516
Stu	–	3	7	24		–		256	Stu	–	3	9	13	–	942
Stu	–	3	7	25		–		279, 328	Stu	–	3	9	17	–	345
Stu	–	3	7	26		–		279, 328	Stu	–	3	9	19	–	726
Stu	–	3	7	27		–		269	Stu	–	3	9	20	–	248
Stu	–	3	7	29		–		248	Stu	–	3	9	24	+	861, 892, 1114
Stu	–	3	7	30		–		1632	Stu	–	3	9	26	–	219
Stu	–	3	7	31		–		1453	Stu	–	3	9	27	–	456
Stu	–	3	7	32		–		520	Stu	–	3	9	28	–	219
Stu	–	3	8	2		–		1487	Stu	–	3	9	29	+	861
Stu	–	3	8	3		–		502	Stu	–	3	9	30	+	840
Stu	–	3	8	4		–		219	Stu	–	3	9	31	–	223
Stu	–	3	8	5		–		345	Stu	–	3	9	32	–	248
Stu	–	3	8	6		–		242	Stu	–	3	9	33	–	223
Stu	–	3	8	7		–		447	Stu	–	3	9	35	+	587, 613, 922, 963

Stu	–	3	9	36	+	594, 807	Stu	–	3	13	5	–	942
Stu	–	3	10	5	–	554	Stu	–	3	13	7	–	780
Stu	–	3	10	7	+	831	Stu	–	3	13	8	–	361
Stu	–	3	10	14	+	620	Stu	–	3	13	9	–	345
Stu	–	3	10	19	+	361, 561, 744	Stu	–	3	13	11	–	273
Stu	–	3	10	20	–	354	Stu	–	3	13	13	+	661, 831
Stu	–	3	10	26	–	260	Stu	–	3	13	14	+	129
Stu	–	3	10	27	–	578	Stu	–	3	13	27	–	698
Stu	–	3	10	28	–	1021	Stu	–	3	13	28	+	698
Stu	–	3	10	29	–	242	Stu	–	3	14	3	–	486
Stu	–	3	10	30	+	456, 861	Stu	–	3	14	7	+	942, 1183
Stu	–	3	10	34	+	774, 1051, 1056, 1085	Stu	–	3	14	9	+	469
Stu	–	3	10	35	–	520	Stu	–	3	14	10	–	469
Stu	–	3	10	36	–	358	Stu	–	3	14	11	–	857
Stu	–	3	11	1	–	599	Stu	–	3	14	12	–	493
Stu	–	3	11	2	+	129, 599	Stu	–	3	14	14	–	219
Stu	–	3	11	4	+	840	Stu	–	3	14	18	+	465, 876, 881
Stu	–	3	11	7	–	655, 780	Stu	–	3	14	19	+	198, 242, 840
Stu	–	3	11	8	+	853	Stu	–	3	14	23	–	613
Stu	–	3	11	13	–	260	Stu	–	3	14	25	+	486
Stu	–	3	11	14	+	759	Stu	–	3	14	30	+	807, 861
Stu	–	3	11	19	–	47	Stu	–	3	14	31	+	1039, 1114
Stu	–	3	11	20	+	686	Stu	–	3	14	34	–	756
Stu	–	3	11	26	+	433	Stu	–	3	15	1	–	469
Stu	–	3	11	28	–	433	Stu	–	3	15	2	–	219
Stu	–	3	11	29	+	1186	Stu	–	3	15	4	–	309
Stu	–	3	11	33	–	1667	Stu	–	3	15	5	–	502
Stu	–	3	11	34	–	1832	Stu	–	3	15	7	–	361
Stu	–	3	12	2	+	433	Stu	–	3	15	8	–	242
Stu	–	3	12	5	+	698	Stu	–	3	15	13	–	361
Stu	–	3	12	6	+	788	Stu	–	3	15	14	–	334
Stu	–	3	12	10	+	840	Stu	–	3	15	15	+	727, 1005
Stu	–	3	12	17	+	698	Stu	–	3	15	17	–	433
Stu	–	3	12	23	–	698	Stu	–	3	15	18	–	469
Stu	–	3	13	3	+	774	Stu	–	3	15	20	–	1186
Stu	–	3	13	4	+	861	Stu	–	3	15	22	+	1005

Stu	–	3	15	23	+	376, 861, 871
Stu	–	3	15	25	+	248, 698
Stu	–	3	15	26	–	827
Stu	–	3	15	29	+	613, 774
Stu	–	3	15	34	–	334
Stu	–	3	15	35	–	469
Stu	–	3	16	2	+	302, 1122
Stu	–	3	16	4	–	807
Stu	–	3	16	6	–	807
Stu	–	3	16	7	–	248
Stu	–	3	16	9	+	591
Stu	–	3	16	10	–	361
Stu	–	3	16	13	–	620
Stu	–	3	16	18	–	522
Stu	–	3	16	19	–	354
Stu	–	3	16	24	–	807
Stu	–	3	16	25	–	587
Stu	–	3	16	29	–	273
Stu	–	3	16	30	–	456
Stu	–	3	16	32	–	456
Stu	–	3	16	33	–	461
Stu	–	3	16	34	–	827
Stu	–	3	16	35	–	661
Stu	–	3	16	36	–	578
Stu	–	3	17	5	+	1014
Stu	–	4	6	4	+	433
Stu	–	4	6	5	+	699
Stu	–	4	6	6	+	1097
Stu	–	4	6	11	+	807
Stu	–	4	6	23	+	361
Stu	–	4	6	28	+	1183
Stu	–	4	6	30	+	792
Stu	–	4	7	2	–	522
Stu	–	4	7	5	–	45
Stu	–	4	7	8	–	46
Stu	–	4	7	11	+	1151
Stu	–	4	7	13	–	302
Stu	–	4	7	18	–	566
Stu	–	4	7	19	–	366
Stu	–	4	7	25	–	279, 328
Stu	–	4	7	26	+	1191
Stu	–	4	7	32	–	345
Stu	–	4	7	33	–	358
Stu	–	4	7	34	–	309
Stu	–	4	7	35	–	248
Stu	–	4	8	2	+	396
Stu	–	4	8	3	+	582
Stu	–	4	8	4	–	20
Stu	–	4	8	5	–	273
Stu	–	4	8	6	–	302
Stu	–	4	8	7	–	231
Stu	–	4	8	8	–	591
Stu	–	4	8	9	–	311, 326, 584
Stu	–	4	8	10	–	273
Stu	–	4	8	11	–	20
Stu	–	4	8	12	–	376
Stu	–	4	8	13	–	780
Stu	–	4	8	14	–	207
Stu	–	4	8	17	–	161
Stu	–	4	8	20	–	366
Stu	–	4	8	24	–	345
Stu	–	4	8	27	–	321
Stu	–	4	8	28	–	345
Stu	–	4	8	29	–	520
Stu	–	4	8	30	–	248
Stu	–	4	8	31	–	219
Stu	–	4	8	32	–	248
Stu	–	4	8	35	–	516
Stu	–	4	8	36	–	343
Stu	–	4	9	1	–	192
Stu	–	4	9	3	–	219

Stu	–	4	9	4	–	361	Stu	–	4	11	3	–	831
Stu	–	4	9	5	–	302	Stu	–	4	11	4	+	756
Stu	–	4	9	6	–	469	Stu	–	4	11	5	–	376
Stu	–	4	9	8	–	45	Stu	–	4	11	6	–	469
Stu	–	4	9	13	–	343	Stu	–	4	11	9	–	242
Stu	–	4	9	14	–	215	Stu	–	4	11	10	–	317, 318
Stu	–	4	9	15	+	1039	Stu	–	4	11	11	–	548
Stu	–	4	9	18	–	366	Stu	–	4	11	12	+	942
Stu	–	4	9	19	–	302	Stu	–	4	11	13	–	248
Stu	–	4	9	21	+	946	Stu	–	4	11	23	–	219
Stu	–	4	9	23	–	343	Stu	–	4	11	27	–	114
Stu	–	4	9	24	–	114	Stu	–	4	11	28	+	807
Stu	–	4	9	25	–	241	Stu	–	4	11	30	+	302
Stu	–	4	9	26	–	366	Stu	–	4	11	33	–	587
Stu	–	4	9	27	–	345	Stu	–	4	12	1	+	853
Stu	–	4	9	28	–	309	Stu	–	4	12	8	+	840
Stu	–	4	9	29	–	345	Stu	–	4	12	10	+	853
Stu	–	4	9	30	–	433	Stu	–	4	12	11	+	840
Stu	–	4	9	31	–	236, 261	Stu	–	4	12	19	+	788
Stu	–	4	9	32	–	343	Stu	–	4	12	20	+	853
Stu	–	4	9	34	–	718	Stu	–	4	12	32	+	759
Stu	–	4	9	35	–	345	Stu	–	4	12	33	+	634
Stu	–	4	10	1	–	469	Stu	–	4	12	34	+	780
Stu	–	4	10	2	–	184	Stu	–	4	14	3	+	461, 548
Stu	–	4	10	3	–	321	Stu	–	4	14	9	+	433
Stu	–	4	10	4	+	129, 1122	Stu	–	4	14	10	+	236, 250
Stu	–	4	10	6	+	594, 831	Stu	–	4	14	11	+	343
Stu	–	4	10	7	–	248	Stu	–	4	14	12	–	358
Stu	–	4	10	9	–	343	Stu	–	4	15	1	+	686, 871, 942
Stu	–	4	10	11	+	840	Stu	–	4	15	5	–	796
Stu	–	4	10	17	+	853	Stu	–	4	15	6	–	302
Stu	–	4	10	24	–	502	Stu	–	4	15	10	–	840
Stu	–	4	10	25	–	351, 566	Stu	–	4	15	12	–	345
Stu	–	4	10	29	+	1122	Stu	–	4	15	13	+	234, 782
Stu	–	4	10	30	–	433	Stu	–	4	15	14	+	1177, 1191
Stu	–	4	10	33	–	502	Stu	–	4	15	18	+	944, 945, 1198

Stu	–	4	15	20	+	594, 726	Stu	–	4	17	2	+	792
Stu	–	4	15	23	+	861	Stu	–	4	17	4	+	703
Stu	–	4	15	24	+	861	Stu	–	4	17	5	+	516, 545, 612, 1014
Stu	–	4	15	25	+	634, 853	Stu	–	4	17	6	+	827
Stu	–	4	15	26	+	433	Stu	–	4	17	8	+	569
Stu	–	4	15	27	+	535, 756, 1114	Stu	–	4	17	9	+	703, 1106
Stu	–	4	15	29	+	840	Stu	–	4	17	10	+	945
Stu	–	4	15	30	+	1191	Stu	–	4	17	14	+	703, 853
Stu	–	4	15	31	+	578	Stu	–	4	17	17	+	587
Stu	–	4	15	33	+	578	Stu	–	4	17	19	+	1183
Stu	–	4	15	36	+	343, 699, 882	Stu	–	4	17	20	+	502, 749
Stu	–	4	16	1	+	361	Stu	–	4	17	21	+	1089, 1090
Stu	–	4	16	4	–	619, 625	Stu	–	4	17	23	–	619, 625
Stu	–	4	16	5	+	882, 888, 946	Stu	–	4	17	24	–	840
Stu	–	4	16	6	+	554, 888	Stu	–	4	17	24	+	661
Stu	–	4	16	7	–	888	Stu	–	4	17	25	–	520
Stu	–	4	16	8	–	591	Stu	–	4	17	26	–	871
Stu	–	4	16	9	–	613	Stu	–	4	17	27	+	433, 844
Stu	–	4	16	10	+	469, 892	Stu	–	4	17	28	+	307, 554
Stu	–	4	16	11	–	248	Stu	–	4	17	29	+	486, 542, 888
Stu	–	4	16	12	–	639, 840	Stu	–	4	17	30	+	782
Stu	–	4	16	13	–	718	Stu	–	4	17	31	+	343
Stu	–	4	16	14	–	519, 557	Stu	–	4	17	32	+	343, 345
Stu	–	4	16	17	–	749	Stu	–	4	17	33	+	354, 566, 780, 788
Stu	–	4	16	18	–	840	Stu	–	4	17	34	–	569
Stu	–	4	16	23	–	223	Stu	–	5	7	4	+	944, 945, 1183
Stu	–	4	16	24	–	661	Stu	–	5	7	5	–	334
Stu	–	4	16	27	–	634	Stu	–	5	7	6	–	566
Stu	–	4	16	28	–	706, 722	Stu	–	5	7	7	+	375, 422
Stu	–	4	16	30	–	840	Stu	–	5	7	8	+	422
Stu	–	4	16	32	+	925	Stu	–	5	7	9	+	1039
Stu	–	4	16	33	–	726	Stu	–	5	7	10	+	1039, 1142
Stu	–	4	16	34	–	844	Stu	–	5	7	11	+	942, 1050, 1051, 1052
Stu	–	4	16	35	–	361	Stu	–	5	7	13	+	376, 1085
Stu	–	4	16	36	–	502	Stu	–	5	7	17	–	321
Stu	–	4	17	1	+	991, 1069	Stu	–	5	7	24	–	195

Stu	–	5	7	26	+	1056, 1179	Stu	–	5	9	24	+	242
Stu	–	5	7	27	+	273, 535	Stu	–	5	9	26	+	686, 756
Stu	–	5	7	33	+	354	Stu	–	5	9	29	+	840
Stu	–	5	7	34	+	273, 840	Stu	–	5	9	33	+	840
Stu	–	5	7	36	+	807	Stu	–	5	9	34	–	861
Stu	–	5	8	2	–	260	Stu	–	5	10	1	–	248
Stu	–	5	8	4	–	542, 1298	Stu	–	5	10	2	–	522
Stu	–	5	8	9	–	223	Stu	–	5	10	3	–	433
Stu	–	5	8	10	–	475, 691, 692, 989	Stu	–	5	10	5	–	1309
Stu	–	5	8	11	–	345	Stu	–	5	10	6	–	345
Stu	–	5	8	13	–	634	Stu	–	5	10	7	–	774
Stu	–	5	8	14	–	516, 605	Stu	–	5	10	8	–	520
Stu	–	5	8	18	–	302	Stu	–	5	10	9	–	954
Stu	–	5	8	19	+	273	Stu	–	5	10	9	+	1038
Stu	–	5	8	20	–	594	Stu	–	5	10	10	–	302
Stu	–	5	8	23	+	974	Stu	–	5	10	11	–	433
Stu	–	5	8	24	–	594	Stu	–	5	10	12	–	333
Stu	–	5	8	25	+	861	Stu	–	5	10	13	+	807, 853, 946
Stu	–	5	8	26	+	807	Stu	–	5	10	14	+	334, 807, 888
Stu	–	5	8	28	–	469	Stu	–	5	10	19	+	1021
Stu	–	5	8	31	–	1021	Stu	–	5	10	20	+	759
Stu	–	5	8	33	+	888	Stu	–	5	10	23	–	807
Stu	–	5	9	1	–	343	Stu	–	5	10	24	+	219
Stu	–	5	9	2	–	219	Stu	–	5	10	26	–	613
Stu	–	5	9	3	–	516	Stu	–	5	10	29	+	219, 888
Stu	–	5	9	6	–	248	Stu	–	5	10	32	+	343
Stu	–	5	9	7	–	566	Stu	–	5	10	34	+	868, 1137
Stu	–	5	9	8	–	882	Stu	–	5	11	4	+	699
Stu	–	5	9	9	–	302	Stu	–	5	11	10	+	871
Stu	–	5	9	10	–	219	Stu	–	5	11	13	+	1183
Stu	–	5	9	11	–	358	Stu	–	5	11	18	+	753, 1882
Stu	–	5	9	12	–	613	Stu	–	5	11	19	+	1106
Stu	–	5	9	13	–	502	Stu	–	5	11	27	+	718
Stu	–	5	9	14	–	642, 820	Stu	–	5	11	31	–	831
Stu	–	5	9	17	–	726	Stu	–	5	11	33	+	1183
Stu	–	5	9	18	–	399	Stu	–	5	12	12	+	853

Stu	–	5	12	26	+	469	Stu	–	5	17	24	–	361
Stu	–	5	12	32	+	469	Stu	–	5	17	25	–	345
Stu	–	5	13	24	–	361	Stu	–	5	17	26	+	840, 868
Stu	–	5	16	4	–	256	Stu	–	5	17	27	–	469
Stu	–	5	16	5	–	248	Stu	–	5	17	28	–	469
Stu	–	5	16	6	–	248	Stu	–	5	17	29	–	469
Stu	–	5	16	7	–	376	Stu	–	5	17	30	+	703
Stu	–	5	16	8	–	831	Stu	–	5	17	33	+	920
Stu	–	5	16	9	–	861	Stu	–	5	17	36	+	334, 831, 946
Stu	–	5	16	11	–	827	Stu	–	5	18	2	+	396
Stu	–	5	16	12	–	827	Stu	–	5	18	3	–	587
Stu	–	5	16	13	+	782, 1097	Stu	–	5	18	9	+	1046
Stu	–	5	16	17	–	926	Stu	–	5	18	23	+	840
Stu	–	5	16	18	+	722, 724, 855	Stu	–	5	18	28	+	1183
Stu	–	5	16	19	+	1183	Stu	–	5	18	31	+	502
Stu	–	5	16	23	–	361	Stu	–	5	18	33	+	587
Stu	–	5	16	24	+	661, 1014, 1137	Stu	–	5	18	34	–	844
Stu	–	5	16	25	+	699, 1109, 1177	Stu	–	5	18	35	+	726
Stu	–	5	16	27	+	334, 354, 1014	Stu	–	5	18	36	+	273, 840
Stu	–	5	16	28	–	361	Stu	–	6	6	19	+	905
Stu	–	5	16	29	+	840	Stu	–	6	8	1	+	361, 366, 840
Stu	–	5	16	30	–	683, 714	Stu	–	6	8	2	+	554
Stu	–	5	16	31	+	917	Stu	–	6	8	3	+	461, 871
Stu	–	5	16	36	+	620	Stu	–	6	8	5	–	1056
Stu	–	5	17	1	+	502, 718	Stu	–	6	8	7	+	461
Stu	–	5	17	2	+	587, 726, 993	Stu	–	6	8	8	–	223
Stu	–	5	17	3	+	892	Stu	–	6	8	11	–	756
Stu	–	5	17	5	–	807	Stu	–	6	8	13	+	749
Stu	–	5	17	7	+	589, 867, 1132	Stu	–	6	8	14	–	749
Stu	–	5	17	8	–	461	Stu	–	6	8	17	+	578, 594, 599
Stu	–	5	17	10	+	535	Stu	–	6	8	18	+	493
Stu	–	5	17	11	+	587, 882, 1014	Stu	–	6	8	19	+	461
Stu	–	5	17	12	+	587, 1186	Stu	–	6	8	27	+	882
Stu	–	5	17	13	+	589, 624, 867, 1117, 1132	Stu	–	6	8	28	–	256
Stu	–	5	17	14	–	361	Stu	–	6	8	29	+	358, 892, 1179
Stu	–	5	17	19	+	853	Stu	–	6	8	30	+	493

Stu	–	6	8	35	+	248	Stu	–	6	13	34	+	1051
Stu	–	6	8	36	–	433	Stu	–	6	13	35	+	888
Stu	–	6	9	1	+	262, 587, 726	Stu	–	6	14	30	+	1192
Stu	–	6	9	3	–	361	Stu	–	6	15	13	+	1192
Stu	–	6	9	3	+	401	Stu	–	6	16	1	+	1192
Stu	–	6	9	4	–	248	Stu	–	6	16	2	+	1192
Stu	–	6	9	7	–	343	Stu	–	6	16	10	+	840
Stu	–	6	9	9	–	256	Stu	–	6	16	12	+	905
Stu	–	6	9	10	+	831	Stu	–	6	16	19	+	780
Stu	–	6	9	12	+	844	Stu	–	6	16	20	+	698, 853
Stu	–	6	9	13	–	445	Stu	–	6	17	1	+	475, 774
Stu	–	6	9	17	+	882	Stu	–	6	17	2	+	1036
Stu	–	6	9	18	+	853	Stu	–	6	17	4	+	774, 1097
Stu	–	6	9	19	+	1056	Stu	–	6	17	5	+	476, 469
Stu	–	6	9	20	+	486, 853	Stu	–	6	17	8	+	613
Stu	–	6	9	25	–	207	Stu	–	6	17	9	+	774, 807
Stu	–	6	9	31	–	756	Stu	–	6	17	10	+	703
Stu	–	6	9	32	–	161	Stu	–	6	17	11	–	731
Stu	–	6	10	1	+	974	Stu	–	6	17	12	–	219
Stu	–	6	10	2	+	946, 974	Stu	–	6	17	14	–	207
Stu	–	6	10	4	–	634	Stu	–	6	17	36	+	698
Stu	–	6	10	7	+	655, 945	Stu	–	6	18	19	–	942
Stu	–	6	10	8	+	599, 974	Stu	–	6	18	20	+	286, 413, 414, 457
Stu	–	6	10	10	+	1097	Stu	–	6	18	23	+	744, 1014, 1032, 1109
Stu	–	6	10	11	+	343	Stu	–	6	18	28	+	807, 831
Stu	–	6	10	13	–	535	Stu	–	6	18	29	+	286, 326, 360, 433, 831
Stu	–	6	10	14	+	1032	Stu	–	6	18	30	+	433
Stu	–	6	11	3	+	469	Stu	–	6	18	32	+	434, 892
Stu	–	6	11	9	+	469, 1039	Stu	–	6	18	33	+	634, 831
Stu	–	6	11	10	+	469	Stu	–	6	18	34	+	703
Stu	–	6	11	33	+	587	Stu	–	6	18	35	–	831
Stu	–	6	12	1	–	207	Stu	–	6	19	3	+	349
Stu	–	6	12	3	+	942	Stu	–	6	19	4	+	661
Stu	–	6	12	27	+	1007	Stu	–	6	19	8	+	349, 401
Stu	–	6	13	27	+	807	Stu	–	6	19	9	+	349, 401, 1106
Stu	–	6	13	30	+	707, 920	Stu	–	6	19	10	+	1106

Stu	–	6	19	11	+	469, 502	Stu	–	7	17	13	+	888, 1879
Stu	–	6	19	12	+	782	Stu	–	7	17	14	+	1192
Stu	–	6	19	13	+	447	Stu	–	7	17	20	+	433
Stu	–	6	19	14	+	447, 782	Stu	–	7	17	23	+	905
Stu	–	6	19	20	+	726	Stu	–	7	18	2	+	774, 807
Stu	–	6	19	27	+	1052, 1151	Stu	–	7	18	3	+	545, 721, 886
Stu	–	6	19	28	+	882	Stu	–	7	18	4	+	502, 545, 721, 886
Stu	–	6	19	29	+	447	Stu	–	7	18	5	+	545, 611, 639
Stu	–	6	19	34	+	892	Stu	–	7	18	12	+	522, 613
Stu	–	6	19	35	+	1056, 1186	Stu	–	7	18	17	+	831
Stu	–	6	19	36	–	840	Stu	–	7	18	18	+	248, 958
Stu	–	7	9	1	–	334	Stu	–	7	18	24	+	905, 1137
Stu	–	7	9	7	+	396	Stu	–	7	18	26	+	1039
Stu	–	7	9	12	+	807, 861, 882	Stu	–	7	18	27	+	1039
Stu	–	7	9	14	+	599	Stu	–	7	19	2	–	831
Stu	–	7	9	19	+	599	Stu	–	7	19	3	–	1052
Stu	–	7	9	20	+	726	Stu	–	7	19	5	+	434
Stu	–	7	9	23	–	836, 927	Stu	–	7	19	7	+	219
Stu	–	7	9	25	+	599	Stu	–	7	19	8	–	223
Stu	–	7	9	26	+	599	Stu	–	7	19	10	+	219
Stu	–	7	9	29	–	774	Stu	–	7	19	14	+	958, 1052
Stu	–	7	9	32	+	1151	Stu	–	7	19	17	+	434
Stu	–	7	10	2	+	853	Stu	–	7	19	19	–	1114
Stu	–	7	10	9	+	260	Stu	–	7	19	20	–	1039
Stu	–	7	11	12	+	840	Stu	–	7	19	23	+	1021
Stu	–	7	12	13	+	1097	Stu	–	7	19	25	–	1039
Stu	–	7	12	19	+	782	Stu	–	7	19	29	+	892
Stu	–	7	14	6	–	270	Stu	–	7	19	32	+	434
Stu	–	7	14	20	+	1114	Stu	–	7	20	9	+	542, 1089, 1090
Stu	–	7	15	12	+	905	Stu	–	7	20	10	+	542
Stu	–	7	15	14	+	703	Stu	–	7	20	12	+	756
Stu	–	7	15	18	+	456	Stu	–	7	20	23	+	993, 1074
Stu	–	7	15	28	–	566	Stu	–	7	20	24	+	993, 1074
Stu	–	7	15	35	–	566	Stu	–	7	20	25	+	703, 704
Stu	–	7	16	31	+	840	Stu	–	7	20	26	+	469
Stu	–	7	17	3	+	469	Stu	–	7	20	31	+	861, 1039

Stu	–	7	20	33	+	587
Stu	–	7	26	13	+	796
Stu	–	8	9	4	+	861
Stu	–	8	9	8	+	1032
Stu	–	8	9	9	+	1005
Stu	–	8	9	11	–	683, 944, 945
Stu	–	8	9	29	+	882
Stu	–	8	9	30	+	1151
Stu	–	8	10	1	+	1114
Stu	–	8	10	2	+	950
Stu	–	8	10	3	+	223
Stu	–	8	10	5	+	683, 944, 945
Stu	–	8	10	12	+	376, 892
Stu	–	8	10	14	+	433, 469
Stu	–	8	10	20	+	759, 905, 1192
Stu	–	8	10	21	+	897
Stu	–	8	10	23	+	835, 901, 1097
Stu	–	8	10	24	+	587, 1097
Stu	–	8	10	26	–	917
Stu	–	8	10	28	+	827, 1151
Stu	–	8	10	33	+	861
Stu	–	8	10	34	+	831
Stu	–	8	11	2	+	958
Stu	–	8	11	7	–	683
Stu	–	8	11	7	+	917, 1118
Stu	–	8	11	8	+	780, 861
Stu	–	8	11	10	+	1122
Stu	–	8	11	13	–	223
Stu	–	8	11	14	–	223
Stu	–	8	11	17	+	861
Stu	–	8	11	18	+	903
Stu	–	8	11	20	+	876, 881
Stu	–	8	11	23	+	876, 881, 1106
Stu	–	8	11	33	–	639
Stu	–	8	11	33	+	1122
Stu	–	8	11	34	+	882, 1183
Stu	–	8	11	35	+	1039, 1106
Stu	–	8	12	27	–	840
Stu	–	8	12	29	+	260, 469
Stu	–	8	12	32	+	302
Stu	–	8	12	33	+	561, 744, 876, 881, 1032, 1141, 1186
Stu	–	8	12	34	+	1151
Stu	–	8	12	35	+	670, 944, 945, 1099
Stu	–	9	9	2	+	703
Stu	–	9	9	3	+	703
Stu	–	9	9	4	+	703
Stu	–	9	9	–	5	603
Stu	–	9	9	–	6	603
Stu	–	9	9	–	8	603
Stu	–	9	9	11	+	630
Stu	–	9	9	14	+	707, 876, 881, 1191
Stu	–	9	9	–	22	703
Stu	–	9	9	23	+	703
Stu	–	9	9	–	26	703
Stu	–	9	10	23	+	302
Stu	–	9	10	27	+	655, 917, 1085, 1157
Stu	–	10	1	–	4	703
Stu	–	10	1	–	5	703
Stu	–	10	1	–	6	703
Stu	–	10	1	–	9	703
Stu	–	14	15	18	+	1043
Stu	–	14	17	2	+	630
Stu	–	19	15	17	–	52
Stu	–	21	7	7	–	37

UNIDENTIFIED LAND OFFICE DISTRICT

Unk	–	1E	1N	20	+	1134
Unk	–	1E	1N	21	+	1134
Unk	–	2	2	3	5	187

Unk	–	2	2	3	6	187
Unk	–	2	2	3	7	187
Unk	–	2	2	3	15	187
Unk	–	2	2	3	16	187
Unk	–	2	2	3	17	187
Unk	–	3	1	1	–	26
Unk	–	3	1	1	10	187
Unk	–	3W	2N	15	–	982
Unk	–	3W	2N	–	22	982
Unk	–	3W	2N	–	27	982
Unk	–	3	7	1	–	766
Unk	–	3	7	22	–	51
Unk	–	3	11	19	–	51
Unk	–	3	16	3	–	984
Unk	–	4E	2N	3	+	1134
Unk	–	4E	2N	11	+	1134
Unk	W	4	4	–	–	518
Unk	W	4	5	–	–	518
Unk	–	4	8	3	+	656
Unk	–	4	11	10	–	368
Unk	–	4	15	17	+	803
Unk	–	4	15	18	+	1158
Unk	–	4	17	5	+	803, 1166
Unk	Pre	5	2	17	–	2189
Unk	–	5	5	30	+	543
Unk	–	5	7	33	+	342
Unk	–	5	17	4	+	458
Unk	–	6	2	30	–	56
Unk	–	6E	3S	–	15	1045
Unk	–	6	9	8	–	55
Unk	–	6	10	3	+	762
Unk	–	6	18	4	–	458
Unk	–	6	18	29	–	393
Unk	–	6	19	28	+	458
Unk	–	6	19	33	–	458
Unk	–	7	9	7	–	769
Unk	–	7	9	13	–	769
Unk	2E	8	3	34	+	874
Unk	–	9	9	–	26	961
Unk	–	10	1	–	5	961
Unk	–	10	1	–	6	961
Unk	–	10	5	9	+	1064
Unk	–	10	12	15	+	1048
Unk	–	10	12	27	–	971
Unk	–	10	12	27	+	1047
Unk	–	10	12	33	+	1196
Unk	–	13	7	1	–	28
Unk	–	13	7	4	–	28
Unk	–	13	15	6	+	1180
Unk	–	13	15	12	+	1172
Unk	–	14	15	5	–	285
Unk	–	14	15	9	+	1139
Unk	–	14	15	14	+	285
Unk	–	16	1	31	+	581
Unk	–	16	2	4	–	171
Unk	–	17	7	1	16	177, 178
Unk	–	17	14	7	+	1075
Unk	–	18	15	28	+	464
Unk	–	18	16	13	+	933
Unk	–	19	12	30	–	254
Unk	–	20	12	7	+	1083
Unk	–	20	12	18	+	1083
Unk	–	20	15	13	–	932
Unk	–	20	15	27	+	636
Unk	–	22	4	11	–	913
Unk	–	"in lots"	3			1081
Unk	–	"in lots"	5			1081
Unk	–	"in lots"	20			1081
Unk	–	"out lots"	5			1081
Unk	–	"out lots"	26			1081
Unk	–	"out lots"	52			1081

			VINCENNES LAND OFFICE DISTRICT				

Vin	*	–	–	–	25		632

*Militia Donation Tract.

Vin	–	3E	4S	2	+	739, 884
Vin	–	3E	6S	–	4	2087, 2090
Vin	–	3E	6S	–	5	2087, 2090
Vin	–	4E	3S	30	+	772
Vin	–	4E	4S	4	+	797
Vin	–	4E	6S	15	+	854
Vin	–	5W	1S	3	+	854
Vin	–	7W	2N	5	+	890
Vin	–	7	3N	–	–	1655
Vin	–	7	4N	–	–	1655
Vin	–	7	5N	–	–	1655
Vin	–	9	1N	–	–	1655
Vin	–	10	1N	–	–	1655
Vin	–	10	1S	–	–	1655
Vin	–	10W	6S	8	+	890
Vin	–	11W	2S	–	–	1661
Vin	–	11W	3S	6	+	890
Vin	–	13W	4S	3	+	675
Vin	–	13W	8S	–	29	675
Vin	–	13W	8S	30	–	675
Vin	–	14W	8N	–	18	675
Vin	–	14W	8S	20	+	778
Vin	–	14W	8S	21	+	675, 778

WEST PEARL RIVER LAND OFFICE DISTRICT

WPR	–	Bayou Pierre				808, 1030
WPR	–	1E	1	30	–	1965
WPR	–	1W	1	36	–	1965
WPR	–	1E	2	18	–	1965
WPR	–	2E	3	19	–	1965
WPR	–	2E	6	30	–	1965
WPR	–	3E	1	32	–	1965

ZANESVILLE LAND OFFICE DISTRICT

Zan	–	1	1	1	+	388
Zan Mil	1	1	2	+		1022
Zan Mil	1	1	3	1		1013
Zan Mil	1	1	3	4		1013
Zan Mil	1	1	3	5		1013
Zan Mil	1	1	3	6		1013
Zan Mil	1	1	3	9		1013
Zan Mil	1	1	3	10		1013
Zan Mil	1	1	3	23		1013
Zan Mil	1	1	3	26		1013
Zan Mil	1	1	3	27		1013
Zan Mil	1	1	3	38		1013
Zan Mil	1	1	3	39		1013
Zan Mil	1	1	3	40		1013
Zan	–	1	1	8	+	1087
Zan Mil	1	1	9	+		388, 537
Zan Mil	1	1	10	+		537
Zan	–	1	1	16	+	1087
Zan	–	1	2	4	+	777
Zan Mil	1	2	19	+		537
Zan Mil	1	2	21	+		388
Zan Mil	1	2	22	+		896
Zan	–	1	3	5	+	525
Zan Mil	1	3	24	+		539
Zan	–	1	9	4	+	616
Zan Mil	1	9	11	+		949
Zan Mil	1	9	12	+		1022
Zan Mil	2	1	1	+		1121
Zan Mil	2	1	3	+		1098
Zan	–	2	3	10	+	388
Zan	–	2	7	11	+	772
Zan	–	3	1	20	+	717
Zan Mil	3	1	21	+		709
Zan	–	3	5	–	5	1512
Zan	–	3	5	11	+	1512

Zan	–	3	8	1	+		697	Zan Mil	6	8	3	16		826
Zan Mil	3	8	1	+			979	Zan Mil	7	1	3	+		972
Zan	–	3	8	2	+		697	Zan	–	7	1	9	+	1176
Zan Mil	3	8	2	+			979	Zan Mil	7	1	9	+		1149
Zan	–	3	8	3	+		697	Zan	–	7	1	13	–	826
Zan Mil	3	8	3	+			979	Zan	–	7	1	13	+	733
Zan	–	3	8	9	+		772	Zan Mil	7	1	13	+		887
Zan Mil	3	8	10	+			884	Zan	–	7	3	18	+	777
Zan	–	3	9	1	+		369	Zan Mil	7	4	2	39		626
Zan	–	3	9	8	+		369	Zan Mil	7	4	2	40		626
Zan	–	3	9	11	+		772	Zan Mil	7	4	14	+		940
Zan	–	3	9	13	+		369	Zan Mil	7	4	25	+		539
Zan	–	3	9	18	+		369	Zan	–	7	5	2	+	1077
Zan	–	3	9	20	+		842	Zan	–	7	5	7	+	1077
Zan	–	3	10	12	+	697, 879	Zan	–	7	5	9	+	862
Zan	–	3	10	21	+		842	Zan Mil	8	2	4	+		539
Zan	–	4	4	7	+		777	Zan Mil	8	2	13	+		539
Zan	–	4	8	1	+		562	Zan Mil	8	2	14	+		896
Zan Mil	4	8	3	+			798	Zan Mil	8	2	18	+		539
Zan	–	4	8	4	+		1017	Zan	–	8	4	2	7	826
Zan Mil	4	8	8	+			798	Zan	–	8	4	2	8	826
Zan	–	4	8	12	+		1017	Zan Mil	8	4	3	7		826
Zan Mil	4	8	13	+			798	Zan Mil	8	4	3	8		826
Zan	–	4	15	18	+		860	Zan	–	8	8	6	+	940
Zan	–	4	16	11	+		1022	Zan	–	8	8	12	+	1108
Zan Mil	5	1	1	+			1098	Zan	–	8	8	13	+	1108
Zan	–	5	1	6	+	908, 1197	Zan Mil	9	1	3	23		690
Zan	–	5	1	10	+	794, 795, 902	Zan Mil	9	1	3	24		690
Zan	–	5	1	12	+	915, 916	Zan	–	9	1	12	+	763, 767
Zan	–	5	1	15	+	908, 1197	Zan Mil	9	6	18	+		1011
Zan Mil	6	1	7	+			972	Zan	–	9	7	7	+	1121
Zan	–	6	1	10	+		972	Zan	–	9	8	3	+	537
Zan Mil	6	8	3	5			826	Zaŋ	–	9	8	4	+	824
Zan Mil	6	8	3	6			826	Zan	–	9	8	5	+	616, 873
Zan Mil	6	8	3	7			826	Zan	–	9	8	6	+	949
Zan Mil	6	8	3	15			826	Zan	–	9	8	7	+	1121

Zan	Mil	10	1	20	+	921, 972	Zan	–	14	15	11	+	392
Zan	–	10	6	31	+	1077	Zan	–	14	15	14	+	462, 618
Zan	–	10	6	32	–	1077	Zan	–	14	15	18	+	838
Zan	–	10	8	–	–	737	Zan	–	14	15	26	+	972, 1017
Zan	Mil	10	8	28	+	1098	Zan	–	14	15	27	+	388
Zan	–	10	9	6	+	777	Zan	–	14	15	28	+	388
Zan	–	11	13	10	+	1121	Zan	–	14	15	30	+	365
Zan	–	12	12	–	8	1068	Zan	–	14	15	33	+	717
Zan	–	12	12	17	+	365	Zan	–	14	15	34	+	1059
Zan	–	12	12	–	17	1133	Zan	–	14	16	1	–	1467
Zan	–	12	12	–	20	1133	Zan	–	14	16	13	+	785
Zan	–	12	13	3	+	1135	Zan	–	14	16	18	+	842
Zan	–	12	13	6	+	1120	Zan	–	15	16	5	+	462
Zan	–	12	13	7	+	388, 1120, 1121	Zan	–	15	16	12	+	949, 1022, 1121
Zan	–	12	13	17	+	365	Zan	–	15	16	17	+	717
Zan	–	12	13	28	+	388	Zan	–	15	16	18	+	1011
Zan	–	12	13	33	+	388	Zan	–	15	17	9	+	960
Zan	–	13	10	5	+	842	Zan	–	15	17	10	+	960
Zan	–	13	11	–	4	388	Zan	–	15	17	17	+	596, 674
Zan	–	13	11	5	+	357	Zan	–	15	17	23	+	388
Zan	–	13	11	–	7	972	Zan	–	15	17	24	+	388
Zan	–	13	11	8	–	972	Zan	–	15	17	25	+	388
Zan	–	13	12	2	+	365, 777	Zan	–	15	17	26	+	785
Zan	–	13	12	7	+	365	Zan	–	15	17	27	+	1182
Zan	–	13	12	9	+	1182	Zan	–	15	17	30	+	1121
Zan	–	14	14	4	+	380	Zan	–	15	17	31	+	1022
Zan	–	14	14	9	+	616, 1068	Zan	–	15	17	35	+	616
Zan	–	14	15	2	+	1182	Zan	–	15	18	9	+	862
Zan	–	14	15	9	+	940	Zan	–	15	18	10	+	1144
Zan	–	14	15	10	+	842	Zan	–	15	18	15	+	717, 1144
Zan	Mil	14	15	10	+	1098	Zan	–	18	13	18	–	388